Witchcraft and Magic
in the Nordic Middle Ages

THE MIDDLE AGES SERIES

Ruth Mazo Karras, Series Editor
Edward Peters, Founding Editor

A complete list of books in the series
is available from the publisher.

Witchcraft and Magic in the Nordic Middle Ages

Stephen A. Mitchell

PENN

UNIVERSITY OF PENNSYLVANIA PRESS

PHILADELPHIA · OXFORD

Publication of this volume was aided by a gift
from the Royal Gustavus Adolphus Academy.

Published by
University of Pennsylvania Press
Philadelphia, Pennsylvania 19104-4112
www.upenn.edu/pennpress

Printed in the United States of America on acid-free paper
10 9 8 7 6 5 4 3 2 1

Library of Congress Cataloging-in-Publication Data

Mitchell, Stephen A., 1951–
    Witchcraft and magic in the Nordic Middle Ages / Stephen A. Mitchell.
        p.   cm.
    Includes bibliographical references and index.
    ISBN 978-0-8122-4290-4 (hardcover : alk. paper)
    1. Witchcraft—Scandinavia—History.   2. Magic—Scandinavia—History.   I. Title.
BF1584.S23M58   2011
133.4'309480902—dc22   2010022016

To my very supportive family and friends

Contents

Preface

This study examines the responses in the legal, literary, and popular cultures of the Nordic Middle Ages to the belief that there existed people capable of manipulating the world through magical practices. To date, there have been no comprehensive evaluations of Nordic witchcraft beliefs between 1100 and 1525, whereas studies of Scandinavian witchcraft in the eras both before and after this period abound. The reasons for this situation are many. In large part, it is explained by the tendency for many of the late medieval materials, such as the Icelandic sagas, to be appropriated to discussions of the much earlier Viking Age; moreover, there is a view among some specialists that nothing much happened with respect to Scandinavian witchcraft before circa 1400.[1]

I argue, on the contrary, that much was happening and that an evaluation of this important meeting ground of church doctrine and vernacular belief systems in the period between the Viking Age and the early modern era has long been a desideratum, both for the study of witchcraft in Scandinavia itself and for the study of witchcraft in Europe more broadly.[2] The current work thus presents an account of developments in witchcraft beliefs throughout Scandinavia in the later Middle Ages, of how elite and nonelite, native and imported constructions of witchcraft evolved during the centuries before the Reformation, an era of profound and widespread changes that set the stage for the early modern crazes.

A phrase like "Nordic witchcraft," especially when framed by specific dates, suggests a highly bounded entity, a set of orthodox views held by a homogenous culture, but nothing could be further from the truth. What we know and what we can reconstruct about the world of Northern Europe from the early Iron Age through the Middle Ages says that it was always a heterogeneous and dynamic world, and, importantly, seen from the perspective of the people we tend to think of as "Scandinavians" or "proto-Scandinavians," a world in which their neighbors, the Sámi, with their shamanic practices, played significant roles, as recent research has emphasized.[3] More-over, as the Nordic world expanded during the Viking Age, leapfrogging its way across the North Atlantic islands, Norse settlers and travelers came into contact with yet another shamanism-practicing culture when they established colonies in Greenland, western outposts that lasted throughout the Middle Ages. Likewise, their eastward expansion brought them into greater proximity to Finnic and other peoples, whose cultures too had echoes of shamanism.[4] And it should be borne in mind, as regards the variegated nature of the Nordic cultural region, that these events took place across a stretch of the earth roughly comparable to distances across North America.[5]

At the same time, that Scandinavia was drawn into the Christian ambit by the beginnings of the new millennium meant that the cultural construc-tion of such concepts as magic and witchcraft was increasingly shaped under thinking developed in other parts of Europe. By the later Middle Ages, ideas about such matters reticulated between the local Scandinavian population and adjacent vernacular cultures, especially in Hanseatic-influenced cities with large foreign settlements (e.g., Bergen, Copenhagen, Stockholm). In other words, there is in one sense no such thing as "Nordic witchcraft," but there are recoverable outlines of an evolving set of more or less similar beliefs held by the Scandinavian-speaking peoples of the Middle Ages, and it is in that sense that I intend the phrase "Nordic witchcraft," even when I have not elaborated the problematic nature of the expression.

The time frame 1100–1525 is naturally both artificial and subjective but does reflect certain important criteria that tend to bundle around these boundaries: in the European context, the dates capture the legal reforms that took place circa 1100 and the early thirteenth-century shift in the church's thinking about the nature of witchcraft and magic and the relationship of these phenomena to diabolism and heresy (e.g., the oft-cited *Vox in Rama* of Pope Gregory IX in 1233); at the other end, the date reflects the beginnings of the Reformation (e.g., Martin Luther's excommunication in 1521).[6] Within the Scandinavian context, Christianity is reasonably well established in elite circles—at least—throughout Scandinavia by 1100, and it is first in the thir-teenth century that contemporary Nordic documents become available in large quantities. And, of course, the Nordic region was deeply transformed by the early sixteenth-century Reformation, a period in which major political, religious, and linguistic developments mark a break with the medieval past.[7] I have used the somewhat arbitrary year of 1525, because it is at approximately this point that the dominant political map of Scandinavia is set for the next

three centuries with the establishment of a Swedish kingdom clearly independent of Denmark.

Many of the residents of this region were descendants of the Nordic
pirates and adventurers who traveled, raided, traded, and settled widely
throughout much of the known world during the so-called Viking Age, but
this emphatically is *not* a book about Vikings. It does, however, depend in
large part on a great medieval literature that centers on events—sometimes
factual, sometimes mere literary confections—set in the Viking Age. The
sheer brilliance of these texts, and especially their uncanny ability to make
the medieval world seem so accessible, can be an attractive nuisance, to use
the lawyer's term of art. An extraordinary medieval literature, often well informed by tradition, the sagas are nevertheless not mirrorlike reflections of
the Viking Age but rather something akin to forerunners of the historical
novel.[8] No one would, by way of a parallel, hope to use the weird sisters from
the opening of *Macbeth* (ca. 1605) as source material for eleventh-century
Scottish witchcraft beliefs rather than those of Jacobean Britain. Yet in the
Old Norse field, mining an Icelandic saga known only from post-Reformation
articulations in order to comment on the tenth century does not automatically seem so improbable or problematic.

That is not to say, however, that the remarkable work done in interpreting the sagas in the light of folklore, archaeology, philology, and other frameworks has not done much to encourage our confidence in the sagas as sources
and shown how critically important they are as parts of a larger cultural
puzzle.[9] As a number of earlier studies have carefully combed through these
texts, identifying their testimony to the various qualities the thirteenth and
later centuries attributed to Nordic magic and witchcraft, I have avoided
repeating that process yet again here. Instead, I want to demonstrate how
and to what extent medieval Icelanders actively used the concepts of magic
and witchcraft in their literature and, more narrowly, how witchcraft and its
practitioners are employed to project a sense of the past, of the remote world
of pagan Scandinavia.

Determining the best means for presenting the complicated, interlaced
evolution in clerical and popular cultures about witches in the centuries between the Viking Age and the Reformation presents a challenge. In structuring this monograph I have eschewed the more obvious chronological
approach—its directness appealing at first blush, of course, but fraught with
its own complications—and instead embraced an approach in which the various chapters are organized around specific idea complexes. Thus, although

the chapters are not meant to be limited to, or by, types of source material, they do often reflect concentrations of certain genres—literature, laws, and so forth. Chapter 1 surveys the available materials on, and approaches to, the topic; further, it reviews the status of magic in pagan Scandinavia, as well as its represented value in the conversion of the Nordic region. The nature and usefulness of magic in daily life, in both Christian and pagan contexts, is the subject of Chapter 2, which also reviews the major arenas in which magic was used, namely, romance, fortune, health, weather, and malediction. Chapter 3 examines how medieval Nordic authors represent, and use, witchcraft and magic in narrative materials, not only in the Icelandic sagas, but also in histories and other forms of courtly and ecclesiastical literature. In Chapter 4, I take up late medieval mythologies developed in the Nordic world about the nature, powers, and habits of witches. Chapter 5 examines the rich materials about witchcraft contained in normative documents, such as the provincial laws, as well as the documented cases of witchcraft prosecution from medieval Scandinavia. The complex relationship between gender and the construction of witchcraft in medieval Scandinavia is the subject of Chapter 6. And, finally, in the epilogue I survey the developments in the medieval period in Northern Europe, with a focus on how these changes help establish the framework for the witch-hunts of the early modern era.

As regards nomenclature, it should be noted that there are important differences in the contemporary world between the geographically derived designation "Scandinavian" and the more inclusive "Nordic," an adjective whose usage embraces with greater ease the non-Indo-European cultural and linguistic traditions of the region, Sámi and Finnish in particular, and does not so readily pigeonhole Icelandic and Faroese traditions. On the other hand, the terms are so thoroughly intertwined in standard English usage, and offer such an excellent opportunity for stylistic relief, that I use them interchangeably and mark meaningful differences in materials that are Germanic versus non-Germanic, insular versus noninsular, and so on with explicit designations. Similarly, in the interest of clarity, I have generally used what are strictly speaking anachronistic terms such as Danish, Norwegian, and so on, even where the cultures and polities under discussion were not always consonant with the modern national states. At the same time, I have tried to respect the political realities of the Middle Ages where there have been important postmedieval changes in boundaries (e.g., the modern Swedish regions of Skåne, Blekinge, Halland, and Bohuslän). As regards the spelling of personal names, no single rule works perfectly. I have generally normalized names to Old Norse standards for periods before the mid-fourteenth century or so but, for later periods, regularized them according to rules of the dominant national language, orthographic anachronisms notwithstanding.[10]

No less difficult has been the question of what terms to apply to the phenomena scrutinized in the following pages. The very sensible concerns raised by scholars who prefer employing native terminology like *trolldómr* and *galdr* rather than "witchcraft" and "magic," for example, are not lightly dismissed; yet at the same time, this debate, so familiar to students of folk narratives, has another side, one which argues that although using native terminologies has its advantages, it also removes the Nordic world from the growing international discussion of such topics.[11] Moreover, because this study is keyed to the later Middle Ages rather than the pre-Christian era, and especially given the increasing influence of the church in shaping these issues, employing the vernacular terms, where many of our documents use Latin terms such as *maleficia,* would be forced and anachronistic. In the hope of resolving this issue favorably, and with due attention to both the native traditions and the international context, I have generally used standard English terminology followed by the Nordic or Latin terms in parentheses where the exact phrasing can be deemed significant.

Introduction

Norse mythology, as described by Snorri Sturluson (1178–1241), tells of a story falsely spread by the dwarves about the death of Kvasir, the anthropomorphic representation of knowledge in Norse paganism. The dwarves, who have actually slain the creature themselves, tell the gods that Kvasir died because he was unable to disgorge himself of what he knew: Kvasir has essentially choked on his own knowledge.[1] The diligent student of witchcraft in any European tradition writing in the twenty-first century must necessarily feel uncomfortably at home in this story, as the volume of scholarly literature treating European witchcraft, already vast, has grown especially rapidly over the past forty years or so, reflecting a rekindled interest that is simultaneously both popular and professional.[2]

Certainly witchcraft has been in the spotlight in recent decades, so much so that it has been likened to the rise and fall of the Roman Empire, that is, a field unto itself.[3] Given the volume and diversity of available scholarship, a writer hoping to provide a fully articulated *Stand der Forschung* for the study of witchcraft in medieval Scandinavia, let alone Europe as a whole (or other inkhorn act of hubris), will want to think twice. Still, some observations on trends in this extensive scholarship will be useful in their own right, as well as to situate in the reader's mind my own line of inquiry and the basis for—and biases of—my comments.[4] First, I outline the main currents in scholarship about magic and witchcraft in Europe, and then turn to the issue of the trends within scholarship on this field in Scandinavia. Finally, I examine the basic concepts and vocabulary important to this study.

Very broadly, the development of the church's thinking about witchcraft—the ability to manipulate power due to an individual's innate qualities, to acquired learning, or to a bargain with evil forces—increasingly saw this phenomenon in nearly Manichean terms, characterized by one scholar as the church's "sharp binary division of the spiritual universe into opposing divine and demonic realms. . . ."[5] On the one side stood church doctrine about such matters; on the other, everything else, namely, all that was perceived as opposing that view, notably, paganism as an active force in areas as yet unconverted, the remnants of paganism in those that were, and, increasingly, heresies of various kinds. Throughout the Christian era, witchcraft and other forms of magic are condemned by influential church leaders (e.g., Saints Augustine of Hippo, John Chrysostom, Isidore of Seville) and church councils (e.g., the Council of Paris in 829). At the same time, a critical spirit in some writers cautiously regards these beliefs as unreal, that is, as phantasms and diabolical deceptions, expressed most famously in the early tenth-century *Canon episcopi* of Regino of Prüm and works influenced by it (e.g., the penitential of Burchard of Worms).

The significant changes in legal thinking that came in the twelfth and thirteenth centuries, especially the recovery and reintroduction of Roman law, and with it, an inquisitorial (as opposed to accusatorial) system buttressed by judicial torture,[6] as well as a more robust system of canon law,[7] has led some scholars to conclude that it was at this point that Europe became a "persecuting society."[8] With respect to magic and witchcraft, an important result of this transformation was the tendency to seek out perceived heterodox views. It is hardly surprising that those believed to practice magic would soon fall within the ambit of such a system: thus, for example, in 1326, Pope John XXII published a decree (*Super illius specula*) calling for immediate excommunication of all those who invoked demons in the pursuit of divination or other acts of magic.[9] By the end of that same century (1398), the theology faculty of the University of Paris condemned in broad terms all forms of sorcery, tying acts of magic to the notion of the devil's pact (*pactum cum diabolo*).

In 1437, Pope Eugenius IV wrote all papal inquisitors concerning invokers of demons, enumerating some of the evil deeds of which he understood them to be guilty (e.g., weather magic) and associated these acts with the work of the devil. In fact, throughout the fourteenth and fifteenth centuries, a series of works by a variety of clergymen (e.g., Nicolaus Eymeric, Nicholas von Jauer, Jean Gerson, Johannes Nider, Johannes Hartlieb of Bavaria, Nicholas Jacquier) helped promote similar views.[10] What is perhaps the most famous of the medieval texts to address witchcraft, *Malleus maleficarum*, came into existence only near the end of the Middle Ages (1486). The work mainly of Heinrich Krämer (Institoris), a Dominican inquisitor, with uncertain, and disputed, assistance from his fellow inquisitor, Jakob Sprenger, this so-called hammer of the witches perhaps represents more an outlying view of

women, witches, and court procedures than the norm for which it is sometimes taken; certainly the degree to which it reflects medieval mentalities has
come under attack in recent years.[11]

For many centuries, the church regarded activities associated with witchcraft as mere superstition, simple error that could be corrected through penance and other forms of contrition. By the end of the Middle Ages, however,
those who employed this kind of non-Christian magic were conceived of as
part of an organized diabolical cult, worshippers of Satan who engaged in
gruesome rites and activities and who were generally beyond salvation and
subject to capital punishment.[12] That this came to be so, it has been argued,
resulted from the combination in clerical thinking of two different systems
of magic. One type, practiced among elites as well as nonelites, included
spells and talismans for such purposes as finding lost articles, identifying
thieves, preventing illness, and so on. Those guilty of such activities, it was
thought, had fallen into superstitious ways and were to be corrected. By the
end of the thirteenth century, a less common form of magic appeared, what
came to be called "necromancy," where access to Latin learning was a prereq-
uisite.[13] Magic of this sort has been characterized by one expert as "learned
demonic sorcery [. . .] a highly structured variety of magic limited to a small
clerical elite."[14] The conflation at the end of the Middle Ages of such views
was partly responsible for the caricature of the evil-intentioned hag, setting
the stage for the witch-hunts of the early modern period.[15]

These theological innovations occurred against the backdrop of important historical events, including medieval heresies (e.g., Cathars), the Cru-
sades, and such political and social upheavals as those created by the
extermination of the Knights Templar and the Black Death of the mid-fourteenth-century. And, as one noted scholar in the area reports, despite the
important codification of the church's thinking about witchcraft in the later
Middle Ages, nothing in the fifteenth century compares in importance to the
shifts that transpired in the twelfth and thirteenth centuries.[16] A synthesizing
account of the medieval and early modern European witchcraft phenomenon
suggests that popular traditions about witchcraft and other forms of nonelite
magic in the medieval era evolved, and largely even merged, with elite belief
systems. Thus, age-old slanders—used at first against Christians themselves
and later against the Waldensians and other heretics—were recycled to fit the
emerging image of devil-worshipping witches.[17] The stage was thus further
set for the great witch-hunts of the early modern era.

With the Enlightenment of the eighteenth century, elite society withdrew from the consolidated belief system that had given rise to the "hunts" and was inclined to regard such beliefs as primitive. So changed is this perspective among the upper classes that their disbelief evolves into a kind of fascination with historical episodes of witchcraft that needed to be explained away as delusions, or as the product of a mass hysteria.[18] The seriousness of purpose evident in a text like Hutchinson's famous eighteenth-century critique of witchcraft ideology gives way over time to views in which the idea of witches cannot be taken seriously in elite circles—although we have every reason to suppose that beliefs about witchcraft continued to have vitality in popular opinion.[19] Enlightenment rationalism led to ever greater disbelief toward traditional witchcraft systems. In her splendid study of the shifting views in Sweden, Linda Oja finds what she calls a secularization of attitudes.[20] The subsequent reinterpretation of the early modern witch-hunts gave rise, for example, in Sweden to reproductions of tracts from the seventeenth-century witch-hunts and their presentation of the sabbat scenario.[21] Compilations of this sort satisfied the public's appetite for gothic horror and produced in the book-buying public a lust for texts that centered on witchcraft as a kind of spectacle.[22]

By the end of the Nordic nineteenth century, more sober, if still popular, historical treatments of witchcraft and related topics were increasingly common, sometimes with important considerations for the future use of the social sciences in the study of witchcraft.[23] Studies written from the perspective of intellectual and church history abound in the new century, but at about this time, what might be regarded as a reaction against the top-down view of witchcraft gave way to the possibility of more popular origins for witchcraft beliefs.[24] The most famous work to expound this view was Margaret Murray's *The Witch-Cult in Western Europe* (1921). Its revolutionary thesis that the medieval witches represented the survival of ancient European fertility traditions created, the book's many flaws notwithstanding, increased interest in understanding witchcraft from this popular perspective.[25]

Although Murray principally focused on British data, it did not take long for the book's impact to be felt outside the Anglophone world. Her key notion perhaps found most fertile expression in Northern Europe in Arne Runeberg's sober and still very readable treatment of the topic, *Witches, Demons, and Fertility Magic: Analysis of Their Significance and Mutual Relations in West-European Folk Religion* (1947). Nordic witchcraft scholarship, as exemplified in the work of, for example, Nils Lid, Bente Alver, Gustav Henningsen, Jan Wall, and Kim Tørnsø, continues to value nonelite sources as a means for understanding what witchcraft was believed to be and how the system as a whole functioned.[26]

Hugh Trevor-Roper is widely credited with turning attention away from medieval superstitions, the confessions of accused witches, and other efforts to discover folk beliefs about witchcraft and toward the question of social attitudes, especially the degree to which it was indeed elite members of society, those few powerful political and ecclesiastical figures at the apex of society, whose instrumental roles shaped the nature of European witchcraft.[27] In line with this hierarchical stance, the principal champion of cultural materialism within anthropology, Marvin Harris, introduces his discussion of historical European witchcraft in explicitly class-conscious terms, more or less recycling, if inverting, Michelet's nineteenth-century peasant-revolt hypothesis: "My explanation of the witchcraft craze is that it was largely created and sustained by the governing classes as a means of suppressing this wave of Christian messianism."[28]

A more influential interpretation of the role of class relations in the case of early modern English witchcraft came with Keith Thomas's monumental *Religion and the Decline of Magic.*[29] Similarly, Bengt Ankarloo's breakthrough study of the seventeenth-century witch-hunt in Sweden, *Trolldomsprocesserna i Sverige* (1971), made the case for the importance of carefully sieving the data with such issues as the wealth, gender, and so on of the accused in mind, an influential Nordic example of a much larger tendency within witchcraft studies.[30]

Over the past several decades, scholars coming from differing disciplinary allegiances—history, religion, anthropology, folklore, philosophy, literature, and so on—have put their shoulders to the wheel, occasionally borrowing methodologies from other fields, often anthropology.[31] Particularly powerful in structuring this inquiry has been the opportunity to understand the European experience against the backdrop of important observed *comparanda* from such regions as sub-Saharan Africa and the Americas.[32] Few scholars have had a deeper influence in this regard than Victor Turner, whose dynamic, incident-specific approach became, and remains, a widely imitated method.[33] It was at this point that the observations of anthropologists on the African experience began to be turned to the historical European situation.[34]

The suitability of the analogical ethnographic argument to historical Western European documents, although generally well regarded, has not been without its difficulties.[35] One obstacle has been the frequently insurmountable differences between the realities of village-level observations and the uncertainties of reconstructed large-scale events, with their attendant ex-tralocal factors such as the strategies of the national secular and supranational religious authorities. A further complication has been the proliferation of theories looking to interpret the data, many of them exceedingly helpful but almost always presented with a certain intellectual hegemonic quality. Historians have certainly felt the pinch that comes with interpretations that dare to rely on multiple theories for getting at some central truth, as Robin Briggs rightly reminds us.[36]

Yet after several decades of debate, the bipartite summary proposed by Macfarlane of the phenomena necessary for the formation of accusations of witchcraft in specific instances—"firstly, the presence of some tension or anxiety or unexplained phenomenon; secondly, the directing of this energy into certain channels"—remains useful, tempered, as another scholar notes, by a newfound "emphasis on the need to reconstruct holistically the mental world of the participants in the trials, and a perception of the enhanced importance of folklore studies and psychology in the interpretation of the Hunt."[37] That scholars often find themselves struggling against the confines of disciplinary walls is natural enough: after all, scholarship does not always fit into neat categories, and any claims that suggest otherwise must be ad-justed by an appreciation for the realities of the synthesizing human mind.[38]

Much of the scholarship on Scandinavian witchcraft, whatever its theo-retical orientation, has tended to focus on the post-Reformation situation, where the extent of the witch craze outbreaks is great, the imprint of elite witchcraft ideology imported from the Continent readily apparent, and the documentation substantial.[39] Witchcraft in the Viking period and the early Middle Ages, on the other hand, has long fascinated scholars but proved to be an elusive topic for earlier generations, only slowly precipitating out of the evidence as much more than a shadowy survival of Norse heathendom.[40] Lately, however, there has been a veritable flood of research on magic and witchcraft during the Viking Age.

Among the many works to have appeared on pre-Reformation Nordic witchcraft and magic, several important monographs stand out. Perhaps no other work tackles the question of magic as represented in the medieval Ice-landic sagas with quite the same vigor as does François Xavier Dillmann's extraordinary 1986 Caen dissertation, *Les magiciens dans l'Islande ancienne: Études sur la représentation de la magie islandaise et de ses agents dans les sources littéraires norroises*, recently revised and republished.[41] In this dense and richly textured study, Dillmann argues for the historical value of the Icelandic sagas as repositories of earlier magical traditions. From his detailed observations, Dillman draws a number of intriguing conclusions about both the function of magic in the pre-Christian Nordic world and the social status of its practitioners.[42]

The erudition and learning of its author notwithstanding, the book is necessarily limited by the fact that it largely allows the surviving medieval Icelandic sagas to define both the range of its inquiry and the nature of its evidence.[43] Brilliant though they are, the sagas are first and foremost testimony to how thirteenth-century Christian Icelanders understood—and used—their forebears' conduct and beliefs; to that must be added the fact that we possess, of course, only a fraction of the saga materials that once existed, a factor that further limits our perspective. Reconstruction from such data is possible but fraught with difficulties. Yet, within this confined range of sources, Dillmann ably and exhaustively demonstrates how the image that emerges of the magico-religious world of the Viking Age might be characterized as one that retains a functional magical component (power to divine, protect, and alter the weather, for example, but, curiously, relatively uninterested in influencing fertility), as well as, more revealingly, the reception and perception of those who practice it among their fellow Icelanders. This is tricky terrain, not least because here Dillmann attempts to rescue for the ninth, tenth, eleventh, and twelfth centuries the attitudes of the public toward magic and the psychological profiles of those who practiced sorcery through works written and recorded in the thirteenth and later centuries. I am sympathetic to the mission and impressed by the author's insights and industry but am less inclined than he, as will become clear, to place faith in just how far we can utilize these late medieval narratives to reveal the mentalities of the Viking Age (as opposed to the later Middle Ages themselves).

Of a very different attitude toward the sources is Catherine Raudvere's *Kunskap och insikt i norrön tradition: Mytologi, ritualer och trolldomsanklagelser.*[44] Writing from the standpoint of the history of religions, Raudvere undertakes a source-critical review of many of the same Icelandic sagas and eddic texts on which Dillmann's study focuses. Raudvere, however, is more skeptical about the prospect of teasing from these delicious late medieval narratives insights into the magical world of Viking Age Scandinavians. That is not to say that she does not believe it possible to draw conclusions about these beliefs, like Dillmann, largely basing her views on the products of Icelandic literary enterprise. But in this instance Raudvere cautiously distinguishes between what she regards as faux and echt testimony, seeing in some saga examples "authentic" witness to pagan practices, but elsewhere Christian interpolations and propaganda; moreover, Raudvere is careful to draw into her discussion such adjacent disciplines as archaeology. In addition to magic and witchcraft, she takes up their relationship to the all-important arena of fate and presses to new heights the possibility of precipitating ritual practice and other performances out of the narratives.[45]

Working from their perspectives as archaeologists, but with a deep knowledge of the textual materials, two archaeologists published studies in 2002 with a focus on magic and the question of gender. Brit Solli's *Seid: Myter, sjamanisme og kjønn i vikingenes tid* argues for an understanding of Viking Age magical practices from the perspective of queer studies, specifically the social construction, rather than a biological designation, of gender, a key factor in the consideration of Óðinn's purported role in the practice of *seiðr*.[46] The evidence of material culture is certainly important to Solli's conclusions but perhaps secondary to her theoretical explication and ruminations, which are powerful. Solli focuses on the Norwegian world and relies for much of her archaeological evidence on the so-called sacred white stones, with their apparent gender ambiguities, traits for which she plausibly posits analogues within Old Norse mythology, such as the question of Nerthus-Njǫrðr.[47]

Although also concerned with these vexing questions of gender construction, violence, and cognitive archaeology, but less dependent on a specific theoretical orientation and more reliant on the material and textual data, Neil Price's *The Viking Way: Religion and War in Late Iron Age Scandinavia* represents a saltation event in our understanding of Viking Age mentalities.[48] Interested not only in the specific issue of magic and the practice of *seiðr* but also in recapturing for Scandinavian history and archaeology the vital role of the Sámi in the cultural evolution of the region, Price explores in both a Sámi-specific and more broadly circumpolar context the likely shared ideologies and practices of shamanism among the indigenous Sámi peoples and their North Germanic-speaking neighbors.[49]

Price's is a study that looks to provide a unified explanation for the paradox represented by Norse magic, with its apparent reliance on gender-bending practices (*ergi*) carried out in the context of perhaps history's most explicitly homophobic culture. The answer, he argues, is to be found in the Vikings' need to produce effective battle magic through such shamanistic practices, praxes that at the same time resulted in "nothing less than a view of the nature of reality itself."[50] This ritualized aggression came at a cost, one that under normal circumstances would have been shameful and unthinkable within Norse culture, but that in the specific context of the practice of war and what he terms the "supernatural empowerment of violence" was understood to be worth the cost one had to pay. *The Viking Way* breaks new ground in assessing that world, extensions of our knowledge and methodologies not easily captured in a short summary, one of which is surely its artfully balanced appreciation for evidence of many different types from many different disciplines and regions. It also makes clear that the various modern debates from the past seventy years about the question of shamanism in Norse religious practice raised important issues for which equally important and revealing answers are now being formulated.[51]

Despite their diverse areas of interest, differing approaches, and varied receptions by the scholarly community, these recent monographs touching on witchcraft in medieval Scandinavia share one feature: they are all principally concerned with the Nordic world during the early Middle Ages, that is, the Viking Age (ca. 800–1100). These studies, complemented by the often magisterial studies on sixteenth-, seventeenth-, and eighteenth-century Scandinavian witchcraft mentioned earlier, thus form two "bookends" in the study of Nordic witchcraft. What has largely gone missing concerning this important meeting ground of church doctrine and vernacular belief systems is the period between them, roughly the years from 1100 to 1525, the subject of this monograph. It is, after all, as noted earlier, precisely during these four centuries that we witness the accommodation of native views about magic, sorcery, and the supernatural to church teachings on witchcraft, and it is from these years that we first possess contemporary texts on these issues. The excitement over the possibilities of recovering the magical worldview of Viking Age Scandinavia, on the one hand, and the concern to account for the disturbing witch-hunts of the early modern era in the Nordic region, on the other, have generally led scholars to ignore or devalue the post-Conversion era.

In fact, there has been a strong tendency among scholars of Nordic witchcraft—despite the evidence suggesting that developments in the twelfth and thirteenth centuries were more important to the conceptualization and prosecution of witchcraft and other forms of magic in Europe than those of the fifteenth century—to regard the understanding of magic in that era as relatively unchanged for much of the Middle Ages, with the principal shift in thinking about witchcraft and magic in medieval Scandinavia coming about in the fifteenth century.[52]

To be sure, these fifteenth-century developments were important, but it is manifestly not the case that a relatively unaltered perspective on pagan witchcraft and magic was suddenly transformed at the very close of the Nordic Middle Ages, as important and dramatic as some of these newly introduced changes were. The process had already begun centuries earlier as both secular and ecclesiastical authorities strove to gain, maintain, and exercise control and power, as well as to ensure the spiritual and physical well-being of their communities. Of course, these changes were often made as a direct result of clerical thinking flowing from the Continent. Thus such important considerations of magic, sorcery, and witchcraft (and often also of inquisitorial practice) as Pope Alexander IV's decretal, *Quod super nonnullis* (1258), Bernard Gui's *Practica inquisitionis* (1320), Nicolas Eymeric's *Directorium inquisitorum* (1376), and Johannes Nider's *Formicarius* (1437–38) help shape Nordic views about magic and its practitioners. Likewise, the canonical and penitential writings of such important figures as Ivo of Chartres and Burchard of Worms were well known in Scandinavia.[53] On the other side of the diaphanous membrane separating elite from nonelite attitudes were, of course, complex systems of traditional beliefs. These magical practices and views were by no means uniformly distributed with respect to region, livelihood, gender, status, or personal predilection, nor were they immutable entities: the charm magic and other activities of Nordic "witches" were as subject to mutation and renewal over time as are any set of customary rites, especially ones that are not monitored by a centralized authority.

The degree to which specimens of medieval magic are to be understood as residues of paganism has been much bruited about in recent years.[54] The notion that "all tradition is change" is widely accepted in folklore studies, and the truth of that idea is as relevant to the study of post-Conversion relics of Old Norse religion as it is to other areas of customary behavior.[55] If such practices do not continue to be relevant, why would anyone continue to perform them, as one noted scholar in the field has asked, and the student of medieval folklore would do well to keep that thought in mind as much as does the student of contemporary folklife.[56]

Still, in the case of the medieval Scandinavian world, although one may reasonably debate the accuracy with which a particular Old Norse belief or practice has been described and preserved, or the way modern scholarship has interpreted such phenomena, that there existed well into the Middle Ages practices and narratives whose roots can be traced back to pre-Christian times seems so far beyond question as to be well outside the grasp of even the most ardent Christian triumphalist or other skeptic.[57] At the same time, it would be naïve to assume that elements of pagan magic, sorcery, and witchcraft simply continued to exist for centuries, completely unaltered by their Christian contexts, or, more especially, by the Christians, even if only nominally so, who used such charms or passed other sorts of numinous knowledge along to subsequent generations.[58] Neither chunks of undigested paganism nor fantasies cut from whole cloth, magic and witchcraft in the Nordic Middle Ages were constructed both "from below" by a populace (including elites) that regularly employed them in their daily lives and "from above" by church authorities and others who feared, described, defined, and prosecuted them—and from whom, anything but incidentally, we get much of our information.

As to the terms used in this study, the broadest is surely "magic." As will precipitate out of many of the discussions that follow, I am hard-pressed to see in exoteric terms much essential difference between the magic elite members of society believed was being used by their social inferiors,[59] even though they may have preferred to call these activities "superstitions," "errors," and so on, and the kinds of magic they themselves venerated, which they would call "miracles."[60]

Naturally there were critical differences between these two categories, critical at least in the minds of church authorities, based on the source of power that made them effective. A truism, as appropriate to the medieval way of thinking as it is of much modern scholarship, is that practitioners of magic—sorcerers, witches, cunning folk, and so on—manipulate that power, command it, ordering the source of power to do the performer's will, whereas the religious person comes as a supplicant, praying to the source of power. Writing of the first type, Valerie Flint notes, "Magic may be said to be the exercise of a preternatural control over nature by human beings, with the assistance of forces more powerful than they."[61]

The latter part of Flint's formulation conforms to the idea that the magical practitioner commands these forces and hints at one of the most important aspects of the Catholic Church's perspective on magic as a theological issue in the Middle Ages: the *daemones*, those morally ambiguous spirits of antiquity, have been collapsed with the biblical notion of the fallen angels.[62] The devil (*diabolus*) is principal among them and thus the prince of demons.[63] In the minds of the church, these demonic forces become the source of power for medieval magicians and thus also the source of most accusations of witchcraft, where it is equated with heresy.[64] Occasionally, the juxtaposition is quite straightforward: in an Old Swedish legendary, translated from foreign sources, for example, a pagan magician confronting a Christian commands (*biudher*) his devils to bind the saint, whereas the saint prays (or asks [*badh*]) for help from God's angels.[65]

Indeed, as we will see, formulations among surviving Nordic charm magic fit the "manipulation versus supplication" model, with the imperative form of the verb, not asking but rather commanding. So, for example, "I exhort you, Óðinn, with heathendom, the greatest of fiends; assent to this; *tell me . . .*," as one Norwegian sorcerer carves in runes in attempting to discover the identity of a thief.[66] The command to "tell me" (*seg mér*) is repeated no fewer than three times in the inscription. The question is not purely the technical matter of what form of the verb is used—after all, the imperative can certainly be seen in Christian runic inscriptions as well (e.g., part of N 289 M reads, "Lord Jesus Christ, who is both God and man, *hear* my invocation . . ." [*drottinn jesus kristr sa er bæði er guð ok maðr heyr akall mitt . . .*]), and such forms were common in the Latin mass.[67] The use of honorifics and introductory phrases (*Te rogamus*), however, indicate a marked if ineffable difference in expectation and attitude.

Distinguishing between magic, on the one hand, and religion, on the other, by reference to this notion of "commanding" versus "imploring" is one held within the church from the time of the patristic writers (e.g., Augustine). It is also the most frequent means that scholarship of the last century and a half has used to distinguish the two categories. The modern parameters of this discussion were set in the late nineteenth and early twentieth centuries with an eye toward the interrelated character of magic, science, and religion.[68] Frazer, one of the most influential figures in the discussion, in extending Tylor's earlier views, argues that these concepts were to be understood historically with an evolutionary perspective: magic is perceived as a kind of faulty reasoning about causality, which over time is replaced by religion, and that, in turn, gives way to science.[69]

A different approach can be seen in the more socially oriented perspective taken by Malinowski, in line with the earlier work of Durkheim and Mauss. Famously living among the Trobriand Islanders, Malinowski urges an understanding of magic that is less evolutionary and that focuses instead on function. Toward that end, he sees magic as a result of anxiety: in situations where danger is present, technology stressed, and the outcome uncertain, magic addresses a psychological need. Magical beliefs, spells, and so on fill, as he wrote, "those gaps and breaches left in the ever imperfect wall of culture which [man] erects between himself and the besetting temptations and dangers of his destiny."[70]

Considerations of the magic-religion-science triad have since the early twentieth century been carried out with these two opposing perspectives, Frazer's and Malinowski's, keenly in mind. Writing in the influential *Encyclopedia of the Social Sciences*, Ruth Benedict argues, "Magic is essentially mechanistic; it is a manipulation of the external world by techniques and formulae that operate automatically. Frazer names it therefore the science of primitive man. Both magic and science are technologies, capable of being summed up in formulae and rules of procedure [. . .] although both magic and science are bodies of techniques, they are techniques directed to the manipulation of two incompatible worlds. . . ."[71] By two incompatible worlds, of course, Benedict refers to the natural world and the supernatural world. Writing in the successor encyclopedia three decades later, Nur Yalman insightfully captured the essence of the debate by noting, "The core of the magical act rests on empirically untested belief and is an effort at control—the first aspect distinguishes it from science, the second from religion."[72]

I find compelling a proposal made by Rosalie and Murray Wax that, I believe, fits the evidence of medieval Scandinavian notions of magic: in a series of articles, the Waxes proposed a different kind of paradigm to account for the category we call "magic."[73] In their "The Magical World View," the Waxes make a case for viewing the continuum of magic-religion in a manner quite different from the traditional manipulation versus supplication division: "Has our understanding been advanced by the attempted distinction between manipulation and supplication? We think not. The facts are that the cultic practices of the magical world exhibit a variety of relationships to beings of Power. Sometimes these are supplicative; sometimes manipulative; sometimes a forthright embodiment of kinship reciprocities; and so on."[74] Their basic premise, that the relationship to "Power," is what matters, strikes me as a highly relevant concept in considering the lingering acts of paganism, perceptions of syncretism, and so on that we witness in the medieval Nordic record. Power, here essentially synonymous with effectiveness, is surely what magical practitioners sought, not theological purity.

With respect to the third member of this group, science, it is important to bear in mind that, in the Middle Ages, what was understood as a form of natural science does not always appear that way to modern observers. In that context, Kieckhefer concludes that "intellectuals in medieval Europe recognized two forms of magic: natural and demonic. Natural magic was not distinct from science, but rather a branch of science. It was the science that dealt with 'occult virtues' (or hidden powers) within nature. Demonic magic was not distinct from religion, but rather a perversion of religion. It was religion that turned away from God and toward demons for their help in human affairs."[75]

Finally, a brief word or two about the terms "sorcery" and "witchcraft": one can, following a well-established tradition in anthropological usage, argue that the basis of the former has to do with its uses of the magical toolkit, its learned character, and so on while the latter is associated with those who possess a more intuitive power to harm others.[76] I believe, however, that when these terms are used in standard English, it is very difficult to escape a certain gender bias: in our hearts, we recognize that a sorcerer "is" a man and a witch a woman, historical realities, our intellectual dispositions, and a stream of scholarship notwithstanding.[77] The point is that it is difficult for us to escape the way we use these terms in contemporary speech. I have for the most part looked to acknowledge the gender questions involved by using the two terms, if not as equivalents, then at least with keen awareness of this problem, noting gender marking in the original languages where it is important. In my mind, a witch, or a sorcerer, whatever her or his magical kit, was an individual who in the minds of contemporaries had and used special knowledge that allowed him or her access to abnormal or increased amounts of Power (to employ the Waxes' orthographic convention). The definition of witchcraft is, in the end, a dynamic human perception rather than a bounded entity; that is, its meaning derives most importantly from behaviors that were regarded as acts of witchcraft rather than from the appearance or other attributes of individuals believed to be witches. To do otherwise, of course, leads to all the stereotypical portrayals of witches—the hag, the seductress, conical hats, black cats, and all that—a perspective that also has its place in discussions of this sort, to be sure.

A useful definition of witchcraft takes its principal cues from the social interactionism associated with Victor Turner's work in Africa.[78] At its core, a definition based on this perspective is, to exploit Turner's evocative expression, dynamic rather than static, that is, one might say that it is composed of verbs rather than adjectives and nouns—"she killed," "he cursed," or "they poisoned," rather than assemblages of "eye of newt and toe of frog" and other ingredients or personal and often physical characteristics such a pendulous breasts.

And this view comports well with medieval perspectives too: in an Old

Swedish translation of Bernhard of Clairvaux (1091–1153), for example, it is said that the sin of witchcraft and witches, specifically female witches, is resistance or opposition (*genstridh*) to obedience, underscoring the idea that it was behavior rather than articles or attributes that defined the term.[79] Similarly, medieval Latin usage commonly employed the term *maleficium* to designate witchcraft, a term that derives from 'evil doing.' The same fundamental pattern accounts for many of the words used in Old Norse for those who practice magic, male and female (e.g., *fordæðumaðr, gerningakona*), which are often built on *dáð* 'deed' or *gerning* 'act, doing, deed' (> *gerningar* 'witchcraft'). Exactly what medieval Nordic witches, sorcerers, and cunning folk were thought to do, for good or for ill, both by their communities and by church authorities, is the topic of the rest of this study.

Chapter 1

Witchcraft and the Past

What sort of information is useful for the study of medieval witchcraft? More to the point, perhaps, what sort of evidence is not? Church statutes, amulets, court records, runic inscriptions, pictorial representations of witches, and so on all have their parts to play. Interpreting bygone cultures clearly requires us to have access to "data," the information-laden detritus that history capriciously bequeaths to us. Having collected it, scholars grandly organize these materials into what we trust are sensible taxonomies and refer to the results with all-too-obvious high hopes as "databases" and the like. And as we sift for meaningful patterns in what are more realistically called our "data *middens*," mounds of serendipitously preserved intelligence, what images of magic and witchcraft precipitate out?

Frankly, the very randomness of our information can create peculiar pictures. To take an example from our own world, how might a future group of scholars, many millennia from now, understand the state of Christianity in the twenty-first century if their "data midden" consisted solely of several fundamentalist hymnals, assorted Orthodox icons, a collection of papal bulls, a Christmas wreath, a recording of the *Missa Luba*, Thomas Aquinas's *Summa Theologica*, a well-preserved cathedral, a King James translation of the Bible, a U.S. dollar bill with the legend "In God We Trust," Anton LaVey's *The Satanic Bible*, and a decorated Easter egg? Would our future colleagues not be tempted to force some contrived interpretation on these diverse and eclectic materials, torturing them into a harmonious narrative that might make sense to them (and appear to be consistent with the data), but strike any living observer today as absurd?

An impossible example? Perhaps, but the problem it presents very much resembles our situation in dealing with aspects of spiritual life in medieval

Scandinavia. In the case of the present study, the resources available to us are not unlike the situation faced by our hypothetical future students of twenty-first-century Christianity in that, like them, we are dealing with a chorus composed of many different voices, with a far less centrally harmonized libretto in the pre-Christian era. Studies of medieval popular culture, and medieval popular religion in particular, frequently note different sociological layers—generally bifurcated into elite versus nonelite. Even this view, which sees, as one scholar summarizes it, "two distinct cultures, the one clerical and bookish, the other popular, oral and customary, the first accessible through traditional intellectual and spiritual categories, the second mainly through cultural anthropology and comparative religions," fails to appreciate adequately the complexity of the systems under discussion.[1] How then do the religious systems and demographics of medieval Scandinavia impinge on our—and its—understanding of witchcraft?

The Cultures, the Sources, and the Method

Given the monolithic stereotype of Scandinavia, it is important to underscore the rich diversity of the medieval Nordic world, an area that spanned much of Northern Europe, including Greenland, Iceland, and the Faroes, of course, but also Shetland and parts of insular and coastal Scotland; it also included modern-day Norway, Denmark, and Sweden, and Gotland to be sure, but also parts of coastal Finland and other areas around the Baltic littoral, and extended south into modern Germany. Complex not only in geography but also in cultural terms, late medieval Scandinavia possessed both Alpine and maritime economies, rich farmlands, mines, courts, international trading centers, remote valleys, and isolated farms, and the people, foreign-born and native, speakers of various Germanic, Finnic, and Balto-Slavic dialects, to go with them.[2]

In brief, the political history of Scandinavia in the later Middle Ages can be characterized as one in which a period of growing Norwegian influence becomes one of rapidly expanding Danish hegemony, followed by a century-long effort by Sweden-Finland to free itself from this arrangement, a feat finally managed in the 1520s.[3] By the late thirteenth century, a muscular Norway had control of Iceland, Greenland, the Faroes, Shetland, and Orkney and wrestled with Scotland over its continued possession of the Hebrides—it is indicative of the period that King Hákon Hákonarson died in Orkney in

1263, following a mostly inconclusive invasion of Scotland over the very issue of the Hebrides. Marriages arranged between the various Scandinavian royal houses led to the birth of Magnus Eriksson, son of the powerful Swedish duke, Erik Magnusson, and Ingibjǫrg, the daughter of King Hákon of Norway.

Magnus thus technically became king of Sweden and Norway throughout much of the fourteenth century, followed by a brief period during which Sweden was governed by Albrecht von Mecklenburg. Growing German influence, especially from cities like Lübeck through their role in the Hanseatic League, was an important factor in many of the political, linguistic, and cultural developments of late medieval Scandinavia, rivaled in significance only by the mid-fourteenth-century arrival of the Black Death. Through dynastic marriage arrangements, political upheavals, and a series of deaths, claims to all three Nordic crowns could be made toward the end of the fourteenth century by Margarethe of Denmark, under whose influence the so-called Union of Kalmar was forged in 1397, in theory creating a united political entity of Scandinavia under a single monarch. The history of the fifteenth century is largely framed by the struggles of Sweden-Finland to wrest its independence from the Danish crown, something finally accomplished under Gustav Vasa's leadership in 1523.[4]

The impignoration to Scotland of Orkney in 1468, followed in 1469 by the similar mortgaging of Shetland, further diminished the Danish empire and removed from the Nordic world the last vestiges of its former possessions in the British Isles. By the end of the medieval period, the Nordic world thus consisted of a Swedish-Finnish kingdom and a still very impressive Danish kingdom, including Norway, Iceland, and the Faroes. Although certain provinces were hotly contested, especially border areas such as Skåne and Bohuslän, for the most part these areas did not take their present places on the political map until the seventeenth century; Gotland, traditionally a broadly autonomous region within the Swedish orbit, fell to Denmark in 1361 and did not come under Swedish rule again until 1645.[5]

Trade ensured lively communications between such increasingly important Nordic emporia as Bergen, Copenhagen, and Stockholm, and their Dutch, British, German, and other Baltic counterparts.[6] With the conversion to Christianity came the rapid growth of a church infrastructure and religious houses, and Scandinavia too took its place among the recently converted in venerating local saints—for example, Saint Knútr and Saint Knútr Lavard in Denmark; Saint Magnús in Orkney; Saint Þorlákr in Iceland; Saint Óláfr in

Norway; Saint Sigfrid, Saint Botvid, and Saint Erik in Sweden; and Saint Henry in Finland—as well the remarkable Saint Birgitta of Sweden (1303–37), who was officially canonized.[7] The image of daily life that emerges from, for example, the original and translated (and almost always also transformed) literature of the Nordic Middle Ages is extremely rich and can give modern readers a vibrant sense of that world.[8]

For all the diversity apparent in the Nordic world, there exists a modern tendency to divide its population along simple lines into a ruling elite, on the one hand, and an unlettered peasantry, on the other, institutional versus noninstitutional entities (also often vicarial representatives for Christian and pagan, one suspects, and a host of other dyads necessary for the description of medieval Scandinavia, such as noninsular and insular). Although not without its advantages, this view of the Middle Ages tends to assume, for example, that a medieval fisherman believed in and practiced magic, whereas a monk did not. In all likelihood, both of them did.

This elite versus nonelite model of the medieval world has been criticized and challenged in recent years, and instead of a simple bifurcation between clerical and lay, elite and popular, and so on we should bear in mind that a more nuanced and synthetic image comes by envisioning individuals in terms of their relation to a number of factors, not just those two poles.[9] The results provide a more rounded and realistic view of lived lives and do not automatically slot individuals into proscribed behaviors, allowing us to see from our materials that priests, princes, and wealthy merchants, for example, were just as capable of a "magical worldview" as farmers, laborers, and prostitutes.[10]

In fact, the Nordic world is rich in resources for the student of medieval popular culture, perhaps especially where witchcraft is concerned: a wide array of nonnormative texts provide insights into how the image of the witch was constructed in the Scandinavian world, providing opportunities for us to see realities that go beyond condemnations of magic and its practitioners by authors representing church and state.[11] Broadly speaking, we look to either material objects, such as paintings and talismans, or narratives, that is, texts and monuments in one sense or another, for our knowledge. About all of these materials—laws, literature, historical chronicles, synodal statutes, letters, skaldic poems, sermons, charms, prayers, the visual arts—the same questions need to be asked: not just when and where they were written, but also for whom, to what purpose, under what sponsorship, and so on. Among the documents most influential in shaping attitudes toward witchcraft, of course, were those authored by, for, and within the church. Prohibitions against witchcraft and magic were developed and promulgated first and foremost by this tissue-thin—if deeply influential—segment of society, together with secular authorities, and it is overwhelmingly their views that inform standard visions of medieval Nordic witchcraft. But in addition to these institutional images of witchcraft, it is important to keep in mind opportunities to discover additional perspectives and attitudes, ones that reflect the full spectrum of society, not just its apex of educated elites.[12]

Despite modern assumptions about the uniform vision that Christianity had of witchcraft, ecclesiastical works are no more monolithic than other forms of narratives. Hagiographies, spiritual literature in the vernacular, homilies, miracle collections, prayer books, synodal statutes, and penitentials collectively suggest trends in medieval thinking about magic and witchcraft among learned ecclesiastics but do not present a uniform impression. For their part, legal texts represent an area with considerable overlap between church and state: the reticulation between these two poles of authority was great at the time the materials were codified, and many of the medieval Nordic law codes specifically include sections relating to religious life (e.g., kyrkobalker).[13]

An attractive nuisance I hope to have avoided in working with these materials is the assumption that the more official the source of our information, the more its data should be trusted. Scholarship has found this caution to be especially true of such presumed gateways to truth as court documents, whether ecclesiastical or secular, to which a modern audience naturally attaches significant probative value.[14] In addition to these official narratives, a diverse network of unofficial sources of information exists, a designation not intended to deny the influence of the church, either direct or indirect, on the materials. Paramount among these sources are the Icelandic sagas, to which may be added a wide array of other resources, including runic inscriptions and other evidence of charm magic. In many respects, the goal of reconstructing medieval mentalities has advantages over studies that want to establish historical facts, as for our purposes even texts patently invented and fabulous can be of great interest; moreover, their lack of historical verisimilitude need not only fail to concern us but can even be a help, insofar as they allow us into the thought world of medieval Northern Europe.[15]

With the possible exception of the archaeological record, perhaps our best and most direct indication of prevailing, popular views of witchcraft and magic in the immediate post-Conversion era is to be found, not among the justly celebrated literary texts of medieval Iceland (in which category one might reasonably include large numbers of the mythological works), but rather among the early laws of Scandinavia. None of these codes, at least in the form in which we have them, is old enough to provide direct testimony on the eleventh century, but several of them may have originated soon after the Conversion. Many of them specifically legislate against pagan practices and may be among our most reliable opportunities to see the raw data of early Nordic witchcraft, that is, views about this world that have not been masticated by the brilliance and narrative purposes of later Icelandic saga writers.

Thus, for example, the statutes governing the western fjord area of Norway, *Gulaþingslǫg* (*The Law of Gulaþing*), preserved mainly in thirteenth-century manuscripts but believed to have been recorded first a century earlier and to have even older oral roots, hint broadly in this direction. In a section called "Concerning Prophecy and Witchcraft" (*Um spár oc um galldra*), the law declares that people should believe in neither "soothsaying, witchcraft nor maleficence" (*spám ne golldrum ne gerningum illum*) and goes on to enumerate penalties for those who harbor such beliefs or practice them.[16]

Admonitions of this sort, despite their general wording, are nevertheless a good indication of the negative attitudes held by elite society in medieval Christian Norway toward the practice of witchcraft and sorcery but in themselves detail little about the nature of such beliefs and behavior.[17] Something closer to such an itemized litany of practices appears in the law code for the Oslo fjord area, the Borgarþing laws, which are, like the Gulaþing code, datable to the mid-twelfth century, although preserved only in later, mainly early fourteenth-century, manuscripts:

> II. 25. But if a woman bites off a finger or toe from her child and does that [in order to secure] long life, she is fined 3 marks. The worst witch is she who destroys a man or woman or child or cow or calf. And if sorcery is found in bedding or bolster, the hair of a man, or nails or frog feet or other talismans which are thought wont in witchcraft, then a charge may be made[. . . .] That is a felony if one sits out and rouses trolls thereby. That is a felony if one kills oneself. That is also a felony if one journeys to Finnmark for soothsaying.[18]

This and related texts are taken up in later chapters, but at this juncture suffice it to say that this enumeration of charges connected with the practice of *fordæðuskapr* 'witchcraft', 'sorcery' is striking, especially given the specificity of the charges. It suggests an active tradition of manipulating the universe through charm magic and rituals.

To reiterate an earlier point, the existence of a law of this sort from the early era of Christianity in Norway against such behavior does not guarantee that such activities were actually practiced in the earlier pagan world or that they continued to exist in the post-Conversion world of medieval Norway. Still, few would doubt that we can indeed read out of these texts practices and beliefs (whether "real" or invented) that were current at the time the text was written—and that a well-developed witchcraft complex existed already in the earliest periods from which we possess reliable textual data from medieval Scandinavia.[19]

A further important window onto that world, and one that inherently nullifies the problems of contemporaneousness and cultural distance that attach themselves to textual sources, is provided by the archaeological record. And the attention of archaeologists is increasingly turning to matters of spiritual culture in the Nordic world.[20] Finally, after years of working in relatively atomistic parallel universes, such necessarily interrelated fields as folklore, history, philology, and archaeology are once again recognizing the advantages of a comprehensive approach to such subjects as witchcraft, magic, and religion, what Neil Price, in the most important study of this phenomenon to date, calls "an archaeology of the Viking mind."[21]

Yet those interested mainly in texts are not entirely without a direct, if often enigmatic, material image of pagan spiritual life, namely, the runic inscriptions that hark from both the pre-Christian and Christian eras. But these sources, if direct, are nevertheless not without their troubles, as specialists in the field are wont to remind us.[22] Key to our understanding is the fact that although the content of certain inscriptions may correctly be understood as relating to the magico-religious world of pre-Christian and Christian Scandinavians, the writing itself is no more or less "charged" than it would be if it were written in a Latin script on vellum.

The inference that certain runic inscriptions derive from magical practices does not require great leaps of faith: to take a Viking Age example, the ninth-century Nørre Nærå stone (DR 211), from the Danish island of Fyn (Odense amt), is one of a number of so-called grave binding runic inscriptions. Its imprecation apparently calls on the dead to remain still and not to wander: "Make good use of the monument! Þormundr."[23] No mere bit of well-wishing or celebration of a relationship to the deceased, this monument intends to prevent the dead man from coming back and haunting the living.

It is a form of charm magic writ large. The practice of charm magic can also be seen in a small twelfth-century amulet from the Swedish province of Västergötland: "(I) practice witchcraft against the spirit, against the walking (spirit), against the riding, against the running, against the sitting, against the sinking, against the travelling, against the flying. Everything shall [lose] its vitality and die."[24] The linguistic and runic forms of the amulet suggest that it comes from the same era as the Christianization process in this region of Sweden; moreover, it was found in the cemetery of a church likely to have been contemporary with it.[25] Thus it is important to recognize that we cannot know for certain whether we are here dealing with a charm that should be understood against a pagan or Christian background. Very likely it is a transitional monument, that is, one whose basic form harks back to the pagan era but whose user may well have been a Christian, an appropriately ambiguous state of affairs as we consider the complexity of medieval Nordic society and the resources it offers us for research.[26]

So, how should we approach such confoundingly ambiguous medieval evidence? Modern interpretations of European witchcraft have naturally been formed in their own intellectual context, often reflecting the views of the period in which a given study is produced.[27] Thus early students, who found the possibility of witchcraft actually existing impossible, could see in the witch-hunts little more than mass hysteria, yet more recent views have increasingly teased out of the same accusations of witchcraft the empowerment of early modern women.[28] A social context for knowledge is natural, and certainly in recent decades, studies of historical witchcraft have needed to be cognizant of a variety of factors that condition our understanding.[29]

An area of inquiry particularly well suited to an investigation of this sort, of course, is folklore. Maximizing the opportunities offered by this fertile intersection of the humanities and social sciences has not been without its challenges in modern scholarship, especially to the degree that folklore (or folkloristics, as some prefer) is often pared away from its adjacent fields. This problem is common in Anglophone scholarship, but by no means limited to that world. Indeed, this debate is one that has had far-reaching effects in the Nordic world, a cultural region that has itself played a critical role in the shaping of folklore studies.[30] In the context of a study largely concerned with medieval folklore, especially Nordic concepts of magic and witchcraft, a collection of essays by the preeminent Nordic folklorist concerned with this issue, Dag Strömbäck, is worth noting. Published as *Folklore och filologi* (*Folklore and Philology*), the author introduced the collection with the comment that they, and he, belonged to that folklore school which traced itself back to Moltke Moe in Norway and Axel Olrik in Denmark.[31] Strömbäck subsequently spelled out what he meant by noting his dedication to "the Scandinavian philological discipline and the critical-historical method," which he describes as "the approach which interweaves historical fact, philological interpretation and textual criticism. . . ."[32]

That one can approach the folklore of the bygone Scandinavian world, the medieval period in particular, through the tools of contemporary folkloristics is, as Strömbäck notes, an important issue.[33] The history of folklore scholarship in Scandinavia, a region beset by issues of colonialism and postcolonialism, has been one conditioned by nation-building and nationalism, most obviously in the cases of Finland, Iceland, and Norway, but also true elsewhere.[34] And, indeed, many, perhaps even most, cultural institutions and academic pursuits at the end of the nineteenth century were harnessed to the same nationalistic yoke, even the seemingly rarified disputes about such topics as the character of Icelandic saga origins (i.e., the so-called *Freiprosa* vs. *Buchprosa* debate), the nature of the Nordic ballad, and the dissemination of folktales. Out of the subsequent exchanges surrounding these issues, von Sydow noted that "collaboration between philology and the study of folklore is of supreme importance. Philologists can produce much material of very great value to folklore research[. . . .] But the oral material is no less important for placing the contents of the ancient sources in the living whole to which they belong. . . ."[35] This dictum is of obvious importance to the study of medieval witchcraft, with its copious and highly variegated sources of information.

On the current relationship between folklore and philology, Richard Bauman suggests the philological model of the past as one possible charter for the future of folklore: "The enduring importance of the intellectual problems that the philological synthesis was forged to address constitutes a productive basis on which we as folklorists might orient ourselves to our cognate fields and disciplines."[36] In a characteristically more strident manner, von Sydow argued much the same thing when he wrote that it was, after all, philologists who had discovered folklore's scientific value and that mutual cooperation ought to be the standard relationship between the two disciplines, especially as they are each other's "necessary assistants."[37] One can easily imagine that the same thing is true of "ancillary" fields such as history, sociology, and anthropology.

Perhaps best represented by Jacques Le Goff—in particular his inclusive view of how folklore should figure into our understanding of the Middle Ages—we have in recent decades entered into a new understanding of the field of medieval folkloristics.[38] It can no longer be understood as merely a branch of textual criticism but as something of an archaeology of past mentalities and a recontextualization of performance practices.[39] This highly transdisciplinary view, which looks to integrate the methodologies and strategies of a number of fields, is the modern understanding I take to what the field of folklore can mean to the study of medieval witchcraft and magic and, more generally, medieval cultural history.[40]

Pagan Scandinavia and the Conversion

Magic in pagan Scandinavia, as it has been reconstructed from the writings of foreign observers, the archaeological record, and—not least—the texts written in cultures tracing their ancestry back to the Viking world (most prominently, Iceland), suggests that many people were able to call on, and even command, supernatural powers. After the Conversion, Christian observers associated these activities with the church's evolving image of witchcraft and sorcery. Beyond such simple assumptions, however, there is little we can be certain of regarding the belief complexes, religious practices, and mythological systems from this early period, as they overwhelmingly come to us from several hundred years after the acceptance of Christianity. What sort of picture can we confidently draw about the world of Nordic magic before the widespread adoption of Christianity? And beyond the attempt to reconstruct Scandinavian paganism, how does magic "work" in the medieval Christian world, not only in the most transparent sense of the term, but also in the way in which magic itself becomes a kind of metalanguage for communicating perceptions and important ideas about what it meant to be a pagan or a Christian?

This problem of perception, especially where the so-called Frazerian triptych is concerned (i.e., magic, science, and religion), can be illustrated by a few examples drawn from medieval Nordic leechbooks.[41] One recommends that the gall of a black dog, or of a particular kind of fish, be burned in a wooden vessel and used as a remedy against witchcraft and diabolical influences.[42] A Danish formula against wantonness calls for a potion made of the leaves of a plant mixed with liquid, although what makes it stand out is the instruction that the brew should be blended while the *Pater noster* is being "read."[43] Modern readers naturally assume that recipes of this sort are a form of magic.

But how would medieval users have understood such practices? If a practitioner were to intone phrases invoking a pagan god or the Christian deity while burning the fish gall, for example, would we understand it as a religious practice? Or if the fumes of the gall were believed to have a specific chemical or pharmacological purpose, should we then understand this practice as a kind of primitive science? And are the answers we give to these queries merely elusive matters of perspective, or are they in fact hard and fast conclusions, as true in the modern context as they would have been in pre-Christian Scandinavia?

And for that matter, just what is pre-Christian Scandinavia? Christian missionary efforts in the Nordic world were diverse with respect to their points of origins and successful only over a long period of time. Taking the Swedish area as an example, the conversion effort begins by at least the early ninth century, with Ansgar's missionary ventures to Birka, but Christianity cannot be said to have been the dominant religious culture until well into the eleventh century, perhaps even later.[44] In 1075, for example, the heathen Swedes are said to have deposed their Christian king and replaced him with his pagan brother-in-law, "Sacrifice-Sveinn" (Blót-Sveinn). Traditions about events of this sort eventually gave rise to an Icelandic literary portrait of Sweden in later centuries as a backward, heathen holdout.[45] Although we may look with deep suspicion on the reliability of these later accounts, just how long the deep-rooted pre-Christian practices associated with such tales may in fact have continued in remote districts will no doubt remain an area of unresolved dispute for some time to come.

After all, it is precisely from the image of rural—and thus, from the perspective of the dominant society, culturally peripheral—inhabitants that the two words most commonly used in English for people holding on to their pre-Christian religion are often said to be fashioned: "pagan" (derived ultimately from Latin *pāgus* 'country, rural district') and "heathen" (possibly derived from Old English *hæð* 'untilled, uncultivated land').[46]

Language is vital but cannot, of course, tell us everything. Archaeology, and its focus on material culture, has certainly shown itself to be of paramount importance and is providing exciting and valuable new vistas from which to view witchcraft and related magical practices in these preliterary periods.[47] So too have recent investigations utilizing the subsequent textual record,[48] perhaps especially when that record is examined comparatively, against the important backdrop of adjacent cultures, the Sámi in particular.[49] Although we assume that the complex set of late medieval Nordic beliefs relating to witches and magic evolved from (and within) native traditions under heavy influence from imported views brought by Christianity, it is important to recognize as well the probable roles played by the various Finnic peoples of Scandinavia.[50] What, then, did magic look like in the Nordic world at the time of Christianity's arrival? Although no attempt at a full account of witchcraft in those earlier periods is intended here, it is certainly helpful to have a grasp of these pre-Christian traditions. Toward these ends, this section briefly reviews several of the main deities from Norse paganism connected with magic, as well as examples of missionary efforts in Scandinavia and the ways in which the metalanguage of magic figures into them.

The modern image of pre-Christian religion in Scandinavia is one that has been drawn from non-Icelandic sources, such as Saxo's *Gesta Danorum* (*History of the Danes*), and, principally, from the literary traditions of Icelanders several centuries after the Conversion—the *Poetic edda, Snorra edda,* and the sagas, as well as the tradition of skaldic poetry (e.g., *Haustlǫng*).[51] It is difficult not to be drawn to these rich materials, with their vivid story lines and memorable characters, but at the same time, few scholars today accept at face value that these mainly thirteenth-century texts mirror with accuracy the actual belief systems of the farmers, traders, raiders, concubines, and kings of the Viking Age. Many layers of selection, interpretation, and obfuscation lie between us and that world, just as they did for the medieval Icelanders.

Thus, for example, much of the mythological material preserved in literary tradition, almost all from Iceland, focuses on the numinous and sexual exploits of Óðinn, but a variety of reasons—tied to sponsorship, the medieval Icelanders' perceptions of their history, and, not least, Óðinn's close relationship to poetry and chieftainship—may account for his popularity in these later traditions that color so greatly our perception of his importance in the lives of everyday people in the pagan world. Despite the near omnipresence of Óðinn in the texts, the evidence of theophoric place names from throughout Scandinavia, for example, strongly suggests that other gods and goddesses, including some who do not emerge distinctly from the literary sources, were very significant in the religious lives of people throughout Viking Age Scandinavia. Hence, for example, Ullr is mentioned in eddic poems and *Gesta Danorum,* but whereas he is a rare figure in the texts, the name so often forms part of the built landscape of parts of Sweden and Norway as to suggest that his worship may have extensive.[52] The lesson here is that we must constantly bear in mind the possibility that we possess a highly skewed version of Norse paganism.

Still, the preserved stories tell us something, and they frequently concentrate on the exploits of the gods Óðinn and Þórr against the *jǫtnar* 'giants' and other representatives of the Otherworld, such as the World Serpent. We are often told of the attempts by the giants to possess various goddesses, Freyja in particular. Other narratives describe such events as Freyr's acquisition of Gerðr; how the gods' citadel is built; how the two families of gods— the Vanir and the Æsir—resolve their dispute and exchange hostages; how the soteriological figure of Baldr comes to be killed; and the defeat of the current generation of gods at the final battle, *Ragnarǫk* 'fate of the gods'. Magic, too, emerges from these tales and is associated, as we shall see in detail later, with two figures in particular, Óðinn and Freyja.

Briefly, the sources paint a portrait of Óðinn as the master of magic: he shape-shifts, awakens and speaks with the dead, sees into other lands, works charms, knows how to use the magic called *seiðr* (which allows him to look into the future and inflict death, misfortune, and other harms on men), and knows the whereabouts of treasures and how to retrieve them. Freyja is portrayed as a female counterpart to Óðinn, a great offerer of sacrifices and the one who teaches the Æsir *seiðr*, a form of magic common among the Vanir. So certain does the relationship between Viking Age women and magic seem that several scholars have even sought to apply to the magical traditions of the Nordic region in the Viking Age the much earlier statement by the Roman commentator Tacitus (*Germania* 8) to the effect that women held a marked prophetic status among the various Germanic peoples, a view also reflected in Caesar's *Gallic Wars* (1.50).[53] Against a seemingly highly patriarchal pantheon, dominated in the extant narrative materials by the lusty sexual adventures and arcane knowledge confrontations of Óðinn, Þórr, and other male deities (and, where magic is concerned, spiced with the possibility of shamanistic influences), the role of females in the world of gods and humans has become an area of increased attention by scholars.[54] Of female deities, only Freyja (to a lesser degree, Frigg and Iðunn) receives much attention in the surviving texts. In assessing the saga reports about those Icelanders who practiced magic in this earlier period, some scholars have seen the gender ratio as being roughly equal; other researchers focusing on the mythological materials have emphasized the role of female deities endowed with magic as well as of saga women who wield magical powers.[55]

A telling indication of Freyja's prominence in Nordic paganism is reflected in a bit of poetic rhetoric from the history of the Conversion: just as the debate between paganism and Christianity reaches a crescendo in Iceland (AD 999), Hjalti Skeggjason publicly assails the old religion by making up a ditty, which he concludes by saying, "I consider Freyja a bitch."[56] For his blasphemy, the Icelanders outlawed Hjalti. The connection between Freyja's more frightening attributes and subsequent constructions of the witch figure is readily made, as are the transfer of her positive aspects to the Virgin Mary.[57] Although the somewhat slender mythological materials treating the goddesses may prove to be an important resource on Nordic witchcraft, the reality of later Christian mediation in selecting what has been preserved and how it is presented clearly represents an awkward impediment against employing these medieval literary texts as a direct window onto the Viking Age itself before the Conversion.[58]

A more direct view of pagan practice may be offered by recovered material objects, although these items are no more free from problems of interpretation than are texts: they are more or less randomly preserved, often recovered alternatively in paradoxically very precise and very imprecise ways and always "read" according to human designs.[59] Since the earliest recognition that such things as serendipitously discovered artifacts bore a relationship to the preserved Norse mythological texts, scholarship's understanding of pre-Christian Nordic religion has relied on archaeology. Conclusions drawn from modern scientific research at cult sites (e.g., Uppåkra in Skåne) and Icelandic temple-farms (e.g., Hofstaðir, Hrísbrú) seem to confirm just how thoroughly magic and its rituals formed part of not only pagan worship but also daily life.[60] With respect to magic in the Viking Age, recent archaeological interpretations have focused on gender, and especially transgressive gender roles, as key elements in its practice.[61]

Wary, one suspects, of the museum-*cum*-warehouse approach to archaeology and ethnography, Neil Price's exemplary study of magic and warfare in Viking Age society looks to move the discussion of daily religious life in that period well beyond a catalogue of the bric-a-brac of magic, the serendipitously preserved incunabula of day-to-day magic, and place his field closer instead to realizing what has been termed cognitive archaeology.[62] Following a close inspection of the ritual form of magic, much referred to in our later literary sources, called *seiðr*, Price compares this reconstructed magic ritual with an analogous Sámi practice called *noaidevuohta*.[63] He examines both of these rituals in the broader context of shamanism (itself a much debated term, especially when presented as a single bounded entity), of which *noaide-*

vuohta is surely an example and *seiðr* might well be, and finds confirmation for this perspective in everything from the material remains of the graves of sorceresses (*vǫlur*) to written Arabic and Norse accounts. Price argues that the magic of the Viking Age and the aggression it helped channel were bound up in the mythological figure of Óðinn, making this curiously Viking-specific form of shamanism a kind of "battle magic" and a view of reality.[64]

Price's synoptic study also offers us an explanation for one of the stranger aspects of Viking Age magic, namely, the evident use of practices with significant gender implications (*ergi*) in a society notably hostile to such notions. He reasons that acquiring effective battle magic through such gender-challenging shamanistic practices resulted in "The Viking Way" of his title.[65] Price provides us with a detailed image of what place magic had and what its practice might have looked like in the pagan era—or to put it another way, what the face of magic may have looked like when the missionary efforts in Scandinavia began in earnest.

Dating the conversion of the various regions of the Nordic world to Christianity tends to be a matter of providing the year in which ruling monarchs or leading statesmen accepted the new religion—between 965 and 985 for Denmark, around 1000 for Norway, and the same for Iceland. Although Sweden had a Christian king as early as 1008, even enthusiastic partisans would not claim it as a Christian nation for nearly another century.[66] This tendency is natural enough, for these are the dates that history, and especially those who wrote history in the Middle Ages, have bequeathed to us. But the truth is that the conversion process began much earlier than any of these dates and was surely not fully articulated throughout the Nordic world until after many more generations had passed.

No one knows with certainty, for example, the name of the first Scandinavian who actually received the *prima signatio* or converted fully to Christianity.[67] On the other hand, we can say with authority who finally, some earlier efforts notwithstanding, brought Christianity to the Nordic world: Ansgar (801–65), the so-called Apostle of the North.[68] According to his vita, Ansgar undertook his missionary activities at the behest of Scandinavian rulers, first to Denmark and then to Sweden. Perhaps the most notable aspect of Ansgar's efforts among the Danes was the education of young natives, resulting in a school with a dozen or so boys. Taking careful advantage of both political and commercial opportunities to promote Christianity, Ansgar received permission from the Danish king to build a church in Hedeby, very likely also the site of the school. Importantly, Rimbert notes that the presence of a priest brought much delight to those Danes who were already Christians, that is, he specifies, those who had been baptized in towns such as Dorstadt and Hamburg, and that this Christian entree into the Nordic world eased the prohibition against Christian merchants plying their trade in the pagan world.[69]

Ansgar's reception and missionary work in the Swedish trade center of Birka in 829 and thereafter is given detailed treatment by Rimbert, who vividly portrays the confrontation between the native and foreign faith systems. The Swedish king receives Ansgar's company well and grants them permission to preach the gospel. Their work finds favor among the Christian slaves held in Birka—their presence no doubt a key reason for the mission—as well as among some of the pagan natives, most notably an official of the town, Herigar. So devout does this convert become that Herigar is said to have had a church built on his own land. Ansgar departs, leaving behind a small, but apparently vibrant, congregation of Christians. Years later, however, pagan resentments—ascribed by Rimbert to the devil—lead to an uprising, during which one of the Christian priests is killed and the others driven away. The vita then employs several vignettes to illustrate the tribulations involved in working with the northern pagans.

In one of them, Rimbert relates a Job-like story in which miraculous, or magical, events have a central role. It concerns an important pagan's son who had taken part in the attack on the mission and secreted his portion of the loot in his father's house. Thereafter the father's fortunes decline, his herds decrease, and his son, wife, and daughter die, one after the other. Feeling that he must have offended one of the gods, the man follows local custom and consults an oracle, who casts lots and discovers that it is the god of the Christians who is angry with him because of what turns out to be a purloined book taken from the mission, a manuscript he goes to some lengths to get back into Christian hands.[70]

After several years' absence, Ansgar sends a representative to Birka, and with Herigar's help, Christian services begin anew. Now, however, there are more direct if less violent confrontations between Norse paganism and the new religion: at an assembly meeting, for example, praise for the traditional gods is mixed with reproach for Herigar for his having separated himself from the community by adopting the foreign deity. Through an important series of miracles—that is, what must have seemed to the pagan Swedes, like the earlier story of the stolen book, to be Christian magic—Herigar demonstrates the greater power of his religion.[71]

Yet, despite the tenacity of this Christian outpost, another century and a half would pass before we hear of a Swedish king being baptized; moreover, the Svea region itself would not be Christianized until some 250 years after Ansgar's mission. This point underscores a key element in the present discussion: Conversion dates presumably reflect the behavior and decisions of a few elite members of society. Given the preference of the missionaries to work top down, changes of faith and practice among the populace as a whole must have filtered in only very slowly.

An imposing monument to the conversion process is the tenth-century assemblage of rune stones and other materials at Jelling in Jutland.[72] One of the rune stones proclaims that King Haraldr made the Danes Christian.[73] However true this statement may be in the broad sense, there is little likelihood that its assertion that the king "made" (or declared legally or the like) the Danish people Christian actually speaks to the conversion experience of large numbers of Viking Age Danes: perhaps they simply followed the crown's declaration of Christianity as empty ritual observations lacking personal meaning, but just as likely, they were motivated by economic or other nonspiritual opportunities, or perhaps the Nordic experience in Anglo-Saxon England,[74] or even by opportunities for personal spiritual growth, possibly especially for women in the community.[75] Or perhaps it was none of these possibilities; perhaps the average Jutlander simply ignored the whole thing.

But one thing we do know: narratives in the Middle Ages about the conversion experience of the Danes emphasize the moment when Christian magic—a miracle—tipped the scales in favor of that religion. According to this story, as given first in Widukind's history of the Saxons, the tenth-century Danish king Haraldr Bluetooth challenges the view that Christ is the only god. Poppo accepts the challenge and is reported to have carried glowing hot iron in his hands and then shown the king that he remained unharmed. By virtue of this feat, the king converts, ordering that his subjects should thenceforth reject idols.[76] In fact, magic, often dueling pagan and Christian magic, is a frequent phenomenon in conversion tales.

The key role played by pagan magic and its practitioners in the confrontation between heathenism and Christianity, such as Rimbert describes at Birka and Widukind for Jutland, is highlighted in the life of the Norwegian missionary ruler, Óláfr Tryggvason, king of Norway from 995 to 999 (or 1000). Óláfr had been a renowned Viking in the British Isles before returning to Norway and becoming one of the figures most closely tied to its conversion to Christianity, at least in Icelandic and Norwegian traditions.[77] But among the oldest sources of information about Óláfr is Adam of Bremen's Latin history of the Hamburg-Bremen archbishopric, the see charged by the Catholic Church with the conversion of Scandinavia. Basing his narrative not only on the archives available to him in Bremen and such written sources as Rimbert's *Vita Anskarii* but also on personal interviews with King Sveinn of Denmark in the late 1060s, Adam gives us a picture of Óláfr some sixty-odd years after his death.[78]

Adam's Óláfr in *Gesta Hammaburgensis ecclesiae pontificum* (*History of the Archbishops of Hamburg-Bremen*) is a dissolute apostate, angry at God for having allowed him to be driven into exile. Not only is Óláfr's embrace of Christianity depicted as questionable, but in Óláfr's necrologue, Adam maintains—with a churchman's eye toward the topic—that the king was himself a practitioner of pagan magic, specifically an augur, a reader of lots, and a diviner of bird behavior, and known by the cognomen, Cracabben (presumably from Old Norse *krakabein* 'crow bone [or leg]').[79] Indeed, Adam reports that not only was Óláfr himself an adept of the "magical arts" (*artis magicae*), but also allowed his household to be composed of witches (*maleficos*).[80]

By contrast, later West Norse sources portray Óláfr as utterly resolute in his determination to promote Christianity in his homeland and to wipe out paganism, especially to the extent that the vitality of the heathen world can be gauged by the practice of pagan magic. In Snorri Sturluson's *Óláfs saga Tryggvasonar* (*The Saga of Óláfr Tryggvason*), for example, King Óláfr declares that all those who traffic in magic must leave the country,[81] and he then has the area searched for such *men*.[82] Having brought the sorcerers together, the king provides them with strong drink at a feast and then has the building set ablaze. All of the sorcerers are killed except for Eyvindr kelda, whose grandfather, Rǫgnvaldr réttilbeini, had also been a witch and had been likewise killed through a "burning in."[83] Eyvindr, described as a practitioner of *seiðr* and very learned in witchcraft (*seiðmaðr ok allmjǫk fjǫlkunnigr*), tauntingly sends word of his escape back to King Óláfr.[84]

Later, as the king is about to celebrate Easter, Eyvindr arrives with a fully equipped warship manned by a crew composed entirely of witches (*seiðmenn ok annat fjǫlkyngisfólk*). They approach the king's quarters under the cover of magic, but as they do so dawn breaks, and the magical darkness that had made them invisible now envelopes and confuses them.[85] King Óláfr's troops capture the sorcerers, and the king orders that they be taken and bound on a skerry, where Eyvindr and the other witches are drowned with the incoming tide. It should be noted that from a narrative perspective, the principal importance of this incident is to establish the framework for the immediately following episodes, in which the king is first confronted by, and defeats, the pagan deity Óðinn and subsequently compels the recalcitrant franklins of Þrándheimr to accept Christianity. Essentially the same story about Eyvindr and Óláfr—with an even more heightened confrontation between paganism and Christianity than in Snorri's version—is recounted in the *Óláfs saga Tryggvasonar en mesta* (*The Longer Saga of Óláfr Tryggvason*).[86] The image of King Óláfr as a fierce missionary hero thus emerges in many West Norse sources, including *Ágrip af Noregskonunga sǫgum* (*A Synoptic History of the Kings of Norway*) and *Fagrskinna*, another panorama of Norwegian history.[87]

It would be difficult indeed to reconcile the distinctly disparate images of Óláfr Tryggvason textual history offers us.[88] If we are to coax meaning out of the dislocation created by the dueling pictures of Óláfr the grudging apostate and Óláfr the fiery zealot, we may want to take a page from anthropology's field notes: ethnography long ago demonstrated how, given similar instances of opposing narratives among living peoples, reconciling antipodal points of view can be perhaps precisely the wrong approach. Writing of exactly this kind of conundrum in Kachin society with competing origin myths, Edmund Leach notes, "Neither of these versions can be said to be more correct than the other [. . . .] Now, in the past, Kachin ethnographers have never appreciated this point. They have regarded tradition as a species of badly recorded history. When they have found inconsistencies in the record, they have felt justified in selecting that version which seemed most likely to be 'true' or even in inventing parts of the story which appeared to be missing."[89]

How often do philologists, historians, folklorists, and other scholars working in nonliving traditions commit this same crime against their data by imposing a unifying meaning without recognizing either the implicit debate involved or, as in this instance, the idiom of that argument?[90] In the case of the Kachin, Leach is able to show how the conflicting narrative traditions of competing clans are not usefully explained if they are merely viewed as factual errors in need of straightening out, but rather shed light only when they are understood as part of a larger dialogue: "It is a language of argument, not a chorus of harmony."[91]

The element common to both Adam's eleventh-century presentation and the later Icelandic tradition is the way both narratives seize on and valorize pagan magic as a means of demonstrating Óláfr's relationship to Christianity, tepid as it is in the one case in which Óláfr is a magician, and zealous as it is in the other when he rids the land of such people.[92] It is a fair supposition that neither the West Norse nor the Dano-German portrayal of Óláfr reflects deep concern for historical verisimilitude, and we can safely assume that both portraits tell us less about the historical Óláfr than they do about how the various authors responded to complex cultural forces. What matters here is the idiom the two traditions have selected for this implicit debate—the metalinguistics of witchcraft and magic.

Magical acts, whether Christian miracles or pagan divination rituals, draw, after all, on a common experiential foundation, what one noted scholar characterized as "a region in which the evidently real and the imaginary seem to overlap . . . ," an area where prospective converts and evangelists shared concepts, beliefs, and perhaps even language.[93] Magic may not only have been useful when it was believed to have invoked the supernatural or "worked" in other ways, but was, as the examples of Herigar, Óláfr Tryggvason, and many other conversion histories show, also valuable for its implicit communicative value. Or, as one might express this idea, magic is not only good to practice but also good to think with.[94]

In Christianity's confrontation with paganism, magic was fraught with possibilities, and by no means were all of them negative from the church's point of view. True, its practice was a palpable embodiment of heathen worship, and as such, magic, at least magic that called on the old gods, needed to be eradicated. Yet the concept of magic also embodied a kind of discourse, or at least the possibility of discourse, between pagan and Christian, a metalanguage that could communicate complex ideologies on a high plain.[95] Magic as the basis for a system of communication between pagans and Christians should not be surprising. In fact, the binary character of the Christian magic–pagan magic dyad represented a highly productive way to think about the special nature and value of magic and religion in the no-man's-land of turn-of-the-millennium conversion activities.[96]

Like other paired cultural categories that constitute society's system of signs, pagan and Christian magic overlap significantly yet also differ markedly. Speaking to how cultures employ such conceptual categories, Leach elsewhere notes, "Certain binary concepts are part of man's nature—e.g., men and women are alike in one sense yet opposite and interdependent in another; the right hand and the left are, likewise, equal and opposite, yet related."[97] The value of such binaries derives from the fact that they are critical to humanity's capacity for symbolic thought. A miracle about a drenching rain storm, such as Rimbert recounts, during which the pagans are soaked and the Christian Herigar remains dry, is thus not a flaccid story of meteorological one-upsmanship, as it may seem to modern readers, but rather stands for a broad range of pairings, beginning (and ending) with the one Herigar himself is said to have pointed out, the beings the pagans call gods versus his Christian deity: "Let us prove who the more powerful is by a miracle, the many whom you call your gods or my one, the Almighty Lord Jesus Christ. Look, it is going to rain. . . ."[98]

Little wonder then that reports of missionary efforts often center around competitions between Christian magical acts (*miracula*), on the one hand, and whatever magic the worshippers of native gods can muster, on the other. At one level, naturally, such tales offered prospective converts the possibility of tapping into a more powerful source of magical authority, of gaining authority and might, but these contests were also exchanges of ideas. Stories about the varying efficacy of pagan and Christian magic were a form of communication, where magical acts represent the competing faiths and competing deities; where, contrary to modern Western aversion to the reality of magic, the actuality of magic is readily accepted and only its source of power is debated; where pagan and Christian practitioners could exchange examples of their magic and, most important, the power of their deities, just as individuals exchange words in verbal duels.[99] The conversion to Christianity was not just a struggle about *what* was to happen, but also about *how* it was to come about.

Thus, with an almost modern scientific sense for experimentation, the author of *Brennu-Njáls saga* (*Njal's Saga*), writing centuries after Rimbert, sets up the following test in his presentation of the conversion of Iceland: knowing that a warrior, a so-called *berserkr*, is coming, the Christian missionary, Þangbrandr, challenges his still-pagan hosts to test the powers of their differing faiths. They will light three fires, he suggests, one that the pagans will consecrate (*vígja*), and one to be consecrated by Þangbrandr, while the third "control" fire will remain unconsecrated. If the *berserkr* is frightened by Þangbrandr's fire but unafraid of the pagan fire, then they must adopt the new faith.[100] Predictably, when this fearsome warrior arrives, he moves untroubled through the pagan-hallowed fire, but when he gets to Þangbrandr's fire, he dares not cross it and says that he is burning all over. Þangbrandr strikes the *berserkr*'s arm with his crucifix and a great miracle takes place (*varð jartegn svá mikil*), in which the *berserkr* drops his sword and is dispatched.

As a result of this magical competition, Þangbrandr's host and all of his household are baptized.[101] Importantly, Þangbrandr proclaims beforehand, as had Herigar, that he is offering the pagans the chance to test which faith is better (*at þér skuluð reyna, hvár betri er trúan*). Although we have little reason to accept the historicity of the scenario as it relates to the tenth century, its widespread use in saga literature notwithstanding, it is easy to see how thirteenth-century authors employ the idea of magic as a way to praise Christianity and demean paganism.[102]

Magic used as a metalanguage lasted for a long time: with respect to its value as a means of expression, it hardly seems to matter whether the text is from the ninth or thirteenth century, consumers of this kind of story continue to understand the message. The key element in a scene of this sort is the display of God's power over that of the pagan gods: for all we know, Þangbrandr and his pagan competitors may have hallowed the fires by similar, even identical, technical means, but what was important was the source of the power they invoked to affect the ends they sought—a fact that will gain importance as the Middle Ages progress.[103] The fire-consecration competition between Þangbrandr and the pagans come near the end of his missionary activities in Iceland: it is true that he has previously, with some success, converted a few Icelanders by persuasion, but he has also fought a duel about the competing faiths, using a crucifix for his shield,[104] been subject to attack by sorcery,[105] and had a pagan woman "preach" (*boða*) to him at length about the native gods, who, she claimed, had been the ones responsible for his earlier shipwreck.[106]

If magic in its abstract form constituted a special system of signs in lofty pagan-Christian dialogues about religion, it was also at a mundane level central to a wide variety of everyday activities—protection from illness, shelter from supernatural forces, assistance in childbirth, foresight about weather and harvests, recovery of lost articles, and so on. Christianity looked to supplant many of these purposes with its own devices—with saints' relics, holy water, crucifixes, devotional medals, and the like—but it could neither do so immediately nor expect to supersede entirely long-standing traditions used for the same purposes.[107] The persistence of various indigenous practices in Scandinavia lay in part with the unwillingness, inability even, of the population to relinquish them, as well as the fact that throughout the era of missionary activity, the church showed itself willing to accept, or to adapt, native practices to its own ends when it could not decisively deal with them more expeditiously.[108] How this practice influenced the character of Nordic witchcraft and magic in the later Middle Ages is integral to our story.

Given Western historiography's tendency toward Christian triumphalism—with, as it is often presumed, its complete, uniform, and evenly distributed spiritual hegemony over all postmillennial events, institutions, and regions in Scandinavia—the possibility of pagan beliefs having survived for long periods after the Conversion in the north has generally been dismissed out of hand. Admittedly, the terms used in the languages of medieval Scandinavia for the change of faiths may appear to strengthen this impression: *réttsnúning, siðaskipti, umvändilse,* and so on build, like their English counterpart, "conversion," on the idea of turning away from one faith and toward another one.[109] Implicitly such language gives rise to the impression that the "turn" is a quick one, although there is nothing in the data that demands such an interpretation. The alternative position, one that accepts a more gradual shift in popular attitudes toward a Christian norm, including significant reinterpretation of past practices within the emerging dominant cultural paradigm, has not been an easy one, not least because of the often unreasonable and far-reaching claims of its early advocates.

Still, the notion of a generations-long process is exactly the image that emerges from the widely cited pronouncement in Icelandic saga literature about the Conversion, in this instance, like the earlier examples, drawn from the thirteenth-century *Brennu-Njáls saga.* The text says that, after the discord created by Þangbrandr's mission to Iceland, at the next national assembly the Christian and pagan Icelanders, after naming witnesses, withdrew the protection of the law from each other.[110] Bedlam follows, but in the end, the Icelanders select the pagan priest (*goði*) Þorgeirr frá Ljósavatni to declare how they should proceed. In what is perhaps the most famous scene in all of medieval Scandinavian literature, Þorgeirr spends an entire day with a cloak over his head without anyone speaking to him.[111] When he reaches his conclusion, Þorgeirr asks for and gets sureties from both parties that they will abide by his decision and then declares that henceforth the Icelanders shall believe in one god—father and son and holy ghost—and forsake all idolatry (*skurðgoðavilla,* lit., 'carved image heresy'). Þorgeirr then specifies two other pagan practices that will also have to be renounced—the exposure of infants and the consumption of horse flesh. He further enumerates how the question of feast days should be resolved. And, importantly, Þorgeirr adds the following codicil: it will be considered a matter worthy of outlawry if anyone openly practices the old heathen ways, but if they are done secretly (*leynliga*) the act will go without punishment.[112] The saga's author then adds that within a few years all heathenism is forbidden, whether practiced openly or secretly.[113]

Naturally the sentiment expressed here and elsewhere about the possibility that post-Conversion Icelanders continued to worship the pagan gods in secret has occasioned a great deal of speculation about how fully and how quickly Christianity replaced the worship of Óðinn, Þórr, Freyr, Freyja, and so on. It is impossible to know today how accurately the statement attributed to Þorgeirr reflects possibly tolerant views on this issue in eleventh-century Iceland, but it is clear that later historians and saga authors felt it vital to include the idea so as to demonstrate the unity displayed by the Icelanders and the reasonableness they showed at the point of the *réttsnúning*.

Moreover, there were, as one scholar has remarked, "bridges" in cult, custom, and worldview between the old and new faiths that could, and did, serve the Christianization process.[114] Among the best known of these opportunities are the widely discussed uses of the pre-Christian gods and heroes well into the Christian era. That a representation of Gunnar in the snake pit, for instance, a scene drawn from the legend of Sigurðr the Dragon-slayer, should decorate a number of medieval Nordic churches and baptismal fonts may baffle a modern observer at first blush, but clearly such appropriations made a great deal of sense to their contemporary audiences.[115] Pagan rituals were even sometimes incorporated into Christian worship and given a Christian interpretation: it has been argued that pagan traditions of feasting, beer brewing, and ritualized beer consumption are adapted into Christian observance (see Chapter 2).

The tendency has been, however, to assume that this portrayal of a slow, and, if correct, tolerant and perceptive, Christianization process cannot be accurate, and there has been a general disinclination on the part of academics to venture back into this hotly debated arena. Yet after a prolonged period of relative obscurity, and nearly embarrassed silence, the twin questions of pagan survivals and pagan-Christian syncretism have risen again to positions of respectable scholarly debate.[116] It needs to be noted, however, that not all questions of "survivals" and so on are the same. A very helpful contribution to this question is the distinction made between different types of syncretism: one kind of syncretism takes place at the level of elements, that is, individual aspects of an old religion that have been accommodated to the new faith, whereas the other type of syncretism functions at the level of systems, where whole segments and ideologies have been transferred.[117] In the case of the Nordic materials, as far as scholarship has been able to make out, we are overwhelming faced with the former rather than the latter, and, if anything, syncretism at the level of systems has probably been imposed onto the pagan

Nordic religion in the centuries before the Conversion rather than the other way around.

Influences could run in both directions, as the well-known embrace of the Germanic-derived terms "God" and "hell" into the Christian vocabulary amply demonstrates. Surely some dramatic changes accompanied the adoption of Christianity in the various Nordic cultures, but just as the belief that some elements of the old religion may have survived the Conversion does not argue for a tradition of underground worship, secret cults, or the like, neither does the Christianization of the Nordic world necessarily lead to the conclusion that all vestiges of the old faith were suddenly eliminated.[118]

Certainly Nordic sources themselves support this case: the annals of the Icelandic settlement, *Landnámabók* (*Book of Settlements*), comment on Helgi "the Lean," a Norse settler said to have been fostered in the Hebrides and reared in Ireland, that he was a man of mixed faith, being a Christian but calling on the pagan god Þórr when making sea voyages or when in difficulties.[119] That we are told these details about Helgi depends, of course, on the continuation of the entry about Helgi, which serves to cast doubt on the usefulness of Þórr's assistance. As Helgi approaches Iceland, he inquires of Þórr (*gekk hann til frétta við Þór*) about where to land, and sails further north. Helgi's son then asks whether he would be willing to sail all the way to the Arctic if Þórr showed him the way.[120] The scenario this episode poses—that some Norsemen may have attempted to fold Christ into the pagan pantheon or otherwise accommodate both faiths—*may* reflect the genuine experiences and attitudes of some early Nordic Christians, but as our oldest attestation of the story comes from the thirteenth century, prudence demands that we understand it rather as an attempt to show the foolishness of putting faith in the old gods rather than as a mirrorlike reflection of an actual conversion biography.

Significantly, several redactions of *Landnámabók* conclude by noting widespread apostasy in early Iceland. A number of Christians were among the settlers, most having come from the British Isles, but although some of them remained Christian until death, that was uncommon in most families. Among them, their sons built temples and sacrificed, and the country was fully heathen for nearly 120 years.[121] We can only speculate, of course, but one wonders if, to the degree this view is accurate, the early settlers in this first new world colony did not find the everyday rituals and magic of paganism more comforting than their Christian counterparts.

Chapter 2

Magic and Witchcraft in Daily Life

Bronislaw Malinowski, one of the principal shapers of scholarly debate about the function of magic, bluntly wrote early in the last century, "There are no peoples however primitive without religion and magic."[1] Despite the lack of consensus about such so-called universals, few observers would disagree that spiritual life—religion, magic, and so on—represents an area where human beings demonstrably share common impulses across time and space.[2] And the desire to influence events, to look into the future and manipulate it, is the beginning point of what for some is the defining evolutionary pattern in human history, moving from magic to religion to science.

Key to understanding this human instinct is what has famously been called the "magical world view," that is, belief in causation, a world where nothing is accidental but rather the result of the actions of others, stimuli that can be interdicted and altered.[3] Not only does this ideology bear directly on the nature of witchcraft, but it is also intimately related to virtually all areas of daily life in the Middle Ages. Indeed, it is not difficult to understand the power of this satisfying view of life and why the theory of causation is not merely a useful analytic tool for scholars. It is central to the cultural construction of witchcraft because the "magical world view" allows for the discovery of how individuals and communities are beleaguered and by whom. Once identified, the community can deal with them through various socially sanctioned means, such as countermagic, exile, or execution. But it is important to realize that the same theory of causation that can identify witches and expose them to justice also provides supplicants with power, with the possibility of securing their health, of improving their financial circumstances, of preventing accidents, of coaxing better production from their fields and herds—in short, of managing their fates, not merely being subject to them.

Historical accounts, archaeological evidence, poetry, prose, and every other means of understanding the Nordic Middle Ages tell us that the "magical world view" was, in fact, its dominant *Weltanschauung*, both before and after the conversion of Scandinavia to Christianity. Yet the language used by the dominant Christian culture to describe many of the magical practices of everyday life associated with the past—what in English is called 'superstition' but more transparently termed *hindrvitni* 'hinder knowledge', *vantrú* 'unbelief', and so on in the Nordic languages—inclines modern observers to assume that magic had relevance only in the lives of nonelites.[4] But nothing could be further from the truth.

With respect to nomenclature, many terms in the older Scandinavian dialects describe what we would today broadly regard as charms, magic, and so on. But their use is not evenly distributed. Icelandic sagas and other narrative sources typically employ a very wide array of locutions in referring to incantations and spells (e.g., *álag, ákvæði, atkvæði, galdr, taufr*) and their use (e.g., *magna, síða, taufra, trylla, vitta*), verbs meaning 'to enchant', 'to charm', 'to bewitch'. But such descriptions as we get from legal and other less literary sources tend to be more restrained, usually mentioning only something like a person being apprehended in an act of witchcraft, as when, for example, the late thirteenth-century Swedish laws of Uppland call for a homicidal witch to be taken to the assembly for trial "together with the articles of her witchcraft," or when the Danish laws of Jutland blandly talk of homicide "through witchcraft."[5]

Yet even here the distribution pattern of terms is unequal, as the Norwegian laws often use a more explicit range of activities than those of Sweden and Denmark. Thus the Norwegian Gulaþing laws talk not only about not engaging in "soothsaying, incantation, or wicked sorcery,"[6] but in a supplement from the early fourteenth century, add a wide array of activities, including being a "troll-rider," a soothsayer, a believer in the land spirits, and one who "sits out" to discover the future.[7] And within the Swedish tradition, the further back in time the law, the more diverse and colorful the language that is used, as in the famous passage from the early thirteenth-century *Äldre Västgötalagen* (*The Older Law of Västergötland*) concerned with the gate-riding hag.

Whether these patterns demonstrate an increasing adherence within Nordic jurisprudence to evolving European norms, both legal and with respect to the nature of witchcraft and away from native traditions, or merely demonstrate the more restrained nature of the codifiers' language, the rhetoric of those who dealt semiprofessionally with acceptable evidence within the Nordic legal system, is difficult to know. But as this chapter explores, there can be little doubt but that medieval Scandinavians were every bit as subject to Malinowski's observation as any group he had in mind when he wrote that there exist no peoples without magic.

Pagan and Christian Magic

Christianity may have changed Scandinavia forever, but it did not change it overnight. As the history of missionary activities in the previous chapter makes clear, no cultural saltation event precipitated an immediate and absolute dividing line between old and new throughout Nordic society, whatever the impression generated by modern timelines of the conversion process. To pursue the biological metaphor further, gradualism rather than saltation is the process that emerges from the evidence. If, for example, some magical practice were believed to be effective before the dominance of Christianity, would it automatically have been discarded after the Conversion? And if a handy bit of heathen magic remained in use after Christianization, adapted to the new faith, would we recognize it today?[8] In all likelihood, the answers here are "no" and "maybe."

An example of the sort of transformation that may have been common, and of the difficulties that face us, comes from the Christian law section of the Norwegian Gulaþing laws. This law is concerned with beer brewing and the celebratory consumption of the brewer's art at specific times of the year, which, the law says, is to be done as a means of giving thanks to Christ and Mary for abundance (i.e., abundant crops) and peace (*til árs ok til friðar*).[9] This very same tradition appears to have been widespread already in pagan Scandinavia and figures prominently in various sagas and other historical sources: in his thirteenth-century edda, for example, Snorri Sturluson notes of the god Freyr that he is a deity to whom it is good to pray "for abundant harvests and peace" (*til árs ok friðar*), precisely the formulation used in the Gulaþing Christian laws.[10] In *Hákonar saga Aðalsteinsfóstra* (*The Saga of Hákon Aðalsteinsfóstri*), Snorri enlarges this image by describing a great heathen sacrifice at yuletide, during which toasts in honor of the various gods are drunk, including one to Freyr using that same phrase, "for abundant harvests and peace" (*til árs ok friðar*).[11] That a tradition of brewing ale for the purpose of celebrating pagan deities at festivals was adjusted to fit the

Christian milieu is widely accepted by modern scholarship. It is a form of syncretism, a special kind of "cultural loan shift," representing not, of course, the continuation of paganism as such, but an adaptation of old customs to new conditions and new interpretive frameworks.[12]

Supporting the likelihood of such continuities, or loan shifts, is the fact that many issues—health and sexuality, for instance—transcend the conversion from paganism to Christianity: they were of the same central concern to one group as to the other. So too with respect to care for the dead—and the living: where a pre-Christian pagan inscribes a memorial for a dead man with such protective words as "May Þórr hallow this mound,"[13] or "May Þórr hallow the runes. . . . ,"[14] Christian Scandinavians formulate the same idea instead as "May Michael protect his spirit,"[15] or "May God and the holy maiden protect his [scil., soul]."[16] And where a Christian might hope to safeguard his health by bearing an amulet with the inscription, "May God protect the one who carries me. . . . ,"[17] a pagan's periapt declares, "May Þórr protect him. . . ."[18]

The structures and mentalities of these passages are broadly comparable, although the pagan entreaties focus on the tangible, whereas the Christian prayers tend to focus on the soul of the departed. And clearly the powers to whom the prayers appeal differ. The wording of all such invocations embodies the purpose of every type of magic, whether pagan or Christian. It is, as one venerable scholar in the field observes, "to impose the human will on nature, on man or on the supersensual world. . . ."[19] But the difference to the Christian observer is the context as well as the powers called on. Although essentially the same magical paraphernalia are sometimes used, the evaluations of such items are strikingly dissimilar and entirely framed by whether they are thought to be connected with pre- or post-Conversion Scandinavia.

So, for example, the medieval Norwegian laws denounce the use of poppets made of dough and clay and make it clear that the practice is condemned because it is a vestige of homeopathic magic belonging to the old pre-Christian religion (til hæidins sidar).[20] Yet when a very similar object plays a role as part of a saint's life, it is equally clear that praise and glory are intended. Thus, according to a miracle attached to the vita of Saint Katarina (d. 1381), the first abbess of Vadstena cloister and daughter of Saint Birgitta of Sweden, when a resident of Arboga falls gravely ill, his friends promise that he will go on a pilgrimage to Katarina's grave and there present the image of a human being made from wax (de cera). Through Katarina, the sick man miraculously improves and is able to make the pilgrimage, and the episode concludes with the man's praise of God's work through Katarina.[21] Again, the pagan poppet and the Christian anthropomorphous image are obviously analogous practices (perhaps even historically connected), but because of the sources of the powers involved, one set of circumstances leads to condemnation, the other to the declaration of a miracle.

As these examples demonstrate, the differences between what might be considered "village-level" superstition, charm magic, and witchcraft at one extreme and the activities associated with the "high" magic of elite and often clerical culture at the other are not always easy to gauge. In fact, a debate raged throughout the thirteenth and subsequent centuries among the neo-Platonists about the precise dividing line between such activities as goeteia (or theurgy), *maleficium*, and simple charm magic, such as the wearing of amulets.[22] A fine example, known in Scandinavia and elsewhere in Northern Europe, combining elements of all the traditions—Christian, pagan, learned, and so on—is the advice to write on lead the opening words of the Gospel of John ("In the beginning was the word . . .," known as the *In principio*) as a charm against elves, apparently to be carried as an amulet.[23] To most medieval Scandinavians, however, as a practical matter, the critical distinction where magic was involved must surely have been one thing and one thing alone—efficacy. Terminological and taxonomic debates concerned with high and low magic would no doubt have been meaningless to them, even if refashioned as questions of natural magic versus demonic magic. Nor were pagan and Christian worldviews in opposition in every way: both perspectives benefited from what might be termed practical magic. The Conversion stories in which pagan magic competes with Christian magic suggest that the membrane separating them was often diaphanous indeed, having mostly to do with the source of their power.

Still, if medieval Scandinavians were principally concerned with the efficacy of magic, they were also aware of the differences between the two types, a fact underscored by the vocabulary for magic and witchcraft. A complete inventory of terms for magic, witchcraft, and so on shows that the lexicon could be broad, as when Saint Birgitta lists magical practitioners of different sorts, including witches, pharmacognosists, and soothsayers of both genders (*trolkonor ok lifkonor ok spakonor älla spamän*), conjurers who trouble people with "devilish arts and give themselves to the devil for worldly things."[24] Most frequently, however, non-Christian magic is typified by its relation to the supernatural or the old religion. Thus they often play on its connection to the world of the trolls (e.g., Old Swedish *troldomber* 'witchcraft, sorcery'

< troll-ness) or to the world of the past, with expressions such as Old Icelandic *fornspjǫll* 'old lore' and *fornfrœði* 'old learning'. Tied to this image of magic as a special kind of learning is the term *fjǫlkyngi* 'manifold knowledge'. And it seems that magic was indeed knowledge, something in the medieval Nordic world one consciously acquired as part of a learning process, not an innate ability. Thus we routinely encounter practitioners of witchcraft who attribute their knowledge to those who have taught them specific practices, as well as literary texts that paint the picture of something like apprenticeships, in which individuals study the magical arts.[25]

Church statutes (e.g., the Arboga statute of 1412) and other ecclesiastical writing (e.g., *Fornsvenska legendariet* [*The Old Swedish Legendary*], *Jacobs saga postola*) in Scandinavia often cite the existence of grimoires (*fjǫlkyngisbœkr, galdrabœkr*) and other learning aids associated with high magic, and it is useful here to recall that the image of goetic books plays an important role in the New Testament.[26] When Paul's missionary work in Ephesus leads many citizens to repent their use of magic, "a good many of those who had formerly practiced magic collected their books and burnt them publicly" (Acts 19:19). References to books of this type increase notably throughout Western Europe from the late thirteenth century onward.[27] Necromantic writings take on new dimensions in particular at the court of Pope John XXII: he both approves of a commission to look into the misuse of such books and is himself subsequently said to be the object of necromancy.[28] Such texts as *Lemegeton* (also known as the *Lesser Key of Solomon*) and other pseudo-Solomonic works figure regularly in learned discussions of witchcraft and sorcery thereafter.

A well-developed narrative about such a magic book from the Icelandic Middle Ages comes in the story of Jón Halldórsson, a Norwegian cleric who studied in both Paris and Bologne.[29] In the tale, the young Jón—who would later serve as bishop of Skálholt from 1322 to 1339—has recently taken up his studies in Paris. One day, the master is gone and leaves his book out. As the young man hurries to read from his master's text, a furious storm begins. Jón hears the master returning and rushes back to his seat. As the master walks in, he swears an oath, saying that if the storm continues until evening, it will dry up all the lakes in France. Then it occurs to him that perhaps someone has been fooling about with his book while he was gone. Jón confesses to the deed, and the master hastens to his book and proceeds to read a section of it. Soon the storm subsides, and the episode concludes with Bishop Jón commenting that such things demonstrate what "arts" live in books (*hverjar listir lifa í bókunum*). This image, one of learned clerics dabbling in the magical arts, ran deep in the Middle Ages: several late medieval Danish statutes, for example, prohibit clerics from engaging in magic, because of its inevitable connection with the devil.[30]

Learned magical books of this sort (e.g., *Rauðskinna*) are frequently, and prominently, mentioned in legends,[31] but suggestions of medieval Nordic grimoires notwithstanding, extant copies mainly date near the early modern period.[32] What they would have been like we can mostly infer from the very rich Nordic charm materials from more recent centuries,[33] often post-Reformation materials from the sixteenth and seventeenth centuries resembling those of the Greek magical papyri or of Anglo-Saxon tradition, complete with carefully detailed utterance instructions.[34]

Learning and magic are also blended in medieval texts with important connections to the grimoire, namely, the medical treatise. Thus a Danish leechbook from the mid to late 1300s, for example, exhibits strong interest in the occult sciences amid its various pharmaceutical recipes.[35] It notes that to discover whether a sick man will recover or not, one should take a woman's milk and steadily drop it into his urine. If the milk sinks, he will die; if it floats, he will live.[36] In a similar vein, if one wants to know whether a woman is carrying a male or female baby, "Take a vat of clean spring water and drop into it a woman's milk. If the milk floats in the water, then it is a son; if the milk sinks, then it is a daughter."[37] It recommends, underscoring the connection between magic and religion, that if one wants to ensure that thieves, robbers, and wolves not steal ones livestock, one should inscribe a particular Latin prayer on the doorpost where the animals go out.[38] "If you don't want your wife,"[39] it helpfully suggests, "to take another man, take the liquid of the 'common houseleek',[40] and smear your penis with it, and then lie with your wife, and after that, while you are alive, she will not have 'sexual relations' with another man."[41]

The text also provides the remedy for wantonness,[42] a cocktail made of the juice of the gladiola (*Gladiolus*) mixed with wine or water and given to the afflicted person with atramenta or other liquid.[43] But what makes this otherwise rather ordinary recipe notable is its injunction that the brew should be blended as the *Pater noster* is being "read" (*læs,* in the imperative in keeping with the nature of the recipe). And here, of course, we see again the power of a practice that draws on all three elements of the magic-science-religion triptych, the sort of symbiosis that leads the editor to comment, "We have in this leechbook a good example of so-called clerical medicine [lit., 'monk medicine'] with its raw empiricism, its ignorance and superstition."[44]

Learned clerics, in fact, were keen to pursue "natural magic," although there is little direct medieval Nordic evidence for a knowledge of alchemy, such data as we have all point to its knowledge having been restricted to the clerical community.[45] The early fifteenth-century bishop of Århus, Bo Mogensen, apparently had some knowledge of it: in documents relating to the disposition of the bishop's property, Archbishop Peter notes in 1420 that the late bishop had engaged in "some peculiar arts" (*noger besynnerlik konst*), including alchemy, medicine, and geometry.[46] A century earlier, when the former Danish archbishop, Jens Grand, dies in Avignon in 1327, "a little book about alchemy" (*Quidam libellus Arquimie*) is listed in the inventory of his library.[47] And a Swedish poem from 1379 connected with the Birgittine community at Vadstena also appears to display a knowledge of alchemy, a finding in line with Sten Lindroth's conclusion that already those Swedish clerks who studied abroad from the thirteenth century onward probably became acquainted with the basics of alchemy.[48] By the end of the fourteenth century, the church begins to question seriously the goals and role of alchemy, and its relation to the church changes significantly.[49]

Another important form of learned thaumaturgy in the Nordic Middle Ages derives from Jewish magical tradition. Dror Segev, in particular, has argued for the largely overlooked importance of this branch of magic for the Nordic materials.[50] Thus, in addition to such standard elements of learned magic in Europe as *AGLA*, with its Jewish background, and the *Sator Arepo Tenet Opera Rotas* palindrome, both found on a number of medieval Scandinavian rune carvings, Segev draws attention to such interesting issues as the possible influence of the Jewish Solomonic tradition on the treatment on biblical topics in Old Norse and the likelihood of isolated words in magical formulas, for example, being of hitherto unrecognized Hebrew origin.[51]

Attributes of the church were common elements in the everyday magic of the Nordic Middle Ages. Typical of these, for example, is a Latin hymn or encomium to Saint Dorothea and Christ found on a piece of paper dated to the late fifteenth century and thought to have been used as part of a charm or as an amulet.[52] Similarly, the Latin text of John 1:1–14 written on parchment, bearing on the reverse a further Latin inscription beginning, "Sanctus sanctus sanctus . . ." with several circles around it, was almost certainly borne as a protective amulet peddled to its owner by a traveling monk.[53] Among the runic inscriptions from medieval Scandinavia, those from the Norwegian city of Bergen play a special role and include a number of amulets, or talismans, variously calling on God in Latin and the vernacular to protect the bearer and so on.[54] An amulet with the popular Saint Anthony's "brief" puts the protective magical nature of European Christianity in a medieval Nordic context—a Latin-language inscription in runes—when it begins by proclaiming, "Behold the cross of the Lord; flee, you hostile powers. . . ."[55]

A Danish text, described by its editors as a teacher's manual (in the belief that it might have been used at, e.g., a cathedral school), from between 1452 and 1467 is telling in this regard: among the many highly diverse entries in both Latin and the vernacular, mostly addressing grave theological issues, are included charms against fever in oneself, disease, fever in others, and toothache and two charms against theft.[56] The first of the theft charms is especially interesting as it invokes the powers of both hell and heaven (*in nomine dyaboli* [. . .] *in nomine domini ihesu christi*).

Christian magic was not only textual; it could be corporeal as well. It is said in *Þorláks saga byskups* (*The Saga of Bishop Þorlákr*) that, in addition to the help brought by praying to this saintly figure for assistance, if one took earth from his tomb and bound it to various sores, the boils and wounds would heal quickly.[57] This curative cocktail, made of equal parts medicine, religion, and magic, one supposes, says a great deal about the nature of all three areas in medieval Scandinavia, especially the degree to which they form an integrated and interrelated whole. Because the formula represents the perspective of the dominant Christian culture, one reverentially writes "religion" here, although it is not difficult to image a similar pagan scenario where it would be phrased differently: perhaps medicine, superstition, and magic.

Similarly, according to another of the miracles appended to the vita of Saint Katarina, a woman in the Swedish parish of Linderås fell victim to poisoning and was near death. Seeing that she is barely able to breathe, those who are with the woman appeal to Katarina, offering a donation, and suddenly the woman regurgitates a worm from her mouth, followed immediately by fourteen toads (*xiiij buphones*). Thereafter she recovers fully.[58] If we accept the facts as they are presented, as a medieval audience was surely meant to, what were people to think, and, indeed, what must people have thought? As we have seen, the distinction between miracle and magic has as much to do with the observer as with the observed. This story is one of a series of wonders associated with the life and works of Saint Katarina,[59] but it is easy to imagine how if the figure to whom the supplication had been directed had been, say, the pagan goddess Freyja, we would form entirely different conclusions about the character of the event.[60]

Continuity in connection with charm magic of this sort can be traced over long periods in the North. An extraordinary example of this point is a case in which a pagan god is involved centuries after the nominal conversion of the area to Christianity. A late medieval trial for theft and apostasy in Stockholm charges that the accused "had served Óðinn for seven years."[61] The tendency has been to dismiss this reference to Óðinn with the explanation that what is really being referred to here is the satanic figure constructed by late medieval Christianity, but there is evidence suggesting connections to the pagan god through charm magic.[62] Nor is this case an isolated one: some years later, another man is charged in Stockholm with similar crimes and a similar connection to the old heathen god. This man is sentenced to burn at the stake for apostasy, and again the accusation maintains that he served Óðinn.[63] Evidence from the postmedieval period strongly suggests a continuous Swedish tradition in which people appealed to Óðinn for success, especially in financial matters.[64]

But to understand these episodes simply as a question of the struggle of Christianity against paganism, or of the ability of paganism to escape being eradicated by Christianity, is to miss the point. The question as I would style it is not "Who wins the religious war?" but rather the question of how Scandinavians of the Middle Ages addressed their problems in health, romance, misfortune, and so on. Magic, whether Christian or pre-Christian in origin, provided one key response. For most moderns, magic is generally the stuff of gothic novels and Hollywood fantasy, but for its medieval practitioner, magic was by no means all "smells and bells"—it was also the commonplace. Of course, there was nothing quotidian about, for example, the marked language of charm magic, or applying a handful of grave mould, or mixing meadowsweet [meadwort] root in wine, or acquiring a cat's brain. These actions must have had their spiritual dimensions, but such practices were not sequestered from the flow of everyday existence in the lives of sailors, priests, beggars, farmers, laborers, queens and other people making up the complex fabric of medieval Nordic society.

But if people were able to make use of magic for their own beneficial purposes, there was, of course, another side to this story. Although magic, whether connected with local saints' cults or a legacy of pagan folk religion, might in certain circumstances be acceptable, there were also magical practices that were definitely not, and the perception of such unacceptable practices was conveniently summarized under the notion of "witchcraft" (i.e.,

trolldómr, fjǫlkyngi, fordæða, forneskja, fyrnska, etc.). Even if most people practiced some form of magic in their daily lives, that does not mean they did
not fear its power when wielded by others. Many prayer books at the very
end of the Nordic Middle Ages, for example, express fear of witches and
witchcraft.[65] Lapidaries and leechbooks brim with various concoctions useful
against devils and witchcraft: Peder Månsson's early sixteenth-century translation, for example, contains numerous entries useful for protecting against
witches, as one description says.[66] A medical treatise recommends among
other prescriptions fish galls placed in a juniper pail and covered at bedtime
with glowing coals, the reek of which will drive away all witchcraft and devilry; a similar effect can be had with the gall of a black dog, the stench being
so great, that witchcraft loses its power.[67]

Relief through magic and relief from magic were both important means
of addressing the stresses of everyday life in the Middle Ages.[68] One sanctioned way to ameliorate the problems of everyday life was to pray, do hom-
age, go on pilgrimages, or otherwise hope to gain the approval of the church,
perhaps even witness or be the beneficiary of a miracle.[69] The difference
between a miracle and an outcome produced by magic was thin, the great
distinction for the church having to do with the power from which it drew
its vitality—does the supernatural event derive from a kind and benevolent
God interceding on behalf of his people or from demonic powers who use,
or are used by, a human to accomplish these goals? In her treatment of magic
in the early Middle Ages, Valerie Flint comments on this distinction as it
relates to the magical and the miraculous: "Augustine recognizes that magicians and good Christians may do similar things. The difference lies in their
means and ends."[70] It also lies, she might have added, in the interpretative
frameworks of the observer.

In fact, we possess an excellent example of precisely this notion. Or what
would we otherwise think of a supernatural figure who could heal illness and
injuries through song, cure sick cattle the same way, extinguish fires with
mere words, and by using special magical gear heal humans and animals and
with the same equipment protect food stores from the deprivations of vermin? But this is not a figure outside of a Christian context: if he were, we
would assume him to be a pagan god, witch, or sorcerer. The person believed
to be so remarkable was none other than Bishop Þorlákr, declared a saint in
1198: his songs are hymns, his words a blessing, and his magical kit holy
water.[71]

Romance, Fortune, Health, Weather, and Malediction

Saint Birgitta enumerates many of the purposes to which magic was put, saying that both men and women follow the counsel of "accursed witches and sorceresses" (and here she specifies the female gender) in order to conceive children, win love, discover the future, and be healed of illness.[72] Magic of one sort or another touched all aspects of daily life, but we should hardly be surprised to discover that, as in Birgitta's list, romance, attempts to discover one's destiny, and health emerge as the dominant elements of surviving examples of medieval Nordic magic, to which might be added, imprecation.[73] The curious case of weather magic—little in evidence as performed magic, yet much talked about in literature—represents another important area to consider in the materials that follow.

Romance

Among charms, those concerned with love and sex constituted an important part of the magical tradition of medieval Scandinavia, a tradition represented both before and after the Christianization of the area. That such charms persisted in the post-Conversion world may be seen from medieval Nordic religious works of various types—sermons and visions, for example—that condemn people who turn to witchcraft and magic in order to make their paramours love them better.[74] In general, charms associated with men look to seduce—or more accurately, coerce—women into having intercourse with a man (i.e., aphrodisiac charms), while at the other extreme, charms associated with women seek to prevent a couple from having sex (i.e., anaphrodisiac charms). Whether hoping to consummate or prevent a liaison, magic is the medium, and that this particular arena of magical and sociological concern was perceived as a genuine problem is supported by its sober treatment in both medieval laws and ecclesiastical writings and by its role in a number of fourteenth- and fifteenth-century trials from Norway and Sweden.[75]

In fact, we possess a dramatic treatment of this sort of enchantment, what is often euphemistically referred to in the scholarly literature as "love magic," in *Skírnismál* (*The Lay of Skírnir*), a poem preserved from circa 1270.[76] The poem describes Skírnir's wooing of the giantess Gerðr on behalf of his master, the god Freyr. Skírnir's mission is seemingly doomed to fail as long as he merely offers the maid a variety of gifts, nor do its chances of success improve when he simply threatens her and her family's *physical* well-being. But his errand succeeds when he turns to magic and curses her *sexual* well-being, in essence, using an anaphrodisiac curse in order to achieve an aphrodisiac end.[77]

Key to his curse is a magic wand he carries and on which he apparently carves runes. Such wands (referred to in this poem as a *tamsvǫndr* 'taming rod' [v. 26] and *gambanteinn* 'magic wand or rod' [v. 32]) are well known in Norse literature and did in fact exist in the Viking Age as part of the sorcerer's kit.[78] In this case, Skírnir not only carves runes on the wand but also declares that he will "tame" (*temia*) Gerðr to his will after he has touched or struck her with it (v. 26). He then exiles Gerðr to a vile distant region, tells her she will be painfully ugly and will know nothing but sorrow, be bitten by imps, and likens her to a thistle at harvest time. Skírnir explains that he has acquired the wand by going to the forest and then immediately declares that she has angered the gods.

Addressing himself to various races of supernatural beings, Skírnir then denies the pleasure and enjoyment of men to her:

> how I forbid,   how I debar
>   men's mirth to the maid,
>   men's love to the maid. (v. 34)

Having refused to her human males, Skírnir then says a thurs will *have* her (*Hrímgrímnir heitir þurs, / er þic hafa scal* [v. 35]). The phrase he uses (*scal hafa*) can in this instance only mean one thing: Skírnir does not say *eiga* 'own, possess, have for a wife' or some other term that might imply the legal obligations of marriage, but rather *hafa*, almost certainly to be understood as 'use, employ', no doubt with a sexual connotation. He further declares that she will know only "lechery, loathing, and lust" (*ergi oc œði / oc ópola*), emotional states and drives represented by runes that he apparently can manipulate by carving them into the wand. Alternatively, he can also cancel them by obliterating the runes.[79] This threat clinches the deal, and she acquiesces to his demands.

Scholarly attention to the poem's "love magic" has tended to center rather narrowly on the metaphor of the dried thistle at harvest time.[80] The classic interpretation of this image is one according to which it is best understood in light of an Estonian harvest custom in which a rock holds down a thistle, metaphorically containing and controlling the demon within it, and thus preventing the harvest from being spoiled.[81] In recent years, focus has widened to include as well the connections between Skírnir's curse and various other Nordic imprecations, especially since the discovery of a Norwegian runic inscription with important connections to the poem.[82] The fourteenth-century runic text is inscribed on a four-sided wooden stick (wand?) from Bergen that begins, "I cut runes of help; I cut runes of protection; once against the elves, twice against the trolls, thrice against the ogres. . . ."[83] In the middle of the inscription, the carver calls down on the woman who is the object of the text, 'wolfish lechery and lust' (*ylgjar ergi ok úpola*), echoing the phrase in *Skírnismál,* and concludes its Norse portion with a curse that the woman should be subject to unbearable distress and misery, declaring, "Never shall you sit, never shall you sleep," until the woman loves the carver as she loves herself.[84] The language of this inscription and that of *Skírnismál* suggest that they are both part of a much broader tradition of Nordic charm magic, where the object is to compel the subject of the charm to "love" in all senses the one for whom the charm is being done.[85]

Representations of this kind of magic, as in these cases, often suggest that it was more or less the exclusive province of men and their desires. Although there may be some truth in this image, there are also portrayals of it being used by women, in literature in any event.[86] In one of the most famous such cases, Snorri Sturluson, in his early thirteenth-century portrayal of events that supposedly took place in the ninth century, draws a picture of King Haraldr being subjected to just such a form of "love magic" when he visits "the Finns." In Norse tradition, the Sámi, which is what is intended here by Finns, are presented as especially well-endowed magically, so much so that a term such as *finnfǫr* (lit. 'Finn-trip') meant to visit the Sámi in order to inquire about the future.[87] In this case, the king is taken to the beautiful Snæfríðr, who rises to meet him. "She poured a cup of mead for the king, and he took both the cup and her hand; and immediately it was as if a hot fire coursed through his body [lit., 'his penis'], and he desired to lie with her that same night."[88]

This desire is parlayed into a marriage, and so enamored of his new wife is the king that he neglects the kingdom and his responsibilities to it. When Snæfríðr later dies, her corpse does not putrefy, and the king remains beside her for three years in the hope that she will come back to life. Finally his advisors fool him into moving the body and suddenly its corrupt nature becomes obvious: "then stench and foul smell and all kinds of odors of corruption rose from the corpse [. . .] her entire body became livid, and all kinds or worms and adders, frogs and toads and vipers crawled out of it."[89] The degenerate yet apparently wholesome-appearing corpse is no doubt intended to parallel the nature of pagan magic itself; that is, even when it worked—and there is little doubt but that medieval observers believed it could be effective—its nature was corrupt.

In yet another example of "love magic," and here this label seems especially inappropriate, the inscription reads in its entirety, "You will fuck Rannveig the Red. It will be bigger than a man's prick and smaller than a horse's prick."[90] This thirteenth-century phallocentric inscription from Bergen is carved on a wooden stave. There can be little doubt that one of the individuals whose fate was conjured on this charm—its second-person "you"— believed the inscription capable of directing the future (and especially the object of the owner's lust), although we should hold out the possibility that a text of this sort might have been an augury, a device geared toward prognostication. More likely, however, its owner thought that by manipulating the talisman in various specified ways, or perhaps through its very production or purchase, he could direct the future, not merely know it. For her part, of course, Rannveig, the object of all this concupiscent concern, may, if she knew what was going on, justifiably have considered it an imprecation.

Although the topic and wording of this charm will strike many modern observers as crude, it forms part of the larger tradition of love charms evident throughout medieval Scandinavia. As was the case in *Skírnismál*, charm magic of this sort, which looks to seduce, or coerce, a woman into having intercourse with a man, was widespread in the Old Norse world. Not all runic inscriptions treating matters of the heart—or elsewhere, anatomically speaking—are abusive, of course. We can presumably infer that a Norwegian inscription that reads "I love the maiden even better! Even better!" may simply represent a private declaration of hope and emotion or, just perhaps, given the repetition of the phrase "even better," a less violent form of charm magic.[91]

If inscriptions of this sort give us the context for understanding the line "You will fuck Rannveig the Red" (*Rannveig *Rauðu skaltu streða* [alt., *serða*]), how are we to contextualize and interpret the remainder of the text, "It will be bigger than a man's prick and smaller than a horse's prick" (*Þat sé meira enn mannsreðr ok minna enn hestreðr*)? *Vǫlsaþáttr* (*The Story of Vǫlsi*) is an Old Icelandic story that treats a priapic cult—featuring a horse penis—and is known to us only from the late fourteenth-century version of the life of Saint Óláfr in *Flateyjarbók*.[92] The central question about this story has always been the issue of its authenticity: Is it a reflection of ancient practice, or is it a creation of the Christian Middle Ages?[93] For our purposes, perhaps this question does not matter: that a medieval author and audience found this sort of material engaging—and whatever the background of the story, whether invented or inherited, King Óláfr's resolution of the problem of recalcitrant paganism in his kingdom is pricelessly funny—is more than enough. Should the basis for the tale eventually prove to be of ancient heritage, such a finding would simply add additional weight to its testimony and its relevance.

Whether ancient or newly minted, the story is entirely built around the essentialization of the male member, in this instance, a horse phallus (*hestreðr*) although the pizzle is referred to by other names in the tale, such as *vingull*, *beytill*, and *Vǫlsi*.[94] Specifically, the story relates that when the farmer's horse dies, the slave who is skinning the creature cuts off "that limb, which nature has given to animals that conceive by intercourse, and which is named 'vingul' on horses, according to the ancient poets."[95] After its preservation, the pizzle is passed among all those present, who make up verses encouraging the phallus, and the others present, to act in certain, often very suggestive, ways.[96] The choice of an equine phallus to embody the power of the male generative organ is anything but random, and certainly the history of the horse in Nordic religious culture adds further layers of complexity to the story.[97] The notion in the runic charm that "it" would be bigger than a man's penis and smaller than a horse's penis conforms to the typical male fantasy in which penis size is an index of manhood.[98]

A further indication of the complex to which this charm belongs is no doubt seen in the versified imprecation the witch, Busla, casts on the sleeping King Hringr in *Bósa saga ok Herrauðs* (*The Saga of Bósi and Herrauðr*): like the Bergen charm, it begins by calling on the forces of the supernatural world to harass the king, and then on the natural world to do unnatural things:

Trolls and elves
and sorceresses,
goblins and giants
shall burn your halls;
frost-giants shall fright you
and stallions ride you,
straws shall sting you,
storms drive you mad;
may you ever be damned,
unless you do what I want.[99]

The translation is here more polite than the original, which literally says, 'may stallions fuck you' (*hestar streði þik*). This verse is only a part of the longer *Buslubæn* (*Prayer of Busla*) and *Syrpuvers* (*Syrpa Verse*), which, significantly, ends in an enigmatic runic cluster.[100] In other words, although Busla's objective in this curse is quite different, both the specific term used as part of her charm and the broader image of her behavior—the structure of verbal charming apparently leading into, and concluding with, the carving of runic characters—inform our understanding of the background against which the material residue represented by the Rannveig the Red inscription must be keyed.

If we possess clear outlines of a phallocentric tradition of "love magic," we have perhaps even stronger evidence for its equally gendered opposite, namely, a tradition of anaphrodisiac magic, that is, charm magic intended to prevent coitus, usually by removing the strength of the male member.[101] Mentioned both in literary sources and court cases, this form of magic appears to have been common. The most detailed nonnarrative portrayal of such magic comes, as is so often the case, from the Norwegian city of Bergen, where in 1325 a woman is accused of cursing her former lover by elaborate means (discussed in detail in Chapter 5). Under questioning, she admits to having hidden bread and peas in the bridal bed on the first night of the wedding and a sword near the heads of the newlyweds. Having secreted herself in the room, she later uttered an incantation, calling on spirits to bite the accursed in the back and breast and to stir up "hatred and ill-will." The protocol continues, "and when these words are read,[102] [one] should spit upon the one the curse concerned."[103] Having successfully completed this clandestine portion of her spell, the woman, Ragnhildr, might now have waited for the results of her work. But whether through hubris or, as one suspects, because some sort of public declaration represented a final element in the charm, on the second day of the wedding she publicly declares, "My mind rejoices that since [they are] bewitched, Bárðr's genitals will be no more effective for intercourse than this belt rolled up in my hand."[104]

Several thirteenth-century Icelandic sagas—*Kormáks saga* (*The Saga of Kormákr*) and *Brennu-Njáls saga* (*Njal's Saga*) in particular—are helpful in underscoring the apparently widespread popularity in literature of the kind of magic for which Ragnhildr is brought before the bishop. In *Kormáks saga*, a curse placed on the saga's eponymous hero ensures that he and his beloved can never experience intimacy: "Thórveig brought it about by her witchcraft that Kormák and Steingerd should never have intercourse together."[105] Although an attempt is made to undo the curse by another witch, this story of frustrated romance concludes with the malevolent magic successfully keeping Kormákr and Steingerðr apart.

A similar, and far more graphic, example comes from *Brennu-Njáls saga*, when the Norwegian queen, Gunnhildr, curses her Icelandic lover, Hrútr, when he falsely denies that another woman is waiting for him in Iceland. Gunnhildr embraces Hrútr at their last parting, kisses him, and says, "If I have as much power over you as I think, the spell I now lay on you will prevent your ever enjoying the woman in Iceland on whom you have set your heart. With other women you may have your will, but never with her."[106] The situation resembles the story of Ragnhildr tregagás, but the nature of the two curses could not be more different: whereas Ragnhildr claims that her charm will cause impotence in Bárðr, Gunnhildr's curse has the opposite operative consequences for Hrútr, albeit with the same goal of keeping the newlyweds from consummating their relationship. As Unnr, Hrútr's wife now that he is back in Iceland, subsequently explains to her father,

> "I want to divorce Hrut, and I can tell you the exact grounds I have against him. He is unable to consummate our marriage and give me satisfaction, although in every other way he is as virile as the best of men." "What do you mean?" asked Mord. "Be more explicit." Unn replied, "Whenever he touches me, he [lit., 'his penis'] is so enlarged that he cannot have enjoyment of me, although we both passionately desire to reach consummation. But we have never succeeded. And yet, before we draw apart, he proves that he is by nature as normal as other men."[107]

Unnr's reference to Hrútr's ability to reach a climax, despite the couple's inability to engage in coitus, is no gratuitous bit of salaciousness but reflects a serious debate current among the decretists in this period.[108]

Accusations of similar anaphrodisiac curses emerge from Sweden in the late medieval period.[109] Operationally, the magic used by "Crazy Katherine" (*galna kadhrin*) in Arboga in 1471 differs significantly from the earlier cases, even if the intent appears consistent: she will arrange things such that a man leaves his fiancée for another woman through a charm involving a cat's head. But this case introduces a new element, namely, a professional witch, Crazy Katherine.[110] A case from Stockholm in 1490 suggests a similar scenario of hostile female magic. There can be little doubt in this instance as to the nature of the curse, even if it is almost impossible to infer the circumstances of the event: here, a Margit *halffstoop* admits that years earlier she had taken from a particular man "all the strength in his manhood etcetera" while he stood and urinated.[111] Further, she says that she learned this magic (*then trolldomen*), which also includes a cat's head, from another woman in Björklinge, a village north of Uppsala.[112]

"Love magic" is the term by which all charms of this sort are known, but, as these cases make clear, fulfilling one's desire can have both different methods and different meanings. One key lesson to be drawn from the anaphrodisiac, or "antilove," cases is the fact that it is not merely the physiological condition of impotence (or its obverse) in the man that is significant. Rather, causality is the chief issue, that is, that such a condition results from the manifest, informed behavior of an individual with evil intentions. The same, of course, might be said of aphrodisiac magic as well. And, as discussed in Chapter 5, both types of "love magic" bring their users to the attention of the legal authorities.

Fortune

Another theurgical area well represented in the sagas is the quest for foreknowledge by consulting specialists. But as is the case with romance, evidence of interest in vaticination and prognostication comes to us from many different sources, not just the Icelandic sagas. Naturally, in Christian Scandinavia, prophecy of a certain type is regarded as fully acceptable—when it comes in the historical context of the Hebrew Scriptures or other unobjectionable church-sanctioned circumstances. As the thirteenth-century *Konungsskuggsjá* (*The King's Mirror*) notes, building on 1 Corinthians 12:1–11, Saint Paul says that God gives men the gift of the Holy Spirit for a specific purpose, and some "receive a spirit of prophecy."[113] The most common native terms for prophetic sorcery—*spá, spádomr, spásaga, spámæli, forspá*—and those who practice it—*spámaðr, spákona*—are also used in Old Norse to describe prophecy in its Christian context, where it can be discussed with approbation, as well as in the context of what was regarded as superstition, where it was routinely condemned.[114] Another sanctioned presentation of prophecy came in the form of the sibylline oracles, pagan, Jewish, and early Christian prophetesses well known from a wide variety of popular ecclesiastical texts and even church murals in medieval Scandinavia, such as the presentation of the twelve sibyls in Århus cathedral (Figure 1).[115]

Prophecy is portrayed as having played an important role in the conversion process in Scandinavia, as discussed in Chapter 1, and in yet another text depicting the confrontation of the old and new faiths, *Þorvalds þáttr víðfǫrla* (*The Tale of Thorvald the Far-Travelled*), a pagan, Koðrán, declares that the person the Christians call their "bishop" is this faith's *spámaðr* 'prophet'. Koðrán says that he has his own prophet (*spámaðr,* masculine gender) in whom he trusts and who lives in a rock and helps him in various ways, warning him in advance of coming evil, as well as guarding his livestock; moreover, this prophet warns him about the Christians and their ways.[116] Inevitably, in the contest that follows, the bishop's prayers and ceremonies prove that Koðrán should "turn to the most powerful god" (*snúisk til þess ins styrkasta guðs*), with the result that the fiend (*fjándi*) leaves, but not before relating to Koðrán the many things that have happened to him because of the bishop's actions and saying that he has been ill rewarded by Koðrán. Here, in clearly a Christian context, the *spámaðr* retains his prophetic function but appears to have a much expanded range of activities.

Prophecy in the Icelandic sagas classically portrays a female soothsayer engaging in seeing the future, sometimes through the magical practice known as *seiðr*. The sagas are laced with images of such events, for example, *Hrólfs saga kraka* (*The Saga of King Hrolf Kraki*), *Ǫrvar-Odds saga* (*Arrow-Odd's Saga*), *Víga-Glúms saga* (*Viga-Glum's Saga*), *Vatnsdœla saga* (*Vatndalers' Saga*), and *Eiríks saga rauða* (*The Saga of Eiríkr the Red*).[117] The simplest form introduces the topic, as, for example, in *Víga-Glúms saga*, by noting the ability of a certain woman to look into the future, as well as the fact that housewives in the district felt it important to entertain her well, as her opinions reflected the reception she had received.[118] When she has visited one home and made her remarks, a testy exchange follows between the housewife and the woman, after which the prophetess is said to be, in typical saga fashion, *ór sǫgunni* 'out of the saga'.

At the other extreme, there are also quite minute presentations of the process, none more so than the description in *Eiríks saga rauða* of a witch (*vǫlva*) and the practices she engages in (taken up in detail in Chapter 3). Not only is the ritual noted with great care—how, for example, she is seated on a raised dais with women surrounding her, one of whom sings what are called *varðlokkur*, to which many spirits are drawn—but also the dress and other habits of the *vǫlva* are painstakingly recorded.[119] For present purposes, the key information in this scene is near its conclusion, where the saga relates, "Then men went to the prophetess and each asked what he was most eager to know. She was free with her information and few things did not turn out as she said."[120]

Whatever the value of such saga presentations in assessing the archaic traditions of the Nordic cultures—and recent studies suggest they are great—it would be misleading to use these texts as the sole image of such practices among medieval Scandinavians. By way of demonstrating both the contrast and convergence of views represented between the two worlds, commenting on the world of fourteenth-century Sweden, Saint Birgitta describes a Swedish knight who inquired of a prophetess (*spakonu*) whether or not there would be a rebellion against the king, and things turned out as the prophetess foretold. He told the king of these events within the hearing of Birgitta, and as soon as she left, "the bride of Christ" heard a voice that asked if she had heard how the knight asked for counsel of the prophetess and how she told of the coming peace. Birgitta is instructed to tell the king that, because of the people's superstitious nature (*for folksins vantro*), God allows the devil to know about things that will happen. The devil in turn reveals the future to those who ask him for counsel in order to deceive those who are faithful to him "and unfaithful to me" (*oc mik äru otrone*). Those who traffic in such prophecies should be condemned and removed from Christian society, as they have given themselves to the devil and hope to become rich against God's will and thereby allow the devil to gain power over their hearts. To accomplish such evil temptations, the devil sends helpers like witches and other opponents (*trolkonur ok andra tronne genuärdhogha*) through whom humans can be fooled.[121]

In this episode, Birgitta provides us with the basics of the ideological struggle Christian thinking saw in the survival of pagan traditions: How is it that soothsayers working outside a Christian context can sometimes be right? And what is the source of their power? The answers are both clever and tortured: the Almighty allows the devil to know about things that will come to pass because of the superstitious nature of the people; the devil, in turn, wants to fool those who are faithful to him; the devil has emissaries in the form of witches to assist him in these deceptions; and those who have abandoned the true faith and gone over to the devil are to be condemned and dealt with. To the extent that this story provides a window on how even at the highest levels of fourteenth-century Nordic society prophecy was a reliable resource for intelligence, as well as an active force to be reckoned with by church authorities, it is a remarkable testimonial, but it is not especially rich in details about how the prophecies were achieved.

More revealing in this regard is a miracle from circa 1385, in which a couple consult with a man who believes in the devil and conjures him when he wants to know the tidings (*tha han wilde nakur tidhande wita*).[122] A childless couple come to this man to ask whether or not the woman will bear children, and the man, as was his custom, casts a circle and calls his devils, many of whom immediately come to him in different forms. One of these bears a crown on his head, and when a priest goes by with the consecrated host, the devil falls to his knees, removes the crown, and acknowledges Christ's supremacy. As a result, the couple recognize and mend their evil ways, and the devil fails to capture their souls. The scene sketched in this miracle, as typical of European witchcraft norms as it is, is also uncannily like the broad outlines of the scene in *Eiríks saga rauða*, where again a circle to which spirits are drawn is the key feature. This is not to suggest a direct relationship between the texts but rather that these may be yet another example where institutional power has relied in one way or another on folk traditions or, at the very least, seized on the opportunity to exploit the similarities between elite and nonelite images of magic.

Health

Magic is sometimes held in the popular imagination to be a kind of poor man's panacea, yet in the mid-1300s Magnus Eriksson, king of Sweden and Norway, had a stone that he believed would sweat if it came near poison.[123] King Magnus no doubt regarded this stone as both a superior medical discovery and a practical security device, but most modern observers would view the whole business as "mere superstition."[124] Such too must have been the attitude of church authorities, which had already put the stamp of disapproval on such beliefs: the early laws of Iceland declare, "People are not to do things with stones or fill them with magic power with the idea of tying them on people or livestock. If a man puts his trust in stones for his own health or that of his livestock, the penalty is lesser outlawry."[125]

In fact, stones, and especially gemstones, play a very important role in medieval thinking. So, for example, the Old Swedish poem referred to earlier and connected with the Birgittine double monastery in Vadstena, called by its modern editor *Den vises sten* (*The Philosopher's Stone*), tells of a marvelous stone belonging to a *mestare* 'master', the life-giving properties of which restore a man to health, indeed, raise him from the dead.[126] But the stone not only gives him life but also endows the man with "wisdom and understanding," as well as "strength and power."[127] Further, it cures lameness, deafness, and blindness. Much of the poem is concerned with the man's attempts to keep the stone from falling into the hands of the enemy, and by various means he ensures that it does not come into the devil's grasp.[128]

The hermeneutic possibilities are many: perhaps this stone is to be understood against the many metaphorical and physical stone references in the Bible.[129] Or perhaps it should be read against the significant scientific interest in gemstones exhibited in the Middle Ages (e.g., *De Lapidibus* of Bishop Marbode of Rennes), especially where medical applications were believed to be a possibility,[130] a perspective paralleled by their popular allegorical use in a great deal of medieval literature.[131] Moreover, mystics such as Mechthild of Magdeburg and Hildegard of Bingen make frequent use of stone symbolism, as does Saint Birgitta of Sweden herself. And it is also possible that alchemical allusions are being made as well.[132] But whatever the key to understanding this special stone that can cure the lame, the deaf, and the blind and has so many other virtues, it is clearly a magical stone to be desired and does not seem to comport well with the dour pronouncement in the Icelandic laws concerning trusting stones for one's health.

In fact, Nordic magic related to health, like that tied to romance, is another area where the evidence is strong. One rich resource has been the large number of amulets, often bearing runic inscriptions, that survive.[133] These protective articles reflect important aspects of medieval magic in that they are often specific as to desired effect, and frequently in Latin as well as the vernacular. To take one useful example, the whetstone-shaped amber amulet from Dømmestrup on Fyn in Denmark from the later Middle Ages bears a Latin inscription that twice reads 'against all harm' (*contra omnia mala*).[134] That the amulet is shaped like a whetstone may have as-yet unfathomed importance, and certainly the fact that its words are in Latin rather than the vernacular helps demonstrate the probable role of the clergy in the production of such magical instruments and the greater power understood to be possessed by the language of the church.[135] Moreover, recontextualizing the "performance" of the inscription, where the repetitions in the text may suggest ways in which the amulet was more than just an observed object of power—perhaps also a script for private rituals—must be kept in mind.

Another Latin text from Denmark demonstrates the broad connections Nordic charms of this sort had with European conjurations, from its invocation of the seven sisters to its employment of the ubiquitous magical formula *AGLA*:

I invoke you, seven sisters [. . .] Elffrica(?) Affricca, Soria, Affoca,
Affricala. I invoke and call you to witness through the Father, the
Son and the Holy Spirit, that you do not harm this servant of God,
neither in the eyes nor in the limbs nor in the marrow nor in any
joint of his limbs, that the power of Christ Most High shall reside
in you. Behold the cross of the Lord; flee, you hostile powers. The
lion of the tribe of Juda, the root of David, has conquered. In the
name of the Father, the Son and the Holy Spirit, Amen. Christ
conquers, Christ reigns, Christ rules, Christ liberates, Christ blesses
you, defends you from all evil. Agla (= Thou art strong in eternity,
Lord). Our Father.[136]

Similarly, another Latin text from Norway invokes the Gospel writers
and then says, "Peace for the bearer! Health [to the bearer!]" (*Pax portanti!
Salus [portanti!]*).[137] Yet another includes both languages, saying in the vernacular, "For the eyes," and then in Latin, "Tobias heals the eyes of this person,"
and finally concluding with the famous figures from the Hebrew Scriptures,
Shadrach, Meshach, and Abednego, conjoined by "and" in both Latin and
Norse.[138]

In yet another example, a rune-inscribed stick from the Danish town of
Ribe from circa 1300 consists of a prayer for help in curing some malady,
perhaps malaria, which reads,

I pray Earth to guard and High Heaven, the sun and Saint Mary
and Lord God himself, that he grant me medicinal hands and healing tongue to heal the Trembler when a cure is needed. From back
and from breast, from body and from limb, from eyes and from
ears, from wherever evil can enter. A stone is called Svart[r] (black),
it stands out in the sea, there lie upon it nine needs, who shall
neither sleep sweetly nor wake warmly until you pray this cure which
I have proclaimed in runic words. Amen and so be it.[139]

The apparent invocation of the Christian God and the Virgin together
with the sun, earth, and sky is a notable piece of syncretism, and one is
struck by the request by the carver—perhaps also speaker—that he be granted
"medicinal hands and healing tongue."

Weather

Few things are of greater moment to the realities of daily life in Scandinavia—crops, livestock, fishing, and sailing, for example—than weather. Certainly the fact that there existed specific terms to designate the products of this kind of magic, *galdrahríð* 'magic storm' and *gerningaveðr* 'storm raised by witchcraft' (also *gerningahríð*), hints that the concept may indeed have been of significance. Control of the elements is important enough for its attributes to be enumerated among Óðinn's "List of Chants" in *Hávamál* 154:

> That ninth I know: if need there be
>   to guard a ship in a gale,
> the wind I calm,   upon the waves also,
>   and wholly soothe the sea.[140]

And, indeed, the image that emerges from the testimony of the Icelandic sagas suggests that weather magic was in fact regarded as very important.[141] Manipulating storms and other weather-related phenomena play significant roles in such sagas as *Brennu-Njáls saga*, *Gísla saga Súrssonar* (*The Saga of Gísli Súrsson*), *Fóstbræðra saga* (*The Saga of the Sworn Brothers*), *Vatnsdæla saga,* and *Víglundar saga* (*The Saga of Víglundr*).

Frequently the saga writers employ weather magic as a literary device to set a tone or establish an atmosphere (see also Chapter 3). But it is also often portrayed as part of a climatic arsenal, frequently for hire, a weapon to deploy against foes. So, for example, in *Eyrbyggja saga* (*The Saga of the People of Eyri*), Þóroddr arranges with a witch named Þorgríma for her to create a magic storm (*at hon skyldi gera hríðviðri*) against a man crossing a heath.[142] When a family of witches is accused of crimes in *Laxdæla saga* (*The Saga of the People of Laxdale*), the father erects a ritual platform and the entire family mounts it, chanting spells, until they have raised a great storm, directed against their enemies.[143] In one of the more fantastic manifestations of this idea of weather as a tool, a character in *Þorsteins saga Víkingssonar* says that he owns a "weather bag" (*veðrbelgr*), which when he shakes it, causes such cold and fierce wind to blow out of it that a lake freezes.[144] In *Óláfs saga Tryggvasonar* (*The Saga of Óláfr Tryggvason*), Rauðr, a sacrificer very skilled in magic (*blótmaðr ok mjǫk fjǫlkunnigr*), is able, due to his magic, to get a good wind for his warship whenever he wants.[145]

Examples of this sort could be multiplied many times over within the narrative world of medieval Scandinavia, suggesting that such powers may have formed part of the Nordic *Weltanschauung*, but identifying evidence of their practice is another thing altogether. It may be, of course, that Scandinavian charms about weather were of a type that simply left no archival or material footprint. One of the very few examples of charm magic connected with weather phenomena comes from just before the period of this book, the late eleventh century, from Sigtuna in Uppland, Sweden. Parts of this complicated runic inscription appear to call on "mist" and "(sun)shine" as agents to do the magician's bidding.[146] The abiding value of these abilities is readily inferred from the fact that they are attributed to medieval Christian saints as well. Thus, for example, it is said of the Icelandic bishop Saint Þorlákr that he provided aid to those who prayed to him, calming winds and seas, diminishing waves, and quelling storms, sharing many of these talents not only with Óðinn but also with Saint Elmo, the patron saint of sailors, underscoring the continuity of needs and functions within the Nordic area, irrespective of the dominant religion.[147]

Malediction

The language noted earlier of the Ribe rune stick raises an intriguing question, alluded to already several times: the question of performance. How were charms enacted? Something very similar to the Ribe runic charm, if with a very different objective, is presented in a runic inscription from Bergen dated to the late fourteenth century.[148] One of the commonly addressed problems to which magic was put was the discovery of lost property, or of the identity of the person who had stolen them, and this text was arguably part of some more elaborate ritual whose purpose was to find the name of a thief. The text also shows how a pagan god could continue to have vitality, but in a new setting, as the carver invokes not Christian powers in the first instance but Óðinn (*ek særi þik, Óðinn*).[149] Conversely, the broader Christian cultural framework is apparent when the text calls the old god "greatest among devils" (*mestr fjánda*) and invokes Christianity as part of the charm as well (*fyr kristni*).[150] It is surely the residue of a magical performance: although not unproblematic, the language of the text appears to provide us with a remarkable record of a charm actually being worked.[151]

Romance, foreknowledge, health, and weather represent important categories where medieval man could improve his or, as often as not, her lot in life, but magic no doubt touched virtually every aspect of life, including work; thus Birgitta condemns a man for using "witchcraft and other diabolical words" to increase his catch of fish.[152] The Icelandic laws implicitly recognize the differing uses of magic and explicitly detail two levels of witchcraft, saying,

> If someone uses spells or witchcraft or magic (*galldra eþa gørningar. eþa fiolkýngi*)—he uses magic (*fiolkyngi*) if he utters or teaches someone else or gets someone else to utter words of magic over himself or his property—the penalty is lesser outlawry[. . . .] If a man practices black sorcery (*fordæs skap*), the penalty for that is full outlawry. It is black magic (*fordæs skapir*) if through his words or his magic (*fiolkyngi*) a man brings about the sickness or death of livestock or people.[153]

Most of the forms of magic discussed thus far would no doubt have been regarded as more or less venial offenses, but one final area that needs to be mentioned is precisely what the Icelandic laws mean here when they designate "black magic" (*fordæðuskapr*, alt., *fordæsskapr*) as the form of magic that calls for full outlawry.[154] This kind of magic causes death, illness, and madness in others or in their livestock, as in the previous example, and of this sort of magic we have only a few examples.

One of the last recorded events in the Norse colony on Greenland falls into this category and involved so-called love magic. A man is executed in Greenland in 1407 for sleeping with a married woman, having taken her through "the black arts."[155] The inferences to be drawn from this brief entry include the possibility that it is the affair with this man and his subsequent execution that leave her unbalanced or perhaps rather that her mental health is impaired by the man's use of "the black arts," an act of *fordæðuskapr*, which in turn was the reason for his being consigned to such a terrible fate.

In fact, most of the evidence that would seem to bear on the matter of performance involves a malediction. As discussed earlier, such cases as those ostensibly involving anaphrodisiac magic—Ragnhildr tregagás, Margit halffstoop, and perhaps others—include a kind of cursing, but although we do have some specific details, few entries in the trial documents compare with the ways in which cursing procedures are presented in the surviving literary sources.[156] Indeed, the art of malediction often provides for some of the most dramatic moments in the literature of medieval Scandinavia, and in this last section I examine several presentations in our sources detailing individuals laying down a curse, mostly, but not all, from literary sources.

Thus, when in the scene discussed earlier, the witch Busla forces King Hringr to do her will in *Bósa saga ok Herrauðs*, the tripartite presentation of the process reflects the notion that there exist layers of impermissibility: when the author provides several hundred words of her first imprecation, the so-called *Buslubæn*, he says that it consists of evil words that Christians do not need to know. Following these words, the king tells her to go and threatens to have her tortured for her imprecations (*forbænir*), but at this point she has already made it impossible for him to rise from his bed. She then launches into what the author specifies as the second third of her curse (*Busla lét þá frammi annan þriðjung bænarinnar . . .*), about which the narrator further notes that it is less likely to be repeated if it is not written down and therefore he will only provide the beginning of the text.[157] Following her delivery of the chant, the king now partially accedes to her demands, and, unsatisfied, Busla responds to the effect that she must do him one better.[158] She then utters *Syrpuvers*, which the author says is the most powerful sort of magic and which cannot be said after sunset. When she has finished it, including the runic puzzle at the end, the king agrees to do as she wants. The scenario is at one level highly stylized, yet it also hints at what the art of imprecation and its allusive performance practices may have been like in the Nordic Middle Ages.

A similar and, if anything, even more dramatic presentation of how one worked magic, in the eyes of saga writers at least, is given in *Egils saga Skalla-Grímssonar* (*The Saga of Egill Skalla-Grímsson*). Having fallen out with the king and queen of Norway, Egill kills their young son and his men, loots the valuables from the farmstead, and then performs a powerful curse, described in the saga in some detail.[159] Egill goes up on the island with a hazel pole, which he raises on a rock outcropping and on it places a horse head. He then begins to perform an incantation:[160] he declares that he has raised the insult-pole (*níðstǫng*) and that he turns (*sný*) its imprecation on the king and queen. He then turns (*sneri*) the horse head toward the land and says that he turns (*sný*) the imprecation against the land-spirits who dwell in that land, that they should be disoriented and lost until they have driven the king and queen from the land. Egill then shoves the pole into a fissure in the rock and allows it to stand there. He turns (*sneri*) the head toward the land, carves runes on the pole, writing out the entire invocation, and then goes to the ship. We learn subsequently that the king and queen are, indeed, forced to leave the country.

We have no way of knowing just how well, or how poorly, this scene matches what may really have happened in the practice of magic, either at the time when the story's events were supposed to have taken place in the tenth century or, for that matter, at the time they were written down in the thirteenth century, but there are aspects of the narrative that lead us to believe that it comports well with tradition, even if it the historical Egill never did what the story reports. Thus the use of a *níðstǫng* is treated elsewhere in Norse sources as real and as a chargeable offense, the verb *snúa* 'turn' (> *sný, sneri*) in Nordic charm contexts appears to have a deep pedigree, and so on. Simply put, there is much about the scene of Egill's imprecation that feels right, both within Nordic praxis and as compared to wider European traditions of cursing.[161] That is not to suggest that we can recontextualize a performance of this sort with accuracy but rather to note that the saga's portrayal of this execration projects a worldview and a use of the tools of Nordic charm magic in ways that seem entirely plausible.[162]

The use of performance as a key for understanding Nordic charm magic holds great promise and is a perspective that has been heavily mined in other areas of the Old Norse field in recent years.[163] Although the means and methods of these writers have differed, the goal that Old Norse scholarship emphasizing performance shares with parallel research on other cultures and epochs is to return the archaic cultural goods on which we work to the richly textured contexts from which the stories have sprung; to derive from a consideration of performance contexts a deeper understanding of meaning; and to consider whether their findings would be recognizable to the medieval audiences of the works.[164] Performance—at least in the sense modern scholarship intends it—may indeed overlap partially with older arguments about orality but is distinct from it in that the goals and concerns of the two are often quite different. Focusing on performance theory allows us to shift our gaze from a consideration of our medieval texts as determinate entities in themselves and toward their place in a broader tradition of enactments and reenactments.[165]

Although the general nature of the curse in *Skírnismál* has already been discussed earlier as part of Scandinavian traditions of "love magic," it is well worth considering it again in this context, and especially with regard to the rich evidence the poem provides about the process of Skírnir's successful malediction. Thus, part of the reason *Skírnismál* is so compelling to modern

audiences depends on the central paradox that dominates it and its treatment
of the reluctant "bride" Gerðr.[166] The text is appropriately conceived of as
being concerned mainly with sex and consuming desire, and only more ab-
stractly with fertility, but the resolution of the poem's central tension is
achieved specifically by threatening Gerðr's reproductive capacity with an
anaphrodisiac imprecation.[167] A consideration of Skírnir's curse in its entirety
makes clear that when neither gifts nor threats to the physical well-being of
Gerðr's family accomplish his goal, Skírnir turns to magic. In delivering the
curse, he punctuates, or perhaps partitions, the curse with references to the
magic wand he carries, paralleling the way the sword operates in the earlier
section of the dialogue when Skírnir threatens the lives of Gerðr and her
family.

Using the references to the wand as markers partitioning the curse, it is
apparent that the curse consists of, like Busla's curse, three sections: first,
Skírnir says he will "tame" (*temia*) Gerðr to his will after he has hit or
touched her with it, and he then exiles Gerðr to a netherworld, telling her
she will be ugly and will know nothing but sorrow, and compares her to a
thistle at harvest time. Skírnir now makes a second reference to the wand,
and he explains how he got it by going to the forest, and then he declares
that she has angered the gods. Calling on various races of supernatural beings,
Skírnir then denies her the enjoyment and use of men but says that a giant
will have her. Finally, in his third specific reference to the wand (v. 36), he
says that he will write runes "for her," which will give her madness, lechery,
and restlessness. Alternatively, he can cancel these states by scratching away
the runes.

Skírnir's tripartite curse with its mix of oral cursing and runic writing is
consistent with other examples of Norse imprecations, at least as presented
in literary sources such as *Bósa saga ok Herrauðs* and *Egils saga Skalla-Grímssonar*. A performance such as that presented for Skírnir also helps us understand
what is at the heart of the historical data (e.g., the trial of Ragnhildr tregagás)
and some of the surviving rune sticks (e.g., N B257 M). Busla's curse must
be understood as having been presented to the king near its conclusion in a
written runic form, one inconsistent with a purely oral presentation, just as
Skírnir carves runes during his charm. Egill too concludes his ritual by carving in runes the words he has earlier uttered. In the fourteenth-century case
of Ragnhildr tregagás, the records describing events, and particularly the performance of the curse around which the case turns, say at the exact moment
where the curse is to be laid down "and when these words are read" (*oc sidan*

þesse ord ero lesen). Perhaps the wording of the bishop's amanuensis at this juncture is to be taken literally—or perhaps not—but they seem to fit the larger pattern of Nordic cursing.[168]

The degree to which Skírnir, Egill, and Busla are all portrayed as cursing in ways that mix speaking and writing belie the frequent treatment of the two communication modes as being in categorical opposition to one another.[169] This view appears to be codified in the *Gulaþingslǫg* (*The Law of Gulaþing*), for example: when in discussing the penalties for *níð* 'insult', 'libel', 'scorn', the authors of the laws (dated in their current form to the thirteenth century) carefully distinguish between *tunguníð* 'slander' (lit., 'tongue insult', i.e., orally performed defamation) and *tréníð* 'libel' (lit., 'tree insult', i.e., written or carved defamation).[170] Here the law writers are evidently providing the full range of expressive media, oral and written, or that which is formed on the tongue and that which is formed on wood. But in the area of Nordic charm magic, oral and written utterances do not represent so much an opposition as a continuum, seemingly categorical opposites bound together by the fact that both require actuation through performative acts; moreover, despite the apparent oppositional nature suggested by writing and speaking, there exist numerous reticulated relationships between the two as they were used in cursing, as may be readily inferred from our materials.

It is, in fact, of no small consequence that—our embedded literary references aside, such as those in *Skírnismál*, *Egils saga Skalla-Grímssonar*, and *Bósa saga ok Herrauðs*—the evidence for a Nordic tradition of charming consists to an unusual degree of what appear to be the realized end products of a magical process, that is, the detritus of actual magical practices where the utterance instructions usually associated with the grimoires of Anglo-Saxon tradition, for example, have in Scandinavia actually been performed. Thus, although we may lack texts comparable to the prescriptive charms of the Anglo-Saxon *Lacnunga* (BL MS Harley 585), Nordicists may take heart that, instead, we possess such objects as the Bergen rune stick against which to measure texts like *Skírnismál*. This object is no abstract recipe telling its user how to bend a woman to one's will, but rather a demonstration of the power of such a charm captured in flagrante delicto.

Comparing, for example, these three literary portrayals of malediction with the one historical instance we possess from medieval Scandinavia where the art of malediction is drawn in some detail, the trial of Ragnhildr tregagás in Bergen, provides us with an excellent sense of the "actual" nature of how incantation was performed. There is a lot to unpack in this story, including that we begin to see continuities, as in the important phrase *gondols ondu* and the concern in the Norwegian laws for articles of witchcraft being hidden in beds.[171] So, for example, *Borgarþingslog* (*The Laws of Borgarþing*, datable to the mid-twelfth century, although preserved only in later, mainly early fourteenth-century, manuscripts) state, "And if sorcery is found in bedding or bolster, the hair of a man, or nails or frog feet or other talismans which are thought wont in witchcraft, then a charge may be made."[172]

Another important component in this case is the degree to which the declaration of the curse must be public—very public, in fact. Indeed, it is worth repeating the sequence of events here: on the first night of the wedding, Ragnhildr carries out the three fundamental aspects of the curse—hiding the objects in the bed, uttering the actual curse formula, and spitting on Bárðr—but it is as if these action are not operational until she makes her public declaration of the curse. Thus Ragnhildr, the perpetrator of the charm, finds it necessary to go up to her rival at the wedding feast and declare openly that she has made her erstwhile lover impotent—the possibility of revenge from Bárðr and his party, or of accusation from the authorities, seems not to be a consideration for her, so critical an element to the success of the charm does broadcasting the news seem to be. Performance matters, and it is obvious that how things are done is nowhere of greater relevance than in the context of highly prescribed ritualized behavior of the sort one associates with casting a spell.[173]

Much has been made of the fact that *galdr*, one of the most common words in Old Norse for 'magic', 'witchcraft', and 'sorcery' but also more narrowly for 'magic song', 'charm', is historically related to *gala* 'to crow; to chant, sing', the same root that yields in English such words as 'yell', 'yelp', and the last element of 'nightingale'.[174] In fact, the terms used for the witches' spells and charms are frequently based on words having to do with song (or the noise and sound by which incantations are produced), nomenclature that has subsequently attached itself both to the individuals carrying out the performance and the act itself. And this association extends well beyond the Germanic dialects. Thus when the Roman poet Horace describes the incantations of several witches (*Satires* 1.8.25), he says that they, Canidia and Sagana, *ululantem* 'cry out, shriek, yell' (cf. *ulula* 'screech owl'). A whole series of words in Latin, often with modern resonances—*carmen* 'song, charm, ritual formula', *cantus* 'song, incantation, spell', *cantio* 'singing, incantation, spell', *cantare* 'to sing, bewitch'—points to the same association. Sometimes word histories are just derivations, but sometimes, too, they bear profound meaning. In the case of charm magic, the etymologies underscore an important aspect of their practice: performance was indeed a critical component of the production of magic, both its broad social production as well as its more narrowly operative production.

Chapter 3

Narrating Magic, Sorcery, and Witchcraft

Scandinavia's medieval literature is famously rich, and anyone looking to discover Nordic attitudes toward witchcraft in the Middle Ages will naturally want to use it as a witness.[1] After all, it reflects considerable preoccupation with issues of magic and witchcraft, greater than many other Western traditions.[2] But what sort of testimony do the narrative materials from that world provide? Are they to be regarded as statements about what medieval Icelanders and other Scandinavians—or perhaps their forebears—actually thought about magic and witchcraft, or are they tendentious documents written for the very purpose of shaping what their readers and other audience members should think, or yet again, are they some other sort of mediating alternative? Impinging too in significant ways on how these documents should be understood are questions of patronage, authorship, intended audience, relationship to the past, and other issues related to the social production of these texts, important but not always knowable facts.

An illuminating example of this dilemma in the East Norse area is the anthology known as *Fornsvenska legendariet* (*The Old Swedish Legendary*), a vast compilation originally executed in the late thirteenth century, largely built on the *Legenda aurea* (*Golden Legend*) of Jacobus de Voragine, showing knowledge of texts such as the *Chronicon pontificum et imperatorum* (*Chronicle of Popes and Emperors*) of Martinus Oppsaviensis and German works such as *Sächsische Weltchronik* (*Saxon World Chronicle*). More than just an eclectic set of translations, also interfoliated into it are specifically Swedish narratives, such as the vita of the national patron saint, Saint Erik.[3] The legendary is a dauntingly hefty text and offers extraordinary glimpses into clerical thinking about magic, diabolical agency, and witchcraft in the period around 1300. Yet despite many decades of vigorous philological, literary, and cultural analysis, and although we know quite a bit about the native dialect of the translator-author, for example, we know little about—presumably—him; and perhaps even more important, we have no idea who the intended audience for so carefully wrought a work in the vernacular was to have been. Speculation has centered on the Beguine population in Skänninge, or some other female religious community, but to date no clear answer has emerged.[4] Notwithstanding this lacuna in our most basic understanding of the work's background, scholars reasonably, and profitably, look to mine the collection for all sorts of information, not least reflections of church thinking about witchcraft and magic at that time.

Other layers of cultural context can occasionally further cloud our ability to understand medieval Nordic literature, especially the question of a text's relationship to the past and the degree to which, say, a fourteenth-century work informs us, or can inform us, not only about the views contemporary with its composition but also about those from earlier periods. Obviously, medieval textual culture was anything but a perfect mirror of the past, yet it was undoubtedly capable of being informed by traditions about the past, and sometimes even of preserving with accuracy information from the past, although historicity in these instances is a hotly debated topic.[5] One noted scholar in the area, Pernille Hermann, reasonably argues that we regard the literature produced in medieval Iceland as both a preservation of *the* past and the creation of *a* past.[6]

How then are we to understand the considerable literary resources of the later Nordic Middle Ages when looking to interpret attitudes toward magic and witchcraft in that period? In my opinion they represent an extraordinary research opportunity to be neither ignored, at one extreme, nor simply accepted at face value, at the other, but are rather a tool to be used with due caution. Jenny Jochens wisely remarked some years ago that even though they are not spotless mirrors of bygone eras, the Icelandic sagas "can tell us what the thirteenth-century authors wanted their audiences to believe about past behavior. . . ."[7] It is in this sense, as mainly thirteenth-and fourteenth-century uses of the past to express contemporary perspectives, that we should encounter the descriptions of historical sorcerers, witches, and magic.[8] At the same time, however, we need to recall that these phenomena had not died out as active forces within Scandinavian society, meaning that representations of past magical practices sometimes also resonate with contemporary realities.

Also important to bear in mind is that although we as modern readers are naturally drawn to the brilliance of the Icelandic sagas, given their originality, well-told tales, and promise of shedding light on the Middle Ages (especially when set against the comparatively dim wattage of many other medieval literatures), these texts were by no means the only, or even the main, sort of narratives known throughout late medieval Scandinavia. Indeed, many different forms of narrative materials—saints' lives and translated romances, of course, but also histories, moralizing tales, even sermons and private prayer books—also represent important, if generally less original, sources of information. These too are taken up here in order to provide a more complete impression of how magic and witchcraft were presented and shaped in the spiritual culture of medieval Scandinavia.

Icelandic Poetry and Sagas

In discussing magic and witchcraft in medieval Scandinavian narratives, I separate out for special attention the poetry and prose of Iceland. Treating Iceland in this manner, although justifiable, does run the risk of valorizing Icelandic culture in a peculiar way, suggesting, for example, that it was uniquely conservative or culturally isolated, insular in more than simply geographical terms. That, of course, would be nonsense. On the other hand, "Icelandic exceptionalism," as it sometimes called, is not without merit. The notion of medieval Icelandic narrative sensibility and memory being out of the ordinary can be justified initially by turning to the opinions of medieval Scandinavians themselves: Saxo Grammaticus and the author of *Historia de antiquitate regum Norwagiensum* (*The Ancient History of the Norwegian Kings*), Theodoricus, both writing in the late twelfth century, suggest that Icelandic knowledge of Nordic traditions was extraordinary, more so than in the other Scandinavian lands.[9] Moreover, the sheer volume of original materials produced by Icelandic authors dwarfs the literary endeavors of the other Nordic countries. To suggest that there was not something special about the medieval Icelandic situation—or at least the quality and volume of its literary production, in any event—would be equally unwarranted.

Undoubtedly the single most important cultural object to come from the Scandinavian Middle Ages for our understanding of the pre-Christian traditions of Scandinavia is the collection known as the *Poetic Edda*.[10] It is from this remarkable presentation of Norse mythology and heroic literature that we have many of the centerpieces about the role of magic in pre-Christian Scandinavia, such as *Skírnismál* (*The Lay of Skírnir*) and *Hávamál*

(*The Sayings of the High One*). The manuscript of this anthology dates to about 1270, but something like the current collection must have existed already earlier in the century.[11] It is useful to consider the very fact that a thirteenth-century Icelander found assembling, or copying, this manuscript worthwhile. That is not as uncomplicated an idea as it may seem and should raise any number of questions about the value and function of such poetry in Christian Iceland.[12] What, for example, are we to conclude when the poem called *Vǫluspá* (*The Seeress' Prophecy*) appears in the *Poetic Edda* (ca. 1270), as well as in the fourteenth-century collection known as *Hauksbók, and* is extensively cited in the early thirteenth-century *ars poetica* known as *Snorra edda* (the *Younger* or *Prose Edda*)?[13] That is, the poem is recorded, copied, cited—opinions vary but, in any event, used—on three occasions over the course of a century. May we not reasonably suppose that these facts speak not only to the relative popularity of that particular text but also more broadly to the appeal of visionary literature in that period, especially when other kindred works, albeit with a more Christian tone, are considered?[14]

In other words, we need to be aware that these texts, although occasionally harking back to earlier periods, also had their own relevance to the thirteenth and fourteenth centuries and were in all likelihood not merely preserved in them. Although they may represent memories from, or representations of, the past, these poems are hardly likely to have been mere cultural atavisms, recorded only through some reawakened antiquarian interest: they surely meant something to the people who wrote them down and to those who in turn heard or read them. Producing manuscripts of this sort was serious business in terms of economic and social costs, that is, the actual manufacture of vellum, the training of a scribe, the "opportunity costs" (i.e., the loss of labor that could be used in other ways), and so on. Seriousness of purpose lay behind the production of such manuscripts.

Given that fact, how much we know about Nordic mythology is surprising, for, in addition to the eddic poems, a variety of other narratives, such as Snorri's edda, saga texts, and non-Icelandic sources, such as Saxo's *Gesta Danorum* (*History of the Danes*), provides us with the sometimes conflicting outlines of Nordic paganism.[15] Witchcraft and magic as projected in the mythological corpus are complex phenomena in which charms, incantations, and sacrifice play significant roles. These cultural products are heavily tied to the worship of the pre-Christian gods, among whom the use of magic is shown—in eddic poetry in particular—to be common.

The deities Óðinn and Freyja were outlined in Chapter 1. Here I revisit them and, in particular, their connections with magic. Certainly the principal pagan deity tied to magic in the extant poetry is Óðinn, nowhere more clearly so than in *Hávamál*.[16] Structurally, the poem moves from the quotidian (e.g., advice on how to comport oneself as a guest) to the arcane (e.g., claims to knowledge of various spells). Just prior to the so-called *Ljóðatal* (List of Chants, st. 146–64), Óðinn asks if the listener knows certain kinds of arcane things, including how to sacrifice, and then enumerates in the list itself eighteen different charms that he claims to know, covering such areas as illness, courage on the battlefield, weather, countercharms against hostile magic, defense against hags (*túnriðor*), settling discord, communicating with the dead, and seducing women.

And just before this section, *Hávamál* recounts how Óðinn sacrifices himself to himself and in so doing acquires the runes (*nam ec upp rúnar*), "nine mighty songs" (*fimbullióð nío*), as well as fecundity and knowledge (*þá nam ec frævaz / oc fróðr vera*).[17] Óðinn's acquisition of runic knowledge thus allows him to manipulate fertility and wisdom, as we have seen in the case of the charms discussed earlier. It is Óðinn who engages the seeress (*vǫlva*) in the poem called *Vǫluspá* and queries her about the past and future events, as she herself makes clear when she describes him looking into her eyes and addresses him directly.[18] Arguments abound as to how the framing scenario of the poem should be understood, but whether the seeress is awakened from the dead, for example, as some believe, or constrained by Óðinn by other means to tell him what he wants to know, it is clearly he who is the necromancer.

The image of Óðinn, not only as a pagan deity, but also as a magician—indeed, the chief of magicians—is widespread. So, for example, in his early thirteenth-century edda, Snorri Sturluson presents a catalogue of Odinic cognomina and other references to the god in the poetry of the "main poets" (*hǫfuðskáldin*).[19] There, among the various references to Óðinn's connection with the dead, his acquisition of the poetic mead, his coming death at Ragnarǫk, and other stories about him, Snorri cites Kormákr's comment that Óðinn had worked magic on Rindr.[20] This story is connected with the death of Baldr, foreshadowing the passing of the old generation of gods at the final great battle between the gods and the forces of evil.[21] This myth complex, known from disparate sources, provides a fine illustration of Óðinn as necromancer and worker of spells.

According to Icelandic sources, following Baldr's death at the hands of his brother, Hǫðr, Óðinn begets another son, Váli, with Rindr. In the eddic-style poem *Baldrs draumar* (*Baldr's Dreams*), Baldr is disturbed by bad dreams, causing Óðinn, "the father of magic" (*galdrs fǫður*) to ride to Hel.[22] There, in a scene clearly parallel to *Vǫluspá*, he uses *valgaldr* 'charms to raise the dead' to awaken a dead witch.[23] In response to his repeated command, "Cease not, seeress, / till said thou hast," she reveals that he will father a child, Váli, who will avenge his brother, using nearly the same words found in *Vǫluspá* (st. 33).[24] Although Snorri lists Rindr among the goddesses, little is known of her apart from the idea that she is said to bear Óðinn a son who avenges his brother.

In his late twelfth-century *Gesta Danorum* (book 3), the Danish chronicler Saxo Grammaticus provides a very different, albeit related, story, in which Óðinn (Othinus) attempts through a variety of means, including military prowess and producing jewelry, to win the woman, now called Rinda, but to no avail. Finally, in the guise of a female physician, Óðinn seizes his opportunity when she falls ill and instructs that she be tied down, due to the violent reaction the medicine will produce. Once secured, he rapes her. Óðinn's "success" in Saxo is thus the result of his guileful nature, not magic. In fact, here Óðinn is mostly presented as an end user, not a producer, of magic—likewise, at the beginning of the episode, Saxo writes, "Now although Odin was regarded as chief of the gods, he would constantly approach seers, soothsayers and other whom he had discovered strong in the finest arts of prediction, with a view to prosecuting vengeance for his son."[25] Despite Óðinn's relatively slight association with magic in Saxo's version of the Rinda story, he does retain some magical abilities. When at one point Rinda refuses his advances by pushing him so that he falls to the floor, Óðinn responds by touching her with an inscribed piece of bark, which causes her to go mad for a while, but her later sickness, which gives Óðinn his opportunity to sire Váli, apparently has nothing to do with this episode.[26]

When Snorri takes up the figure of Óðinn in *Ynglingasaga* (*Saga of the Ynglings*), the opening text in *Heimskringla*, like Saxo, he too presents a euhemerized Óðinn. The chief of the gods in other sources, he is said to be a human ruler who migrates north with his followers. And here magic is not only a significant feature, but one of its chief organizing principles. Perhaps one of the most intriguing comments Snorri makes is his insistence, repeated several times, that Óðinn's magical practices continued for a long time.[27] Among his magical abilities, Óðinn could make his enemies blind, deaf, or terrified in battle and dull and bend their weapons. Moreover, he possesses the ability to change his physical shape, lying as if dead or asleep, yet moving about in different places in the shape of a bird, animal, fish, or snake.[28] He also possesses the ability with words alone to put out fires, calm the seas, and turn the wind in different directions.[29] These skills he taught "with those runes and songs called incantations," and it is for this reason the Æsir are called sorcerers (*galdrasmiðir*, lit., 'magic-smiths').[30]

The location of buried treasures is known to him, and he knows those songs by which the earth, rocks, stones, and mounds are unlocked and could with words alone bind those who live in them and go in and take what he wanted.[31] And he uses the dead, occasionally waking them up or sitting under the hanged, for which reason he was called lord of ghosts and lord of the hanged.[32] The greatest power of all, however, resides in that art (*þá íþrótt*) which Óðinn knew and practiced, namely, *seiðr*.[33] Through it, he could have knowledge of the fates of men and things that had not yet happened and could cause in people death, bad luck, or illness and transfer wisdom or strength from one person and give it to someone else. But because this form of witchcraft (*fjǫlkynngi*) was followed by so much *ergi*, that is, 'lewdness', 'lust', it was thought shameful for men to practice it, and therefore it was taught to priestesses.[34]

Óðinn is tied closely to magic of all sorts, and the full range of magical activities associated with him and, important for us, known to medieval Icelandic Christian writers included (1) *galdrar* and runic magic, (2) *seiðr*, and (3) other magical skills where the terms *fjǫlkyngi*, *fróðleikr*, and *ljóð* would be appropriate terms.[35] The first group, following Price, included shape-shifting and ethereal travel; control of fires, water, and wind; communicating with the dead; helping spirits such as Huginn and Muninn; travel on the magical ship Skíðblaðnir. The second group included divination, killing, causing sickness, inflicting misfortune, decreasing or increasing the wit of people, and decreasing or increasing the strength of people. The third included revealing what is hidden; opening stones, mounds, and the underground; and binding their inhabitants. Whatever Óðinn's role within the "actual" practice of the pre-Christian religion of the Nordic world—a topic of considerable debate—he was certainly the key figure in the post-Conversion presentations of that mythology where magic was concerned.[36]

It would be difficult indeed to disambiguate the use of magic from the presentation of Óðinn, but other figures too, especially the goddess Freyja, are also associated with enchantment.[37] *Ynglingasaga* states that Freyja teaches *seiðr* to the Æsir, because it was a custom among her people, the Vanir.[38] *Vǫluspá* maintains that magic (*seiðr*) was taught to the gods by a female figure, generally believed to be Freyja.[39] And the argument for her special connection to the magical world is surely strengthened, when in *Hyndluljóð* (*Chant of Hyndla*) Freyja plays a role very like Óðinn's, in that the goddess stirs a *vǫlva* awake and discovers from her what she needs to know.[40] In fact, one scholar has argued that Freyja should be understood as the Nordic resonance of "the great goddess" and thus holds a special relationship to such areas as fate.[41]

The image of magic and those who employ it—witches, prophetesses, gods—that emerges from eddic poetry tells us that these concepts were fundamental to that mythological and heroic world. A verse from *Vǫluspá in skamma* (*The Shorter Vǫluspá* or *Seeress' Prophecy*) lists several types of enchanters, provided with, one suspects, an eye toward gender.[42] In explaining that giants (*hrímþursar*, *jǫtnar*) descend from Ymir, Snorri cites part of the poem: all prophetesses (*vǫlur*), it says, come from Viðólfr, all wizards (*vitkar*) from Vilmeiðr, all practitioners of sorcery (*seiðberendr*) from Svarthǫfði.[43] It is difficult to escape the impression that exactly these terms are selected because the people to whom they refer encompass users who are explicitly both females and males.

The most dramatic presentation of magic being used in eddic poetry is, as discussed in Chapter 2, surely *Skírnismál*, but similar in many ways is the eddic-style poem called *Grógaldr* (*Magic of Gróa*).[44] It is one of two poems in *ljóðaháttr* that make up the work known collectively as *Svipdagsmál*.[45] Extant in several dozens of post-Reformation manuscripts, these works too are thought to be from the mid-thirteenth century. In *Grógaldr*, Svipdagr is given the task of searching for and winning the giantess Menglǫð. He seeks the advice and help of his dead mother, Gróa, who provides him with nine charms. In *Fjǫlsvinnsmál*, Svipdagr encounters a castle surrounded by flames. A watchman starts to send him away, but in their knowledge confrontation, the watchman makes known that Menglǫð is there and awaits a particular hero. When Svipdagr reveals his true name, the gates open, and he is received by the maiden. *Grógaldr* highlights two aspects of magic as it is portrayed in presentations of the pagan world—the importance of knowing charms and the use of necromancy. In that sense, the poem is very similar to the "List of Chants" section of *Hávamál* (albeit the number of charms is reduced to nine from eighteen) and shares with *Baldrs draumar*, *Vǫluspá*, and other texts the motif of the awakened witch or seeress.

A further poetic genre, peculiar to Iceland, should be mentioned in this context, the *rímur*. This form of epic poetry is not in evidence before the very late fourteenth century, quickly becoming one of the most productive types of Icelandic literature over the next half millennium.[46] Often based on *fornaldarsǫgur*, romances, and other texts, these popular works use highly stylized diction and elaborate metaphors and combine traditional alliterative meters with end rhyme. Frequently reworked from sagas and other literature, the *rímur* often reflect the original text's presentation of the magical world, one in which sorcerers and sorceresses play the role of adversaries to the hero, along with, as Vésteinn Ólason notes, "cruel Vikings," giants, and dwarves.[47] So, for example, in *Friðþjófs rímur*, the *rímur* form of *Friðþjófs saga frækna* (*The Saga of Friðþjófr the Bold*), the hero's enemies employ two transvecting witches (*hamhleypur*) who try to work their magic against Friðþjófr, very much, but not exactly, as in the saga.[48]

Among the original *rímur*, the most famous, *Skíðaríma* (*Skíði's Rímur*), is a parody, in this instance of both vision literature and the old gods.[49] In it, the hero is a tramp who has a dream in which he goes to Valhǫll, where he is to help make peace. There he meets many of the figures from the mythological and heroic world, including Óðinn, Þórr, Baldr, Heimdall, and Freyja. But rather than quelling disturbances, Skíði causes them, especially when he cannot refrain from referring to the Christian God in front of the old gods (st. 110–11), including making the sign of the cross (*Skíði gǫrði skyndikross*, st. 123). As a result, fighting breaks out between the various figures known from Scandinavia's mythological and heroic world. Sharing *Skíðaríma*'s interest in the pagan god, *Lokrur*, for example, recounts the story known from Snorri's edda in which Þórr and Loki visit Útgarða-Loki.[50] These *rímur*, as well as the pagan theophanies in some of the sagas, make it apparent that knowledge, and use, of the old gods was continuous throughout the Icelandic Middle Ages.

Magic unattached to the pre-Christian gods also plays an important role in these texts. A typical example comes from a *rímur* tied to the European tradition about Virgil.[51] The hero hopes to seduce a king's daughter, but she soon proves herself to be more than his equal. When they meet, the two discuss "book-learning and all kinds of tricks."[52] One might expect the term translated here as "tricks" (*bragð*) to refer to a physical ruse, but as the *rímur* makes clear, the tricks here and elsewhere are more than just sleight of hand.[53] In fact, Virgiles says that if she will not do as he asks, he will have to use some *listar* [sg., *list*] 'art, craft, skill', a word often employed to refer to magic. But it is she who outsmarts him, asking him to transform himself into a horse, which he does, at which point she rides him all over the countryside.[54]

Magic also plays an important role in the saga literature of medieval

Iceland. For the scholar approaching the topic from the point of view of a modified cognitive realism, there is little comparable to these medieval narratives.[55] As noted earlier, the relationship of the past to the present, and how medieval Icelanders used the one to comment on the other, is of paramount importance to our consideration of the presentation of witchcraft in the sagas. More broadly, the historical worth of these narratives has been at the center of scholarly activity for centuries. A complex debate evolved around the question of cultural realism in these medieval prose texts, formulated in the earliest periods by the view that the sagas might be understood as history rather than as historical fiction and, more recently, as testimony to the history of mentalities.[56] The evolution of this debate develops around the central question of just what sort of cultural documents we have in the sagas, with the key issue being the degree to which they can be trusted to present in a reliable form ethnographic data.[57] The questionable verisimilitude of these works did not, for example, stop generations of early modern nationalist writers from exploiting their contents to bolster competing claims to territory and prestige, especially in the context of seventeenth-century Dano-Swedish antagonisms.[58] That is not to say that these early modern polemicists did not have reasons to see the sagas and other medieval texts as rich resources holding out the possibility for recovering the past. After all, some of the best-known legendary cycles of medieval Northern Europe are based on history: Icelandic sagas about Alexander the Great, Charlemagne, Theodorik, and Saint Óláfr are all, at whatever remove and however thinly, informed by traditions inspired by actual events.[59] Moreover, the fact that the very word *saga* itself meant 'story', 'history', and 'account', as well as the specific literary genre its use conjures nowadays in almost all modern languages, added weight to the view that the events contained in them were based on reality reasonably well preserved.[60]

But as those early uses of medieval literature, and the charged political and nationalist debates to which they were tied, receded into the past, the historical accuracy of the medieval sagas took on new meaning. The soft skepticism of earlier historians working to promote their respective homelands' claims to political and cultural hegemony in Northern Europe gave way in the nineteenth and twentieth centuries to a new literalist phase, styled Freeprose-Bookprose by one of the debate's participants.[61] As an intellectual matter, this discussion looked to explain the compositional techniques used in the production of the sagas. In broad terms, Freeprose advocates believed in texts of such strong oral character that their form became memorized and fixed. That fixed form, in turn, was understood to convey from generation to generation highly accurate historical information. Bookprose partisans argued instead for something similar to modern authorship, often using the belief in the sagas' historical accuracy as a means of demonstrating the flaws in their opponents' views.[62] To the degree the sagas reflected individuals, places, and events verifiable through other kinds of evidence, they supported the Free-prose position; to the degree that the sagas could be shown to be filled with unhistorical matter, foreign borrowings, and imagined details, on the other hand, they could be shown to be Icelandic texts composed, mainly, in the thirteenth century.

At another level, this academic debate was a proxy war of words for a different issue that can only be understood in the context of the Nordic world's long history of inter-Scandinavian colonialism, as sentiment for political independence grew in Norway and Iceland. To the degree that the sagas were seen to be specifically Icelandic products, they bolstered Icelandic claims to autonomy, but to the degree that these wonderful medieval texts were understood to be the end products of a literary form developed and refined already in Norway, and brought by its emigrants to Iceland during the settlement era, then they helped support Norwegian claims of cultural maturity and thus a ratification of its demands for political independence.[63]

It was thus against a complicated background that a neoliteralist position began to emerge several decades ago. More subtle than that label perhaps suggests, it is a view that appreciates the arguments and concerns of previous generations about reading too much historicity into these manifestly literary works but at the same time refuses to dismiss the possibility of cautiously mining the medieval sagas for historical data that can be used in combination with other cultural monuments to shed light on the medieval period.[64] Naturally, progress in this regard was not made in a vacuum. Among the most important developments in refining our thinking about treating historical sources in the years intervening between the earlier discussions and the current situation may be seen in the rise of such methodologies as ethnohistory and microhistory,[65] as well as a more subtle notion of how studies of orality can help us understand the social production of the sagas.[66] Of equal importance has been the consideration in recent years of different kinds of memory in shaping the sagas.[67]

The sheer number of sagas makes some sort of organizational scheme in discussing them advisable. Although many attempts at establishing classificatory schemes have been made over the years,[68] one idea scholarship has widely applauded (if not always embraced), which has evident relevance to this discussion, is the proposal by Sigurður Nordal that rather than accepting traditional genre designations we adopt a system that disregards such features as the nature of the hero and focuses instead on the very tangible element of the sagas' "pastness."[69] This term is not one he uses but is easily teased out of his work and suggests a novel scheme for organizing medieval Icelandic literature. The argument proposes dividing the sagas into three categories, based on the distance from the cultural moment they treat and the time that gave the saga birth.[70] Thus he proposes categories for sagas that (1) deal with the distant past, before the settlement of Iceland (i.e., mainly the so-called *fornaldarsǫgur* [mythical-heroic, or legendary sagas] and *riddarasǫgur* [chivalric sagas], but also such works as *Ynglingasaga*); (2) are concerned with events during the first centuries of the settlement of Iceland, from the mid-ninth century to circa 1100 (i.e., many *íslendingasǫgur* [family sagas], some *konungasǫgur* [kings' sagas]); and (3) are more proximate to the thirteenth century, a category that includes most of the various texts that make up the synoptic history of Iceland known as *Sturlunga saga*, as well as some kings' and bishops' sagas. Although some of these latter texts are truly contemporary, some, for example, would treat twelfth-century events but are held to be based on observations and reports of those living at the time. He labels these groups *oldtidssager*, *fortidssagaer*, and *samtidssagaer*—that is, sagas of antiquity, sagas of the past, and contemporary sagas.

This temporal, and notably past-oriented, approach is particularly helpful here, for, as is frequently noted, there is relatively little witchcraft in the contemporary sagas.[71] Indeed, it was almost always understood in relationship to paganism and to the problem of lingering pagan superstitions. Continental views about the nature of witchcraft naturally gained acceptance over time in the Nordic world and certainly shaped its understanding of the phenomenon, but the association with heathenism was rarely far away. And, as will be discussed later, witchcraft and magic became convenient signs with which authors might indicate a sense of the text's remoteness and connection to the hoary past. With this tripartite system in mind, I take up in the following the role of magic and witchcraft in selected examples of medieval Icelandic sagas.[72]

In dealing with the earliest period, before the settlement of Iceland and the so-called sagas of antiquity (*oldtidssager*), an obvious place to begin is the thirteenth-century *Ynglingasaga*, both because of its relatively certain date of composition and because of the famous position it occupies in discussions of

Norse magic. It is situated as the first narrative in Snorri Sturluson's comprehensive history of the Norwegian kings, *Heimskringla*.[73] Partially based on an earlier scaldic poem, *Ynglingatal*, assigned by tradition to the poet Þjóðólfr úr Hvin, whom Snorri quotes generously, *Ynglingasaga* presents its audience with the earliest traditions of the royal houses of Sweden and Norway—the arrival in the north of the "gods" and the descent of the Ynglings.[74]

Once magical power is introduced among the Ynglings, it haunts them: indeed, several of the early Yngling rulers die in ways that appear to mimic the possibilities of what the saga earlier says about Óðinn's dark knowledge. Thus, where Óðinn can calm the seas with his magic, King Fjǫlnir drowns in a beer-brewing vat; where Óðinn knows the charms by which the rocks and stones are unlocked, King Svegðir enters a stone, never to return; and where Óðinn can send his spirit out in the shape of various animals as he lies in a sleeplike state, King Vanlandi is "ridden" to death in his sleep by a nightmare, trampled in the most literal sense, as Þjóðólfr suggests, by the troll-woman.

This last episode suggests another frequent theme in the sagas, the degree to which magic is attached to the idea of "the other."[75] Thus Freyja is said to have brought magic in the form of *seiðr* to the Æsir from her people, the Vanir, and the projection of magical abilities onto differing peoples has many resonances in the Nordic materials.[76] King Vanlandi's adventures illustrate this idea. He spends a winter "in Finland" (*á Finnlandi*), where he acquires a wife, Drífa.[77] He promises to return, and when, after ten years, he has not, Drífa contacts a witch named Hulð, whom she instructs to make Vanlandi return to Finland; failing that, she is to kill him. When Hulð performs her magic, Vanlandi senses a great desire to go to Finland but is advised against it by his friends and advisors, who say that his urge must be due to the magic of the Finns (*fjǫlkynngi Finna*). He now falls asleep and is trampled to death by a night-mare, that is, Hulð in the shape of a horse, or what in other contexts would be called an incubus. As Þjóðólfr says,

> A vile witch
> caused Vanlandi
> to visit
> Vili's brother [i.e., Óðinn in Valhǫll; 'to visit Vili's brother' = to die],
> when that trod
> the troll-woman,

wicked wench,
the warrior king;
was he burned
on bank of Skúta,
noble prince, whom
the nightmare killed.[78]

Of a very different character, although its composition is also separated by many centuries from its cultural moment, is *Friðþjófs saga frækna*, documented only in post-Reformation manuscripts and in the *rímur* tradition. Although not preserved in any directly medieval manuscript, it is thought to have been composed in the later Middle Ages, presumably in the postclassical era.[79] It is perhaps the best-known saga of the non-Icelandic nineteenth century due to its rewritten and modernized form in Swedish as *Fritjofs saga*, a poem reportedly translated into every European language.[80]

Friðþjófr is the son of Þorsteinn Víkingsson, himself the subject of a saga known from late medieval manuscripts, *Þorsteins saga Víkingssonar* (*The Saga of Þorsteinn Víkingr's Son*), which forms a prequel to *Friðþjófs saga frækna*.[81] These two sagas, which recount the adventures of three generations of heroes—Víkingr, Þorsteinn, and Friðþjófr—from Sognefjord in western Norway, are set in a period before the Viking Age, some six or seven centuries before the time from which the texts derive. Both simply brim with magical activity, and specifically, the malefic actions of sorcerers and witches, especially where weather magic is concerned.

By far the more complex of the two tales, *Þorsteins saga Víkingssonar* tells the stories of Þorsteinn and Víkingr, Friðþjófr's father and grandfather, as they serially square off against magically empowered enemies. Víkingr battles mainly against the offspring of Kolr, a man said to be as big as a giant and as ugly as the devil, skilled in magic, a shape-shifter, and someone able to transvect on the wind, who kills Tírus "the great" of India and takes over the kingdom.[82] Víkingr later kills Hárekr "iron-skull" (*járnhaus*), one of Kolr's spawn, when the monster attacks the kingdom of King Hríngr and his daughter, Húnvǫr.

Víkingr is subsequently put at risk when he encounters a beautiful maiden named Sólbjǫrt. Víkingr drinks from her horn, lays his head in her lap, and falls asleep, only to awaken, alone, dizzy, and with no recollection of his betrothal to Húnvǫr. He has, in fact, contracted leprosy (*líkþrá*) by drinking from the horn. It is later revealed that the maiden was, in fact, another of Kolr's offspring, the shape-shifter or transvectant witch, Dís (*ham-hleypan Dís Kolsdóttir*), the worst "troll" (*tröll*) in the world.[83]

Yet another of Kolr's children, Íngjaldr, comes to Norway, kills King Hríngr, and takes Húnvör back to India with him.[84] Víkingr is cured of leprosy by a dwarf who acquires the magical horn belonging to Dís. Víkingr and his men take Dís, place a skin bag over her head and stone her to death, proclaiming that they will now go to India. They capture Íngjaldr and bind him, but he manages to escape through means the saga wryly suggests were thought to be due to Ingjaldr's witchcraft.[85] In a subsequent battle with Víkingr and his men, Íngjaldr suddenly disappears, and in his place appears a boar, which attacks Víkingr's men. Víkingr eventually slices the animal along its back, and "they saw that Íngjaldr lay there dead, then they started a fire and burned him to cold ashes."[86]

Víkingr and his sworn brothers, Hálfdán and Njörfi, now settle down. Njörfi and Víkingr each father nine sons. To Þorsteinn, on whose exploits the remainder of the saga focuses, Víkingr gives his magical sword, Ángrvaðill, a weapon that had once belonged to Kolr. Through witchcraft, Kolr had caused it to be the only weapon that could be his children's bane, whereas no other iron could bite them (*lét seiða till þess, at ekki vopn skyldi at bana verða öllu hans afsprengi, utan sverðit Ángrvaðill*).[87]

The principal conflict of the latter portion of *Þorsteins saga Víkingssonar* involves a blood feud between these two families. After the slaying of one of the sons of Njörfi, several of Víkingr's sons, including Þorsteinn, take refuge on an island in Lake Vännern. Jökull, one of Njörfi's sons, prepares an attack on them, and the aquatic defense of the natural moat behind which Víkingr's sons have ensconced themselves is undone when one of Jökull's men volunteers, "I have a certain bag, called a weather bag; if I shake it, then out of it storm and wind blows with such fierceness and cold that within three nights such strong ice will be on the lake that horses can be ridden on it, if you want."[88] This man, Ógautan, is introduced earlier in the saga in a marked way when he and his brother, Gautan, arrive at Njörfi's court in dark blue cloaks.[89] Although Njörfi is ill-disposed toward them, his thoroughly malicious son, Jökull, offers them a place among his followers, seeing them as men with special talents (*íþróttirmenn nokkrir*).

Jökull asks Ógautan whether he cannot through his arts discover (*viss verða með listum þínum*) the whereabouts of Víkingr's sons. Ógautan asks that he and his brother be given a building to sleep in, that no one should come to them before Jökull himself, and that not happen until three days have passed. They are provided with an outbuilding (*skemma*), and when Jökull arrives early on the third day, Ógautan tells him where the sons of Víkingr are hiding, leading to the previously mentioned cold weather remark.

In the ensuing battle, only two brothers from each of the families survive, and the story follows for a while a series of largely incidental magical events (e.g., a fight with one combatant wearing a helmet with a magic stone preventing the wearer from falling in battle). The narrative now turns to Skati, king of the Sogn region, and his son, Beli, and daughter, Íngibjörg, who, the saga helpfully explains, is not then in the kingdom, as she is under a spell.[90] Years before, two Vikings, Gautan and Ógautan, had killed King Skati. Ógautan becomes king and asks Íngibjörg to marry him, an idea she rejects, saying that she would rather kill herself than marry the slayer of her father and someone who looks more like a fiend than a human.

Vengefully, Ógautan curses her (*leg ek þat á þik*), saying she will in size, appearance, and nature be like his sister, Skellingnefja, live in a cave, and not be able to break the curse until he himself is dead and a man of noble birth (*velborinn maðr*) promises to marry her; moreover, his sister will take on her appearance.[91] Remarkably, Íngibjörg attempts a countercurse and declares that Ógautan will only enjoy his kingdom poorly and for a short while. It is, however, Ógautan's imprecation that comes true (*áhrínsorðum*), and Íngibjörg suddenly disappears.

Her brother, Beli, retakes the kingdom, and the brothers, Gautan and Ógautan, escape to King Njörfi's court. Jökull and Beli now vie for the hand of the same woman, Ólöf, and she is asked which of the two she would marry. She is about to select Beli, when "at that moment, Ógautan threw a stick of wood in her lap, and it startled her such that she turned down Beli and married Jökull."[92] Hearing that Þorsteinn is sailing, Jökull consults with Ógautan, asking him to use his talents to raise a storm against Þorsteinn (*ok bað hann reyna listir sínar ok gera veðr at Þorsteini*). Ógautan then creates a great magical tempest (*kyngiveðr*) against Þorsteinn, in which all his men are drowned. Þorsteinn is saved by a hideous woman wearing an ill-fitting leather cloak—too long in front, too short in back.[93]

The text now returns to the homeward journey of Ógautan and Jökull following their successful trip to woo Ólöf. Suddenly, in good weather, a great darkness envelopes the ship, together with a terrible chill, and when the darkness lifts, the men see Ógautan hanging dead from the masthead. Þorsteinn engages in yet another battle with Jökull and, having lost his grip on the sword, Ángrvaðill, is rescued by Skellinefja, who looks, as the saga says, "no fairer than before" (*öngu fegri enn fyrr*). When he now promises to marry her in exchange for her help (including the further need for her to retrieve Ángrvaðill), she reveals that he has now helped release her from the curse Ógautan had placed on her.[94] A series of more mundane battles and a few further encounters with the supernatural conclude the saga.

The story of the third member of this family, the eponymous hero of *Friðþjófs saga frækna* and the son of Þorsteinn Víkingr's Son, is a tale of parted lovers, and it too is partially shaped by the deeds of practitioners of magic, if not quite so thoroughly as the narratives about Friðþjófr's forebears. The basic story here is one in which Friðþjófr incurs the hatred of Íngibjörg's brothers, all three of them the offspring of King Beli. In order to keep the two lovers away from each other, and in order to punish Friðþjófr for having violated the sanctity of Baldr's Pasture (*Baldrshagi*) in having visited Íngibjörg there, the brothers send Friðþjófr on a mission to collect taxes in the Orkneys. Meanwhile, Íngibjörg is married off to the aging King Hríngr, and the brothers raze Friðþjófr's home. Returned to Norway, Friðþjófr is outlawed by the brothers and takes up a Viking's life, nobly slaying only evil men and Vikings and leaving farmers and merchants alone. Eventually he ends up at the court of King Hríngr, whom he serves faithfully, so much so that when the old ruler is about to pass away, he declares Friðþjófr king and gives him Ingibjörg in marriage.

Those are the barest outlines of the narrative, and magic, paganism, and witchcraft clearly play a role but strike the modern reader as often being more ornamental than these same factors are, for example, in *Þorsteins saga Víkingssonar*. There are, however, two central areas where the author uses these important themes in the saga, namely, the pagan site of worship referred to as Baldr's Pasture and the use of witchcraft in an attempt to undo Friðþjófr on his errand to the Orkneys. In the case of the pagan temple at (or called) Baldr's Pasture, we get interesting, and rare, reconnaissance: at one point Friðþjófr enters the "hall of dísir," where the kings are said to be attending to the "dísir ritual."[95] Perhaps even more unusual than the saga's presentation of this house of worship are the references to the activities there: the wooden idols of the gods are being warmed and oiled and wiped down by the kings' wives, a practice that also occasions the burning of the hall when Friðþjófr attempts with disastrous results to wrest from one of the women the ring he had earlier given to Íngibjörg.[96] Thus it transpires that the idol of Baldr that she is warming and that had recently been anointed falls in the fire and in turn catches the building on fire.

Earlier the brothers have deposited Íngibjörg and eight other women in Baldr's Pasture while they are away at war, thinking that not even Friðþjófr would be so brash as to visit her there, implying a prohibition of a sexual sort, an interdiction that is indeed in evidence in other manuscript traditions.[97] And within the text, Björn, Íngibjörg, and others, despite their own willingness to violate this prohibition, treat the issue with seriousness. Clearly the author wants his audience to envision an ancient tradition of sanctity and sexual prohibitions, such as the Vestal virgins, *sacerdos Vestalis,* of Roman mythology, although whether this is a reflection of actual pagan practice in the north or merely a way to present pre-Christian Scandinavia as curious and heathen is impossible to know.

As a punishment for violating the sanctity of Baldr's Pasture, as well as an all too obvious way to get rid of him, Friðþjófr is sent by the brothers to collect overdue taxes from the Orkney Islands. To ensure that he not return, the saga says that they hire two witches (*seiðkonur*) to send a storm against Friðþjófr and his men and that "they performed their witchcraft, and mounted the scaffold with incantations and sorcery."[98] Running into the gale thus produced, Friðþjófr refers in a verse to "old charms" (*galdrar gamlir*) being the cause of it. As the seas and the weather grow worse and worse, Friðþjófr climbs the ship's mast and comes back with important news, "a very wondrous sight" (*mjök undarliga sýn*): a great whale circles the ship, which Friðþjófr understands to be the cause for their dilemma and knows too that King Helgi is responsible for it. Moreover, on the back of the whale, he has seen two women and declares that they have caused the storm with their terrible witchcraft and incantations, and he plans to see which is greater, "our luck or their sorcery."[99] Friðþjófr manages to dispatch one of the shape-shifters (*annari hamhleypunni*), while his magical ship, Elliði, takes care of the other. At the same time, back in Norway, "while the sisters were at their sorcery, they tumbled down from the high sorcery-scaffold and broke both their backs."[100]

As this outline makes clear, these sagas treating three generations of a family from Sogn, all set at some point anterior to the settlement of Iceland, bristle with magic. Indeed, it would be hard to imagine the current *Friðþjófs saga frækna* or, especially, *Þorsteins saga Víkingssonar* without their plots' heavy reliance on magic and those who use it. They are also texts reliant on notions about magical practice popular in courtly literature (e.g., Víkingr laying his head in the lap of Dís and the magical drinking horn, capable of both giving and curing leprosy). It is not difficult to envision how these texts look to present their heroes in the context of what Lars Lönnroth famously termed "the noble heathen," that is, good and moral pre-Christian paladins.[101] But as we have seen, these heroic figures are anything but cut from the same template, although that charge has typically been one of the complaints about them.[102]

In those sagas treating the ancient pagan period, magic, witchcraft, and sorcery are critically important concepts, in that their association with paganism is employed by saga writers as the key defining characteristic of that rough-hewn heathen world, not merely a widely practiced pre-Christian form of religion, but rather a way of presenting and referring to an entirely different manner of thinking. From the perspective of the thirteenth-century saga authors, the heathen world is one devoid of a benevolent creator to whom prayer may be addressed and is instead a world consisting entirely of soulless mechanistic appeals to demons. Turning from the texts set in the remote world of ancient Scandinavia to the sagas set in the intermediate period, the sagas of the past (*fortidssagaer*), that is, from the time since the settlement of Iceland to just before the contemporary period, we see a different role for magic and witchcraft in the hands of Icelandic authors. These phenomena represent a form of pagan resistance to the inevitability of Christianity, introduced within the time frame of the *fortidssagaer*. Witchcraft and all of its associations are no longer a kind of backdrop on which to paint the action, but have often become a focused means for shaping the nature of the hero, where the "noble heathen" becomes an ever more pronounced theme and a plot device of the first water.[103]

The treatment of magic and witches in the life of the tenth-century missionary king of Norway, Óláfr Tryggvason, as presented in Snorri Sturluson's *Heimskringla*, provides an excellent example of this point.[104] As the ruler who oversees the introduction of the new religion to Norway and Iceland, it is unsurprising that his opposition to paganism is one way in which his character is displayed. And as discussed previously, in this saga we do encounter serious and positive uses of one sort of magic, the magic that derives from God and has a Christian purpose.

Thus, while still a pagan Viking, Óláfr, hears of a prophet (*spámaðr*) in the Scilly Islands, and after testing his wisdom, Óláfr visits the hermit, who offers him a "holy prophecy" (*helgum spádómi*), namely, that through him, many men will be brought to the true faith and be baptized.[105] In fact, this very question of what the prophet's source of power might be is exactly the query Óláfr puts to the holy hermit, who says that it is the god of Christian men who reveals these thing to him.[106] After hearing about God's miracles, Óláfr converts and spends time with the prophet learning about his new faith and leaves the islands with both priests and other learned men.

Here the text presents both the superiority of Christian magic and of Óláfr's character, especially so, as this episode contrasts so vividly with the earlier episode in the saga of the conversion of King Haraldr of Denmark. In this case, although Haraldr's conversion is said, essentially en passant, to come about through the miracle of Poppo's bearing glowing iron, the saga also makes it clear that Haraldr's decision is primarily brought about by Emperor Ótta's military successes. Even greater is the contrast between Óláfr and Earl Hákon of Norway, who is forced by Haraldr to accept conversion. But he then becomes an apostate, setting ashore the missionaries meant to help convert Norway and subsequently offers a great sacrifice to Óðinn.[107]

Tergiversation of this sort must have been a very real problem for not only the early missionaries but also for those of later centuries who could see that magic of a type that relied not on the power of the Christian God but on invoking the old pagan gods that continued to hold a prominent place among nominal Nordic Christians. In contrast to the sort of behavior Earl Hákon displays, Óláfr is shown to be not merely an ardent follower of Christ but also a passionate opponent of all who resist the new faith. And those opponents, at least in Snorri's treatment of the Óláfr traditions, are frequently presented as witches, sorcerers, and other wielders of pagan magic.

Corresponding in character, if not in scale, to those villains are saga scenes set in Iceland, where virtuous heroes like Gísli Súrsson are bedeviled throughout their careers by infamously wicked figures such as Þorgrímr nef, a man "full of sorcery and witchcraft, and he was as much a wizard as could be."[108] Occasionally one encounters an entire nest of witches, as in the Hebridean family of Kotkell in *Laxdœla saga*. They raise a great storm against those who attempt to stop their thieving and witchery, drowning all their enemies: the father, mother, and two sons are all said to be great sorcerers.[109] Similar characters are to be found in many sagas, such as Þórdís in *Kormáks saga* (*The Saga of Kormákr*) and Geirríðr in *Eyrbyggja saga* (*The Saga of the People of Eyri*), some of the most memorable secondary figures we encounter in the Icelandic sagas. The case for the "noble heathen" in the sagas, who anticipates the goodness of coming Christianity, is made possible exactly because there are those who are *not* noble.[110] And such ignoble foils are as often as not drawn by saga authors by making them witches and sorcerers.

The old crone whose charm magic undoes Grettir Ásmundarson is surely one of the most memorable witch figures in saga literature. *Grettis saga Ás-mundarsonar* (*Saga of Grettir Ásmundarson*) offers a fascinating glimpse, not only of a fourteenth-century Icelander's view of magic and witchcraft, but also of the later period's perception of the Conversion era and the possibility of paganism being reignited.[111] Incapable of being defeated by normal means, Grettir has survived internal exile on Iceland for years, and in desperation, his enemies look for magical assistance from Þuríðr. When the old crone is introduced, she is described as very old and useless; moreover, it said that when she was young and men were heathens, she had been both *fjǫlkunnig* and *margkunnig* (both terms relating to the manifold knowledge associated with the witchcraft), but it was generally thought she had now forgotten it all. The author further notes that although the country was by then Christian (i.e., in the early eleventh-century setting of the story), there remained nevertheless many heathen sparks (*margir gneistar heiðninnar*), and although it was punishable with the so-called minor outlawry to publicly worship in the old way, doing so in secret was still possible.[112]

Having been introduced in this interesting fashion, Þuríðr subsequently displays cunning, temper, and power as she uses her magical skill to accomplish what Grettir's male adversaries have thus far been unable to do, namely, to defeat him. Despite her great age, the fact that she can hardly get out of bed, and so on, Þuríðr's witchery proves potent indeed.[113] One scene makes this story especially interesting: in order to effect her magic, Þuríðr goes to the seashore where she carves runes into a beached log, rubs her blood into them, recites a charm, and then walks withershins around the object.[114] Here, I think, is a description of charm magic in performance that has the ring of truth about it, a description that maps well onto a charm scenario Óðinn addresses in the *Ljóðatal*.[115]

In Chapter 2, a number of accounts of magical performances were reviewed. So, for example, we saw how Egill Skalla-Grímsson's ability to use magic is exploited to give insights into his character, most famously in his raising the "curse-pole." In the same saga, Egill even corrects poorly executed runic magic, noting that no one should attempt to write runes who does not fully understand their use.[116] Perhaps the single most celebrated description of magic being enacted in Nordic sources is the section of *Eiríks saga rauða* (*Saga of Eiríkr the Red*), which describes in detail the performance of *seiðr*. The saga, composed in the thirteenth century and preserved in fourteenth-century manuscripts, purports to tell of events from around the millennium in the fledgling Greenlandic colony at the settlement on Herjólfsness:[117]

At that time there was a great famine in Greenland. Men who went out hunting for food had little success, and some never came back.

There was a woman in the settlement named Þorbjǫrg; she was a seeress [*spákona*] and was called the Little Sibyl [*lítil-vǫlva*]. She had had nine sisters, all of whom were seeresses [*spákonur*], but she was the only one still alive. It was Þorbjǫrg's habit during the winters to attend feasts, and she was invited most by people who wanted to know their futures, or about the coming season; and since Þorkell was the chief farmer thereabouts, it was thought to be his responsibility to discover when these hard times would come to an end.

Þorkell invited the seeress to his home, and she was well-received there, as was the custom with such women. A high-seat was prepared for her with a cushion, which had to be filled with hens' feathers. And when she came in the evening together with the man who had been sent for her, she was dressed like this: she had on a blue cloak with straps and set with stones all the way down to the hem; she had on a necklace of glass-beads and on her head a black lambskin hood, lined with white catskin; and she held a staff in her hand, which had a knob on it, bound with brass and set with stones below the knob. She had around her middle [a belt of] touchwood and on it a great pouch, in which she kept the charms she needed for her witchcraft [*fróðleikr fróðr* 'knowing, learned, well-informed']. On her feet she had hairy calfskin shoes with long laces which terminated in large pewter buttons. On her hands she had catskin gloves which were hairy and white inside.

When she came in, everyone felt obliged to give her a proper greeting; she accepted these in a manner which accorded with her opinion of the giver. Þorkell took her by the hand and led her to the seat which had been prepared for her. Þorkell then asked her to run her eyes over his home, herd, and household. She had little to say about anything. In the evening tables were set up, and now should be told what was fixed for the seeress. A porridge was made for her of kid's milk and also prepared for her were the hearts of all living animals which were available there. She had a brass spoon and an ivory-handled knife bound with two rings of copper, and the point of it was broken off.

When the tables were taken up, Þorkell went to Þorbjǫrg and asked her what she thought about what she had seen there, about how satisfactory the household and people's behavior there seemed to her, and about how soon she would know [*vís vera*, lit., 'become wise'] about what he had asked her and about which men were eager to know. She answered that she would not say anything until the next morning, when she had slept there overnight first.

And the next day as it got late, she was supplied with what she needed to perform the witchcraft [*seiðr*]. She asked for the aid of women who had that knowledge which was necessary to the witch-craft called "warlock-songs" [*varðlokur* MS variants *uardlokr*, *varð-lokkvur*]. But no such women were found. Then an inquiry was made among the household to see if anyone there knew [them].

Guðríðr says then, "I am neither a sorceress nor a witch, but in Iceland my foster-mother Halldís taught me a song [*þat kvæði*] which she called the 'warlock-songs' [*varðlokur* MS variants *vard lokr*, *vardlokkvr*]."

Þorkell says, "Then you are wise at just the right moment."

She says, "This is the sort of affair I want no part of, for I am a Christian woman."

Þorbjǫrg says, "It might happen that you could be of help to others in this and yet not be a worse woman than before. But I must depend on Þorkell to get what is needed."

Þorkell now pressures Guðríðr, and she says that she will do as he asks. The women now formed a circle around the scaffold upon which Þorbjǫrg sat. Guðríðr sang the song [*kvað . . . kvæðit*] so beautifully and well, that no one who was there believed they had heard more beautifully sung songs [*kvæði kveðit*]. The seeress thanked her for the song [*kvæðit*] and said "many spirits have come here and think it beautiful to hear the song [*kvæðit*] so well delivered [*flutt*], spirits who previously stayed away and would not grant us obedience. And many are now apparent to me which earlier had been hidden from me and many others. And I can say this to you, Þorkell, that this famine will not last longer than this winter and things will improve with the spring. The epidemic which has been on us will improve more quickly than expected. And as for you, Guðríðr, I will reward you right away for your help, for your future is laid out before me. You will make a most distinguished match here in Greenland, although it will not last long, for your paths lead to Iceland[. . . .] And now farewell, my daughter."

Then men went to the prophetess and each asked what he was most eager to know. She was free with her information and few things did not turn out as she said. Then she was sent for from other farms; then she departed for them. Þorbjǫrn was sent for, for he had not wanted to be home while such superstition had been practiced [*meðan slik hindrvitni var framið*].[118]

This famous scene of the performance of *seiðr* has been frequently discussed, not least, of course, with respect to the question of whether this detailed description can be trusted or should be seen as an invention by the author.[119] In fact, this scene of witchcraft, perhaps more than any other, is one where the question of authenticity is more relevant and debated than any other. The sheer amount of detail provided in the saga has struck some as suspicious, immoderate larding of particulars, meant to mask the fact that the scene is indeed invented, in order to demonstrate the sanctity of Guðríðr, who, after all, is the ancestor of two bishops.[120] Strömbäck, for example, is quite doubtful about the authenticity of the so-called *varðlokkur* or, in any event, of the saga writers' understanding of this point, while others argue for the possible correctness of this part of the episode.[121]

Yet others have examined the scene and concluded that, although not every component of it need be correct, the overall impression it provides of witchcraft, that is, of *seiðr*, being performed is likely to be right, or so I infer.[122] Price expands our sense of the scene by suggesting that we regard it as a kind of "ritual reassurance," to the extent that the broader intention of the piece may be one where the *vǫlva* is believed to have "a *genuine* ability to see the future . . ." but is expected to adjust her vision to fit the needs of her audience.[123] This functional argument is a helpful way to view the scene and perhaps one with resonances heard as loudly in the thirteenth century as in the tenth. And the scene is one of the most dramatic confrontations we witness in the sagas between pagan magic and Christianity, notwithstanding such famous episodes as those involving red hot iron being borne, slowly drowning *seiðmenn*, and other more violent clashes. Here the saga writer gives the specter of a Christian woman who quite simply as a matter of conscience does not want to participate in a ritual she rightfully associates with the old religion.

Finally, the so-called contemporary sagas (*samtidssagaer*), dealing as they mostly do with events from the thirteenth century (and the very late twelfth century) when they were composed, might be expected to reflect medieval man's perceived preoccupation with diabolical agents and their uses of magical power to work ill.[124] Yet the contemporary sagas tend to show connections with the magical worldview in only two regards: a deep-seated concern with seeing the future, often presented in the form of dreams and other premonitions, and with imprecations, in both a general and, I argue, more narrow, specific sense.

But what we do not see in these texts dealing with contemporary and near-contemporary events is any sort of decisive intrusion by sorcerers, witches, or magical practices to set the course of the narrative or turn the tide of events. How unlike the sagas treating earlier periods! No Þuríðr helping dispatch Grettir; no magical acts by Egill exiling the king and queen and setting the stage for future actions; no Busla offering to teach the black arts; no magic potions of forgetfulness such as that administered to Sigurðr by Grímhildr; and so on. The world projected by the *samtíðarsǫgur* is largely one of power politics, human cruelty, and human frailty, but interestingly, indeed even suspiciously, never one where witches or witchcraft play a significant role.

That is not to suggest that there is no interest in the supernatural world in these texts concerned with contemporary events, but rather that such interest very rarely takes the form of witchcraft. In fact, there is an explicit association with magic in *Sturlu saga* (*The Saga of Hvamm-Sturla*), when a man called Þorir "the witch" (*Þorir inn fjǫlkunnugi*, lit., knowledgeable in manifold arts) is captured by his adversaries. Subsequently, the question of his possible release is raised. To that idea, Helgi the priest responds, saying that it would never do to release a thief and someone thus empowered with magical knowledge (*at láta lausan þjóf ok fjölkunnugan mann*).[125] And that brief exchange, for all of its approximately one quarter of a million words,[126] is just about all *Sturlunga saga* has to say on the subject of witchcraft per se.[127]

Sturlunga saga's evident fascination with premonitions and the prediction of things to come has been the subject of much discussion. Its *Hrafns saga Sveinbjarnarsonar* (*The Saga of Hrafn Sveinbjarnarson*),[128] for example, opens with a section in which there are many prophecies with the remark, "In the West Fjords there were then many kinds of dreams and visions."[129] Three prophetic events follow, two of them visions that hint at Christianized references to Óðinn. In the first dream, a man named Þórðr is visited by a grim, black figure (*svartr ok illiligr*). He says in *ljóðahattr* verse that he is of an ancient lineage, a constant traitor to peace, a bringer of death and an eater (or user?) of corpses.[130] In naming himself in *Sturlunga saga*, this sinister figure calls himself Faraldr, 'epidemic, plague, pestilence,' presumably playing on his subsequent comments about bringing death.[131] Then a man named Guðbrandr is visited in a dream by a large and grim man (*mikill ok illiligr*) who likewise says in verse that he takes pleasure in terror, and that he is traveling south with a troop, apparently early testimony to the fusion of Christian views about the devil with pagan traditions.[132] A third man is subsequently visited in a dream, and he is told by a stranger that he sees the sinful souls of men, their spirits quivering at the serpent's mouth, presumably a reference to medieval fondness for showing the gate to Hell as the mouth of a serpentine monster into which the souls of evildoers are marched (Figure 2).[133]

Against a scholarly tradition that has not chosen to see this passage in this way, I find the sinister, diabolical creatures who appear in the first two dreams—dark, large, and bloodthirsty—difficult to disassociate from Christianity's interpretation of Óðinn, a cross between the old pre-Christian god and the satanic figure of medieval Catholicism.[134] Frequently referred to in the noun phrase "the devil Óðinn" (e.g., *dyeffuolen Oden*), the figure is neither wholly Christian nor wholly pagan by the close of the Middle Ages.[135] In one post-Reformation Swedish source, for example, Óðinn has retained many of his heathen characteristics, but in a manner also consistent with his increasing identification with the devil of Christianity, he is everywhere associated with the color black: he visits humans accompanied by big black dogs and servants on black horses, riding in a coach drawn by black horses, all with eyes that burned like fire.[136]

Underscoring this interest in the one-eyed chief of the pre-Christian gods in the *Sturlunga saga* compilation is a curious passage in *Sturlu saga*, in which a woman, displeased with a dispute in which her husband is engaged, runs up to the leading opponent, holding a knife, and says, "Why shouldn't I treat you most like the figure you want to be—and that is Óðin?, and attempts to gouge his eye out."[137] The effect of this sort of *interpretatio Christiana*, the melding of a heathen god with the Christian idea of the devil, is one means by which, despite his continued function in certain contexts, the pre-Christian deity is fashioned throughout the Middle Ages to become the greatest of demons, *mestr fjánda*, as one rune-carving sorcerer calls him (see Chapter 2).

Among the various *Sturlunga saga* texts, it is *Íslendinga saga* that demonstrates the greatest interest in prognostication.[138] That this will be the case is foreshadowed early on in the saga, when one brother challenges another by asking whether he thinks he is a seer (*spámaðr*), to which the other brother responds that he is not.[139] This interest in prophecy is made manifest later in the saga, just before the decisive battle at Ǫrlygsstaðir (chaps. 132–36), at which point the saga is filled with portents about impending disasters, mostly in the form of dreams. Typically, men and women appear in these dreams and speak in verse to the dreamer, the style of these lists of future events often echoing the catalogue-like effect of miracle collections (jarteinabækur).

Indeed, one senses that the author is even aware of this characteristic and conditions the reader for it. Earlier in the saga, one character, after hearing of his interlocutor's quick recovery, says, "That must seem to you like a miracle," to which the other responds, "I call such a thing an event, not a miracle."[140] In a stream of vaticinations, with one prophetic moment coming after another, the overall impact is a little mind-numbing and seems likely to have been built on the model of the miracle collections and hence is better understood in terms of its emotional rather than aesthetic effect. Sturla himself seems to sense the tendency toward overkill, concluding the discussion by writing, "Many other dreams, although they are not all written down here, were recounted at this time; men thought them fraught with great tidings and portents."[141]

By contrast with the great pile of prophetic events that make up this section, a much more delicately balanced treatment of similarly portentous dreams comes near the end of Íslendinga saga in a dream sequence by a young woman named Jóreiðr. In these phantasms, she is visited by a series of figures, including no less a character than Guðrún Gjúkadóttir from the Vǫlsung cycle.[142] It is revealed then that "they intended with their wickedness to bring heathendom to the whole country."[143]

Sturlunga saga also provides insights into the use of curses and imprecations. Occasionally, these utterances seem little more than expressions of frustration and outrage. Thus, when an irritated Loftr says, "The devil take their jokes!" (Djǫfullinn hafi þeira hróp), the comment will strike modern readers as mild, perhaps ambiguous at worse.[144] But when we see him add to that introductory execration, "May they never thrive, and may things turn out so that not everybody seeks their friendship!" we understand, as surely the audience of the saga was meant to, that something else was, quite literally, at work.[145] This statement is no longer simply an angry outburst but rather a desire to affect the future, if still far short of ritualized charm magic as such.

Reports that touch on this desire to control or have an impact on future events in this way map heavily onto the dreams sections mentioned earlier. The verses the various phantasms deliver often come in the context of what

Finnur Jónsson refers to as a "dream- and warning verse" (*drömme- og varsel-svers*).[146] Although built on a different meter, its similarity to "magical meter," or *galdralag*, such as is Skírnir's curse of Gerðr discussed earlier (Chapter 2), through the repetition of phrases or whole lines, generally with mild variation, is apparent. *Íslendinga saga* reports of one of the portents before the battle of Ǫrlygsstaðir:

There was a man named Snæbjǫrn who lived in Sandvík out from Hǫfðahverfi. He went out one night before Christmas, in the winter before the battle at Ǫrlygsstað. Then a woman came into the home-field; she was big and strong, dreary and red of face. She wore a dark blue kirtle, and a linked belt; she spoke this verse, turning toward him:

Slayer of men will I here become.
Savage the strife throughout the land.
A plague I will be now for you
As vengeance for many impels me.
Death and destruction will not miss our foes
But come ever closer to all who are fighting.
The voice of the dead calls out loudly;
The voice of the dead calls out loudly.

And this she also recited:

Raging I fare away
To savaging battles.
I wing over holt, over heath
in the path of black ravens.
I come to the vale where all is dark.
The valley of death which awaits me.
Sorrow-harmed I hurry ahead
To endure the torment of famine,
The torment of famine my fate.[147]

In this passage, we perhaps see a combination of various deadly female figures from Norse tradition, the valkyrie, the fetch, the Norn, the ogress, and something much closer to the witch image, for here is a woman whose behavior parallels what we might expect in a scene of performed magic.[148]

First of all, this woman, "big and strong, dreary and red of face," does not, like the other speakers in this prophetic sequence, appear in the context of a dream but rather walked (*gekk*) into the more workaday world of the home field, albeit at night, when the man has gone outside. On the other hand, that the incident takes place in a home field (*tún*, originally the hedge that defined the field) is very suggestive: one Norse term for "witch" is *túnriða*, that is, 'hedge rider'.[149] I think the parallel here is more than accidental; moreover, the narrator describes the woman as wearing two specific items, a dark blue dress (*dǫkkbláum kyrtli*) and a 'linked belt' (*stokkabelti*). Dark-hued clothing in the sagas almost always indicates impending violence, usually death, and the curious detail of a particular sort of belt brings to mind that the meticulous description by the author of *Eiríks saga rauða* of the Green-landic *vǫlva* 'sibyl, prophetess', also referred to in the text as *spákona* 'seeress, soothsayer'. And, indeed, two of the items enumerated in the saga's descrip-tion of her are her dark-hued clothing and a special belt.[150]

Nor is it insignificant that the author does not merely say that she spoke the verses but rather that "she spoke (*kvað*) this verse, turning (*ok snerist*, lit., 'and turned herself') toward him." 'Spoke' is the normal translation of *kveða* 'speak' (cf. archaic English 'quoth') but the word also encompasses 'recite' and 'sing' and is the term used, for example, when in the case of the scene in *Eiríks saga rauða*, it is said that Guðríðr sang the so-called warlock song (*kvað . . . kvæðit*).[151] More to the point, if one has entered a field and gone over to a man standing in it, what is the necessity of turning toward him? In fact, the text carefully specifies such movement with a clear sense that these actions are done in a sequence.[152] The use of *snúa* 'turn' here is very much in keeping with other descriptions of a charm being delivered in the Old Norse world (see Chapter 2). I believe we here see a curse being performed, one that may have included conducting the verbal portion while facing away from the object of the curse, or more to the point, with the curser's anus toward to the object of the curse.[153]

On the one hand, medieval Christian writers in Iceland generally thought, and wanted their audiences to think, that witchcraft and magic in earlier eras, or in far-off places, was rife. On the other hand, they did not much see such phenomena as having the same sort of major role in the course of events in their own day. Writing in a parallel context, about the authentic-ity of the 'blood-eagle' rite, Roberta Frank noted some years ago, "Medieval men of letters, like their modern counterparts, could sometimes be over-eager to recover the colourful rites and leafy folk beliefs of their pagan ancestors."[154] It may be a strong indication that something of this sort is also true of our area of inquiry when texts placed to the earliest periods are filled with magical behavior and yet so little of it appears in the sagas set in more contemporary times.

As reasonable as this perspective may be, it can also be overemphasized, a view that assumes, of course, a lack of agency on the part of the saga writers, and might seem to suggest something of a haphazard and naïve relationship to the material, that is, that they simply could not help themselves. I detect a more serious pattern and purpose to how magic and witchcraft were used. If, following Victor Turner, we focus on the genealogical or intergenerational dimension of those texts that come as a sequence, we see the same dominant pattern.[155] Just as the three types of sagas enumerated by Sigurður Nordal become more filled with magic and witchcraft, the greater the distance between the time of composition and the setting of the saga, so too within smaller groupings does the same pattern occur. Thus, if we plot the three generations of *Þorsteins saga Víkingssonar* and *Friðþjófs saga frækna*, discussed in detail earlier, that is, Víkingr-Þorsteinn-Friðþjófr, it is apparent that, as one moves forward in time, although magic still plays a role, that role lessens. One might argue the same, I think, with respect to the multigenerational saga of the men of Hrafnista, *Ketils saga hængs–Gríms saga loðinkinna–Qrvar-Odds saga* (*The Saga of Ketill 'Trout'–The Saga of Grímr Hairy-Cheeks–Arrow-Odd's Saga*). Or even, albeit to a much lesser degree, within *Sturlunga saga*, for example, *Geirmundar þáttr heljarskinns–Þorgils saga ok Haflíða–Sturlu saga* (*The Tale of Geirmundar Hell-skin–The Saga of Þorgils and Haflíði–The Saga of Sturla*).

In other words, in all of these instances, I believe we see a learned class, wittingly or not, ascribing magic, sorcery, and witchcraft primarily to earlier periods, using it to represent from their point of view the very essence of what that world was like before the introduction of Christianity.[156] That is, although they acknowledge the reality of miracles, which we might, from a modern theologically neutral vantage point, regard as just one more form of magic, medieval saga writers intuitively understood pagan works of wonder to be a very different sort of phenomenon. That they saw and used this difference is not to say that there existed a rigid programmatic approach according to which every saga was composed, but that there was a tendentious approach to the idea of witchcraft that led to many, even most, of the saga authors to be willing to see pagan magic and witchcraft at every turn in the ancient pre-Christian world but much more modestly present in their own time. By no means do I want to suggest that we discard the evidence to be had from the sagas, but it is obvious that their testimony must be sipped cautiously. Can the Icelandic sagas inform us about the nature of witchcraft in the Nordic Middle Ages? Most definitely, but sometimes, as in the case of the *Íslendinga saga* verses, they may tell us most exactly when they do not know they are doing it. And when they are aware that they are informing their audiences about the magical practices of bygone eras, it would be wise to have our critical senses sharpened as much as possible, for surely we see their intentions on display at least as much as their knowledge.

Ecclesiastical and Court Literature

In discussions of medieval Scandinavian literature, Old Icelandic spiritual culture understandably tends to overshadow the traditions of the other Nordic regions. This situation is easy to fathom but should not mask the fact that Icelandic sagas and poetry are not the only important narrative materials we have.[157] Moreover, by breaking out Icelandic as a separate entity for the purpose of these discussions, I do not mean to imply that Icelandic writers would not have been aware of or participated in the same waves of innovation that gave rise to the narratives taken up here, and, as we will see, there are areas of overlap. Broadly speaking, in the following I take up the materials by types—historical writing, legendaries, sermons, moralizing texts, and so on—and incorporate where possible a chronological scheme.

After discussing the Icelandic materials of medieval Scandinavia, whatever oxygen is left in the room is generally consumed rapidly by the towering image of Saxo Grammaticus, the Danish cleric who wrote of the "deeds" or history of the Danes (*Gesta Danorum*) in sixteen imposing books.[158] Begun around 1190 and not completed until sometime after 1208, Saxo's remarkable synoptic history of the Danes incorporates much of "the same" mythological material as that known to Snorri and other Icelandic writers, albeit with his own attempts to work it all into an acceptable framework, and with some very different perspectives and understandings from those in the Icelandic sources.[159] Fundamentally, however, he shares with other Christian writers the need to explain why it is appropriate to discuss pagan topics, as well as the tendency to resort to euhemerism for his explanation.

In order to show that he is not making up his history—so Saxo reassures his audience early on—he reveals that there were three types of sorcerers who practiced magic (1.5.2):[160] the first, giants; the second, sorcerers; and the third, a hybrid of the first two.[161] The first group was characterized by its size and strength, the second by its skill in divination and the practice of magic, which apparently allowed them to subdue the giants in their constant warring. Although neither as powerful in body nor as crafty in their arts as the parent groups, the third type was misunderstood by people to be gods and worshipped as a false religion, a topic to which he returns repeatedly.

The vision of, and attention to, sorcery presented in Saxo's *Gesta Danorum* is comprehensive and includes most of the forms of magic we can tease out of the various other Nordic sources. So, for example, Saxo describes necromancy being practiced by Harthgrepa (1.6.4); Ollerus engaging in magical transvection (3.4.12); a *niðstong* being raised (5.3.7); Othinus (i.e., Óðinn) working charm magic (3.4.4); and a witch transmogrifying into a horse and then turning herself and her family into marine mammals (5.16.2). And he describes a Swedish champion whose seven sons exhibit what are clearly *berserkr* behaviors, such as biting their shields and so on, but are also associated by Saxo with sorcery (7.2.7). In fact, magic and those who practice it are generally associated with most of the ills of mankind in *Gesta Danorum*.

Magic is especially connected with the earliest period of history, when people were duped by magic into falsely worshipping humans whom they believed to be gods, most of all Othinus (i.e., Óðinn). To a lesser extent we also hear of Thor (i.e., Þórr), but as one scholar notes, these two deities aside, there is little attention to the other pre-Christian gods in Saxo's work.[162] Very often, however, mentioning Othinus and the old gods generically comes exactly in this context of Saxo's maintaining that it was magic that allowed them to be understood as deities. So, for example, he writes, "At one time certain individuals, initiated into the magical arts, namely Thor, Odin and a number of others who were skilled at conjuring up marvellous illusions, clouded the minds of simple men and began to appropriate the exalted rank of godhead. Norway, Sweden and Denmark were ensnared in a groundless conviction, urged to a devoted worship of these frauds and infected by their gross imposture."[163]

It has been argued that *Gesta Danorum* is constructed according to a pattern in which the first four books cover the pagan era; the second four, the non-Danish Christian era; the third four, the conversion of the Danes; and the last four, the era of the Danish archbishops.[164] Magic is a recurrent topic in the history, especially the earliest parts of it, because Saxo, like the Icelandic saga writers, uses magic most often in connection with the lost bygone world of paganism. It is for Saxo one means for a Christian Scandinavian to explain how the worship of false gods came about.[165] And, like the Icelandic writers, he sees far less of it in the era after Conversion.

There is another pattern at work here too, and that is Saxo's treatment of women in his history. This question is not unconnected to the issue of magic in that it has been suggested that women are presented as significant actors in the heathen part of his history, but thereafter, with the Conversion, become less important.[166] The heathen women's connection to power, one scholar has argued, comes from their use of magic, where "we meet comparatively more women than men," as she writes, adding that magic begins to fade after the ninth book.[167]

Saxo's *Gesta Danorum* is unique in medieval Nordic literature, an extraordinary work that lacks, as has been said, both prototype and imitation, but it is far from the only history written in that period.[168] Indeed, in many ways, history writing accounts for much of medieval Scandinavian literary activity, including the sagas, as has been pointed out many times. Magic, witchcraft, and sorcery as a means of identifying or characterizing in such a context that which was understood to be foreign, distant, or "other" appears to be a common theme in all of them. We have seen how this tendency frequently attaches itself to the pagan past as one vehicle by which Christian writers could offer an explanation for the heathenism of their ancestors: that is, as the sleight-of-hand trickery, the magic, of the individuals later euhemerized and believed to be deities, those who fooled the populace into worshipping them. But it was also a convenient tag for otherness, for the practices of cultures that were alien.

This tendency may nowhere be more pronounced than in the treatment of the so-called Finns, or Sámi.[169] The author of the mid-twelfth-century *Historia Norwegie* (*History of Norway*), for example, comments extensively on the perceived magical practices of the Sámi,[170] saying, "A person will scarcely believe their unendurable impiety and the extent to which they practice heathen devilry in their magical arts. There are some who are worshipped by the ignorant masses as though they were prophets. . . ."[171] Then follows a passage everything about which suggests that it partially describes a shamanic séance: in it, the hostess suddenly falls forward, being perceived as dead by the Christian traders, but the Finns tell them that she is not dead, "merely pillaged by the gands of her adversaries."[172] A magician then prepares himself with spells and other items and, after considerable chanting and leaping, throws himself on the ground where he expires. Consulting with another magician, who goes through similar preparations, the hostess subsequently arises in good health and "he" (referring to the third sorcerer) tells them that the second magician's "gand" had been harmed while in the shape of a whale and that that harm manifested itself in the real magician's death.[173]

When in the *Vetus Chronica Sialandie* (*Older Sealandic Chronicle*), its Danish author focuses on the supposed widespread nature of magic in Norway, it is surely exactly because of the large Sámi population there. That is, the chronicler's comments are more likely born of racial and cultural factors than those connected with political or national rivalries when he notes how many magicians live in Norway, listing among such monsters, as he calls them, diviners, augurers, mages, enchanters, "and other followers of the Antichrist," which he further explicitly connects with demons.[174] Here, of course, is something new, as this kind of magical practice is no longer typified as simply odd, frightening, or bizarre—although it may still be all of these—but now being associated in explicitly religious terms with the enemies of the church.[175]

An area where there is very little interest in this question is Old Swedish historical writing. Sensitivity to the question of lingering paganism no doubt colors the way historical mythmaking in Sweden treats the Conversion, especially when set against its strong tradition of historical rhymed chronicles. Medieval West Norse sources were fond of presenting the Swedes as pagans and reluctant, even backsliding, Christians; well-known examples include *Hervarar saga*'s epilogue concerning the deposing of the Christian King Ingi, who refuses to perform the traditional pagan sacrifices, in favor of his brother-in-law, 'Sacrifice-Sveinn' (Blót-Sveinn), who commits himself to such rituals. And Snorri's *Magnússona saga* (*Saga of the Sons of Magnús*) presents the crusade of the Norwegian king, Sigurðr the Crusader, together with the Danish king, Níkolás, against the heathen Smålänningar and other Swedes, who are said to be still mostly heathens or only superficially Christian.[176]

The foundational narrative about Sweden's Christianization process is, as we saw earlier, the life of Saint Ansgar by Rimbert. *Vita Ankarii* (*The Life of Saint Ansgar*) details the steady if slow growth of the church in Sweden and frequently uses the dramatic confrontation between pagan and Christian magic as a means of illustrating the story. Importantly, Rimbert's *Vita Ankarii* was translated into the vernacular by one of Ansgar's great admirers, Nils

Hermansson (1325–91), bishop of Linköping, at the end of the fourteenth century, providing the narrative with a broader audience.

Otherwise, however, original vernacular literature in medieval Sweden, most notably the quintessentially historical genre of the "rhymed chronicle" (*rimkrönika*), simply does not take up the country's shift in faith—the significance of this fact is more obvious if one compares this reluctance to treat the subject to the valorization of the same event as found elsewhere in medieval Nordic literature, such as *Kristni saga* and *Brennu-Njáls saga* (*Njal's Saga*). In fact, one of the earliest medieval Swedish-language texts to treat this theme is the so-called *Vidhemsprästens anteckningar* (*The Vidhem Priest's Commentary*) from about 1325.[177] An appendix to the provincial laws of Västergötland, the text is an early example of both the kings' and bishops' list. Given its placement at the end of the West Gautish laws, these notes tend to privilege the primacy of that region as often as possible.[178]

This commentary tells of how the first Christian king of the Swedes and Goths was baptized in the spring at Husaby in Västergötland by the English bishop Sigfrid.[179] Here the Vidhem priest is following established local tradition, as codified in the *Legend of Saint Sigfrid* (ca. 1200), but there are alternative versions (e.g., Saxo 10.11.6).[180] One of the arguments being made by this presentation of historical "facts" in *Vidhemsprästens anteckningar* would seem to be the relatively steady, unbroken rule of Christianity in Sweden, traceable back to the baptism of Olof Skötkonung in that spring in Västergötland.[181] Notably there is, contra Icelandic tradition, no mention of a pagan insurrection or a "Sacrifice-Sveinn." Instead, *Vidhemsprästens anteckningar* discusses briefly the martyrdom of the second bishop, Unni, deleting Sveinn entirely from the list of Sweden's monarchs.[182]

Despite the relative scarcity of surviving conversion scenes in Old Swedish, it is hardly the case that the Swedes did not recognize that their ancestors had been pagans, and we do occasionally see the same tendency toward viewing the pre-Christian gods as the (often-euhemerized) figures falsely worshipped by pagan Swedes. So, for example, *Fornsvenska legendariet* reports about the missionary activities of Saint Philip: "Philipus preached for twenty years i 'sithia' which is now called Sweden, from the eastern lands to Öresund. The heathens captured him at last and took him to the temple in Uppsala and coerced him into making sacrifices to Mars, whom the Swedes call Óðinn."[183]

In a miracle vaguely reminiscent of the deeds of great Theseus-like characters of the Bǫðvarr-Bjarki sort in the sagas, Philip vanquishes a dragon and saves the people from a plague, resulting in the country's becoming Christian.[184] This narrative, part of the great cycle of Old Swedish legendary materials from circa 1300, is preserved in a manuscript from a half century or so later, Codex Bureanus.[185]

In fact, it is useful to discuss *Fornsvenska legendariet* in the context of history writing, as with its organizational scheme and many references to popes, emperors, early martyrs, and Nordic saints and the work of the church toward the Christianization of Scandinavia, it represents an ecclesiastical world history, integrating Scandinavia into the chronology of the church.[186] In it, a kind of magic is often presented that is different from the sort of paganism and pre-Christian worship of false gods discussed thus far, the occasional references to native themes in the local saints' stories, as in the case of Saint Philip, notwithstanding. Overwhelmingly, however, the images of magic that emerge from the collection are of two types. One is the story of the learned magus in direct confrontation with the saint, so in that sense this image is rather like the Nordic conversion contests discussed earlier in which magic functions as a shared form of communication between the rivals. The other scenario typically involves a foolish figure who makes a rash and subsequently regretted promise, often to the devil, and who is subsequently saved through the intervention of a saint. In the first case, conversion scenes commonly employ miracles and other wonders, of course, and often enough as the representatives of the two camps—the Christian and the unconverted—contest the power of their respective faiths. We have seen how, in the treatments of missionary activities in Viking Age Scandinavia, these scenes always involve the old pagan gods and their followers. In *Fornsvenska legendariet*, however, the representatives of this perspective tend to be learned magicians and Jews.

So, for example, against the proselytizing miracle of the gift of tongues, two magicians (*koklara*), Zoroes and Arafaxat, come with murderous, fire-breathing dragons.[187] But when Matthew slays them and is subsequently able by calling on Christ's name to do what the magicians cannot—bring to life the king's recently deceased son—the king thankfully falls at the missionary's feet. A similar scene plays out with Zambri, a Jewish *mæstari* 'master', 'learned man', 'teacher', perhaps here meant as 'rabbi', representing the opposition to conversion. He and Pope Sylvester compete to see who can bring a bull back to life. Sylvester wins by calling on the name of Jesus Christ, whereas Zambri fails when he intones into the bull's ear what Sylvester characterizes as the name of the worst devil.[188] In an extended confrontation between Saint Jacob and the Jewish mage, Hermogenes, the power of Christian and non-Christian magic are again set side by side. Hermogenes conjures his devils and commands them to bind the saint, but the curse is reversed, and instead it is the magician who is fettered. When he converts, the magician says that he knows the temperament of the devils and asks for protection, which Jacob gives him in the form of his staff. Hermogenes brings to him all of his grimoires with the intention that they be burned, but Jacob, fearing the smoke would do harm, says that should be buried instead.[189] These few examples illustrate what transpires in a number of the narratives in *Fornsvenska legendariet*, in which the two sides, one Christian, one not, contend for moral, spiritual, and importantly, physical supremacy (e.g., raising the dead) by using opposing magics.

The other scenario involves the so-called diabolical pact, or *pactum cum diabolo*, a belief of enormous importance for the shaping of European witchcraft mythology (see Chapter 4). A concept whose consolidated form is most closely associated with the later Middle Ages and Reformation eras, the roots of this idea are to be seen in church documents from very early on. And it is of no small consequence that we find them in Scandinavia already by circa 1300. Thus the life of Saint Basil in *Fornsvenska legendariet* tells of how as a result of his lust for a woman a young man dedicates himself to the devil (*han gaff sik diæflenom*). The devil, feeling that Christians are an untrustworthy lot, demands that he renounce God and commit himself to the devil in writing. But the saint saves him in the end, of course.[190] Similarly, in the legend of Saint Cyprian and Saint Justina, lust and magic again play a heavy role, as does the devil's demand that Cyprian swear him an oath.[191] A story set in more contemporary surroundings is told of a knight who in order to become rich promises himself and his wife to the devil. It is only through the intervention of the Virgin Mary that his wife is saved.[192] And, of course, the most famous of these tales, the story of Theophilus, lays out the idea of the written diabolical pact and of how Mary's intervention saves him.[193]

Religious literature of this kind was prevalent in all the Nordic tradition areas, of course, and it is hardly surprising that ecclesiastical texts are among the oldest surviving Norse texts.[194] Intended to inspire faith in their audiences and to confirm its truth, such texts were, together with such contacts as came through the education of clerics at schools on the Continent, pilgrimages, royal marriage arrangements, and trade, including the increasingly large foreign populations in Hanseatic communities, significant channels for importing continental ideas northward.[195] Just who would have access to the kind of writing represented in *Fornsvenska legendariet* and other vernacular religious texts, and how it would have been communicated to them, is an intriguing question. In the case of *Fornsvenska legendariet*, in particular, the question of whether it might have been intended for a female religious community has been suggested, where, one assumes, it would have been read aloud. But how did the views of the church reach broader, less privileged audiences?[196]

Certainly one means by which the church's views were broadcast was through the quintessential narrative art, preaching, a phenomenon that increased markedly beginning in the thirteenth century with the rise of the mendicant orders and their dedication to the art, a process likely to have been the most important channel for exchange between the church and large numbers of nonelites, especially in urban areas.[197] On the other hand, as one expert in the field has remarked, we have no idea of how frequently sermons were preached, only that surviving documents by bishops and other authorities often urge that it be done frequently.[198]

What sorts of topics are covered in the surviving homiletic literature from Scandinavia?[199] Certainly the topics taken up with vigor, regardless of whether the sermons are from the thirteenth, fourteenth, or fifteenth centuries, include magic and witchcraft. "Sermo ad populum," in *The Old Norwegian Homily Book* from the early 1200s, for example, lists as the principal sins, church theft, manslaughter, rancor, envy, and a variety of other antisocial activities, including "belief in 'women's pharmacopoeia' or witchcraft or prophecy," referring to them as "diabolical."[200] Similarly, "Sermo necessaria" from the same collection lists among those sins to avoid, pride, slander, and murder, various types of witchcraft, and magic.[201]

Among the sermons in the early fourteenth-century *Hauksbók* (*Haukr's Book*), a sort of "gentleman's library" belonging to an Icelandic lawman, Haukr Erlendsson (d. 1334), who spent much of his career in Norway, one is of special interest here.[202] Derived from an Anglo-Saxon original, the text has been judged to be as much an adaptation as a translation, with some of the longer theological discussions abbreviated and with a more emphatic treatment of the question of witchcraft.[203] It condemns, for example, women who prepare what is clearly sexual magic for their men in the form of a potion to ensure that they should as a result love them well. And the text is very specific in its warnings against such diabolical activities as those that constitute witchcraft, speaking "of witches and sorcerers, those who traffic in magic or in 'pharmacopoeia' or in prophecy, for that is a fiendish heresy [*fianda villa*] and Satanic service [*diofuls pionasta*]."[204]

Fifteenth-century sermons sometimes recycle the same concerns, even the same language, of earlier texts, such as the idea that the sin of witchcraft is its struggle against obedience[205] or that witchcraft is among the principal sins to be on guard against, specifically, "belief in witchcraft and 'pharmacopoeia' and sorcery and other heresies. . . ."[206] Another sermon sets more or less the same phrase into a more dogmatic context: "Your wickedness will bring you reproach and your turning away from God and the proper faith to witchcraft and 'pharmacopoeia' and sorcery and other diabolical arts shall bring you reproach."[207] Yet lingering still in the sermons of the late Middle Ages, however, are views one is tempted to associate with paganism. Thus a sermon for the second Sunday in Lent tells the story of a woman whose daughter is possessed by the devil. The key here is that the mother prays to the Lord for help and does not turn to magic for relief; specifically, "neither to *rwnakarla* nor male witches."[208] *Rwnakarl* (or *runokarl*, as one might expect) literally, if inelegantly, means a 'rune man', that is, a 'male charm worker who uses runes', and suggests a reference to the sort of activities noted in Chapter 2.

This growing concern in the fifteenth century about witchcraft is mentioned more and more frequently in the sermons.[209] Another change is in the works as well, for no longer do the sermons merely chide listeners about their own moral and spiritual obligations; instead the concerns become more defensive, especially where the miracle-working goods of the church itself are concerned. Thus the fire-brand preacher of mid-fifteenth-century Ribe, Peder Madsen, preaching in Latin to a different sort of audience, needing a different type of admonition, warns against the possibility that water from baptismal fonts might be used for witchcraft and that the consecrated host might likewise be put to similar use.[210]

An unusually multilayered perspective on magic and witchcraft comes to us from the fourteenth century in the various works associated with Saint Birgitta, especially her "Revelations."[211] At once very personal but also highly public and deeply influential in the Nordic countries and elsewhere in Europe, Birgitta's visions comment on these themes several times. Given that she lived the last decades of her life in Rome (except for brief pilgrimages), it is sometimes difficult to know whether the conditions reflected in her observations and views are about Scandinavia, or Italy, or perhaps somewhere else. On other occasions, however, Birgitta could not be clearer. So, for exam-

ple, in a text directed to Archbishop Bernard of Naples, she comments extensively, and explicitly, on local issues, including the status and conditions of
infidel female slaves, such as the failure to instruct them in Christianity and
their frequent use as harlots, which Birgitta labels the first sin. Birgitta then
goes on to give a catalogue of the way she sees magic being misused: there
are those, she says, who use "malignant sorcerers and diviners and the most
evil of enchantresses" (*malignos sortilegos et diuinatores et aliquas pessimas
incantatrices / forbannadhom trolkonom ok gallirkonum*) in order to conceive
children. Others employ incantations in order to make certain men and
women fall in love with them. Still others use them to discover the future,
and some to heal sicknesses. But all those who use such witchcraft or magic
are cursed by God.[212]

In the story concerning a Swedish knight who consults a prophetess
(*phitonissa / spakona*) about the future, Birgitta is told by the voice of the
Lord that the devil uses his knowledge of the future through such assistants
as witches (*phitones / trollkonur*) to ensnare those who are unfaithful to
God.[213] A similar sentiment is implicit in the tale of a fisherman who uses
magic to increase his catch.[214] In a different kind of tale, she prays for the
release of a priest from a witch (*trollkona*) who has enchanted the cleric for
the purpose of fornication.[215] Occasionally her comments are of the most
generic kind, as when she condemns Saul's use of a medium[216] or equates a
sorcerer with the devil.[217]

Literature intended to provide moral instruction is one of the most common genres of the later Middle Ages. As an example, *Siælinna thrøst* (*The
Consolation of the Soul*), a Swedish translation of a German original, also
known in Old Danish,[218] is clearly intended as a moralizing work, a text that
blurs the line between standard biblical exegesis and the sort of framed narrative one associates with collections such as *The Thousand and One Nights*.[219]
It is, of course, not merely a translation but has been expanded by using, for
example, biblical and legendary material already in Old Swedish. With a
framing device constructed around the Ten Commandments, it is both a
commentary and an occasion for brief tales of the sort one encounters in
texts of *The Seven Sages* type, as well as in saints' lives and miracle collections,
Icelandic *þættir*, and other short tales.[220]

Siælinna thrøst shines a bright light on the sorts of ideas from abroad
then streaming into Northern Europe, both feeding into, and being fed by,
popular traditions. In one of its most complete, if sometimes puzzling, sections in which the issues of witchcraft and magic are addressed, the following

excerpt comes, significantly, in the context of the first commandment, "Thou shalt have no other gods before me" (Exod. 20:3):

> My dear son, if you would keep the first commandment, then you should not enchant or work witchcraft, nor advise nor perform it. You should not allow yourself to be healed with pharmacopoeia or other [magical] herbals, [although] you may certainly accept medicine which does not involve heresy or superstition. You shall not prophesy or have prophecies made. You shall not have yourself measured with rope [*bast*] or red thread or with anything else.[221] You shall not have wax or lead poured for you. You shall not believe in bird song [as a form of prophecy], not in the cukoo when he calls, not in *prusta*,[222] not in itching in your ear, not in itching in your hand or anything like that. You should not believe in dreams, nor that it is more fortuitous to meet one person than another, or for one animal to meet one than another.[223] You should not believe in hand-luck,[224] nor in amulets[225] or other magical inscriptions. You should make no incantations or exhortations whether over iron or anything else. You should not set the Psalter in motion as students do or anything like it.[226] You should not have books in which magic is written. Some people have matted hair and are thus superstitious, for you should cut it off and guard your soul as superstition and heresy are manifold and of many types which I cannot describe in this book.[227]

Although the writer does not explicitly mention the devil, the fact that this discussion comes in the context of the first commandment makes it clear that the all-important late medieval understanding of the diabolical pact controls the author's thinking, so thoroughly, it would seem, that the diabolical connection can simply be taken for granted. And it needs to be underscored that this list does not represent native thinking but rather mostly reflects the inventory in the source text.[228]

In fact, much of the concern in *Siælinna thrøst* about magic and witchcraft comes in association with this commandment, and so it tells again the story from the legend of Saint Basil, known already in Sweden in *Fornsvenska legendariet*, of the young woman whose husband has arranged their union by bargaining for his soul with the devil and who is saved through the intervention of Saint Basil.[229] But now the story has an interesting twist missing from the earlier version: in the Old Swedish legend from circa 1300, the young man offers himself directly to the devil. In this later multiform, it is indeed the devil who stirs up the young man's lust, but his reaction to this emotion is worth noting: "he searched until he found a male witch (*trulkarl*) and was counseled by him. The male witch (*Thrulkarlin*) said, 'Do as I say and things will be as you desire.'"[230] Thus it is now the intervention of a male witch that subverts the young man and channels his desire in such a way as to bring about the diabolical pact. If the devil represents the opposite of God in such tales, then the witch begins to take on the role of the opposite of the saint, interceding on behalf of evil rather than goodness.

In a similar tale of seduction into the secret society of devil-worshipping users of magic in *Siælinna thrøst*, a priest who "practiced the black arts [and] used witchcraft and magic" attempts to dupe a young man into pledging himself to the devil in exchange for riches.[231] But when he is on his knee before this "king" seated on a throne of gold and told that he must abandon and foreswear the Holy Trinity, he instead recommits himself to Father, Son, and Holy Ghost, "and instantly the king and his castle and all his company sank down into Hell's abyss, and the priest as well. So go all who practice witchcraft and devilry."[232] Elsewhere the text urges that its audience not behave like the heathens (*som hedhnugane*) by believing in fate (*skepnolagh eller ødhno*).[233]

In addition to the texts associated with the clerical culture of the High Middle Ages in Scandinavia, court life in the Nordic kingdoms guaranteed the development of strong interests in chivalric and other elite literatures of the Continent.[234] How quickly and to what extent the worlds reflected in these works percolated out to those beyond the demographically small group who constituted the ruling elite is a vexing problem. Among the stories translated into the various Nordic vernaculars were a number of tales concerned with such heroes as, for example, Charlemagne, Arthur, and Dietrich.

In one such poem, *Konung Alexander* (*King Alexander*), the history of Alexander the Great, we see an impressive image of the medieval court wizard.[235] Nectanabus is often called *magus* 'magician', 'astrologer' and *sortilegus* 'diviner', 'witch' in the texts of other traditions. In many respects, he represents the canonical learned practitioner of high magic. Nectanabus and his fellow Egyptian "masters" (*mästara*) are described as having a knowledge of future events from astrology, their reading of the stars, and heavenly satellites.[236] As Nectanabus himself is introduced (ll. 50–51), we are told he is full of devilry. When King Artarexes of Persia is about to attack Egypt, Nectanabus goes to a secret chamber in the palace, takes a bronze vat and fills it, and into it—showing his knowledge of the diabolical arts (*diæwls fund*, l. 63)—he eventually places wax models of two ships from which he foresees the outcome of the battle. That he knows how to do this is a result of a learned relationship to magic, drawn from a book that his diabolical wisdom allows him to read (*swa las ha*n *innen sinne book / mz diæwls konst thy han war klook*, ll. 91–92). Understanding that he is destined to lose the battle, Nectanabus disguises himself and prepares to flee to Ethiopia, from which he will in accordance with a prophecy go to Macedonia. Through his magical arts, which allow him by turns to transform himself into a dragon, a man, and then back into himself (ll. 274–77), he sleeps with the queen. He thus fathers Alexander with Olympiadis and subsequently becomes his son's teacher—until, that is, Alexander challenges his prophetic abilities through the use of astrology (l. 490), and Nectanabus becomes the victim of his offspring.

As this all too brief review demonstrates, common to virtually all the narrative materials is the inclination to see in the distant past a world where magic has a dominant, even defining, role.[237] The contemporary world of the medieval writers tends to be far more staid in its deployment of magical actors. Narrative materials touching on witchcraft come in widely varying packages, native and imported, prose and poetry, themes both elevated and low, and so on, but that consistent pattern in which the bygone world was seen to be more magical than the writer's own persists throughout. Magic and its practitioners were in that sense often yet another tool in the writer's kit—hence the title of this chapter, intended to underscore the reticulated source-resource nature of the materials. That they were useful tools is not to say that contemporary understandings of magic and witchcraft cannot be teased out of our medieval narratives but that caution is very much in order. Taken in isolation, such presentations might skew our understanding of Scandinavian perceptions. Supplemented by what we can also learn from medieval popular and legal traditions, these artfully composed presentations of magic and the magical world can indeed give us a purchase on evolving Nordic views of magic and witchcraft.

Chapter 4

Medieval Mythologies

Most people love myths, but we may not realize that we live them in our daily lives. In common parlance, of course, a "myth," when the word is not being co-opted to mean 'lie', is understood as being 'a story about the gods'; in the West, that typically implies compendia of Greek and Roman—or even Norse—sacred texts, often "retold for children." But myths are much more than that, of course. It is no coincidence that when the renowned, if controversial, student of mythology, Joseph Campbell, published a collection of his writings on the topic, he used the title, *Myths to Live By.*[1] His choice of words was certainly felicitous insofar as they remind us of the real nature of myths: they are often doctrinal, normative statements of belief, with currency in the culture. Myths are alive, and they resonate in the lives of the individuals who hear, tell, know, and use them. In other words, they are more than just words on a page about the characters and tales from a society long since gone.[2]

Early in the past century, Bronislaw Malinowski articulated the now virtually canonical view that myths express belief and enforce morality, concluding, "Myth is thus a vital ingredient of human civilization; it is not an idle tale, but a hard-worked active force; it is not an intellectual explanation or an artistic imagery, but a pragmatic charter of primitive faith and moral wisdom. . . ."[3] Malinowski reached this conclusion in a world where such declarations were made about others—after all, he begins his remarks by stating, "Myth fulfills in *primitive* culture an indispensable function . . ." (emphasis added). Today we recognize more readily that his comments are as true about our own situation as they were for the Trobriand Islanders among whom he lived. And we realize that they are just as true for medieval Europeans no less than for Pacific Islanders or modern readers.

For the world of the European Middle Ages, where the church wielded enormous power and authority, it is all too easy to imagine that a myth would necessarily be a product of medieval Catholicism. As this chapter discusses, it could be, but that was hardly a requirement, as the church itself often became a user of such materials. In the following, I take up several important myths about witchcraft that had currency in the Scandinavian Middle Ages, views shared by many tradition areas and whose roots can often be traced back in Northern Europe to earlier eras. By the time of our evidence, the myths have frequently been massaged by clerical thinking. In other words, these materials reflect neither elite nor nonelite views exclusively but rather reticulated re-workings, moving back and forth between different segments of society.

For one set of myths, those treating the diabolical connections of witch-craft in the eyes of the church, a great deal of documentation exists. In the other instances, although we have visible evidence and some recoverable tex-tual data, we must mostly reconstruct the myths without the assistance of church documents. Thus, for example, the milk-stealing witch, a myth com-plex that gave voice to worries about perceived injustice—about advantage, disadvantage, and envy—is mostly based on visually communicated materi-als. With that in mind, an important notion for us is "cultural competence," that is, parallel to the notions of linguistic or communicative competence, we must try to "learn" the cultural codes of medieval Northern Europe; we need to be able to see and hear in ways that would make sense to the people who inhabited that world.[4] The acid test for this proposition, of course, is the degree to which we can understand the curious and unequal fragments of that universe that are passed on to us by random preservation. In other words, proof comes to the degree we can recover the mythical worlds of late medieval Scandinavians.

In the Devil's Service: The Pact and the Journey to Blåkulla

Although it is sometimes useful to discuss the medieval Nordic world as a single entity based on a variety of well-known political, religious, and cultural realities, there are always important regional differences to be considered, and these patterns become pronounced in considering the materials at hand. In the case of the diabolical contract or bargain, the so-called *pactum cum diab-olo*, the concept took root quite differently in the various tradition areas of the northern world.[5] The idea of the Faustian bargain, its best-known manifestation, eventually became a widespread, and even canonical, aspect of witchcraft ideology in much of Western Europe by the end of the Middle Ages (as expressed in, e.g., *Malleus maleficarum*, pt. 1, quest. 2 et passim). That was also true throughout most of Scandinavia, where it was often called by a variety of terms implying a bargain with the devil (e.g., *djävulspakt, djävulsförbund*). But the *djöfulssamningur* or *sáttmáli við djöfulinn*, although known, was not a common legal accusation in the early modern era in Iceland or, some have suggested, Norway.

So learned an authority as Jacob Grimm speculated about the primary source in Northern Europe for this story—heathendom or Christianity? As frequently noted, the roots of the diabolical pact are both anterior to, and outside of, Christianity (e.g., Lucan, Firdusi).[6] It was in the context of what becomes the devil's pact that patristic writers, Jerome, in particular, interpreted such biblical passages as Isaiah's warning to the rulers in Jerusalem: "We have made a covenant with death, and with hell are we at agreement" (Isa. 28:15).[7] Exegesis on this passage suggests to many observers an embryonic sense of the *pactum cum diabolo*. But it is especially in the miracle associated with the fourth-century Saint Basil that the concept becomes well formulated, as discussed in Chapter 3. The connivances of the devil lead a young servant to become enamored of a senator's daughter, and in order to fulfill his desires, the man agrees to renounce Christ in writing and serve the devil. Having married the servant, the girl observes her husband's apostasy and turns to Basil for help, who is able to break the devil's hold over the servant and destroy the incriminating document. This story was well known from the *Legenda Aurea* of Jacobus de Voragine (1260–75), the source for it in *Fornsvenska legendariet* (*The Old Swedish Legendary*), but the life of Saint Basil was already well established in the Nordic world long before this reworking of *Legenda Aurea*.[8]

The influential, explicit diabolical pact from the life of Saint Basil was further supported in popular tradition by the well-known tale in the Middle Ages of the sixth-century Theophilus, a narrative whose felicitous conclusion reflected the power of the Virgin Mary. In brief, this legend concerns the *oeconomus* of the Church of Adana in Cilicia, who in order to regain a lost office makes a bargain with the devil for its recovery in exchange for his soul, but, having subsequently repented his decision, manages through the Virgin Mary to achieve the miraculous return of the written contract.[9]

The legend is quite specific on the matter of the contract between Theophilus and the devil: it is written in Theophilus's own hand, returned to him after much prayer and fasting through the intervention of Mary, and finally burned by Theophilus shortly before his death. Turned by Paul the Deacon into a Latin text in the eighth century, this story of "Saint Theophilus the Penitent" achieved great notoriety throughout medieval Christendom. It was, for example, an exemplum and the subject of homilies; the object of a wide variety of iconographic and artistic projects; the subject of poetry by Hroswitha, Gautier de Coincy, and others and a play by Rutebeuf; and, perhaps most famously, included by Vincent de Beauvais in *Speculum Historale* and Jacobus de Voragine in *Legenda Aurea*.[10]

Other testimonies to the popularity of the devil's pact theme, especially in the thirteenth century, underscore its increased role in demonological thinking—the story of the prodigal youth who almost concludes his bargain with the devil in book 2, chapter 12 of the *Dialogus miraculorum* of Caesarius of Heisterbach (ca. 1238), and additional legends in the *Legenda Aurea* (i.e., those of Justina and Cyprianus, and of the knight who is also saved by the Virgin from his bargain with the devil), for example. But at what point the devil's pact became a necessary aspect of ecclesiastical thinking about witchcraft is difficult to fix. It is telling that in 1398 the theological faculty of the University of Paris declared that all superstitious observances, where the results were not those one could expect of God or nature, involved an implied pact with the devil.[11] This idea came to be widely accepted, as may be seen from the fact that, in 1437, Pope Eugenius IV wrote to papal inquisitors, warning them of the successes of the prince of darkness, who is gaining adherents and worshippers of demons: "As a sign of this [they] give them a written contract or some other sign, binding themselves to demons."[12] By the late fifteenth century, the diabolical compact was thoroughly incorporated into the inquisitor's manual, *Malleus maleficarum* (pt. 1, quest. II et passim).[13] This theological twist on witchcraft became the principal feature distinguishing European witchcraft ideology from parallel belief systems elsewhere, and by the early modern period the idea of the devil's pact had become widespread in Denmark and Sweden, but less so in Norway and Iceland.[14]

The connections between witchcraft as a crime and such seemingly mundane legal matters as contracts are complex and deep.[15] One way to contextualize the importance of the diabolical pact is to envision its opposite: a written compact with a saint, where the contract is a positive and life-embracing phenomenon. An example of this sort can be seen in a late medieval Icelandic compact, not with the devil, but with the Virgin Mary. The book, written by Jón Þorláksson, was sponsored by a certain Bjarni and given to the cloister at Munkaþverá, with the stipulation that the reward that Mary would give

Bjarni should be delayed and given to him in the next world when his need would be greatest.[16] Crafted in the same form as the *pactum cum diabolo*, the book stands implicitly, perhaps even explicitly, as a counterforce to the diabolical pact.

Tracing the growth of such ideas in medieval Nordic writings is not difficult and is reflected in several of the texts examined earlier in detail: the translation of the Middle Low German *Seelentrost* (*Consolation of the Soul*) into Old Swedish (and from that translation into Old Danish, ca. 1425) contains a number of popular medieval tales touching on the matter of the *pactum*, often reworked versions of stories known from the *Legenda Aurea* and its related literature. Here, for example, are familiar narratives about pacts with the devil being traded for love and for riches.[17]

An Old Swedish miracle collection of circa 1385 is filled with tales of devil worshippers and those required to renounce their baptism and pledge themselves to Lucifer and includes such commonplaces as the story of "The Witch of Berkeley."[18] An Icelandic collection of legendary and hagiographic materials, AM 657a 4to (ca. 1350), also reports such stories: one of its legends treats the story of a man who sells his soul to the devil.[19] And, of course, there are many examples from *Fornsvenska legendariet*, such as a story from the life of Saint Basil, a knight who pledges himself to a devil, the story of Theophilus himself, an analogue to "The Witch of Berkeley," and so on.[20]

Naturally, it is possible to read the idea of the pact into a variety of texts, as illustrated earlier in the case of the book of Isaiah. Along similar lines, some readers see in the story of the Swedish king Eiríkr "the Victorious" (*sigrsæli*), as presented in the translation of Oddr Snorrason's late twelfth-century life of Óláfr Tryggvason, indications of the Faustian bargain.[21] According to the saga, the king becomes "the victorious" only after pledging himself to "Oddiner" (i.e., Óðinn) for ten years.[22] In Snorri's version in *Heimskringla* (*History of the Norwegian Kings*), Oddr the monk's narrative about the bargain is not mentioned. And in the various Icelandic reworkings of sacred writings called collectively *Maríu saga* (*The Saga of the Virgin Mary*), we see very early testimony to the story of Theophilus in the north.[23] The variation in these Theophilus stories is extraordinary, but all of them are unified on the basics of the narrative: the clerk's frustration with his position, the role of the Jewish magician as intermediary, the presentation of Theophilus at the court over which the devil reigns, Theophilus's renunciation of Christianity and his written bargain with the devil (e.g., " 'Ek nita Kristi ok hans modur.' Þar med gerdi hann bref ok inzscigladi med sinu fingrgulli"), and so on.[24] It may be, however, that aspects of the story had currency in Iceland even earlier.[25]

Regarding actual trial materials, especially where the devil's pact is concerned, the evidence for the medieval Scandinavian region is relatively thin. Although specific contracts are not mentioned, several late fifteenth-century trials in Stockholm mention devil worship and apostasy and suggest exactly the sort of environment in which accusations of such contracts no doubt flourished, such as renunciation of Christianity and the embrace of Satan (e.g., "nw affsigx jak tik [addressed to a crucifix] och tagher tienisth aff fänddanom").[26] There appears to be but one medieval Nordic instance of a proceeding involving a clearly articulated diabolical contract comparable to the images projected in all the moralizing tracts just reviewed. And that case comes surprisingly early, and from an unexpected location, the Icelandic convent at Kirkjubær in 1343.[27]

Three Icelandic annals report this incident in slightly conflicting ways, although two of them are in agreement that a written bargain with the devil is at the heart of it:

A nun was burned at Kirkjubær named Kristin who had dedicated herself in writing to the devil. She had also defiled God's body (i.e., consecrated host) and thrown it into the privy and had engaged in intercourse with many laymen.[28]

A nun was burned at [Kirkjubær] who had dedicated herself in writing to the devil.[29]

Item [Bishop Jón Sigurðarson] deprived a nun at Kirkjubær of her orders for blaspheming the pope and then she was burned.[30]

This case represents a startlingly early appearance of the devil's pact in the medieval north.[31] In the eyes of church leaders, apostasy, diabolism, and witchcraft share a common denial of the authority of the church. Events such as those at Kirkjubær do not happen in a vacuum but are often preceded by a lengthy series of troubles and then set off by some notable incendiary event.[32] Just such a sequence appears to be in evidence here as well, there having been astronomical signs (e.g., a solar eclipse, reports of two moons) and cataclysmic episodes (e.g., the eruption of Hekla) in the preceding decade.[33] Reports already in 1336 of strange incidents at the cloister—moaning from under the dormitory flooring—are another such indication,[34] as is perhaps the reputation that attached itself to the cloister at Kirkjubær and its neighbor, the monastery at Þykkvabær, about improper relations between the nuns and monks.[35]

Flateyjarannáll (*The Flatey Annal*), the most detail-rich text in its description of the offenses, reports that Bishop Jón had three monks placed in irons at Þykkvabær in the same year for having assaulted their abbot; the bishop at Hólar had taken some similar action at the monastery at Mǫðruvellir.[36] As an indication of the troubled and unruly times, *Lǫgmannsannáll* (*The Lawyer's Annal*) relates these events, citing the troubles at Kirkjubær among them.[37] Relevant too are the changes in church hierarchy under way in that year: Agatha, the abbess of Kirkjubær, died in 1343 and a new abbess, Jórunn Hauksdóttir, was elected. Likewise, several new Nordic bishops were appointed in 1343, including Jón Sigurðarson to Skálholt and Ormr Ásláksson to Hólar, both of whom, after being consecrated, went to Iceland, which was then in a political and social climate that one noted scholar has described as "turbulent."[38] That the bishops apparently felt compelled to address the laxity and misconduct in Iceland of both the "learned and lay" is suggested by the entry in *Lǫgmannsannáll* for the following year.[39] This scenario—mysterious signs, a charged social and political atmosphere—is the template for accusations of witchcraft, albeit in this instance the designation is entirely in terms of a written devil's pact.

The events of 1343, and the punishment meted out at Kirkjubær in particular, are unique in Scandinavia before the late medieval period—a notable contrast is provided by the incident in Bergen touched on earlier involving Ragnhildr tregagás (1324–25), which demonstrates the opposite temperament from church authorities. When Bishop Auðfinnr, who had trained extensively in France, confronts Ragnhildr over her scandalous behavior, he maintains that she has renounced God and committed herself to the devil and concludes that hers is a case of heresy.[40] Rather than the harsh judgment handed down at Kirkjubær, the woman is simply condemned to a lifetime observance of fasts and the obligation to go on a multiyear pilgrimage outside of Norway. Despite inflammatory homilies and spiritual narratives concerned with the devil's pact of the sort sketched earlier, when faced with actual cases, medieval authorities appear on the whole to have behaved more in the spirit of Bishop Auðfinnr than of Bishop Jón. With the remarkable exception of the execution at Kirkjubær in 1343, it is only in the early modern period that the devil's pact appears to have been used in trials in Scandinavia, and even then, as noted earlier, more so in Sweden and Denmark than in Norway and Iceland.[41]

With the evolution of the *pactum cum diabolo* by the end of the medieval period, a view whose roots are to be seen already in patristic writings, the stage was set in important ways for the witch-hunts of the early modern era. But if the diabolical pact was a central tenet of Christian myths involving the devil, it was not the only one. One of the most widespread, and certainly the one that has received the most attention in modern treatments of witchcraft, whether scholarly or popular, is the notion of witches gathering for orgiastic rites, that is, the sabbath or sabbat. Although the church fully incorporates the sabbat into its witchcraft ideology by the end of the Middle Ages, it is by no means clear that the church created the story, whose popular origins are still being explored.[42]

It is only in the later Middle Ages that the presentation of witchcraft activities on the Continent begins to change from accusations of relatively simple magic to a much more complex image of organized, diabolical activities by witches.[43] But the possibility for this construction of witchcraft had its origins already much earlier in the church's battle against heresies. Thus, for example, in *Vox in Rama,* a decretal letter of 1232 calling for cooperation in purging heretics, Pope Gregory IX describes the activities of devil-worshippers in northern Germany as including an initiation ceremony and a banquet, after which, the participants offer to the hindquarters of a large black cat the so-called obscene kiss. When the ceremony is over, the lights are extinguished and a concluding orgy ensues, with the pope emphasizing especially the often homosexual nature of this lascivious rite.[44] As Norman Cohn has shown, accusations of this type made by church authorities, including gatherings with the worship of an animal-headed god; feasting; child sacrifice; cannibalism; anonymous, promiscuous sex; and incest, were themselves by no means new but had, in fact, already been made a millennium earlier by Roman observers about the early Christians.[45]

The roots of this saturnalian view and its later development as part of the elite understanding of witchcraft in Western Europe were generally thought to have been well understood.[46] This perspective, perhaps particularly regarding the sabbat, has been challenged, or complicated in any event, by Carlo Ginzburg's arguments regarding shamanism and European witchcraft.[47] The core of his thesis is the existence of centuries, if not millennia, of sorcery and magical tradition that continued to flourish in new, adaptive forms long after the introduction of Christianity in Europe. This hidden culture of shamanistic ritual took many forms, he argues, but remained a consistent factor in European popular culture until long after the Renaissance. The pivotal location of the Nordic traditions, adjacent as they have been throughout recorded history to cultures that practiced shamanism, make the question of shamanism, and Ginzburg's argument, especially relevant for Scandinavian beliefs, a possibility a series of studies have taken up.[48]

Between the polar opposites of innovation and continuity, what is the history and nature of Nordic myths touching on the sabbat scenario? In fact, it appears that Scandinavian belief structures concerning witchcraft change markedly already in the years around 1300, as, for example, Norwegian laws that once called for witches to be exiled now demand capital punishment.[49] In addition to the *pactum cum diabolo*, two prominent elite perceptions of witchcraft are well documented at the end of the Middle Ages, namely that of witches flying or otherwise magically transporting themselves (i.e., transvection) to a place of assembly, and that of the conventicles that followed, typified as they were by stereotyped anti-Christian conduct. Both of these elements are incorporated into the myth known in large parts of Scandinavia as the "Journey to Blåkulla" and figure prominently in late medieval church murals (Figures 2, 3, and 4), of which there are a great many in Denmark and Sweden. Images projecting these views of witchcraft and witches provided an important visualization to parishioners about such ideas.

One of the central tenets of the "Journey to Blåkulla" is that the witches travel—usually by flying—to a location variously called Blåkulla, Blaakolden, Bloksbjerg, and so on, often conceived of as a mountain in a distant country or an island in the south Baltic, where they engage in markedly deviant behavior, including lascivious conduct, boast of evil deeds performed, and so on (Figures 3–4).[50] The name itself is generally traced to German place names, usually Brocken or Blocksberg. An early indication of this complex in Scandinavia comes from a Swedish miracle of 1410, a notice concerning how a ship was endangered and then saved in the sound between the mainland and Öland near "Blaakulla," what becomes the traditional sabbat location for Swedish witches: "A ship [of the sort] called a *snekkja*, belonging to Sir Ture Bengtsson [Bielke], sailed from Lübeck to Stockholm, and in the sea-lanes near Blåkulla was imperiled by a great tempest."[51] This event was recorded in the early 1420s as one of the miracles associated with the altar of the Dominican cloister in Stockholm, especially the triptych of Christ being taken down from the cross.[52] The place of Blåkulla as a site of peril is thus

1. Two of the sibylline oracles, Århus domkirke, Århus amt, Denmark
(ca. 1480). Photo by author.

secured at least as early as the first decades of the fifteenth century, although
witches play no overt role—yet.

In fact, it is not until the Reformation era, a century later, that textual
evidence for the "Journey to Blåkulla," in Swedish tradition now firmly identified with the island Jungfrun (the Virgin), is extant with a fully saturnalian
view of devil-worshipping witches assembled in conventicles, exchanging
trade secrets. The earliest clear evidence of this Scandinavian sabbat scenario
is provided by Olaus Magnus, Sweden's last Reformation-era Catholic archbishop, while living in exile in Rome. There he published in 1555 his great
ethnological work, *Historia de gentibus septentrionalibus* (*Description of the
Northern Peoples*). He devotes much of this massive survey to questions of
the supernatural, including what appears to be the "Journey to Blåkulla,"
albeit referred to by the circumlocution Jungfrun:

> Moreover a tall mountain rises near the northern coast of the island,
> which the common sailors, in order to shun an unlucky omen and
> storms at sea, call the Virgin. Those who spend a while in its haven

2. Detail of transvecting witch, Knutby kyrka, Uppsala stift, Sweden (ca. 1490). Photo by author.

have a habit of giving little presents to the girls, for instance, gloves, belts of silk, and such keepsakes, as a kind of friendly gift to concili-ate them. They seem to think that the divinity of the mountain is not ungrateful, for an old tale recalls what happened once: a voice came down from above and someone who had given a present was ordered to change his anchorage to avoid running into danger; by doing this he remained unhurt when others were wrecked. *It is said that at certain seasons of the year a coven of northern witches assembles on this mountain to try out their spells. Any who comes at all late to this devil-worship undergoes a dreadful chastising;* but in these matters it is better to follow one's belief, rather than people's assertions.[53]

Magnus's critical spirit notwithstanding, we are clearly dealing here with a sabbat theme, an image of massed enemies on an island that has parallels

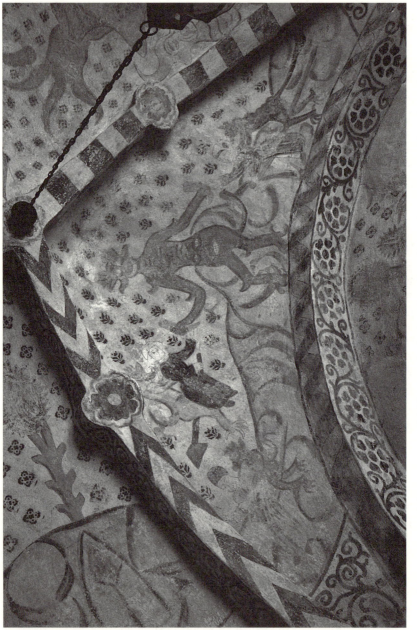

3. Transvection and the journey to Blåkulla, Knutby kyrka, Uppsala stift, Sweden (ca. 1490). Photo by author.

4. Transvectant witches and the devil, Yttergran kyrka, Uppsala stift, Sweden (ca. 1480). Photo by author.

in the north outside the witchcraft orbit. By the end of the sixteenth century, this image of the congregating witch begins to appear regularly in court records as well, as, for example, when one accused witch in Stockholm declares of another, Whore-Geska, that she "had often been in Blåkulla, and is of that society that rides [there] and have the mark in their noses . . . ,"[54] and subsequently says of yet a third accused witch, Brita, that she too "is not of the best kind [*slächted* 'family, race, species'], she was also that sort that usually rode to Blåkulla [. . .] and further, she said that it was not long since she had had sex with the devil. . . ."[55]

Did such a view have currency already a century or more earlier in Catholic Scandinavia? And what is the relationship of this complex to native traditions about witchcraft? First, it must be said that the medieval historical records, such as summaries of trials and other nonliterary documents, give few indications of such beliefs. A number of Nordic trials from the later Middle Ages focus on sex and love, but almost always in the context of love triangles, where passions of the heart are clearly at the forefront, not on indiscriminate, lascivious, orgiastic activities of the sort that so distress Pope Gregory IX in the thirteenth century, or the threat represented by such assemblies.

Regarding the image of massed enemies threatening normal society, separating native and foreign traditions is naturally problematic. Virtually all of Norse mythology as we have it, for example, builds toward the moment when the forces of evil gather under Loki's leadership and launch their all-out assault on the gods. Correspondingly, foreign texts too, including those well known in Scandinavia, frequently employ the image of assembled demons. Thus, *Siælinna thrøst* (*The Consolation of the Soul*), a Swedish translation from Middle Low German (ca. 1430), contains an exemplum from Gregory's *Dialogues* concerning the devils' meeting ("Devils render accounts"), which puts on display a highly sabbat-like, diabolical scene of devils gathering to report their deeds to Lucifer.[56] And, of course, a host of late medieval church murals in Denmark and Sweden make it apparent that this belief complex was known, or becoming known at the very least, at the end of the Middle Ages (Figures 3 and 4).[57]

In native monuments treating Nordic witchcraft, particularly where it relates to the sort of magic understood to have been used in the pagan period, practitioners are frequently presented in surviving narratives as needing assistants, and these texts thus also project the image of individuals gathered together in groups in order to practice witchcraft. The witch (*vǫlva ok seiðkona*) in *Qrvar-Odds saga* (*Arrow-Odd's Saga*) provides an exceptionally provocative example of this sort: "There was a woman called Heid, a witch with second sight [lit., a magic woman and a prophetess], so with her uncanny knowledge she knew all about things before they happened. She would go to feasts, telling people about their destinies and forecasting the weather for the coming winter. She used to have a band of fifteen girls and fifteen boys [lit., She had with her 30 individuals, that is, 15 boys and 15 girls]."[58]

The older, early fourteenth-century manuscript of this saga is more elaborate than the younger, late fourteenth-century main manuscript on two points concerning the assistants: it explains that Heiðr needs this company in order to provide her with chanting ("Þat var raddlið mikit, þvíat þar skyldi vera kveðjandi mikil . . .") and that Heiðr goes outside with this group in order to perform the magic rites ("gekk hon þá út með liði sínu . . . ok efldi seið").[59] The significance of the second point resides in its similarity to historical materials that forbid such activity. Thus, as one example among many, *Gulaþingslǫg* (*The Law of Gulaþing*) mentions "[those who are killed] for [deeds of] murder or for [the practice of] witchcraft or for going abroad at night to call forth evil spirits and to promote heathendom thereby."[60]

This image of the witch surrounded by chanting assistants cannot help but bring to mind the dramatic treatment of similar material in *Eiríks saga rauða* (*The Saga of Eiríkr the Red*) in its presentation of the activities in the Greenland colony (see Chapter 3). There we are told that Þorbjǫrg, the seeress, is one of nine sisters (*níu systr*), all of whom were seeresses. Perhaps we are to understand this comment biologically, meaning simply that there were nine female offspring in Þorbjǫrg's childhood home, but one wonders, given the fact that "sister" (*systir*) can also refer to elective affinities (i.e., 'nun', 'sister of charity'), whether this comment suggested to its audience that Þorbjǫrg is, in fact, one of a group of seeresses.

Þorbjǫrg is said to travel about attending feasts in a fashion comparable to the scene in *Qrvar-Odds saga*, except, of course, that she lacks the traveling band of assistants. The author likely omits this routine feature, as the saga wants to underscore Guðríðr's role in the ceremony, and the lack of companions makes this plot development possible. Þorbjǫrg must ask for such a group to be assembled: "And the next day as it got late, she was supplied with what she needed to perform the witchcraft [*seiðr*]. She asked for the aid of women who had that knowledge which was necessary to the witchcraft [*seiðr*] called "warlock-songs.""[61] After the heroine, Guðríðr, agrees to overcome her reluctance as a Christian and participate in this pagan rite, the saga says that the women formed a circle round the scaffold where Þorbjǫrg was sitting and Guðríðr sings the "warlock-songs.""[62]

Whether these scenes from *Qrvar-Odds saga*, *Eiríks saga rauða*, and elsewhere represent empirical knowledge of pagan practice or, as some have suggested, romantic interpolations is uncertain, yet their testimony assures us that the image of the congregating witch, especially of female witches, was already in use by the fourteenth century at least and that the fourteenth century's interpretation of the past, whether accurately or not, understood such conventicles to be one of the activities associated with witchcraft.

Transvection and assembly are brought together too in *Ketils saga hœngs* (*The Saga of Ketill "Trout"*), where the gathering is adapted to native legal traditions of the "assembly," the *þing*. Perhaps composed already by circa 1300, we know this text only from fifteenth-century and later manuscripts, and clearly the extant text must be read in the context of a gathering in the broadest sense, but one that perhaps helps lay the foundation for how the sabbat, a supernatural assembly, was understood in Northern Europe:[63]

One night he was awakened by a great crack in the woods. He
jumped up and saw a witch [*sá tröllkonu*], and her mane fell to her

shoulders. Ketill asked, "Where are you off to, mother?" She stiffened at him and said, "I am going to the witch-assembly [*til tröllaþings*]. Skelkingr, north out of Dumbshaf, king of the witches [or trolls, *konungr trölla*], and Ófóti from Ófóti's Firth, and Þorgerðr Hörgatröll and other great wights [*stórvættir*] from the north of the country are going there. Don't detain me. I don't like you. You're the one who did in [the giant] Kaldrani." And then she waded out into the water and then to the sea. There was no shortage of witch-rides [*gandreiðir*] among the islands during the night, but Ketill wasn't harmed. . . .[64]

Moreover, in the immediately preceding episode, Ketill encounters, and apparently kills, another *tröllkona* 'witch', 'troll', who also appears to be on the move, having just come, "black as pitch," up out of the sea, and who tries to return to it in the shape of a whale.[65]

This idea of the *gandreið* (as a verb phrase, *renna gand* [or *gǫndum*]) usually implies a witch going out, often in a noncorporeal sense, to gather information, as opposed to the sabbat-like association of *Ketils saga hængs*. When, for example, the witch Þórdís awakens in *Fóstbrœðra saga* (*The Saga of the Sworn Brothers*) after being observed having a troubled night's sleep, she reports on the activities and whereabouts of her enemy, saying, "Afar have I ridden the witch-ride this night."[66] In a slightly different vein, the sighting of a witch-ride can portend great events, as when Hildiglúmr has a vision before the burning-in in *Brennu-Njáls saga* (*Njal's Saga*), which is interpreted by others as a witch-ride.[67] Other terms, such as *kveldriða* 'evening-rider' and *myrkriða* 'dark-rider', are used for the practitioners of this phenomenon, and *trollriða* 'witch-ridden' for those subjected to it.[68]

These materials suggest an evolution in the concept of the witch-ride, since *Brennu-Njáls saga*, *Fóstbrœðra saga*, and other relevant sagas are preserved in manuscripts already from the early fourteenth century. *Ketils saga hængs*, with its more continental view of the witch-ride, on the other hand, is known only from fifteenth-century manuscripts. Another fifteenth-century manuscript tells of Þorsteinn bæjarmagn, one of King Óláfr Tryggvason's retainers, who, on a trip to Finland, sees a boy on a mound. The boy calls out: "'Mother [. . .] hand me my crooked stick and gloves, I want to go for a witch-ride [*gandreið*]. They're having a celebration down below in the Underworld.' Then a crooked stick, shaped like a poker, was thrown out of the mound. The boy put on the gloves and sat astride the stick and started riding it, as children often do."[69]

Þorsteinn too acquires a stick from the woman in the mound, follows the boy to a feast in the Otherworld, and returns, after a near misadventure, with various treasures from the "world below," which has been presided over by its own king and queen. There is no question here of a witches' sabbat in the sense it is meant in later periods, but rather of a very traditional visit to the world of the elves and assorted otherworldly creatures often made in Nordic (and Celtic) folklore.[70] On the other hand, this tale of transvection on a *krókstafr* 'crooked stick' to a great celebration in a topsy-turvy world like—yet unlike—our own is suggestive, an association made explicit by the author's use of the term *gandreið* 'witch-ride'. Importantly, then, changes are afoot: in the two later, fifteenth-century manuscripts, 'witch-ride' is used to designate physical transvection to the site of an assembly or feast, whereas earlier manuscripts use the term to designate a generally less corporeal, and noncongregating, image of the solitary witch undertaking a specific mission.

Of course, there is nothing in these texts that *absolutely* demands that such concepts as the *gandreið* need be understood as native in origin rather than imported—there rarely is. That magical arch-villain of medieval theology, Simon Magus, claims, in the early fifteenth-century Swedish *Siælinna þrøst*, for example, that he can fly.[71] The same collection of moralizing tales tells the story of Saint Germanus, the interpretation of which, within the broad scope of international witchcraft beliefs, would appear to relate to the notion of nocturnal vectitation, although in the exemplum itself, the tale is specifically used to moralize against secret pagans and other unfaithful miscreants.[72] As the story is part of a commentary on the first commandment, that is hardly surprising.

According to the tale, Bishop Germanus takes lodging overnight and sees the housewife setting the table, just as everyone is going to bed. Germanus asks who will eat the food, and she answers that "sprites" (*tompta gudhane*) come at night and that she must do as she does in order for her livestock to thrive. Germanus immobilizes the creatures and ascertains that they come in the shape of the woman's neighbors. When a messenger is sent and reports that he has visited the homes of these neighbors and discovered them asleep in their beds, the "sprites" admit that they are really devils sent to plague those who do not follow the right faith. Germanus sends them away in shame, and the housewife and her household are converted from

their unbelieving ways ("Oc hustrun oc folkit vmwændos fran thera wantro
oc diæfwlslike willo").

The sabbat-like scene, the motif of the transvectant spirit out traveling,
feasting, and stealing food from neighbors, is a common element of witchcraft beliefs, extending far outside the European orbit.[73] One might be
tempted to accept these features as simply part of the Christian ideology that
gives rise to the Saint Germanus tale. Still, these texts are relative latecomers,
and there exist early indications of a Nordic belief in conveyance by unusual
means. Perhaps the most suggestive testimony of all with respect to assembly
and transvection is the famous passage from *Hávamál* 155, from the thirteenth-century *Regius* manuscript:

> That tenth I know,   if night-nags sporting
>   I scan aloft in the sky:
> I scare them with spells   so they scatter abroad,
>   heedless of their hides,
>   heedless of their haunts.[74]

Interpretations of this passage vary, but central to all readings is the idea
of the "Wild Hunt," or *die wilde Jagd* (E501).[75] This complex is well known
from the *Canon episcopi* of Regino of Prüm (ca. 900), which had currency in
medieval Scandinavia:[76] "It is said in holy books that night-riders or transvecting witches (*kveldriður eða hamleypur*) are believed to travel with the goddess
Diana and Herodias for a while over the great sea riding on whales or seals,
birds or animals, or over the great land, and they are thought to travel in the
flesh, but books affirm that this is a lie."[77]

Thus does the author of *Jóns saga Baptista* (*The Saga of John the Baptist*),
circa 1300, attempt to explain the nature of Herodias—and ultimately her
daughter, Salome—just before the beheading of John the Baptist.[78] Here
the writer, more or less directly influenced by Regino or one of that text's
subsequently inspired works, such as the tenth-century penitential of Burchard of Worms, maintains Regino's rationalist point of view, one that he has
in turn taken from Saint Augustine: there is no divinity other than God, and
those who believe in such things are allowing themselves to be deceived by
the devil.[79]

The image of the night-riding hag is well known elsewhere in Nordic
sources. Already *Äldre Västgötalagen* (*The Older Law of Västergötland*), from
the early Swedish thirteenth century, describes a famous slander that can be

uttered of a woman: "I saw that you rode the 'witch-ride' [lit., 'the pen-gate'], with your hair loose, and in a witch's shape, 'caught' between night and day" ("Iak sa at þu reet a quiggrindu löfharæþ. ok i trols ham þa alt var iamrift nat ok daghér").[80] Perhaps this picture of a supernaturally empowered female figure riding an unusual object is correctly tied to the frequent, and often quite archaic, projection of valkyries, female trolls, witches, ogresses—indeed, apparently the entire range of supernatural female figures—astride wolves, a picture referred to in many different early Norse media, runic inscriptions, picture stones, and mythological prose and poetry.[81]

The image of transvectant females, albeit in the much more conventional setting of religious pilgrims, is fused with that of assembled, Nordic females threatening society in one of the legends associated with Saint Ingrid, the founder of the Dominican convent in Skänninge, Sweden, a story we know only from the mid-sixteenth-century *Historia de gentibus septentrionalibus* of Olaus Magnus (1555, 217 [book 6, chapter 19]). When Ingrid and her companions (*virginibus comitibus*) return from the Holy Land, the devil is said to have ridden into the city in the form of a mighty lord with a troop of knights and convinced the citizens that these women were, in fact, a group of terrible witches (*pessimarum incantatricum*). When the crowd begins to cross itself, the devil and his host suddenly disappears, the truth about Ingrid and her traveling companions is revealed, and they are welcomed into the town and presented with gifts. No earlier evidence of this tale is known, and it has been reasonably suggested that Olaus Magnus himself knew this tale, not from any written source, but rather from oral traditions in Skänninge.[82]

The reputation of Saint Ingrid, great in the Nordic Middle Ages, has largely been eclipsed by her vastly more famous compatriot, Saint Birgitta.[83] Indeed, the similarities between these two Swedish women, separated by a century, with their shared experiences of traveling to Rome to convince the church to establish gynocentric religious houses in Sweden, has led some scholars to conclude that Ingrid's and Birgitta's biographies, and the stories associated with them, have on occasion been conflated. This idea is noteworthy in the context of the present discussion, for among Birgitta's *Revelationes Extravagantes* (preserved in fourteenth-century manuscripts) is the story of the saint's arrival in Rome at a time when her ecstatic religious experiences were still without official sanction or interpretation. Confronted with her extraordinary visions and even more extraordinary claims, some of the roused populace of Rome assault Birgitta, saying that they want to burn her alive and that she is a witch.[84] The strong parallels between these two stories make it probable that the story of Ingrid's return from the Holy Land has been influenced by—or perhaps has influenced—the story of Birgitta's arrival in Rome. The legend of Saint Ingrid further substantiates the proposition that the concept of assembled witches was familiar in medieval Sweden.

Were transvection and assembly traditional aspects of Nordic witchcraft then, or were they imported into Northern Europe in the later Middle Ages as part of an elite continental view of witchcraft? In all likelihood, both imported elite traditions and native popular traditions played important parts in shaping the story. Certainly Nordic belief systems about witches and the supernatural appear to have long included an element of vectitation and, by the close of the Middle Ages if not earlier, of witches assembling.[85]

Witch-rides, however, appear in the older sources to have had a different purpose than the one imagined in the continental view of witchcraft, a purpose that seems consonant with witch beliefs in their broader international perspective. One imagines that this native belief complex about the witch's journey to discover information, or to attack individuals, became an obvious candidate for inclusion in the continental construction of the witches' sabbat as that image made its way into Scandinavia, and was assimilated to it, especially in elite paradigms of the witch.[86]

Furthermore, the sexuality associated with native traditions of *seiðr* and witchcraft in the pagan period (*ergi* 'unmanliness') does not seem to map well onto the diabolical and orgiastic sexual debauchery described in later testimonials concerned with the "Journey to Blåkulla."[87] This idea, at least, may be best accounted for as a borrowing from the elite continental model of sabbat activities. But as already Sahlgren understood, a further element in the development of the complex in Northern Europe may have been the fact that there existed additional, separate concepts concerning abduction by otherworldly creatures (so-called *bergtagningar*), especially where these tales involved elements from the Mountain of Venus motif (F131.1), that "hollow mountain otherworld where men live a life of ease and lustful pleasure in company with beautiful women."[88] In other words, the sabbat complex that emerges at the end of Nordic Middle Ages was likely heavily reticulated with elements from both native and foreign understandings of witchcraft.

The Milk-Stealing Witch and Other Myths

These myths about the diabolical pact, assembly, and transvection are connected through a shared discourse about the nature of evil, the source of its effectuation (i.e., the devil), and so on to several additional tradition complexes. In this instance, however, we have far less textual evidence from the Middle Ages and must instead reconstruct the myths by coordinating the medieval materials with data from later periods. That, of course, does not make them less interesting to the medieval period, but it does affect what we can know. And it offers us the interesting opportunity to test the concept of cultural competence.

What, for example, do we understand as we enter the antechamber, *vapenhus*, of a Swedish parish church and find on one side of the door an image from the later Middle Ages of a diabolical figure holding a very long pole stretched over the top of the doorframe to the other side of the door, where at the other end of the pole stands a woman? On closer inspection, it is apparent that she is receiving a pair of shoes from the pole. Or can it be that she is giving them? Can we discover what such a medieval image meant, and, more significantly, why it would matter that parishioners should see it last among the many images as they leave the church?

In fact, thanks to the industry of several scholars, we know quite a bit about this mural and its purpose.[89] With roots stretching back to at least the thirteenth century (and well into the modern era), it is a Nordic particularization of the international tale type known as *The Old Woman as Troublemaker* (AT 1353).[90] The woman is known as Sko-Ella ('Shoe'-Ella), sometimes Titta-Grå, and known as the "woman who was worse than the devil." According to postmedieval traditions, the devil had long hoped to stir up trouble between a married couple and engages Sko-Ella as this helper, implying some sort of relationship with him. Her reward is to be a pair of shoes. She tells the wife in the couple that her husband has been unfaithful and that the wife can prevent future philandering if she cuts off a lock of his beard at night.[91] Sko-Ella then tells the husband that his wife is planning to kill him at night with a knife. He is thus prepared when she approaches him at night to clip his beard and kills her. The devil, given that he believes Sko-Ella is actually worse than he, fears giving her the reward and does so only at the end of the long pole.[92]

The story of Sko-Ella is, then, a moralizing tale about the evils that come from slander, gossip, and loose talk, as well as, of course, from intercourse with the devil (although it should be noted that in the story as we have it, Sko-Ella pays no price for her actions).[93] Most noteworthy is that the scene's frequent placement around the door functioned as a final warning about proper behavior to a parishioner, female parishioners in particular, one imagines, before leaving the church (see Chapter 6). Thus the meaning of our mural is not only intelligible and sensible but spoke to its intended audience about the hierarchy of social codes in medieval Sweden: rancor and discord born of slander, meddling, and gossip are works of the devil. Our cultural competence, our ability to "fill in the blanks" about the context of the mural, is in fact high in this instance.

A more widespread myth complex involving violations of the social codes is that of the milk-stealing witch, a belief system known in several European tradition areas.[94] In his influential eleventh-century *Decreta*, Burchard of Worms, citing an earlier penitential, makes explicit reference to the complex: "Have you as certain women believe they have done with the help of the devil through their bewitchments and spells (*fascinationibus et incantationibus*) and taken from their neighbors' overabundance of milk and honey for themselves and their animals or for whomever they want?" he asks.[95]

Something very similar, combining the understanding of a Regino and a Burchard about the devil's power to deceive people into believing his power is real, together with the idea of the milk-stealing witch, is found in an important Swedish text of the fourteenth century, Magister Mathias's *Homo conditus* (1330–50). A sourcebook for preachers to the laity, it was written by one of the most influential Swedish clergymen of the century.[96] Here Magister Mathias takes up the concept of the milk-stealing witch and not only verifies that the myth was known to him already in the early fourteenth century but also ties it to the view stated explicitly in such works as the *Canon episcopi*, namely, that such ideas are only deceptions of the devil, not real phenomena.[97] Specifically, the tradition he knows suggests that there existed women who made bags into which they could gather milk from their neighbors' cows.[98] Naturally, his long residence in Paris makes entirely plausible the possibility that he has learned this tradition from non-Nordic sources— Jan Wall, for example, makes a credible case for the potential of British influence on Magister Mathias.[99] And we have seen in instances such as the fifteenth-century story about Saint Germanus from *Siælinna thrøst*, the idea of food theft by way of supernatural interventions was widespread and often used by the church itself toward its ends.

These many references to the milk-stealing witch in the works of learned clergymen, foreign and domestic, would appear to suggest that this belief system was wholly imported from abroad, but I am by no means convinced that such was the case. Evidence for a similar idea complex—supernaturally purloined food—predating by a century *Homo conditus*, for example, comes from the following scene in *Heimskringla*'s *Hálfdanar saga svarta* (*The Saga of Hálfdan the Black*):

> King Hálfdan was entertained at a Yuletide banquet in Hathaland. Then on Yule eve there occurred a strange incident: when they had sat down to the table—and a very large number were assembled there—all food and all ale disappeared from the table. With a heavy heart the king remained sitting, but all the others went to their homes. Now in order to find out what had caused this event, the king ordered a Finn to be seized who was reputed to be skilled in many hidden things [*er margfróðr var*], to make him confess the truth. He tortured him, yet got nothing out of him. The Finn turned to the king's son Harald for help, and Harald asked the king for mercy, but in vain. Then Harald let him escape, braving the king's anger, and accompanied him himself. They came to some chieftain's house where a great feast was being celebrated, and they were to all appearances welcomed there. And when they had remained there till the spring, one day this chieftain said to Harald, "A mighty great affront your father thinks it that I took some food from him, this winter; but I shall reward you with some joyful news: your father is dead now, and you must return home. Then you have as your own all the realms he ruled, and all of Norway besides."[100]

This scene, of course, distinguishes itself from the later tales of the milk-stealing witch in several ways, including the marked occasion (Yule) and the gender of the thief. Perhaps especially significant is the plot-driven purpose the theft serves in the saga, yet the fundamental similarity between tales of this sort and the myth of the milk-stealing witch also suggest that the history of the complex may be more intricate than it at first appears.[101] Moreover, the motif in which food magically disappears and reappears is well known in more recent Nordic folklore, although usually associated in modern tales with the activities of the *huldrefolk* 'elves' and other supernatural creatures.[102] The ability of the "Finn" here is clearly tied to his magical abilities (*margfróðr* < 'much knowing', of magic). That Snorri appropriated popular materials in composing sagas has been demonstrated elsewhere, and there is little reason to doubt that something of the same sort has transpired here.[103] But, of course, from the point of view of those who knew, believed, and used these myths in the Middle Ages, their precise origins would have been of little

5. Milk theft and churning, Tuse kirke, Holbæk amt, Denmark (1460–80). Photo by author.

value anyway: the two strands—if that is what they are—of supernaturally purloined foodstuffs were no doubt mutually supportive.

In the case of the later milk-stealing witch, she—and now it is always she—steals, or has her demons steal, the milk of other people's cows or sometimes other foodstuffs as well, typically, in addition to milk, grain products to be used in brewing beer (cf. Figures 5, 6, 7, 9, and 10).[104] One of the most remarkable aspects of this myth is how well-attested it is in the mural paintings of late medieval and early modern churches in Northern Europe—but its distribution is not even throughout the area.[105] Here we begin to see strong differences between various Nordic areas, with this specific configuration of the milk-stealing witch primarily figuring into the church iconography of Denmark and Sweden.[106] According to one study, there are some sixty churches with images of this myth: forty in Sweden, four in Finland, sixteen in Denmark, and three in northern Germany.[107]

Although all of these scenes can be reasonably connected with this complex, there are regional treatments of the materials. In Denmark, various devils typically bring the milk to churns where it will be turned into butter. On Gotland, a woman milks the cows but with assistance of, or in the company of, devils. In Sweden itself, a devil often holds the cow while it is suckled by another animal, whereas in Finland, a devil holds the cow while it is milked by a woman.[108] A further seventy-three churches show scenes of butter churning associated with this story, while there are thirteen with scenes of women being taken to Hell with attributes suggesting they too are part of this complex. All told, Wall reckons that there are 143 scenes of this myth in various churches, reflecting strong testimony to the popularity of the myth, as well as the importance pictorial communication channels played in the medieval period.

This evidence suggests an impression of the myth's age and distribution and if our only source of information were the murals, we might be tempted to believe that this complex properly belonged only to the very late medieval and Reformation eras. But there are a number of indications that this myth had currency already much earlier and was being influenced by Church doctrine, developing a view of witchcraft that, on the one hand, drew on local traditions, while, on the other, was also informed by elite views imported from the Continent. It is not difficult to imagine how the church might push back against such "local" beliefs, as in their appearances in the penitentials suggests, yet at the same time appropriate them for their own larger purpose as a warning about trafficking with the demons and falling into the power of the devil.

Very sensibly, the myth of the milk-stealing witch is explained, or perhaps even explained away, by noting how such a tale addresses such basic human emotions as envy and jealousy: Why does that person have more than I do? And do they have more because they have taken something away from me? These materialist explanations appear to motivate everything from some of the best-known witch-hunts, such as Salem in 1692, to modern political debates.[109] Exploring this psychological dimension edges us closer to the inner meaning of these myths, I believe, but in emphasizing the implicit concern with "lack" in the story, we should not discount either the outrage that the idea of theft itself must have engendered or the fear the possibility of supernatural powers being active in the community must have created.

Myths of this sort—not only that of the milk-stealing witch but the other narratives as well—have had strong explanatory and psychological power, but at the same time we recognize this purpose, we should also realize that members of medieval society were not as interested in brooding about the nature of things, I suspect, as they were in taking effective countermeasures, and these myths helped point the way.

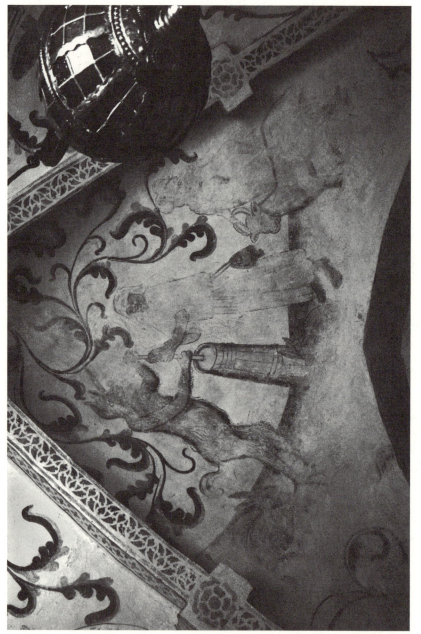

6. Milk theft and churning, Övergran kyrka, Uppsala stift, Sweden (ca. 1480). Photo by author.

7. Milk-stealing witch bearing a "butter-mound" (*smörtopp*) and devils, Dannemora kyrka, Uppsala stift, Sweden (ca. 1520). Photo by author.

To look at the function of such myths in the same perspective in which non-European witchcraft traditions are often assayed, as noted earlier, medieval Nordic society surely held to a "magical worldview" as much as any other society, a worldview that does not recognize the possibility of accidents or randomness: in the magical worldview everything is logically connected in a chain of causation.[110] And importantly, the magical worldview, by its nature, allows "normal" society an outlet for its fears and emotions about suspected cases of magic and witchcraft. If there are bad things happening in the community—a cow is underproducing, for example—then such things are being caused by someone (a witch), and having identified that person, the community has been informed by tradition about the means by which to fix its troubles.

The existing evidence means that we know very little about such occurrences of witchcraft accusations in medieval Scandinavia. Once in a great while we see, I suspect, glimpses of social conflicts that bubble up in such a way as to draw the attention of elite society and thus be recorded (e.g., fifteenth-century Arboga), but for the most part, to the extent that such things took place, they happened in ways that did not make them celebrated enough to enter the records, or if they did, then the cases were handled by the authorities (e.g., Ragnhildr tregagás).[111] Either way, we know very little about accusations concerning what is sometimes called village-level witchcraft in the Nordic Middle Ages. Yet unless nonempowered society in that time and in that place was very unlike any other we know or has been written about, their myths were not unidirectional. In other words, although it is generally understood that there is a connection between belief and myth, the assumption seems to be that belief feeds myth, but not the other way around. In that view, myths are a kind of terminal dumping ground for received opinion, but the truth is far different.

In the real world of medieval Scandinavia, one can readily imagine, the question often came up regarding what one should do when witchcraft is abroad in the community. In fact, there is a strong argument to be made that myths of the sort under consideration here do not merely reflect anxieties and beliefs but also help set the terms for behavior. Acting out the beliefs implicit in traditional narratives, what one folklorist describes as the dramatic extension of legend complexes into real life, is a factor frequently cited in the context of contemporary rumor or moral panics concerned with the sort of scenario one can imagine must have happened on a few occasions in the Scandinavian Middle Ages.[112] When such behaviors—such acts of ostension—occur, they represent reticulations between beliefs, on the one hand, and behavior that helps constitute these phenomena, on the other.[113] Ostension gives individual actors the power to control, or at least the sense that they can control, their lives; the chain of causation allows them to do something about their situations, not merely be victims of them.

In that context, I return to an idea raised in the early pages of this book, namely that what is important in defining witchcraft and magic is most of all what their practitioners do or were thought to do. In other words, what matters is not just the static view of what witchcraft was, in the whole "eye of newt" sense, but rather how witches conduct themselves and what they do, to the extent, for example, that they *make* diabolical pacts, they *steal* food, they *cause* discord, they *dry up* cows, and so on. For the medieval "everyman," witchcraft is not "merely" a theological issue but a practical problem requiring practical solutions. For the residents of the Nordic Middle Ages, not only was the pact with the devil about a source of power for troublemakers, but it was also a resolute contract to be disharmonious and disruptive, to be an agent of evil within the community. But understanding the nature of witchcraft in this way also provided them with the means for fighting against it.

Chapter 5

Witchcraft, Magic, and the Law

The appellation "medieval" in English and other modern European languages has an almost exclusively pejorative sense.[1] If we add to this already negative view the inherent prejudices that we assume attach themselves to accusations of witchcraft, we are tempted to imagine a foreordained "guilty" outcome to any trial in the period of this study. Yet however unlikely the idea of justice within the court systems of medieval Northern Europe may seem, readers of the medieval Icelandic sagas, for example, will appreciate the possibility of "medieval justice" being both fair and real, if also susceptible to manipulation.

A valuable defense against accusations of witchcraft, at least in the world before the witch-hunts of the early modern era, was an upstanding reputation, and individuals went to some lengths to preserve their good names. Thus the laws and court records of medieval society reflect grave sensitivity about accusations of witchcraft, as when witnesses appear before the justices in Stockholm in 1485 to testify that they have heard a man call a certain widow a witch (*trullkona*).[2] Bearing in mind this issue of reputation, as well as the broader question of medieval legal process, it is helpful to consider the following case: in Stockholm, on June 23, 1478, a woman named Sigrid admits that she has called the apparently troublesome Ragnhild 'gray goose' (*graagaas*) a heretic (*kiätterska*) because Ragnhild and her daughter had slept with the same man.[3] A week—and the oath of five good men as to Ragnhild's innocence—later, the council was on the verge of giving Sigrid a serious sentence (possibly the death penalty), when the pleas of the "better women" (*dande quinnor*) convince them merely to exile her from the city. If she enters the city again, she is to be pilloried (*tha skal hon stupas*).[4]

This case, although not directly tied to accusations of witchcraft, underscores several significant aspects of medieval justice, including what happened when witchcraft came before the law—namely, the overwhelming importance of reputation as a defense; the related need to clear one's name; and the corresponding charge of slander against the person who made the accusation, an actionable offense.[5] It is certainly no coincidence that much of our understanding about witchcraft-related legal thinking and sanctions derive from the care with which the law codes address slander. And the case also emphasizes the great care with which trials were undertaken in the Nordic Middle Ages, despite modern, popular perceptions of a capricious rather than careful medieval judiciary.

Legal thinking, not just with respect to criminal cases, but also regarding inheritance, property, and most other aspects of daily life, were matters of careful deliberation in the Nordic Middle Ages, although opinions about the quality and usefulness of these records vary greatly.[6] Synthesizing many decades of debate about the nature of jurisprudence in medieval Scandinavia, a noted historian asks in a recent essay whether laws were held to exist from the beginning and could thus only be identified rather than legislated in the Norwegian Middle Ages.[7] One of his conclusions is that the transformative thirteenth century witnesses the emergence of a new kind of individual, one who understands legal principles and possesses specialized knowledge not available to ordinary people, a key ingredient in making possible the unified, hierarchical nations then being formed.[8]

There are, of course, a number of questions that need to be asked of the Nordic laws, as of all sources: Who created them and for what reason? Why and by what means have they been preserved? Are they representative? What power relationships gave rise to them? Do our consequent attempts to understand such empirical evidence—and impose meaning on it—shed useful light? Most significantly, do our readings result in views that would be recognized by the producers and consumers of our evidence?

Most researchers would agree on the value of these and related questions but probably not find themselves in agreement about the answers. The early laws raise many irresoluble puzzles, but certain facts emerge: all of the medieval Nordic law texts we possess demonstrably spring from the Christian era, meaning that in their extant forms they are all overtly Christian in tone and attitude. This point may seem obvious to us today, but the valorization of these texts as a window onto ancient Germanic culture by earlier generations often resulted in a very different view. Still, although modern scholarship cannot be certain that it comprehends the medieval Nordic view of magic and witchcraft at such a level that we catch every reference that a tradition bearer might recognize as being connected with these areas, sketches of spiritual life in the Scandinavian Middle Ages, and regulations of significance to our topic, do precipitate out.[9]

An important aspect of witchcraft prosecutions is that the legal rituals involved reassured a concerned public that someone was doing something to remedy a perceived problem in the community. Curative functions of this sort largely depend on the "magical worldview."[10] Witchcraft in this sense, as a logical cultural construct meant to deal effectively with the world, was classically formulated through the study of African witchcraft, in a conscious refutation of a view that regarded magic as unintelligible to logical thought. In addition to the conclusion that the living world of magic and witchcraft is anything but illogical, this approach has helped us recognize important social functions of witchcraft and helped develop better, more dynamic, incident-specific interpretive frameworks for assessing witchcraft trials, as the following sections describe.

Regulating Magic and Witchcraft
Secular Laws

A remarkable resource for the study of medieval Nordic life is its secular legal system, not only the national law codes from medieval Denmark, Norway, Sweden, and Iceland, but also earlier collections of regional laws. Together these texts provide fascinating insights into how witches and witchcraft were perceived in the centuries after the conversion to Christianity. Commenting on the central problem of exploiting such normative sources, whether secular or ecclesiastical, one noted scholar in this field neatly summarizes the key conundrum as "whether any of the early medieval written laws and even the penitentials and the *indiculi superstitionum* deal with activities that were contemporary with the texts that describe and denounce them or simply conventionally repeat earlier material."[11] The source value of the Nordic laws has been clouded somewhat by several interlocking scholarly debates concerned with nativist and antinativist arguments about the origins and context of these laws.[12] Early commentators, such as Montesquieu, Hegel, and Grimm, believed they were able to find in the earliest Germanic law codes pristine reflections of pre-Roman (and thus *echt*) Teutonic social regulations.[13]

Influenced by this perspective, nineteenth- and twentieth-century Nordic philology and historiography developed a particular view about the presumed oral nature of the laws before they were written down, a process that begins in earnest in the twelfth century in Scandinavia: for example, the *Annales Ryenses* (*Annals of Ryd*) state for the year 1170 that "the laws of the Danes are published."[14] Even earlier, *Íslendingabók* (*The Book of the Icelanders*) says that the Icelanders decide in 1117 that their laws would thenceforth be written down and not merely "declaimed."[15] Before the written laws, medieval testimony suggests that they were recited orally (*sagði lǫg upp* and so on) at the various assemblies. This image is most vividly presented in the Icelandic sagas, which are filled with scenes at the Alþingi where the reader witnesses the vital role the "law speaker" (*lǫgsǫgumaðr*) has as the preliterate keeper of the culture's legal codes.[16]

Other testimony—such as the references in some of the Old Swedish laws to a custom of "law recitation" (*laghsagha*, a term that over time came to define the law's geographical application)—strengthens the established impression of a tradition of oral law recitation being supplemented by private, desultory notes on the oral laws—what have been famously called "folk law books" (*folkelovbøker*)—which in turn gives way over time to organized, systematic, and written codifications of the laws, which were officially sanctioned and approved by the monarchy.[17] Although this view, and its assumptions, has not been without critics,[18] it has certainly been the dominant perception of the early medieval secular laws in the Nordic countries, a twelfth- and thirteenth-century world seen as existing at the moment of transition from a predominantly oral to a predominantly written elite culture.[19]

Against this nativist view, some scholars have argued for the significant influence of non-Nordic legal models, such as Mosaic law and other legal traditions.[20] There have even been disputes about the degree to which one can reasonably take an essentially Durkheimian view about the fundamental relationship between cultural institutions and the culture that gives rise to the laws.[21] Connected to this issue is the question of age: given the overarching importance of the law codes for understanding developments in the medieval Nordic world, one might expect a carefully worked out chronology, but such a scheme has proved elusive. There is broad consensus, for example, that the oldest of the Norwegian laws may have been written down as early as the twelfth century, but most manuscripts derive from the thirteenth and later centuries.[22] Thus the oldest fragment from *Gulaþingslǫg* (*The Law of Gulaþing*), for example, is sometimes dated to the twelfth century, but the oldest complete manuscript is roughly a century younger.[23] Moreover, it is in their nature that as legal codes were updated, different sections reflect different periods: some passages might be conservatively preserved, others cut from whole cloth, and still others based on older materials but modified here and there in order to bring them up-to-date.[24] In general, the secular and ecclesiastical law materials discussed in this chapter are arranged according to a broad typology that examines laws (a) composed before the late thirteenth century, (b) those from the late thirteenth century, and (c) those after circa 1300.[25]

Mindful of the important part played by reputation in witch trials in later periods, it is perhaps not so surprising that the laws' concerns about witchcraft frequently arise in the context of slander; indeed, accusations of witchcraft and witchlike behavior are so tied to this concept that these characteristics are regularly mentioned in the section of the early secular laws that deal with actionable insults, so much so that one wonders whether imputations involving such activity were not a steady source of friction in the communities.[26] In the Gulaþing laws of western Norway, for example,[27] witchcraft is explicitly mentioned among the words of gross insult for which compensation could be sought (fullrétti).[28] Similar provisions appear throughout the Norwegian laws.[29] The defense for those who bring such a charge raises interesting questions: if through judicial torture—bearing hot iron for a man, plunging her hands into a boiling kettle for a woman—a person accused of witchcraft is found innocent, then the accuser should be considered a slanderer. This judgment, however, can be averted if the accuser can defend himself with the fact that "this view is commonly held" (lit., 'home verdict').[30] Reputation clearly matters in this early period as much as it does in the later periods.

The image of witchcraft in the Nordic world that precipitates out of such laws is not always so clear-cut as this statute from Gulaþingslǫg, however, and can sometimes be bewildering. Or how else do we approach a passage such as the following famous lines Äldre Västgötalagen (The Older Law of Västergötland) from the early thirteenth century?

§ 5. These are the slanderous words about a woman. "I saw that you rode the 'witch-ride' [lit., 'the pen-gate'], with your hair loose, and in a witch's shape, 'caught' between night and day" [= twilight? equinox?]. [If it is] said of her that she is able to destroy a woman or cow, these are slanderous words. [If it is] said of a woman that

she is a harlot [*hortuta*], these are slanderous words. [If it is] said of
a woman that she has [had intercourse with] her father, or has
aborted her child, or has murdered her child, these are words of
abomination. § 6. All these sins should first be discussed with the
priest and not flare up in rancorousness or rage. . . . [31]

This passage comes from a part of the code that deals with various sorts
of lawlessness and is immediately preceded by a parallel discussion of slanders
against men, namely insults of various kinds and accusations of cowardice,
homosexuality, bestiality, and incest.[32] Clearly these segments conjure in gendered terms the most despised and serious vices the medieval Nordic mind
could imagine, one of which, scholarship has inferred, says a great deal about
witchcraft in western Sweden in the thirteenth century.

But what exactly is it saying? First of all, in discussing this form of
slander, the text provides a hypothetical case in which a person maligns a
woman by claiming to have actually witnessed her engaged in a particular
activity.[33] There is no question here of the implied association with witchcraft
being based on untestable evidence, such as secret pacts with the devil or the
like; rather, the claim rests on the affirmative assertion of having literally
seen the individual corporeally participating in conduct with certain cultural
associations. Second, the woman's appearance and behavior are marked in
the extreme: she has been seen riding (*reet* 'rode') a gate in the form of a
"troll" (*i trols ham*).[34] Both the time and place of her conduct are carefully
specified, and both have important cultural connections: she is said to have
ridden the gate at a liminal point in time, "when all was even [between]
night and day" (*þa alt var iamrift nat ok daghér*), either at the equinox or at
twilight or at some combination of the two times.[35]

Liminality is also the hallmark of the location where she engaged in this
apparently odious behavior: by its very nature and purpose, a gate represents
a boundary between areas and therefore also a threshold from one domain
into the other. Gates and pen fences underscore the fact that the act has
taken place in the shadowlands between two areas, metaphorically perhaps
also two different worlds; in any event, that she is said to have been specifically on a pen gate (*a quiggrindu* < *qui,* f. 'pen, fold') would appear to
suggest, and recognize, other dichotomies familiar to modern audiences, such
as nature-culture and so on.[36]

The most alluring phrase to our eyes is the one that says the woman has
been in the shape of a "troll." As discussed earlier, *troll* 'a monstrous, evil-

disposed being, not belonging to the human race; a human being having the nature of a troll' is a very productive element in compounds for practitioners of witchcraft—in Old Swedish, *trolkarl*, *trolkona*, and *trolkärling*, for example. Does this phrase then mean that the woman has an appearance the slanderer associates with witches or, more literally, that she has taken on a monstrous form?[37] Comparanda from throughout the Nordic world, as well as later developments in it, all suggest that this scene is part of a native tradition according to which witches were able to fly (see Chapter 4).[38] Examination of the later redaction of these laws, *Yngre Västgötalagen* (*The Younger Law of Västergötland*; composition 1281–1300, manuscripts from the fourteenth century) sheds further light on what is meant. Philological details aside, the utterance is, with one exception, the same. To the unkempt coiffure of the woman has now been added a further sign of her unwillingness to accept social norms: she is not only loose-haired but also *lösgiurþ* 'loose-girdled'.[39] Taken together, the image of a 'loose-haired' and 'loose-girdled' woman was one intended to portray a female willful and impertinent, perhaps sensuous as well.[40] Everything about the description, which, after all, comes by way of providing an example of an actionable slander, suggests that we are hearing how some thirteenth-century Swedes thought witches behaved (and how decent women did not), and very likely the accusation that follows about being able to destroy a woman or cow is also part of the total witchcraft package.

The bundling of slanders in the Old Swedish provincial laws offers invaluable insights into how witchcraft was perceived: *Gutalagen* (*The Law of Gotland*) places witchcraft (*fordeþsciepr*) together with such deeds as theft, murder, and whoredom.[41] The Bjärkö Laws (Old Swedish *biærköarætter*; Old Danish *biærkeræt*; Old Icelandic/Norwegian *biarkeyarréttr*), or municipal laws, known in Sweden from Lödöse in the west from circa 1345, although believed to have originated in Stockholm in the previous century, are even more cosmopolitan in their treatment of accusations of witchcraft.[42] As with *Äldre Västgötalagen*, these laws begin by discussing actionable slanders against men—thief, murderer, liar, arsonist, "son of a bitch" (*hwnzæmæ son*), or the son of a thrall if he is a freeman's son. The list of male insults also includes *herriæns son*, 'son of Herjann', it has been suggested, one of the many cognomina for the pagan god Óðinn.[43] The law then continues with the slanders for which a good woman, as this law specifies, may bring charges: whore, harlot, witch, or sorceress.[44]

Although the earliest Icelandic law texts possess interesting information on witchcraft, these passages fall in the church law section. What the secular Icelandic laws do not say is of equal interest. According to tradition, toward the end of the settlement period in the tenth century, an Icelander named Ulfljótr brought the laws to Iceland from Norway.[45] In the twelfth century, the Icelanders proclaim their intention to keep written law codes, at which time they also plan to replace with new laws that which would seem to them an improvement on the old laws.[46] *Íslendingabók* adds that the revised laws met with much acclaim. Although we cannot be certain that we possess precisely these resulting laws, it has generally been believed that the diverse materials that make up the Icelandic laws from the period of the commonwealth (which ends 1262–64) are probably close to them.[47] These laws from before the unification with Norway were never codified in any normal sense and have been preserved in a variety of manuscripts, sometimes closely resembling one another, sometimes quite different. Collectively, the laws have come to be known as *Grágás* (lit., 'Gray Goose').[48]

As we have seen, in the early Norwegian and Swedish secular laws, witchcraft typically comes up amid enumerations of slanders and the cases that can be brought against rumormongers. Surprisingly then, especially given the link between the *Grágás* materials and the Norwegian legal tradition, is the fact that in the sections on slander, witchcraft is not raised at all. Indeed, one can read *Grágás* and come away with the impression that women were never slandered in early medieval Iceland—or if they were, it was of no great concern, for the lists of slanders is highly phallocentric. This apparent inattentiveness might be taken for just that and little more, but it plays into an important point about the possible regional differences in conceptions of witchcraft and magic in medieval and early modern Scandinavia. In Iceland, as one important author notes, words are the tactile realization of magical ability, but the source of that power is knowledge, a relationship that helps explain why the typical early modern Icelandic witch was male: "Knowledge or wisdom (*fræði*, *fróðleikur*) was associated with men, at least after the introduction of Christianity and the emergence of a new kind of literati or *kennimenn*."[49]

On the other hand, after the end of the Icelandic Commonwealth, the Icelandic legal system is consciously brought more in line with the Norwegian legal system, first with the much disliked laws called *Járnsíða* (1271–81) and later with the long-lasting *Jónsbók* (1281).[50] The writers of *Jónsbók* used the national laws of King Magnús as their model, although the two codes are by no means identical everywhere. One senses this similarity immediately, when lists of offenses drawing on the magical world are enumerated—witchcraft, soothsaying journeys, and sitting out to awaken trolls, by which heathenism is promoted.[51] And the slander provisions in the two countries now closely resemble one another. In most of the several hundred manuscripts of *Jónsbók*, no mention of magic or witchcraft is made in the section on slander; however, witchcraft is specified in four manuscripts, which list as actionable insults being called a traitor, a thief, a pilferer, a whore's son, and so on, and being called a *fordæða* 'witch'.[52] Perhaps more in keeping with the tradition of *Grágás* is the way slander is brought up obliquely in *Jónsbók* in the section on poetic composition, when the laws note the possibility of bringing suit if one is said to be guilty of larceny or witchcraft (*fordæðuskap*).[53] Especially noteworthy is the wording of the direct slanders, which makes clear that it is an insult to men to be called by these terms. Women are simply not mentioned.[54]

In a similar vein, the early secular laws from Denmark are relatively quiet on questions of witchcraft:[55] surprisingly, the laws of Jutland of 1241 do not take up the topic at all, although a century and a half later they will address the question in detail.[56] Conversely, the Scanian Municipal Laws of 1328 specify that if a man destroys (*forgiør*) a woman, or a woman a man, or a woman a woman through witchcraft or other sorcery, so that the person dies, a man should be sent to the wheel, a woman burned.[57] The terms *firigæra*, *fyrirgera*, *forgöra*, and so on—'destroying' or 'killing'—are generally associated, as here, with witchcraft, a correlation frequently made in the Old Swedish provincial laws as well. Thus *Äldre Västgötalagen* states that if a woman does in (*firigær*) a man, she can be declared an outlaw and killed.[58] The same law maintains that a woman may not be killed for any crime other than witchcraft (*utæn firi trolskap*).[59] One suspects that poisoning may be the specific kind of witchcraft the law has in mind, as has been argued in detail by at least one scholar.[60] The interpretation generally fits well, especially as *intoxicatores* 'poisoners' are sometimes collocated with witchcraft in suggestive ways in later texts.[61] Moreover, the possibility of poisoning is treated as a very real threat in the West Gautish tradition: a later addendum to the laws tells of King Ingi, who was killed by an evil drink in Östergötland and died from it, although there is no overt suggestion in this instance that witchcraft is involved.[62]

It is also telling that in a late medieval Latin translation of the Old Swedish phrase *meþ trulldom ælla andrum forgerningum* 'by witchcraft or other means',[63] a canon in Uppsala, Ragvald Ingemundsson, uses the phrase *veneno aut arte magica* 'poisoning or magical arts'.[64] Undoubtedly, verbs such as *firigæra* and so on, as one famous scholar has said, are used to designate all sorts of injury that cannot be explained by obvious violence; witchcraft is one of its forms, poisoning another.[65] *Yngre Västgötalagen* implies malice of just this sort when it states that a woman taken in the act of "destroying cow or cattle, woman or man" forfeits her life.[66] This sense is strengthened by laws predicated on constructions that specify, as in the case of *Upplandslagen* (*The Law of Uppland*, 1296), that if a woman gives a man something destructive, she should be placed in fetters and taken to the assembly, and with her the same destructive articles, presumably witchcraft paraphernalia, clearly so that they can be used as evidence in the case.[67]

What should not be overshadowed by the details of these early secular laws, however, is the tendency for them, like the old Roman tradition, to single out for capital punishment only witchcraft that produced actual physical harm.[68] By contrast, women who were merely guilty of superstitions, for example, were fined in *Yngre Västgötalagen*.[69] That is not to say that the secular laws were entirely practical about misfortune: obviously they too were influenced by the ideology that shapes the church law sections concerned with the maintenance of Christian probity and sometimes mimic the themes and language of the ecclesiastical laws.

Just who controlled the writing of the laws was a matter of gravity: when, for example, in Norway the revisions of the individual provincial laws began, a process that eventually led to a national law, King Magnús and Archbishop Jón met in 1269 at the Frostuþing where the issue was resolved.[70] The decision, ratified by the assembly, declared that the king might address all secular issues and those connected with the monarchy, but the clear implication is that the Christian laws should be the under the archbishop's jurisdiction.[71] Even so, among the criminals condemned to outlawry in the miscellaneous provisions of *Frostuþingslǫg* (*The Law of Frostuþing*) are listed those who are guilty of murder, witchcraft, soothsaying-journeys, and sitting out at night in order to awaken trolls and thereby promote heathendom, language that would be adopted in the Icelandic *Járnsíða* and *Jónsbók*.[72] Much the same language is found in the Norwegian municipal laws, which join to the crimes of soothsaying and sorcery the offense of sacrificing to heathen spirits (*á heiðnar vættir*) and say that all these acts are worthy of outlawry.[73]

As the laws were amended, changes in the attitude toward witchcraft became apparent, all the more so as they were eventually worked into national codes—first in Norway and then, after the end of the commonwealth, in Iceland, followed by Sweden.[74] The relatively benevolent tone calling for outlawry for the practice of witchcraft, for example, began to shift. An amended text of the *Gulaþingslǫg* lists the familiar collocation of those women charged with "using magic and witchcraft" (*fara með golldrum. eða með gerningum*), who are still, as in previous codes, to be outlawed and driven into exile if found guilty.[75] But the text goes on to say that if a woman is imputed with being a 'troll-[woman]' (i.e., witch) and a man-eater (*En ef þat er cono kennt at hon se troll. oc manneta*) and found guilty, she should be taken to the sea and hewn in the back (*þa scal fǫra hana a sæ ut oc hoggua a rygg*). Several key points arise from this passage: first of all, if the editors' dating of the manuscript fragment to the late twelfth century is correct, this phrase would be early testimony indeed to the idea of the anthropophagic witch in the Nordic region. As a comparable phrase (*Enn ef þæt er kent kono at hon se trolkona eða manæta*) is used in one of the later church laws,[76] one might be tempted to dismiss the image of the "man-eater" as the result of imported continental views, where the association of cannibalism and witchcraft had a long tradition (e.g., the sixth-century Salic laws; the penitentials of Burchard of Worms).[77] Yet the Icelandic sagas know of the anthropophagic witch,[78] and in native tradition there exist a wide array of ogreish Otherworldly creatures eager to eat humans.[79] Foreign and indigenous views on anthropophagic witches may have found in each other mutually supportive parallels. But what is certainly the case—whether the *mannæta* is of foreign origin or an indigenous character, or some combination of the two—is that the laws here envision both a special kind of crime and a different kind of punishment than had been the case in earlier codes.[80]

Similarly, the secular portions of the earliest Swedish provincial law, *Äldre Västgötalagen*, bring up witchcraft in the section dealing with bodily injury (*þättä är bardaghä*) and again list the accusation of witchcraft among other slanders that in toto comprise an overview of the society's cardinal sins.[81] But still, that leaves the secular treatment of witchcraft in *Äldre Västgötalagen* as one that positions the topic among accidental ax blows, defaulted loans, and escaped slaves. How differently the topic appears to be handled a century or so later in the national law code of circa 1350, *Magnus Erikssons Landslag* (*Magnus Eriksson's National Law*). Witchcraft is taken up twice in the section that deals with the most serious of crimes (*Höghmälisbalker*, lit., 'high case section'): murder, infanticide, bigamy, poisoning stepchildren (for the purpose of denying them their inheritance), rebellion, treason, arson.[82]

Clearly the attitude toward witchcraft, and the sort of threat it represents to society, was changing, as was the penalty: women found guilty of witchcraft are to be burned at the stake (some manuscripts call for them to be stoned), and men tortured and executed (*stegla*).

An addendum to the Danish Jutlandic law from the later Middle Ages, usually dated circa 1400, "Concerning Witchcraft," rather blandly comments that if someone is charged with having killed an individual through witchcraft and denies the charge, certain rights of defense are available to him.[83] Of course, given the loss of so much material, including many medieval administrative texts, during the great Copenhagen fire of 1728, it is difficult to gauge how representative the extant legal codes are for the Danish Middle Ages, but it is often noted how infrequently witchcraft is mentioned in the medieval Danish laws, and when it is, the context often seems to be an enumeration of the rights of defense. In many ways, the projection of witchcraft and its legal situation in medieval Denmark stands apart from the scenario projected by the law codes of the other three Nordic polities. The explanation may be, as has been suggested, that Denmark was simply further along in working out the relationship between secular law and canon law, and there was thus no reason to address witchcraft from an additional perspective.[84]

Magnus Erikssons Landslag was reworked under King Kristoffer and confirmed in 1442 and suggests further shifting attitudes in the late medieval period. For the most part, they reflect the attitudes toward, and even the wording about, witchcraft as found in *Magnus Erikssons Landslag*. They discuss witchcraft in the context of homicide (*VI. ¶ Forgör nokor androm meth trull doom*) with the same penalties: burning at the stake for women and torture and execution for men.[85] Of note, however, are the regulations about slander, whether involving a man or a woman, which have been altered slightly in that the list of accusations has been expanded to include not only the usual array of thieves, whores, and whore's sons but also a male witch (*trulkarl*) or a female witch (*trulkonna*) and equally, and explicitly, gender-inclusive murderers and heretics: thief, murderer, robber, heretic, whore's son,[86] male witch, whore, female murderer, female heretic, or female witch (*tiufuer, mordare, röfuare, kettare, horenszon, trulkarl, horkonna, moordherska, ketterska eller trulkonna*).[87] Always condemned, the perception of witchcraft changes palpably over time in the laws, increasingly in the later Middle Ages placed in the various laws among the most serious and damning offenses.

Ecclesiastical Regulations

The image of Nordic witchcraft that emerges from the normative documents largely produced by and for the church is more suggestive, and more colorful, than the somewhat spare visage offered by the secular laws.[88] As we have seen, the secular laws were primarily, although not exclusively, interested in witchcraft and related topics in connection with homicide and the loss of social harmony brought about by slanderous, and provably false, accusations. Medieval Christian ordinances in Scandinavia add to these practical concerns their own deep suspicion of lingering pagan practice among the populace, fear of heretical beliefs of all sorts that might undermine the church's authority, and, more fatefully, a suspended critical spirit with regard to the character and effects of witchcraft.[89]

A cautionary corrective may be in order at this juncture: the apparition of a monolithic Roman Church dominates contemporary perceptions of medieval Christianity in the West, but realistically, no such phenomenon existed in the Middle Ages. Considerable diversity existed within the church itself, and especially in its various regional entities and bishoprics, and in their relationships both with the larger church and with local authorities. The tendency toward uniformity throughout an archbishopric and the regularization of national church statutes with canon law is one of the chief guiding principles one witnesses in the Nordic world.[90]

Already by the mid-twelfth century, a metropolitan see was established in the Norwegian city of Niðaróss, and church laws with broad national application were developed, eventually leading to the volume called *Gullfjǫðr* (*Gold Feather*), which sought to bring Norwegian church rules in line with the canon laws of Gratian's *Decretum*.[91] With regard to governance, church leaders found it necessary to negotiate with secular authorities over the extent of their influence, and while there are some general trends, it is important to recall that the situation differed from area to area, and from period to period.

Thus, under the Norwegian king Magnús Erlingsson, for example, the church achieved a degree of success concerning authority over the jurisdiction of church property and its clergy and the appointment of bishops. These changes were denied to the church by King Sverrir Sigurðarson (1177–1202), who caused a stir by arguing for a return to the king's leadership in important church matters. When King Magnús Hákonarson met with Bishop Jón in 1277, he ceded to the bishop most of the same privileges that had been granted to the church under King Magnús, only for these rights to be challenged by the aristocracy a few years later during the minority of Eiríkr Magnússon.

The relations between church and secular leaders became so strained in the period of the 1280s that the archbishop and two bishops were exiled.[92] And thus the testy and changing relationships between the national and ecclesiastical institutions continued over the decades and across the vast space that constituted Scandinavia in the Middle Ages. Indeed, one history of the medieval Nordic world consists of the intense power struggles that took place over questions of ecclesiastical immunities and privileges, all the many wide-ranging negotiations necessary between the secular government, on the one hand, and a religion that saw in itself an institution both distinct from, and independent of, that government, on the other.[93] And in medieval Scandinavia this potential for ecclesiastical particularism is apparent in the differing treatments of witchcraft in the early church laws.

Most of the provincial and national legal codes of Iceland, Norway, and Sweden begin with so-called Christian or church laws (e.g., *kirkiu balker*); the Danish situation stands apart, although they too have church laws, of course.[94] The treatment of witchcraft in these statutes is highly variegated: in the West Norse area—that is, in Iceland and Norway, whose legal systems were historically intertwined by heritage and politics—witchcraft, sorcery, and magic play a major role in the Christian laws. By contrast, in East Scandinavia, witchcraft and related topics have only a minor part in the Danish church laws, and none to speak of in the church laws of the earliest Swedish provincial laws, appearing only after circa 1300. Typical of the early church laws in the West Norse area is the passage from *Grágás* that calls on citizens to trust in God and his saints and not to worship heathen spirits. It goes on to state that if one employs witchcraft, sorcery, or magic (*galldra eþa gørningar. eþa fiolkýngi*), lesser outlawry is the sentence.[95] The law then carefully specifies what it means by this sort of witchcraft (*fiolkyngi*): "if he says it, or teaches it, or causes it to be said for himself or his property (alt., livestock)." From the wording, the reference is apparently to a form of apotropaic charm magic, and thus the censure associated with it, motivated by belief in superstition. The law further defines the typology in effect: if, by contrast, one uses a harmful form of witchcraft (*fordæs skap*), then full outlawry is called for. It is this kind of witchcraft, the law specifies, if through one's words or magic illness or death is visited on people or livestock. In both cases, prosecution requires a twelve-man jury.[96] Following this discussion, the laws spell out several forms of magic—for example, endowing stones with power—the practice of which, because of the "superstition" (*hindr vitni*) involved, calls for the penalty of lesser outlawry. Set against the general austerity of the secular laws, with their emphasis on the tangible act of murder and on accusations of witchery that could be demonstrated to be false, it is not difficult to see that there are fundamental differences between the approaches the two different kinds of laws take to the subject of witchcraft, a perception that only increases the more one examines Icelandic, Norwegian, and, later, Swedish texts.

Thus the church laws of the *Gulaþingslǫg* dedicate an entire section to questions of witchcraft and soothsaying:

> The next is this, that we must pay no heed to soothsaying, incantation, or wicked sorcery. And if a man is accused and convicted of having practiced soothsaying or having told fortunes, he shall be an outlaw and shorn of all personal rights; and all his chattels to the last penny shall go, one-half to the king and one-half to the bishop. And if any man gives heed to soothsaying and the charge is proven, he shall owe a fine of forty marks, one-half to go to the king and one-half to the bishop. And if a man practices sorcery and witchcraft, and he is accused and convicted of it, he shall depart from the king's dominions, for men must give no heed to such doings. But whosoever does pay heed [to such things] has forfeited his chattels to the last penny; and his [only] choice shall be to go to confession and do pennance. If the bishop or his deputy accuses a man of practicing soothsaying or sorcery or witchcraft and he denies the charge, a method of defense has been provided. If a man is accused of practicing soothsaying, let him refute [the charge] with a sixfold oath: let twelve men of his own rank be selected, and let him choose one of the twelve; he himself shall be the second; his nearest kinsman shall be the third and [there shall be] three others, men who can be held to account for pledge and promise; and if the oath fails, the failure leads to outlawry[. . . .] If a woman is accused of practicing sorcery and witchcraft, let six women be appointed, housewives whom men know to be good [women], three to stand on either side of her; and they shall bear witness that she knows neither sorcery nor witchcraft. But if this testimony fails, she becomes liable to outlawry, and the king shall have one-half of her property and the

bishop one-half. And her heir shall convey her out of the king's dominion.[97]

The sections that immediately follow this one—addressing heathen sacrifice and bestiality—underscore the moral outrage with which the church regarded these depraved errors. And in this passage, the enumerated penalties make clear that to engage in any act of witchcraft, whether as the performer, or even as the beneficiary, was regarded as sinful behavior. For consumers of this kind of magic, the penalties are severe: fines for listening to prophecies and the loss of property and penance for anyone paying heed to the other forms of witchcraft mentioned.

But agency carries a much higher penalty: outlawry and the loss of rights and property for fortune-telling and exile for the one who practices witchcraft and sorcery (*sa annarr er ferr með galldra oc gerningar*). Of particular note too is the slight but significant gendered difference in the nature of proving one's innocence: if a man is accused of engaging in soothsaying (*er þat kent at hann fare með spár*), he must prove he has not done it by a sixfold oath, whereas if women are imputed with practicing witchcraft and sorcery (*En ef þat er konom kent at þær fare með golldrum oc gerningum*), she must prove by her existing reputation among good women that she *knows* no witchcraft or sorcery (*þær scolo vitni bera at hon kann eigi galldra ne gerningar*). In other words, unlike an accused male, the threshold of innocence for a woman is not merely that she is not responsible for a specific deed, but rather that her reputation is such that she is regarded by her peers as being incapable of doing it. Perhaps the same reliance on reputation is envisioned in the case of a man charged with witchcraft, but the language of the law suggests there is a difference based on gender in the way the cases are adjudicated.[98]

Borgarþingslǫg (*The Law of Borgarþing*) the early laws from the Oslofjord area, offer impressive insights into the nature of witchcraft practices in the centuries following the conversion to Christianity—or at least what church authorities thought these practices were.[99] The felonies (*ubota værk* lit., 'deeds which cannot be atoned for with money') it cites provide a veritable catalogue of the forms witchcraft-related crimes could take. First, the law declared it a felony to "sit out," a ritual connected with the practice of witchcraft.[100] Then the law forbade prophecy in the specific form of making "Finn-trips," or journeys to Finnmark, in order to consult with the Sámi about the future.[101] It assessed a three-mark fine for a woman who might bite off a finger or toe from her child in order to secure longevity.[102] The same fine was to be leveled for rearing a child as a heathen.[103] It then stated that "the worst (female) witch" is the one who destroys "cow or calf, woman or child" ("Su er fordæða uærst er firer gerer ku eða kalve kono eða barne").[104] And it noted that it is witchcraft (*fordæðo skapr*) if human hair or nails or frog's feet or other things usually reckoned as sorcery (*till gærninga*) are discovered in bed or bolster.[105] Significantly, the law goes on to discuss a woman who is charged with "witchery" (*trylzka*)—she should have six women testify on her behalf that she is not a witch. Again, it is a communal judgment about a woman's reputation rendered by other women that counts, not a defense of her specific behavior at a particular time and place.[106] The section closes by noting that men ought to believe in God, not in imprecations and idolatry (*æigi a boluan eða a blot skapp*), but if someone engages in heathen sacrifice, as is forbidden in canon law, then he should pay a fine of three marks.[107]

This entire section of the law is also found in various places in subsequent iterations of the *Borgarþingslǫg* as well as in the *Frǫstuþingslǫg*.[108] Modest modifications aside—for example, instead of the "worst witch" being she who destroys cows or calves, women or *children*, the other laws generally have the somewhat less frightening (and more gender- and generationally equitable) phrase "woman or *man*"—the key difference is that each of the other versions amplifies the expression "sit out" by noting that one sits out and thereby "awakens (the) troll(s)."[109] Indeed, the concatenation of elements witnessed here—sitting out to awaken troll(s), sorcery, prophecy, the promotion of paganism, and so on—are often found bundled in the Norwegian laws, whether secular or church laws.[110] And as noted earlier, even though most of our direct evidence comes from the thirteenth century and later, the laws themselves suggest that they are older. In line with many of the rules we have seen thus far, for example, the *Frǫstuþingslǫg*. mandate the use of ordeals for charges connected to paganism, prophecy, and witchcraft:

> If a man sacrifices to heathen gods or practices sooth-saying or sorcery, or if a man gives credence to such a one or harbors him for such purposes, he shall be outlawed like a banesman and the bishop shall have his property to the last penny. If he denies [the guilt], let him carry the hot iron, or, [if a woman], let her go to the hot kettles. And the one who accuses any man of this [and the man is cleared], shall be rated a slanderer, if witnesses are called to take note of it, unless he can produce witnesses to common rumor.[111]

Despite the relatively late date of the manuscript, judicial torture (Latin *ordalium*; Old Norse *skírsl*) was abolished in Norway, as in the other Nordic countries, with the visit of the papal legate, Cardinal William of Sabina, in 1247, so this passage is widely held to be traceable back much further than the earliest manuscript fragments.

A similar situation obtains for many of the Norwegian church laws: the origins of the *Eiðsivaþingslǫg* from the Oppland area are confidently placed by some to the twelfth century but are known only in manuscripts from the later centuries.[112] These laws display deep concern with the realm of magic, as they forbid anyone from having in their home a wand or heathen altar, charm materials or poppet, or anything considered part of pagan practices.[113] Similar prohibitions are repeated later in the same church laws, but to these proscriptions against belief in witchcraft, charms, idolatry, and other heathen customs is added belief in "Finns" and traveling to the "Finns," that is, the common notion of seeking soothsaying among the Sámi.[114] And, these church laws from the Eiðsivaþing say that a woman charged with "riding" a man or one of his servants may defend herself by swearing an oath.[115]

According to the Icelandic annals, in the year 1267 the revisions of the Gulaþing laws undertaken at the behest of King Magnús Hákonarson, known as "law mender" (*lagabœtir*), were accepted, although the extant manuscripts date from the early 1300s.[116] If anything, the allusions to witchcraft and magic appear to grow both more frequent and more lurid in this modernized text. The law explains that people are obliged to believe in "that faith we have pledged to God" and that the king and the bishop must with great care ensure that people are not engaging in a powerful heresy or in heathen beliefs.[117] These falsehoods include such things as charms (*galdrar*), witchcraft (*gerningar*), transvection (*trollriðu*), prophecy (*spadomar*), and belief in spirits inhabiting the land, howes, and waterfalls.[118] Also included in the enumeration of these false ways is the practice of sitting out in order to be informed about the future and searching for treasure or otherwise becoming knowledgeable, as well as attempting to awaken ghosts (*draugha*) or cairn-dwellers (*haughbua*).[119]

Shortly after the revision of the Gulaþing Christian laws, probably in the years 1269–73, a Norwegian church law meant to have national authority was composed, described by its early editors as essentially a compilation of the church laws of the Gulaþing and the Frostuþing.[120] Through a misreading of the first item in the main manuscript—a codex attributed to Þorgeirr Hákonarson, a scribe from the reign of King Eiríkr Magnússon (1280–99)—

these church laws have mistakenly come to be connected with the name of King Sverrir, hence the title *Kong Sverrers Christenret* (*King Sverrir's Christian Law*).[121] It carries over much from *Gulaþingslǫg* concerning witchcraft and soothsaying,[122] as well as the Gulaþing reference to the anthropophagic witch.[123] It also forbids, as does one of the later supplemental laws to *Gulaþingslǫg*, the raising of a special pole for charm purposes.[124] Specifically, it forbids idolatry and sacrifice to heathen spirits, to heathen gods, to cairns, and to mounds. Following this impressively complete list, the law demands the loss of property, the obligation to confess and atone with Christ (or failing that, exile) for anyone who "raises a pole and calls it a scald-pole" (*ræisir stong oc kallar skaldzstong*).[125]

For their part, the Iceland law codes offer intriguing insights into how witchcraft was understood and treated. One text of much-debated age lists in one section several powerful items connected with witchcraft, such as a man or a woman performing *seiðr* or "raising" trolls to ride men or livestock.[126] In another section, it provides an augmented list of such activities, including pursuing prophecy through witchcraft or sorcery, awakening trolls or spirits, or committing any other sort of heresy that is opposed to God and the Christian faith.[127] Whereas this part of the law declares the evildoer a heretic and sentences him to be outlawed, the first section cited calls for the condemned to be taken out to sea and drowned.[128]

After such evocative glimpses into the world of witchcraft in the West Norse region, the church materials from the East Norse area in the early periods seem thin gruel by comparison. The Danish church laws, presumably among the oldest we have, are more like the secular laws in the early periods, as they tend to raise matters of witchcraft mainly in the context of homicide. Both the Sealandic Church Law and the Scanian Church Law mention, more or less in passing, the possibility of a man or a woman acquiring a reputation for witchcraft or sorcery (*trulldom æller fordæper*), but even there the references seem like afterthoughts on the heels of discussing homicide and are cited in order to provide examples of defense through oaths and ordeal.[129] With a few exceptions from the late medieval period, these brief glimpses are about all that comes from the medieval church laws in Denmark, which stand apart from the trend in the rest of Scandinavia.

Perhaps surprisingly, in the earliest periods the Swedish church laws are largely silent as well: the Christian sections of *Äldre Västgötalagen* and *Yngre Västgötalagen* address witchcraft not at all. When *Upplandslagen* was ratified in 1296, it became a model for a number of subsequent legal codes in Sweden.

Its church section, *kirkiu balker*, is again relatively quiet with regard to witch-craft, commenting only on individuals who believe in superstitions (*ællr mæþ wiþær skipi farit*).[130] Passing references of this sort are typical, as when the *kirkiu balker* of *Östgötalagen* (*The Law of Östergötland*; manuscript from the mid-1300s), lists witchcraft among a series of crimes for which a certain type of oath may be used in defense.[131]

More revealing is the paragraph in the church section of *Dalalagen* (*The Law of Dalarna*) devoted to female witches—significantly, tucked between passages on bestiality and infanticide.[132] Like the Norwegian *Borgarþingslǫg*, the Dala church laws enumerate some of the materials a witch might be expected to have in her possession, although it is unclear whether the law envisions a witch caught in the act of using these items or simply has in her possession "horn and hair, quick and dead, that may well be termed witchcraft. . . ."[133] The phrases used here—*horn oc haar quict oc döt*—correspond to, and presumably help elucidate, the parallel passages in other Old Swedish laws that call for incriminating witchcraft materials to accom-pany an accused witch to the assembly (e.g., "ok þe samu forgiærningær mæþ hænni").[134] Given the context of the phrase and the wide, nearly univer-sal, use of both hair and nail clippings in sympathetic or, more narrowly, contagious magic, *horn* has generally been understood as referring to nail clippings. The idea that the charm ingredients consist of both living and dead is again best understood against the backdrop of magic beliefs documented elsewhere.

Charm magic demands all sorts of materials—and here the "Eye of newt and toe of frog, / Wool of bat and tongue of dog" aspect of witchcraft is highly relevant—and, as discussed earlier, Nordic evidence suggests that ev-erything from peas to cat brains to human effluvia could figure into the formulae. For the practitioner, the omnibus character of the ingredients meant that they were easily available, but the same thing was true for those interested in proving witchcraft: almost anything found in the average house-hold could be fitted to such a scheme, living or dead, whether wildlife, do-mestic animal, herbs, virtually any article. The sentence for a woman convicted of witchcraft and unable to pay a heavy fine—*wari stens mattit oc stranda* 'let her be meat for stones and strand'—has occasioned much debate, although the sense of it would seem to be that she should be taken to the shore and stoned to death.[135] Both the manner of execution and the apparent dereliction of the corpse are intended to underscore the severity of the crime (for poor women, at any rate).

What is generally referred to as *Smålandslagen* (*The Law of Småland*), of which only the church law section has been preserved, has language similar to *Dalalagen*.[136] Among the principal moral outrages that it claims should be adjudicated by the bishop are the murder of an unbaptized child, incest, and witchcraft. This rule is to apply to witchcraft (*trolldomb*er), the law continues, whether the individual is taken "within yard and gate, with horn and hair," terms that naturally bring to mind the corresponding nail and hair phrase of *Dalalagen*.[137] In addition, of course, the use here of *grind* 'gate', perhaps also *garper*, in the context of witchcraft reminds one of *Äldre Västgötalagen* and its peculiar image of the gate-mounted witch.[138]

Under the auspices of the metropolitan see in Niðaróss, which, in addition to the bishoprics in Bergen, Stavanger, Oslo, and Hamar had authority over suffragan bishops in various locations throughout Norway's Atlantic empire, including Garðar in Greenland, Skálholt and Hólar in Iceland, Kirkjubøur in the Faroe Islands, and Kirkwall for the Orkneys and Shetland, a number of statutes were declared by the provincial councils, which met on an irregular basis. In an episcopal ordinance relating to confession (*skriptaboð*) from 1326 (preserved in fifteenth-century manuscripts), witchcraft is again included in the same section as incest and other sexual crimes in a now-familiar pattern of "sitting out," promoting witchcraft, or performing *seiðr* or other heathen activity.[139] Under Archbishop Páll Bárðarson of Niðaróss (1334–46), who had studied Roman and canon law in Orléans and held the title of *professor utriusque juris*, a number of statutes were promulgated at provincial councils.[140] The ordinance known as *Archbishop Páll's Third Statute,* preserved both in Norway and in Iceland, addresses witchcraft several times and extends our vision of what the concept encompassed in the fourteenth-century Nordic world.[141] It warns against what it calls "herbs, runes and magic" (*lif runir oc galldra*), noting that these are but delusions and mockeries of the devil.[142] Other manuscripts add *taufr*, another term for magic, to the list of errors, and still others "artifices" (*velar*) to the devil's subterfuge.[143] Later the ordinance includes in a list of fornicators and other malefactors, "*notorious* prophets or magicians" (emphasis added), perjurers, and heretics.[144]

Although we know that runes figured prominently in traditional charm magic (see previous discussion, Chapter 2), they have not been legislated against earlier as a source of magic and witchcraft, so far as we know. They had, together with herbs and other medicines, become part of the witchcraft kit as understood from the pulpit: as we have seen, sermon after sermon ties these items together. Now, however, the collocation acquires formal legal status, when in about 1347 a new statute is promulgated under Páll's successor, Archbishop Árni Einarsson; it now includes runes among the many sins associated with witchcraft and magic. Indeed, its list of activities to avoid has expanded to include not only runes, but witchcraft and sorcery, herbs, superstitions, and any other creed not taught by the church.[145] To do otherwise is to be a cursed heretic.[146]

Synodal statutes in the East Norse area are, at about this same point (i.e., mid-fourteenth century), relatively silent on this issue but in time also expand the range of witchcraft associations, albeit not in exactly the same direction as the West Norse area. On the other hand, the oldest Swedish penitential materials, from Skara in Västergötland (manuscript from ca. 1335), do not even raise the topic of witchcraft, a situation that might be explained, as one expert has suggested, by the fact that the provincial laws were believed to have already adequately provided for it.[147] A document from the diocese of Strängnäs from the mid-1300s, however, now lists *veneficia* 'poisoning; magic, sorcery' and *sortilegia* 'soothsaying, prophecy' among such great sins as homicide and sacrilege.[148] Indeed, exclusion from communion for witchcraft-related peccancies becomes routine in Swedish church law, as ever more detailed lists of such sinners indicate what late medieval church authorities in Sweden deemed constituted witchcraft and associated crimes.

A number of these items are attributed to Nils Hermansson (also known as Nicolaus Hermani), canon of Uppsala cathedral from 1350, archdeacon in Linköping from 1360 and bishop of Linköping from 1374 to his death in 1391, although probably best known to posterity for his important connections to Saint Birgitta.[149] Before these appointments, he had studied theology in Paris and canon law in Orléans. In what is apparently the earliest of the ordinances promulgated by him, he condemns poisoners, murderers, church thieves, witches (*incantatrices*), and anyone who summons demons.[150] In another list of those forbidden to take communion, usurers are classed together with 'workers of magic', enchanters, and enchantresses.[151]

Building on this view of witchcraft are passages from a number of fifteenth-century Swedish penitentials: some reflect the combination of previously mentioned magic and demon-invocation, sometimes augmenting the list with a reference to the use of auguries. Like the West Norse codes, these penitentials also forbid belief in the efficacy of such methods: a penance of seven years is called for in all these cases.[152] Often these texts, as already the earlier Swedish materials suggest, touch on concerns more akin to a learned court's view of the magical world than the charmingly homey, if all too brief, mentions of herbs and runes in the Norwegian statutes. Despite possible broad prototypes, there are no known direct foreign antecedents and thus little reason to believe other than that the information reflects Swedish conditions, as Bengt Ankarloo has noted.[153]

The central concerns of these texts, which date from a church meeting in Arboga in 1412, are prophecy; incantations; soothsaying; the interpretation of dreams; writing with characters and words not found in sacred texts, which some superstitious people believe to be potent against fire, water, sword, disease, and other threats; all writing on lead meant as a defense against toothache, fevers, and all manner of diseases of men and beast; all means used to discover stolen goods that have been hidden; and the observation of so-called Egyptian Days (a calendric system for divining fortunate and unfortunate days).[154]

The late fifteenth century also provides several very interesting items from Denmark: in a statute titled simply "Concerning Magic," priests and other clerics are forbidden from engaging in any sort of magic, since such things are always part of the devil's secret administration.[155] And from the same period, parish priests are warned to keep the Eucharist and holy oil under proper locks because of the potential harm from both magic and "threatening dangers."[156] The latter decree apparently has older roots: very similar rules were articulated in a statute from Strängnäs in Sweden, dated by one authority to the mid-1300s, cautioning priests to protect the holy water fonts against magic and impurities.[157] In the cases calling for protection of holy water, holy oil, and the Eucharist, priests are surely being warned to ensure that the articles are not stolen in order to be used in various charms, as this was a common concern.

Prosecuting Witchcraft and Related Crimes

Proscriptive cultural monuments such as legal statutes are inherently hypothetical and how much we can learn from them suspect—unless, of course, there exist actual cases from which to form judgments. And what do we know about those brought to trial for witchcraft or related activities in the Nordic world in the centuries before the Reformation?[158] Given the data set, even if every case can be successfully identified, it is difficult to imagine, due to the small number of trials, anything like the subtle and meaningful statistical readings a number of scholars have managed to tease out of the early modern period for the various national situations.[159] After all, it might be argued that our data consists entirely of what statisticians would regard as "outliers," cases that fall outside the norm and thus skew our impressions.

Conversely, however representative—or not—the cases are, they can provide important profiles of witchcraft-related crimes in the Nordic world. Looking at the incidents as a group, several parallel and telling patterns are clear. On the one hand, the precipitating crisis in cases where a female is charged tends to involve sexuality; when the women are charged, the accusation generally includes witchcraft and its associated activities, especially aphrodisiac and anaphrodisiac charms; and the women are nearly always either acquitted or lightly sentenced. In the cases involving male defendants, on the other hand, the charge is routinely apostasy and devil worship, with additional accusations of theft (often from churches) being commonplace, and in every case where we know the court's disposition the sentence is capital punishment.[160] Strictly speaking, these two groups have little in common, as the specific charges tend to differ. Despite this distinction, indeed, largely because of it, the comparison of these two groups creates the chance to understand the question of gender in Nordic witchcraft cases.

In addition to the relatively well-documented cases discussed in detail later, there are indications of other trials and persecutions as well. In 1080, for example, Pope Gregory VII urges the king of Denmark not to hold certain women accountable for life's misfortunes; there can be little doubt that the pope is referring to female witches.[161] And a famous European case involving a key Nordic figure shows that in elite circles accusations of witchcraft could be a potent political tool as well: the history of the marriage in 1193 of Ingeborg of Denmark to King Philipp II Augustus of France is well documented, suggestive, and, to say the least, bizarre.[162] In brief, King Philipp claims that he has been bewitched by his new Danish queen on their wedding night, a story repeated by some contemporary chroniclers.[163] Despite the volume of material relating to this case, whether the cause is personal distress on the king's part (brought about by impotence, as many have believed), or is part of some political stratagem (as has also been suggested), or some combination of the two (as seems plausible) remains unresolved.

So, although we can suppose there were other instances, the first documented case of witchcraft to take place in the Nordic world comes from the Norwegian city of Bergen in the winter of 1325, when Bishop Auðfinnr reports having a problem.[164] How was he to respond to growing rumors about the behavior of a certain Ragnhildr, who, it was reliably and widely reported, had renounced God, fallen into heretical beliefs, and used magic in an attempt to preserve her adulterous and incestuous relationship with her cousin Bárðr? Bishop Auðfinnr further notes (a) that gossip about Ragnhildr's lapses and character had been heard week after week; (b) that he could not with a good conscience allow such public discussion to continue without investigation; and (c) that although she denied the allegations in January 1325, when later confronted with witnesses who swore that Ragnhildr had in November 1324 freely confessed to her crimes, she admitted that she had concealed in Bárðr's and Bergljót's bridal bed on the first night of the wedding a sword and other items and uttered an incantation.

When examined again, Auðfinnr continues, Ragnhildr admitted (1) that the testimony of the witnesses was correct; (2) that she had, while her husband was still alive, four times had carnal relations with Bárðr, to whom she was related; (3) that she had denied God and given herself over to the devil in order to sow discord and rancor between Bárðr and Bergljót; (4) that she, at the incitement of the devil, had recited this curse—"I cast from me Gandul's spirits. May one bite you in the back; may another bite you in the breast; may the third stir up in you hatred and ill-will" (*Ritt ek i fra mer gondols ondu. æin þer i bak biti annar i briost þer biti þridi snui uppa þik hæimt oc ofund*)—after which one was to spit on the individual concerned; (5) that due to Ragnhildr's actions, Bárðr rejected Bergljót and went to Hálogaland, whence Ragnhildr prepared to go as quickly as she possibly could; (6) that her claims to have power over Bárðr's life and death if he failed to follow her will in everything was due to the fact that her husband would kill him for his adulterous and incestuous relationship with her; (7) that she, on the second day of the wedding, in mockery of the bridegroom had an outburst, expressing her happiness that because of witchcraft Bárðr would be impotent, telling the bride in front of everyone that his penis would be as much use to her as the woven belt she held rolled up in her hand; (8) that she, on the first night of the wedding and without the knowledge of the bride and bridegroom, concealed herself in the bedroom next to the bed; and (9) that she had learned the heretical incantations in her youth from Sǫrli Sukk.

The sentence Auðfinnr gives Ragnhildr is restrained. Bishop Auðfinnr concludes that Ragnhildr's crimes center on her use of a charm and the heresy thereby involved, as well as on her attempts to destroy Bárðr's marriage to Bergljót. He notes that Ragnhildr has long been kept imprisoned in fetters, where, after fasting and prayers, she looks for an appropriate punishment.

Auðfinnr then notes that he is told by reliable individuals that at the time of the crimes Ragnhildr was not in full command of her faculties. Due to these factors, he will soften his judgment, as his fellow clerics have urged, citing the admonition from Ezekiel 18:23. Assured by her oath that she will abandon such activities, the bishop orders her to observe a set of fasts (several a week) for the rest of her life and to go on a seven-year pilgrimage to visit holy sites outside of Norway. If Ragnhildr fails in any respect, she is to be regarded as having relapsed in heresy and turned over to the secular courts.

As explored earlier in relation to the myth of the diabolical pact, the burning of a nun from Kirkjubær in Iceland in 1343, although largely unnoticed in witchcraft literature, is of particular significance. According to three of the Icelandic annal traditions, all belonging to what Gustav Storm and others have viewed as the middle group, that is, those written at the end of the 1300s, a nun at Kirkjubær was burned to death by order of the bishop, Jón Sigurðarson.[165] The three entries differ slightly as to the nature of her crime. According to *Lǫgmannsannáll* (*The Lawyer's Annal*), she was guilty of defaming the pope. *Skálholtsannáll* (*The Skálholt Annal*) claims that she had in writing given herself to the devil (*er gefiz hafði pukanum með brefi*), and *Flateyjarannáll* (*The Flatey Annal*) enumerates three interrelated sins: the nun had given herself in writing to the devil, she had mistreated the body of Christ by throwing it into the privy, and she had had intercourse with many laymen.

Also preserved in the Icelandic annals, and as grim as the previous instance, is a sentence meted out in the Norse colony in Greenland in the early fifteenth century. According to *Lǫgmannsannáll*: "In this same year [1407] a man in Greenland named Kolgrímr was burned because he had lain with a certain man's woman named Steinunn, the daughter of Hrafn the Lawman, who died in the avalanche north in Lǫnguhlíð. At that time, Þorgrímr Sǫlvason had her to wife. That man got her will with the black arts, and was later burned after the judgement. The woman was never the same again and died a little later."[166]

One scholar has suggested that in addition to a finding implying the use of witchcraft, the sentence "probably was a face-saving device for a high-born Icelander whose wife had succumbed to the charms of a social inferior."[167] Steinunn's demise, and Kolgrímr's execution, have been much discussed over the years, but with respect to understanding Nordic witchcraft, the key issues in this curious case are threefold: the proposition that Kolgrímr used some sort of "love magic" to bend Steinunn to his will; the fact that a number of people appear to accept its efficacy, even if the reason is to save face; and the use of the term "black arts" to describe the charms Kolgrímr presumably employs. This fixed phrase might be explained by the secret nature of its practice or the widespread image of the devil as a black man, but it was by this time well-attested in religious literature in the Nordic world.[168] The wording of the passage invites speculation: for example, a reading of "pursuant to the sentence" (i.e., *eptir dómi*, with the dative) might be more sensible, and even expected, here, but the phrase "ept*ir* dom" (i.e., with the accusative) demands 'following the judgment'. This temporal sense may strike a reader as oddly out of place unless, as one might reasonably suspect, the point being made is that Kolgrímr was spared vigilante justice—after all, his "victim" is the daughter of a lawman and the wife of a prominent man—and given a proper trial.[169]

In 1471, a Danish case combining church theft and the hording of the communion host, presumably for use in witchcraft just as the ecclesiastical regulations warn against, takes place. Not only is the man said to have been burned alive, but his hands are cut off in advance of this horrible death.[170] In that same year, a familiar instance of witchcraft takes place in the Swedish town of Arboga involving a woman who seems to be the stereotypical village "wise woman" or witch. On November 18 of that year, Birgitta Andersdotter appears before the court and says that a woman she calls "Crazy Katherine" (*galna kadhrin*) had suggested using a cat's head and an ox horn filled with water as part of a complicated charm in which a certain man would abandon one woman and love Birgitta instead. Birgitta provides these materials and is advised to take the horn and throw it and its contents against the man's door. Several men (one of whom is presumably her father) step forward and promise on her behalf that she will never again be found in possession of any witchcraft (*forgerningha*) and that she will never disturb the marriage with any witchcraft (*medh nokra forgerningha*).[171] Although Crazy Katherine was supposed to appear before the court as well, she did not.[172] Of great interest is an earlier case in August, in which a "Wise Katherine" is brought to the courts for the theft of a silver spoon.[173] Importantly, the November entry for *galna kadhrin* was originally written as "Wise Katherine" (*visa kadhrin*), but the word has been struck through and "crazy" written in above it. Either we are dealing with two Katherines with opposite cognomina as a means of keeping the two apart, or perhaps we witness here an ongoing reevaluation of just what kind of person Katherine represented to the community over time.[174]

Another Swedish trial, also concerned with sex, takes place in 1490 in Stockholm. A woman named Margit is accused of having made a man impotent years earlier. She is further charged with having learned this witchcraft (*then trolldomen*) from a woman variously referred to as "Anna the singer" (*Anna singerska*) and "Anna the Finn" (*Anna finszka*).[175] It is supposedly this Anna who had administered, as we must assume it to be meant, to Hans Mille in some fashion cat brain, apparently, as in the case of Crazy Katherine, part of the charm. Margit admits that she not been shriven in five years, the relevance of which may largely have to do with assessments of her character.[176]

Against these images of so-called love magic in action, the late fifteenth-century records also reveal more tenebrific cases, such as that of a certain Jens in Stockholm in 1478, who, according to a witness, addressed an image of the crucifix (presumably hanging upside down), saying, "I have long served you; now I renounce you and serve the devil."[177] Other cases from the late 1400s in Stockholm are laced with the familiar sound of apostasy. In 1484–85, two men are accused of having stolen from various churches on numerous occasions, but one of them—to whom the cognomen "Óðinn's man" (*Odinskarl*) is attached—confesses that "he has served Óðinn for seven years."[178] In 1492, a servant named Erik Claueson is sentenced to death for apostasy and other crimes. He is said to have recanted his confession of renouncing God and all his holy company, traveling withershins on nine Thursday nights in the churchyard and accepting the devil Óðinn for the sake of money.[179] He is also guilty of having stolen both money and silver, for which crime he is sentenced "to the fire," but because of his apostasy, Erik is to undergo torture, the wheel, and the rope.[180]

Conclusion

Laws are the ultimate normative documents, in that they dictate the parameters outside of which people will be prosecuted in real-world social experiences, while at the same time they are also philosophical statements about the nature of society. Paradoxically, the actual cases history has bequeathed us are typically fragmentary and frustratingly incomplete, jagged, with curious details, yet generally lacking larger social contexts. The laws suggest that both men and women can be witches, but the trial materials, modest in number as they are, suggest that it is women who are accused of *maleficium, trolldom, galdr*, and so on, whereas men are typically charged with heresy, apostasy, and other crimes against the authorities. The precipitating crisis where a female is charged tends to involve sexuality. When the women are charged, the accusation includes witchcraft and its associated activities, especially aphrodisiac and anaphrodisiac charms, and, although we do not know the resolution of every case, the women are usually either acquitted or sentenced to exile. From Ragnhildr tregagás in the fourteenth century to the various women who appear in the Swedish *tänkeböcker* at the close of the Middle Ages, the pattern is much the same. In the cases involving male defendants, conversely, the charge is routinely for apostasy and devil worship, with additional accusations of theft (often from churches) being commonplace.[181] The one exception to the trend for males to be accused of apostasy and so on is the case of Kólgrímr, who is found guilty of having used "the black arts" in seducing a woman and is burned for the crime. But what is consistent is that in every case where we know the court's disposition, the sentence for men is capital punishment, frequently by fairly grim methods. Two very different patterns, but patterns that may say much about Nordic attitudes toward witchcraft, as the next chapter explores.

Chapter 6

Witchcraft, Sorcery, and Gender

To modern observers, the word "witch" evokes a female image: the statistics profiling European witchcraft prosecutions in the postmedieval era of the great witch-hunts of the sixteenth and seventeenth centuries prove that women were indeed the primary, albeit not the exclusive, targets of witchcraft accusations. Given the predominance of women among the accused, it is surprising that generations of talented scholars generally ignored the gendered character of the early modern witch-hunts.[1] In fact, Scandinavian scholars were among the very first to ask the obvious: Why women?[2] In recent decades, the early modern witch-hunts as a war on women has become a standard component of scholarly discussions, and a series of analyses has shown how fruitful a fundamentally gendered approach to the topic can be.[3] Certainly, these gender-focused strategies have transformed our understanding of the past, not merely by recognizing the place of women in it, but by appreciating the significance of the construction of male and female roles and the processes societies use to perpetuate their perceptions of these relations.

The question of gender and witchcraft in the pre-Reformation north, especially for the period up to the Conversion, has attracted considerable attention in recent years.[4] Thus, for example, in her careful examination of the various Norse literary sources (e.g., heroic poetry, sagas), Jenny Jochens traces the development of the witch figure as one of four conventional female stereotypes among the Germanic peoples. In line with the earlier work of Fogelklou Norlind, Jochens interprets the seeresses and sorceresses of Icelandic literature as reflecting a social reality, one in which there was a gradual displacement under Christianity of female practitioners by males: "Women were the original and remained the most powerful magicians, whereas men gained access only later and never attained parity with women, either in numbers or power."[5] Indeed, Jochens argues that the entire range of activities associated with wisdom—ritual magic, divination, and so on—had once been dominated by women.

The conclusions reached by a number of scholars about women's roles in magic often rely on their confidence in Iceland as a repository of pre-Christian views.[6] Understandably, they hope to push our knowledge from the period of saga writing into the Viking Age (ca. 800–1100). Against this view, one might set the recent conclusions of archaeologists who, although differing from each other on many points, consider the role of gender (as opposed to biological sex) in the magico-religious, and martial, worlds of the Viking Age and reach different conclusions.[7] The cultural moment of this study, of course, differs in that it explores witchcraft in the centuries after the conversion of Scandinavia to Christianity; moreover, it examines witchcraft in a pan-Nordic context, one that certainly includes the important information to be gleaned from the Icelandic sagas, but also looks for answers in non-Icelandic and nonnarrative resources. What, then, can we say about late medieval Nordic magic, witchcraft, and sorcery in the context of gender?

Saints, Sinners, and the "Evil Woman"

A proverb well attested in late medieval Denmark and Sweden runs, "An evil woman is the devil's door nail" (*ondh quinna ær diæwlsins dura naghil*).[8] One of the many questions that curious expression brings to mind is just what would have been meant by the expression "an evil woman", a phrase fraught with meaning for how we understand "witch" and other gender-related questions in medieval Scandinavia. Although the place of women in the Nordic Middle Ages has been the subject of much attention in recent years,[9] scholarly focus has tended to center on literary images, with their sometimes real, sometimes stereotyped roles (e.g., mothers, valkyries, "inciters").[10] To understand the mentality that gave rise to how the "evil woman" was conceived, we need to look at the entire spectrum of possibilities and recognize that the theme of evil women, especially evil women whose behavior corrupts men and challenges male society, features prominently in that world.[11]

To be sure, saga literature provides us with more than a few examples of such women. One need only think in passing of such strong and difficult female types as Freydís in *Eiríks saga rauða* (*The Saga of Eiríkr the Red*),

Hallgerðr in *Brennu-Njáls saga* (*Njal's saga*), and Queen Gunnhildr in a variety of texts to envision such characters.[12] So malevolent is Gunnhildr's behavior that she has been labeled by one scholar as the prototypical "Destructive Prima Donna."[13] But these are, after all, "only" figures from Icelandic literary sources, and the extent to which late medieval nonelites elsewhere in Scandinavia would have known about them is uncertain. In addition to such stereotypes and other literary cutouts, occasional historical figures emerge from our materials who might likewise be considered—especially by male observers—"evil women," in particular women who subvert dominant power relationships.

Ragnhildr tregagás from fourteenth-century Bergen springs to mind as an example of a woman accused of using charms to work her will and who is in any event our best historical image of someone using magic in medieval Scandinavia.[14] We only learn about her when her activities become notorious in town, and if there is one constant in modern witchcraft research, it must surely be that judicial action tends to be the culmination of a lifetime of having been a troublesome presence, an evil woman in the community, rather than because of some unique event.[15] Reliable, nonliterary evidence is obviously hard to come by, but we are occasionally allowed the furtive glimpse into such lives in the late medieval period.

The records of the Swedish town of Arboga provide one such possibility, where one witnesses activities of the following sort as they unfold over a period of years. In June 1466, witnesses testify that they heard Ælseby, Per Haraldsson's wife, call Laurits Håkonsson a wretch (*skalk*), the son of a whore (*een horins*on), and a "pillory-bird" (*kaakslage*re, i.e., someone subjected to punishment in the pillory).[16] Three years later, a witness swears that he has heard Ingeborg of Helle say to Ælseby that she is a tramp (*landløpirska*) who wishes her husband dead.[17] On March 5, 1470, a witness testifies that the same Ingeborg came running into the home of Per Haraldsson and begged him to control his wife, Ælseby, who was going to hit her mother. At that point, Ælseby arrives and confronts the other woman in the doorway. She begins to hit Ingeborg, who responds by knocking Ælseby down.[18] Although a more complete knowledge of Ælseby's situation than that which can be inferred from these documents might exonerate her in our eyes, as seen by her contemporaries at least, what precipitates out of officialdom's logs clearly says that she represents a disruptive force in the Arboga community. Ælseby's conduct, and the reaction of others to her, brings her and those around her to the attention of the courts; in other words, she is an outstanding example

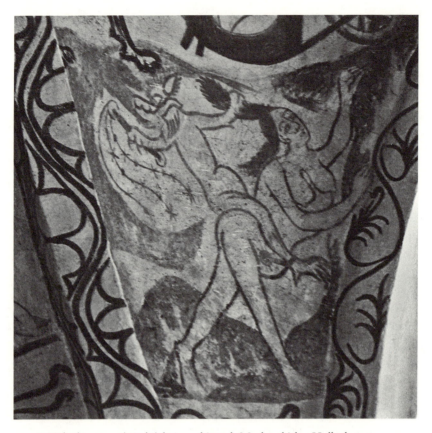

8. Naked woman (witch?) being whipped, Mørkøv kirke, Holbæk amt, Denmark (1450–75). Photo by author.

of someone who was regarded as contentious, outspoken, troublesome, and "uppity"—and therefore, as her contemporaries would no doubt have believed, an evil woman.[19]

Troublemaking women of the sort Ælseby seems to be might be said to have had their own patron "antisaint" in the Middle Ages, the woman discussed earlier called Sko-Ella or Titta-Grå in Swedish tradition, a figure well known in medieval popular culture, AT 1353 *The Old Woman as Trouble Maker*, who sows the seeds of discord between a man and his wife.[20] As noted earlier, this scene is often found in late medieval church murals and is also a widely attested exemplum, known in Europe since at least the 1200s.[21]

The Sko-Ella type is but one misogynistic and stereotypical view of women that permeated most arenas of public discourse in late medieval Europe, not least in art forms sponsored by and for the church. In this context, we might consider a related set of artworks from the Swedish fourteenth century. Both are pieces of decorative ironwork from churches in Götaland, widely attributed to the same artisan (or his school) and to a period in the late 1300s.[22] In one instance, that of a large chest from Rydaholm church, has a scene of Eve in the Garden of Eden being tempted by the serpent to eat the fruit of the Tree of the Knowledge of Good and Evil. The serpent is presented in a monstrous, even dragonlike form, and Adam is notably absent—the scene clearly represents the temptation of Eve, leading to the Fall of Man. Although Nordic representations of the Fall often include both Adam and rather less demonic images of the serpent (e.g., Tingsted church), the meaning of these images, as in so many others in the Middle Ages, is abundantly clear: it is, as Tertullian wrote already in the third century, through a woman that humanity experienced the Fall—the absence of Adam in this work inevitably focuses the onlooker's gaze on Eve's culpability. And it is worth noting too, that this same insubordinate act—in which a female plays the central role—leads God not only to cast Adam and Eve out of the Garden and to command that henceforth the serpent should crawl on its belly but also to ordain that women should suffer in childbirth, be subordinate to their husbands, and experience—as a gender—*wantonness and sexuality*. This is the real meaning of original sin.

God says explicitly to Eve that, as a result of her behavior, "You shall be eager for your husband."[23] According to this myth, it is thus through Eve's transgressive behavior that woman validates society's patriarchal structure and calls upon herself a deistic proclamation of lasciviousness. The misogyny inherent in this foundational myth nowhere bears more bitter fruit than in the *Malleus maleficarum*; indeed, it is no exaggeration to say that much of that witch-hunting handbook, including the whole of part 1, question 6, rests on this biblical image, as in the following passage:

> It is also clear in connection with the first woman that they have less faith by nature, since in response to the serpent's question as to why they did not eat of the tree of paradise, she said, "From every . . . lest we may die" [Gen. 3:2–3]. In this she shows that she is doubtful and does not have faith in the words of God. All this is demonstrated by the etymology of the noun. For the word *'femina'* [the Latin word for woman] is spoken as 'fe' and 'minus,' because she

has and keeps less [Latin '*minus*'] faith [Latin '*fidem*'] [. . .] Woman, therefore, is evil as a result of nature because she doubts more quickly in the Faith. She also denies the Faith more quickly, this being the basis for acts of sorcery.[24]

The *Malleus* later summarizes this view, saying that everything is governed by carnal lust, which is insatiable in women.[25] The extreme attitudes projected in the *Malleus* are a good reflection of late medieval elite mentalities, as the line between witchcraft and the general, biblically validated view of woman as the weaker vessel grew thinner and thinner throughout the later Middle Ages.[26]

These oft-quoted examples of medieval misogyny help us understand the other piece of artwork, decorative ironwork from the door of Rogslösa church. Here too one sees the images of the Tree of the Knowledge of Good and Evil, of Eve in her sinful act, and of the serpent. Adam is again missing, and now the consequences of the Fall are lavishly illustrated. Illustrated not, however, as we in the modern world are used to imagining that scene of the casting out of mankind from the Garden, with its inevitable use of "the cherubim and a sword whirling and flashing to guard the way to the tree of life" (Gen. 3:24), but rather by showing a cocklike demon, complete with spurs and comb, torturing a woman with a spurred instrument that would appear to match what is referred to in discussions of torture as a *járnkambr* 'iron-comb' or a *járnkrókr* 'iron-hook', both having as their function to rend the flesh.[27] This scene is often associated with witchcraft by way of the presumed inferiority and culpability of women and ties in with such widely repeated views as Bernhard of Clairvaux's position that the main sin of witchcraft is the desire to struggle against obedience, a view repeated by the authors of the *Malleus*. Within this scene on the door of Rogslösa church is contained the entire complex of misogynistic ideas that shape the connection between women, evil women, and witchcraft in the Nordic world by the end of the Middle Ages. Witches were surely not the only sort of evil women medieval Scandinavians knew, but they perhaps became the prototypical evil women of that world.

Eve's role in the Fall is also cited in Genesis as the reason for the existence of patriarchy—because of her behavior, Eve's husband will rule over her. Any behavior that subverts this hierarchy thus threatens divinely ordained social order, and any woman who assisted in this transgressive activity was seen ipso facto as an evil woman. This idea manifested itself in various ways in the later

Middle Ages and became the stuff of parish church murals. An extreme example comes from Villberga church in Uppland, Sweden, circa 1450, which presents two instances of inverted social order: one, with the wife holding the shovel and the man stirring the kettle; the other, with the wife shown beating the husband.[28]

These ideas are fundamental to the story of the "Battle over the Pants" in its various manifestations.[29] In fact, such secular images of transgressive women are relatively common in church murals, especially the woman-devil dyad (e.g., Mørkøv; Figure 8 in the present volume). Indeed, few sources can compete with what we see, quite literally, in church murals and other plastic representations of woman and witchcraft from this same world. They provide us with a special opportunity to understand the emerging mentalities of the Middle Ages with respect to evil women and witchcraft.[30] The argument is generally made that the walls of medieval parish churches were intended as a kind of *biblia pauperum*, the poor man's opportunity to see what he could not read, "pages" in full public view on which worshippers could contemplate images of the flight to Egypt, the Virgin Mary, the nativity of Christ, Cain slaying Abel, the slaughter of the innocents, Jesus in the temple, the story of Samson and Delilah, and myriad other tales drawn from the scriptures.[31] Yet not every theme surrounding worshippers was drawn from the Bible, and depictions of women and demonic figures are commonplace. Scenes showing a devil being ridden by a woman, his tail being pulled and his buttocks apparently being thrashed by the woman are well documented (e.g., Åstrup church), as are corresponding scenes showing the same theme the other way around, that is, a naked woman being ridden by a devil, who is pulling her hair and whipping her buttocks with a vicious-looking lash (e.g., Mørkøv church, Figure 8 in the present volume).

It seems probable that these images are intended as admonishments, observations on witches interacting with the invisible world of demons. An association of just this sort can be seen from the paintings in Västra Vemmerlöv church, where the figure of a woman holds the tail of a devil and beats its arse with what appears to be a branch. The right-hand part of the painting shows a milk-stealing witch.[32] That females beating devils, as in this scene, should be associated with witchcraft can be confirmed when we look broadly at the paintings of Nordic church murals in this late medieval period. Vejlby church (Figure 9) on Jutland also displays the milk-stealing witch but with important differences: it shows a central female figure churning butter; to her left two devils advance bearing what is likely to be milk stolen from the cows

9. Milk theft and churning, Vejlby kirke, Århus amt, Denmark (1492).

10. Beer theft, Tuse kirke, Holbæk amt, Denmark (1460–80). Photo by author.

in the neighborhood to be used in the preparation of the butter, and hanging onto the right side of the churn is a small devil, looking backward at yet another woman. It is she who captures the attention of the viewer, as both of her breasts are exposed, and it is on them the little devil's gaze appears to be focused; moreover, she holds in her hands two whips, one resembling a branchlike instrument, the other, presumably a whip. This figure is thus central to holding together the well-developed complex of the milk-stealing witch with the other images of women and devils with whips: there is every reason to interpret the women in these images as witches.

Frequent as the occurrence of the demon-witch-whip triptych is, the milk- and beer-stealing witch scenes are both more numerous and more widespread (e.g., Tuse, Söderby-Karl). In these paintings, we see various imps, demons, and devils attending and assisting the witches in the theft and preparation of food. But there is sometimes much more than that in these pictures: in the case from Tuse church (Figure 10), one sees that two devils assist the woman, one of whom clearly leers at her; moreover, the same winged demon is pressing from behind a tube of some sort (a spigot?) into the woman's genitals, perhaps to be interpreted in a straightforwardly sexual way, perhaps

11. Devils tormenting woman, Marie Magdelene kirke, Randers amt,
Denmark (1475–1510). Photo by author.

as though he is tapping her soul. Either way, we are here and elsewhere
confronted with scene after scene detailing exactly the misdeeds associated
with witchcraft, including lustful behavior, disobedience, and trafficking with
demons.

The concept of punishment—presumably also of a witch—is displayed
in the most graphic way in the grotesque mural from Marie Magdalene
church (Figure 11): a woman's dress is pulled up, her legs and posterior exposed, and she, as in so many other images of witches, holds a whip in her
hand. As a bird pecks at her eye, she spews into a glass held by a hermaphro-
ditic and multi-specied demon holding a cudgel of some sort, while another
devil (with a gallows on his head) penetrates her anus or vagina with a burning brand and licks his fingers; finally, a cat, perhaps representing the devil,
looks on while preening itself and licking its own rear. At least one interpretation holds that we see here a witch who has had sexual relations with the
devil and is now at the Final Judgment.[33]

If ever we are presented with an image of what late medieval Scandinavia must have regarded as an "evil woman" (*ondh quinna*), certainly this one is it. And yet these often lurid murals surely had more purpose than merely to provide variously titillating and terrifying images to the unwashed peasantry attending mass. In the context of his discussion of art as a cultural system, anthropologist Clifford Geertz notes, "To be of effective use in the study of art, semiotics must move beyond the consideration of signs as a means of communication, code to be deciphered, to a consideration of them as modes of thought, idiom to be interpreted."[34] In that vein, the discussion turns now to the larger meaning of such paintings and the notion of social space in an effort to discover what "mode of thought" is at work here.

One way to approach the problem is to envision what these church images meant in the lives of medieval women and men. Among the quintessentially Nordic aspects of church architecture is the so-called *vapenhus*, a vestibule that functioned as a cold-trapping antechamber and a place where weapons were to be left. But it also represents the transitional or liminal space between the outside secular world and the marked holy area of worship. Indeed, one can easily envision a whole series of oppositions mediated by the liminal space of the *vapenhus*, such as exterior-interior, armed-disarmed, dark-light, secular-holy, and so on. Important in that context, whereas the murals of the church interior—of the choir, the nave, and the chancel—tend overwhelmingly to be covered with scenes drawn directly from the Bible, the walls of the *vapenhus* frequently sport secular scenes as well as religious images. But, of course, even these secular images appear to bear religious purpose.

Our modern archival systems are necessarily atomizing and tend to obscure the continuity of images that the arrangements themselves sometimes exhibit. Seen in situ, however, a subtle interweaving of themes among the topics suggests a pedagogical and didactic intentionality at work, even in small parish churches.[35] The scenes do not always relate directly to one another, but they do display an important, meaningful pattern at work in the selection of topics. One scholar finds that murals containing devils are among the three most common types in the Uppland churches.[36] Indeed, the very large number of murals dealing with devils and witchcraft themes in Swedish and Danish churches is striking: here are scenes from the journey to the sabbat; of the milk-stealing witch making her butter; of the story of Sko-Ella; of the Final Judgment as witches approach the gates of hell; of the devil riding a woman; of a woman riding a devil, sometimes whipping him; and so on (Figures 2–12). According to Swedish inventories, for example, a partial

12. Devils conveying monks, bishops, kings, and a woman (witch?) to hell,
Tuse kirke, Holbæk amt, Denmark (1460–80). Photo by author.

list of Swedish churches includes five with scenes of the journey to Blåkulla
and more than three dozen churches with that of the milk-stealing witch.[37]

If we consider these scenes in situ, that is, what they look like in context
and in relation to one another, there can indeed be a tendency for these
pictures to be bundled into coherent iconographic packages. In the fifteenth-
century church at Vamlingbo on the island of Gotland, for example, the
following four scenes are placed in such a way as to suggest a nearly chronological, narrative quality to the tableau, using familiar witchcraft iconography: milk-theft, churning butter with the stolen milk, devils conveying a
woman to hell, and a presentation of hell itself.

In a similar manner, standing inside the *vapenhus* of Dannemora church
in northern Uppland in Sweden, and facing its massive exterior door, as one
is about to leave the building, a worshipper would have seen the following
murals facing him—or, of more than simply politically correct inclusiveness,
her, pronominal attentiveness of genuine importance here: to the left, the
wheel of fortune; a devil and a witch churning butter; two devils driving to
hell a naked witch holding a butter mound (Figure 7); and to her right, two
women fighting over a kettle.[38] Seen together, it is impossible not to believe

that one is indeed viewing the equivalent of a large open book concerned with social conduct for women—a didactic message to the female congregants about how they should behave or, more accurately, how they should not behave.[39] Nudity, querulous shrews, milk-stealing witches, lewd behavior, envy of the well-provisioned by those poor in foodstuffs, women trafficking with demons—certainly the themes of these pictures would have conjured images of the most feared and unwelcome aspects of human society where women played a role.

In the context of the proverb cited earlier, "an evil woman is the devil's door nail," surely such figures were the very evil women it envisions; that the devil's assistants should be presented in such transitional space as the *vapenhus* usefully reminds us of the remainder of the proverb. The passageway worshippers necessarily took out of the church thus provided a regular opportunity to see, inspect, and recall this visual conduct literature for women as they transitioned from the site of worship to the mundane world outside. We moderns tend to examine these pictures as evidence of the church's fears and its construction of a diabolical witchcraft belief system, as well we should, but it is useful to recall that, seen from the village level, these pictures represent a powerful, and from the parishoners' perspective, hopefully prophylactic, reminder of how women should, and should not, behave, in particular how they might avoid being evil women.

Collectively, these murals suggest the antithesis of the presentations of female behavior to be found in the church itself, often dominated by female saints and images drawn from the tradition of Marian piety (e.g., the resplendent Virgin Mary in the nave of Dannemora church). These two polar opposites, the Virgin of the nave and the diabolical witch of the *vapenhus*, were, of course, the alpha and omega of how late medieval society viewed women and how it thought they might conduct themselves. Much has been made in recent years of the "male gaze" in the Middle Ages, but we have perhaps given too little attention to the idea of the female gaze, especially where it was a reflexive one, whether the standard of perfection was imposed by male society or not.[40] After all, one of the great engines of social control of women was, in fact, other women (cf. the role of women as accusers in the post-Reformation witch-hunts). In this context, it is useful to recall the section from *Äldre Västgötalagen* (*The Older Law of Västergötland*, ca. 1225) in which a Swedish version of the night-riding witch is described, and especially that this important monument to Norse witchcraft comes to us in the context of an enumeration of actionable slanders that can be said of women, including accusations of whoredom, infanticide, incest, and abortion.

At the end of this list of social horrors—inversions of acceptable, normal society, defining what was meant by an "evil woman"—the statute notes in a significant comment rarely included in discussions of the passage, "All these sins should first be discussed with the priest and not flare up in rancorousness or rage. . . ."[41] The purpose of such a phrase might generously be said to avoid gossip and the administration of unsanctioned local justice, but one cannot easily avoid the conclusion that the passage is also meant to exert control by promoting spying on others and reporting suspected misdeeds to church authorities.

One is reminded here of how in his influential treatment of spectacle and control, Michel Foucault exploits the metaphor of Jeremy Bentham's Enlightenment Age prison design, the Panopticon.[42] Bentham's twin means of control—isolation and surveillance—were seized upon by Foucault as a vivid metaphor for social control and the less corporeal, but no less dread possibilities for oppression in the information age, but at its root, panopticism is largely concerned with employing social space as a means of social control. This understanding has obvious application to our materials, with the intersection in the later Middle Ages of social control, women, women's conduct, and witchcraft. At Dannemora and a few other parishes, at least, within the liminal space of the *vapenhus*, between the "wonder," or *mira*, of what occurs in the celebration of the Eucharist within the church and the "evil," or *malum* (exemplified by the idea of *maleficia* 'witchcraft'), of the outside world, female congregants were in plain text reminded of the dichotomy they were literally and metaphorically transgressing. As they passed through the door of the narthex to the outer door of the *vapenhus*, the reality of the belief that "an evil woman is the devil's door nail" reverberated all about them.

Because of its extreme views on the subject of witchcraft, especially its exploration of the "fact" that these enemies of God and man are so frequently women, *Malleus maleficarum* (1486) is usually cited in this regard. But as suggested earlier, the rush to vilify the *Malleus* risks misunderstanding the degree to which it principally echoes rather than forms common late medieval thinking about women. Thus, for example, in 1483, three years before the publication of this notorious codification of gynophobic thinking, the first book printed in Sweden appeared: Maynus de Mayneriis's *Dyalogus creaturarum optime moralizatus*. One is immediately struck by what this text suggests about prevailing elite views of women at the close of the Middle Ages, notions easily transferred to ideas about magic and witchcraft. According to *Dyalogus creaturarum* (citing other authorities), man is a soul incarnate, a silhouette of his time, an explorer in life, a slave of death, a wayfarer in transit, a guest and a stranger, a dejected soul, and a temporary habitation; woman, by contrast, is the bewilderment of man, an insatiable creature, a constant concern, an incessant strife, the slave of man, and a pitfall for the abstinent man.[43]

Gender and Power

How does this reading of medieval attitudes about the nature of the sexes, and women in particular, affect how witchcraft was constructed? Is this view static, or does the relationship between gender and witchcraft in the Nordic region in the four centuries before the Reformation evolve? The previous chapters examined the various resources available for answering those questions, that is, narrative sources, such as the sagas and court literature; normative texts, especially secular and ecclesiastical law codes, such as the provincial laws and synodal statutes; folk beliefs and popular mythology; and documentary sources, particularly the transcripts, protocols, and other testimony of actual trials. I return here briefly to each of these areas with the specific question of gender in mind.

All of these types of source materials are useful in assessing perceptions of male and female roles in witchcraft, but they are not equal. Narrative texts, for example, are more likely than other types of evidence to reflect a single individual's idiosyncratic views (albeit drawing on broader cultural norms). And even if occasionally "clouded" by these individual points of view, such representations can nevertheless provide a much more fleshed-out picture of witchcraft than the sort of enigmatic entry one often finds in an annal or other record. The testimony of legal thinking implicit in law codes and trials, on the other hand, is more likely to express the prevailing normative views of the empowered elite sector of society that had the principal hand, and an interest, in crafting them. Trial records and other documentary notices, for their part, yield shadowy information in this period and are sometimes so cryptic as to forgo any reasonable attempt at interpretation. The attempt to rescue popular traditions from obscurity, the belief systems that gave meaning to the images on the church walls, for example, perhaps brings us closest to what "everyman" understood about witchcraft.

Literary presentations of witches, witchcraft, and magic differ from the other sources in another very important way—it is only there that one occasionally finds positive representations of these phenomena, especially when they can be used in the service of the hero. Thus, for example, in *Bósa saga ok Herrauðs* (*Saga of Bósi and Herrauðr*), it is through magic that the witch Busla manages to secure the release from prison of her foster son, and the saga's hero, Bósi.[44] The attitude toward magic and witchcraft in *Bósa saga ok Herrauðs* is, however, anything but uniform: when Busla utters her charm, the author goes to some length to make his disapproval apparent.[45] And at an earlier point in the saga, he writes, "There was an old woman named Busla, who had been Thvari's concubine, and fostered his sons for him. Busla was highly skilled in magic. She found Smid more amenable than his brothers and taught him a great deal. She offered to tutor Bosi in magic as well, but he said he didn't want it written in his saga that he'd carried anything through by trickery instead of relying on his own manhood."[46]

That anyone in Western Europe in the early fourteenth century could be so ambiguous—even directly playful—about the topic of witchcraft is surprising but reflects one aspect of "Icelandic exceptionalism," namely, its special relationship to the Nordic past.[47] Yet in this apparently lighthearted dismissal of magic as a would-be weapon in the hero's arsenal, one also senses an important and meaningful opposition between that which is "manly" or virtuous (*karlmenska* 'manhood, valor' < *karl* 'man (male)' plus *menska* 'human nature'), on the one hand, and magic, on the other (*sleitum*, lit., 'through subterfuge', in Bósi's rejection but *taufr* 'sorcery, charms' in Busla's offer).[48] That this distinction was operative appears to be borne out by the fact that, among the many male practitioners of magic to be found in medieval Icelandic literature, male witches are overwhelmingly portrayed as villainous characters set in opposition to the hero, generally a Christianizing king or a dowdy native son, rather than as dabblers in love magic and so on.

Thus, in Snorri Sturluson's early thirteenth-century *Óláfs saga Tryggvasonar* (*The Saga of Óláfr Trggvason*), King Óláfr is said to have had all the sorcerers—all those "who were known to be guilty of practicing magic and sorcery or who were *seiðr*-men"—in Norway rounded up and to have attempted to execute them.[49] Then follows the king's conflict with one of the most powerful sorcerers in Norway, Eyvindr Kelda, who engages in activities that project a highly militaristic image, including mustering a "levy" (*leiðangr*), a term freighted with martial associations, and closing in on the king's army, in "a warship fully manned with warlocks only and other kinds of sorcerers."[50]

Tales of this sort in the saga portray obstinate and studied resistance to the king and his new religion, with the military-like use of magic to prevent the Christianizing king from advancing his hold on Norway. The picture Snorri paints lumps pagan practices together with witchcraft in order to portray an organized, pagan-led resistance to the conversion of Norway.[51] And again, it is noteworthy that those who champion witchcraft and paganism in opposition to the heroes of the kings' sagas are exclusively males—massed supernatural females were part of Nordic tradition, yet Christianizing kings in the sagas do not face bands of female sorcerers and witches in their attempts to convert the country to Christianity.[52]

In the family sagas, virtuous heroes like the eponymous Gísli Súrsson of *Gísla saga Súrssonar* (*The Saga of Gísli Súrsson*) are bedeviled by male witches such as Þorgrímr nef. According to several scholars, there is a slight preponderance of female witches in the sagas: of sixty-two identified witches and sorcerers, twenty-nine are men, thirty-three are women.[53] Among them is, to be sure, the occasional female witch like Þuríðr in *Grettis saga Ásmundarsonar* (*Saga of Grettir Ásmundarson*) who stands in direct and life-threatening opposition to the hero, but many female witches, such as Þórdís in *Kormáks saga* (*The Saga of Kormákr*) and Geirríðr in *Eyrbyggja saga* (*The Saga of the People of Eyri*), are linked to the hero through such issues as sexuality and romance. Male witches, by contrast, tend to intersect with the heroes in more martial terms.

Magic wielded by females has a special function in these sagas, where, conceived of as a literary device rather than an atavism, it arms saga women who otherwise have no direct conduit to institutional puissance within a phallocentric system. The careful use of magic thus fulfills plot-and character-driven purposes in the narratives. As Jóhanna Katrín Friðriksdóttir writes, through magic "a female desire for power, autonomy and subjectivity operates in a patriarchal world dominated by male violence and a legal system to which women had no formal access."[54] She regards this magical empowerment as being used by saga women principally to maintain or restore honor, keep peace, and gain financial advantage. The image that emerges from the representation of magically empowered figures in medieval Nordic narrative sources is then anything but uniform. Magic was not necessarily an impediment to being a virtuous, or at least beneficial, character in either native or imported literature (e.g., Busla, Merlínús), but was generally treated as an evil attribute to be shunned, and such exceptions that exist are few and far between. Solitary witches and sorcerers, male and female, are often presented as significant or even insurmountable obstacles for otherwise undefeatable saga heroes, but when witches and sorcerers are shown in massed, armylike scenarios in opposition to Christianizing kings, they are male.

If we turn to the treatment of gender in legal and ecclesiastical codes, a substantially different image emerges, changes that are somewhat surprising. Charges of witchcraft were widely held to be slanderous if unproven, and this principle is occasionally phrased in the law codes to suggest a gendered reality. So, for example, *Äldre Västgötalagen* (*The Older Law of Västergötland*) begins its remarkable commentary on witches with the statement, "These are the slanderous words about a woman. . . ."[55] Two centuries later, *Kristoffers Landslag* (Sweden's *National Law of King Kristoffer*, ca. 1442), at the other extreme, appears to go out of its way to give parallel masculine and feminine sets of charges for slander, marked morphologically and semantically, saying that a man or woman is guilty who calls another *tiufuer, mordare, röfuare, kettare, horenszon, trulkarl* . . . 'thief, murderer, bandit, heretic, whore's son, male witch,' or *horkonna, moordherska, ketterska eller trulkonna* . . . 'whore, murderer, heretic, or female witch. . . .'[56]

The gender complexity of the legal texts is notable in some of the provincial and national law codes. For their parts, the Danish and native Icelandic laws are relatively disinterested in the problem of witchcraft, compared to the detail and the frequency with which it is treated in the corresponding Norwegian and Swedish documents. The Danish laws consistently present witchcraft as a phenomenon of which both men and women are capable: texts from the twelfth-century Scanian Church law through the famous fifteenth-century addendum to the Jutlandic Secular law display this gender-neutral view, although no text seems to be more painfully aware of the dyadic possibilities than the fourteenth-century Scanian secular law:[57] "If a man poisons a woman, or a woman a man, or a woman a woman through witchcraft or other poison, so that he or she dies of it, then [if it is] a man, he shall be drawn and quartered, and [if it is] a woman, she shall be burned, if there are adequate witnesses."[58] Icelandic law from the era of the commonwealth generally reflects an ungendered character, expressed through the unmarked masculine pronoun used: "If one [*maðr*, i.e., 'man' or, as here, 'a person'] uses magic or witchcraft . . ."[59]

Although some of the laws from the Scandinavian peninsula itself assert the same sort of gender-blind condemnation of witchcraft found in the Danish and Icelandic codes, things are of a very different order on closer examination. For example, the portion of *Eiðsivaþingslǫg* (*The Law of Eiðsivaþing*) concerned with witchcraft draws a picture of evenhanded justice that makes clear that witchcraft was something of which both men and women were capable.[60] Yet this apparently fair-minded and impartial section on witchcraft is in the same law code (and in the same manuscript tradition) only a few sections later undermined by the declaration, "If it is known of a woman that she has ridden a man or his household . . ."[61] Indeed, there is an entire substrate in the Norwegian laws which appear to assume that, although witches can be males, witchcraft is principally something women engage in; thus, *Kong Sverrers Christenret* (Norway's *King Sverre's Christian Law*) remarks, " 'But if it becomes known of a woman that she is a witch or a man-eater . . .' "[62]

The Swedish laws exhibit a great deal of concern with one of the oldest arenas of witchcraft, poisoning, and for the most part, this attention comes in an entirely gendered fashion.[63] Typically, the laws read as in this example from *Upplandslagen* (*The Law of Uppland*): "If a woman poisons a man and she is taken in the act, then she shall be fettered and taken to the thing (court) and the (articles of) poison with her [. . .] if she is found guilty, then she shall be burned on the pyre."[64]

With the codification of the various Swedish provincial laws under Magnus Eriksson in the mid-fourteenth century, however, this section is carefully reworded so as to make clear that if a man or a woman engages in such activities, it will lead to capital punishment.[65] And while the mid-fourteenth-century national authorities place witchcraft in the realm of human, and not just female, activities, the various earlier provincial laws are quite unambiguous about how the concept was viewed. *Dalalagen* (*The Law of Dalarna*), for example, baldly states, "If a woman is taken (in an act of) witchcraft, with horn and hair, alive and dead, that may well be called witchcraft."[66]

Perhaps surprisingly, especially against the background of increasingly misogynistic writings on the Continent, there is scant evidence in such local ecclesiastical texts as penitentials and synodal statutes to suggest that Nordic church leaders pushed for an a priori association of witchcraft with women, despite an ever more detailed and ever more lurid sense of the crime.[67] On the other hand, nonjuridical ecclesiastical writings in Scandinavia—that is to say, texts that reveal the attitudes of church leaders but lack the power of law—are quite outspoken in their association of women with witchcraft.

Among the most important testimonies in this regard are the writings of

Saint Birgitta, who devotes an entire vision to the topic of witchcraft, which she condemns (in particular, its efforts to control love, fertility, and health and to see into the future), decrying the fact that men and women turn to it. Birgitta specifically says that it is wrong for them to follow the counsel of these deplorable *female* practitioners of witchcraft.[68] And although Birgitta elsewhere mentions males who use magic (both as practitioners and customers), she mainly casts females in the role of active witches.[69]

In this context, where gender, power, and the image of women are all central, it is useful in the Nordic context to reflect on the role of Saint Birgitta. Known for her prophetic visions, she established a female religious community, the Ordo Sanctissimi Salvatoris. The monasteries of the Order of Saint Bridget (as it is known in the Anglophone world) were to consist of two locally separate, but proximate and institutionally unified convents composed respectively of sixty nuns and twenty-five monks, deacons, and lay brothers that would on secular issues be under the leadership of an abbess jointly selected by the two groups. Birgitta envisioned this monastery as an institution principally for nuns, and the supremacy of the abbess in worldly matters extended even to the head of the monks' section, the confessor general.

Birgitta was under no illusion as to the difficulties the order would encounter: women, she opined in a visionary discussion with the Virgin Mary, would have no trouble submitting to the order, "but it will be difficult to find men willing to submit themselves to the rule of a woman."[70] Her concern was in one sense well founded, for although there were many men who became devoted and active members of her order, there was also consistent, and vocal, opposition, especially noticeable at the church councils of the early 1400s. The growth of her order in Scandinavia, England, Estonia, the Netherlands, Italy, and elsewhere in the later Middle Ages is striking. And in the context of shifting Nordic perceptions of women, power, and witchcraft, it is useful to recall the issue that inevitably, and properly, attaches itself to the study of witchcraft, well framed by Christine Larner's rhetorical question, "To what extent, then, was the European witch-hunt [. . .] a response to a perceived threat to the social order through some change in the status or power of women?"[71]

The church had always had a place for women, but as it experienced them not only in the context of Marian piety, of noble female converts such as Clotilda and of suffering female martyrs such as Saint Lucy, but also as capable women administrators, as ecstasy-experiencing Christians, and as

members of a thriving female-led cult with fast-growing possessions and influence, and particularly in the context of women's governing not merely
other women but also men, troubles seem to have developed. A dynamic and
fast-growing institution such as the Order of Saint Bridget may at some level
have reinforced fears of a gynococracy, of an organized society of women. In
this connection, it is worth noting that the opposition faced by the Birgittine
Order at the Council of Constance (1414–18)—and to a lesser degree again
at the Council of Basel (1431–49)—was due not only to the interpretation of
Birgitta's visions by many as heretical but also to a very high degree to the
order's apparent status as a "double monastery."[72] Proof of subsequent structural conflicts of the sort that worried many church leaders can be seen in
the problems that arose at Vadstena and other Birgittine monasteries in the
early fifteenth century, at least partially to be accounted for by the genders of
the participants.[73]

Beyond tensions of this sort, more striking still is the fact that the sometimes feverishly negative responses to Birgitta—both by nonelites and by
elites—tended to rely on constructions of the witch image: when she first
arrived in the Eternal City at midcentury, the Roman crowds reportedly
wanted to kill her, condemning her as a witch, and she likewise endured
accusations of witchcraft by the aristocracy.[74] The whole issue of female spirituality, and thus the religious authority of such women, was put to the test
at the Council of Constance when Jean Gerson considered the gift of the
Holy Spirit and female mysticism, with a focus on Birgitta's recent canoniza-
tion.[75] As one scholar succinctly summarized these developments, "Birgitta's
boldness and controversial prophecies aroused suspicions, and her detractors
accused her of heresy and witchcraft."[76] The *Malleus maleficarum* remarks
that among the three qualities that typify those women especially subject to
witchcraft is ambition; it also applauds the view that a man who would allow
a gynococracy within his own house, who would permit his wife to govern
him or impose laws on him, is the vilest of slaves; moreover, it approves
heartily the view that the root of all women's vices is greed.[77] One cannot
help but wonder what the author(s) of the *Malleus* thought of women mystics
like Birgitta and female-run monasteries like those of the Ordo Sanctissimi
Salvatoris.

Gerson's treatise was far from the first indication of such inquiry: in a
recent study, Dyan Elliott painstakingly outlines the gradual criminalization
of women's religiosity in the later Middle Ages, a process whose beginnings
she traces to the time of the Fourth Lateran Council in 1215.[78] That the

general character of women (as well as Elliott's argument about "proof" and "proving") found fertile ground in the Nordic world as well can be seen in a Danish text about the bad character of women. It is from the same fifteenth-century collection of materials (AM 76, 8to) discussed earlier and character-ized by its editors as a teaching manual, presumably for a cathedral school. After describing how a woman can with her false arts bring a man to grief, the writer declares that her words should be tested (*prøue*) and concludes the piece by noting that Solomon, despite his cunning and wisdom (*Salomon war bode viss och klog*), was deceived by a woman.[79] Translated religious litera-ture in the northern world shows many examples of males who have sold themselves to the devil for material gain or sexual gratification but generally assumes that witches are women.[80] This is a widely held view and can be traced from at least the late thirteenth-century Icelandic interpretation and presentation of the *Canon episcopi*'s views, mirrored in the Old Icelandic life of John the Baptist.[81]

How, then, do such considerations play out if we turn to the issue of those people who were actually brought to trial before the Reformation?[82] Given the character of the records, even if every case is successfully plucked from the archives, it is difficult to imagine, based on the small size of the data set, anything like the subtle and meaningful statistical readings some scholars have managed to tease out of the early modern period for the various national situations. Conversely, and with due appreciation for the fact that there ex-isted individual circumstances that have led to each of these cases, interesting profiles do begin to emerge from the pre-Reformation data.

Such evidence as we have, clustered largely in the late fifteenth century suggests several parallel and telling patterns, the outlines of which can be traced all the way back to the late twelfth century. Witchcraft charges against women most often arise from cases involving sexuality and the women seem to be judged lightly. From Ragnhildr tregagás in the fourteenth century to the various women who appear in the Swedish *tänkeböcker* at the close of the Middle Ages, the pattern is the same. Although theoretically eligible for the charge of witchcraft, men rarely stand accused of this crime but rather of related offenses, such as apostasy and devil worship. And in each of these cases, the men suffer the ultimate penalty, execution by such grim methods as being burned alive.

From a strict point of view, these two groups have nothing to do with each other because the charges are different. But despite this distinction—indeed, perhaps better still, *because* of it—the comparison of these two groups is of great interest if we are to understand the question of gender in late medieval Nordic witchcraft cases. Clearly, women are more likely to have been charged with witchcraft in pre-Reformation Scandinavia, but at the same time they seem to have been treated with relative leniency, especially to the extent that there is no evidence of capital punishment among women charged. The impression also emerges that the courts were quite scrupulous about the charges being brought. In the case of Ragnvald Odenskarl, who is accused of having stolen from four different churches and of having served Óðinn for seven years, he has an accomplice in the thefts, Jon Land. Yet Land is never charged with anything other than the thefts themselves, a fact that is striking, given the promiscuous use of the charge of the "Journey to Blåkulla" in post-Reformation trials.[83] The one exception to the trend for males to be accused of apostasy and so on is the case of Kólgrímr, who is found guilty of having used the "black arts" in seducing a woman and is burned for the crime.

What image emerges when we lay these pictures of gender and late medieval witchcraft one on top of the other? Is it consistent, or is there nothing but chaos and irrationality? In fact, there is a great deal of unity in the way witchcraft is treated in our sources: the normative materials suggest the theoretical possibility of witches being either male or female, yet the secular laws seem to suggest that in the early period women were more likely to have been suspected and accused. With respect to the documentary materials, we might be content to say that every accusation that actually mentions witchcraft involves a woman, but if we open the lens just a little wider and not only include the cases where the specific terms *maleficium, trolldom, galdr*, and so on are used but also look at related trials where devil worship and other acts that threatened church and civil stability were adjudicated, we come much closer to understanding the core reality of late medieval Nordic witchcraft, especially the essentially gendered way in which the northern legal authorities approached the topic. Women were generally tried for magical acts that had to do with the manipulation of sexuality, and only the case of Kólgrímr has a similar nature among the men.

In the cases involving males, the men were tried for more openly rebellious acts against the church—heresy, devil worship, apostasy, and church theft. And recalling Snorri's thirteenth-century presentation of witches and sorcerers at the time of the conversion to Christianity, we see this archetype reflected already, namely, in the image of massed sorcerers wielding not only magical power but also military might in opposition to the church and the state. In fact, overall in the narrative materials, while witches may again be either male or female, their roles differ, and it is the male witches who tend to be cast as the direct opponents of the missionary kings and the native heroes, whereas the female witches generally govern the realm of romance and sexuality.

In line with Jochens's view that the roles of witch and sorcerer become *de*creasingly female and *in*creasingly male over time in the north, as noted earlier (Chapter 5), conceptions of witchcraft—as reflected in the organization of the laws about it—evolve throughout the Middle Ages. In the early provincial codes, such as those for Gulaþing, witchcraft statutes are located just before such topics as heathenism, incest, and bestiality.[84] There is little doubt but that witchcraft is conceived of here as being a perversion, and its relation to sexuality is hardly to be doubted. By the mid-fourteenth century, however, the Norwegian *Third Statute of Archbishop Pål* (written between 1336 and 1346) has altered slightly its placement of witchcraft and now puts fornicators, perjurers, and heretics (*villumen*) together with sorcerers and witches (*spamen eða galdrmenn*).[85] The sexual connection is not lost, but witchcraft is also being put on a par with those crimes that threaten social order—perjury and heresy.

The earliest Old Swedish provincial laws (e.g., *Äldre Västgötalagen*, *Upplandslagen*) situate witchcraft statutes in whatever section seems sensible—those about superstition among the church laws, those about poisoning among the criminal statutes, and so on. But by the time of the mid-fourteenth-century codification of the Swedish laws (*Magnus Erikssons Landslag*), witchcraft is addressed among laws of a very different sort. *Höghmala balker* (*The Section on High Crimes*) evinces the following order: different forms of murder (of spouses, children, and so on), witchcraft (*Forgör [. . .] meþ trulldom ælla andrum forgerningum*), the death of stepchildren, traitors who would raise an army against the king (*Huilkin sum reser hær a mot kununge ælla riksins hærra*), those who would bring a foreign army against their homeland and rightful lord (*Nu æn man leþir a fosterland sit hær vtlænzskan, bær auoghan skiold amot sinum rættum hærra*), the murder by servants of their masters, arson, rape, and poisoning (usually understood as a witchcraft statute).[86]

That witchcraft should now be thought of as having something in common with such high-stakes topics as treason and armed rebellion as well as with important civil crimes that also threaten social order such as murder and rape appears to be more than simple reorganization of the codes. The changes represent, it would seem, a reevaluation about just what sort of threat witchcraft was understood to be: it is no longer simply a perversion but represents a serious danger to social stability.

It should be remembered that Bernhard, Bonaventura, Peder Månsson, and many other writers saw as the real problem of witchcraft its disobedience of, and resistance to, God's law and the church's authority.[87] Similar accusations of heresy and devil worship had been constructed earlier by the church and its secular allies against the Knights Templar.[88] And at the very end of the Nordic Middle Ages, although the motivation and effects are more clearly political, heresy is exactly the charge brought against the Swedish leaders in what has come to be called Stockholm's Bloodbath.[89] That this charge was used is often interpreted as a legal sleight of hand by Kristian II and the bishops, as heresy was not covered in the parties' previous agreement; however, we should consider the possibility that there was more meaning and tradition to the charge, and less legal maneuvering, than is sometimes supposed. Heresy was the logical accusation in a period that had increasingly found this charge to be a useful tool for continuing the domination of the church and state. Heresy was also one of the charges made against Birgitta.

Witchcraft is sometimes defined as religion operating outside the structures and strictures of the orthodox religious hierarchy. With that definition in mind, it is not difficult to see how the legacy of Birgitta might have been understood, not as witchcraft per se, but, given her claims to direct, prophetic connections to Godhead, as operating outside the orthodox religious hierarchy.[90] The obverse of this same gendered concern may be seen in the native Nordic perception of witchcraft as being fundamentally effeminate, that is, the view that *seiðr* 'witchcraft' was too womanly for men.[91] And here Bósi's judgment about how he wants to rely on his *karlmenska* 'manhood, valor' rather than on using magic (*taufr*, *galdr*) and trickery (*sleita*) may usefully be recalled. In other words, witchcraft and magic had a great deal to do with how "maleness" and "femaleness" were constructed in late medieval northern thought. This native view was further reinforced over time by the pan-European feminization of witchcraft, which held that only the weak-minded and weak in faith would be duped by the devil, traits long associated by learned society with women.[92]

The gendered character of witchcraft in medieval Scandinavia—the fact that when women are accused of the crime the charges have to do with sexuality, whereas men are typically charged with heresy and similar crimes, yet in theory witchcraft is something both men and women practice—is critical for our grasp of Nordic belief systems in that period. Yet the relationship between gender and Nordic witchcraft in the later Middle Ages is exceedingly complex exactly because it does not seem to follow any simple rules about how witches are portrayed or treated in literature, law, and legal documents. Without a doubt, the relationship is more than a question of power, but power is part of the equation. It is more than a question of theology, but theology unquestionably has a powerful role too. And it is more than a question of attitudes and beliefs surviving from the pre-Christian period, yet these holdover views are also important in how such phenomena are shaped. All of these potent issues help shape Nordic witchcraft in the late medieval period, a cultural and legal construction with particularly important ramifications in the centuries that follow as Scandinavia enters into the era of the early modern witch hunts.

Epilogue

The Medieval Legacy

The preceding chapters have in different ways all addressed a single, central issue: What happened in Catholic Scandinavia as Christian ideology, with its own developing views of witchcraft and demonic magic, encountered and merged with native Nordic traditions of sorcery? How did these cultural categories meld and evolve in the four centuries before the Reformation? Inevitably, research of this sort has traveled discursively into such areas as popular culture, theology, legal thinking, and so on, and among other issues investigated are the following:

- magic's role in the pre-Christian era, at least as represented in Christian writings;
- the relationship between Christian and pagan magic and their potential as shared discourse;
- the consequences of the fact that the Conversion was accomplished only over a lengthy period, with some functions within the magical orbit shifting from pagan forms to Christian counterparts;
- the variety of learned strains of magic in medieval Scandinavia, including not only elite Christian thinking but also Jewish magical traditions and alchemy;
- the evidence of both regional and pan-European traditions of charm magic in medieval Scandinavia;
- the operational aspects of charm magic, arrived at through close readings of the material evidence and literary presentations (e.g., *Skírnismál*);
- how a spectrum of objects—from unique to quotidian, from gemstones to breast milk—could be used in charm magic to influence

romance, weather, and health; to peer into the future; and to curse;

- how the presentation in native texts of *seiðr*, *galdr*, and other forms of magic can sometimes preserve historical data;
- how these texts also employ magic as a "mere" literary device, to, for example, suggest differences between the contemporary world of the writer and the ancient pre-Christian world;
- how the same tendency toward using magic as a cipher for the past is also true of native Latin works and translated texts from abroad;
- how mythologies about witchcraft—the diabolical pact, the sabbatic journey to Blåkulla, the milk-stealing witch—evolved in the Nordic Middles Ages;
- how the secular laws—of Sweden and Norway in particular—treat witchcraft beliefs, frequently in the context of slander, underscoring the importance of reputation as a defense against accusations of witchcraft;
- how the legal codes suggest differences from our earliest records in the treatment of witchcraft in the differing national polities;
- how church laws focusing on superstition, magic, and witchcraft map onto presentations of these practices in sagas, trials, and other sources;
- how the arrangement of the laws, especially the crimes with which witchcraft is associated, changes over time;
- how medieval Nordic trials involving witchcraft and related crimes demonstrate a pattern in which females are charged with witchcraft involve sexuality and given relatively light sentences, whereas men are charged with more serious crimes and executed;
- how witchcraft is best understood in a gendered context, underscoring that the central idea of the witch as "evil woman" provided social control to various communities; and
- how the cultural construction of witchcraft affects our understanding of Nordic attitudes toward gender, power, and issues of masculinity and effeminacy.

What are the consequences of these evolving attitudes toward witchcraft and magic as Scandinavia moved into the post-Reformation world? A seemingly minor incident provides an illuminating example, in part due to its apparently uncontroversial nature. Writing at the height of the Thirty Years' War, a century after the Reformation had transformed Scandinavia, the Swedish agent in Zürich, Carl Marinus, contacted Sweden's prime minister, Axel Oxenstierna, and expressed concern for how the contest between the Protestant and Imperial forces for Rheinfelden would end, given the fact that one of the enemy had, under torture, informed the Protestants that four hundred of their opponents in the Catholic stronghold had entered into a pact with the devil.[1] That the matter is taken seriously demonstrates the extent to which this concept of the diabolical pact had by now become an important form of shared discourse, a European-wide metaphoric language that happily employed images of humans as agents of the devil. This same idea was, of course, the cornerstone of the European witchcraft belief system that had emerged from the Middle Ages.

Here in a seventeenth-century Europe in the midst of one of its bloodiest and most destructive eras, Catholic and Protestant archenemies "talk" through a shared, metaphoric language: the captured Imperial prisoner claimed that his fellow soldiers had entered into a diabolical pact in order, perhaps, to intimidate the opposition or perhaps to escape further torment. The agent in turn passed the information on as a serious matter. Beyond the fact that opposing forces could apparently communicate through a shared metalanguage built on fear, it is also remarkable that the concept of the diabolical pact is so easily accepted as part of "lived life," a fact with such terrible consequences in the sixteenth and seventeenth centuries.[2]

Some decades later, from 1668 to 1676, Sweden experienced what was Scandinavia's most pronounced example of witchcraft mania, as many individuals, mainly women, were accused of practicing witchcraft, in large measure demonstrated through their purported participation in the orgiastic concept of the journey to Blåkulla, a mythology whose roots, like the pact, had their origins in the Middle Ages.[3] Similar profiles can be drawn for the other Nordic countries: Denmark experienced as many as one thousand witchcraft executions and, in a 1617 ordinance defining the crime of witchcraft, officially tied it to the diabolical pact, an offense for which burning was deemed the appropriate penalty.[4] Although with far fewer incidents, Norwegian trials too, as recent research has demonstrated, were profoundly shaped by the concept of the diabolical pact.[5] Even Iceland, a famous outlier in mainly executing male witches during the post-Reformation period, could not entirely escape the effects of the pact ideology.[6]

How very different this conspiratorial view of witchcraft seems when compared to the relatively benign view of witchcraft in the Nordic Middle Ages, when such issues as lingering paganism and the occasional malefic witch dominated church and state thinking about practitioners of magic. By the end of the medieval period, witches and the power of witchcraft were seen, heard, and believed virtually everywhere in Scandinavia. A late fifteenth-century Swedish sermon indicates what the faithful were directed to believe: it compares the devil with a wolf coming to harm the soul, "secretly egging fools to sin or heresy and unbelief, fooling them with false teachings, with magic herbs, with witchcraft, and with the devil's sorcery. . . ."[7] In a similar vein, but targeting a different audience, Peder Madsen, a mid-fifteenth-century priest in Ribe, Denmark, rails widely against various forms of witchcraft in his Latin sermons, warning against the possible subversion of Christianity's magical kit—that is, baptismal water and the host—for use in charm magic.[8]

Prayer books of the period likewise display serious concern about witchcraft. In a Danish prayer book from the early 1500s, for example, the owner-nun prays to be protected "from all destruction and from all poison and from witchcraft and from all that which can do harm either in body or soul."[9] Other Danish prayer books show a similar pattern, for example, "protect (me) . . . from poisoning and from other witchcraft and from false tongues . . ."; "protect and hide me [. . .] from blows, from fire, from water, from all sorts of witchcraft, from treason . . ."[10] The prayer book of Birgitta Andersdotter, a Swedish nun at Vadstena in the early 1500s, amplifies the prayer considerably, listing many other possible forms of harm, including witchcraft. And the company witchcraft keeps in these litanies of potential ills is notable: not only witchcraft of every type but also weapons, fire, water, treason, captivity, evil of every sort, or anything that can harm her life, soul, reputation, or honor.[11]

At the same time that we recognize how widespread the fear of witchcraft had become by the time of the Reformation, it is important not to emphasize such dread to the degree that we lose perspective on the actual extent of accusations about this particular crime during the late medieval period. To take as a possible example of the rate of witchcraft trials at the close of the Middle Ages, in the Stockholm protocols for the period 1471–92 there are only two capital cases of witchcraft, less than 0.1 percent of the total crimes recorded.[12] And to return momentarily to the remarkably interior Nordic prayer books, the list of frightening potential harms by which Birgitta Andersdotter feels threatened is so lengthy and the witchcraft entry so relatively "unmarked" that it provokes an important question: Just how serious in real terms was the fear of witchcraft among the populace, even among such theologically well-informed individuals as nuns? After all, among the many hundreds of prayers that have been preserved from the Nordic Middle Ages, only a handful specifically mention witchcraft.

Still, a growth in concern for witchcraft is noticeable, as we have seen, in the Danish laws of Jutland, which contain a famous paragraph concerning witchcraft, indeed, its only statement on the topic. The date of the section is uncertain, with some arguing that its origins are in the thirteenth century, while others maintain that it came about roughly at the time of the manuscript, circa 1400. It reads in its entirety, "Concerning Witchcraft. If one knows of someone that he has killed one of his people through witchcraft and the accused does not confess but rather denies it, and the accuser confirms the charge against him, then the accused should defend himself with a committee (drawn from) the parish, face to face with the accuser as with the Bishop."[13] As scholars have long noted, whatever the date of the statute, it is clearly more concerned with process than with definitions or enumerations of witchcraft activities; moreover, defense against the charge, rather than accusation or definition, is the critical element.

By the time of Kristian II's national Danish law of 1521, on the other hand, a very different perspective had developed.[14] In it, the law specifies the nature of witchcraft, tying it both to the reputation of individuals in the community and to such empirical markers as their behavior on, for example, Maundy Thursday and Walpurgis Night.[15] As in the cases examined earlier of conversion narratives using magic as a form of communication and as a way for saga writers and other medieval Nordic authors to project a sense of antiquity, this law code uses witchcraft as a means of communication, in this case as a proxy or forum for debate between the church and the monarchy. Who will, in fact, define what witchcraft is and how it should be punished, the crown or the clergy?

Early sixteenth-century focus on such issues was itself perhaps more an indication of the changes that had been taking place in Scandinavia over the previous four centuries than it was a shaper of them. Ideologies worked out throughout the Nordic Middle Ages—the consolidated myths about magical theft and the journey to Blåkulla, together with deep belief in the diabolical pact, especially as these ideologies became fixed in the eyes of both secular and ecclesiastical authorities—set the stage for the hunts of the early modern period. These myths were ostensive narratives that both explained life's dark events and offered solutions to them: against the threat of witchcraft stood the promise offered by Christian prayer—"protect me [. . .] from all sorts of witchcraft"—as well as the full prosecutorial weight of both church and state.

Despite the break with the Catholic Church represented by the sixteenth-century Reformation, witchcraft's trajectory changed little in the Protestant era.[16] There were those who objected, of course: the Danish bishop, Peter Palladius, for example, complains at midcentury about the "popishness" he believes to be behind the fear of witches.[17] That view was not the dominant one, however, and did not stop large numbers of Danish citizens from being executed for the crime in the early modern era. Clearly, perceptions of witchcraft had evolved dramatically over the previous centuries, from a time when in the early fourteenth century Bishop Auðfinnr sentenced a confessed practitioner of magic to nothing more draconian than fasts, pilgrimages, and exile, what one observer has characterized as "an enlightened and rational cultural figure's opposition to the superstitions of the period."[18] If modern scholarship is correct, not so many centuries before the bishop's finding, the practice of magic may well have been an instrument of Nordic warfare and an integral part of Viking Age society.[19] Much, indeed, changes over the interim, as the presumably socially approved, and even lauded, magic of the Viking world is transformed throughout the Middle Ages into Scandinavia's Reformation-era vision of witchcraft. With its images of the milk-stealing witch, the participant in the diabolical and sexually charged events at Blåkulla, and the evil woman in league with the devil this much altered conception of witchcraft forms the necessary predicate for the formidable Nordic witch-hunts that will play out in the early modern era.

Notes

PREFACE

1. See, e.g., Ankarloo 1984 and Raudvere 2003, 32.

2. Cf. Eriksson 1994, 40.

3. So, e.g., Tolley 1996; DuBois 1999; Price 2002; and Tolley 2009. This connection has a long history in scholarship in the area (e.g., Fritzner 1877).

4. See Davidson 1976 and Siikala 2002.

5. As a crude comparison, modern-day Nuuk, Greenland, lies some 2,400 miles (approximately 3,800 kilometers) from Helsinki, Finland; the distance between Montreal, Canada, and Mexico City, Mexico, or between Montreal and Los Angeles, California, is about the same (approximately 2,300 and 2,500 miles, respectively).

6. See, e.g., Bailey 2008.

7. The Reformation was accomplished only slowly. By way of example, for Sweden alone, one might justifiably argue that 1526, 1527, 1529, and 1544 each mark the break with Catholicism, even though Lutheranism was not confirmed as the official state religion until the Uppsala Synod of 1593.

8. Cf. the forceful argument in Harris 1986.

9. For fine examples drawing on adjacent fields, see Gunnell 1995; Price 2002; Gísli Sigurðsson 2002, 2004; and Jochens 1996.

10. Thus the Viking Age Norwegian ruler Eiríkr Hákonarson would appear in that form, but a corresponding name in fifteenth-century Sweden, for example, would be given as Erik Håkonsson.

11. Cf. Raudvere 2001 and 2003, 22–23.

INTRODUCTION

1. "Dvergarnir sogþv asvm, at Kvasir hefþi kafnat imanviti, firir þvi at engi var þar sva froþr, at spyrja kyni hann froþleiks." Finnur Jónsson 1931, 82.

2. Cf. such periodic assessments as Midelfort 1968; Behringer 1996; and Rowlands 1998.

3. "The European witch-hunt of the sixteenth and seventeenth centuries is one of

those events, like the decline and fall of the Roman Empire, which is so complex and resonant that its historiography has almost become a field in itself." Whitney 1995, 77.

4. Although I have not followed any one design faithfully, this discussion has been influenced by the organizational schemes used by several distinguished scholars, such as Ankarloo's 1971 breakthrough study of seventeenth-century Swedish witch-hunts (Ankarloo 1984). Others include Kieckhefer 1976, 1–4; Ankarloo and Henningsen 1993, 1–15; Whitney 1995; Sörlin 1998, 3–12; Cunningham 1999; and Oja 1999, as well as the review of scholarship in Briggs 1996b, 431–40. On anthropological approaches in particular, see Marwick 1967 and Macfarlane 1991, 240–53; cf. my discussion in Mitchell 2004, on which some of these comments are based.

5. Bailey 2008, 28. Excellent English-language discussions and orientations can be found in Russell 1972; Cohn 1975; Kieckhefer 1976, 1989; Bailey 2003, 2007. A rich anthology of primary texts in translation is available in Kors and Peters 2001.

6. See esp. Peters 1978, 1996, 2001; Bartlett 1986; Bailey 2008; and Brundage 2008, 75–125.

7. Cf. Brundage 1995.

8. "Some scholars argue that the intellectual shifts that supported this revolution, particularly the increasingly bureaucratic nature of governments and courts, helped transform Europe into a 'persecuting society' at this time." Bailey 2008, 10; see as well his review of the literature there.

9. Almost certainly aimed at necromancy and learned magic associated with the clergy, the decree would eventually extend to witchcraft as well. See Peters 2001, 220–22, and Bailey 2007, 122–23.

10. For a general treatment of many of these works, see Russell 1972, 202–10 and 346–50. For a thorough examination of perhaps the most influential of them, Johannes Nider, see Bailey 2003.

11. On the question of authorship, see Mackay's considered comments (Institoris 2009, 2–6). As to how representative the views in *Malleus* are, see Broedel 2003 and the substantial literature reviewed there.

12. E.g., Russell 1972; Cohn 1975; Kieckhefer 1976, but as regards the sea change in attitudes beginning in the fourteenth century, see esp. Ginzburg 1984, 1985.

13. Necromancy (< *necromantia*) should refer only to divination through the use of the dead (cf. Greek *nekros* 'corpse'), practices so often associated with Óðinn in Nordic sources and with such figures as the witch of Endor in the Bible (1 Sam. 28), but confusion, intentionally or through happenstances, with *nigromantia* 'black arts' led to their equivalence. See Kieckhefer 1997, 4 and 19.

14. So Bailey 2001, 965–66. Cf. Fanger 1998, vii–viii, who further splits the world of medieval ritual magic into "demonic" and "angelic" forms, operationally dissimilar.

15. Cf. Bailey 2002.

16. "Christian authorities persisted in framing magic almost entirely in terms of their faith's ancient competition with paganism. New paradigms emerged in the legal and intellectual revolutions of the twelfth and thirteenth centuries. While other important

changes occurred in the fifteenth and sixteenth centuries, no line that can be drawn around 1500 seems quite as fundamental for the history of magic as that drawn around 1200." Bailey 2008, 28.

17. See Cohn 1975, 1–32. This argument has, however, been challenged in Ginzburg 1991; see also Ginzburg 1993a and 1993b. This phrasing perhaps masks the diversity that exists in the scholarly literature: some would, for example, see in Russell 1972 a strong emphasis on folk traditions, whereas a work such as Peters 1978 focuses more on the scholiast view.

18. Examples of this point are found in treatments concerned with the New World's most celebrated witch-hunt, that in Salem in 1692: one written on the eve of the American Revolution, the other seventy years later. Both Hutchinson 1870 (from the 1760s) and Upham 1832 regard, and to some extent look to explain away, the event as a "delusion."

19. Hutchinson 1718. The seismic shift in thinking is one I have explored in a case from the early nineteenth century. See Mitchell 2000c, 2004.

20. Cf. Oja 1999, 33–34 et passim.

21. E.g., Walberg 1815; Kröningssvärd 1821; Annell 1840; Norlin 1858.

22. E.g., Berg 1981.

23. E.g., Bætzmann 1865; Lehmann 1920.

24. E.g., Linderholm 1918a.

25. Murray 1971. To the extent they are still needed, useful critiques are provided in, e.g., Cohn 1975; Simpson 1994; and Hutton 1999.

26. Runeberg 1947; Lid 1950; Alver 1971; Henningsen 1969; Wall 1977–78; and Tørnsø 1986. Ginzburg's findings (1985) have resulted in renewed interest, and confidence, in such a scenario.

27. Trevor-Roper 1967; cf. Trevor-Roper 1969.

28. Michelet 1862; Harris 1974, 193.

29. Thomas 1971. In his review, Midelfort (1973, 434) comments that "Thomas has written one of the most important books of recent times."

30. Ankarloo 1984. Cf. similarly fine statistical analyses, and materialist arguments, in such works as Midelfort 1972; Boyer and Nissenbaum 1974; and Næss 1982.

31. Anthropology as a "modern" point of comparison is misleading—already well before Evans-Pritchard's landmark study of Zande witchcraft (Evans-Pritchard 1937), Kittredge 1929, 26 et passim, drew on contemporary ethnographies in his exhaustive survey of Anglo-American traditions.

32. The best example of this synergy may be Macfarlane 1991, the preface to which was written by E. E. Evans-Pritchard. The application of anthropology to history, and the study of witchcraft in particular, has been of such influence that some have even suggested that its moment may have passed (e.g., Nedkvitne 2000).

33. Cf. Turner 1967. For a useful example of this dynamic approach, see Turner 1972, 148–53.

34. Most prominently, Thomas 1971 and Macfarlane 1991, but also Douglas 1970b, xiii, signals this sea change: "Historians and anthropologists have a common interest in

the subject of witchcraft, but until very recently their outlooks have diverged[. . . .] Now this difference is being narrowed: the historians who have contributed to this volume have succeeded in delving into material very comparable to that used by anthropologists and the latter are gradually improving the time-scale of their observation."

35. See Douglas 1970a, and the other contributions in the volume, esp. Thomas 1970.

36. "There are indeed historians who claim that there is something illegitimate about offering multiple explanations for simultaneous occurrences of a general kind. . . ." Briggs 1996b, 397.

37. Macfarlane 1991, 231; Hutton 1996.

38. Cf. Briggs 1996a.

39. E.g., Alver 1971, 2008; Ankarloo 1984; Siglaugur Brynleifsson 1976; Næss 1982; Jensen 1988; Sörlin 1998; Ólína Þorvarðardóttir 2000; Östling 2002; Van Gent 2008.

40. An earlier generation of scholars (e.g., Bætzmann 1865; Lehmann 1920; Bang 1896; Gering 1902; Gadelius 1912–13; Linderholm 1918a, 1918b; Ólafur Daviðsson 1940–43) did yeoman's work in assembling materials. These early works have largely been eclipsed by emerging new techniques and views, such as the reintegration of archaeology and philology provided in Price 2002 and others, and by detailed examinations of the sagas (e.g., Dillmann 2006). In a class by itself is Dag Strömbäck 1935, a study of (mainly) literary representations of divination and "black magic," whose continued importance was recently reassessed by Almqvist 2000 and Mebius 2000. Many of the relevant primary materials on early Nordic magic are conveniently anthologized in McKinnell, Simek, and Düwel 2004.

41. Dillmann 1986, 2006. 1986 was also the year in which Regis Boyer's more popularly oriented *Le monde du double: La magie chez les anciens Scandinaves* appeared. Cf. Boyer 1981.

42. Any attempt to distill in a few lines the nearly eight-hundred-page results of many decades of research will naturally fall far short of perfection. For a thorough review, see Jochens 2006.

43. With respect to the sagas, see my remarks below in Chapter 3, as well as Mitchell 2000a; however, these texts remain useful, indeed indispensible, to the study of late Iron Age Scandinavia. See, e.g., the argument in Andrén 2005.

44. Raudvere 2003. Many of Raudvere's views are also available in her earlier English-language discussion of witchcraft (*trolldómr*) in Raudvere 2001.

45. This question, and the conflict between the heroic ethos and the idea of fate, was the subject of an earlier monograph, Wax 1969.

46. Solli 2002.

47. Several studies have taken to Viking Age witchcraft and magic the issues of gender, social roles, and feminism, e.g., Morris 1991 and Jochens 1996.

48. Price 2002.

49. This formulation is, of course, a matter of great debate within Nordic archaeology, a topic Price (2002) is at some pains to discuss.

50. Price 2002, 393.

51. E.g., Strömbäck 1935; Ohlmarks 1939; Buchholz 1968, 1971; Tangherlini 1990, but already in the nineteenth century similar questions were being raised (e.g., Fritzner 1877). Major contributions in recent years include DuBois 1999; Siikala 2002; and Tolley 2009. Cf. the vigorous analysis in Schnurbein 2003 concerning shamanism and Old Norse culture.

52. So, e.g., Alver 1971; Ankarloo 1984; and a host of other scholars. Also see Raudvere 2003, 32, and the literature cited there. On the broader context, see Kieckhefer 1989, 38–40, and Peters 2001, as well as the detailed study in Bailey 2001.

53. See Edsman 1982b, 662.

54. E.g., Flint 1991, whose demonstration of a "middle way" concretizes some of this debate.

55. Cf. the discussion in Mitchell 1991b, 15–16, 44–46.

56. Santino 1994, xvii, with specific reference to holidays.

57. Advocates of these two extremist positions—the one uncritically romantic, the other skeptical to the point of intellectual nihilism—have talked past each other for decades; see the review in Lindow 1985.

58. See Mitchell 2009a for an example.

59. Cf. Jansen 1959, although it should be obvious that the obverse, the esoteric perspective, renders a very different judgment.

60. Cf. Flint 1991, 33. Increasingly large numbers of clerics practiced learned forms of magic; on this point, see esp. Kieckhefer 1989.

61. Flint 1991, 3. For a valuable summary of perspectives, see Cunningham 1999 as well as Styers 2004, who argue for a more socially constructed understanding of magic as a category developed in the context of the colonialist expansion of the West (see esp. 25–68).

62. Cf. Russell 1972, 17–20, and Kieckhefer 1997, 154–62. On Augustinian demonology and its influence over church thinking on such matters, see Fleteren 1999.

63. Russell 1972, 18, divides the medieval demons into three groups: minor demons, major demons (e.g., Beelzebub), and "the Devil himself." On the medieval conception of "the devil," see Russell 1984 and the literature cited there.

64. By the end of the Middle Ages, of course, this mythology also incorporated the idea of the devil's pact (*pactum cum diabolo*). On this phenomenon in medieval Europe generally, see Russell 1972, 18–19, 59–60, 65 et passim; and for medieval Scandinavia, Mitchell 2008b and the discussion in Chapter 4.

65. "Hermogenes kallar sina diæfla: Ok biudher them binda *sanctum* jacobum [. . .] Jacobus badh gudz ængil læta them løsa . . ." Stephens and Dahlgren 1847–74, 1:164. *Biudha (biuþa)* is here understood as "bjuda, befalla. med personens dat." See Söderwall and Ljunggren 1884–1973.

66. "ek sœri þik, Óðinn, með heiðindómi, mestr fjanda; játa því; seg mér . . ." I am here following the normalized text provided in MacLeod and Mees 2006, 31, as well as their translation, with my emendations.

67. Cf. the similar formulation, *Te rogamus, audi nos* 'we ask you, hear us', of the *Missale Romanum*. The transliteration and translation of runic inscriptions here (and elsewhere, unless otherwise noted) follows *Samnordisk runtextdatabas* (Elmevik and Peterson 1993–; see also the comments in Peterson 1994). Tags of the sort "N 289 M" are used to identify inscriptions, generally by place and item (although usages vary somewhat), in this instance, *N*orway 289 *M*edieval.

68. Many of the great figures in anthropology and sociology have debated this relationship (e.g., Tylor, Durkheim, Mauss, Parsons). In addition to the texts already cited, see the roundtable debates in *Current Anthropology* (e.g., Wax and Wax 1963; Rosengren 1976; Winkelman 1982). For an excellent overview deconstructing many of our implicit assumptions, see Tambiah 1990.

69. See Frazer 1890, as well as the "canonical" third edition, Frazer 1915.

70. Malinowski 1948, 62.

71. Benedict 1937, 40.

72. Yalman 1968, 527.

73. Wax and Wax 1963; Wax and Wax 1962, 1964.

74. Wax and Wax 1962, 187. Cf. Hammond 1970, 1355, who concludes, "Magic is not an entity distinct from religion but a form of ritual behavior and thus an element of religion." The hag-oriented view (cf. Daly 1978), although useful, is far from a majority perspective; cf. Stark 2001, 114, who writes, "Magic differs from religion because it does not posit the existence of Gods, does not offer explanations either of its own domain or address questions of ultimate meaning, does not offer 'otherworldly' rewards, and is unable to sanctify the moral order, while religion does all of these. Magic and religion also differ in that the former is subject to empirical falsification, while the latter need not be."

75. Kieckhefer 1989, 9.

76. Cf. Evans-Pritchard 1937; Turner 1967; and Mair 1963, 27, for example.

77. See, e.g., the excellent discussion on this topic in Apps and Gow 2003, as well as in Kent 2005. Likewise, modern English usage of the term "warlock" lends itself to strictly gendered use, on which, see Mitchell 2001.

78. Cf. the approach by Russell 1972, 4–5, using Venn diagrams to illustrate how in the standard, overlapping "religion-magic (now divided separately into high and low varieties) -science" triptych witchcraft maps onto and overlaps with both religion and low magic.

79. "Thy at genstridh är swa som trolskaps älla trollkona synd, och afgudha dyrks onzska, är at ey wilia lydha . . ." Wieselgren 1966, 65.

CHAPTER 1

1. Van Engen 1986, 529, characterizing the positions of Le Goff and Schmitt. See, e.g., Le Goff 1967 and 1978. On the division between an essentially ecclesiastical medieval culture and a more popular, oral culture in the Nordic world, see Lönnroth 1964 and Mitchell 1991b, 1–6 et passim. Boglioni 1977, 699, suggests a tripartite system for conceiv-

ing religious folklore: (1) "true pagan survivals" (i.e., paganism intact as a religious system), (2) "pagan folklore" (i.e., heterogeneous remnants of heathenism), and (3) "Christian folklore" (e.g., cults centered on healing beliefs about local saints).

2. Still useful are Troels-Lund's monumental portrait of sixteenth-century Scandinavia (Troels-Lund 1880–1901) and Hans Hildebrand's charming if dated review of medieval Sweden (Hildebrand 1983, originally published from 1879 to 1903). More recent scholarship has tended to focus on the role of women in medieval Scandinavia (e.g., Skyum-Nielsen 1971; Jacobsen 1986, 2007; Jochens 1995).

3. I make no pretense to completeness in this survey but intend only to provide an orientation for those not already familiar with the topic. For excellent English-language discussions of Nordic history in this period, see Sawyer and Sawyer 1993 and Helle 2003.

4. These inter-Nordic rivalries gave rise to a great historiographical tradition in the North, mostly in the form of rhymed chronicles. On the genre as a whole, and specifically on the Swedish tradition, see Jansson 1971; on the Danish rhymed chronicle, see Hermann 2006 and 2007b.

5. On the Gotlandic assertion of autonomy, see Mitchell 1984.

6. See Gelsinger 1981, esp. 181–94. So great was this international connection that, despite a supposed trade monopoly, the Icelandic fifteenth century is called "the English Age" (*Enska öldin*); see Björn Þorsteinsson 1970.

7. For excellent presentations, see the entires in DuBois 2008.

8. For English-language surveys, see the medieval chapters in the national volumes that make up *A History of Scandinavian Literature* (Rossel 1993–2007). With the important, and dominant, exception of the Icelandic sagas, the medieval materials have largely remained untranslated and thus tended to remain the province of specialists.

9. E.g., Brown 1981; Flint 1991; Gurevich 1988.

10. Cf. Wax and Wax 1962. The elite-nonelite dyad remains a convenient intellectual tool and underscores the relationship between learned, "global" discourses on witchcraft and local folk belief—how, for example, the elite community appropriates local belief for its own ends. See the discussions in Birkhan 1989; Mitchell, Collins, and Tangherlini 2000; and Watkins 2004.

11. On "medieval popular culture," see Rosenberg 1980, who notes the proclivity to insert into the Middle Ages our own atomistic approaches, specifically such notions as "elite," "popular," and "folk."

12. The possibility of discovering history's hidden voices, "history from below," has given rise to such fields as subaltern studies, microhistory, and ethnohistory.

13. "Overlap" should not obscure the fact that the Christian law sections often indicate a power struggle between church and state about the authority to formulate these sections of the codes.

14. Cf. the negative assessment in Russell 1972, 245.

15. E.g., Ginzburg 1992.

16. Keyser and Munch 1846–95, 1:17.

17. Cf. Bagge 1998, 103–6.

18. "En ef kona bitr fingr af barne sinu eda to ok gerer þat til langlifis hon er sæck .iij. morkum. Su er fordæda vest en firir gerer manne eda kono eda barne. ku eda kalfe. En ef fordædoskapr verdr funnin i bædium eda bulstrum manna har eda nægl eda frauda fôtr. eda adrer þæir lutir e[r] uenir þickia til gærninga. þa ma sok gefa [. . .] þat er vbota verk ef madr sitr vti ok væckir troll up. Þat er vbota verk ef madr tynir ser sialfr. Þat er ok vbota verk ef madr fær a fin merkr at spyria spa." Keyser and Munch 1846–95, 1:362.

19. On the prospects of such legislative texts as the basis for teasing out folk practices and beliefs, see Thyregod 1895–96 and Palme 1969; a wider Germanic perspective is represented in Vordemfelde 1923. On the broader European situation, see, e.g., McNeill 1933 and Oakley 1940 (esp. his cautionary remarks, 215–16).

20. E.g., Hjørungdal 1989; Price 2002.

21. Price 2002, 47.

22. E.g., Bæksted 1952; Düwel 1992. Cf. Page 1995, 105: "Epigraphists are often tempted to interpret as magical the inscriptions of which they can make little straightforward sense. This is particularly true of runologists, since they may be influenced by the theory of rune-magic." Recent useful anthologies include McKinnell, Simek, and Düwel 2004 and MacLeod and Mees 2006. Cf. Lindquist 1923.

23. For the original text and a review of earlier scholarship, see Jacobsen and Moltke 1941–42, 254–56. Cf. the sensible suggestion by Nielsen 1983, 75, who objects that rather than the name of the rune carver, the Þormundr is more likely to be the name of the deceased: thus, "Make good use of the monument, Þormundr!"

24. Jungner and Svärdström 1940–70, 396, normalizes the inscription as, "Gal anda viðr, gangla viðr, riðanda við(r), viðr rinnanda, viðr s[it]ianda, viðr sign[and]a, viðr f[a]randa, viðr fliughanda. S[kal] allt fy[r]na ok um dø[i]a." '(I) charm' might be preferred to '(I) practice witchcraft', as it is closer in form and meaning to the original gal (cf. gala 'crow; chant, sing [= spell]'). On this charm, see Jungner and Svärdström 1940–70, 394–403; on its dating, 402–3.

25. According to Adam of Bremen, Skara was the site of a bishop's seat already in the eleventh century (Book 2, 56 [Pertz 1846, 89–90]).

26. On the role of runic inscriptions during this period, see Sawyer 2000, 124–45, esp. her observation that these monuments represent "a transitional stage, when many new converts tried to bridge the gap between their, and their kin's, pagan past and their own—Christian—era." See also Williams 1996a on the absence of conflict between pagan and Christian in Swedish rune stones of this period.

27. A phenomenon generally known as "Whig history" (or "present-centeredness"), in which "the historian, in seeking to study, reconstruct and write about the past, is constrained by necessarily starting from the perceptual and conceptual categories of the present," as Ashplant and Wilson 1988, 253, write. Butterfield's (1931) *The Whig Interpretation of History* is generally regarded as the first work to identify directly this anachronistic approach to history, but cf. Cosgrove 2000, 147: "Butterfield's critique was hardly a flash of lightning in a cloudless sky."

28. Kittredge 1929 is an excellent example of the first tendency, Purkiss 1996 of the second.

29. See, e.g., Purkiss 1996, 7–29.

30. A full account of the key role played by Nordic folklorists remains unwritten, but a sense of their significance can be found in Boberg 1953 and the essays in Strömbäck 1971. See Mitchell 2000a, on which some of these remarks are based.

31. "den folkloristiska forskningsskola, som en gång i tiden grundades av Moltke Moe i Norge och Axel Olrik i Danmark och som jag är förmäten nog att räkna mig själv till . . ." Strömbäck 1970, 5. The title reflects a scholarly debate about the medieval materials. Cf. the differing, and polarized, evaluations in the exchanges in *Folkminnen och folktankar* (e.g., Finnur Jónsson 1922; von Sydow 1922a, 1922b).

32. Strömbäck 1979b, 10–11.

33. See his remarks in Strömbäck 1979a, esp. 13. With respect to this relationship and the role of sacrifice, see Jón Hnefill Aðalsteinsson 1997, 11–31.

34. Cf. Alver 1980; Honko 1989, 18; Holbek 1992, xix. See also Chapter 3.

35. Von Sydow 1965, 241.

36. Bauman 1996, 17.

37. "Det var filologen som upptäckte folkminnenas vetenskapliga betydelse, och det är naturligt att ett ständigt samarbete bör råda mellan filologi och folkminnesforskning, i det *de är varandras nödvändiga hjälpvetenskaper*." von Sydow 1944, 32 (emphasis added).

38. Most apparent in Le Goff 1978.

39. On the possibilities here, see, e.g., Bauman 1986 and Mitchell 2002a.

40. Cf. the remarks in Canadé-Sautman et al. 1991, 6–7.

41. On these cases, see also Chapter 2. Debate about Frazer's (1915) arguments has raged, and although his cultural significance cannot be denied, not everyone greets that fact with approbation; see, e.g., Murmel 1991; Beard 1992; and Leach 1985.

42. This example is from Klemming 1883–86, 438. See Kieckhefer 1989, 8–17, and Flint 1991, 49–50 et passim, for considerations of this question, as well as the very full treatment in Tambiah 1990, 1–15, 111–39. An early but still useful account of medieval theories of magic is Thorndike 1915.

43. Såby 1886, 47. Or perhaps lechery or adultery.

44. On the available resources, see the Gräslund 1996a; Hallencreutz 1996; and Williams 1996b. Cf. Sawyer and Sawyer 1999.

45. See the excellent summary of these views in Lönnroth 1996.

46. So too Old Norse *heiðinn* 'heathen'. See Fritzner 1973, 752–53, and de Vries 1961, 216–17. Cleasby and Vigfusson 1982, 247, specifically reject the "heath" etymology in favor of a New Testament Greek origin. The *Oxford English Dictionary* (Simpson and Weiner 1993) likewise expresses doubt about the "heath" etymology for English.

47. E.g., Poulsen 1986; Price 2002.

48. Among the most notable publications in this regard are Dillmann 1992; Jochens 1996; Raudvere 2001, 2003; and Dillmann 2006 (cf. Dillmann 1986).

49. So, e.g., Buchholz 1968, 1971; Tolley 1994, 1996; DuBois 1999; Drobin and Keinänen 2001; Hultkrantz 2001; Price 2002; Siikala 2002; and Tolley 2009.

50. In addition to the works just cited, see Zachrisson 2008 for an orientation to the medieval Sámi situation.

51. In these remarks, I intend only to give some impression of the deities inhabiting the mythological world of pagan Scandinavia; more detailed comments on the relationship of these figures to magic and witchcraft are treated separately in Chapter 3.

52. See Elgqvist 1955 in particular.

53. E.g., Morris 1991, 30–31; Jochens 1996, 114. Cf. Quinn 1998.

54. There are many excellent introductions and guides to Old Norse mythology (e.g., Turville-Petre 1964; Clunies Ross 1994, 1998; and Lindow 2002); on the role of the female element in pagan Norse religion, see, in addition to Ström 1954, esp. Näsström 1995; Jochens 1996; and Davidson 1998. With respect to gender and the conversion to Christianity, see Karras 1997 and Gräslund 1996b.

55. Cf. Morris 1991; Jochens 1996; Helga Kress 2008; and Jóhanna Katrín Friðriksdóttir 2009. See Chapters 3 and 6 in this volume for discussions of figures such as Queen Gunnhildr and Þorbjǫrg.

56. "grey þykki mér Freyja." The line is found in *Íslendingabók* (Jakob Benediktsson 1968, 15) and more fully in a number of sagas (e.g., *Brennu-Njáls saga* [Einar Ól. Sveinsson 1954, 264]).

57. Cf. Näsström 1996.

58. Cf. the comments in Lindow 1985, 22–23. On the important question of the kinds of memory employed and the implications of this process for our preserved texts, see Hermann 2009.

59. I have in mind here the contrast between the accidental discovery of an important find when it turns up under a farmer's plow versus the carefully articulated designation of test pits dug at a known site according to an algorithm formulated to yield randomness.

60. On the remarkable Scanian site, see the many volumes now published as part of the monographic series *Uppåkrastudier*; see, on the Mývatn district farm, McGovern et al. 2007, on Hrísbrú, Byock et al. 2005

61. Price 2002; Solli 2002.

62. Cf. the incisive remarks on this problem in Kirschenblatt-Gimblett 1991.

63. An extensive literature on this relationship dates back to at least Fritzner 1877, properly including not only Sámi but also Finnish traditions. See, e.g., the treatments in DuBois 1999, 122–38 et passim, and Siikala 2002.

64. Price 2002, but cf. Tolley 2009, 390–93.

65. See his comments in Price 2002, 393.

66. Cf., for example, Jones 1968, 73–74.

67. On "prime signing" in the Nordic Middle Ages, see Sandholm 1965. On the conversion process in Scandinavia, see, e.g., Ljungberg 1938; Paasche 1958; Jones 1968, 106–8 et passim; Roesdahl 1982, 159–83; Sawyer 1982, 131–43; and Sawyer and Sawyer 1993. For recent reevaluations of the Christianization of Sweden, see the essays in Nilsson 1996b, esp. the editor's synthesizing remarks (Nilsson 1996a), and, for Norway, Skre 1998 and Schumacher 2005.

68. Missionary attempts before Ansgar include those by Bishop Willibrord (d. 739;

see the short life by Alcuin) and by Archbishop Ebbo of Reims in 823. The principal source of information on Ansgar's mission to Scandinavia is the vita written by his protégé and successor, Rimbert (Waitz 1977, trans. as Robinson 1921). On Ansgar's conversion efforts, see Jahnkuhn 1967; Hallencreutz 1982; and esp. Busk Sørensen 2004.

69. On the methods used by missionaries among the northern barbarians, see Sullivan 1953 and Reu 1998. On the mercantile aspects of early conversion contacts and the fact that trade centers figure so prominently, see Olsen 1966, 116, as well as Sandholm 1965. Schmidt 1939 argues for a patterned sequence of conversion activities among the Germanic peoples: early cultural contacts, including trade (*Kulturmission*); advocacy through preaching and other persuasive means (*Wortmission*); and, finally, recourse to coercive and violent methods (*Schwertmission*). Molland 1982b suggests that, for Scandinavia, archaeological evidence from Kaupang in Vestfold, Norway, fits Schmidt's *Kulturmission*; the work of Saint Ansgar, Schmidt's *Wortmission*; and Óláfr Tryggvason's extreme techniques, examples of a *Schwertmission*.

70. Waitz 1977, 38–39. The historical worth of this story, given its resemblance to the Job story, an influential tale in the early Middle Ages (cf. Besserman 1979, 66–75), is less than its metaphorical value.

71. Miracles as Christian magic has been at the core of a long debate. Even *The Catholic Encyclopedia*'s wording supports the equation: "Latin *miraculum*, from *mirari*, 'to wonder' [. . .] wonders performed by supernatural power as signs of some special mission or gift and explicitly ascribed to God." See Knight 2003. The proximate character of miracles and magic is, of course, at the heart of the legend of Simon Magus; cf. Acts 8:9–24 and the comments on this legend in Flint 1991. For an excellent review of miracles in saints' lives as a form of "white magic," see Loomis 1948. Thomas 1971, 25–50, offers an assessment of the role of the church and magic in daily life in medieval England. On the Nordic situation, see the survey in Edsman 1982b, as well as Mitchell 2009b.

72. This site has generated an enormous body of literature; excellent orientations are provided in the contributions to Nielsen et al. 1974 and in Roesdahl 1982.

73. "King Haraldr ordered this monument made in memory of Gormr, his father, and in memory of Þorvé, his mother; that Haraldr who won for himself all of Denmark and Norway and made the Danes Christian." Elmevik and Peterson 1993–. See also Jacobsen and Moltke 1941–42, 79.

74. Commenting on pagan Scandinavian burial mounds in Derbyshire, Wainwright (1975, 281) remarks, "There are scraps of evidence that they adopted Christianity eagerly and early and that heathenism had ceased to be a powerful force among them by *circa* 900. . . . " Cf. Whitelock 1937–45. Dahlerup (1993, 84) after noting the early missionary efforts, remarks, "Of more lasting importance was the conversion of several Viking settlers on the British Isles, and the continual contacts between the Danelaw Vikings and their relations at home had a significant impact."

75. See Gräslund 1996b, esp. 327–32.

76. On this episode, see Cusack 1999, 145. A number of later texts tell similar tales (e.g., *Chronicon* of Thietmar of Merseburg; the *Annales Ryenses* and *Annales Ripenses*; *Óláfs*

saga Tryggvasonar en mesta). Cf. the less miraculous narratives in, e.g., Adam of Bremen and *Historia de antiquitate regum Norwagiensium*. This episode in its various forms is carefully examined in Jackson 2006.

77. *Íslendingabók* says of Óláfr that he brought Christianity to Norway and Iceland and sent to Iceland the priest Þangbrandr (Jakob Benediktsson 1968, 14). On Óláfr, see the bibliography in Jón Viðar Sigurðsson 1993.

78. For an orientation to Adam of Bremen, see the entries in Bolin 1982 and Buchner 1968–.

79. Cf. Lind 1920–21, cols. 217–18.

80. "Quare etiam cognomen accepit, ut Olaph Cracabben diceretur. Nam et artis magicae, ut aiunt, studio deditus omnes, quibus illa redundat patria, maleficos habuit domesticos, eorumque deceptus errore periit." Book 2, 38; Pertz 1846, 77.

81. Bjarni Aðalbjarnarson 1962, 311–12. Snorri enumerates several different types of witchcraft and sorcery: "þeir menn allir er kunnir ok sannir yrði at því, at fœri með galdra ok gørningar, eða seiðmenn, þá skyldu allir fara af landi á brot." On Snorri's "program" vis-à-vis the Conversion, see Weber 1986.

82. *mǫnnum*. Like its English counterpart, *maðr* 'man', pl. *menn* 'men', can be understood as a collective including members of both sexes (i.e., the equivalent of 'people'), but the context in this story clearly suggests that masculine gender is intended.

83. Bjarni Aðalbjarnarson 1962, 138–39. On Rǫgnvaldr, one of the sons of King Haraldr inn hárfagri, and the episode about him, see Mitchell 2000b.

84. An abbreviated version of this tale is related, for example, by Theodoricus monachus, which reads in part, "Illuc ergo rex adveniens invitavit ad se omnes illos, qui arctiori vinculo diabolicarum falsitatum irretiti fuerant et vulgari locutione dicuntur *seithmen*, et quia illos perspexit insansabiles, ne novellæ plantationi nocerent, collectos in domum dæmonibus dedicatam una cum simulachris igni cremari jussit; quorum fuisse ferunt numerum octoginta promiscui sexus." Storm 1973, 18–19. On the complex relationship between Theodoricus's *Historia de antiquitate regum Norwagienium*, the *Historia Norwegiae*, and Icelandic saga writing, see Bjarni Guðnason 1977.

85. "Gerði Eyvindr þeim huliðshjálm ok þokumyrkr svá mikit, at konungr ok lið hans skyldi eigi mega sjá þá" [lit., Eyvindr made for them a "hidden helm" and such a great murky fog that the king and his troops would not be able to see them]. The term *huliðshjálmr* (also *hulinshjálmr*) is often glossed as 'hidden helm' (Cleasby and Vigfusson 1982, 292) or 'hiding helmet' (Zoëga 1975, 215); more expansively, Fritzner 1973, 2:90, writes, "Hjelm som gjør den usynlig, der bærer den paa sit Hoved [. . .] men i Almindelighed betegnes derved ethvert Trolddomsmiddel, som anvendtes til at gjøre en Person usynlig." Cf. de Vries 1961, 266, who glosses it as *tarnhelm*, noting its connection (through *hylja*) to *hel*.

86. When, e.g., Eyvindr and his fellow sorcerers are to be killed, Snorri writes simply, "Síðan lét konungr taka þá alla ok flytja í flœðisker ok binda þá þar. Lét Eyvindr svá líf sitt ok allir þeir." Bjarni Aðalbjarnarson 1962, 312. By contrast, in *Ólafs saga Tryggvasonar en mesta*, King Óláfr delivers a lengthy disquisition to Eyvindr, laced with references

to Christ, and offers Eyvindr and his men the opportunity to "trua vm siðir aa sannan guð" (91). The Eyvindr episode as a whole is found in Ólafur Halldórsson 1961, 2:82–91; cf. Finnur Jónsson 1932. Tales about Óláfr Tryggvason have provided rich materials for medieval Nordic authors: Oddr Snorrason, a monk of the Þingeyrar monastery, wrote a Latin life of Óláfr, circa 1190. His fellow monk, Gunnlaugr Leifsson, also wrote a Latin life, probably before 1200. Although now lost, Oddr's text is known from an Old Norse translation from about 1200. Oddr's saga, together with the heritage about Óláfr in the skaldic tradition, were probably used by Snorri in composing his saga of Óláfr; Gunnlaugr's text is thought to have been used by the author of *Ólafs saga Tryggvasonar en mesta*. See Bjarni Aðalbjarnarson 1962, xiii-xiv, and Bjarni Aðalbjarnarson 1936, 55–135, as well as the overview in Ólafur Halldórsson 1993. On Óláfr against the "Powers of Darkness," see Simpson 1973.

87. Bjarni Einarsson 1984, 21–22, 145. *Ágrip* is thought to have been used in the composition of a variety of subsequent texts; the issue here is not a question of independent source value but rather of attitudes.

88. Cf. Lindow 2008 on Óláfr's complicated presentation in the literature.

89. Leach 1965, 266–67.

90. Cf. Leach 1982.

91. Leach 1965, 278.

92. On the wide array of historical and textual sources, and their various perspectives on Óláfr Tryggvason, see, e.g., Bagge 1991, 131–40.

93. Caro Baroja 1964, 13. Cf. the illuminating comments situating Caro Baroja's contributions in Clark 2001, 1–9.

94. Readers will recognize that I am intentionally parodying one of the most famous things Claude Lévi-Strauss did *not* say—or did not exactly say. It is sometimes bruited about that the famous French anthropologist had once written something like, "Food is not only good to eat, but also good to think with." As far as I can determine, he never wrote those words (or their French equivalent), although he did note, "We can understand, too, that natural species are chosen [for totemic purposes] not because they are 'good to eat' but because they are 'good to think'" (Lévi-Strauss 1963b, 89), a remark that has occasioned a variety of thoughtful responses (e.g., Tambiah 1969). The pseudo-Lévi-Straussian remark is admittedly not the same thing as the original, but the reformulation has taken on a life of its own in scholarship and popular culture (e.g., Bloch 1998) and offers its own interpretive possibilities.

95. See, e.g., the confrontation over "real" and "commodified" magic in the case of Simon Magus in Acts 8.

96. The most obvious line of inquiry on this issue—the human faculty for symbolic interpretation—is that associated with Ferdinand de Saussure and subsequent structuralist thinking within anthropology influenced by it (the works of Claude Lévi-Strauss most famously), but it should be noted that this view also has roots in the writing of Émile Durkheim as well. An excellent overview of Lévi-Strauss's contributions is provided in Leach 1989, 35–56 et passim.

97. Leach 1989, 44, following Lévi-Strauss.

98. Mellor 2008, 48; "probemus miraculis, quis sit maioris potentiae, vestri multi quos dictis dii, an meus solus omnipotens dominus Iesus Christus. Ecce tempus adest pluviae." Waitz 1977, 40 (chap. 19).

99. In one of the best-known statements about the implications of his findings, Lévi-Strauss 1963a, 61, writes that he is looking to analyze "marriage regulations and kinship systems as a kind of language, a set of processes permitting the establishment, between individuals and groups, of a certain type of communication. That the mediating factor, in this case, should be the *women of the group,* who are *circulated* between clans, lineages, or families, in place of the *words of the group,* which are *circulated* between individuals. . . . "

100. "Vér skulum gera elda þrjá; skuluð þér heiðnir menn vígja einn, en ek annan, en inn þriði skal óvígðr vera. En ef berserkrinn hræðisk þann, er ek vígða, en vaði yðvarn eld, þá skuluð þér taka við trú." Einar Ól. Sveinsson 1954, 267–68. An analogous biblical story is the pyromantic confrontation between Elijah and the prophets of Baal in 1 Kings 18:22–39.

101. Similar narratives are found in *Kristni saga* and elsewhere. See the many examples from Icelandic literature listed under "V331.1. *Conversion to Christianity through miracle*" in Boberg 1966. Many of the narratives dealing with the conversion of Iceland are addressed in Sveinbjörn Rafnsson 1977, while a more ethnographically situated study of the process is laid out in Jón Hnefill Aðalsteinsson 1978.

102. Cf. Sveinbjörn Rafnsson 1977.

103. Cf. Flint's comments (1991, 33) on the differences between the two as understood by Saint Augustine: "In these chapters of the *City of God* we have a summary of where lay, for Augustine, the dividing line between condemnable and essential magic. 'Veneficia,' 'maleficia,' 'malefici' diminish, defraud, give pain. In league with demons, they conceal the true good from humankind. 'Mira' and 'miracula,' on the other hand, overcome fear and pain, and encourage hope and open happiness. Yet, undeniably, they contain magic of a kind."

104. "þá bar Þangbrandr róðukross fyrir skjǫldinn . . . " Einar Ól. Sveinsson 1954, 258.

105. "Maðr hét Galdr-Heðinn [. . .] keyptu heiðnir menn at honum, at hann skyldi deyða Þangbrand ok fǫruneyti hans, ok fór hann upp á Arnarstakksheiði ok efldi þar blót mikit." Einar Ól. Sveinsson 1954, 259.

106. "hon boðaði Þangbrandi heiðni ok talaði lengi fyrir honum . . . " Einar Ól. Sveinsson 1954, 265.

107. Cf. the remark by Reu 1998, 14, that "the old forms were given new content: the numerous saints could to a large extent take over the functions of the pagan gods and demigods; relics were used as amulets; some Christian prayers and the sign of the cross served henceforth as formulas to ward off evil, while Christian festivals were by preference celebrated on the same days as earlier pagan feasts."

108. Sentiments along these lines are most famously associated with Pope Gregory's

instructions to Saint Augustine as reported in Bede's *Historia ecclesiastica gentis Anglorum* (chap. 27). On pagan survivals in the Christian calendar in the Middle Ages, see Russell 1972, 50–52. Largely concerned with this phenomenon of Christian interpretations of pagan ritual and magic is Flint 1991, 254–328.

109. English "conversion" ultimately derives from Latin *convertere* 'to turn around', Old Icelandic *réttsnúning* from *réttr* 'law, right, due' and *snúa* 'to turn', *siðaskipti* from *siðr* 'custom, habit, conduct, faith' and *skipta* 'to shift, change', and Old Swedish *umvändilse* and Old Danish *omwendelse* from *vända* 'to turn'. Other terms, such as Nynorsk *truskifte* and Bokmål *trosskifte* are similarly constructed.

110. "Um daginn eptir gengu hvárirtveggju til lǫgbergs, ok nefndu hvárir vátta, kristnir menn ok heiðnir, ok sǫgðusk hvárir ór lǫgum annarra . . . " Einar Ól. Sveinsson 1954, 271.

111. "Þorgeirr lá svá dag allan, at hann breiddi feld á hǫfuð sér, ok mælti engi maðr við hann." Einar Ól. Sveinsson 1954, 271. This literary presentation of Iceland's conversion has been remarked on many times; see the evaluation of the oracular character of this scene in Jón Hnefill Aðalsteinsson 1978. A comprehensive and detailed consideration of the church's extension of authority into daily life in Iceland is provided in Orri Vésteinsson 2000.

112. "skal fjǫrbaugssǫk á vera, ef víst verðr, en ef leynliga er með farit, þá skal vera vítislaust." Einar Ól. Sveinsson 1954, 272.

113. Cf. the wording in Ari's *Íslendingabók*, which after detailing a similar list of customs to be abandoned, reads, "Skyldu menn blóta á laun, ef vildu, en varða fjǫrbaugsgarðr, ef váttum of kvæmi við. En síðarr fám vetrum vas sú heiðni af numin sem ǫnnur." Jakob Benediktsson 1968, 17.

114. "I kult og sed og forestillingsverden var det broer mellom det gamle og det nye." Molland 1982b, 707.

115. Cf. Byock 1990 and Mitchell 1996, 7–8.

116. As noted earlier, this debate has a long and important place in discussions of Nordic cultural history. In addition to the works cited earlier, see the reviews in Ström 1969 and Sigurður Líndal 1974, 239–88, as well as Jakob Benediktsson 1974, 192–96; Foote 1984; Boyer 1975; and Hultgård 1992. For broader European considerations of the possibilities and problems, see, e.g., Karras 1986; Jolly 1996; the articles in Milis 1998; and the enthusiastic (but also thought-provoking) assessments in Jones and Pennick 1995.

117. See Berner 2001, 502–4.

118. For an excellent examination of the consequences of the conversion for Icelandic intellectual and spiritual life, see Gísli Sigurðsson 2002 (trans. 2004).

119. "Helgi var blandinn mjǫk í trú; hann trúði á Krist, en hét á Þór til sjófara ok harðræða." Jakob Benediktsson 1968, 250. *Landnámabók* exists in five redactions and occupies a critical position with regard to Icelandic history and historiography. For an orientation, see Jakob Benediktsson 1982a, and for a detailed analysis, see Jakob Benediktsson 1968, l–cliv.

120. "þá spurði Hrólfr son hans, hvárt Helgi mundi halda í Dumbshaf, ef Þórr vísaði

honum þangat . . . " Jakob Benediktsson 1968, 250. The fact that Helgi later puts ashore two swine, which multiply greatly, might imply a connection with the Vanir gods as well, although the section on Helgi concludes by saying that he believed in Christ and called his homestead after him (252).

121. "ok heldu þeir sumir vel kristni til dauðadags. En þat gekk óvíða í ættir, því at synir þeira sumra reistu hof ok blótuðu, en land var alheiðit nær hundraði vetra." Jakob Benediktsson 1968, 396.

CHAPTER 2

1. Malinowski 1948, 17. Other prominent contributors to this discussion include Edward Tylor and James Frazer, whose *The Golden Bough* (Frazer 1890, and many subsequent revisions, esp. Frazer 1915) was deeply influential in formulating the nontheological study of religion. The change of subtitle from *A Study in Comparative Religion* to *A Study in Magic and Religion* suggests Frazer's growing recognition of the important place of magic in such a study.

2. Cf. Brown 1991; Cournoyer and Malcolm 2004. For a survey of earlier literature, see the review in Kearney 1975.

3. This phrase is widely associated with Wax and Wax 1962, 183, who summarize the essence of the argument by noting, "It is we who accept the possibility and logic of pure chance, while for the dweller in the magical world, no event is 'accidental' or 'random,' but each has its chain of causation in which Power, or its lack, was the decisive agency."

4. Providing an adequate translation for the prefix *van-* can be elusive: 'lacking' and 'under' (as in Zoëga 1975) are close. Cf. Hellqvist 1957, "prefix med upphävande el. förringande betyd. av samma slag som ty. *miss-*, *un-*, *ver-* . . . " The same can be said of *vid-* in Old Swedish *vidskipilse* 'superstition', of which Hellqvist notes, "i pejorativ betyd., ungef. likbetyd, med van-i t. ex. vantro . . . "

5. "þe samu forgiærningær mæþ hænni . . . " Schlyter 1822–77, 3:149–50; "mæth troldoom . . . " Brøndum-Nielsen, Jørgensen, and Buus 1920–42, 2:1, 506.

6. "spám ne golldrum ne gerningum illum . . . " Keyser and Munch 1846–95, 1:17. The translation is from Larson 1935, 56.

7. "trollriðu. spadomar. oc trua at landuetter se i londum. haughum æða forsom. Sua oc utisættur at spyria forlagha . . . " Keyser and Munch 1846–95, 2:326–27.

8. See, e.g., Mitchell 2009a.

9. "En þat ol skal signa til krist þacca. ok sancta Mariu. til árs. oc til friðar." Keyser and Munch 1846–95, 1:6. Cf. Molland 1982b, 707–8. On the Norwegian setting of this practice and its broader legacy, see Nordland 1969, 11–12, 56–61, 138–42, and 266–73; and Nordland 1982. On a similar accommodation of old customs to the new religion, see Granlund 1982; Thunæus 1968. The phrase "for abundant harvests and peace" appears frequently in both the Old Norwegian and Old Swedish laws; see the entries cited in Ström 1982.

10. "ok ahann er gott at heita til ars ok friþar." Finnur Jónsson 1931, 31.

11. "ok Freys full til árs ok friðar." Bjarni Aðalbjarnarson 1962, 168. The same phrase appears in *Ólafs saga Tryggvasonar*. Bjarni Aðalbjarnarson 1962, 316. Cf. Celander 1955 and Árni Björnsson 1961.

12. In using "cultural loan shift," I am building on "loan shift," a "makeshift expression," as Einar Haugen called his sociolinguistic neologism, meant to describe the fact that "they appear in the borrowing language only as functionalist shifts of native morphemes." Haugen 1950, 215. On the various forms of syncretism, see Berner 2001, as well as the discussion in Chapter 1. Religious syncretism has been at the center of a lively debate, ably portrayed in the essays in Stewart and Shaw 1994, as well as in the editors' introduction, pp. 1–26. Although Jolly (1996, 11–12, 102–3) intends the concept more expansively than syncretism alone (and to an extent subsumes it), her notion of "middle practices" has obvious relevance here.

13. Normalized as *Þor wigi þæssi kumbl* (the Virring stone, DR 110), Jacobsen and Moltke 1941–42, cols. 147–48. Here and throughout, see also Elmevik and Peterson 1993–. On the phenomenon of the so-called Thor-påkaldelser, see Jacobsen and Moltke 1941–42, col. 1012.

14. Normalized as *Þor wigi runaR* (the Sønder Kirkeby stone, DR 220), Jacobsen and Moltke 1941–42, cols. 269–71.

15. Normalized as *Mikael gæti and hans* (the Ängby stone, U 478), Wessén and Jansson 1940, 2:2, 297–99.

16. Normalized as *guð gæti hans ok hinn helga mær*. See Olsen and Liestøl 1957, 181–82, and Elmevik and Peterson 1993– for N 368 M.

17. *Guð gæti þess er mik berr(?) ok(?) . . .* See Elmevik and Peterson 1993– for N A323 M.

18. *Þorr gæti hans . . .* See Elmevik and Peterson 1993– for Öl 52. This inscription comes from the Öland "fish amulet," the subject of much debate, although about this particular phrase there is general agreement. See Nilsson 1976; Westlund 1989; Grønvik 1992; and Louis-Jensen 2001; as well as Fuglesang 1989; cf. Lindquist and Holm 1987, although Lindquist's reading has not met with widespread approbation.

19. Butler 1998, 3.

20. "Nu ef blot er funnit i husi laslausu, matblot. eda læirblót gort i mannzliki. af læiri. eda deigi . . ." Keyser and Munch 1846–95, 1:383.

21. Lundén 1981, facsimile leaf 83 (unnumbered) of Bartholomeus Ghotan's 1487 edition, one of Sweden's oldest printed books. The Swedish translation is on p. 95. Offerings of wax, a much sought-after commodity, are frequent in Nordic miracle collections.

22. Cf. Peters 1978, esp. 110–12, and Flint 1991, which is devoted to perceptions of beneficial and harmful magic in the early medieval period. Protective amulets were likely to have caused only small alarm among the authorities; see Flint 1991, 243–48.

23. "Contra elphos hoc in plumbo scribe." See Gjerløw 1982, 430.

24. "Huru christus hiudhir fordärua aff rikeno ok landino trolkonor ok lifkonor ok spakonor älla spamän som plägha suika siälana mz tholke diäfulzlike konst ok giua sik diäflenom for värlz thing." Klemming 1857–84, 3:395. Cf. "Christus grauiter reprehendit

hic credentes spiritui phitonis predicenti futura, quia hoc operatur dyabolus ex subtilitate nature permissione Dei propter infidelitatem et cupiditatem hominum." Bergh, Aili, Jönsson, and Undhagen 1967–98, 6:243. Regarding the "herb, medicine woman," several scenes in medieval Nordic literature show women as healers (e.g., *Óláfs saga helga* [Bjarni Aðalbjarnarson 1979, 391–93]), but typically the appellation in such instances is *læknari*, *læknir* 'physician'. *Lyf* suggests both medicine and witchcraft (e.g., "kraftig Middel, der benyttes til et eller andet Øiemed saasom Lægedom, Troldom" [Fritzner 1973, 2:575]; cf. *læknislyf* 'a medicine'). The term is frequently found in collocations that imply that its association, or perhaps its contrast, with witchcraft was common (e.g., ecclesiastical laws [Keyser and Munch 1846–95, 3:285–86], sermons [Eiríkur Jónsson and Finnur Jónsson 1892–94, 168]). Thus one sermon describes a woman stricken with epilepsy: "*ok* enga læcning lyf *eða* galldra cvað hon sér at hialpum verða." Indrebø 1931, 123.

25. Among historical examples of such confessions: e.g., in a Norwegian case from 1324–25, a woman says she has learned a curse from a man (Unger and Huitfeldt 1847–, 9:114); in a Swedish case from 1490, a woman says she has learned a charm from another woman (Carlsson 1921–44, 418). The Icelandic sagas brim with representations of witchcraft being learned by younger people from more seasoned practitioners: e.g., Gunnhildr's apprenticeship with the Sámi in *Haralds saga ins hárfagra* (Bjarni Aðalbjarnarson 1962, 135), Busla's offer to teach magic to Bósi in *Bósa saga ok Herrauðs* (Rafn 1829–30, 3:195–96); Gunnlaugr's visits with Geirríðr in *Eyrbyggja saga* (Einar Ól. Sveinsson and Matthías Þórðarson 1957, 28). See Mitchell 2003c.

26. Gummerus 1902, 30–31; Stephens and Dahlgren 1847–74, 1:165; and Unger 1874, 531, 525. I infer a reference to grimoires (and other magical writings) from the Arboga statue's rejection of "quascunque litteras et scripturas cum characteribus et vocabulorum ignotorum in sacra scriptura non expressorum inscripcionibus" (30). Although I do not maintain the distinctions often clustered around the ideals of high and low magic, I do occasionally, as in this instance, refer to the dichotomy—this choice is not intended to gainsay the excellent work of other scholars in keeping this categorization in plain view, but on the whole, I find myself agreeing with Peters 1978, 166–70, with respect to these questions.

27. Cf. the older reviews in, e.g., Lehmann 1920, 1:185–219, and more recent treatments, such as Peters 1978, 63–84, 110–37; and Kieckhefer 1997, 1–21.

28. Cf. Kieckhefer 1997, 1.

29. Guðrún Ása Grímsdóttir 1998, 445–47. *Index Exemplorum* lists this episode as no. 737: "A student caused a storm when he read his master's book of magic. When the master returned and read a chapter in the book of equal length, the storm ceased. [*Islendsk Æventyri*] #23," but this description in Tubach 1969 hardly gives a full impression of this variation of the popular "Sorcerer's Apprentice" story, which is evidently a multiform of AT 325* *Apprentice and Ghost* (Aarne and Thompson 1961). The essence of the story is at least as old as the *Philopseudes* of Lucian (AD 125–80) but is no doubt best-known to modern audiences through Goethe's poem, *Der Zauberlehrling*, which was taken up a century later in *L'apprenti sorcier* by Paul Dukas. That work was in turn made famous in Walt Disney's animated sequence in *Fantasia* (1940).

30. E.g., Thorkelin 1781, 118. This same idea is at the heart of the well-known international story, *Escape from the Black School* (ML 3000 in Christiansen 1958; cf. the post-medieval Icelandic text in Jón Árnason 1954–61, 1:469–70), aspects of which are found in connection with Sæmundr the Wise already in the older version of *Jóns saga helga* (Sigurgeir Steingrímsson, Ólafur Halldórsson, and Foote 2002, 339–43). The broad outlines of the story are already present in the medieval text, but in the later tradition, the dark character of the tale has been developed and embellished: the all-knowing astrologer as master has evolved into the devil himself, the *Svartaskóli* "Black School" is now fully articulated, and so on; at the same time, the more modern version eliminates Jón's role and considerably reconfigures the nature of Sæmundr's escape. On the legendary career of Sæmundr the Wise, see Halldór Hermannsson 1932; Turville-Petre 1953, 81–87; and Jón Hnefill Aðalsteinsson 1994; on the tradition more broadly, see Benedikz 1964 and Jón Hnefill Aðalsteinsson 1996 and the literature cited there.

31. See, e.g., Jón Árnason 1954–61, 1:473–74, 572 et passim.

32. Hødnebø 1982b, 671, notes that there are no existing pre-Reformation grimoires intended to help make contact with evil spirits, but of a tradition using various forms of sympathetic magic, there are traces. The so-called Vinje book from Telemark (published as Garstein 1993; individual charms also in Bang 1901) survives from the late fifteenth or early sixteenth century (pace Hødnebø 1982b, 672, who places it to ca. 1520; Garstein 1993 calls for a decades older date). Mostly filled with medical and religious materials, often learned, some items, such as the charms for discovering a thief or bending a woman's will, reflect precisely the issues taken up here. One of the best known early modern Scandinavian charm collections is Lindqvist 1921 (trans. as Flowers 1989).

33. See, e.g., the collections in Bang 1901; Ohrt 1917–21; Lindqvist 1921; and Matthías Viðar Sæmundsson 1996.

34. On this aspect of the Old English charms, see esp. Nelson 1984 and Stuart 1985; for a consideration of the tradition more broadly, see Jolly 1996.

35. AM 187, 8to. Såby 1886, iii, claims that the book as a whole derives from the fourteenth century but adds that it "without a doubt" goes back to an older, now lost original. Assuming, he notes, that *mæster gislebertus* (p. 86) is the thirteenth-century English physician, Gilbertus Anglicus, "have vi her en grænsebestemmelse for bogens alder." Brix 1943, 36, also dates it to the mid-1300s and associates its contents with the "common European" tradition of folk medicine, further suggesting that it may be based on a Latin original. On Nordic leechbooks, see the extensive review in Sørensen 1982.

36. "Om thu wilt widæ, om siuk man ganger undæn æller æy, Tac quinnæ melch oc drøp maglekæ i hans urinal. siunker melchæn nethær, tha dør han. flyter hun oppæ, tha lefær han." Såby 1886, 88.

37. "Om thu wildæ widæ, om quinnæ, thær barn hauer, om hun ær mæth søn æller doter, Tac eet kar mæth reent keldæ watn, oc drøp quinnæ melch thær j. flyter melchæn upa watnet, tha ær thæt søn. siunkær melchæn nethær, that ær thæt doter." Såby 1886, 96.

38. "Om thu wilt, at thiufæ tachæ æy thit fæ oc æy ransmæn oc æy ulwæ tachæ thæt, tha scrifh thætte ofæn dyrnæ træt, thær the gangæ wt: Domine, qui creasti equos, porcos,

boues, uaccas *et* oues in adiutoriu*m* ho*minu*m, crescant op*er*a tua, et defende animalia tua
de dentib*us* lupo*rum et* de manib*us* inimico*rum*. *cristus* illa ducat, *cristus* illa reducat *et* p*er*
intercessionem *sancti* eustachij defende illa de lupis *et* latronib*us, amen.*" Såby 1886, 88.

39. *thijn quinnæ* can refer to wife or to a woman (i.e., lover) more generally.

40. *barbe iouis os* 'the liquid of the barbe iouis', apparently refers to *Sempervivum tectorum*, or common houseleek (widely known as "hen and chicks").

41. "*Vt tua mulier non possit cum alio adulterari,* Om thu wilt, at thijn quinnæ tachær
æy annen man, Tac barbe iouis os, oc smør thin pintel thær m*æth,* oc lig thaghær m*æth*
thijn quinnæ. oc thær æfter, mæthæn thu leuær, tha ma hun æy annen man nytæ." Såby
1886, 94. The term here, *nytæ,* while normally indicating 'exploitation', 'use', and so on is
specifically glossed by Såby (154) for this citation as "have legemlig omgand med (oldn.
njóta)."

42. 'Against the Devil's Arrows' (*Contra sagittas dyaboli*) might refer to elf shot, or, as
I assume here, wantonness and adultery. Cf. the Middle English *Ancrene wisse* (*Anchoresses'
Guide*), and its phrase, *The echnen beoth the forme arewen of lecheries prickes,* "The eyes are
the first arrows of lechery's pricks," Hasenfratz 2000, ll. 127–34.

43. "Tac gladioli os oc blathæn af hænnæ, the høgstæ, the thær wændæs nithær
aiorthæn, oc læs pate*r* n*o*ste*r* i the stund, th[u] writher ofæn th*ær* af, oc blandæ m*æth* wijn
æller m*æth* watn oc gijf thæ*n* siukæ at drickæ m*æth* canap oc atrame*n*t oc uinella." Såby
1886, 47.

44. "Vi have i denne lægebog en god prøve på den så-kaldte munkemedisin med
dens rå empirisme, dens uvidenhed og overtro." Såby 1886, vi.

45. See Kieckhefer 1989, 9, and Bailey 2001.

46. Wegener et al. 1864, 357.

47. Munch 1860, 174. As Grand had lived outside of Denmark for several decades
when he died, this fact may not reflect directly on Nordic conditions. Still, the king's
charges against the archbishop while he was still in Denmark include the accusation that
Grand possesses a book about raising the dead, or possible necromancy in the more general sense (*liber necromanticus*). See Krarup and Norvin 1932, 170, as well as the comments
in Riising 1969, 331.

48. See Mitchell 2008c and Lindroth 1989. On the study trips that form the basis
for his belief, see esp. Lindroth 1989, 53–63, 119–26. Contra Lindroth's view, Åström
reasons that, although the topic was generally well known in Europe, it was mostly unknown in Sweden ("I Sverige däremot synes alkemin ha varit i stort sett okänd" [Åström
1995, 309). Cf. Garboe 1982, col. 576.

49. One of the most renowned medieval alchemists, John Dastin, praises the power
of elixir, saying that it should be sought by all (cf. Holmyard 1990, 151–52), but attitudes
take a negative turn when, during the rule of Pope John XXII (1316–34), a decretal is
issued condemning alchemy, insofar as it led to the production of counterfeit precious
metals. See Holmyard 1990, 148–50; cf. Ganzenmüller 1942, 329, who argues that it is
their critiques of the church, rather than the actual practice of alchemy itself, that caused
the alchemists to run afoul of the church. By the end of the fourteenth century, however,

not only are the questionable material practices of alchemy under attack, but so too are its broader goals. In 1376, the *Directorium inquisitorum* of Nicolaus Eymericus, the inquisitor in Aragon, specifically associates alchemists with other magicians who succeed through their use of demons; see Ogrinc 1980, 116–17.

50. See Segev 2001.

51. In addition to Segev 2001, see also MacLeod and Mees 2006, 134–39, 143–44, 188–90, 192–95 (on *AGLA*) and 139–40, 149–52, 189 and 198 (on *Sator* etc.); on the formulas in a general European context, see Kieckhefer 1989, 73, 85, and 159, and 77–78, respectively. *AGLA* is believed to stand for *Ata Gibor Leolam Adonai* 'Thou art mighty for ever, O Lord' in Hebrew. *Sator Arepo Tenet Opera Rotas* forms a square that can be read the same in four directions.

52. "vistnok benyttet som Trylleformular eller Amulet . . . " Unger and Huitfeldt 1847–, 12:239–40, from Hallingdal.

53. The full text on the back reads, "Sanctus sanctus sanctus dominus deus sabaoth pleni sunt celus et terra gloria tua osanna excelsis agyos ys[ter]os tetragramaton. Jesus Nazarenus rex Judeorum. benio. bio buo bio." See Unger and Huitfeldt 1847–, 7:440–41, who note, "Brevet, der uden Tvivl har været forfærdiget og benyttet i overtroisk Öiemed, er sandsynligvis solgt til Gunnulf Gunnarssön af en eller anden omreisende Munk [. . .] Brevets stærke Sammenlægning og Bogstavernes Aftrykning paa den nærmest liggende Flade af samme synes at vise, at det har været baaret som Amulet."

54. A fire in part of the city's Hanseatic wharf area in 1955 led to the unearthing of extraordinarily rich numbers of runic inscriptions; see Herteig 1959 and Liestøl 1964 for early overviews.

55. "Behold the cross of the Lord; flee, you hostile powers [. . .] Ecce crucem Domini, fugite partes adversæ [. . .]" N 248 M in Elmevik and Peterson 1993–. This statement is connected with a thirteenth-century miracle when the saint is said to have helped a possessed woman find relief.

56. See text nos. 38a, 38b, 38c, 47b, 47c, and 47d in Kroon et al. 1993, 121, 433–34.

57. "ok ef menn bundu mold ór leiði hans við mein, sulli eða sár þá batnaði skjótt." Ásdís Egilsdóttir 2002, 98. Cf. D1503.12. *Magic earth heals wounds* (Thompson 1966) and related motifs.

58. Lundén 1981, facsimile leaf 48 (unnumbered); for the Swedish translation, see pp. 67–68.

59. Cf. esp. Fröjmark 1992, 50–66.

60. Worth noting is the apparent continuity between this miracle and the story of King Óláfr the Saint and his men, who upon destroying the idol of the god Þórr, find that all manner of vermin run out of the broken image: "ok hljópu þar út myss, svá stórar sem kettir væri, ok eðlur ok ormar." Bjarni Aðalbjarnarson 1979, 189. Cf. Tubach 1969, nos. 2738, 4890.

61. "ath han hade tiänth Odhanom j vij (7) aar . . . ." Carlsson 1921–44, 2:66–67.

62. See Mitchell 2009a for a detailed discussion of this and related cases.

63. "widerthagit dyeffuolen Oden fore peninga schull." Almquist 1930, 3:18

64. In *En Swensk Cröneka*, Olaus Petri writes, "Men lijkare är thet at the haffua dyrkat honom för rijkedomar skul, at the skulle få godz och peninga noogh, Och ther aff pläghar man än nw seya, at *the tiena Odhenom, som monga peningar och rijkedomar sammanslagga*." Hesselman 1917, 11 (emphasis added): "But it is more probable that they worshipped him for the sake of riches, that they should gain wealth and money, and that's why people still say that *they serve Óðinn who amass a lot of money and riches*." A court case from Småland in 1632 relates a tradition in which people would surrender themselves to Óðinn, or the devil, in order to get money. Uppvidinge häradsrätts arkiv A Ia, Domböcker och protokoll vid ordinarie ting, volym 2, for February 6, 1632 in the Uppvidinge district (Kronobergs län), cited in Hyltén-Cavallius 1972, 1:218–19. I take this opportunity to thank Claes Westling, Landsarkivet i Vadstena, for his helpfulness in providing copies of these documents. Similarly, Petter Rudebeck describes in 1693 how Óðinn visits on Thursdays to make people rich. See Liljenroth and Liljenroth 1997, esp. 294–95.

65. See Kristensen et al. 1945, 3:170, 4:252. and 4:336, 462, as well as Geete 1907–9, 502 and 504, as well as the discussion of prayer books in the Epilogue.

66. "Lignites är en sten fagher som glas hängis han pa halsen aff barnom, them beskermar före trölkärlingom . . . " Geete 1913–15, 480; cf. the similar entries on pp. 457, 459, 461, 466, 468, and 474. Månsson occasionally cites stones and gems that are useful in "the black arts," as he writes at one point ("Anancithidus är en sten til swarthakonstena tyänar at kalla diäffla . . . " Geete 1913–15, 462). See also 470–71, 472, 476, and 490.

67. "Jtem tak gallan aff eno*m* fisk so*m* hethe*r* saringina oc läth j ena bysso so*m* giord är aff ene trä, oc tha tw gaar j sängh, läg pa glödhe*r*na aff the*m* gallano*m*, oc the*n* röken fördriffw*er* alla*n* tröldom oc dyäffwulskap aff the hwseno, Jtem gallen aff eno*m* swarto*m* hwnd lwktar swa mykith illa ath han fördriffwer diäfwllen borth aff hwseno, oc hwar han stänkes vm hwsith kan jnge*n* troldom haffwa makth . . . " Klemming 1883, 438.

68. Cf. Næshagen 2000, 315, after a review of medieval Norwegian edifying literature, opines that among medieval Norwegians "a moderate religiosity in the sense of both inclination to magic and feelings of spiritual transcendence seems a reasonable conclusion."

69. Medieval theologians such as Thomas Aquinas regarded a miracle in strict terms, arguing that it must (1) consist of an extraordinary event that transcends the normal order of nature, (2) be perceptible to the senses, and (3), most important, be produced by the interventions of God in a religious context (cf. Cross and Livingston 1997, 1091).

70. Flint 1991, 33; see also her comments cited in Chapter 1 regarding *veneficia*, *maleficia*, and *malefici* versus *mira* and *miracula*. On theories of "wonder," see Bynum 1997.

71. "Margir gengu þeir heilir af hans fundi, þá er hann veitti þeim blezan ok yfirsǫngva, er með ýmsum meinum kómu á hans fund. Mart bar þat annat honum til handa er margir virðu þá þegar til jarteina. Sá atburðr varð þá er hann var þar staddr at eldr kom í hús, en þá er Þorlákr kom til ok bleizaði þá slokknaði eldrinn. Ef fénaðr sýkðisk, þá batnaði ávallt við hans yfirsǫngva, ef lífs var auðit," etc. Ásdís Egilsdóttir 2002, 60–61. On Bishop Þorlákr, including a translation of this passage (pp. 266–67), see Wolf 2008.

72. "Nw äru mange män oc qvinnor som leta raadh aff forbannadhom trolkonom ok gallirkonum, stundom ther til at the maghin afla barn oc födha Somlike at the maghin faa thäs meere älskogha oc hiärtelikin kärlek aff nokrom mannom ok qvinnom Somlike at the maghin faa vita kommaskolande thing Somlike at the maghin faa helbrygdho aff sinom siukdom Thy alle the som tholik thing göra älla nakra andra galdra älla troldoma oc the som halla oc hysa tholka j sinom husom älla tro thom äru hatughe ok forbannadhe . . ." Klemming 1857–84, 3:293–93.

73. "Romance" as used here includes desire and a wide range of often coerced sexual activities, as well as magically induced sexual dysfunction.

74. E.g., Klemming 1857–84, 3:292–93. An explicit example in *Hauksbók* condemns whoredom, illegitimate births, diabolism, and witchcraft, including a reference to women who employ aphrodisiacs on men "that they should then love them well" ("En þer ero sumar konor er gera drycki oc gefa gilmonnum sinum. til þess at þær skili þa unna þeim væl" [Eiríkur Jónsson and Finnur Jónsson 1892–94, 168]).

75. On these trials, and the general problems associated with this branch of "hostile magic," see Chapter 5, and Mitchell 2000b.

76. Due its centrality in discussion of Nordic love magic, this text is taken up here, rather than in Chapter 3. Called *Fǫr Scírnis* (lit., 'Skírnir's journey') in most editions of the *Poetic edda*, the poem is also widely known as *Skírnismál*, the title I use here.

77. See Neckel and Kuhn 1983, 69–77, for the text of the poem, as well as a prose multiform in Finnur Jónsson 1931, 40–41; translations follow Hollander 1986. For interpretations of the curse, see Reichardt 1939; Harris 1975; Lönnroth 1977; Mitchell 1983; Steinsland 1991, 130–71 et passim; and Mitchell 1998, 2007b, on which some of the present remarks build. For orientations to the poem, see Harris 1985; Mitchell 1993; and von See et al. 1997.

78. Perhaps the best-known example is the *seiðstafr mikill* 'large wand' referred to in *Laxdæla saga* (chap. 76). Price 2002, 175–204, demonstrates that such objects were indeed part of the material kit of Nordic magicians. With respect to the tool Skírnir holds, Price concludes, "The *gambanteinn* thus emerges as a particularly terrible weapon, employed by the highest levels of the sorcerous hierarchy within a narrow range of sexual and violent functions" (180).

79. Hollander's (1986) generally felicitous translation may here yield something to metrical considerations. "ergi oc œði / oc óþola" might more accurately be translated as 'lechery, madness, and restlessness.'

80. "ver þú sem þistill, / sá er var þrunginn / í ǫnn ofanverða." Neckel and Kuhn 1983, 75.

81. Olsen 1909.

82. See the entry in Elmevik and Peterson 1993– for N B257 M. On the stick, see Liestøl 1964, 41–50; cf. Mitchell 1998.

83. Elmevik and Peterson 1993– provide the following translation: "I cut runes of help; I cut runes of protection; once against the elves, twice against the trolls, thrice against the ogres [. . .] against the harmful 'skag'-valkyrie, so that she never shall, though

she ever would—evil woman!—(injure) your life[. . . .] I send to you, I look at you (= cast on you with the evil eye): wolfish evil and hatefulness. May unbearable distress and 'ioluns' misery take effect on you. Never shall you sit, never shall you sleep, [. . .] (that you) love me as yourself. [Latinate magical words] and [magical words]."

84. I am here glossing the phrase *ylgjar ergi ok úpola* using the same terms as those for the comparable and linguistically equivalent section of the curse in *Skírnismál* ("ergi oc œði / oc ópola"), but note that Elmevik and Peterson 1993– translate it as 'wolfish evil and hatefulness'.

85. Other examples include the runic inscriptions at Borgund church, the ninth-century Gørlev runestone in Denmark, and the eleventh-century Ledberg runestone in Sweden, as well as the so-called *Syrpuvers* in *Bósa saga ok Herrauðs*, an Icelandic saga preserved in three fifteenth-century manuscripts. See Mitchell 1998 for a review of interpretations. For Gørlev, consult Jacobsen and Moltke 1941–42, esp. the text volume, cols. 292–94 and 812–15. The Ledberg inscription is reproduced in Brate 1911, 174–76, although Brate's interpretation runs counter to subsequent readings. For the *Buslubæn*, see Rafn 1829–30, 3:202–7. Additional monuments noted by Thompson 1978—all Norwegian—include inscriptions from Lomen, Nore, and Bergen.

86. I know of no unambiguous examples from medieval Scandinavia of women using this sort of magic outside the realm of literature, so even those instances we have may, in fact, be male fantasies.

87. On the portrayal of the Sámi in Norse sources, and especially on the question of Sámi-Norse religious exchanges, see DuBois 1999; Hermann Pálsson 1997, 1999b; Price 2002, 2004, 2008; Siikala 2002; and Tolley 1996, 2009.

88. "Þar stóð upp Snæfíðr, dóttir Svása, kvinna fríðust, ok byrlaði konungi ker fullt mjaðar, en tók allt saman ok hönd hennar, ok þegar var sem eldshiti kvæmi í hörund hans ok vildi þegar hafa hana á þeiri nótt." Bjarni Aðalbjarnarson 1962, 1:126. The translation is from Hollander 1991, 80–81.

89. "þá slær ýldu ok ópefani ok hvers kyns illum fnyk af líkamanum. Blánaði áðr allr líkaminn, ok ullu ór ormar ok eðlur, froskar ok pöddur ok alls kyns illyrmi." Bjarni Aðalbjarnarson 1962, 1:127. The translation is from Hollander 1991, 81.

90. *Rannveig *Rauðu skaltu streða* [alt., *serða*]. *Þat sé meira enn mannsreðr ok minna enn hestreðr*. This text is not taken up in Liestøl 1964, nor yet in *Norges innskrifter med de yngre runer*. The National Library's entry (available at www.nb.no/baser/runer/fullpost .php?bnr = B628 [accessed February 23, 2009], NB: N B628 M = BRM110/03490) gives the age of this four-sided stick, now in six pieces, as "before 1248" and transcribes the text as follows:

-ranniuæh rauþ(ou)sk [. . .] usirþ
-þat:semæira:in:ma(nn)s[.]æþr:ok:mi(nn)a:en
-hatræþr

See also the entry for it in Elmevik and Peterson 1993–, whose normalization and translation I follow here.

91. *Unna ek meyju(?) enn betr. Enn betr.* See Elmevik and Peterson 1993– for N A258 M. The choice of verbs also makes clear the very real differences between the different types of traditions.

92. See esp. Steinsland and Vogt 1981, as well as the survey in Simek 1993. On *Flateyjarbók*, see Rowe 2005.

93. See, e.g., Ström 1954 and Steinsland and Vogt 1981, and the literature cited there.

94. Turville-Petre argues that a key element in all such discussions, the name to which the participants pray, Mǫrnir, is attested as a sword name and thus likely to be yet another phallic reference, comparable to the other terms used, *vingull*, *beytill*, and *Vǫlsi*. See Turville-Petre 1964, 256–58.

95. "þann lim sem eftir skapan natturunnar hafua þesskyns kuikende til getnadar sem ǫnnur dyr þau sem aukazst sin a mille ok eftir þui sem fornnskalldin visa til heitir uingull a hestum." Guðbrandur Vigfússon and Unger 1860–68, 2:332.

96. E.g., *þrif þu vid Volsa* '(you) take hold of Vǫlsi'; *þrystu at þer Vǫlsa* 'thrust Vǫlsi up yourself'. Guðbrandur Vigfússon and Unger 1860–68, 2:334. This episode may be compared to the modern Faroese custom of *at senda drunn* or *irkja ivur Drunnin*, on which see Matras 1957, 1958; Coffey 1989; and Joensen 2003.

97. On this point, see Turville-Petre 1964, 256–58.

98. Cf. the difficulties Hrútr encounters under Gunnhildr's curse in *Brennu-Njáls Saga*.

99. Hermann Pálsson and Edwards 1968, 67. "Tröll ok álfar / ok töfranornir, / búar, bergrisar / brenni þínar hallir, / hati þik hrímþursar, / hestar streði þik, / stráin stangi þik, / en stormar æri þik, ok vei verði þér, / nema þú vilja minn gerir." Guðni Jónsson 1954, 3:294. It should be noted that not every manuscript shows *streða* (e.g., "hestar troði þik." Rafn 1829–30, 3:206).

100. See n. 85 above and the literature discussed there.

101. Cf. Mitchell 1998. *hǫrundfall* (cf. *sinfall* [lit., 'penis-fall']) is typically glossed as 'impotence', but the term perhaps implied a wide range of sexual dysfunctions, including frigidity. See the argument in Mundal and Steinsland 1989. On the broader medieval European context of this problem, see Brundage 1982 and Rider 2006.

102. The translation of *oc sidan þesse ord ero lesen* as 'and when these words are read', although accurate, may mask an important ambiguity. The semantic range of *lesa* is broad. It includes 'read' in the modern sense, but also 'gather', 'grasp', 'cast', 'embroider', and 'talk' (typically with a preposition in the latter sense; cf. modern English expressions of the sort. 'The book said that . . . '). Possibly *lesa* could be understood here as 'said', but based on the comparanda, 'read' seems preferable. On the larger context of this issue, see Mitchell 1991b, 92–104, and esp. Bjarni Guðnason 1977.

103. "Ritt ek i fra mer gondols ondu. æin þer i bak biti annar i briost þer biti þridi snui uppa þik hæimt oc ofund, oc sidan þesse ord ero lesen skall spyta uppa þan er till syngzst." Both records concerned with this trial are found in Unger and Huitfeldt 1847–, 9:1, 112–15. On this episode, see esp. Mitchell 1997c, 1998, 2003c, on which parts of this chapter build. On the legal aspects of this case, see Chapter 5.

104. "Jtem quod secundo die nupciarum sponsum subsannando in hec verba pro-rupit, arridet *meus mens quod genitalia Barderi ut maleficiata non plus valerent ad coi-tum quam zona ad manum meam revoluta." Unger and Huitfeldt 1847–, 9:1, 112–15.

105. "Þórveig seiddi til, at þau skyldi eigi njótask mega." Einar Ól. Sveinsson 1939, 223; the translation is from Hollander 1949, 24. A parallel motif, M443.2* *Curse: Conti-nence in marriage*, is found in *Bragða-Ǫlvis saga* (Hooper 1932, 52), preserved only in seventeenth- and eighteenth-century manuscripts. As in *Ála flekks saga*, the curse is cast at the bridal bed itself. The situation in *Bragða-Ǫlvis saga* also parallels the Bergen case of 1324–25 in that the curse is delivered by a rejected suitor who is a "witch" (*fiolkunnigr maþr*). Akin to the situation in *Kormáks saga* is T591 *Barrenness or impotence induced by magic* in *Ambales saga*, preserved in seventeenth-century manuscripts, where the witch's revenge is the primary motivation for the fact that they have no children: "hún mundi um hann til qvenn manna búid hafa." Gollancz 1898, 170–71: "she had perchance bes-pelled him with regard to women." This motif finds no place, however, in Saxo's version of the Hamlet story in books 3 and 4 of his *Gesta Danorum* and may well be a late or even postmedieval addition. Cf. T321.5 *Magic sickness (discomfort) prevents lover from raping woman* in *Ambales saga*, where Fástínus experiences the pain "heldst um þíng sín og þarma." Gollancz 1898, 42.

106. "Ef ek á svá mikit vald á þér sem ek ætla, þá legg ek þat á við þik, at þú megir engri munúð fram koma við konu þá, er þú ætlar þér á Íslandi, en fremja skalt þú mega vilja þinn við aðrar konur." Einar Ól. Sveinsson 1954, 21. The translation is from Magnus-son and Hermann Pálsson 1966, 49.

107. "Ek vilda segja skilit við Hrút, ok má ek segja þér, hverja sǫk ek má helzt gefa honum. Hann má ekki hjúskaparfar eiga við mik, svá at ek mega njóta hans, en hann er at allri náttúru sinni annarri sem inir vǫskustu menn." "Hversu má svá vera?" segir Mǫrðr, "ok seg enn gørr." Hon svarar: "Þegar hann kemr við mik, þá er hǫrund hans svá mikit, at hann má ekki eptirlæti hafa við mik, en þó hǫfum vit bæði breytni til þess á alla vega, at vit mættim njótask, en þat verðr ekki. En þó áðr vit skilim, sýnir hann þat af sér, at hann er í œði sínu rétt sem aðrir menn." Einar Ól. Sveinsson 1954, 24; the translation is from Magnusson and Hermann Pálsson 1966, 52, with my emendations. This curious passage might be explained as a scribal error, in which *svá mikit* "so large" has been written for *svá miukt* "so soft"; if correct, Njáll's would be a case of impotence. See Örn Ólafsson 2000.

108. See Brundage 1988 for a review of the competing theories about marriage con-summation and impotence, including this question.

109. On these cases, see esp. Mitchell 1998, 2000b, as well as the detailed discussions in Chapter 5 of this volume.

110. Noreen and Wennström 1935–, 1:360.

111. Carlsson 1921–44, 418. The cognomen *halffstoop* is perhaps best understood as a half-empty stoup 'font for holy water; drinking vessel' (Old Norse *staup* 'cup'), which in Swedish also implies a measure; thus she may be 'Margit half-tankard' or 'Margit half-pint', one possibility referring to her social habits, the other to her stature. The text itself

subsequently uses this name in the definite: *halffstopit*, 'the half-stoup' or 'the half-pint'. In addition to Mitchell 1998, 2000b, see Schück 1951, 434–35, and Witt 1983, 118.

112. The recurrence of cats' heads in Arboga and Stockholm is paralleled by German charm materials, including love magic; see Bächtold-Stäubli and Hoffmann-Krayer 1987, cols. 75–77 and 1115–17. At the close of the Middle Ages, Peder Månsson translates into Swedish from a Latin lapidary, the *Speculum lapidum* of Camillus Leonardis, explaining that "doriatides" is a stone found in the head of a cat, when the head is cut off and ants are allowed to eat the flesh and reveal the black stone. Significantly, "Its virtue is to help accomplish all desire" ("hans dygdh är at hiälpa til ath fwlkompna all begärilse" [Geete 1913–15, 470]). On the question of cat heads and brains and their association with magic in Old Swedish contexts, see Lidén 1933, 323, and Noreen 1941, 18–19.

113. "hljóta sumir spáleiks anda . . . " Keyser, Unger, and Munch 1848, 120.

114. By way of example, prophecy is regularly condemned in the Norwegian laws. Keyser and Munch 1846–95, 1:17, 152, 182, 265–66, 318, 350–51, 362, 372, 429–30; 2:51, 212, 307–8, 326–27, 381; 3:271; 4:18, 160 and 62–63; and 5:56. The semantic range of this term in Old Norse is explored and documented in Dillmann 2006, 30–34, a point also explored, on an international basis, in Tedlock 2001, whose typology demonstrates just how wide-ranging the notion of divination can be in different contexts.

115. In general, see the entry in Knight 2003; on medieval Scandinavia, Edsman 1982a; and on the Århus arcade, Saxtorph 1997, 256. I use the now outdated *Amt* system here, as the authoritative collection of inventories, *Danmarks Kirker*, is keyed to it.

116. Sigurgeir Steingrímsson, Ólafur Halldórsson, and Foote 2002, 61–62.

117. See also Chapter 3. The treatment of such scenes in the Icelandic sagas has been thoroughly explored in Dillmann 2006.

118. "bað hana spá nǫkkut . . ." The example used here is the portrayal of Oddbjǫrg in *Víga-Glúms saga*. Jónas Kristjánsson 1956, 41.

119. Few descriptions of magic in the Norse world have occasioned more commentary than that of Þorbjǫrg lítilvǫlva. See the discussion and literature cited in Chapter 3.

120. "Síðan gengu menn at vísindakonunni, ok frétti þá hverr þess, er mest forvitni var á at vita. Hon var ok góð af frásǫgnum; gekk þat ok lítt í tauma, er hon sagði." Einar Ól. Sveinsson and Matthías Þórðarson 1957, 208–9.

121. Klemming 1857–84, 3:395–96. This vision is in book 8, chap. 38 in Old Swedish, book 6, chap. 82 in Latin.

122. Klemming 1877–78, 5–9.

123. See Bø 1982, 131. Among the possessions of Magnus Eriksson at Båhus castle was part of serpent's tongue, an object generally held to be of magical significance. See Bø 1982, 131–32.

124. Magic stones play a major role in court cultures throughout the later Middle Ages, and certainly the Latin lapidary tradition was well known in Scandinavia (e.g., *Alfræði íslenzk* [Beckman and Kålund 1908–18, 1:40–43]; *Speculum lapidum* [Geete 1913–15, 455–98]). On the Nordic context, see Foote 1956 and esp. Foote 1982, which reviews the various texts.

125. "Men*n* sc*o*lo eigi fara me*þ* steina. e*þ*a magna *þ*a ti*l* *þ*ess at binda á menn e*þ*a a fé man*n*a. Ef me*N* trva a steina ti*l* heilindis s*er*. e*þ*a fé. oc var*þ*ar f*io*r*b*avgs Gar*þ*." Vilhjálmur Finsen 1974a, 23. The translation follows Dennis, Foote, and Perkins 1980–2000, 1:39.

126. Old Swedish *mästare* encompasses not only 'teacher', 'master', 'master craftsman', and so on but also 'a learned man' in general. The poem is published in Geete 1900, 3–8; on the manuscript, see Andersson-Schmitt and Hedlund 1991, 592–600 (596 on *Den vises sten*). Interest to date has mainly focused on Geete's brief notes on the poem's association with the ordained Vadstena monk, Sturkarus Thurgilli (but cf. Mitchell 2008c). On Sturkarus Thurgilli, see also Gejrot 1988, 171.

127. *vit oc skiel* (1⁵); *krapt oc sterke* (1⁶) in Geete 1900.

128. This artfully detailed image of the devil fits well with the era's heightened fear of a more palpable incarnation of evil, on which see Russell 1984, 208–9.

129. Most famously the stone that seals the Holy Sepulchre and later rolled back (*et accedens revolvit lapidem* in the Vulgate, Matt. 28:2) or the words of Jesus when he responds to Peter's foundational confession, saying that on "this rock" he will build his church (*et super hanc petram aedificabo ecclesiam meam* in the Vulgate, Matt. 16:18), perhaps the most thoroughly debated pericope of the Bible. And, of course, Jesus is himself referred to as a "living rock" (*lapidem vivum*), the corner- or foundation-stone of the church, "ad quem accedentes lapidem vivum ab hominibus quidem reprobatum a Deo autem electum honorificatum." 1 Pet. 2:4. See further 1 Pet. 2:6–8; cf. Isa. 28:16. Indeed, the number of stone references in the Bible is staggering, and any one of them might contribute to the central motif of this poem.

130. On this point, see the survey in Bø 1982. Of course, Icelandic saga tradition also mentions healing stones, e.g., the *lyfsteinn* of *Kormáks saga* and the *náttúrusteinn* of *Karlamagnúss saga*.

131. For a thorough survey, see Meier 1977, esp. 89–138.

132. See Mitchell 2008c for details on all these points.

133. Comprehensive surveys are provided in Bø 1982; Moltke 1938; Fuglesang 1989; MacLeod and Mees 2006; and Zeiten 1997.

134. In addition, it reads once *contra . . . malorum*. On this object, see Kiær 1982, 684.

135. On this point, see Simpson 1979 and Mitchell 1985b.

136. "Coniuro vos, septem sorores [. . .] Elffrica(?) Affricca, Soria, Affoca, Affricala. Coniuro vos et contestor per patrem et filium et spiritum sanctum, ut non noceatis [i]stam famulum Dei, neque in occulis neque in membris, neque in medullis, nec in ullo comp[ag]ine membrorum eius, ut inhabitat in te virtus Christi altissimi. Ecce crucem Domini, fugite partes adverse, vicit leo de tribu Juda, radi[x] David. In nomine patris et filii et spiritus sancti, amen. Christus vincit Christus regnat Christus imperat, Christus liberat, Christus te/et benedicit, ab om[n]i malo defendat. Agla. Pater noster." See Elmevik and Peterson 1993– for DR AARB1987, 205 M.

137. "Johannes, Marcus, Lucas, Matthias. Pax portanti! Salus [portanti!]." See Elmevik and Peterson 1993– for N A77 M.

138. "Við augum. Tobias sanat oculus istius hominis . . . Sidrak, Misak et auk Abdenago." See Elmevik and Peterson 1993– for N 633 M.

139. "Iorþ biþ ak uarþæ ok uphimæn, sol ok santæ Maria ok sialfæn Guþ drottin, þæt han læ mik læknæshand ok lif-tungæ at liuæ biuianda er bota þarf or bak ok or bryst, or likæ ok or lim, or øwæn ok or øræn, or allæ þe þær ilt kan i at kumæ. Svart hetær sten, han stær i hafæ utæ þær ligær a þe ni nouþær, þær [. . .] skulæ huærki søtæn sofæ æþ uarmæn uakæ førr æn þu þæssæ bot biþær, þær ak orþ at kæþæ ronti. Amen ok þæt se." The dating and interpretation here follow Moltke 1976, 396–400. See Elmevik and Peterson 1993– for DR EM85, 493 M, as well as MacLeod and Mees 2006, 123–24. With respect to the so-called needs, see Mitchell 2008a.

140. Hollander 1986, 39. In the original:

Þat kann ec iþ níunda,   ef mic nauðr um stendr,
  at biarga fari míno á floti:
vind ec kyrri   vági á
  oc svæfic allan sæ. (Neckel and Kuhn 1983, 43)

141. On this topic, see Ogilvie and Gísli Pálsson 2003 and Ogilvie and Gísli Pálsson 2006.

142. Einar Ól. Sveinsson and Matthías Þórðarson 1957, 109.

143. "Síðan lét Kotkell gera seiðhjall mikinn; þau fœrðusk þar á upp ǫll; þau kváðu þar harðsnúin frœði; þat váru galdrar. Því næst laust á hríð mikilli. Þat fann Þórðr Ingunnarson ok hans fǫrunautar, þar sem hann var á sæ staddr, ok til hans var gǫrt veðrit." Einar Ól. Sveinsson 1934, 99.

144. Rafn 1829–30, 2:412.

145. "Rauðr hafði jafnan byr, hvert er hann vildi sigla, ok var þat af fjǫlkyngi hans." Bjarni Aðalbjarnarson 1962, 325.

146. Elmevik and Peterson 1993–, U AST1, 166 M. Cf. MacLeod and Mees 2006, 121–22.

147. "Ef menn váru staddir á sjó eða á landi, í hvers konar háska sem váru, þá fengu skjóta bót sinna vandræða þegar hétu á hann, svá at vindr lægðusk en sjór kyrrðisk, eldsgangr slokknaði, vǫtn minnkaði, hríðir fellu . . . " Ásdís Egilsdóttir 2002, 98.

148. See Elmevik and Peterson 1993– for N B241 M.

149. This and other uses of the pagan gods in runic inscriptions from Bergen are addressed in Knirk 1995. Cf. the survey of such cases in Lassen 2006, who has a more restricted view of their utility.

150. This case is not unique, and use of pagan gods in charms continues into the early modern period, as in the case of the so-called fart charm from an Icelandic grimoire, or *galdrabók*. It invokes a host of powerful spirits, Judeo-Christian, learned, pagan, and so on, at its conclusion: "i dinu Mechtigste Naffne Herre Guð Ande wercke(re) Oden tor frelssere Freg Frege Oper Satan Belsebub med hielpere till storrkende Guð wernd med Filgere Uteo(s) Morss (N)okte vitales." Lindqvist 1921, 74, translated in Flowers 1989, 79–80: "In your mightiest name Lord God, Spirit (?), Creator, Óðinn, Þórr, Savior, Freyr,

Freyja, Oper, Satan, Beelzebub, Helpers, Mighty God, you who protect your followers, Uteos, Morss, Noht, Vital."

151. "I exhort you, Óðinn, with heathenism, greatest among devils. Agree to it. Tell me the name of the man who stole. For Christianity. Tell me now (your) evil deed. One I scorn, (the second) I scorn. Tell me, Óðinn! Now (multitudes of devils?) are called forth with all (heathenism). You shall now acquire for me the name of the one who stole. (Amen)." My translation, following Elmevik and Peterson 1993–; Knirk 1995; and Mac-Leod and Mees 2006, 31–32.

152. *galdra ok somlik diäfwlzlik ordh* . . . Klemming 1857–84, 3:196.

153. "Ef maþr ferr með galldra eþa gørningar. eþa fiolkýngi. þa ferr hann með fiol-kyngi. ef hann queðr þat eþa kennir. eþa lætr queða. at ser eþa at fe sinv. þat varþar honvm *fiorbavgs Garþ*. [. . .] Ef maþr ferr með fordæs skap. þat varþar *scogGang*. þat ero fordæs skapir. ef maþr gérir i orðvm sinvm. eþa fiolkyngi sott eþa bana. fe eþa mavnnvm." Vilhjálmur Finsen 1974a, 23. The translation is from Dennis, Foote, and Perkins 1980–2000, 1:39.

154. In Indo-European languages, that which can be done, that is, the ability of a witch to accomplish certain deeds as an exercise of power, often forms the basis for the vocabulary. Cf. Buck 1988, 1495, 1496, and 1498. In the Nordic context, this pattern accounts for many words for those who practice magic, male and female; typically built on *dáð* 'deed' or *gerning* 'act, doing, deed' (> *gerningar* 'witchcraft'), these terms are among the most negatively charged in the entire lexicon (e.g., *fordæðumaðr, gerningakarl, gerningamaðr, gerningavættr, fordæða, gerningakona, gerningavíf*). In addition to those who practice magic, the terms may also indicate the results of such witchcraft; e.g., *gerningahríð* and *gerningaveðr* 'storm raised by witchcraft'; *gerningasótt* 'sickness caused by sorcery'.

155. Storm 1888, 288–89.

156. Unger and Huitfeldt 1847–, 9:1, 112–15; Carlsson 1921–44, 418.

157. "ok mun ek láta þat um líða at skrifa hann, því at þat er öllum þarfleysa at hafa hann eptir, en þó má svá sízt eptir hafa hann, at hann sé eigi skrifaðr. En þó er þetta þar upphaf á . . . " Guðni Jónsson 1954, 3:294.

158. The term in the text is *þula*, which is often glossed as 'rhapsody', 'rote', and 'rigamarole', but cf. its connection to *þulr*. De Vries 1961, 82 (and *þylja* 'to chant'?).

159. Sigurður Nordal 1979, 171, but also all of chap. 57.

160. The phrasing here, "Síðan veitti hann formála . . . ," may harbor directly performative components, with *veita* understood in that specific sense (cf. Fritzner 1973, 3:898, "8) gjøre, forrette, udføre noget").

161. The Icelandic law code, e.g., remarks, "en þat er níð ef maðr skerr tréníð manni eðr rístr eða reisir manni níðstöng . . . " (Grág. i. 147, cited after Cleasby and Vigfusson 1982, 455); on *snúa*, see Mitchell 1998, 2003c. With respect to Egill's curse in its European context, I note, e.g., that it follows the structure outlined in Bozóky 2003 (e.g., conjuration, naming of the adjuvant powers, actualization, dramatization).

162. Cf. Mitchell 2002a.

163. So, e.g., Lönnroth 1971, 1978; Bauman 1986, 1992; Harris 2000a, 2000b, 2003;

and Mitchell 2002a. It is critical to note that "performance," as it is intended here, has little to do with the desiccating Freeprose-Bookprose debate that long dominated Old Norse studies, on which, see my remarks in Mitchell 2003d. My comments here are based on the detailed presentation in Mitchell 2007b.

164. Milman Parry, the iconic figure in the field of oral poetics, phrased this central question as follows: "My Homeric studies have from the beginning shown me that Homeric poetry, and indeed all early Greek poetry, is oral, and so can be properly understood, criticized, and edited only when we have a complete knowledge of the processes of oral poetry; this is also true for other early poetries such as Anglo-Saxon, French, or Norse, to the extent they are oral. This knowledge of the processes of an oral poetry can be had up to a certain point by the study of the character of a style, e.g., of the Homeric poems; but a full knowledge can be had only by the accumulation from a living poetry of a body of experimental texts. . . . " Quoted in Mitchell and Nagy 2000, ix.

165. Performance theory as formulated in, e.g., Bauman 1975. As one scholar has expressed the impact of this view, "Attention to the formal attributes of verbal art and its essence as live performance has revivified the study of ethnographic *and ancient texts*, as scholars recognize poetic structuring and dramatic action in texts formerly conceived of as *only* prose narratives." Sawin 1998, 498 (emphases added). On *Skírnismál*, performance, and staging, see also Gunnell 1995; cf. Gunnell 1993.

166. Reichardt regards the curse as an interpolation but views the curse itself as an authentic example of Nordic "love magic": "die Liebesbeschwörung unseres Liedes ein Stück magischer Poesie aus altnordischer Zeit darstellt, welches sehr wohl verwendet worden sein kann, um einen Liebeszauber an einer Frau realiter durchzuführen." Reichardt 1939, 484.

167. Cf. Larrington 1992 and Heinrichs 1997.

168. Verbs indicating acts connected with written texts are notoriously equivocal, as they are in English, e.g., "It *says* in the newspaper that . . . " On such verbs as *lesa* and *heyra* (and their possible synonymy), see Bjarni Guðnason 1977.

169. On this point, see Brink 2005. Commenting on nonelite and elite cultural spheres, Brink notes, "For hundreds of years (c. 1100–1350) the two cultures lived side by side in Scandinavia, the oral culture with runic carvings for visual messages and the *thing* assembly as the focus and fundamental social arena, and the literacy culture with the Latin script for visual messages and documentation, and the church as focus and fundamental social arena" (118). Cf. Lord 1991.

170. Keyser and Munch 1846–95, 1:57. Fritzner 1973, 3:719 specifies that *treníð* refers to raising a *níðstǫng*, but it can also refer to the slander that comes in the form of some sculpted defamation, such as famously occurs in *Gísla saga Súrssonar*; see also n. 161 above. On all aspects of *níð* and versified magic, see Almqvist 1965. For an excellent recent discussion of the various types of insults, *ýki* as well as *níð*, see Finlay 2001.

171. A substantial literature exists on this and similar phrases, on which, see Mitchell 2003b; an important recent dissertation, Heide 2006, has taken up the complex as a whole. There exist some very near analogues to the wording of Ragnhildr's curse; see

Björn K. Þórólfsson and Guðni Jónsson 1972, 243; Ásdís Egilsdóttir 2002, 266; Einar Ól. Sveinsson 1954, 447; and Finnbogi Guðmundsson 1980, 91–92.

172. "En ef fordædoskapr verdr funnin i bædium eda bulstrum manna har eda nægl eda frauda fötr. eda adrer þæir lutir e[r] uenir þickia til gærninga. þa ma sok gefa." Keyser and Munch 1846–95, 1:362. The text has *en* here, but all other comparable statutes (e.g., Keyser and Munch 1846–95, 1:350–51, 1:372, and 4:62–63) show *er*.

173. See my comments in this regard in Mitchell 2007b.

174. Cleasby and Vigfusson 1982, 187, note "prop. a song [. . .] but almost always with the notion of a *charm* or *spell*." Similarly, Fritzner 1973, 1:540, says of it in this sense, "Sang, især Tryllesang, Trolddomsformular," adding "hvad der gjøres til eller anvendes som Trolddomsmiddel."

CHAPTER 3

1. By "literature" in this instance, I refer primarily to the Old Icelandic sagas and eddas, but I consider a wide range of narrative materials, not only those that map easily onto modern literary genres.

2. Remnants of pagan superstitions are, of course, found in other traditions (e.g., Anglo-Saxon poetry), but commenting on recently converted cultures, several authorities have noted the relative paucity of such materials. Thus, e.g., Hen 1995, 206, concludes, "Merovingian society, although recently converted, was clearly a Christian society after all, and the so-called 'pagan survivals' and 'superstitions' can be acknowledged as an insignificant and marginal part of its culture." Similarly, Filotas 2005, 359, after canvassing the evidence of pastoral writings from AD 500 to 1000, estimates that some two thousand passages survive that relate to pagan survivals and superstitions, concluding, "This is not much, considering the extent of time and expanse of space covered: over 500 years and most of Western Europe."

3. For an English-language orientation to *Fornsvenska legendariet*, see Mitchell 1996, 15–16; on Saint Erik, see the commentary and translation in Sands 2006.

4. The original work dates to between 1267 and 1307, but the term *Fornsvenska legendariet* covers a number of related texts. For recent assessments, see Carlquist 1996 and Haugen and Johansson 2009, 20–23. Still very useful, despite their age, are Schück 1884 and the comprehensive examination in Jansson 1934.

5. See, e.g., Andersson 1964. We think first and foremost of the Icelandic sagas in this regard, but such texts as Saxo's *Gesta Danorum* and the Old Swedish rhymed chronicles also figure in the construction of postmedieval pseudohistories. On the latter, see Jansson 1971 and Mitchell 1996.

6. Hermann 2009, who examines the kinds of memory available and in evidence in the Icelandic context and how memory factors into writing. Cf. Clunies Ross 1998, 83–85, including her view that in medieval Icelandic literature the past and the present form a "meaningful and coherent historical continuum" (85).

7. Jochens 1980, 378. Cf. the similar sentiments in Einar Ól. Sveinsson 1937–38, esp. 78–79.

8. Cf. Mitchell 1985a and 1991b, 114–36.

9. Davidson 1979, 5–6; Friis-Jensen 2005b, 1:74, 76 (*praefatio*, 1, 4).

10. Strictly speaking, this title refers only to the poems in a single Icelandic manuscript, the Codex Regius of the Elder Edda (Gks 2365, 4to). Over time, similar poems have been added to the canon, so that, as Gunnell 2005, 82, writes, "The term 'eddic poetry' essentially covers those anonymously transmitted 'poems' [. . .] that deal with the myths and heroic world of the Nordic countries. . . . " Among these additional poems, particularly important in the current context are *Baldrs draumar* (*Baldr's Dreams*, also called *Vegtamskviða* [*Lay of Vegtamr*]) and the poems known together as *Svipdagsmál* (*Words of Svipdagr*), that is, the *Grógaldr* (*Magic of Gróa*), and *Fjǫlsvinnsmál* (*Words of Fjǫlsvinnr*), perhaps also *Hrafnagaldur Óðins* (*Óðinn's Raven-magic*). Based on recently acquired manuscript testimony, Lassen (forthcoming) argues (pace earlier conclusions) that the poem represents an antiquarian enterprise built on such well-known sources as *Snorra edda*, rather the fourteenth-century text for which it has sometimes been taken.

11. For an orientation to the eddic materials, see Gunnell 2005, as well as the detailed reviews of scholarship in Harris 1985 and Lindow 1985. For an expansive annotated bibliography, see Lindow 1988.

12. A point famously pursued by many scholars. Thus, e.g., a poem like *Þrymsqviða* (*The Lay of Þrymr*) can be understood as Christian propaganda in which the principal protective god of the pagan pantheon, Þórr, is mocked by his dressing up like a bride. In his comprehensive study of the poem, de Vries 1928 concludes that the poem was composed in the thirteenth century. On dating the poems, see the comprehensive review in Fidjestøl 1999.

13. On this point, and on the reception and use of these mythological materials throughout the entire medieval period, see Clunies Ross 1998, esp. 22–43.

14. So, e.g., a work such as the *Sólarljóð* (*Song of the Sun*), on which, see Attwood 2005, 61–62, and Amory 1993.

15. On modern scholarship's predilection for creating its own smooth version of the materials bequeathed to us by capriciously uneven preservation, see the enlightening and intellectually pugnacious comments in Leach 1982.

16. Given its heterogeneity, *Hávamál* has occasioned much debate, ranging from those who, like Lindquist 1956, would reassemble the "original" poem, to von See 1981, who sees an explicitly learned background to the poem (cf. von See 1972). Very useful for its attempt to place *Hávamál* in the context of similar "wisdom poetry," such as *Grógaldr*, is de Vries 1934.

17. St. 139–41, Neckel and Kuhn 1983, 40. This episode has frequently excited the question of Óðinn's relationship to *seiðr* and shamanism as elements of pre-Christian religion in the Nordic world. An extensive secondary literature has developed on this topic, reviewed in meticulous detail in Price 2002, 76–91. In addition to Price 2002 (also Price 2001, 2004), see esp. Tolley 1994, 1996, 2009, as well as the work of earlier scholars

(e.g., Pipping 1928; Strömbäck 1935; Davidson 1943, 1964; and Buchholz 1968, 1971). Cautious perspectives (Tolley, for one, is by no means convinced of the comparison's full applicability) come from among others, Georges Dumézil (1970), whose thesis about the Indo-European heritage of Norse mythology is clearly at risk in such a context. Perhaps the most assertive rejection of the shamanic comparison comes from Fleck (1971a, 1971b), who, based on a formal definition of "shamanism," argues that none existed in Germanic tradition. The work of Jens Peter Schjødt (e.g., Schjødt 2001, 2008) is very helpful in sorting out these conflicting views: with his source-critical perspective, he cautiously analyzes the materials and, although he allows for the possibility of shamanic influence, principally sees in these instances the numinous results of initiation. Thus, e.g., regarding the wisdom features of *Vǫluspá* and *Baldrs draumar*, he writes, "It can be seen that they are both variants of a structure and an imaginative world that has deep roots in pagan thought processes, in a way of thinking that is fundamentally foreign to Christianity, with its relationship between the living and the dead, with its emphasis on the feminine as a source of knowledge and its insistence upon Óðinn himself needing to acquire knowledge from dead women" (Schjødt 2008, 223–24).

18. St. 28, Neckel and Kuhn 1983, 7.

19. For an orientation to the so-called *Prose edda* of Snorri Sturluson, see Faulkes 1993; Schier 1977; and, situated in Snorri's biography, Ciklamini 1978. With regard to Snorri's knowledge and use of, and attitude toward, the heathen past, see Baetke 1950; Holtsmark 1964; Faulkes 1983; Clunies Ross 1994, 85–102 and 1998.

20. *Seið Yg*r til Rindar, Finnur Jónsson 1931, 166. Here Snorri is citing Kormákr's *Sigurðardrápa*, a poem thought to have been composed in the mid-tenth century.

21. On all aspects of this myth, interested readers should consult the thorough analysis and bibliographic treatment in Lindow 1997. See also McKinnell 2005, 157–62.

22. Neckel and Kuhn 1983, 277–79. Included in all modern editions of the edda, the poem is preserved in AM 748, 4to.

23. Þá reið Óðinn   fyr austan dyrr,
    þar er hann vissi   vǫlo leiði;
    nam hann vittugri   valgaldr qveða,
    unz nauðig reis,   nás orð um qvað: (Neckel and Kuhn 1983, 277)

24. "Þegiattu, vǫlva! / þic vil ec fregna," the opening lines of st. 8, 10, and 12. Cf. 1 Sam. 28 and its presentation of the dead prophet as a raised *draugr* foretelling the future.

25. Davidson 1979, 76. "At Othinus, quamquam deorum precipuus haberetur, diuinos tamen et aruspices ceterosque, quos exquisitis prescientie studiis uigere compererat, super exequenda filii ultione sollicitat." Friis-Jensen 2005b, 1:204 (3:4, 1).

26. Davidson 1979, 77; Friis-Jensen 2005b, 1:206 (3:4, 4).

27. "kendu íþróttir þær, er menn hafa lengi síðan með farit," and "hefir þaðan af dreifzk fjǫlkynngin víða ok haldizk lengi." Bjarni Aðalbjarnarson 1962, 17, 19–20.

28. "Óðinn skipti hǫmum. Lá þá búkrinn sem sofinn eða dauðr, en hann var þá fugl eða dýr, fiskr eða ormr, ok fór á einni svipstund á fjarlæg lǫnd at sínum ørendum eða annarra manna." Bjarni Aðalbjarnarson 1962, 18.

29. "Þat kunni hann enn at gera með orðum einum at sløkkva eld ok kyrra sjá ok snúa vindum hverja leið er hann vildi . . . " Bjarni Aðalbjarnarson 1962, 18.

30. "með rúnum ok ljóðum þeim, er galdrar heita." Bjarni Aðalbjarnarson 1962, 19. I have translated *galdrar* in its sense as 'charms' or 'magic songs' here, but note that the term, esp. when in the plural, could simply be glossed as 'witchcraft' or 'sorcery'.

31. "Óðinn vissi um alt jarðfé, hvar fólgit var, ok hann kunni þau ljóð, er upp lauksk fyrir honum jǫrðin ok bjǫrg ok steinar ok haugarnir, ok batt hann með orðum einum þá, er fyrir bjoggu, ok gékk inn ok tók þar slíkt, er hann vildi." Bjarni Aðalbjarnarson 1962, 19.

32. "en stundum vakði hann upp dauða menn ór jǫrðu eða settisk undir hanga. Fyrir því var hann kallaðr draugadróttinn eða hangadróttinn." Bjarni Aðalbjarnarson 1962, 18.

33. "Óðinn kunni þá íþrótt, svá at mestr máttr fylgði, ok framði sjálfr, er seiðr heitir . . . " Bjarni Aðalbjarnarson 1962, 19.

34. "En þessi fjǫlkynngi, er framið er, fylgir svá mikil ergi, at eigi þótti karlmǫnnum skamlaust við at fara, ok var gyðjunum kend sú íþrótt." Bjarni Aðalbjarnarson 1962, 19.

35. I am here following Price 2002, 93–94.

36. The argument that Óðinn is a late addition from the outside to the Nordic pantheon has frequently been made (so, e.g., Ödeen 1929–30; Helm 1946; Briem 1963). For useful introductions, see Halvorsen 1982 and Turville-Petre 1964, 35–74.

37. Cf. the argument for a truly substantial role for Freyja in Näsström 1995; see also Raudvere 2003, 99–101.

38. "Dóttir Njarðar var Freyja. Hon var blótgyðja. Hon kenndi fyrst með Ásum seið, sem Vǫnum var títt." Bjarni Aðalbjarnarson 1962, 13.

39. On the connection between the enigmatic figure of Gullveigr in *Vǫluspá* and *Ynglingasaga*'s presentation of Freyja, see Clunies Ross 1994, 203–4.

40. Holtsmark 1982b suggests that *Hyndluljóð*, although generally treated as a mythological poem, but might just as well be counted among the heroic poems. On Freyja's possible roles in the larger mythology as understood from this poem, see esp. Näsström 1995, 151–77.

41. Cf. Näsström 1995.

42. The poem was known to Snorri Sturluson, who quotes part of it in *Gylfaginning* (and also provides us with the name by which it was known to him), as well as a longer interpolation in *Hyndlujóð* (st. 29–44) in the late fourteenth-century *Flateyjarbók*. As Gunnell 2005, 92, comments, *Hyndlujóð* "is probably a combination of two *fornyrðislag* poems" (i.e., The Shorter *Vǫluspá* and what is regarded as *Hyndlujóð* itself).

43. Here from *Hyndluljóð*:

Ero vǫlor allar   frá Viðólfi,
vitcar allir   frá Vilmeiði,
enn seiðberendr   frá Svarthǫfða,
iǫtnar allir   frá Ymi komnir. (Neckel and Kuhn 1983, 293)

44. See, e.g., Reichardt 1939; Gunnell 1993; and Mitchell 2007b.

45. Bugge 1867 argues that the two poems present a single narrative, a view generally accepted by scholarship. Following a lead from Svend Grundtvig, Bugge demonstrated that the poems are related to Danish and Swedish ballads about Ungen Svejdal (*Types of the Medieval Scandinavian Ballad* A45) and probably formed the basis for the later ballad tradition. See Holtsmark 1982c.

46. The oldest recorded example is *Óláfs ríma Haraldssonar* in *Flateyjarbók*. See the following English-language orientations: Craigie 1952; Hughes 1978, 1980; Vésteinn Ólason 1982, 52–82; and Vésteinn Ólason 2006, 55–62.

47. Vésteinn Ólason 2006, 58.

48. Finnur Jónsson 1905–22, 1:425. "Gjǫrðu þær af gǫldrum seið / geystiz hrǫnn og bylgja."

49. Finnur Jónsson 1905–22, 1:10–40. For orientation, see Homan 1975. Although the poem only exists in post-Reformation manuscripts, it is generally thought to have been written in the late Middle Ages.

50. Finnur Jónsson 1905–22, 1:290–309.

51. *Virgilessrímur* (*Rímur of Virgil*), thought to have been composed between 1300 and 1450, is perhaps most notable within the medieval Virgilian tradition for its violent sexual imagery. See Gísli Sigurðsson and Mitchell 2008.

52. "Bóka nám og brǫgðin ǫll / bæði frá eg þau greina . . . " Finnur Jónsson 1905–22, 2:845 (v. 14)

53. *Bragð* 'trick, scheme, device' can also indicate a sudden motion (and may even be used to describe wrestling moves, according to Cleasby and Vigfusson 1982).

54. For the texts of *Virgilessrímur*, see Finnur Jónsson 1905–22, 2:843–58, and Kölbing 1876, 234–40, translated in Gísli Sigurðsson and Mitchell 2008. On *Virgilessrímur*, see Jakob Benediktsson 1982b and Jón Þorkelsson 1888, 179–80.

55. See the comments by Lindqvist 1992, 6.

56. Historically, Old Norse scholarship has avoided the term, but one senses an increased interest in the question of "mentalities" in the sagas. Cf. Knuuttila 1995, 18: "From the standpoint of cultural studies in folkloristics the concept of mentality is problematic in a different way from the way it is in historical research." See also Knuuttila 1993, 121.

57. Kirsten Hastrup (1990) has applied to the Icelandic materials the principles of historical anthropology. Coming from the philological direction, Preben Meulengracht Sørensen (Meulengracht Sørensen 1977, 1980, trans. into English as Meulengracht Sørensen 1993, 1983) was among the first to take a most directly anthropological approach to the Icelandic sagas. Cf. the critique in Lindqvist 1992, 10–11, 14–15, and Mitchell 2003c.

58. On this point, see, e.g., Mitchell 1991b, 32–36, and Byock 1992.

59. *Alexanders saga, Karlamagnús saga ok kappa hans, Þiðreks saga af Bern.* Cf. de Vries 1963, 194–209, on this point.

60. Cognate with English "saw" (i.e., "saying"), the word in some Nordic dialects, such as Swedish, means 'fairy tale' unless designated an Icelandic saga.

61. Andreas Heusler coined the phrases *Freiprosa-Buchprosa* to capture the two poles of the debate. On its history, see Andersson 1964, 65–81.

62. Cf. Sigurður Nordal's famous 1940 examination of *Hrafnkels saga Freysgoða*. Modern approaches are vastly more subtle in their framing of the problems and the possible solutions, e.g., Gísli Sigurðsson 2004. See also my comments in Mitchell 2003d.

63. On the history of the Nordic world in this regard, see the survey in Byock 1994; on the Icelandic case, see the essays in Gísli Sigurðsson and Vésteinn Ólason 2004, esp. "Bring the manuscripts home!" (171–77).

64. In considering the use of sagas as historical sources and their potential for informing us about the periods in which they themselves were written, Jochens (1980, 378) concludes that they will be inconsistent in both regards. See her further discussions in, e.g., Jochens 1990, 1993, and 1996, 9–10. Karras 1988 represents another important milestone in the restoration of the sagas' status as historical sources. This newly won credulity has its limits, however, as when, e.g., Jochens's otherwise positive review of Dillmann 2006 opens with evident concern: "For many of the afficionados of the Icelandic family sagas who remain nostalgic for the days when these narratives could be read at face value— that is as evidence of conditions in ancient Iceland before the arrival of Christianity—this book will be greeted with enthusiasm." Jochens 2006, 488.

65. Most famously, Carlo Ginzburg's remarkable 1992 investigation into the worldview of a sixteenth-century peasant burned for heresy. Other key players in formulating this interpretation of "history from below," as it is sometimes called, include Clifford Geertz's (1973) seminal essay on "thick description," and the field of ethnohistory, on which, see the helpful survey in Chaves 2008. In the modern Icelandic context, cf. Sigurður Gylfi Magnússon 1997.

66. See the comments and bibliographies in, e.g., Acker 1998; Bauman 1986; Byock 1984; Gísli Sigurðsson 2002, 2004; Harris 1983; Mitchell 2002a and 2003d.

67. E.g., Glauser 2000; Byock 2004; Glauser 2007; Hermann 2007a.

68. See, e.g., Mitchell 1991b, 9–32, and Clunies Ross 1998, 44–58, and the literature cited in them on the genre question.

69. See Sigurður Nordal 1953, 180–82.

70. Specifically, Sigurður Nordal 1953 sets against the prevailing genre system, which categorizes the texts according to topic or protagonist (i.e., kings, bishops, etc.), a system that categorizes the sagas "efter afstanden mellem begivenheder og optegnelser" (181).

71. E.g., Gísli Pálsson 1991; cf. Raudvere 2001, 161.

72. The materials cited are, of course, intended to be representative but by no means exhaustive. As that task has already been accomplished elsewhere (see esp. Strömbäck 1935; Price 2002; Raudvere 2003; and Dillmann 2006), I refer readers to these studies for systematic and complete examinations of the references to witchcraft in the sagas.

73. For English-language orientation to this important work, see Andersson 1985, 219–22 et passim; Bagge 1991; and Ármann Jakobsson 2005.

74. Active in the late ninth and early tenth centuries; see Magerøy 1982. The poem informs parts of *Historia Norwegiae* as well as, albeit only passingly, *Íslendingabók*, in addition to *Ynglingasaga*.

75. Cf. McKinnell 2005 and Raudvere 2001, 130–31. Especially relevant is the thorough analysis of giantesses (and to the extent Norse *trǫllkona* and other elements of its vocabulary ambiguously also indicate witches) in Schulz 2004, 231–51.

76. On this point, see Strömbäck 1935; DuBois 1999; Price 2002, 2004; and Tolley 2009.

77. By "Finland," Snorri no doubt means lands inhabited by the Sámi.

78. En á vit

Vilja bróður

vitta véttr

Vanlanda kom,

þás trollkund

of troða skyldi

líðs grímhildr

ljóna bága,

ok sá brann

á beði Skútu

menglǫtuðr,

er mara kvalði. (Bjarni Aðalbjarnarson 1962, 29)

The translation follows Hollander 1991, 17. The interpretation of individual kennings has been subject to considerable debate, although not the general interpretation of the verse; see the notes in Bjarni Aðalbjarnarson 1962, 29–30.

79. *Friðþjófs saga frækna* is one of the texts included in Rafn 1829–30, 2:63–100, and was subsequently edited, together with the *rímur*, in Larsson 1893. The saga is discussed in Finnur Jónsson 1920, 2:812, and de Vries 1964, 2:490–93.

80. Cf. Wawn 2005, 331–32.

81. Rafn 1829–30, 2:383–459. On the saga, see Finnur Jónsson 1920, 3:810. The saga is preserved in several fifteenth- and early sixteenth-century manuscripts, but Rowe 2004 has cogently argued for an original composition in the late thirteenth century.

82. "hann var stórr sem jötun, ljótr sem fjándinn, ok svá fjölkunnigr, at hann fór í jörðu ok á, ok límdi saman stóð ok stjörnur; hann var svá mikil hamhleypa, at hann brast í ýmsra kvikinda líki; hann fór ymist með vindum eðr í sjó." Rafn 1829–30, 2:390.

83. Rafn 1829–30, 2:395–96.

84. Íngjaldr's cognomen, *trana* 'crane', can hardly be right, as the text explicitly says, "hit fjórða barn þeira hét Íngjaldr, vǫr hans hin efri var álnar laung frá nefi, því var hann kallaðr Íngjaldr trana." Rafn 1829–30, 2:391. Perhaps there is some confusion here with *trjóna* 'snout', which would make sense in light of his subsequent transmogrification into a *göltr,* 'boar, hog'—unless there exists some ornithological detail here more apparent to the medieval mind than to mine.

85. "þótti Íngjaldr hafa sýnt trölldóm sinn." Rafn 1829–30, 2:400.

86. "Sáu þeir, at Íngjaldr lá þar dauðr, tóku þeir síðan eld ok brendu hann upp at koldum kolum . . . " Rafn 1829–30, 2:403.

87. Rafn 1829–30, 2:391. The sword had been inherited by Kolr's son, Björn blátönn, who had lost it in a fight with Víkingr.

88. "ek á einn belg, þann er veðrbelgr heitir, en ef ek hristi hann, þá stendr úr honum stormr ok vindr með svá stórri grimd ok kulda, at innan þriggja nátta skal lagðr svá sterkr ís á vatnit, at ríða skal mega hestum, þótt vill." Rafn 1829–30, 2:412. *Belgr* can mean 'bellows' or 'bag' (< 'skin'), as I have translated it here due to the text's use of the verb *hrista* 'shake', which seems the most sensible collocation.

89. This well-known color scheme suggests that trouble and death comes with them. The brothers' names apparently mean 'Babbling' and 'Not Babbling'.

90. "hún hafði fyrir álögum orðit." Rafn 1829–30, 2:431.

91. Rafn 1829–30, 2:432.

92. "en í því varpaði Ógautan kefli í kné henni, en svá brá henni við þat, at hún neitaði Bela, en gekk at eiga Jökul." Rafn 1829–30, 2:434.

93. This type of interaction between an apparent giantess and a human hero is the subject of a special study, McKinnell 2005, and also plays an important role in the discussion of giantesses in Schulz 2004.

94. "en þó hefir þú þetta fullu launat mér, þvíat þú hefir komit mér úr álögum þeim, er Ógautan lagði á mik." Rafn 1829–30, 2:438.

95. "Síðan gekk Friðþjófr inn, ok sá, at fátt fólk var í dísarsalnum, voru konungar þá at dísablóti, ok sátu at drykkju . . . " Rafn 1829–30, 2:86. Any observations about the *dísir* and other female agents of fate naturally begins with Ström 1954. See Raudvere 2003, 61–69, for an updated review.

96. "sátu konur þeirra við eldinn ok bökuðu goðin, en sumar smurðu, ok þerðu med dúkum." Rafn 1829–30, 2:86.

97. The manuscript tradition used in Guðni Jónsson 1954, which also refers to Baldrshagi as a sanctuary (*griðastaðr*; 3:77, 80), is explicit in this view: "ok skyldi þar ekki saman koma konur ok karlar" (3:80).

98. "þær efldu seiðinn, ok færðust á hjallinn með göldrum ok gjörningum." Rafn 1829–30, 2:72.

99. "hvort meira má, hamingja vor, eða tröllskapr þeirra . . . " Rafn 1829–30, 2:79.

100. "en er þær systr voru at seiðum, duttu þær of anaf seiðhjallinum, ok brotnaði hrygginn í báðum." Rafn 1829–30, 2:84.

101. Lönnroth 1969.

102. See my comments on the eclectic nature of this type of saga (Mitchell 1991b, 44–90), as well as the remarks in Schlauch 1934.

103. Cf. the excellent argument concerning magic as a literary device in the *Íslendingasögur* in Jóhanna Katrín Friðriksdóttir 2009.

104. Cf. Ármann Jakobsson 2005, as well as the discussion in Chapter 1, on these traditions.

105. Bjarni Aðalbjarnarson 1962, 266.

106. "Einsetumaðr segir, at sjálfr guð kristinna manna lét hann vita alt þat, er hann forvitnaðisk . . . " Bjarni Aðalbjarnarson 1962, 266.

107. Bjarni Aðalbjarnarson 1962, 260. See the excellent analysis in Jackson 2006.

108. "fullr af gørningum ok fjölkynngi ok var seiðskratti, sem mestr mátti verða . . ." Björn K. Þórólfsson and Guðni Jónsson 1972, 37.

109. "ǫll váru þau mjǫk fjǫlkunnig ok inir mestu seiðmenn." Einar Ól. Sveinsson 1934, 95.

110. Cf. Lönnroth 1969.

111. *Grettis saga* is dated to 1310–20. See Guðni Jónsson 1964, lxix–lxx.

112. "hon var mjǫk gǫmul ok til lítils fœr, at því er mǫnnum þótti. Hon hafði verit fjǫlkunnig mjǫk ok margkunnig mjǫk, þá er hon var ung ok menn váru heiðnir; nú þótti sem hon myndi ǫllu týnt hafa. En þó at kristni væri á landinu, þá váru þó margir gneistar heiðninnar eptir. Þat hafði verit lǫg hér á landi, at eigi var bannat at blóta á laun eða fremja aðra forneskju, en varðaði fjǫrbaugssǫk, ef opinbert yrði." Guðni Jónsson 1964, 245.

113. Although Þuríðr's witchcraft achieves its end, the saga writer uses the fact that Þorbjǫrn has employed witchcraft in defeating Grettir as one way to underscore the hollowness of his victory. See Guðni Jónsson 1964, 265. Not only does his behavior earn Þorbjǫrn condemnation and a charge at the Alþingi that he has illegally employed witchcraft and sorcery (*galdr ok fjǫlkynngi*; Guðni Jónsson 1964, 268), but the saga further maintains that it is a result of this case that all witches are outlawed in Iceland: "Var þá í lǫg tekit, at alla forneskjumenn gerðu þeir útlæga." Guðni Jónsson 1964, 268–69.

114. "Nú var svá gǫrt, sem hon beiddi, ok er hon kom til strandar, haltraði hon fram með sænum, svá sem henni væri vísat til. Þar lá fyrir henni rótartré svá mikit sem axlbyrðr. Hon leit á tréit ok bað þá snúa fyrir sér; það var sem sviðit og gniðat ǫðrum megin. Hon lét telgja á lítinn flatveg, þar gniðat var; síðan tók hon kníf sinn ok reist rúnir á rótinni ok rauð í blóði sínu ok kvað yfir galdra. Hon gekk ǫfug andsœlis um tréit ok hafði þar yfir mǫrg rǫmm ummæli. Eptir þat lætr hon hrinda trénu á sjá ok mælti svá fyrir, at þat skyldi reka út til Drangeyjar, ok verði Gretti allt mein at." Guðni Jónsson 1964, 249–50.

115. *Hávamál* 151, "Þat kan ec it sétta / ef mic særir þegn / á rótom rás viðar." Neckel and Kuhn 1983, 42. "That sixth I know, / if me someone wounds / with runes on gnarled root written." Hollander 1991, 38.

116. "Skalat maðr rúnar rísta, / nema ráða vel kunni." Sigurður Nordal 1979, 229–30.

117. The relevance of this saga and *Grœnlendinga saga* (*The Saga of the Greenlanders*) to the question of Norse explorations of the North American littoral has subjected it to intense scrutiny. On the manuscripts and the testimony of the two sagas, see Jansson 1945. For discussions and updated literature, see Seaver 1996 and Gísli Sigurðsson 2004.

118. Einar Ól. Sveinsson and Matthías Þórðarson 1957, 206–9, my translation. It should be noted that the term I gloss here as "song" (*kvæði*) also means 'poem'.

119. E.g., Strömbäck 1935, 49–60; Raudvere 2003, 122–24; Price 2002, 71–73, 114, 169–70 et passim; Dillmann 2006, 69–70, 131–33, 202–5 et passim; Tolley 2009, 1:159–60, 174–76 et passim.

120. Writing in 1935 in his masterful study of *seiðr*, Strömbäck (1935, 59) came to this

conclusion: "Såsom ovan framhållits uppfatta vi hela kapitlet såsom en av sagaförfattaren uppbyggd framställning syftande till Guðríðs glorifiering."

121. In Mitchell 2001, I connect this term with "women's calling songs." Cf. Strömbäck (1935, 60), who suggests that this part of the scene, at least, should be viewed "med avgjord misstro." Anticipating my comments below, it should be fairly apparent that I too regard the scene as an important source of information, although I am wary of taking everything in it too literally.

122. However one feels about the text's authenticity, it is impossible to ignore: thus, e.g., Strömbäck (1935, 49–60) treats it with considerable finesse and concludes that the author must have had a good understanding of what he was writing about despite his tendentiousness ("I det stora hela har han varit väl underrättad om hithörande ting . . . " 60). The respectful treatment given the data in this episode in Dillmann 2006, 131–33, 369, 595, et passim, suggests that he too regards this information as reliable. Perhaps the most troubled among recent scholars by the scene in *Eiríks saga rauða* are Raudvere (2003, 122–24), who takes up this case, but does so, as she writes, "med viss tveckan" (122), on the sensible grounds that it is all too often used as though it were an anthropological description of a ritual involving a *vǫlva*; and Tolley (2009, 1:511–12), who devotes an entire section to "the deceptive allure of verisimilitude."

123. Price 2002, 114. Cf. his additional comments (71–73, 169–70 et passim).

124. Although much mined by scholars interested in historical matters, through his many examinations of *Sturlunga saga* Úlfar Bragason has reminded us that these texts too are narratives and susceptible to literary analysis. On this genre, see esp. Úlfar Bragason 2005 and the literature cited there.

125. Guðni Jónsson 1948, 1:114.

126. So Hallberg 1993, 616.

127. Several entries in Boberg 1966 are misleading in this regard. "Troll-woman" is often ambiguous as an abstract term but not always so in situ. Thus, in *Prestssaga Guðmundar Arasonar*, an episode designated by Boberg as G271.2.2. *Witch exorcised by holy water* clearly concerns, not a witch, but rather a supernatural being closer to a giant. Likewise, the case of the *grýla* 'ogre' in *Íslendinga saga*—G219.8.1. *Witch with fifteen tails.* See the perceptive discussion in Ármann Jakobsson 2009 and the bibliography cited there on this point.

128. An independent *Hrafns saga Sveinbjarnarsonar* also exists, in two versions, as well as the *Sturlunga saga* version, representing roughly half of the saga. On the manuscript traditions and their relationship, see Guðrún P. Helgadóttir 1987, esp. pp. cviii–cxvi.

129. McGrew and Thomas 1970–74, 2:213; "Þá urðu í Vestfjörðum mörg kyn bæði í sýnum ok draumum." Guðni Jónsson 1948, 1:417. Already Finnur Jónsson (1920, 2:555) concluded that the many dreams and portents in this saga, and the author's belief in them, pointed toward a cleric as the author: "Forf. er gejstig [. . .] Forf. tror på onelser, varsler og drömme, og meddeler en mængde sådonne . . . "

130. Faraldr ek heiti,
ferk of aldar kyn,

emka ek sættir svika.
Döprum dauða
ek mun drengi vega
ok nýta mér nái. (Guðni Jónsson 1948, 1:418)

The use of *ljóðaháttr* in such a dream verse is otherwise unknown. As Guðrún Helgadóttir notes, "Its use here may have been prompted by *ljóðaháttr* exchanges between human and supernatural characters in which self-identification, boasts, and threats play a part, such as are found in *Helgakviða Hjǫrvarðssonar*, 12–30, and in *Ketils saga hængs*[. . . .]" Guðrún P. Helgadóttir 1987, 108.

131. *Sturlunga saga* shows *Faralldr*, but in the *Hrafns saga* traditions it is variously given as *Farvalldr* and *Þǫrvalldur*. On this point, Guðrún Helgadóttir (1987, 108) remarks, "A compound *fárvaldr*, 'mischief-causer', is not otherwise known. There is a neuter word *farald*, with a basic sense of 'journey, that which travels', and in modern Icelandic *faraldur* meaning 'pestilence' is attested, cf. *L[exicon] P[oeticum]*, Fritzner, and Blöndal, s.v. The St[urlunga saga] reading has consequently been taken by some to give the right form of the name, glossed in *L[exicon] P[oeticum]* as 'som farer om, især for at stifte ulykke'. In that case *fer ek of aldar kyn* in the next line plays heavily on the name's sense and form." The fact that the name is masculine would seem to lend weight to its association with 'plague, epidemic, pestilence', as does the remainder of the verse, with its heavy connection to death, disease, decay, and the morbid thought of 'using' corpses (on which theme, see Mitchell 2008a). McGrew's gloss of the appellation as 'Far-traveler' is justifiable based on the non-*Sturlunga saga* manuscripts. On the other hand, *faraldur* in modern Icelandic is attested as epidemic (*umgangsveiki*), as the corresponding *faraldr* was in Old Norse (cf. Norn *far*, Norwegian *farsott*, Danish *farsot*) and is the form in at least one of the manuscripts. Moreover, in addition to the *faraldr* entry cited earlier in Guðrún Helgadóttir from *Lexicon Poeticum*, it is to be noted that the same work lists for neuter *farald*, "egl. 'hvad der farer omkring, er almindeligt, rammer mange, især om smittende sygdomme,'" Finnur Jónsson and Sveinbjörn Egilsson 1966, 123. The association with tragic and widespread disease thus strikes me as much the likelier meaning here.

132. Historically, the connection between the "Wild Hunt" (E501 *die wilde Jagd*) and Óðinn has been problematic (e.g., Höfler 1934), and often rejected (e.g., de Vries 1962), but can be adduced in the context of late medieval mythology. An enduring study of this tale type, esp. in the context of specifically Scandinavian evidence, is Celander 1943.

133. On this motif, one widespread in Nordic church murals, and its origins in the British context, see Schmidt 1995, esp. 41–45.

134. See, e.g., Russell 1984 and Wolf-Knuts 1991 on the various permutations of this figure in medieval theological and modern folklore traditions. In Mitchell 2009a, I argue that Óðinn retained essential functions in Nordic charm magic well after the Conversion.

135. In this instance, from a late fifteenth-century Swedish trial, Almquist 1930, 3:18. See, e.g., the discussion in Brilioth 1941, 779.

136. *Forna Rijdghiöta eller Smålendske Antiqviteter [. . .] aff Petter Rudebeck Anno 1693.* See Liljenroth and Liljenroth 1997, 295.

137. McGrew and Thomas 1970–74, 1:107–8; "'Hví skal ek eigi gera þik þeim líkastan, er þú vill líkastr vera,—en þar er Óðinn?'" Guðni Jónsson 1948, 1:174. Cf. the scene in *Egils saga Skalla-Grímssonar* where Egill similarly disfigures an opponent, making him one-eyed; Sigurður Nordal 1979, 227–28.

138. On this point, see esp. Glendinning 1974 and Heinrichs 1995.

139. "'Sighvatr tók undir í gamni ok með nökkurri svá græsku: 'Hvárrgi okkar þarf nú at bregða öðrum elli,—eða hvárt gerist þú nú spámaðr, frændi?' Þórðr svarar: 'Engi em ek spámaðr.'" Guðni Jónsson 1948, 2:276–77; "Sighvatr took this in jest and said mockingly, 'Neither of us should reproach the other with age. Or do you pretend to be a seer, brother?' Þórð answered: 'I am no seer . . .'" McGrew and Thomas 1970–74, 1:295.

140. "'Þat mun þér þykkja jartegn', segir Sighvatr. Arnórr segir: 'Slíkt kalla ek atburð, en eigi jartegn.'" Guðni Jónsson 1948, 2:82; the translation follows McGrew and Thomas 1970–74, 1:170. On the use of miracle collections, and their style, in secular sagas, see Lönnroth 1999 and Mitchell 2009b, and the literature cited there.

141. "Margir váru aðrir draumar sagðir í þenna tíma, þó at hér sé eigi ritaðir, þeir er tíðindaværir þóttu vera, svá ok aðrir fyrirburðir." Guðni Jónsson 1948, 2:326; the translation follows McGrew and Thomas 1970–74, 1:327.

142. On this episode and its relation to then contemporary concerns regarding familial responsibilities, see Meulengracht Sørensen 1988 and Bergljót Kristjánsdóttir 1990, 247–51, who emphasizes its connection to medieval visionary poetry.

143. "Þá ætla þeir með illvilja sínum at koma heiðni á allt landit." Guðni Jónsson 1948, 2:489; the translation follows from McGrew and Thomas 1970–74, 1:432.

144. Guðni Jónsson 1948, 2:304; McGrew and Thomas 1970–74, 1:313.

145. "'ok þrífist þeir aldri, ok mun þeim at öðru verða en allir menn muni til þeira stunda.'" Guðni Jónsson 1948, 2:304; McGrew and Thomas 1970–74, 1:313

146. See Finnur Jónsson 1920, 181–83 et passim.

147. McGrew and Thomas 1970–74, 1:330–31. In the original: "Maðr hét Snæbjörn. Hann bjó í Sandvík út frá Höfðahverfi. Hann gekk út um nótt. Þat var fyrir jól um vetrinn fyrir Örlygsstaðafund. Þá gekk kona í túnit, mikil ok þrýstilig, daprlig ok rauðlituð. Hon var í dökkbláum kyrtli. Stokkabelti hafði hon um sik. Hon kvað þetta ok snerist við honum:

Gríðr munk gumnum heðra.
Grand þróask margt í landi.
Sótt munk yðr, þvíat ættak
efni margs at hefna.
Urðr mun eigi forðask,
at kemr fár, es várar,
dauðs, munu, dolgum órum,

dáins raddar þá kvaddir,
dáins raddar þá kvaddir.

Enn kvað hon þetta:

Eisandi ferk unda
undrsamliga funda.
Líðk of hól ok hæðir
hart sem fugl inn svarti.
Kemk í dal, þars dyljumk,
dánarakrs til vánar.
Harmþrungin fórk hingat
Heljar ask at velja,
Heljar ask ferk velja"

(Guðni Jónsson 1948, 2:331–32).

148. On the interrelated character of these female figures connected with fate, see the excellent discussion in Raudvere 1993, as well as Damico 1984.

149. Cf. Old High German *hagazussa*, possibly Old English *hægtesse* (on which, see Hall 2007), as well as the Old Swedish law referring to a 'witch' riding on the gate to a pen, presumably also in proximity to, or part of, the home field, "Iak sa at þu reet a quiggrindu . . . " Schlyter 1822–77, 1:38. On this law, see Chapter 5 in this volume.

150. "at hon hafði yfir sér tuglamǫttul blán[. . . .] Hon hafði um sik hnjóskulinda, ok var þar á skjóðupungr mikill, ok varðveitti hon þar í tǫfr sín, þau er hon þurfti til fróðleiks at hafa" (Einar Ól. Sveinsson and Matthías Þórðarson 1957, 206), that is, "she had on a blue cloak[. . . .] She had around her middle [a belt of] touchwood and on it a great pouch, in which she kept the charms she needed for her witchcraft [*fróðleikr*]" (my translation). The word *blá* implied a dark hue, variously translated as 'black' and 'blue', much like the English terms used in burnishing weapons (i.e., 'to blue a gun barrel'). The curious belt Þorbjǫrg wears has occasioned much discussion, given the relative infrequence and marked character of the *hnjósku*-element (cf. *fnjóskr*, as well as modern Swedish *fnöske*, *fnas*), usually translated as 'touchwood', indicating "wood or anything of woody nature, in such a state as to catch fire readily, and which can be used as tinder," and further, "The soft white substance into which wood is converted by the action of certain fungi, especially of *Polyporus squamosus*, and which has the property of burning for many hours when once ignited, and is occasionally self-luminous." *Oxford English Dictionary*, 2nd ed., s.v. "touchwood." This latter characteristic of self-luminescence, and perhaps the idea of combustive longevity as well, surely accounts for the fact that the belt is specified as being composed of this material. In order to fabricate a belt of such insubstantial stuff, a "linked belt," that is, a series of connected small plates, seems an obvious, and practical, fashion choice.

151. Cf. Faroese *kvøða* 'sing, chant'. Einar Ól. Sveinsson and Matthías Þórðarson 1957, 208.

152. Cf. Cleasby and Vigfusson 1982, 576, "*snúask at e-m, í móti e-m, við e-m*, to turn upon, face about, to meet an attack or the like."

153. Cf. the argument in Heide 2006.

154. Frank 1984, 337.

155. Turner 1971.

156. Cf. the parallel argument regarding the use of giantesses in Schulz 2004, 65–69, 225–31, 256–93. Bruhn 1999 similarly notes the tendency for the distant past to be more detail filled.

157. Interest in the Old Swedish area has been especially keen in recent years. Marking the beginning of this modern resurgence were the research surveys published several decades ago (Dahlbäck 1987b), the response to which may be seen in such recent anthologies as Bampi and Ferrari 2008 and studies such as Bampi 2007, Layher 2008, and Sands 2010, all of which stand in contrast to the historical tendency for the East Norse area to be of interest only within national discourses. The Old Danish area too has lately witnessed invigorating fresh perspectives (e.g., Hermann 2007b) such that we begin to have a more comprehensive image of cultural life throughout the Nordic area.

158. On Saxo's life, training, and relationship to Bishop Absalon, see esp. Friis-Jensen 1989. Cf. the comments and literature in Friis-Jensen 2005a, Johannesson 1978, and Davidson 1980, as well as the essays in Friis-Jensen 1981.

159. This point has been a matter of some debate; see, e.g., Skovgaard-Petersen 1981. On the question of Saxo's worldview, see esp. Johannesson 1978. By placing quotation marks around "the same," I intend to signal here that although Snorri and Saxo may discuss similar materials, they are no more copies of one another than when one Bosnian singer sings "the same" epic as another: the hero, the basic plotline, and so on may be similar, and modern scholarship may provide both texts with the same title for the sake of cataloguing, but that cannot be understood to mean that the narratives duplicate one another. See Mitchell and Nagy 2000 and esp. Lord 2000. And importantly, as Bjarni Guðnason 1981, 91, emphasizes, the relationship between Saxo and Icelandic traditions is by no means unidirectional, but rather reciprocal.

160. "triplex quondam mathematicorum genus inauditi generis miracula discretis exercuisse prestigiis." Friis-Jensen 2005b, 1:104 (1:5, 2). All references to Saxo's *Gesta Danorum* are to this edition.

161. Cf. Genesis 6:4, which seems to parallel on several fronts Saxo's view of prehistory.

162. "Bortset fra enkelte omtaler om Frøj, Frigg og Balder består det nordiske panteon for Saxo af Odin og Thor . . . " Skovgaard-Petersen 1987, 82.

163. Davidson 1979, 170–71. "Olim enim quidam magice artis imbuti, Thor uidelicet et Othinus aliique complures miranda prestigiorum machinatione callentes, obtentis simplicium animis diuinitatis sibi fastigium arrogare coeperunt. Quippe Noruagiam, Suetiam ac Daniam uanissime credulitatis laqueis circumuentas ad cultus sibi pendendi studium concitantes precipuo ludificationis sue contagio resperserunt" (6.5.3).

164. See Skovgaard-Petersen 1975, 26, an idea taken up in Johannesson 1981. Cf. Kaspersen et al. 1990, 377–78, and Dahlerup 1998, 2:72–76.

165. The pattern Skovgaard-Petersen finds also helps explain the changes in Othinus in the text: "Endnu i 7. bog hævder Odin sig som den øverste gud, men i 8. bog falder for hver episode et nyt slør og røber hans sande væsen." Skovgaard-Petersen 1987, 87.

166. "In the heathen part they play historically important parts, but thereafter their influence is insignificant. However, the influence that women exert in the heathen times is often of a negative kind: they then represent the power of Evil." Strand 1981, 151. See also Strand 1980.

167. So Strand 1981, 151, who says further, "It is in the first nine books that we meet the efforts of the constantly faithless female Matter to overthrow the cosmic system. With the introduction of Christian faith the power of Matter is broken—and from the 9th book the magic, too, fades away. . . . "

168. Bjarni Guðnason 1981, 79, writes, "Foreign learning and a native cultural heritage are combined in so unique a manner in *Gesta Danorum* that Saxo's monumental work has neither prototype nor imitation in the literature of Scandinavia."

169. Old Norse *Finnr*, appearances notwithstanding, usually glosses the Sámi or so-called Lapps. See Hermann Pálsson 1999b.

170. The text and translation here follow Ekrem, Mortensen, and Fisher 2003, who date the text to the middle of the twelfth century: "There is much to suggest that *Historia Norwegie* was conceived before the archdiocese was established in 1152/1153 . . . " (225). Various dates have been suggested for the composition of *Historia Norwegie*, some as early as the date proposed by Ekrem, Mortensen, and Fischer, some as much as a half century later; see the survey in Holtsmark 1982a.

171. Ekrem, Mortensen, and Fisher 2003, 61. "Horum itaque intollerabilis perfidia uix cuiquam credibilis uidebitur, quantumue diabolice supersticionis in magica arte exerceant. Sunt namque quidam ex ipsis, qui quasi prophete a stolido uulgo uenerantur . . . " (60).

172. Ekrem, Mortensen, and Fisher 2003, 63. "sed a gandis emulorum esse depredatum . . . " (62).

173. On this episode, see esp. Tolley 2009, 288–91, as well as Tolley 1994.

174. "Nam et diuini et augures et magi et incantatores ceterique satellites Antichristi habitant ibi, quorum prestigijs et miraculis infelices anime ludibrio demonibus habentur." Gertz 1917–18, 2:20–21. Given the many sources from which its author has drawn, the text is called *et levende blandningsværk* in one literary history (Kaspersen et al. 1990, 206).

175. The value of this statement is blunted by the fact that although the text is often placed to the mid-1200s, no medieval manuscripts exist. We cannot be certain at what stage this comment was introduced or whether it was, in fact, part of the original formulation.

176. Rafn 1829–30, 1:511–12; Bjarni Aðalbjarnarson 1979, 263. For a review and evaluation of the West Norse presentations of the Swedish conversion, see Lönnroth 1996.

177. Schlyter 1822–77, 1:285–347.

178. Cf. the similar function of *Guta saga* as articulated in Mitchell 1984.

179. "Olawær skotkonongær. war fyrsti. konongær sum cristin war .i. sweriki. han

war döptær .i. kyældu þerræ wið hosæby liggær. oc heter byrghittæ. af sighfriði biscupp. oc han skötte þaghær allæn byn till staffs oc stols." Schlyter 1822–77, 1:298. Cf. "Sighfriðær war fyrsti byskupær sum hær com cristnu .a. han ffor aff ænglandi. oc hingæt. oc mærhtti hær þre kyrkyustæðhi oc wighþi. þre kyrkyugarðþæ." Schlyter 1822–77, 1:304.

180. Fant et al. 1818–71, 2:344–76.

181. The favoritism shown Västergötland by the author is most apparent when, in discussing King Stenkil, the list states that he loved the Västgötar above all others in his realm: "Fæmti war. Stænkil konongær. han ælskæðhi wæstgötæ. vm. fram allæ þe mæn .i. hans riki waru." Schlyter 1822–77, 1:299.

182. But cf. the note on the second bishop: "Annar war vnni ærchibiscupær. han wighis .i. ænglanði. oc sændis swa hingat. þa wildi hær swa noðhoght folk wið cristnu takæ. oc þer toko biscupin. oc tyrffðhu till banæ. mæð stenum. sidþæn tok guð wið sial hans. oc hælghir mæn." Schlyter 1822–77, 1:305.

183. "Philipus prædicaþe tiughu ar .i. sithia. som nu callar suerike. fra østarlandom ok tel ørasund ¶ heþne gripu han vm siþe ok drogho tel mønstar .i. opsalom. ok cuskaþo han tel at ofra marti som suæiar calla oþen." Stephens and Dahlgren 1847–74, 1:199.

184. "ænghen sa þæn draka siþan fra þøm dagh ¶ philipus gaf þær næst allom siucom helso [. . .] ok cristnaþe alt þæt land ok rike." Stephens and Dahlgren 1847–74, 1:199. Cf. similar devices elsewhere in the legendary, as in the story of Zoroes and Arafaxat (Stephens and Dahlgren 1847–74, 1:226).

185. See Tjäder 1993, as well as Jansson 1982 and Mitchell 1996, 15–16, for orientations. For a detailed authoritative discussion, see Jansson 1934, as well as the introduction to Jansson 1966. Of *Fornsvenska legendariet* proper, that is, not including such later items as the *Linköping Legendary* from circa 1500 (published as the third volume of the edition called *Ett Forn-Svenskt Legendarium*), there are three main manuscripts: Codex Bureanus (SKB A 34) from circa 1350 or somewhat later; Codex Bildstenianus (Upps. C 528) from the first half of the fifteenth century; and Codex Passionarius (Skokloster 3, 4to) from the mid-fifteenth century or somewhat later. A fragment, SKB A 124, may be the oldest surviving testimony to the legendary.

186. On the legend, see esp. Gad 1961, as well as Gad 1982 and Wolf 1993. Note DuBois 1999, 63, who comments, "Some of the traditions or devotions formerly associated with pagan deities became attached to 'legendary saints,' sometimes with little alteration."

187. "At ther munde koma coclara(na) mz thwem størstom drakom som blæsa brænnastens (eldh) wt aff thera munnom. ok næsum. Ok dræpa folkit mz siukom røk . . . " Stephens and Dahlgren 1847–74, 1:226.

188. "Siluester sagdhe værsta diæwls nampn næmde zambri ok ey guz ok thz wil iak prøfua [. . .] Siluester stodh fiærren ok øpte ok reste wp thiwrin mz akallan namps ihesu christi." Stephens and Dahlgren 1847–74, 1:85–86.

189. "Hermogenes sagdhe til jacobum Jac kiænner diæfla lund: tha the vordho wredhe: Ok ey læta the mik lifwa vtan jak nywte thin. Ok thu gifwer (mik) thina wærio (mz nokro) tekne: Jacobus fik hanom sin staff: til wærio for diæflum: hermogenes bar atir alla sina bøker for jacobum: at brænna: jacobus sagdhe. ey (vilia) gøra vædhrit siukt af

thera røk. Ok bødh hermogenem sænkia them til grunda." Stephens and Dahlgren 1847–74, 1:164–65.

190. Stephens and Dahlgren 1847–74, 1:603–4.

191. "Diæfwlin badh han først swæria sik edha." Stephens and Dahlgren 1847–74, 1:448.

192. Stephens and Dahlgren 1847–74, 1:18–20.

193. "Juþen com þøm saman diavulin ok þeophilum. oc at þeophil*us* viþar sagþe guþ ok guz moþor. ok cristo trolouan. ok skref þær iuir bref mz sino bloþe. ok satte firi sit insigle. ok fik diæflenom insighlat . . . " Stephens and Dahlgren 1847–74, 1:29.

194. Holm-Olsen 1982, 177, notes that this honor may fall to AM 655 IX, 4to, from the second half of the 1100s. For an important and still valuable survey of the critical role of Christian writings as part of the foundation of Icelandic saga writing, see Turville-Petre 1953.

195. See, e.g., the reviews in Lindroth 1989 and Ferm 2001.

196. For a review of research, see Krötzl 2001. For detailed recent studies touching on religion in daily life in medieval Scandinavia, see Fröjmark 1992; Cormack 1994; Krötzl 1994; and Sands 2009.

197. After all, the Order of the Friars Preachers, that is, the Dominicans, founded in the early thirteenth century, was dedicated to this activity. On the recent literature in this area, see the survey in Muessig 2002. Regarding the cultural context of the medieval Nordic situation, see Bagge 2003 and Svanhildur Óskarsdóttir 2005. On the tradition in the various regions, see, for Denmark, Riising 1969; Petersen 1970; and Langkilde 2007. For Norway, see Molland 1982a; and for Sweden, see esp. Andersson 1993 and 2006.

198. Riising 1982, 427: "Det er ikke muligt at konstatere hvor meget der faktsik blev prædiket."

199. See Sandal 1996.

200. "o*k* trva a lif q*u*enna eða ge*r*ningaR. eða a spa-saogur. þ*at* er allt diofuls craftr." Indrebø 1931, 35. *Lif qvenna*, translated here as 'women's pharmacopoeia', is more literally 'women's herbs' (*lyf*, n. 'herb') and relates to the often combined use of drugs and magic. Cf. Old Swedish *lif*, n. *läkemedel, trollmedel, trolldom, incantiones*.

201. "við fordæðuscap. við gaoldru*m*. við ge*r*ningu*m*." Indrebø 1931, 87.

202. Eiríkur Jónsson and Finnur Jónsson 1892–94, 167–69. On the details of the manuscript, or manuscripts, for it now exists as three separate ones, see Gunnar Harðarson and Stefán Karlsson 1993 and the literature cited there.

203. The original is Ælfric's "De augeriis" but may have gone through many iterations before being recorded in *Hauksbók*. On the Anglo-Saxon source texts and Nordic sermons, those in *Hauksbók* in particular, see Turville-Petre 1960; Taylor 1969; Kick 2006; and Abram 2007.

204. "af galdra monnom eða af gernínga monnum. þeim er með taufr fara eða með lyf eða með spar þui at þat er fianda villa oc diofuls þionasta." Eiríkur Jónsson and Finnur Jónsson 1892–94, 168. The semantic range of *villa* includes not only 'heresy' but also 'delusion' or 'error'. Although Cleasby and Vigfusson 1982, e.g., gloss *fjánda-villa* as

'fiendish heresy', that the expression was intended less technically as simply 'fiendish delusion', should not be discounted. With the admittedly hyperbolic (and intentionally ambiguous, as in the original) 'Satanic service' for *diofuls pionasta*, I mean to underscore the parallel between that phrase and *Guðs þjónusta* (lit., 'God's service'), the divine service, the Eucharist or Mass, as I expect would have been in the minds of those hearing the words, while at the same time recognizing that the expression might also simply be rendered by the considerably more anodyne translation 'service to the devil' or the like.

205. "ok trolskaps synd är at stridha mot gudz budhi . . . ," here from Klemming, Geete, and Ejder 1879–, 2:160, but cf., e.g., Wieselgren 1966, 65, and Geete 1904, 137.

206. "troande a truldom och liff ok galra oc andra villo . . . ," here from Klemming, Geete, and Ejder 1879–, 1:17–18. Cf. 1:146 and 2:85 in the same series. The same question noted earlier regarding the best gloss for *villa* also attaches itself to the cognate Old Swedish form, whose range in Söderwall and Ljunggren 1884–1973 includes (a) *galenskap, raseri, sinneförvirring*; (b) *galenskap, dårskap*; (c) *vilsekommet, förvillelse, förvillelse, villfarelse*; (d) *förvirring, oro*; and (e) *bländverk, gäckeri, trolldom*. Perhaps even more to the point, Old Swedish *villo man* means both 'heretic' and 'witch' (*magus*).

207. "Thin ilzska scal awita tik, oc thin frauända fran gudhi oc rätte tro til troldom oc liff oc galdra ok andra diäfwls konstir scal awita tik." Klemming, Geete, and Ejder 1879–, 1:146.

208. "hwaske til rwnakarla eller trolkarla . . . " Klemming, Geete, and Ejder 1879–, 3:103. Cf. the same phrase in 5:207. In a slightly larger context: "J thesse hälghe läst äro mangh thingh märkiande, Först är thesse quinnan som kärdhe sinna dotters nödh oc wanda, ther dyäwlin bedröffdhe oc pinte [. . .] thes war thenna saliga quinnan niutande, serdelis fore fem dygdher skyld som hon haffdhe, Som först war stadheliken tro oc rätfärdoghet, ffor thy hon lot sik til engen annan, hwaske til rwnakarla eller trolkarla at bedhas hielpp sinne dotter som dyäwlin war wtj, wtan hon badh til war herra ihesum christum, som hon trodhe mektoghan wara at fordriffua dyäwlin oc hans wald . . . "

209. Cf. the remarks in Riising 1969, 339, concerning the expansive attention paid to this issue by Peder Madsen in Ribe in the mid-1400s.

210. See Riising 1969, 342. A statute from Strängnäs in Sweden displays similar concerns about baptismal water: "Fontes sub cooperculo modo consueto et custodiantur propter immundicias et sortilegia." See Gummerus 1902, 88, who puts the statute to the mid-1300s.

211. On Saint Birgitta, see the excellent English-language introductions in Morris 1999 and Sahlin 2001.

212. Book 7, chap. 28. See Bergh, Aili, Jönsson, and Undhagen 1967–98, 7:201–7, for the Latin text, and Klemming 1856, 3:291–93, for the Old Swedish.

213. Book 6, chap. 82. See Bergh, Aili, Jönsson, and Undhagen 1967–98, 6:243, for the Latin text, and Klemming 1856, 3:395–96, for the Old Swedish.

214. Book 6, chap. 76. "at thässa husins inbyggiare hawir tw ond thing Först vantro thy at han tror al thing styras j skäpnom ok lykko Annantidh nytia han galdra ok somlik diäfwlzlik ordh at han maghe faa manga fiska j siönom . . . " Klemming 1856, 3:196.

215. Book 6, chap. 3. Klemming 1856, 3:5; Bergh, Aili, Jönsson, and Undhagen 1967–98, 6:61.

216. Book 5, chap. 11. "tho gik saul olydhog*i*r fran mik sino*m* gudh oc spordhe raadh aff trolkono*n*ne . . . " Klemming 1856, 2:305.

217. Book 1, chap. 21. "Hwar är thä*n*ne koklarin vtan diäfwllin hulkin som äggiar ok radh*i*r ma*n*nome*n* til likamlikin lusta ok hedh*i*r hulkin som ey äru vtan fafäng ok forganglikin." Klemming 1856, 1:62.

218. *Seelentrost* has been described by Beckers 1977 as a collective title for "Lehr- und Exemplewerke in mnd. Prosa (2 Hälfte des 14. Jh.)." The editor places it to the middle of the fourteenth century; see Andersson-Schmitt 1959, 124.

219. *Seelentrost* was translated into the Old Swedish *Siælinna thrøst* (surviving in a manuscript from ca. 1430), and then from it into the Old Danish *Siæla trøst*. Some argue that the translation occurred as early the late fourteenth century, others at a time more contemporary with the manuscript. See Lundén 1967, 216–17, for an overview, as well as the detailed discussions in Thorén 1942; Henning 1954; and Henning 1960. On the Old Danish text, see Kaspersen et al. 1990, 573–80. *Sju vise mästare*, the Old Swedish articulation of *The Seven Sages* tradition, was translated into Old Swedish three times, on the first occasion in the late fourteenth century, and the other two times thereafter. All three translations are complete and preserved in manuscripts from the 1400s. On all aspects of this project, see Bampi 2007.

220. On the nature, value, and composition of miracle collections in medieval Scandinavia, see esp. Krötzl 1994 and Dahlerup 1998, 1:254–63.

221. Ejdestam 1975 refers to the phrase, but only in its common usage, but see the discussion in Heide 2006, 235–40. Presumably the connection between spinning technology and foretelling future events explains the current reference. In an eighteenth-century collection of Swedish superstitions (Wikman 1946), several use thread for purposes of, e.g., cursing (#1158) and protection against theft (#1228), and one (#294) in a way that would appear to tie in with the myth of the milk-stealing witch, taken up below. None, however, specify red thread.

222. Apparently a reference to the plant, *helleborus lin*, which as a topical application was used to relieve itching.

223. So Söderwall and Ljunggren 1884–1973 for this passage: "thy (för thu) skalt ey thro oppa dröma, ey oppa moth ellir footh, oc thro ey ath een människia hafwir bätre moth än annor (att det är bättre el. lyckligare att möta en menniska än en annan)."

224. Söderwall and Ljunggren 1884–1973 remark about this passage, "det som lemnas i handen, gåfva. thu skalt ey thro oppa hantzal (gelowen . . . off quader hant gif; härmed syftas på folktron att en under stillatigande utan begäran lemnad gåfva kunde bota vissa sjukdomar)." Cf. Ejdestam 1975, 60: "Handsöl, vanligen de första pengar som en försäljare fick in på dagen. Ordet är inte besläktat med 'öl' utan kommer av ett fornsvenskt *handsal* som betyder 'gåva' i handen. *Man borde spotta på handsölet för att få tur i dagens affärer*" (emphasis added). The phrase here surely points to this kind of belief system concerned with luck and good fortune.

225. Cf. Svenska akademien 1893–: "SVÄRDS-BREV. [fsv. *swärdhbref;* jfr fd. *svärd-brev,* mlt. *swertbref*] (förr) ss. amulett använd (om halsen buren) skriven besvärjelseformel som ansågs göra innehavaren osårbar."

226. Typically a lower cleric, a deacon, *djäkn* can also refer to students and other young people.

227. "Min kære son wilt thu thz første budhordhit wel halda / tha skalt thu engin thrylla eller mz truldom willa / Oc ey [gifwa] radh æller fulbordh [ther] til Thu skalt ey lata thik mz liff bøta / eller annan lifia / Thu math wel lækedom taka then som engin willa eller wantro blandas vthi / Thu skalt ey spa ellir lata spa / thu skalt ey lata thik mæta mz bast eller rødhum thradh eller mz nokro andro / Thu skalt ey wax æller bly lata ofwir thik gyuta / Thu skalt ey thro oppa fughla sang / Ey oppa gøkin tha han gal Ey oppa prustan ey a ørna kladha eller handa kladha eller nokot tholkit / Thu skalt ey thro oppa drøma / ey oppa moth eller footh / Oc thro ey ath een mænniskia hafwer bætre moth æn annor / Oc ey at nokot dywr hafwer bætra moth æn annat / Thu skalt ey thro oppa hantzal Ey oppa swerdhbreff eller annor galdra breff / Thu skalt enga handa beswerning ellir maning gøra hwarte ofwir iern eller nokot annat / Thu skalt ey saltarin lata løpa som diekna plægha ella annat slikt / Thu skalt ey hafwa the bøkir ther tøfri ær scrifwat vthi Somlika menniskior hafwa haar saman walkat oc hafwa ther wanthro til thz skalt thu aff skæra oc wakta thina siel om thu wilt / for thy wantro ok willa ær mangskona oc wardher mangom lundum hwilkit iak kan ey alt bescrifwa i thenna book." Henning 1954, 24–25.

228. See Andersson-Schmitt 1959, 17–18. Conversely, we sometimes find glimpses of native views of the supernatural in *Siælinna thrøst* as well: where the German original lists various otherworldly beings consistent with its cultural environment (pp. 16–17), the Old Swedish has "tha skalt thu ey thro vppa tompta gudha ælla oppa wætter / ey oppa nek / æller forsa karla / ey oppa skratta eller tompt orma / Thu skalt ey thro oppa maro eller elfwa / oc oppa enga handa spook eller willo ffor thy thz er enkte annat æn diefwlsins gab mz hwilko han swiker folkit som ey hafwa fulla oc stadhugha throo." Henning 1954, 23.

229. Henning 1954, 20–23; cf. Stephens and Dahlgren 1847–74, 1:603–4.

230. "han søkte swa længe [at] han fan een trulkarl oc hafdhe sit radh mz honom / Thrulkarlin saghdhe / Wilt thu gøra som iak sighir / thz wardher wel æpter thinom wilia." Henning 1954, 20.

231. "Thz war een prester som plæghade øfwa swarta konstena [han] foor mz throldom oc galdrom . . . " Henning 1954, 18.

232. "Oc genstan j samo stwnd foor konugen [!] mz borghinne oc allo sino herskap nidher j hælfwitis affgrund Oc førdhe Prestin mz sik / Swa skulu alle the fara som troldom oc diæfwlskap øfwa." Henning 1954, 19.

233. "thu skalt ok ekke thro oppa skepnolagh eller ødhno som hedhnugane gøra hwilke som sighia hwat skepnan hafwer mannom skapat ont eller goth thz skal honom io ændelika ofwer gaa hwat thz ær heller sælikheth eller ysæld." Henning 1954, 25.

234. On the impact of this fact, see, e.g., Mitchell 1997b and Layher 2000, 2008.

235. One of the best-known tales of medieval Western Europe, the story of Alexander was translated circa 1380 into Old Swedish as *Konung Alexander* but known already a

century earlier in Iceland as *Alexanders saga*. The Old Swedish rhymed version is based on the prose *Historia de preliis Alexandri Magni*, whereas the Old Icelandic prose translation builds on the *Alexandreis*. *Konung Alexander* is connected with Bo Jonsson Grip (d. 1386). See Pipping 1943, 77–79; Ståhle 1967, 89–93; and Ronge 1957. All references here are to Klemming 1862. With respect to this image of the prophetic high magic sorcerer, already in the early thirteenth century, the Icelandic monk, Gunnlaugr Leifsson (d. 1218 or 1219), of Þingeyrar monastery, translated Geoffrey of Monmouth's *Prophetiæ Merlini* into verse as *Merlínúspá* ([*Merlin's Prophecy*] on which, see Frank 1982 and Marold 1993). Gunnlaugr generally refers to Merlin with the native *spámaðr* 'prophet' (e.g. *spár spakligar spámanns* 'the prophet's wise prophecies'; Finnur Jónsson 1973, 2:11), the term most often also used of biblical prophets, but sometimes he employs the calque *prófeti*. But even when the poem uses this term and takes up learned forms of "magic" (e.g., vv. 95–96 of *Merlínúspá* II), nothing quite like the sense of the high magic practitioner one gets of the Nectanabus of *Konung Alexander* emerges from the poem. Gunnlaugr even goes so far as to describe him as being held dear by Christian people (*kærr vas hann kyni / kristnu þjóðar*, v. 2)!

236. On the differences between high and low magic in the Middle Ages, see Russell 1972, 2–14, and Kieckhefer 1989. A similar figure of this sort in the northern world may be seen in Simon Magus, mentioned earlier. The Christian context of his story and of the sin associated with his name (simony), meant that Simon Magus, the court prestidigitator, was probably better, and earlier, known to the Nordic populations than either Merlin or Nectanabus; cf. Flint 1991, 338–44.

237. An additional narrative form that no doubt played an important role in the culture of late medieval Scandinavia in fashioning and disseminating images of witchcraft and magic was the ballad. Although there is much to be said about the tremendous, with respect to both size and quality, Nordic ballad corpus, I do not take them up in detail here for the simple reason that we do not have so much as a single complete ballad text from the Nordic Middle Ages. Good evidence for their existence exists, but what specific information they contained is impossible to know. I do not, as I have argued elsewhere (e.g., Mitchell 2002b, 2007a) subscribe to the view that the ballads were fixed texts frozen in time, allowing us to access the medieval form by citing the later transcriptions. For introductions to the Nordic ballad in its Danish context, see Colbert 1989 and Dahlerup 1998, 1:191–210, 2:113–213. On the relations between the various Nordic genres, see Jonsson 1991 and Mitchell 1991b, and on the same topic, with particular reference to the importance of the later ballad evidence, see Mitchell 2003a.

CHAPTER 4

1. Campbell 1972. Concerned with the reception of the native mythological materials in Christian Iceland, Clunies Ross 1998, 22–43, employs the same locution, "Myths to live by," to capture how pagan materials were reconfigured into an acceptable worldview for the emerging post-Conversion society. It is precisely in this sense of invented, renewed, actualized, and "narrativized" dogma and *Weltanschauung* that I intend the phrase here.

2. Highly enlightening on this point is Leach 1982, who argues convincingly that although myths are often "doctrinal, normative statements of belief," they are never mere affirmations of cultural hegemony, but can also be contentious articulations of difference.

3. Malinowski 1954, 101, from comments originally published in 1926.

4. By "cultural competence," I mean deep knowledge of a culture's codes. "Cultural competence" was developed as a calque on the idea of linguisitic or communicative competence, as in, e.g., Hymes 1972, and esp. the essays in Gumperz 1982. Kellogg 1991, 96–97, extends the term to distinguish between articulated narrative matter in performance versus an underlying knowledge of the signs that give it meaning.

5. This component of witchcraft ideology has a long scholarly history: for orientations, see "Teufelspakt" in Bächtold-Stäubli and Hoffmann-Krayer 1987, 3: cols. 1842–43, and "Abschwörung" in 1: cols. 120–21. Synoptic reviews are offered in Rudwin 1973; Seiferth 1952; Nuffel 1966; Lazar 1972; Russell 1984; and Boureau 2006, 68–92; on the evolution of demonologists' thinking about the *pactum cum diabolo,* see Clark 1997.

6. Grimm (1966, 3:1019) wonders whether such traditions "were taken over from christian stories of the devil, or had their ground in heathen opinion itself." Rudwin (1973, 169–70) argues that the story is "of Oriental origin," having come from Persian sacred writings, and suggests an evolution from these origins through Jewish traditions (e.g., the Book of Enoch) to Christian belief.

7. Several patristic writers touched on this issue, none more critically for future developments than Saint Augustine, whose "On the Divination of Demons" was to become key, especially as this treatment influenced the thinking of Thomas Aquinas in *Summa Theologica* (pt. 2, quest. 95, "Superstition in Divination"). On this point, see Fleteren 1999 and the literature cited there.

8. Regarding *Basilíus saga*, see following discussion; the translations in AM 225 fol. do not include the life of Saint Basil. On the complicated relations between the texts, see Tveitane 1968, 13–25.

9. Cf. the entry in Knight 2003.

10. See Tubach 1969, nos. 3565–72, on the exempla; and Cothren 1984 on the visual evidence. Many of the Northern European texts are printed in Dasent 1845.

11. Indeed, so significant is this consideration that it is placed third in a list of twenty-eight errors. See Thorndike 1944, 261–66.

12. Quoted in Bailey 2003, 37.

13. A century later, Jean Bodin articulates this view in detail, suggesting that the devil's pact encompasses nine separate offences against God. Cf. Clark 1997, 675.

14. See Mitchell 2008b. In her comprehensive study of postmedieval Icelandic cases, Ólína Þorvarðardóttir (2000, 129–30, 175–84) finds that with minor exceptions (i.e., Sveinn lögmaðr Sölvason), the *djöfulssamningur* is not a common legal accusation in Icelandic witchcraft trials. Hans Eyvind Næss (1982, 134) sees the devil's pact as an insignificant factor in early modern Norwegian cases, as does Bente Alver (1971, 37); however, Rune Hagen (2002) suggests that the focus of earlier scholarship may not have adequately considered northern Norway and the trials involving the Sámi. Cf. Knutsen 2003. The

seats of empire, Sweden and Denmark, actively engaged in this sort of prosecution: Linda Oja's splendid consideration of magic in the Swedish seventeenth and eighteenth centuries notes a large number of cases where the *djävulsförbund* played a primary role. See Oja 1999, 322, and Edsman 2000. On Denmark, where the devil's pact was incorporated into the legal consideration of witchcraft in 1617, arriving at precise tallies is difficult; see Johansen 1993, 344–45, resp. 355.

15. I have argued (Mitchell 2000b) that the placement of witchcraft-related crimes within the later medieval laws is directly connected with this idea.

16. "*med þeim* skilmála ad þau laun *sem* Maria uill h*onu*m un*n*a hi*er* fyr*ir* uill h*ann* an*n*ars heims hafa þa h*onu*m ligg*r* mestá . . . " Kålund 1884–91. AM 80, 8° is dated to 1473.

17. Henning 1954, 20–23, 18.

18. Klemming 1877–78, 1:5–9, 13–16, 47–48, 127–28.

19. Gering 1882, 1:154–60. Note Gering's comment (2:138) that whatever differences may exist between this tale and the Theophilus legend, and they are great, "Die verwantschaft zwischen unserem *æventýri* und der legende ist unverkenbar . . . "

20. Stephens and Dahlgren 1847–74, 1:603–4; 1:18–20; 1:28–29; 2:766–67.

21. E.g., Grimm 1966, 3:1018–19.

22. "Í þann tíma er ríkði yfir Noregi Hákon jarl var Eiríkr konúngr í Svíþióð. Oc eptir þá hina frægia orrostu er hann hafði átt við Styrbiörn oc feck sigr með þeim hætti, at Oddiner gaf honum sigrinn, en hann het því til at hann gafsc Oddineri til eptir hit Xda ár, oc sípan var hann callaðr Eiríkr hin sigrsæli." *Fornmanna sögur eptir gömlum handritum* 1825–37, 10:283; cf. 5:250.

23. Unger 1871, 64–69, 402–21, 1080–90, 1090–1105, on which, see Jorgensen 1994. Regarding the dating of the manuscripts used in Unger's edition of *Maríu saga* (1871), see Widding 1996. On the Theophilus legend in medieval Denmark, see Gad 1961, 139–42.

24. Unger 1871, 1093.

25. *Basilíus saga*, partially preserved in AM 655 VI 4° (ca. 1200–1225) and AM 238 II fol. (ca. 1300–1350), almost certainly presented stories from the saint's life; see Morgenstern 1893. The manuscript dating here follows *Ordbog over det norrøne prosasprog: A Dictionary of Old Norse Prose* 1989, 34. Narratives drawn from folk tradition too may be very telling, and here one thinks most especially about such tales as those attached to Sæmundr fróði and the Black School (ML 3000 *Escape from the Black School*), particularly those already part of the early eighteenth-century materials in Árnasafni that specify such concepts as the bartered soul ("Inn mátt þú ganga, töpuð er sálin") and even state that the devil had concluded a contract with Sæmundr ("Síðan kom fjandinn til Sæmundar og gjörði kontrakt við hann . . . "). See Jón Árnason 1954–61, 1:469–70; on Sæmundr and witchcraft, cf. Ólína Þorvarðardóttir 2000, 253–55 et passim. Some tales employ these motifs for comical effect, such as that of Hálfdan prest and the *kölski* in "Grímseyjarförin." See Jón Árnason 1954–61, 1:502–3 for multiforms of M 210. *Bargain with devil* and M211. *Man sells soul to devil*. See also Thompson 1966.

26. Carlsson 1921–44, 2:148 and 3:18.

27. These events gave rise to local legends that have continued into modern times. See Jón Árnason 1954–61, 2:77, and Finnur Jónsson and Hannes Finnsson 1772, 2:100. The folklore tradition is by no means a mirrorlike reflection of the annals, although it agrees on the main points; see Mitchell 2008b. These events form the background to Vilborg Davíðsdóttir's 1997 historical novel, *Eldfórnin*.

28. "brend syst*ir* ein i K*i*rkiubæ er Kristin het e*r* gefiz hafdi pukanu*m* m*ed* brefi. ho*n* hafdi *ok* misfa*r*it m*ed* guds likama *ok* kastad aftr v*m* naadahustre laagiz m*ed* morgu*m* leikm*onnum*," from *Flatø-Annaler*, Storm 1888, 402. *Naadahustre* has generally been treated by Jón Árnason and others, due to its sensitivity, as the *door* to the privy, but *tré* is intended here in its sense as 'seat', specifically 'the seat of a privy'.

29. "Brend systir ein i k*i*rkiu er gefiz hafði pukanu*m* m*eð* brefi," from *Skálholts-Annaler*, Storm 1888, 210 (n.b., k*i*rkiu, "Feilskrift for K*i*rkiubæ").

30. "J*t*em degr*a*derade h*a*nn [Bishop Jón Sigurðarson] syst*ur* j K*i*rkiubæ v*m* p*a*ua blasphemia*m*. ok sida*n* var ho*n* brend," from *Lögmanns-annáll*, Storm 1888, 274.

31. Cf. Ólafur Daviðsson 1940–43, 14; Ólína Þorvarðardóttir 2000, 121; and Magnús Rafnsson 2003, 10–12.

32. This point has been made in many modern studies of witchcraft; see, e.g., Macfarlane 1991 and Demos 1982.

33. On the relationship between such signs and subsequent witchcraft outbreaks, see Hall 1990 and the literature cited there. On the astronomical features, see *Skálholtsannáll* for 1339 and 1340, Storm 1888, 208.

34. *Skálholtsannáll* for 1336: "Heyrðiz stynr mikill í skalanu*m* i K*i*rkiu bæ. sva s*em* siuks m*a*n*n*z af allri alþyðu miok optliga langan ti*m*a suma*r*s en*n* ecki fa*nn*z þo at leitað væri." Storm 1888, 207. Cf. *Gottskalksannál* and *Flateyjarannáll*, Storm 1888, 349, 399.

35. Jón Árnason 1954–61, 2:77–78, comments, "En snemma lagðist sá orðrómur á að munkarnir vendu þangað komur sínar meir en góðu hófi gegndi til að fífla systurnar," and relates several tales in support of the assertion. But as stories of this type are common and the sources all postmedieval, we cannot, of course, be certain that the accusation reflects medieval views.

36. "Jon*n* bysku*p* fangadi Arngr*i*m Eystein *ok* Magn*us* brædr i Þyckua bæ fyr*ir* þat e*r* þe*i*r hofdu bart a Þo*r*laki abbo*t*a sinu*m*. þeir vrdu *ok* opinbe*r*ir at saurrlifi sum*ir* at barn eign. var Arngr*i*mr settr i taa iarn en*n* Eystein*n* i hals iarn. Hola bysku*p* fangadi .iij. brædr a Modru vollu*m* ok iarnadi fyr*ir* þær sak*ir* h*a*nn gaf þ*eim*." Storm 1888, 402.

37. "J*t*em þa kom *ok* vt Jon bysko*p* Sigu*r*dar son. tok h*a*nn Arngr*i*m *ok* Eyrstein ad corr*e*cc*i*on*em*. brædr j Vere j Þyckkuabæ. fyr*ir* þat e*r* þ*ei*r bordu aa Þo*r*lake abota sinu*m*. var Arngr*i*mr setrr j taaj*a*rn. en Eyrsteinn j hallsiarn J*t*em degr*a*derade h*a*nn syst*ur* j K*i*rkiubæ v*m* p*a*ua blasphemia*m*. ok sida*n* var ho*n* brend. J*t*em Orm*r* bysko*p* hafde *ok* j vblidu brædr aa Modruuollu*m*. *ok* kastade suma j myrkua stofu." Storm 1888, 274.

38. "Báðir biskuparnir voru vígðir 1343 og héldu til Íslands sama ár. Varð þá þegar róstusamt." Magnús Stefánsson 1978, 250.

39. "A þui aare g*er*duzt bysko*p*ar hardir miogh vidr lærda *ok* leika aa Isl*a*nde." Storm 1888, 274.

40. "Jtem quod divine protectioni abrenunciavit et se dyabolo commendavit . . . ";
"Jtem quod super excitatione dyaboli ad perficienda predicta verba que subintrant cum
incantatione pestilenti recitavit . . . " See Unger and Huitfeldt 1847–, 9:1, 112–15.

41. Cf. the case in 1634, when a resident of Odense, Christen Pedersen, was discovered in a field with a detailed, written *pactum cum diabolo*; see Henningsen 1969, 191.
Actual Danish (1721), Swedish (1727), and Norwegian (1705) examples of the devil's pact
continue into the eighteenth century; see, e.g., Henningsen 1969, 194–95; Edsman 2000;
and Alver 1971, 37. In Iceland, a man was executed who was said to have (or whose acts
were interpreted as his having) made a pact with the devil in his sleep; see Ólína Þorvarðardóttir 2000, 137, 143, 146, 182, 188, and 372.

42. With reference to the pact, the sabbat, and the diabolical conspiracy, Pócs 1999,
26, notes that "the popular devil images and the folklore roots of the 'conspiracy' are
missing from the studies. . . ." See Pócs 1991–92, as well as, e.g., Runeberg 1947; Henningsen 1991–92 and 1993. The sabbat's history is not attested as well or as early as once
thought, the result of Cohn 1975 and Kieckhefer 1976. I have argued for pre-Christian
traits contributing to these myths in the Nordic world (Mitchell 1997a), on which these
remarks build.

43. The full bibliography is enormous; excellent English-language reviews are provided in Cohn 1975; Kieckhefer 1976; Flint 1991; and Bailey 2003.

44. Martène and Durand 1717, 1:950–53, available in translation in Kors and Peters
2001, 114–16.

45. Cohn 1975 uses the example of Minucius Felix writing in the second century CE,
describing what the Roman world thought Christians themselves practiced, to make his
point.

46. In addition to Cohn 1975, cf. Russell 1972, 23, 100, et passim.

47. Ginzburg 1991, anticipated already in his classic study decades earlier, Ginzburg
1985. See also Ginzburg 1984, 1993a, and 1993b. Cf. the review in Bailey 1996.

48. The classic study is Strömbäck 1935, and before him, Fritzner 1877; recent studies
focusing on shamanism and the question of Nordic spiritual life include DuBois 1999;
Price 2002; Siikala 2002; and Tolley 2009.

49. Keyser and Munch 1846–95, 1:17; 4:18; see my remarks in Mitchell 2000a.

50. E.g., the Norwegian trial against Helle Joensdatter, 1652, printed in Alver 1971,
135–36. Although the accusations against witches in the various Nordic countries involved
different locations (e.g., the Norwegian witches to Blocksberg and Lyderhorn; the Danish
witches to Blocksberg, or Hekkenfelt in Iceland, or Bredsten in Norway; the Swedish
witches to Blåkulla in the Baltic), the overall pattern is generally the same. On the origins
and nature of *Blåkullafärden*, Sahlgren 1915 remains useful, if dated; see also Mitchell
1997a; Sörlin 1997; and Östling 2002.

51. "Nauis quedam dicta snekkia domini Thuronis Ben[c]tson militis, de Lubek
versus Stokholm velificans, in via prope Blaakulla grande tempestatis periculum subit."
Lundén 1950, 14. The owner of the ship, Ture Bengtsson [Bielke], was a strong supporter
of the Brigittine Vadstena Abbey, having been responsible in 1412 for bringing Saint Bir-

gitta's reliquary-shrine (*skrin*) to Sweden. See the entries for July 1, 1412, January 14, 1415, and August 8, 1431 in Gejrot 1988. See also Lindblom 1963, 19–20. Cf. *Karlskrönikan*, which mentions Sir Ture (l. 168) and says of this year a scant twenty lines later, "Genstan ept*er* litla stundh / öpedes at*er* onth manga lundh" (Klemming 1866, ll. 202–3; "Soon after a little while / evil was again loosed in many ways").

52. Lundén 1950, viii–ix, 4.

53. Magnus, 1996–98, 121–22 (emphasis added). "Præterea prope Aquilonare littus eius exurgit mons excelsus : quem nauticum vulgus vitandi infelicis ominis, & marinæ tempestatis gratia, Virginem vocat : atoß in eius portu manentes certis munusculis puellis dari soltis, vtpote chirothecis, sericeis zonis, & similibus, eas tanquam amico munere placant. Nec ingratum montis numen sentire videntur, prout aliquando factum meminit antiquitas, voce lapsa iussum fuisse donantem mutare portum, ne periclitaretur : & ita faciendo saluus factus est, vbi alij sunt periclitati. *In eo monte certis anni temporibus dicitur esse conuentus Aquilonarium maleficarum, vt examinent præstigia sua. Tardius ministerio dæmonum accedens, dira afficitur correptione.* Sed hæc opinioni, non assertioni cedant." Magnus 1555, 85 (bk. 2, chap. 23; emphasis added).

54. "hade åfta warit i Blåkulla, och åhr vtaf th*et* sälskapet, som ride*n*de åhro, och hafuer märket i näsenn . . . " Almqvist 1939–51, 2:166.

55. "åhr icke vtaf th*et* bäste slächted, honn war och th*et* slaget som pläga rida til Blåkulla [. . .] och åhnn mera sade honn, th*et* åhr icke länge sädenn at hon hade boolet medh diefwulenn." Almqvist 1939–51, 2:167.

56. Translations of Gregory's *Dialogues* into West Norse date already from the mid-twelfth century; see Turville-Petre 1953, 135–37. The Old Swedish text is published in Henning 1954, 226–27. Cf. Tubach 1969, no. 1663, for evidence of the tale's popularity in the Middle Ages. For Gregory's original text, consult Migne 1849, cols. 230, 232; a translation is provided in Zimmerman 1959, 121–23.

57. On the dating of the murals, see Tuulse 1963, 469.

58. Edwards and Pálsson 1970, 4, with my emendations. "Kona var nefnd Heiðr. Hún var vǫlva ok seiðkona; hún vissi fyrir úorðna hluti af fróðleik sínum. Hún fór á veizlur ok sagði mǫnnum fyrir forlǫg manna ok vetrarfar. Hún hafði með sér xxx manna, þat váru xv sveinar ok xv meyjar." Boer 1888, 11.

59. Boer 1888, 11.

60. Larson 1935, 58; "oc sva firi morð oc fordæðo skape. oc utisetu at vekia troll upp. at fremia heiðrni með þvi . . . " Keyser and Munch 1846–95, 1:19.

61. "En um morgininn, at áliðnum degi, ver henni veittr sá umbúningr, sem hon þurfti at hafa til at fre*m*ja seiðinn. Hon bað ok fá sér konur þær, er kynni frœði þat, sem til seiðsins þarf ok Varðlokur hétu." Einar Ól. Sveinsson and Matthías Þórðarson 1957, 207. My translation.

62. Einar Ól. Sveinsson and Matthías Þórðarson 1957, 208.

63. E.g., AM 343a, 4t°; AM 471, 4ᵗº; cf. Konrað Gíslason et al. 1889–94, 578, 654–55.

64. "Þat var eina nótt, at hann vaknar við brak mikit í skóginum; hann hljóp út, ok sá tröllkonu, ok fell fax á herðar henni. Ketill mælti: hvert ætlar þú, fóstra? hún reigðist

við honum, ok mælti: ek skal til tröllaþings, þar kemr Skelkingr norðan úr Dumbshafi, konungr trölla, ok Ófóti úr Ófótansfirði, ok Þorgerðr Hörgatröll ok aðrar stórvættir norðan úr landi; dvel eigi mik, því at mér er ekki um þik, síðan þú kveittir hann Kaldrana; ok þá óð hún út á sjóinn ok svá til hafs; ekki skorti gandreiðir í eyjunni um nóttina, ok varð Katli ekki mein at því . . . " Rafn 1829–30, 2:131. As noted previously, *tröll* is often of ambiguous meaning, although the *tröllkona* here is certainly a witch. Whether *tröllaþing* is a 'witch-assembly', as I have translated it, or something else is an open question. Cf. assembly and sacrifice in *Bárðar saga*: "they made sacrifices for their good fortune at a place now called Trolls' (Witches') Church . . . "; "þá blótuðu þeir til heilla sér; þat heitir nú Tröllakirkja." Þórhallur Vilmundarson and Bjarni Vilhjálmsson 1991, 111.

65. Rafn 1829–30, 2:127.

66. "víða hefi ek gǫndum rennt í nótt." Björn K. Þórólfsson and Guðni Jónsson 1972, 243.

67. "Hjalti mælti: 'Þú hefir sét gandreið, ok er þat jafnan ávallt fyrir stórtíðendum.' " Einar Ól. Sveinsson 1954, 321.

68. E.g., *Helgaqviða Hiǫrvarðzsonar*, 15; *Hárbarðlióð*, 20, both in Neckel and Kuhn 1983; Einar Ól. Sveinsson and Matthías Þórðarson 1957, 29, 93.

69. Hermann Pálsson and Edwards 1985, 259. "Móðir mín [. . .] fá þú mér út krókstaf minn ok bandvetlinga, þvíat ek vil á gandreið fara, er nú hátíð í heiminum neðra; þá var snarat út úr hólnum einum krókstaf, sem elzskara væri, hann stígr á stafinn, ok dregr á sik vetlingana, ok keyrir sem börn eru vön at gjöra." *Fornmanna sögur eptir gömlum handritum* 1825–37, 3:176.

70. Cf. Feilberg 1910.

71. "Jak kan flygha j wædhreno." Henning 1954, 95.

72. Henning 1954, 23–24. Cf. Tubach 1969, no. 1648, for examples from other traditions, including the Middle Low German *Seelentrost* from which the Swedish version is translated.

73. Many cultures bring these motifs together. Of the Nyakyusa of Tanzania, e.g., it was reported, "The incentive to witchcraft is said to be the desire for good food. Witches lust for meat and milk—the prized foods of the group—and it is this which drives them to commit witchcraft[. . . .] The witches are thought to fly by night on their pythons or 'on the wind'; they attack either singly or in covens; and they feast on human flesh." Wilson 1982, 277.

74. Þat kann ec iþ tíunda,   ef ec sé túnriðor
          leica lopti á:
    ec svá vinnc,   at þeir villir fara
          sinna heim hama,
          sinna heim huga. (Neckel and Kuhn 1983, 43)

The translation follows Hollander 1986, 39. The more literal translation by Clarke (1923, 85) reads, "A tenth I know: if I see phantom riders sporting in the air, I can contrive to make them go bereft of their proper shapes and their proper senses."

75. E.g., Björn M. Ólsen 1916; Läffler 1916.

76. See also Riising 1969, 340.

77. "þar sem finz i helgum bokum, at kveldriður eða hamleypur þykkiaz með Diana gyðiu oc Herodiade a litilli stundu fara yfir stor hof riðandi hvolum eða selum, fuglum eða dyrum, eða yfir stor lond, oc þott þær þikkiz i likama fara, þa vatta bækr þat lygi vera." Unger 1874, 914. Cf. the similarity between the comment here about witches riding on whales and the scene in *Friðþjófs saga frækna* involving the *hamhleypur* hired to kill him; Chapter 3 and Rafn 1829–30, 2:79.

78. The various criteria for the dating (specifically, between 1264 and 1298) are enumerated in Unger 1874, xxviii.

79. Cf. Russell 1972, 75–80, and the literature cited there. The wording used in *Jóns saga Baptista* suggests that it may have been modeled after Gratian.

80. Schlyter 1822–77, 1:38. In translating *a quiggrindu* as 'witch-ride', I am following, e.g., Lidén 1914, 413–16, whose argument would equate the phrase with such Icelandic terms as *túnriða*. See the full discussion in Holmbäck and Wessén 1979, 5:125–26. Almost all authorities agree that the term refers in some sense to the idea of the 'witch-ride'.

81. E.g., the runic phrase from Rök (ca. 800) *histR kunaR* (= Gunn's horse = a valkyrie's horse = a wolf); the famous wolf-mounted figure with snake-bridle on the Hunnestad monument, Skårby parish, Skåne; the similar figure in the thirteenth-century prose that accompanies the eddic *Helgaqviða Hiǫrvarðzsonar*; and the ogress HyRockin riding a wolf to Baldr's funeral in *Snorra edda*, also composed in the thirteenth century. See, respectively, Brate 1911, 239–40; Jacobsen and Moltke 1941–42, 1: ills. 677–78; Neckel and Kuhn 1983, 147; and Finnur Jónsson 1931, 65. Not every observer interprets this tradition in the same way; for an earlier generation of scholars, e.g., the image of the witch on a wolf was considered certain evidence of Hellenistic influence; see Linderholm 1918a, 115–17.

82. Magnus 1996–98, 2:308–9.

83. See Schück 1929 and Lundén 1982.

84. *Revelationes Extravagantes*, chap. 8. "somlike aff them hotadho henne liffuandis bränna wilia, Somlike grabbadho hona sighiande henne wille fara, oc ena trulkärling wara . . ." Klemming 1857–84, 4:57. On the witch-saint relationship, see Kieckhefer 1994.

85. Additional examples are examined in Jón Hnefill Aðalsteinsson 1978.

86. Already Linderholm 1918a, 29, viewed the situation largely along these lines: "I det svenska Blåkullamötet hava skilda förkristna och medeltideskristna traditioner flutit samman," although he specifically suggests the witches' sabbat as a legacy of female worship within a phallocentric fertility cult dedicated to Freyr.

87. The sexual connotations of the effeminacy accusation are of a very different sort than the diabolical orgies of the sabbat. See Meulengracht Sørensen 1980, 1983; Price 2002, 210–23, 395–96; and Dillmann 2006, 444–56, and Solli 2002.

88. Sahlgren 1915.

89. See esp. Gjerdman 1941 and Odenius 1984, as well as Folin and Tegner 1985, whose descriptions I follow here.

90. Aarne and Thompson 1961. Cf. Tubach 1969, no. 5361.

91. The idea of clipping a lock of his beard smacks of charm magic and parallels the popular church art subject of Samson and Delilah.

92. I find it difficult to regard the conclusion to this story as frightening rather than amusing but accept that a medieval audience might. And in either case, it could draw the appropriate moral lesson from the tale.

93. See the discussion in Chapter 6 of this volume, as well as in Bardsley 2006.

94. This topic has been exhaustively covered in Wall 1977–78. See Brandt 1976 on Danish murals with this scene. Davies 1999, 189–90, e.g., discusses the continued popularity of this narrative in the British Isles into modern times.

95. "Fecisti, quod quedam mulieres facere solent et firmiter credunt, ita dico, ut si vicinus eius lacte vel apibus habundaret, omnem abundantiam lactis et mellis, quam suus vicinus ante habere visus est, et ad se et ad sua animalia, vel ad quos voluerint a diabolo adiute, suis fascinationibus et incantationibus se posse convertere credant." Wasserschleben 1851, 660. Burchard, *Drecreta,* bk. 19.

96. On Magister Mathias and his work, see Piltz 1974.

97. "Hec et similia facit et procurat dyabolus deludens eos, qui male credunt." Piltz 1984, 28.

98. "Nonne, sicut quidam dicunt se vidisse, intrant quedam corpora a maleficis mulieribus consuta in modum vtrium, et lac de armentis alienis congerunt?" Piltz 1974, 55.

99. "Möjligheten finns, att magister Matthias kände till Robert of Brunnes *Handlyng Synne* eller eventuella andra äldre verk, där liknande företeelser omtalas." Wall 1977–78, 1:86. See 1:75–86, building the case.

100. Hollander 1991, 57. "Hálfdan konungr tók jólaveizlu á Haðalandi. Þar varð undarligr atburðr jólaaptan, er menn váru til borða gengnir, ok var þat allmikit fjǫlmenni, at þar hvarf vist ǫll af borðum ok alt mungát. Sat konungr hryggr eptir, en hverr annarra sótti sitt heimili. En til þess at konungr mætti víss verða, hvat þessum atburð olli, lét hann taka Finn einn, er margfróðr var, ok vildi neyða hann til saðrar sǫgu, ok píndi hann ok fékk þó eigi af honum. Finnrinn hét þannug mjǫk til hjálpar, er Haraldr var, son hans, ok Haraldr bað honum eirðar ok fékk eigi, ok hleypði Haraldr honum þá í brot at óvilja konungs ok fylgði honum sjálfr. Þeir kómu þar farandi, er hǫfðingi einn helt veizlu mikla, ok var þeim at sýn þar vel fagnat. Ok er þeir hǫfðu þar verit til várs, þá var þat einn dag, at hǫðinginn mælti til Haralds: 'Furðu mikit torrek lætr faðir þinn sér at, er ek tók vist nǫkkura frá honum í vetr, en ek mun þér þat launa með feginsǫgu: Faðir þinn er nú dauðr, ok skaltu heim fara. Muntu þá fá ríki þat alt, er hann hefir átt, ok þar með skaltu eignast allan Noreg.'" Bjarni Aðalbjarnarson 1962, 1:91–92.

101. See the thoughtful insights on this point in Ciklamini 1979.

102. On this motif (D1982.4) and others, such as magical milking with a knife, see Alver 1971, 184–209, and Wall 1977–78, 2:120–36.

103. See Harris 1976.

104. On the dating of the murals in Tuse Church (Figures 5, 10, and 12) and the work of "Isefjordsværkstedet," see Nationalmuseet 1933–2008, IV. Holbæk Amt. 1 Bind, 597. Tuulse (1963, 536) suggests that the murals in Övergran kyrka (Figure 6) were the

gifts of Archbishop Jacob Ulfsson, whose heraldic crest is found there. These murals, like those at Yttergran, are believed to be the work of Albertus Pictor or his school, on whom see Lundberg 1961 and Cornell and Wallin 1972. On the age of the Dannemora image (Figure 7), see Norberg 1988, 8, and for the mural in Vejlby kirke (Figure 9), see Nationalmuseet 1933–2008, XVI. Århus Amt. 3 Bind, 1466.

105. The rich resource represented by these works has been carefully explored in, e.g., Nyborg 1978; Nisbeth 1985; Nilsén 1986; Kempff 1992; Saxtorph 1997; and Bolvig 1999.

106. Other complications, such as preservation and the costs of mural painting, also factor into this problem. Post-Reformation traditions in Iceland about the *snakkur* or *tilberi*, e.g., suggest that they formed an important part of Icelandic witchcraft beliefs but have left few traces in medieval sources, although perhaps alluded to in the phrase *eda miolk fra monnum* in Jón Þorkelsson and Jón Sigurðsson 1857–1932, 2:224. On the *snakkur*, see Ólína Þorvarðardóttir 2000, 289–91. More broadly, see Wall 1977–78, 1:72–114.

107. Wall 1977–78, 1:56–57. It is useful to bear in mind that these references are to modern national borders. Thus, e.g., semiautonomous Gotland was part of the Swedish diocese of Linköping but, following the fall of Visby to Valdemar Atterdag in 1361, remained in Danish hands until 1645.

108. Wall 1977–78, 1:58.

109. Thus, e.g., the economic argument laid out in Boyer and Nissenbaum 1974.

110. See Chapter 1 in this volume, and esp. the comment in Wax and Wax 1962, 183: "We think of ourselves as the believers in causal law and the primitive as dwelling in a world of happenstance. Yet, the actuality is to the contrary. . . . "

111. I have noted this possibility in Mitchell 2000b.

112. Ellis 2001, 41. The term "ostension" is borrowed by folklorists from the field of semiotics, notwithstanding its venerable use in other fields (e.g., "ostensive definition"). The meaning of the word—'the act of showing; manifestation; revealing; appearance; display; monstrance'—and its etymology (Latin *ostendere* 'to show') underscore its relevance to the sort of situation under discussion. With respect to the applicability of "ostension" and "ostensive action" to folkloristics, see, in addition to Dégh and Vázsonyi 1983 and Ellis 1989, its use in Fine 1991; Ellis 2000, 204, 226, 236, 286–87; and Ellis 2001, esp. 165–85, "Ostension as Folk Drama." I have applied this approach specifically to a nineteenth-century case of witchcraft assault in Mitchell 2004; see also Mitchell 2000c.

113. As this view has famously been summarized, "not only can facts be turned into narratives but narratives can also be turned into facts." Dégh and Vázsonyi 1983, 29. In his discussion of contemporary "satanic" incidents in the United States, Ellis (1989, 218) argues, "Traditional narratives [. . .] are also maps for action, often violent actions." An extreme case, but with sociological parallels to this argument, is presented in Nash 1967.

CHAPTER 5

1. Cf. Robinson 1984.

2. "Eod*em* die witnade Olaff Heming*ss*on ok Ped*er* Olss*on*, swa ath the hördho, th*et*

Staffan Skalme kallade hustr*u* Kate*r*ina, Andr*es* Jonss*ons* epteliffua, ena t*ru*lkona." Carlsson 1921–44, 114.

3. "Sigridh Jenis Boks [hustru] stoodh til fore rettin, ath hon hade kallath Ragnilde graagaas kiätterska, swa ath hon ok hennis dotter skuldo baaden haffua legat medh en man." Hildebrand 1917, 111. On Stockholm in this period, and this case in particular, see Schück 1951, 417. "Ragnil Gr*a*gas" appears frequently in the Stockholm records of the 1490s: Almquist 1930, 50, 173, 277.

4. "ath fore dande quinnor bön skuld tha skal Sigrid, som kallade Ragnilde gragaas ketterska, niwta liffuetoch forsweria stadin och stadzmark. Komber hon i staden igen, tha skal hon stwpas." Hildebrand 1917, 112. *Stupa* implies being restrained (e.g., in stocks) for the purpose of being further punished. Cf. Svenska akademien 1893–, "spö- l. skampåle vid vilken delinkvent bands l. kedja des fast för att utsättas för offentlig vanära o. hudstrykning l. spöslitning . . . "; and Dahlgren 1914–16, "straffpåle, kåk; spöslitning; ris (vanligen vid kåken)." The phrase *dande quinnor*, despite the modern association of the phrase with *allmogekvinnor, bondhustrur*, and so on (Svenska akademien 1893–), at this time implied various forms of responsible, dignified social status—*ärbar kvinna, dygdig kvinna, äkta hustru, matrona*, etc. Cf. Söderwall and Ljunggren 1884–1973.

5. The cognomen "gray goose" suggests several associations, particularly sexual, as Old Norse (and Modern Icelandic) *gás* can refer to the female genitalia. Cf. Fritzner 1973, "Kvindens Avlelem eller Kjønsdele, lat. *cunnus*"; Sigfús Blöndal et al. 1980, "de kvindelige Könsdele." It has been noted on several occasions that geese figure into Norse charm magic—especially "love magic"; see Mitchell 1998. The association here with witchcraft through an individual's epithet, although tenuous, is not unparalleled: e.g., Elin kattahierne in 1477 (Hildebrand 1917, 179); Gr*a*trollit in 1489 (Carlsson 1921–44, 363; but cf. Lidén 1933, 323, "Det kan icke bli mer än en gisning, att 'Gråtrollit' befattat sig med trolldom"); and Tyredh, Tyreth in 1492 (Almquist 1930, 23, 36, 49, 50; cf. Swedish dialect *tyre* 'witchcraft' and *trolltyre* 'a form of charm magic using a cow's stomach' in Rietz 1962). In general, consult Lidén 1933, esp. 322–23.

6. Cf. Norseng 1987, 1991.

7. Bagge characterizes these perspectives as follows: "Two main interpretations confront each other. According to the first one [. . .] legislation in the strict sense of the word was not possible in the Middle Ages. The law existed from time immemorial and could only be 'found,' not made; i.e. any change or addition to existing rules had to be legitimised by reference to what was believed to be 'the good, old law.' The adherents of the second interpretation argue that legislation in the old regional laws was understood as subject to human decisions and consequently was open to change in the real sense. Further, they maintain that the idea of 'the good, old law' from time immemorial was introduced by the monarchy and the Church in order to change existing laws." Bagge 2001, 73.

8. Bagge 2001, 84–85.

9. Cf. Hastrup 1993.

10. My comments here build on the argument laid out in Mitchell 2004.

11. Peters 2001, 189. Cf. Fenger 1987, 50: "Overalt i videnskap—for at ikke sige i

livet—er det således, at sandhedsværdien stiger, når man støder på noget, som man ikke forventer. Kildeværdien af normative tekster bliver høj, når de ikke lever op til vore forventninger."

12. The value of the medieval Nordic laws as testimony to life in Northern Europe has been subject to a lively discussion, on which see Norseng 1991, a reworked and expanded version of his earlier survey (Norseng 1987); also helpful is Fenger 1987. With respect to a topic like witchcraft, where gender plays such an important role, see also Bjarne Larsson 1992.

13. For a critical review of earlier scholarship's enthusiasm for plumbing the medieval laws in pursuit of earlier Germanic traditions, especially the sort of world Tacitus describes in his *Germania*, see Sjöholm 1988, 33–49, which synthesizes many of her earlier arguments (e.g., Sjöholm 1978), including her negative view of the possibilities for discovering textual "layers" in the laws. Although deeply influential, Sjöholm's views have not been without criticism (e.g., Fenger 1979), nor without parallels and predecessors (e.g., Wåhlin 1974). One fairly consistent line of objection is encapsulated by Norseng 1991, 157, when he protests, "Her narrow approach causes her to close her eyes to alternative suggestions. . . ."

14. "Leges Danorum edite sunt." Jørgensen 1920, 1:85. It should be noted, however, that the manuscript of *Annales Ryenses* dates only to circa 1400. In addition to the much vilified views associated with the Germanic school, the epistemological context for the specific question of the means by which the medieval laws were known, passed on, and delivered to assemblies belongs to a broader debate that has focused on the Icelandic sagas (often referred to by the terms, *Freiprosa* and *Buchprosa*), on which, see the assessments in Chapter 3, and in, e.g., Mitchell 1991b, 1–7 et passim; Hermann Pálsson 1999a; Mitchell 2003d; and Gísli Sigurðsson 2004, 1–50. A recent treatment of the medieval Nordic laws, Jón Viðar Sigurðsson, Pedersen, and Berge 2008, confidently remarks, "It is clear that medieval Nordic law was trasmitted orally long before it was written down" (39).

15. Jakob Benediktsson 1968, 23. The Icelanders may have begun the practice already in the late eleventh century with the tithe laws said to have been adopted in 1095; see Foote 1987, 55–56.

16. Cf. Gísli Sigurðsson 2004, 53–92.

17. Taranger 1926. Cf. Liedgren 1982, 231, whose remarks I am partly paraphrasing here. The original sense of *laghsagha* was apparently 'law recitation', although over time it comes to mean something closer to 'judicial district' (on its medieval origins, see Hafström 1982b). Cf. Pope Innocent III's comment in a communication with the archbishop of Uppsala and his suffragan bishops from 1206 (Liljegren et al. 1829–, 1:156–57), which seems to strengthen this view about the function of the assemblies. Ståhle (1982, 51) captures the immediacy of the oral delivery presented in the medieval manuscript, as well as the pivotal role of the lawman, when he writes, "I Ö[stgötalagen] hörs tydligt lagmannens röst; lagen slutar *Nu är laghsagha iþur lyktaþ ok ut saghþ* . . . " The typology *Rechtsbuch— Gesetzbuch* is most closely associated with Konrad von Maurer, whose scholarly production in this area (e.g., Maurer and Hertzberg 1878) remains the source of both admiration and controversy.

18. E.g., Wiktorsson 1981; Norseng 1987, 57; Sjöholm 1988; and Sunde 2005, but in addition to these more recent criticisms, already in 1934, Nyström (1974, 77), attacked the Germanic school's romantic view of the Old Swedish laws by writing, "Dessa lagar, klädda i helt annan rationalistisk dräkt än bondesamhällets magiskt-religiösa normvärld, har inte tillkommit för att bevara bonderätten utan för att upphäva den."

19. "Landskapslagarnas Sverige befinner sig i brytningen mellan muntlig och skriftlig kultur," as Söderberg and Larsson 1993, 121, observe in their important study of diglossia and literacy in the medieval Nordic world. The consequences of literacy for the Icelandic legal system, and the power struggles resulting from its introduction, are carefully detailed in Gísli Sigurðsson 2004, 53–92, which argues that "the tradition of oral learning remained strong at least into the 13th century and was held to be of considerable importance in the world of politics *vis-à-vis* the new technique of writing that had been gaining ground since early in the 12th" (91).

20. Concerning the complex issue of possible models for, and influences on, the secular laws, see, e.g., Sjöholm 1976, 1988; and Foote 1977, 1984. I find myself unsympathetic to Sjöholm's perception of *nedtecknandet* as boogeyman, i.e., her position that much of the problem derives from the assertion that earlier oral versions of the texts were at some point transcribed (see her comments, Sjöholm 1988, 37). Integral to her argument is the view that the laws were composed at relatively late dates and mostly under other influences than oral tradition. Still, on some points, it may be possible to agree, e.g., that the earliest laws are constructions that no doubt represent the interests of those sufficiently rich and sufficiently powerful to have the written codes taken seriously (cf. Mitchell 1996, 10–13). At the same time, the testimony of the texts themselves about the convention of the so-called *laghsagha* 'law recitation', the presentations made elsewhere in Nordic sources about the laws, and the consistent references to the *lǫgmaðr*, *lǫgsǫgumaðr*, and so on cannot simply be ignored and should also be fitted to the scheme, if only to suggest that such accounts may have been meant as propaganda tools during the medieval period itself. Misguided excesses in the past—an attempted reconstruction of a fully alliterative version of *Upplandslagen* stands as a prime example—need not mean that everything associated with that position is easily dismissed, for as Sjöholm (1988, 38) herself notes, "Att rättsutvecklingen i stort gått från sedvanerätt till skrivna lagar är visserligen högst sannolikt." Where I differ with Sjöholm's otherwise practical point of view is in believing that, even if we cannot know what the laws recited at thing-meets in the heathen period consisted of with absolute word-for-word clarity (i.e., that those who wrote the laws were something other than stenographers snatching words from the air and putting them on vellum), we can, and do, know something about the general cultural framework within which such recitations took place. The classic study of the language of the laws in support of the view that there existed a tradition of oral delivery is Ståhle 1958, but von See (1964, 84) believes the alliterative patterns in the laws to be accounted for by the medieval fondness for this feature, especially in ecclesiastical contexts.

21. E.g., Sjöholm (1988, 26) finds it necessary to write, "Allmänt gäller att normerna naturligtvis refererar till en social verklighet, annars skulle de vara meningslösa." Cf.

Winberg 1985, 19–20. The many strands of this issue, which goes directly to the question of just what sort of document a law from this period represents, are sometimes—rather dismissively to my outsider's eyes—lumped together as a question of legal positivism (*rettspositivisme*). This perspective has been characterized by Sunde 2002, 117, as "the theory of law where one tends to focus on law as tied to, produced and applied by institutions according to proscribed procedures, and as formally made laws with a binding character both for the legal subjects in general and the courts specifically."

22. See Jón Viðar Sigurðsson, Pedersen, and Berge 2008, 42, and the literature cited there.

23. See the comments and reviews of literature in Halldór Hermannsson 1911; Knudsen 1982c; and Rindal 1993, and the more specific remarks in Hødnebø 1995, 9–35. One of the best overviews of the development of the Norwegian laws in general remains Helle 1964, 36–44 et passim, and on the laws of the Gulaþing specifically, Helle 2001. Cf. Sunde 2002. Within Icelandic historiography (i.e., in Ari inn fróði's *Íslendingabók*, from ca. 1122–33; Jakob Benediktsson 1968, 6–7), *Gulaþingslǫg* is said to have been the basis for the Icelandic legal codes passed at the Alþingi in AD 930.

24. So, e.g., *Gulaþingslǫg*; not only are the normal codicological difficulties in play, but the principal manuscript also appears to be an amalgamation of two revisions of the laws, a so-called Óláfr-text (Óláfr Haraldsson, king 1015–28) and a so-called Magnús-text (Magnús Erlingsson, king 1161–84). Cf. Fenger 1987.

25. I have generally relied on the dating in Norseng 1991, as well as judgments by specialists in such areas as palæography (e.g., Rindal 1983), keeping in mind Norseng's cautionary remark (1991, 16) that such datings are based on very old research that has not been recently evaluated. The newly established Nordic Medieval Laws project (directed by Stefan Brink) will, one hopes, bring some much-needed clarity to this problem.

26. The reality of this situation has been the subject of much discussion in the materials from the early modern period (e.g., Briggs 1996b); reputations mattered, and legal action against accused witches often came after, and in response to, years of rumors (cf. Macfarlane 1991). Tracing the development of such antagonisms within a community is naturally much easier in the modern period (cf. Mitchell 2000c, 2004), but that the same basic blueprint would have been true in the medieval period does not seem to me too great a leap of faith.

27. In the tenth and eleventh centuries, Norway was divided into four legal districts: Gulaþing in the west, Frøstuþing in the more northerly area around modern-day Trondheim, Eiðsifaþing in the inland east, and Borgarþing in Oslofjord. The laws may have been written down already in the late eleventh century, although the oldest complete manuscripts date only to the thirteenth century. For an overview, see Rindal 1993.

28. "æða kallar hann troll. æða fordæðo . . . " Keyser and Munch 1846–95, 1:70.

29. E.g., Keyser and Munch 1846–95, 1:273, 321; 3:101, 104.

30. "En ef dyl. bere karlmaðr iarn firir. en kona take i kætil. En sa er þessor mal kennir manni þa værðr hann af þui fiolmæles maðr ef skirskotat er. nema hann hafe firir ser heimilis kuiðiar vitni." Keyser and Munch 1846–95, 1:152 (cf. 1:318). It should be noted

that this passage comes from the church, rather than the secular, law section of the *Laws of Frǫstuþing*. Ordeals such as bearing hot iron were abolished in Norway from 1247 through the interventions of the papal legate, Cardinal William of Sabina.

31. "§ 5. Þættæ aru vkvæþins orþ kono. Iak sa at þu reet a quiggrindu löfharæþ. ok i trols ham þa alt var iamrift nat ok daghér. kallar hanæ kunna firigæræ kono ællær. ko. þæt ær. vkuaþins ord. kallær kono hortutu. þæt ær vkuaþins ord. kallar kono haua at faþur sin ællær strukit hava barn sit fra sær allær hava myrt sit barn. þættæ æru firnær orþ. § 6. All þassi synda mal skal fyrst uiþ præst sin talæ ok eigh braþæ vp *mæþ* awund ællær vrez uiliæ . . . " Schlyter 1822–77, 1:38. This passage has occasioned much discussion, largely reflected in the notes in Holmbäck and Wessén 1979, 5:124–28. *Äldre Västgötalagen* is believed to have been composed in the early 1200s, although the oldest manuscript evidence is from later in the century. Cf. Holmbäck and Wessén 1979, 5:xi–xxxvii. Hafström 1965 remains a useful overview of the Swedish laws; see the survey of more recent literature in Andersson 1987, 124–28, including his comment that the laws are to be seen, not as reflections of ancient *Germania*, but as a "spegel av det medeltida samhälle i vilket de redigerades och nertecknades." On the translation of *quiggrindu,* see Chapter 4, n. 79, as well as n. 34 and n. 36 in this chapter.

32. *retlosä bolkär*. The meaning of *rätlösa*, f., has been widely discussed; despite various ingenuous suggestions, the interpretation first offered by Schlyter continues to be the standard: *rättlöshet, laglöshet, orätt*. See the discussion in Holmbäck and Wessén 1979, 5:114–17. Old Swedish *balker/bolkär* (Modern Swedish *balk*) 'section' is used for the various divisions in all the Old Swedish laws, e.g., the inheritance section, the section on injuries, and so on.

33. This sort of vignette is a characteristic rhetorical device in the Old Swedish laws, which delight in providing examples, often with considerable detail.

34. It has been suggested by some that the phrase does not necessarily imply riding in the sense that the gate is moving or flying but—as indicated by an intense investigation of dialect forms and regional praxis in southwestern Norway—rather perhaps that she simply sits astride the gate. See Lidén 1914, as well as the counterargument in Linderholm 1918b, 141–42. Pipping 1915, 68–71, arrives at the same conclusion as Lidén but gets there by way of an interesting sexual image: *kviþer*, m. 'kved, moderliv' and *grind*, f. 'öppning, springa' (cf. the verb *grina* 'stå i sär, gapa'); thus, *apertura uterina, cunnus*, indicating, as the editors delicately phrase it, "den kroppsdel, på vilken kvinnan vilade, då hon red grensle." Holmbäck and Wessén 1979, 5:126. Few recent observers have not seen a connection between this law and aspects of transvection and the Nordic sabbat (see Chapter 4).

35. Cf. Holmbäck and Wessén 1979, 5:126.

36. Cf. Icelandic *kví*, Gutnish *qviär*. As a concept, liminality possesses a physical as well as a psychological dimension, here referring both to liminal space and the marginality of the woman being described. Famously devised by Arnold van Gennep in describing the *rites de passage*, the term is widely used in describing cultures and behaviors; see, e.g., the discussion in Turner 1977, 94–96 et passim. I have explored the issue of Nordic witchcraft and liminal space in Mitchell 2005. In folklore, liminal spaces such as gates and

other passageways are often portrayed as openings into the Otherworld (e.g., F91. *Door [gate] entrance to lower world*; F59.3 *Gate to upper world*), and along the same lines, cross-roads are also often associated with magical abilities (cf. D1768. *Magic power at cross-roads* and related subtypes, where a wide array of supernatural creatures—ghosts, fairies, and participants in the Wild Hunt—both gain and lose power), the point being that these explicitly "betwixt-and-between" areas are widely believed to be magically significant. On such motifs, consult Thompson 1966 and such area-specific indexes as Boberg 1966. See also the discussion in Chapter 3 concerning the woman who curses Snæbjǫrn of Sandvík.

37. Nothing demands that we understand the passage as being about witchcraft activity, although it is difficult not to agree with Holmbäck and Wessén (1979, 5:126) when they posit, "Att det är fråga om något slags blåkullafärd, torde vara otvivelaktigt." Cf. a phrase like *troll. oc manneta* (Keyser and Munch 1846–95, 2:495; cf. 4:6). Presumably *troll.* here abbreviates *trollkona*, but the form underscores the ambiguity and interchange-ability of these terms. On the usefulness of this ambiguity, see Schulz 2004, esp. 45–46, and Ármann Jakobsson 2009.

38. Cf. *kveldriða* 'night-hag, witch, evening rider'; *myrkriða* 'night-rider, hag, witch, dark rider'; and esp. *túnriða* 'witch, ghost' < *tún*, properly, as Cleasby-Vigfusson notes, a hedge, and secondarily, a hedged or fenced plot, enclosure; the farmhouse with its buildings.

39. Cf. the entry in Söderwall and Ljunggren 1884–1973. It should be noted, how-ever, that Icelandic, *gjörð* (f. pl. *gjarðar*), in addition to the sense of 'girdle', 'belt', also means 'a kind of lady's head-gear, in western Icel. a kerchief wrapped round the head' (Cleasby and Vigfusson 1982); perhaps this change in the younger law does not add new information but rather amplifies the original 'loose-haired'. Cf. Horace's use in the context of a prayer to Venus (*Carminum* Liber 1:xxx) of *solutis Gratiae zonis*, 'with loose-girdled Graces'. The similarity of the Latin image to the Old Swedish phrase may suggest an enduring representation across time and space of voluptuousness, promiscuity, and so on in this association. See Holmbäck and Wessén 1979, 5:125–26 and n. 40 in this chapter.

40. There is a long tradition in Western thinking about women's hair and sensuality. See, e.g., Stevenson 2001, 140: "A woman's long hair, pinned up neatly and covered was seen as indicative of virtue, which (literally) distinguished her from loose (haired) women as well as from men; witches, e.g., have usually been depicted pictorially as having wild and unkempt hair. Unpinned, tumbling or dishevelled, hair is infused with sexual power."

41. Schlyter 1822–77, 7:79.

42. Cf. Holmbäck and Wessén 1979, 5:xcii–xcvi.

43. Cf. Falk 1924. This phrase is found in other Old Swedish laws (e.g., *Södermanna-lagen*) and continues to be used up through *Swerikes Rijkes Stadz Lagh* of 1613.

44. "æller kallær goþæ kono horkono. skykiu. trollkono æller fordæþu." Schlyter 1822–77, 6:127. The same pairings are subsequently incorporated into *Magnus Erikssons Stadslag*: "eller kalla godha kuno forwnna hoorkono, eller forwnna skökio, ella forwnna trullkonu, eller forwnna fordædho." Schlyter 1822–77, 11:285.

45. "En þá es Ísland vas víða byggt orðit, þá hafði maðr austrœnn fyrst lǫg út hingat

ýr Norvegi, sá es Ulfljótr hét; svá sagði Teitr oss; ok váru þá Ulfljótslǫg kǫlluð . . ." Jakob Benediktsson 1968, 6–7. Cf. Sigurður Líndal 1969, who questions the historicity of this account.

46. "Skyldu þeir gǫrva nýmæli þau ǫll í lǫgum, es þeim litisk þau betri en en fornu lǫg." Jakob Benediktsson 1968, 23.

47. Recent assessments have sounded a less unassailable note. See the detailed discussion in Norseng 1991, 141–42, which concludes, "It is uncertain to what extent the stipulations in the surviving laws of independent Iceland are derived from *Hafliðaskrá.*"

48. An old version of the Norwegian Frǫstuþing laws was referred to as *Grágás* (Rindal 1993, 385), and the name later came to be used as a collective title for the Icelandic laws: "Navnets oprindelse kendes ikke; det forekommer for første gang på en inventarliste fra bispestolen i Skálholt i 1548." Ólafur Lárusson 1982a, 410.

49. Hastrup 1993, 388.

50. That *Járnsíða* was unpopular was probably due to what has been called its "remoteness from the Icelandic legal tradition." Sandvik and Jón Viðar Sigurðsson 2005, 227. A now-lost version of the *Gulaþingslǫg* from 1267 may have been the model for *Járnsíða*; see Ólafur Lárusson 1982b, 567.

51. "ok svá fyrir morð eða fordæðuskap ok spáfarar allar ok útisetur at vekja trǫll upp ok fremja heiðni með því . . ." Ólafur Halldórsson 1970, 38. Cf. Keyser and Munch 1846–95, 1:19, 182, 265; 2:51 and 212; as well *Járnsíða*, Þórður Sveinbjörnsson 1847, 22–23. Ólafur Halldórsson 1970, xli–lvii, lists some two hundred manuscripts of *Jónsbók*, the oldest of which date to circa 1300.

52. "En ef maðr kallar mann drottinssvikara, fordæðu, morðingja, þjóf, hvinn, pútuson, hórkonuson eða ǫnnur jafnskemmilig orð . . . " Ólafur Halldórsson 1970, 65. Cf. the corresponding sections of the Norwegian laws that show the same gendered language, e.g., Keyser and Munch 1846–95, 1:273, 2:270.

53. "Nú mál hvert er maðr mælir við annan mann svá at honum horfir til hneyxla, eða kennir honum hvinnsku eða fordæðuskap . . ." Ólafur Halldórsson 1970, 66.

54. I make this assertion realizing that unmarked Old Norse *maðr* 'man; people' and so on (cf. *mannkyn* 'mankind') includes females, but as the laws often go out of their way to specify categories of maleness and femaleness, this wording does not appear to be inclusive.

55. Cf. the remark by one Danish scholar bemoaning the scant legal evidence from actual cases, although one senses that his comments have broader application: "We are left with the fact that, as far as Denmark is concerned, we do not know, owing to the lack of sources, how the courts dealt with the crime before the sixteenth century." Johansen 1993, 339.

56. At a recent research seminar at Aarhus Universitet, Per Andersen argued, based on the index of the older code, that this section, or something like it, was in fact part of the original thirteenth-century law.

57. "Forgiør mand konne eller konne mand eller konne konne med troldom eller andre forgiøringer, saa at hun eller hand døer deraff, da schall mand steyles och konne

brendes, om schellige widne ere till." Kroman 1951–61, 4:338. The precise measure meant by *steyle, stegla*, and so on has been much debated and may not have been carried out in the same way in every region. What it certainly meant was that the individual was tortured before his inevitable, and public, demise. See the discussion and bibliography in Meyer 1982, as well as Merback 1999, 158–97.

58. "Kona firigær manni. fællir hana lukt hærasznæmd. þa skal hun haua griþ til skogs. dax ok nattær. þa skal latæ dömæ hanæ. vgill. firi arva. ok eptimælændæ ok dræpæ þær næst." Schlyter 1822–77, 1:22. See the extensive discussion of this passage in Holmbäck and Wessén 1979, 5:69.

59. Schlyter 1822–77, 1:55.

60. Hemmer 1947.

61. See, e.g., Reuterdahl 1841, 63.

62. "hanum war firi giort mæð ondum dryk .i. östrægötlanði. oc fek. aff þy banæ." Schlyter 1822–77, 1:300.

63. Schlyter 1822–77,, 10:276.

64. Cf. Holmbäck and Wessén 1962, 5:219, as well as the glosses in Sleumer and Schmid 1990, "1. Gift, Gifttrank, Zaubertrank. 2. Unheil, Verderben."

65. I am here paraphrasing Ankarloo's insight: "Förgörning används som beteckning på all slags skadegörelse som inte kan förknippas med yttre våld. Av förgörningen är trolldom en art, förgiftningen en annan." Ankarloo 1984, 35.

66. "Firi giær cona ko *æller* bo. cono *æller* bonde. warþer hun takin viþ. giælðe lif sit firi." Schlyter 1822–77, 1:153.

67. "Bær konæ forgiærningær manni wærþær bar ok a takin. þa skal hanæ takæ ok .j. fiætur sættiæ. ok swa til þinx föræ. ok þe samu forgiærningær mæþ hænni." Schlyter 1822–77, 3:149. Among the Old Swedish provincial laws, see also Schlyter 1822–77, 4:159 and 5:149–50.

68. Cf. Ankarloo 1993, 286.

69. "Far konæ me þ wiþskiplum. böte þrenni sæxtan ortug*her* enar biscupe. ok tuar hærraþe oc kononge." Schlyter 1822–77, 1:153.

70. See esp. Jón Viðar Sigurðsson, Pedersen, and Berge (2008) on this issue, which they outline for medieval Norway, Iceland, and Denmark, concluding that, in the late twelfth century, "the king's control over the law-making process underpinned his superior position in society" (56), with the church attempting to sever that connection and make laws in line with the Gregorian reform.

71. "Magn*vs konvngr ok* Jón erchiby*skv*p vórv á Frostv þingi. Þá *fekk* Magn*vs konvngr* samþyct allra Frostvþingsma*nn*a at skipa *sva* Frostv þings bók *vm* alla lvti þá s*em* til v*er*alldar héyra *ok konvng*dómsins. s*em honom* sý*nn*diz bezt bera." Storm 1888, 138.

72. "oc svá fyrer morð oc fordæðu scapi oc spáfarar oc útisetu at vecia tröll upp oc fremia heiðni með því." Keyser and Munch 1846–95, 1:182. The *Frostuþingslǫg* is known from paper copies made in modern times, before the great Copenhagen fire of 1728 destroyed the originals, believed to have been written in the years 1260–69; some manuscript fragments of these laws date to as early as 1220–25. See Knudsen 1982b, col. 657. *Járnsíða*

reads, "oc sua fire morð oc fordæðo skap oc spafarar oc utisetor, at vækia troll upp, oc fremia heiðni með þui . . . " Þórður Sveinbjörnsson 1847, 22. Cf. the nearly identical phrasing of *Jónsbók*'s "Um níðingsverk" in Ólafur Halldórsson 1970, 38.

73. "Ef maðr blótar á heiðnar vættir. eða ferr hann með spásögur eða með görningum. sá maðr er því hlýðir ok þann mann húsar til þess. hann er svá útlægr sem manns bani." Keyser and Munch 1846–95, 1:318.

74. Several attempts to forge a national law code were made in Norway under kings Magnús Erlingsson, Hákon Hákonarson, and Magnús Hákonarson. A national law, with some regional variations, was finally adopted by 1276 (see Rindal 1993; cf. Keyser and Munch 1846–95, 2:1–178). The Icelandic Commonwealth had been ruled by a variety of laws (e.g., *Kristinn réttr forni*) called in modern times by the collective title *Grágás*. With the loss of independence to Norway (1262–64), the Icelanders were briefly governed by the laws called *Járnsíða* (1271–81), and then by a long-lasting and oft-amended code called *Jónsbók*; see Fix 1993. Following the writing of the numerous Swedish provincial laws, a national law (*Magnus Erikssons Landslag*) was written circa 1350 and revised in 1442 as *Kristoffers Landslag*. A corresponding municipal code (*Magnus Erikssons Stadslag*) was also composed in the mid-fourteenth century. Although among the earliest Nordic countries to record its laws, as one expert notes, "Except for coronation charters, peace regulations, and privileges for the towns, Denmark in the late Middle Ages is deficient in laws." Fenger 1993, 384. Not until the early sixteenth-century attempts by King Kristian II (1521–22) do we see a comparable attempt to create a national law code.

75. Keyser and Munch 1846–95, 2:495.

76. Keyser and Munch 1846–95, 1:434, one of the so-called Christian laws (*Kong Sverrers Chistenret*), with which the passage has an obvious strong relationship.

77. Cf. Russell 1972, 23, 50 et passim; and Morris 1991, 155–69.

78. See the entries under G11.3. *Cannibal witch* in Boberg 1966. Obviously, the fact that such creatures appear in the sagas need not mean that they too could not have been borrowed from a variety of literary and encyclopedic sources (cf. my comments on "Learned Lore" in Mitchell 1991b, 73–88), but given the totality of such presentations in Nordic literature and lore, viewing such monsters as part of the native Northern European "fiend kit" seems to be an excellent fit with the "law of parsimony."

79. See the insightful remarks in Kiessling 1968.

80. That is, in relation to other statutes addressing witchcraft: elsewhere, the laws use this image of burial—or, more closely, disposal—of the bodies of executed evildoers on the seashore and so on in other special cases, such as suicide. Cf. Keyser and Munch 1846–95, 1:13, 391–92, 431; 2:296, 314, 330. See also the cases of *Dalalagen* and *Västmannalagen* (*The Law of Västmanland*) later in this volume.

81. On the explanation of the seemingly truncated *þättä är bardaghä*, see Holmbäck and Wessén 1979, 5:63.

82. The nature of the law itself remains more or less as it had been in many of the provincial laws: "Forgör maþer manne ællæ kunu, kona kunu ællæ manne, meþ trulldom ællæ andrum forgerningum, sua æt han ællæ hon faar döþ af, miste liif sit for þolika

gerning; man skal stæghla ok kunu stena, ok viti þet meþ hæræz næmd sum för ær sakt." Schlyter 1822–77, 10:276, and "Bær kona ællæ man forgerninga manne, varþer bar ok atakin, þa skal hona take ok i fiætur sætia ok sua til þings föra, ok þe samu forgerninga meþ hænne [. . .] fælla þe hona, þa a hon bale brinna . . . " Schlyter 1822–77, 10:281–82. Along the same lines, a few years later, the municipal laws are also codified as *Magnus Erikssons Stadslag*, often mirroring the organization and language of the national law. This is certainly true of the witchcraft statutes in its *Höghmälisbalker*, which again are placed among the same most serious threats known to society. Cf. Schlyter 1822–77, 11:285, 323–24.

83. "Um troldoom. Aff man witær annæn. at han hauær fforgørth. aff hans *mæth* troldoom. oc gangær han æi with. thær sæktæth war. num dyl. oc føør hin thz hanu*m* a hand. thær sækthær. tha wæri han sik. thær saak giuæs *mæth* næfnd i kirki sokæn. bathæ ffor hin thær sæktær. oc swo fforæ biscop." Brøndum-Nielsen, Jørgensen, and Buus 1920– 42, 2:506. The Jutlandic materials are sometimes held to have been intended as a national code, as opposed to the Scanian and Sealandic laws, which are thought to have been more for the private use of powerful individuals, on which, see Jón Viðar Sigurðsson, Pedersen, and Berge 2008.

84. Personal communication with Per Ingesman, May 2009. See, e.g., Fenger 1983; Foote 1977 and 1986.

85. Schlyter 1822–77, 12:302.

86. Explaining the curious appearance in this list of what is otherwise simply an insult, Schlyter comments "ett oqvädinsord som tillkommit genom misförstånd af o. hæri- ansun," tying the word back to the phrase *herriæns son* 'son of Herjann' in *Äldre Västgötala- gen* and elsewhere. See n. 43 in this chapter.

87. Schlyter 1822–77, 12:403. The remedy in 1442 for a false accusation includes a fine, public confession of lying, striking oneself on the mouth, and walking backward around the meetinghouse (*gange baaklenges af tingzstugu*).

88. The genre divisions among the many different types of church materials are anything but clear-cut, but by "normative," I mean here principally *jus ecclesiasticum*, in essence, all directives adopted by the ecclesiastical authorities. But beyond the more obvi- ous items (e.g., penitentials), I also have in mind such materials as the various *kirkiu balker*, *kristinsdómsbálkr*, and so on, that is, the church laws, with which so many of the provincial and national law codes open.

89. It is useful to recall that despite modern regard for subtle distinctions within the magical world, the church tended not to promulgate such taxonomies, but rather the opposite, that is, to group them together as heresy. As Edsman 1982b, 661, rightly notes, "För medeltida teologi är det icke någon grundläggande skillnad mellan häxeri, t[roll- dom], och magi. De tre begreppen får tillsammans också karaktären av kätteri . . . " Cf. Haack 1939a, 1939b.

90. On the relationship between civil and religious laws in Norway, and the implica- tions for dating the regional laws, see Iversen 1997.

91. See Knudsen 1982d.

92. See the review in Magnús Stefánsson 1993. A detailed examination of this struggle—*regnum et sacerdotium*—in Norway is provided in Joys 1948.

93. For an orientation to the principles of church organization and the projection of ecclesiastical authority, see Dahlerup 1993; Gallén 1982; Iuul 1982a; Magnús Már Lárusson 1982b; and Magnús Stefánsson 1993; also see Inger 1982; Iuul 1982b; and Seierstad 1982.

94. "Fyrste bolken i gno. lover er *kristinsdómsbǫlkr.* Her står k[ristenrettar] (*kristinn réttr*), kyrkelova [. . .] Same plass som i desse lovene har *kristinsdómsbálkr* i *Jónsbók* [. . .] Også i dei sv. lanskapslovene står *kirkiu balker* el. *kristnu balker* fyrst [. . .] Dei da. landkskapslovene har derimot ikkje moko tilsv. stykke." Bøe 1982, 297. Cf. Magnús Stefánsson 1993, 88: "The provincial laws included special church laws with provisions governing the relationship between the Church and the people, as well as religious life generally[. . . .] The Church still did not have any inner legislation based on the universally recognized canonical principles."

95. In the Icelandic Commonwealth, two forms of outlawry were common: lesser outlawry (*fjǫrbaugsgarðr*), which was punishable by a three-year exile from Iceland and the confiscation of property, and full outlawry (*skóggangr*), punishable by permanent exile, the loss of property, the denial of inheritance rights to children, disqualification for burial in hallowed ground, and deprivation of the law's protection, that is, he could be killed anywhere by anyone. See Hastrup 1985, 136–45.

96. "Menn scolo trva a einn Gvð oc ahelga meN hans. oc blota eigi heiþnar vættir. þa blötar hann heiþnar vættir. ef hann signir fe sitt oþrvm enn Gvþi. eþa helgvm mavnnvm hans. Ef maðr blotar heiþnar vættir. oc uarþar þat fiorbavgs Garþ. Ef maþr ferr með galldra eþa gørningar. eþa fiolkýngi. þa ferr hann með fiolkyngi. ef hann queðr þat eþa kennir. eþa lætr queða. at ser eþa at fe sinv. þat varþar honvm fiorbavgs Garþ. oc scal honvm heiman stefna. oc sækia við .xij. qvið. Ef maþr ferr með fordæs skap. þat varþar scogGang. þat ero fordæs skapir. ef maþr gérir i orðvm sinvm. eþa fiolkyngi sott eþa bana. fe eþa mavnnvm. þat scal sekia við .xij. qvið." Vilhjálmur Finsen 1974a, 22–23. Cf. the similar language in other manuscript traditions: e.g., Vilhjálmur Finsen 1974b, 25. This passage is from the so-called Older Christian Law (*kristinn réttr forni*), the formulation of which some authorities believe may date to the period 1122–32; see Magnús Már Lárusson 1982a, 305. Witchcraft is mentioned as a special case in the church law section of *Grágás* with respect to the naming of jury panels: if a man is charged with witchcraft (*vm fiolkyngi*), then his chieftain (*góði*) is to name a twelve-man panel rather than a nine-man panel; Vilhjálmur Finsen 1974a, 36.

97. "Þat er nu þvi nest at ver scolom eigi lyða spám ne golldrum ne gerningum illum. En sa er kunnr oc sannr verðr at þvi. at hann segir spar. æða ferr með spám. þa er hann maðr utlagr oc uheilagr. oc hverr penningr fiár hans. þat a halft konongr. en halft biscop. En sa annarr er spám lyðir. oc verðr sannr at þvi. þa scal sa beðta .xl. marca. þat a halft konongr. en halft biscop. En sa annarr er ferr með galldra oc gerningar. oc verða at þvi kunnir oc sanner. þeir scolo fara or landeign konongs várs. þvi eigu menn eigi at lyða. En ef þeir lyða. þa hava þeir firigort hverium penningi fiár sins. En þeir scolo kost eiga at ganga til skripta oc beðta við Krist. En ef þat mælir biscop. æða hans ærendreke at maðr

ferr með spár. æða galldra. æða gerningar. en þeir kveða við þvi nei. þar ero syniar mæltar firi. Ef manne er þat kent at hann fare með spár. syni með settar eiði. nefna menn .xii. iamgoða hanom. þar scal hann einn hava af þeim .xii. monnum. En hann scal sialfr annarr væra. hinn [þriði] nanaste niðr. En þeir þrir ar firi orde oc eiði kunni hyggia. fellr til utlegðar. ef feller [. . .] En ef þat er konom kent at þær fare með golldrum oc gerningum. þa scal þar nefna konor .vi. þriar a hvara hond henne huspreyjur þær er menn vitu at goðar se. þær scolo vitni bera at hon kann eigi galldra ne gerningar. En ef henni þat vitni fellr. þa fellr til utlegðar. þa a konongr fe hennar halft. en biscop a halft. En hana scal ervingi fóra or landeign konongs várs." Keyser and Munch 1846–95, 1:17; the translation is from Larson 1935, 56–57.

98. The elided portion of the quoted passage offers some insight, in that it is a later addition—part of the so-called Magnús-text—detailing the penalties if either the accused or his defenders swear false oaths: "En ef maðr verðr at þvi kunnr oc sannr. at hann vinnr eið usórann. æða leiðir aðra menn með sér. þa er hann sialfr seccr .xv. morcom. en .iiij. morcom firir hvern er svór með hanom ef þeir vissu eigi at usórt var. En ef þeir vissu at usórt var. fyrr en þeir vynni. þa giallde hverr .xv. mercr. sem hann." Keyser and Munch 1846–95, 1:17.

99. The church law section of the Borgarþing law has come down to modern times, whereas the secular laws, some manuscript fragments aside, have not. See Keyser and Munch 1846–95, 1:xi.

100. "Þæt er ubota værk at sitia uti." Keyser and Munch 1846–95, 1:350. On this practice, see Hermann Pálsson 1997, 123–30; Solli 2002, 137–38; and Price 2002, all of whom in varying degrees see in reports of this custom a shamanistic element, developed under the influence of Sámi practices. Jón Árnason 1954–61, 1:422–24 ("Útisetur á kross-götum") not only details the medieval sources but also notes that the custom was known in Iceland beyond the medieval period.

101. "þæt er ubota værk at gera finfarar. fara at spyria spa." Keyser and Munch 1846–95, 1:350–51 (n.b., one manuscript specifies "at fara a Finnmork").

102. "Ef kona bitr fingr eða to af barne sinu till langlivis. bóte morkum .iij." Keyser and Munch 1846–95 1:351.

103. "En ef kona fóder barn hæiðit . . . " Keyser and Munch 1846–95, 1:351.

104. Keyser and Munch 1846–95, 1:351.

105. "En ef fordæðo skapr værðr funnin i bæðium eða bolstrom manna hor eða frauða fóder manna næghl eða þa luti er uener þikkia till gærninga . . . " Keyser and Munch 1846–95, 1:351.

106. "Ef kono er trylzka kend i herade. þa skal hon hava till .vi. kuenna vitni at hon er æigi trylsk. sygn saka ef þætt fæz. En ef hon fær þæt æighi. fare brott or heraðe með fiar luti sina. ækki vældr hon þui siolf at hon er troll." Keyser and Munch 1846–95, 1:351. Worth noting are the semantic associations of *kenna*, which, in addition to the more restricted sense of 'charging' or 'accusing', include 'to know, recognize'; 'to assign or attribute'; 'to feel, perceive'; and 'to show, bear witness of' (here following Zoëga 1975). The polysemy implied by the phrase *er kent . . . i herade* is relevant, i.e., both 'is charged . . . in the district with . . . ' and 'is known . . . in the district for . . . '

107. "A gud skulu menn væll trua en æigi a boluan eða a blot skapp. En ef maðr uærðr at þui sannr at han fær með hæiðin blott þau er firerboden ero at bok male. han er sæckr .iij. morkum." Keyser and Munch 1846–95, 1:351.

108. Cf. Keyser and Munch 1846–95, 1:362, 372; on the *Frostuþingslog*, see Keyser and Munch 1846–95, 4:62–63.

109. "Þat er vbota verk ef madr sitr vti ok væckir troll up." Keyser and Munch 1846–95, 1:362; "Þet er vbota uærk. er madr sittær vti. oc vækkir troll up." Keyser and Munch 1846–95, 1:372; "Tatt er vbota mal et wærk, eff mader sittær vtj et vækkir troll vpp." Keyser and Munch 1846–95, 4:63.

110. In addition to those listed in the preceding note, cf. Keyser and Munch 1846–95, 1:182; 2:51, 212, 307–8, 326–27; 4:18, 160; 5:56, although these passages do not necessarily possess independent source value.

111. "Ef maðr blotar a heiðnar uetter eða fer hann með spasogur eða með gerningum sa maðr er þui lyðir oc þann mann husar til þess. hann er sua utlægr sem manz bane. en biskup a huern pening fear hans. En ef dyl. bere karlmaðr iarn firir. en kona take i kætil. En sa er þessor mal kennir manni þa værðr hann af þui fiolmæles maðr ef skirskotat er. nema hann hafe firir ser heimilis kuiðira vitni." Keyser and Munch 1846–95, 1:152; the translation is from Larson 1935, 251.

112. Hertzberg (1905) argues that with the exception of sections on tithing and the selection of bishops, the *Eiðsivaþingslog*, and those of the other older laws, presumably much as we have them, were written in the period before 1111–20: "Resultatet af den forudgaaende Drøftelse tør erkjendes at være, at de 3 os foreliggende, ældste norske Kristenretter, Gula-, Borgar-, og Eidsivathings, i sin oprindelige Skikkelse er bleven nedskrevne før Indførelsen af den Tiende [. . .] altsaa før Tidsrummet 1111–1120" (111–12; see also his comments on 116–17). Still, I note that in the absence of *documented* earlier testimony, even if that assertion is correct, we cannot know what changes may have been introduced in the intervening centuries. Of the two old manuscripts, the so-called longer and shorter texts, the best text (longer) is also the oldest (ca. 1320). See Knudsen 1982a, 527.

113. "Engi maðr skal hafa i husi sinu staf eða stalla. vit eða blot. eða þat er til hæiðins siðar uæit." Keyser and Munch 1846–95, 1:383. On the archaeological and literary evidence for the existence of wands, see Price 2002, 175–204.

114. "Engi maðr a at trua. a finna. eða forðæðor. eða a vit. eða blot. eða rot. eða þat. er til hæiðins siðar hoyrir. eða læita ser þar bota. En ef maðr fær til finna. oc uærðr hann sannr at þui. þa er hann utlægr. oc ubota maðr . . ." Keyser and Munch 1846–95, 1:389–90; cf. 1:403.

115. "Ef þat er kænnt kono. at hon riði manne. eða þionom hans. ef hon uærðr sonn at þui. þa er hon sæk .iij. morkum. Ef hon næitir firi. þa skal hon uinna setar æið. En ef sa æiðr fællr henne. þa fællr til .iij. marka .vi. alnar oyris. En ef æi er fe til. þa fare hon utlæg." Keyser and Munch 1846–95, 1:390; cf. 1:403.

116. "Logtekin Gvlaþingsbók sú er Magnús *konungr* lét setia." Storm 1888, 137. Due to the dispute between King Magnús and Archbishop Jón about the ecclesiastical laws, the national law code of 1274 lacked any specific church laws; indeed, some years later,

the archbishop began to promulgate statutes at the ecclesiastical provincial councils. This practice halted in 1290, when the king and archbishop agreed to abide by the old church laws. See Helle 1964 and Magnús Stefánsson 1993, 90–91, who captures the complexity of the situation when he notes, "In practical terms, the situation was unclear, however, with the existence of several concurrent versions of church law."

117. N.b., *villa*, translated here as 'heresy', can also be rendered simply 'falsehood', 'error', 'delusion', so the sense I use, although likely, is not the only possibility, a matter of some importance given the timing.

118. Specifically, the law says here that it is part of the heathen way "if one calls another a troll-rider." This may be an important distinction for our understanding of the practice (or belief) that was to be a *trollriða*.

119. "En af þui at menn ero skyldugir at halda þa tru er uér hafum heitið guði i skirsl váre oc aðr uar upp told. þa a konong(r) oc byskup með myklu gaumgæue at ransaka at menn fare eigi með ofmykilli uillu ok heiðnum átrunaðe. En þessir lutir hóyra til uillu ch heiðins atrunaðar. galdrar oc gerningar oc þat ef maðr kallar annan mann trollriðu. spadomar. oc trua at landuetter se i londum. haughum æða forsom. Sua oc utisættur at spyria forlagha. oc þeir en segia af hendi ser guð oc heilaga kirkiu til þes at þeir skuli fe i haugum finna. æða aðra leið æða nokors uisir uerða. Sua oc þeir er freista draugha upp at ueckia æða haughbua. Nv ef nokor maðr uerðr kunnr æða sannr at han fer með þeima atrunaðe oc heiðni uillu æða samþyckir þeim er með sliku fara. þa er sa vtlægr oc fe hans alt. þat a halft konongr en halft byskup. En ef þat mæler konongs umboðzmaðr æða byskups at maðr fer með þeima atrunaðe oc fór han eigi loglæga sannat a hendr honom þa syni sa með tylftar æiði. fellr til vtlægðar." Keyser and Munch 1846–95, 2:326–27; cf. 2:307–8 and 5:56, which notably alters *æða aðra leið æða nokors uisir uerða . . .* to *eda adra læid rikir værda eda nokors visir. . . .*

120. "egentlig blot en Compilation af Gulathings- og Frostathings-Christenretter." Keyser and Munch 1846–95, 1:xii.

121. Called *Kong Sverrers Christenret* in *Norges gamle Love indtil 1387*. See Bøe 1982, 301.

122. Keyser and Munch 1846–95, 1:17; cf. 1:429–30.

123. Keyser and Munch 1846–95, 2:495; cf. 1:434.

124. Keyser and Munch 1846–95, 2:496.

125. "Blott er os kuidiat at ver skulum æigi blota hæiðnar vetter. oc æigi hæiðin guð ne hauga ne horgha. En ef maðr værðr at þui kunnr eða sannar at han læðr hauga eða gerer hus oc kallar horgh. eða ræisir stong oc kallar skaldzstong huern lut er han gerer þæirra þa hæfir han firergort huerium pæningi fear sins. han skal ganga till scripta oc bóta við Crist. En ef han vill þætt æigi þa skal han fara or landæign konongs vars." Keyser and Munch 1846–95, 1:430. On this passage, *niðstǫng* and *trénið*, see Chapter 2.

126. "ef þat verdr kent korllvm eda konvm at þau seide eda magne troll vpp at rida monnum eda bvfe . . . " Jón Þorkelsson and Jón Sigurðsson 1857–1932, 2:223.

127. "Jtem ef karll edur kona fremia spadom j golldrvm edur giorningvm sem dæmmt er. eda uillv. eda vekia vpp troll. eda lannduæt[t]ir j forsvm eda havgvm. eda villa

svin eda miolk fra monnum. edur nockurs kyns uillu. þa sem moti gudi ok kristinne trv er . . . " Jón Þorkelsson and Jón Sigurðsson 1857–1932, 2:224.

128. Jón Þorkelsson and Jón Sigurðsson 1857–1932, 2:223, 224.

129. The Scanian Church Law reads, "Swa oc um trulldom ællær fordæþær. æn um antwigiæ man ællær kunu far rop um swa urþit mal. skæræ sic mæþ iærne um ængin wil henne a hand swæria." Schlyter 1822–77, 10:369. Cf. the Sealandic counterpart in Thorkelin 1781, 17, as well as other versions of the Scanian law, in Thorkelin 1781, 8–9.

130. Schlyter 1822–77, 3:71.

131. "Ok alle þe eþa sum firi þessin mal gangas. þæt æru iorþa delu manhælghis mal: þiupta mal. rans mal. ok þe eþa sum firi trulldoma suerias . . . " Schlyter 1822–77, 2:13. The widely accepted dating of the extant *Östgötalagen* to the late thirteenth century (in any event, to before 1303; see Ståhle 1982, 51–52) has been challenged by Sjöholm (1988, 242–44), who argues that the current text may be from the mid-1300s.

132. The disposition of manuscript B 54 of Kungliga Biblioteket, Stockholm, has become a celebrated *tvistfråga* 'bone of contention' within Swedish historiography. That it is a fourteenth-century legal document in Old Swedish is about all that is agreed on: there is general consensus that this document represents a law with application in a Swedish district somewhere broadly west of modern Stockholm, although whether that district was Dalsland, Dalarna, Västmanland (in which case, this law would be perhaps best understood as an early version of *Västmannalagen*), or, as has most recently been suggested, *Värmland*, has been the subject of much discussion. Holmbäck and Wessén 1979, 2:xiii–xxiv, provides a thorough review of the evidence and theories (see also Hafström 1982a); Wessén 1964, 17, lays out the argument for why, despite the age of the manuscript, the text may, in fact, be quite old; however, these perspectives are challenged by the ingenious argument of Sjöholm 1988, 321–31, that B 54 be understood in the context of the early fourteenth-century semiautonomous region established by Dukes Erik and Valdemar in their struggle against King Birger. Erik and Valdemar sought to build a (mainly) west Swedish area united with Norway, and Sjöholm reasons that these historical conditions, together with some of the similarities of *Dalalagen* to Norwegian legal tradition, account for B 54: "Slutsatsen blir att B 54 är en Värmlandslag." Sjöholm 1988, 329.

133. "Warþir kuna takin meþ truldom. meþ horn oc haar quict oc döt þæt ma wel truldom heta . . . " Schlyter 1822–77, 5:10.

134. Schlyter 1822–77, 3:149.

135. Cf. the extensive discussion in Holmbäck and Wessén 1979, 2:18–19. A similar judgment for witchcraft is made in one of the emended versions of *Gulaþingslǫg* and is deemed appropriate for other selected crimes in the Norwegian laws. Among Old Swedish laws, this punishment appears only in *Dalalagen* and for the theft of crops in *Västmanna-lagen*.

136. It is also known as *The Law of Tio District*, apparently referring to the "ten" (*tio*) regions that made up this *laghsagha*. Cf. the reference to the district in a letter of 1266 as *legifer decem provinciarum*, Liljegren et al. 1829–, 1:437. On this law, see Hafström 1965; Holmbäck and Wessén 1979, 5:lxxv–lxxxiv; and Sjöholm 1988, 90. Cf. Sjöholm 1993,

387: "There is a canon law for the Växjö diocese as an addition to a MS of the state law. This canon law is generally referred to as the ecclesiastical section of the 'Law of Småland' (*Smålandslagen*). However, no MSS of this law have been preserved."

137. "Thætte ær förste dulsak hethit morth, annurær mothna hæfth., thrithi ær trolldomber., wather takin innæn garz oc grindæ. m*eth* horn oc hari. t*et* scal a næfnd koma." Schlyter 1822–77, 6:109. The semantic range of coordinating conjunctions, most famously *en*, is broad in the older Nordic dialects; translating *oc* in both instances as 'or' might yield better sense in English.

138. The alliterative phrase *innæn garz oc grindæ* (alt., *innan gardz ok grindha* and so on) is widely used in Old Swedish, probably comparable in its traditionality (although not in its meaning) to a fixed phrase such as "over hill and dale" in English. *Garþer* implies both that which encloses as well as that which is enclosed, that is, both fence and protected space. English *yard* and *garden* are related terms. In West Norse, *grind* similarly means that which encloses as well as that which is enclosed (in the plural), that is, both gate and pen, although I have found no irrefutable evidence for this polysemy in Old Swedish. On the special connection of these terms with witchcraft, see the discussions in Chapter 3 and earlier in this chapter.

139. "edr sitr madr vti til frodleiks. eda fremr madr galldra. eda magnar madr seid. eda heidni . . ." Jón Þorkelsson and Jón Sigurðsson 1857–1932, 2:604; cf. 2:599.

140. According to the Icelandic annals (*Lögmannannáll*) for 1334, "he*r*ra Paall canceler kosinn til erkeb*ysko*ps j Nid*aro*se. *ok* for ad *cu*riam ok var þar vigdr" Storm 1888, 271. *Annales regii* (*Konunungsannáll*) gives the year as 1333 and refers to him as "Meist*i* Pall" (154).

141. *Erkebiskop Paals tredie Statut* in Norwegian; *Skipan Páls erkibiskups hin þriðja* in Icelandic.

142. "Warizst men oc lif runir oc galldra. þui at þet er ekki vtan fiandans villa oc hans darscapir." Jón Þorkelsson and Jón Sigurðsson 1857–1932, 2:750. This collocation, or elements of it, becomes fairly common. Thus, e.g., from a Swedish collection of sermons (all from Klemming, Geete, and Ejder 1879–): "troande a truldom och liff ok galra oc andra villo . . . " (1:17–18); "älla kättara oc otrona villara villande mz falsom kännedom. lifwo*m* troldom oc dyäfwls galdrom . . . " (2:85): and "oc thin frauända fran gudhi oc rätte tro til troldom ok liff ok galdra ok andra diäfwls konst*ir* . . . " (1:146).

143. Keyser and Munch 1846–95, 3:285–86; Jón Þorkelsson and Jón Sigurðsson 1857–1932, 2:762.

144. E.g., "Jtem openberir spamenn eða galdrmen. Jtem meineiðamen. Jtem villumen." Jón Þorkelsson and Jón Sigurðsson 1857–1932, 2:753. *Opinberr* glosses a range of similar terms, including—in addition to 'notorious'—'open', 'manifest', and 'public'. Some manuscripts show *taufrmenn eða galdrmenn*; cf. Keyser and Munch 1846–95, 3:287, and Jón Þorkelsson and Jón Sigurðsson 1857–1932, 2:763.

145. "Gðymir eðir firir runum. galdrum oc gerningom. lifiom. hindirviti oc ollum atrunadhe þeim sem heilog kirkia kennir iðir eigi . . . " Keyser and Munch 1846–95, 3:300; cf. Jón Þorkelsson and Jón Sigurðsson 1857–1932, 2:843.

146. "Huar sem oðruuiss gerir. þa er han sem villumadhir i gudz bannæ." Keyser and Munch 1846–95, 3:300; cf. Jón Þorkelsson and Jón Sigurðsson 1857–1932, 2:843.

147. Ankarloo 1984, 40. The texts are printed in Gummerus 1900, V–IX.

148. Gummerus 1902, 90, 93.

149. On his life, see the overview in Klockars 1967, 1:198–200, as well as the more detailed presentations in Brilioth 1959 and Schück 1959.

150. "Item intoxicatores vel aliquando mortiferum procurantes seu consilium adhibentes, item sacrilegos et incantatrices, et quoscunque demones invocantes . . . " Reuterdahl 1841, 63. Cf. the slightly altered version, Reuterdahl 1841, 81: "17. Item sacrilegos et incantatores, et quoscunque dæmones invocantes, seu pro furto explorando, seu pro mulieribus, seu pro quocunque alio corpore Christi abutentes." Ankarloo 1984, 39, makes the argument that these and other passages are directly parallel to sections of a miracle collection following English and Continental models, translated at Vadstena in 1385 (see Klemming 1877–78, 7, 15–16, 23, 44–45, 127–28).

151. "Quinto, quod usurarii, sortilegia facientes, incantatores vel incantatrices, non accedant." Reuterdahl 1841, 73.

152. "Item siquis uel siqua diuinaciones, auguria, incantaciones dyabolicas fecerit uel eis crediderit, VII annos peniteat." Gummerus 1900, XVIII; cf. XVI Here from late fifteenth-century Skara in Västergötland.

153. Cf. Ankarloo (1984, 40), whose views I paraphrase here: "Likheterna är emellertid aldrig direkt verbala och det finns ingen anledning att betvivla, att aktstycket speglar svenska förhållanden."

154. One example, here from *Statutum Johannis Jerechini 1412, Arbogæ*: "23. Item dampnamus et reprobamus sortilegia incantaciones, divinaciones, sompniorum interpretaciones et quascu[m]que literas et scriptas cum caracteribus et ignotorum vocabulorum in sacra scriptura non expressorum inscriptacionibus, qua quidam supersticiose valere estimant contra ignem, aquam et gladium et alia mortis et morborum pericula, et similiter omnes scripturas, que in plumbo, oblatis aut parietibus, contra dolorem dencium aut febres vel alios quoslibet, morbos hominum, vel iumentorum. Item omnes modos quibus nituntur homines occulta furta quomodolibet investigare. Item observatores dierum Egypciacarum pro operibus inchoandis et alia huiusmodi deliramenta que non possunt plene explicari, que si quis inventus fuerit agere, scribere vel portare tanquam pro gravi mortali peccato puniatur, et si ea ut licita defenderit ab ingressu ecclesie suspensus publica penitencia puniatur, cum pena trium marcharum." Reuterdahl 1841, 108–9, but cf. the very similar passages from 1412 to ca. 1475 in Silfverstolpe 1875–, 2:544; Reuterdahl 1841, 115, 189; and Gummerus 1902, 30–31.

155. "De Sortilegiis. Item inhibemus ne qvis Sacerdos vel Clericus se intromittat ad aliqvid sortilegium, qvia in talibus semper est occulta diaboli administratio." Thorkelin 1781, 118. This rule is attributed to Archbishop Johannes of Lund, presumably Jens Brostrup (1472–1497). Cf. his letter of June 4, 1482, which likewise begins, "Johannes, dei gratia archiepiscopus Lundensis, Suetie primas et apostolice sedis legatus . . . " Nielsen 1872–87, 4:172. On heresy, superstition, and witchcraft in late medieval Denmark, see the review in Riising 1969, 330–44.

156. "De Evkaristia & oleo sancto. Item qvod presbyteri parrochiarum habeant corpus dominicum & oleum sanctum sub debita clausura propter sortilegia & alia pericula
imminentia sub pena Canonis." Thorkelin 1781, 108.

157. "[10.] Fontes sub cooperculo modo consueto et custodiantur propter immundicias et sortilegia." Gummerus 1902, 88. Cf. his remarks (p. 23) that although the manuscript dates to the 1400s, the materials "tyder på tiden omkr. 1350. . . . "

158. I include only such charges as were adjudicated in the courts, not, e.g., episodes
associated with saints' lives (e.g., the priests who practice sorcery as told in the miracles of
Knut Larvard [e.g., Gertz 1908–12, l. 243, sec. 7]) or literary sources, especially where the
action appears to consist of private retribution (e.g., the story of Þórir þursasprengir in
Landnámabók, as related in Jakob Benediktsson 1968, 257–58). My comments here extend
the arguments in Mitchell 2000b.

159. E.g., Ankarloo 1984; Næss 1982; Johansen 1991. Henningsen's (1992) critique of
Johansen and the need to distinguish carefully between different kinds of magic and their
practitioners are appropriate here as well, but there is little likelihood that the medieval
materials will yield themselves to that level of scrutiny. Cf. Edsman 1982b, 661.

160. There are two exceptions to this principle, the Greenlandic burning of Kolgrímr in 1407, insofar as the case involves sexuality, although the outcome conforms to
the pattern, and the burning of the nun at Kirkjubær in 1343, where both the accusation
and the punishment resembles the pattern for males.

161. "Preterea in mulieres ob eadem causa simili immanitate barbari ritus damnatas
quicquam impietatis faciendi uobis fas esse nolite putare. sed potius discite diuine ultionis
sententiam digne penitendo auertere. quam in illas insontes frustra feraliter seuiendo. iram
Domini multo magis prouocare." Afzelius et al. 1938–, ser. 1, 2:43.

162. A full treatment is provided in Davidsohn 1888; for excellent, although much
briefer, accounts, see Skyum-Nielsen 1971, 235–39, and Skyum-Nielsen 1994 (see also my
comments in Mitchell 2000b). For the documents relating to the case, see Afzelius et al.
1938–, for June 3, 1202; June 30, 1205; November 18, 1207; and May 29, 1208.

163. Cf. the account by Rigord, which reads in part, "Sed mirum! eodem die, insti-
gante diabolo, ipse rex, quibusdam, ut dicitur, maleficiis per sorciarias impeditus, uxorem
tam longo tempore cupitam, exosam habere cepit . . . " Delaborde 1882, 124–25.

164. Unger and Huitfeldt 1847–, 9:112–14. The documents consist of Bishop Auðfinnr's original "proclamation" (*De quadam lapsa in heresim Ragnilda Tregagaas*) and his
subsequent "sentence" (*Alia in eodem crimine*), preserved in transcriptions of the bishop-
ric's "protocol-book." The protocol-book (*Liber ecclesiæ Cathedralis Bergensis*) containing
these texts was evidently lost in the great Copenhagen fire of 1728, but two direct copies
of it are preserved. They differ only on minor points of orthography. On Auðfinnr's
training in France, see Johnsen 1952, and on the political intrigues he faced once back in
Bergen, see Bagge 1970. I have attempted to flesh out aspects of this case in Mitchell
1997c, 1998, 2000b, 2003b, some of which I reiterate here.

165. Jakob Benediktsson 1993, 15, summarizes both the value and the uncertainties
of the Icelandic annals, writing that they "are very important historical sources, but the

analysis of their interrelationships and their relation to the various sources is far from complete." See Chapter 4 in this volume for details on the case.

166. "þetta ed sama (aar) v*ar* bren(d*ur* e)in*n* m*adur* j Grænl*an*di e*r* Kolg*r*im*ur* hiet fyrir . . . ok at hann la ein*n*a m*annz* kvin*n*v er Ste . . . hiet dott*ir* Hrafns logm*annz* er liest (j skr)idvn*n*e n*or*d*ur* (j Launguhl)id. atte h*an*a þa þ(orgri)m*ur* Solva son. (Fieck þessi) m*adur* he*n*nar vilia med. sv*ar*ta kuon(stu*m* oc sijd*an* br)end*ur* ept*ir* dom. v*ar* kuin*n*an (oc alld*ri* m*ed* jafn)ri sin*n*u oc ad*ur*. oc deydi þ(ar litliu sijd*ar*." Storm 1888, 288–89. Another manuscript (AM 420C 4to) of Lǫgmannsannáll, gives the woman's name as Sigrijd*ur*.

167. Seaver 1996, 153–54; cf. 315. Seaver also makes the interesting point, contra Berglund 1982a, 1982b, that "although witchcraft presumably was an offense against the church, Kollgrim was not tried and executed at Gardar [the bishop's seat in Greenland] but at Hvalsey [. . .] one of the four big Eastern Settlement church farms with a festal hall."

168. Cf. Burriss 1936, 138: "Because of their hidden, mysterious nature the rites are occulta, arcana, secreta. Magic rites are called nocturna sacra . . . " Regarding the devil as a black man, see the discussions in Russell 1972, 113–14, and Cavendish 1967, 325–38.

169. Cf. the comments in Seaver 1996, 152–54, and the materials reviewed there.

170. "Anno 1471. Ein verruchter, Gottslästerer Räuber und Mörder, von Adelicher Extraction, ward in diesem Jahr zu Slagelse in Seeland lebendig verbrannt, weil er, nebst andern Schandthaten, viele Kirchen beraubet hatte. Als das Todes-Urtheil ihn vorgelesen ward, zog er eine irgend aus der Kirchen gestohlene Büchse mit geweiheten Hostien aus seinen Busen, und sprach: Ich habe in zehen Jahren kein Sacrament empfangen, alzo will mirs selbst ertheilen. Darauf nahm er eine Oblate, sprechend: Das ist fürs erste Jahr, bey der zweyten, das ist fürs zweyte, und so ferner. Heinrich Menstrup, Königlicher Lehns-mann auf Raarsöer, ließ ihm alsbald beyde Hände abhauen, und aufs Feuer werffen, darnach ward der ganße verfluchte Cörper denselben Weg gesandt." Pontoppidan 1741, 2:653–54. Cf. Riising 1969, 343.

171. "bi[r??]g*ir*tha and*irs*sadotth*ir* stodh i*n*ne før rettin och sagde adh galna kadhrin ko*m* til he*n*na och badh he*n*ne fa sik eth kattohoffwudh och eth oxahorn iak vil se til ath iak ka*n* skilia pedh*ir* belta*re* och hans festh*ir*mo ||aath tha sagde birg*it*ta iak froktar føre ath thu forgiffw*ir* them ney sagde kadrin iak vil fly th*et* saa ath ha*n* skal giffwa pikone øffu*ir* och haffwa kærlegh til thin tha stodh birg*it*ta til ath hon høgh hoffw*u*dith aff enne katto och fik he*n*ne och tez lik*is* eth oxahorn och sagdhe til birgittho iak far tik horn*it* fult medh vatn sla th*et* pa hans dør oc se i*n*the ath*ir* æpth*ir* tik tha thu borth gaar [. . .] and*irs* ingemars*on* vnge bænkt tesse loffwadhe før birg*it*to and*irs*sadotth*ir* i tesso mattho ath hon skal aldregh biffi*n*nas m*edh* nokra forg*er*ningha tez lik*is* ath hon skulle aldregh forhind*ra* ell*ir* qwælia the*ris* hionalagh medh nokra forg*er*ningha." Noreen and Wennström 1935–, 1:360.

172. "mat*is* i bo bilaten pa x mark før eth lyffe han lofwadhe føre galna kadrin ath hon skulle komma før rettin oc ko*m* ey." Noreen and Wennström 1935–, 1:360.

173. Noreen and Wennström 1935–, 1:354, 355.

174. See Noreen and Wennström 1935–, 1:354, 355; 1:360n66.

175. Carlsson 1921–44, 632, suggests that singerska might refer to a woman who practices witchcraft.

176. "ath hon hade thakit Hans Mille allen sin förlich bort pa sin mandoms wegna *etcetera*, huilkit hon widerkendes at hon tet giort hade V (5) aar sidan pa then stad ther han hade standit och giort sit watn fran sig. Samme dach widerkendes halffstopit, ath Anna finszka hon lerdhe henne then trolldomen, som war her Laurense deyja j Börchlinge wiid Vpsala. Sade hon, tet Anna singerska [sångerska?] gaff Hans Mille kattahiernan, at hon tet for henne hade til standit. Samma dach bekendes forscriffne Margith, tet hon sigh ey hade scriptat eller beret j V (5) aar." Carlsson 1921–44, 418. Cf. the comments on this case in Witt 1983, 118.

177. "Eodem die vitnade Laurens tymberman, ath han hörde, thet Jenis forköpare sagde til eth beläte, crucifixum malath vppa ena taffla, som hängde vppa wäggenä: jach haffuer länge tiänth tik, nw affsigx jak tik och tagher tienisth aff fänddanom." Hildebrand 1917, 148.

178. "Jn profesto beatorum apostolorum Symonis et Jude tha kendes Ragvald Odinskarl, ath han stuleth tesse kirkioner [. . .] Thermeth kendes han och, ath han hade tiänth Odhanom j vij aar ok ath Joan Land hade warith meth honom j raadh oc daath ok sälskap, tha forscripna kirkior staalos." Carlsson 1921–44, 66–67. In the margin, the case is identified as that of "Óðinn's Ragnvald" (*Odens Ragwal*). Cf. Carlsson 1921–44, 79, 81. On this trial, see my comments in Mitchell 2009a.

179. "Erick Clauesson, Hans Perssons tienere j Wermdøø, fødder j Wendelle sokn, widerkendes, ath han hade Gudj widersacht ok allt hans helga selscap jx reser om jx torsdaga afftana om kirkiagarden ansylis ok widerthagit dyeffuolen Oden fore peninga schull." Almquist 1930, 18. I translate *kirkiagarden* as 'the churchyard', but it also implies the church cemetery. The choice of adverbs invites speculation: *ansylis* (Modern Swedish *ansyls*, but also without fronting—*ansols*) is used here, as with Old Norse *andsælis*, to mean 'against the sun', 'withershins', and the context of this word is almost always related to witchcraft or magic. Cf. the Swedish laws' remedy for false accusation in 1442, which includes "walking backward" (*gange baaklenges*) around the meetinghouse but notably not *ansylis* 'withershins'. Schlyter 1822–77, 12:403.

180. "Fframdelis kendis han haffue stolit sin egen hosbonde aff och vndandolt bade peninga och sølff en godh deel, som han hade vpborit aff hans landboor och vndandolde, ffore huilkenne zacher han wort dømpder til eldhen for then høgxta zachen, som han Gudj ok war schapere giord j moth och sina saliga siel. Och the andra twa zacher fordrogx hanom til pynan, som war hiwlit och repith, pie memorie." Almquist 1930, 18 (cf. 333).

181. On the case for casting the net widely in examining the instances involving magic-related charges, see Edsman 1982b, 661. The gendered differences in the legal philosophy of the Old Swedish provincial laws, and the greater gender neutrality of the national codes, is carefully examined in Ekholst 2009.

CHAPTER 6

1. E.g., Kittredge 1929. I am not suggesting that early scholarship was unaware of the fact that women accounted for the vast majority of the accused but rather that gender often fails to play any prominent role in the analyses offered. For a thorough and thought-

provoking consideration of witchcraft and gender in the early modern period, see Apps and Gow 2003.

2. E.g., Fogelklou Norlind 1942. Because Fogelklou Norlind tended to endorse Margaret Murray's thesis of holdover pagan cults, her views do not today receive much attention, but her opening sentence will give a broad impression of how forward looking her thinking and, indeed, even her vocabulary were: "Fristående kvinnor, som icke genom det patriarkalt kyrkliga äktenskapet underordnades mannen eller genom klosterkulturens nya bildningstyp ställdes utanför moderskapet, behöllo under medeltiden något av typen prästinna eller 'klok kvinna', utan att i populäruppfattning deg.enereras till den asociala karaktär som betecknas med orden sköka och häxa." Norlind 1942, 180 ["Independent women, who were not subjugated to men through the patriarchal church's [institution of] marriage or who were not placed outside of motherhood through the new model of the cloister culture, retained something of the priestess or 'wise woman' type, without in popular thought degenerating into the asocial character designated with the words 'prostitute' and 'witch'"].

3. Daly 1978; Larner 1987; Labouvie 1990; Clark 1991; Hester 1992; Oja 1994; Brauner 1995. With respect to gender, witchcraft in early modern Scandinavia generally follows the trends elsewhere. Iceland is a famous exception, where overwhelmingly men were executed rather than women (involving, however, very small numbers, twenty men and one woman), on which, see Hastrup 1993 and Ólína Þorvarðardóttir 2000. On the similar Finnish situation, see Nenonen 1992 (with an English summary), Nenonen 1993, and Heikkinen and Kervinen 1993.

4. E.g., Morris 1991; Jochens 1991 and 1996; cf. Dillmann 2006, as well as Mitchell 2000b, on which some of these comments are based. Morris 1991, e.g., employs literary, linguistic, and legal iconography from throughout the Germanic world to argue for an evolution from the beneficial sorceress figure portrayed in Tacitus and other early writers to the later diabolical witch stereotype, seeing her book as "a kind of case study on how the change in the medieval religious *Weltanschauung* (from pagan to Christian) affected the role of women and magic" (7).

5. Jochens 1996, 130–31; cf. 124: "Although men were clearly active and in a few cases equal to women, their overall performance was weaker, thus suggesting that they were latecomers and that their complete integration into the profession of magic was not yet complete."

6. In addition to Morris and Jochens, Dillmann (2006) suggests a particular confidence in the sagas in this regard.

7. E.g., Price 2002; Solli 2002.

8. On this proverb, see Mitchell 2005. The usual Danish locution was *Onth qwinne ær helwedz dørs nafflæ* "An evil woman is Hell's door nail".

9. E.g., Skyum-Nielsen 1971; Jacobsen 1986; Jesch 1991; Sawyer 1992; Jochens 1995, 1996; and the various essays in such anthologies as Gunneng 1989 and Sellevold, Mundal, and Steinsland 1992. In a series of works (culminating in her 2010 study), Agnes S. Arnórsdóttir has outlined the economic and political shaping of gender in the Nordic Middle Ages region, especially with respect to canon law.

10. E.g., Damico 1984; Jochens 1987, 1996.

11. On "mentalities" and saga literature, see Mitchell 2000a.

12. For a consideration of this issue with respect to both Nordic and, more broadly, European contexts, see Ney 2004.

13. Lönnroth 1976, 76; cf. Sigurður Nordal 1941.

14. Unger and Huitfeldt 1847–, 9:1, pp. 112–24.

15. E.g., Macfarlane 1991; Demos 1982.

16. Noreen and Wennström 1935–, 1:243.

17. "tw esth een landløpirska," she says, "och thu vulte at thin bonde var slagen i hell." Noreen and Wennström 1935–, 1:313. *Landløpare, landløpirska* are usually glossed as '*landstrykare, landstrykerska*', but to the extent we have evidence of the term, it frequently is bundled with other accusations, such as murderer and whore, as when one woman calls another *horo ok landløpirsko* (Noreen and Wennström 1935–, 1:121 [1460]). Cf. the accusation that Ælseby would like her husband dead. Ælseby's profile elsewhere in the town records (Noreen and Wennström 1935–, 1:243, 324) makes her appear a stereotypical quarrelsome figure who would easily fit the profile of an accused witch.

18. Noreen and Wennström 1935–, 1:324; cf. Noreen and Wennström 1935–, 1:346; 2:129–30.

19. Albeit from a much later period, cf. the Scottish case of Margaret Lister of Fife in Larner 1987, 85. A review of the literal and metaphoric image of the "evil women" in late medieval and Renaissance art is provided in Grössinger 1997, 94–138; cf. Bardsley's fascinating 2006 examination of the role of gossip and scolding in late medieval English society, a pattern that seems to fit Ælseby nicely.

20. Aarne and Thompson 1961, 402. Typically, the devil and Sko-Ella are painted on either side of the church's exterior door.

21. Tubach 1969, no. 5361; cf. Odenius 1984.

22. See Lindhe 1978, 98–107, and Romdahl 1914.

23. Gen. 3:16. It is with reference to this passage that Tertullian (1951, 14) makes his comments cited earlier.

24. Institoris 2009, 165–66.

25. Institoris 2009, 170.

26. As Mackay remarks, "Even if the *Malleus* is not misogynistic in a narrow sense, the work is clearly permeated with a hostile and negative view of women as a whole" (Institoris 2009, 26). That the *Malleus* is more idiosyncratic than typical in its views is argued in, e.g., Broedel 2003.

27. See Hødnebø 1982a for a review of torture in medieval Scandinavia.

28. See esp. Rodin 1984; cf. Kilström 1957.

29. A vast literature concerns itself with *der Kampf um die Hose*. In addition to Metken 1996, see the helpful *Forschungsbericht* in Bock and Zimmermann 1997. The classic study of the evil woman is Brietzmann 1912; for a very interesting review of the idea's manifestation in Scandinavia, see Rodin 1984.

30. See, e.g., Nisbeth 1985; Kempff 1992; Bolvig 1994; Nisbeth 1995; and Bolvig 1999, but cf. the more skeptical view in Lawrence 1989.

31. The term is intended here as a calque on the *Biblia Pauperum*, or *Biblia Picta*, a block-printed pattern book, showing the life of Jesus and how it was prefigured in the stories drawn from the Hebrew Bible. Known in manuscript form already by circa 1300, the printed versions were popular models in the late medieval period for use by artists working in exactly such place as the Nordic churches.

32. See Wall 1977–78 and Brandt 1976, as well as the discussion in Chapter 4.

33. On this mural, see Haastrup 1992. On the larger question of *kalkmålningar*, see Nyborg 1978, esp. 5–10 and 31–37.

34. Geertz 2000, 120.

35. E.g., Morkarla kyrka. Cf. the views in Lundberg 1961, 52–63, and Nilsén 1986.

36. Pegelow 1976. The other two are scenes of the Crucifixion and *momento mori*.

37. That is, those in Antikvariskt-topografiska arkivet of Riksantikvarieämbetet in Stockholm. These catalogues cover all Swedish churches, including those in provinces that were Danish during the medieval period (e.g., Skåne). Cf. Wall 1977–78, 1:56–57. The comments here about the images of the *vapenhus* apply in my experience more to the Swedish situation; in Denmark, the witchcraft images are often inside the church itself.

38. See Norberg 1988, 8.

39. See the parallel argument in Byock 1990.

40. Cf. Caviness 2001.

41. "All þassi synda mal skal fyrst uiþ præst sin talæ ok eigh braþæ vp mæþ awund ællær vrez uiliæ . . . " Schlyter 1822–77, 1: 38.

42. Foucault 1975. In this vision of what was to be a new and humane prison, solid walls between cells set in a ringlike structure would isolate and block communication between prisoners, while at the same time the backlit cells would allow guards in a second, interior tower at the center of the ring of cells, that is, in the Panopticon, to observe fully and at all times each prisoner. An illuminating study of the church's exercise of social control at the very end of our period is provided in Ingesman 2007.

43. Bernström and Hedlund 1983, 151r [481].

44. Rafn 1829–30, 3:202–5. On the broader context of this curse, see Mitchell 1998.

45. "eru þarí mörg orð, þau sem kristnum mönnum er þarfleysa í munni at hafa . . ." Rafn 1829–30, 3:202.

46. Hermann Pálsson and Edwards 1985, 200. "Busla hét kerling, hún hafði verit frilla Þvara karls; hún fóstraði sonu karls, þvíat hún kunni mart í töfrum. Smiðr var henni miklu eftirlátari, ok nam hann mart í töfrum. Hún bauð Bósa at kenna honum galdra, en Bósi kveðst ekki vilja, at þat væri skrifat í sögu hans, at hann ynni nokkurn hlut sleitum [*other mss:* með göldrum], þat sem honum skyldi með karlmensku telja." Rafn 1829–30, 3:195–96. Similar scenarios, albeit with different results, occur as well, as in *Eyrbyggja saga*: "Gunnlaugr, sonr Þorbjarnar digra, var námgjarn; hann var opt í Mávahlíð ok nam kunnáttu at Geirríði Þórólfsdóttur, því at hon var margkunnig" ["Thorbjorn the Stout's son, Gunnlaug, had a passion for knowledge, and he often went over to Mavahlid to study witchcraft with Geirrid Thorolf's daughter, she being a woman who knew a thing or two"] (Einar Ól. Sveinsson and Matthías Þórðarson 1957, 28; trans. Hermann Pálsson and Edwards 1989, 59).

47. See Mitchell 1991b, esp. 124–36, where I associate the medieval Icelandic fascination with the past with cultural empowerment. More broadly on this issue, see Bagge 1997.

48. Cf. the etymologies of Norse *drengskapr* 'high-mindedness, courage' < *drengr* 'bold, valiant, chivalrous man' and Latin *virtūs* 'manliness, courage, worth' < *vir* 'man'. On the question of *drengskapr* and its place in the heroic sagas, see Mitchell 1991b, 117; in Old Norse society more broadly, see Meulengracht Sørensen 1980, 1983. Helga Kress 2008 notes that a man associated with witchcraft in the sagas is either feminized and described as *argr* 'effiminate' or is related to a witch.

49. Hollander 1991, 201, with my emendations to show the gender marking. "er kunnir ok sannir yrði at því, at fœri með galdra ok gǫrningar, eða seiðmenn." Bjarni Aðalbjarnarson 1962, 311. See also the discussion on these episodes in Chapter 1.

50. Hollander 1991, 201. "langskip alskipat; váru þat alt seiðmenn ok annat fjǫlkynngisfólk." Bjarni Aðalbjarnarson 1962, 311.

51. This comment is not meant to suggest that there were not historical "pagan uprisings" such as the one reported in *Heiðreks saga* (Tolkien 1960, 62–63), but rather that Snorri's intention is of a different sort.

52. Cf. Mitchell 2000b, which I build on and extend here.

53. Jochens 1996, 119–20, 123–24; Dillmann 2006, 143–60. See Helga Kress 2008, who argues that many saga women possess witch characteristics without being identified as such (e.g., Hallgerðr in *Brennu-Njáls saga*).

54. Jóhanna Katrín Friðriksdóttir 2009, 431. She is referring specifically to *Fóstbrœðra saga*, but I believe her comment can be extended to other sagas as well.

55. "Þættæ æru vkvæþins orþ kono . . . " Schlyter 1822–77, 1:38; cf. 1:153.

56. Schlyter 1822–77, 12:403; cf. Keyser and Munch 1846–95, 1:70, 3:104.

57. Schlyter 1822–77, 9:369; Skautrup 1933–41, 2:506.

58. "Forgiør mand konne eller konne mand eller konne konne med troldom eller andre forgiøringer, saa at hun eller hand døer deraff, da schall mand steyles och konne brendes, om schellige widne ere till." Kroman 1951–61, 4:338.

59. "Ef maðr feRR með galldra eða fiolkynngi . . . " Konrað Gíslason et al. 1883, 25. In this instance, from Skálhóltsbók. On the question of the Icelandic, and other, laws as sources, see Norseng 1987.

60. Keyser and Munch 1846–95, 1:389. Here from the "longer" *Eiðsivaþingslǫg*, but the "shorter" version contains much the same language; see Keyser and Munch 1846–95, 1:403.

61. "Ef þat er kænnt kono. at hon riði manne eða þionum hans. . . ." Keyser and Munch 1846–95, 1:390. Although the "longer" *Eiðsivaþingslǫg* are not explicit about this being an activity associated with witchcraft, the "shorter" *Eiðsivaþingslǫg* are and title this section *Vm trol kono* 'Concerning [female] witches'. Keyser and Munch 1846–95, 1:403.

62. "Enn ef þæt er kent kono at hon se trolkona eða manæta . . . " Keyser and Munch 1846–95, 1:434. Cf. the comparable treatment of women as witches elsewhere in the Norwegian laws, Keyser and Munch 1846–95, 1:350–51, 362, 372, 389–90, 429–30; 2:326–27, 495; 4:6, 62–63.

63. An addendum to *Västgötalagen* perhaps explains the level of fear that existed in Sweden about this crime: "hanum [Ingi] war firi giort mæð ondum dryk .i. östrægötlanði. oc fek. aff þy banæ." Schlyter 1822–77, 1:300 ['(King) Ingi was poisoned with an evil drink in Östergötland and died from it'].

64. "Bær konæ forgiærningær manni wærþær bar ok a takin. þa skal hanæ takæ ok .j. fiætur sættiæ. ok swa til þinx föræ. ok þe samu forgiærningær mæþ hænni [. . .] falls hun. þa a hun .j. bali brinnæ." Schlyter 1822–77, 3:149–50. *Upplandslagen* was used as a model for most of the Svea laws; see Norseng 1987, 59.

65. "Forgör maþer manne ællæ kunu, kona kunu ællæ manne, meþ trulldom ællæ andrum forgerningum, sua æt han ællæ hon faar döþ af, miste liif sit for þolika gerning; man skal stæghla ok kunu stena, ok viti þet meþ hæræz næmd sum för ær sakt." Schlyter 1822–77, 10:276.

66. "Warþir kuna takin meþ truldom. meþ horn oc haar quict oc döt þæt ma wel truldom heta." Schlyter 1822–77, 5:10. Cf. the remarks on this passage in Holmbäck and Wessén 1979, 2:18–19, esp. on the phrase *wari stens mattit oc stranda*.

67. See, e.g., Jón Þorkelsson and Jón Sigurðsson 1857–1932, 1:243; Gummerus 1900, XVI, XVIII; Gummerus 1902, 30–31, 63, 76, 88; Reuterdahl 1841, 63, 73, 81, 108, 115, 157, 189; and Keyser and Munch 1846–95, 3:271, 285–86, 287, 300.

68. "leta raadh aff forbannadhom trolkonom oc gallirkonum . . . " Klemming 1857–84, 3:293.

69. For an example of a male so portrayed, see Klemming 1857–84, 3:196. For an incident with a female soothsayer who particularly horrified Birgitta, see Chapter 3 in this volume and Klemming 1857–84, 3:395–96.

70. "Än wansamlika finnas män, som sik wndergiffua wilia enna qwinno foresyn." Klemming 1862, 4:70.

71. Larner 1987, 85.

72. The idea that monks and nuns might constitute a double monastery is nearly as old as the idea of monasticism itself, although there was a lengthy hiatus in the West before the eleventh-century reforms at Fontevrault initiated by Robert of Arbrissel; on the other hand, it has been argued that the leadership role given the abbess in the Birgittine houses was extreme, and the issue of a woman's possessing secular authority over monks represented a thorny issue for the church. Cf. Höjer 1905 and esp. Cnattingius 1963.

73. E.g., the struggles involving the monks, Abbess Ingegärd, and Conservator Lucas Jacobi; possibly even Queen Margareta. Cf. Cnattingius 1963, 47–68.

74. Klemming 1857–84, 4:57; Sahlin 2001, 147–48.

75. See esp. Morris 1999, 154–59, and the literature cited there.

76. Kienzle 2006, 739.

77. Following Cicero in both cases, Institoris 2009, 167–68 and 163.

78. Elliott 2004, whose study is broad and includes not only the now familiar dyad of saints and sinners but also the broader and increasingly important issue of what constituted proof in a theological and legal sense.

79. Kroon et al. 1993, text 56 (pp. 506–7).

80. So, e.g., Stephens and Dahlgren 1847–74, 1:603–4, and Henning 1954, 18, 20–23.

81. Unger 1874, 914.

82. See Mitchell 2000b and Chapter 5 in this volume.

83. Carlsson 1921–44, 2:67, 79, 81.

84. 28) *Um spár oc um galldra*; 29) *Um blot*; 30) *Um udaða menn*. Keyser and Munch 1846–95, 1:17–18.

85. Keyser and Munch 1846–95, 3:287.

86. Schlyter 1822–77, 10:273–82.

87. E.g., the paraphrase of Bernhard of Clairvaux: "trolskaps synd är at stridha mot gudz budhi." Klemming, Geete, and Ejder 1879–, 2:160.

88. See, e.g., Russell 1972, 194–98, and Barber 2006.

89. Stockholm's Bloodbath represents the apogee of the ongoing struggle by Sweden to leave the Union of Kalmar. The various political, ecclesiastical, and economic factors that lead to the event are complex and open to interpretations, perspectives that generally lay the blame on either the Danish king and his advisors or the Swedish archbishop, Gustav Trolle. In brief, in the autumn of 1520, following an agreement between the Swedes and the Danes and the accession to the Swedish throne by Kristian II, more than eighty individuals, mainly Swedish noblemen, clerics, and leading citizens, were executed based on charges of heresy. This incident precipitated the revolt that finally led to a separate Swedish kingdom by 1523, under the rule of Gustav Wasa.

90. Witchcraft and heresy made for a convenient accusation "kit," the medieval equivalent of contemporary accusations of lesbianism and witchcraft in contested child custody cases. Thus, e.g., Joan of Arc's English captors charge her with a variety of misdeeds, including dressing like a man, heresy, and minor sorcery. All of these charges contributed to, and reflect, the view that she and her career were at cross-purposes with nature and with established order. See, e.g., Warner 1981, 101–4.

91. Cf. Strömbäck 1935, 194–96.

92. Cf. Apps and Gow 2003, 118–37.

EPILOGUE

1. "cum quidam captiuorum torturæ subiectus confessus esse dicatur 400 ex obsessis pactum cum Diabolo fecisse." From a letter in Riksarkivet (1634-06-01 Reg. nr. 4141), published in Sondén et al. 1888–. I have also remarked on this case in Mitchell 2008b.

2. Cf. Purkiss 1996 and her consideration of the "dialogue" within the torture chamber.

3. On the great Swedish witch-hunt of 1668–76, see esp. Ankarloo 1983, 1984; Lagerlöf-Genetay 1990; Ankarloo 1993; Lennersand 1997; and Tegler 1997. With respect to the Blåkulla complex, see, e.g., Sahlgren 1915; Mitchell 1997a; Sörlin 1997; and Östling 2002.

4. "Om Troldfolck oc deris Medvidere," where the personal influence of King Kristian IV is surely at work. See Johansen 1993, 345–46; as well as Henningsen 1982, 1983; Johansen 1989, and, more broadly, Johansen 1991.

5. See esp. Knutsen 2003, who, pace Næss 1982, finds the incidence of the pact to be high. Cf. Næss 1983, 1984, and 1990.

6. This anomaly has given rise to a number of theories, on which see Hastrup 1993, as well as Ólína Þorvarðardóttir 2000, 175–84, esp. the degree to which Sveinn lögmaðr Sölvason appears to be an exception to the general thrust of events in Iceland.

7. "lönlika äggiande til synd älla kättara oc otrona villara villande mz falsom känne-dom. lifwom troldom oc dyäfwls galdrom . . . " Klemming, Geete, and Ejder 1879–, 2: 85.

8. See Riising 1969, 339, 342. Cf. Gummerus 1902, 88.

9. "att thw bliffwer forwarett [. . .] fraa alt nedherfaldt oc fraa alle forgifftelße oc fraa troldom oc fraa althet teg kandt skade anthen tiill Siell heller liff." Kristensen et al. 1945, 4:252.

10. "værn [. . .] ffor fförgyfftælsse och ffor annæn troldom och ffor ffalske tvngghær . . . " Kristensen et al. 1945, 4:462; "wernæ och giøm megh [. . .] for hwg for ild for watn for allæ hondæ throldom for fforredelsæ . . . " Kristensen et al. 1945, 4:336. I translate *fforredelsæ/fförrädhilse* in both instances as 'treason', but note that the terms also encompass the less political 'treachery'.

11. "O härra gudh ihesus christus . . . Jak anthwardar mik . . . at thu wärne mik oc göme ffran alt onth Oc fför all handa wapn fför alla mina owener synligha oc osynligha, Oc fför allt thät mik skadha kan, till liff oc siäl, särdelis fför ondh ffal, fför styrt, Oc skot, fföre kast, oc stywngh, fföre hwgh oc slagh, fför eldh oc watn fför aldra handa trwldom fföre fförrädhilse fför ffängilse, oc fför alt thät mik skadha kan til liff oc siäl, til ära, godz, älla rykthe . . . " Geete 1907–9, 502. Cf. the similar language in the prayer book of Ingegärd Ambjörnsdotter: "O *härra* gudh . . . Jak befäller mik j [thin] hälga gudhdom, ath thu mik wärne oc giöme . . . fför watn oc eldh fför troldom oc diäffwlscap . . . " Geete 1907–9, 504. See also Jexlev 1991.

12. Dahlbäck 1987a, 175. On these trials, see Chapter 5 in this volume, where, as elsewhere (Mitchell 2000b), I have argued that several trials that do not specify *maleficium*, *trolddom*, and so on should nevertheless be included in the tally, a factor that, if accepted, would of course increase the percentage.

13. "Um troldoom. Aff man witær annæn. at han hauær fforgørth. aff hans *mæth* troldoom. oc gangær han æi with. thær sæktæth war. num dyl. oc føør hin thz hanu*m* a hand. th*ær* sækthær. tha wæri han sik. th*ær* saak giuæs *mæth* næfnd i kirki sokæn. bathæ ffor hin thær sæktær. oc swo fforæ biscop." Brøndum-Nielsen, Jørgensen, and Buus 1920–42, 2:1, 506.

14. Kristian II's national law of 1521 provides an interesting bookend to the struggles begun in the earliest Christian eras between the bishops and monarchs over control of the law, on which see Lockhart 2007, 59–60.

15. "Om troldom. Mandt eller quinde, som röchte ganger aff, ath the fare meth troldom paa landzbyerne, tha schall vor Embitzmandt lade thage grandgiiffueligen vare paa thennom, om the findes pa sligh steder, som icke sedvonligt er, som hereffter følger, som er om Nattethide, afftenindt syldig, Morgenindt, eller eene vedt rindendis vandt, eller och andre hellige tiider, Skiertorsdag, och Sancti Valburgis Natth, som thet siiges at

brugis meere paa the tiider, endt andre tiider om aaritt . . . " Quoted here from Johansen 1991, 21.

16. In asserting the broad similarities on either side of the Reformation dividing line, I do not intend to mask the real differences that also existed. Kallestrup 2009 closely compares the handling of witchcraft cases in Italy and Denmark, showing, among other things, how relatively humane the supposedly brutal Inquisition was in comparison with the treatment of the accused in Denmark.

17. Cited in Nyborg 1978, 41.

18. Cf. "hans [Auðfinnr's] inngrep overfor Ragnhild Tregagås kan virkelig ses som en opplyst og rasjonalistisk kulturpersonlighets motarbeiding av tidens overtro, en innstill-ning som gjør ham ære." Berulfsen 1948, 52.

19. Cf. Price 2002.

ACKNOWLEDGMENTS

1. Variations of this story have long circulated at Harvard.

2. During this long period of fermentation, to borrow Strindberg's felicitous auto-biographical locution, I note here in general, as I do explicitly throughout, that I have not hesitated to build on the series of essays I have written on this topic over the years.

Works Cited

Characters not used in English follow Library of Congress standards. Icelandic authors are listed by given names with cross-listings from patronymics. Danish cataloging rules are generally suspended, except in a few well-known instances (e.g., Preben Meulengracht Sørensen).

ABBREVIATIONS

ANF   *Arkiv för nordisk filologi*
ARV   *ARV. The Scandinavian Yearbook of Folklore*
CONILC *A Companion to Old Norse-Icelandic Literature and Culture*. Ed. R. McTurk. Blackwell Companions to Literature and Culture, 31. Oxford: Blackwell, 2005.
FFC   Folklore Fellows Communications
ÍF   *Íslenzk fornrit*
KLNM   *Kulturhistorisk leksikon for nordisk middelalder fra vikingetid til reformasjonstid*. Ed. J. Brøndsted et al. 22 vols. Copenhagen: Rosenkilde og Bagger, 1982. Originally published 1956–78.
MScan   *Medieval Scandinavia: An Encyclopedia*. Ed. P. Pulsiano et al. New York: Garland, 1993.
SFSS   Svenska Fornskrift-Sällskapets Samlingar (also: Samlingar utgivna av Svenska fornskriftsällskapet)
SStudies *Scandinavian Studies*
SUGNL   Samfund til Udgivelse af gammel nordisk Litteratur

Aarne, Antti, and Stith Thompson, eds. 1961. *The Types of the Folktale: A Classification and Bibliography*. 2nd rev. ed. FFC, 75 (184). Helsinki: Suomalainen Tiedeakatemia.

Åström, Lars-Åke. 1995. "Vadstenabrodern Peder Månssons latinska traktater om alkemi—vilka var hans källor?" In *Symbolae Septentrionales. Latin Studies Presented to Jan Öberg*. Ed. Monika Asztalos and Claes Gejrot. Runica et Mediævalia. Scripta minora II. Stockholm: Sällskapet Runica et Mediævalia. Pp. 289–315.

Abram, Christopher. 2007. "Anglo-Saxon Homilies in Their Scandinavian Context." In

The Old English Homily: Precedent, Practice, and Appropriation, ed. A. J. Kleist. Studies in the Early Middle Ages, 17. Turnhout: Brepols. Pp. 425–44.

Acker, Paul. 1998. *Revising Oral Theory: Formulaic Composition in Old English and Old Icelandic Verse.* Garland Studies in Medieval Literature, 16. New York: Garland.

Aðalbjarnarson, Bjarni. See Bjarni Aðalbjarnarson.

Aðalsteinsson, Jón Hnefill. See Jón Hnefill Aðalsteinsson.

Afzelius, Adam, et al., eds. 1938–. *Diplomatarium Danicum.* Udg. af Det Danske Sprog- og Litteraturselskab. Copenhagen: Munksgaard for 1938–74; C. A. Reitzel since 1975.

Agnes S. Arnórsdóttir. 2010. *Property and Virginity: The Christianization of Marriage in Medieval Iceland, 1200–1600.* Århus: Aarhus University Press.

Almquist, J. A., ed. 1930. *Stockholms stads tänkeböcker 1492–1500.* Stockholms stadsböcker från äldre tid. 2: a serien. Tänkeböcker, 3. Stockholm: Kungl. Samfundet för utgivande af handskrifter rörande Skandinaviens historia med understöd af Stockholms stad och samfundet Sankt Erik.

Almqvist, Bo. 1965. *Norrön niddiktning: Traditionshistoriska studier i versmagi.* 2 vols. Nordiska texter och undersökningar, 21. Stockholm: Almqvist & Wiksell.

———. 2000. "I marginalen till *Sejd.*" In *Sejd och andra studier i nordisk själsuppfattning av Dag Strömbäck,* ed. Gertrud Gidlund. Acta Academiae Regiae Gustavi Adolphi, 72. Hedemora: Kungl. Gustav Adolfs Akademien för svensk folkkultur/Gidlunds förlag. Pp. 237–72.

Almqvist, Daniel, ed. 1939–51. *Stockholms stads tänkeböcker från år 1592. I. 1592–1595. II. 1596–1599.* 2 vols. Stockholm: Stockholms stadsarkiv.

Alver, Bente Gullveig. 1971. *Heksetro og trolddom: En studie i norsk hekseväsen.* Oslo: Universitetsforlaget.

———. 2008. *Mellem mennesker og magter: Magi i hekseforfølgelsernes tid.* Oslo: Spartacus.

Alver, Brynjulf. 1980. "Nasjonalisme og identitet: Folklore og nasjonal utvikling." *Tradisjon* 10: 5–16.

Amory, Frederic. 1993. "Sólarljóð." In *MScan.* Pp. 607–8.

Andersson, Roger. 1993. *Postillor och predikan: En medeltida texttradition i filologisk och funktionell belysning.* Runica et Mediaevalia. Scripta minora, 1. Stockholm: Runica et Mediaevalia.

———, ed. 2006. *Sermones sacri Suecice: The Sermon Collection in Cod. AM 787 4.* SFSS. Ser. 1, Svenska skrifter, 86. Uppsala: Svenska fornskriftsällskapet.

Andersson, Theodore M. 1964. *The Problem of Icelandic Saga Origins: A Historical Survey.* Yale Germanic Studies, 1. New Haven, Conn.: Yale University Press.

———. 1985. "Kings' Sagas (*Konungasögur*)." In *Old Norse-Icelandic Literature: A Critical Guide,* ed. C. J. Clover and J. Lindow. Islandica, 45. Ithaca, N.Y.: Cornell University Press. Pp. 197–238.

Andersson, Thorsten. 1987. "Svensk medeltid i fornsvenskt pespektiv." In *Svensk medeltidsforskning idag: En forskningsöversikt,* ed. G. Dahlbäck. Uppsala: Humanistisk-samhällsvetenskapliga forskningsrådet. Pp. 119–53.

Andersson-Schmitt, Margarete. 1959. *Der grosse Seelentrost: Ein niederdeutsches Erbauungs-*

buch des vierzehnten Jahrhunderts. Niederdeutsche Studien, 5. Cologne: Böhlau Verlag.

Andersson-Schmitt, Margarete, and Monica Hedlund. 1991. *Mittelalterliche Handschriften der Universitätsbibliothek Uppsala: Katalog über die C-Sammlung.* Acta Universitatis Upsaliensis. Acta Bibliothecae R. Universitatis Upsaliensis, 26:4. C 301–400. Stockholm: Almqvist & Wiksell International.

Andrén, Anders. 2005. "Behind *Heathendom:* Archaeological Studies of Old Norse Religion." *Scottish Archaeological Journal* 27 (2): 105–38.

Ankarloo, Bengt. 1983. "Das Geschrei der ungebildeten Masse: Zur Analyse der schwedischen Hexenprozesse." In *Hexenprozesse,* ed. C. Degn, H. Lehmann, and D. Unverhau. Neumünster: K. Wachholtz. Pp. 172–78.

———. 1984. *Trolldomsprocesserna i Sverige.* 2nd ed. Rättshistoriskt bibliotek, 1:17. Stockholm: A.-B. Nordiska Bokhandeln. Orig. pub. 1971.

———. 1993. "Sweden: The Mass Burnings (1668–1676)." In *Early Modern European Witchcraft: Centres and Peripheries,* ed. B. Ankarloo and G. Henningsen. Oxford: Clarendon Press. Orig. pub. 1990. Pp. 285–317.

Ankarloo, Bengt, and Gustav Henningsen, eds. 1993. *Early Modern European Witchcraft: Centres and Peripheries.* Oxford: Clarendon Press. Orig. pub. 1990.

Annell, Eric. 1840. *Blåkulla-färden skärthorsdagen år 1793 samt djefwulens grasserande uti Römåsen år 1794.* Strengnäs.

Apps, Lara, and Andrew Gow. 2003. *Male Witches in Early Modern Europe.* Manchester: Manchester University Press.

Ármann Jakobsson. 2005. "Royal Biography." In *CONILC.* Pp. 388–402.

———. 2009. "Identifying the Ogre: The Legendary Saga Giants." In *Fornaldarsagaerne: Myter og virkelighed; Studier i de oldislandske fornaldarsögur Norðurlanda,* ed. A. Ney, Ármann Jakobsson, and A. Lassen. Copenhagen: Museum Tusculanum Forlag. Københavns Universitet. Pp. 181–200.

Árnason, Jón. See Jón Árnason.

Árni Björnsson. 1961. "Hjátrú á jólum." *Skírnir* 135: 110–28.

Arnórsdóttir, Agnes S. See Agnes S. Arnórsdóttir.

Ásdís Egilsdóttir, ed. 2002. *Biskupa sögur II. Hungrvaka. Þorláks saga byskups in elzta. Jarteinabók Þorláks byskups in forna. Þorláks saga byskups yngri. Jarteinabók Þorláks byskups önnur. Þorláks saga byskups C. Þorláks saga byskups E. Páls saga byskups. Ísleifs þáttr byskups. Latínubrot um Þorlák byskup.* ÍF, 16. Reykjavík: Hið íslenzka fornritafélag.

Ashplant, T. G., and Adrian Wilson. 1988. "Present-Centred History and the Problem of Historical Knowledge." *Historical Journal* 31 (2): 253–74.

Attwood, Katrina. 2005. "Christian Poetry." In *CONILC.* Pp. 43–63.

Bächtold-Stäubli, Hanns, and Eduard Hoffmann-Krayer, eds. 1987. *Handwörterbuch des deutschen Aberglaubens.* Berlin: Walter de Gruyter. Orig. pub. 1931–32.

Bæksted, Anders. 1952. *Målruner og Troldruner: Runmagiske Studier.* Copenhagen: Gyldendal.

Baetke, Walter. 1950. *Die Götterlehre der Snorra-Edda.* Berichte über die Verhandlungen der Sächsischen Akademie der Wissenschaften zu Leipzig. Philologisch-historische Klasse, 97:3. Berlin: Akademie-Verlag.

Bætzmann, Frederik. 1865. *Hexevæsen og troldskab i Norge: Meddelt til læsning for menigmand.* Oslo: B. M. Bentzen.

Bagge, Sverre. 1970. "Striden mellom kapellmagisteren og biskopen i Bergen 1308–1320." In *Bjørgvin bispestol: Byen og bispedømmet,* ed. P. Juvkam. Bergen: Universitetsforlaget. Pp. 41–54.

———. 1991. *Society and Politics in Snorri Sturluson's Heimskringla.* Berkeley: University of California Press.

———. 1997. "Icelandic Uniqueness or a Common European Culture?" *SStudies* 69 (4): 418–42.

———. 1998. *Mennesket i middelalderens Norge: Tanker, tro og holdninger 1000–1300.* Oslo: Aschehoug.

———. 2001. "Law and Justice in Norway in the Middle Ages: A Case Study." In *Medieval Spirituality in Scandinavia and Europe: A Collection of Essays in Honour of Tore Nyberg,* ed. L. Bisgaard et al. Odense University Studies in History and Social Sciences, 234. Odense: Odense University Press. Pp. 73–85.

———. 2003. "Ideologies and Mentalities." In *The Cambridge History of Scandinavia.* Vol. 1, *Prehistory to 1520,* ed. K. Helle. Cambridge: Cambridge University Press. Pp. 465–86.

Bailey, Michael D. 1996. "The Medieval Concept of the Witches' Sabbath." *Exemplaria* 8: 419–39.

———. 2001. "From Sorcery to Witchcraft: Clerical Conceptions of Magic in the Later Middle Ages." *Speculum* 76 (4): 960–90.

———. 2002. "The Feminization of Magic and the Emerging Idea of the Female Witch in the Late Middle Ages." *Essays in Medieval Studies* 19: 120–34.

———. 2003. *Battling Demons: Witchcraft, Heresy, and Reform in the Late Middle Ages.* University Park: Pennsylvania State University Press.

———. 2007. *Magic and Superstition in Europe: A Concise History from Antiquity to the Present.* Critical Issues in History. Lanham, Md.: Rowman & Littlefield.

———. 2008. "The Age of Magicians: Periodization in the History of European Magic." *Magic, Ritual, and Witchcraft* 3 (1): 1–28.

Bampi, Massimiliano. 2007. *The Reception of the* Septem Sapientes *in Medieval Sweden: Between Translation and Rewriting.* Göppinger Arbeiten zur Germanistik, 744. Göppingen: Kümmerle.

Bampi, Massimiliano, and Fulvio Ferrari, eds. 2008. *Lärdomber oc skämptan: Medieval Swedish Literature Reconsidered.* SFSS. Ser. 3. Smärre texter och undersökningar, 5. Uppsala: Svenska fornskriftsällskapet.

Bang, A. Chr., ed. 1901. *Norske Hexeformularer og Magiske Opskrifter.* Videnskabsselskabets Skrifter. 2. Historisk-filos. Klasse No. 1. Christiania: Jacob Dybwad.

Bang, Vilhelm. 1896. *Hexevæsen og hexeforfølgelser især i Danmark.* Copenhagen: J. Frimodt.

Barber, Malcolm. 2006. *The Trial of the Templars.* 2nd ed. Cambridge: Cambridge University Press.

Bardsley, Sandy. 2006. *Venomous Tongues: Speech and Gender in Late Medieval England.* Philadelphia: University of Pennsylvania Press.

Bartlett, Robert. 1986. *Trial by Fire and Water: The Medieval Judicial Ordeal.* Oxford: Oxford University Press.

Bauman, Richard. 1975. "Verbal Art as Performance." *American Anthropologist* 77: 290–311.

———. 1986. "Performance and Honor in 13th-Century Iceland." *Journal of American Folklore* 99: 131–50.

———. 1992. "Contextualization, Tradition, and the Dialogue of Genres: Icelandic Legends of the Kraftaskald." In *Rethinking Context: Language as an Interactive Phenomenon,* ed. C. Goodwin. Cambridge: Cambridge University Press. Pp. 125–45.

———. 1996. "Folklore as a Transdisciplinary Dialogue." *Journal of Folklore Research* 33: 15–20.

Beard, Mary. 1992. "Frazer, Leach, and Virgil: The Popularity (and Unpopularity) of the Golden Bough." *Comparative Studies in Society and History* 34 (2): 203–24.

Beckers, H. 1977. "Seelentrost." In *Lexikon des Mittelalters,* ed. R. Auty et al. Vol. 7. Munich: Artemis-Verlag. Col. 1680.

Beckman, Natanael, and Kristian Kålund, eds. 1908–18. *Alfræði íslenzk: Islandsk encyklopædisk litteratur.* SUGNL, 37, 41, 45. Copenhagen: S. L. Møllers.

Behringer, Wolfgang. 1996. "Witchcraft Studies in Austria, Germany and Switzerland." In *Witchcraft in Early Modern Europe: Studies in Culture and Belief,* ed. J. Barry, M. Hester, and G. Roberts. Cambridge: Cambridge University Press. Pp. 64–95.

Benedict, Ruth. 1937. "Magic." In *Encyclopaedia of the Social Sciences,* ed. A. S. Johnson and E. R. A. Seligman. Vol. 5. New York: Macmillan Company. Pp. 39–44.

Benediktsson, Jakob. See Jakob Benediktsson.

Benedikz, B. S. 1964. "The Master Magician in Icelandic Folk-Legend." *Durham University Journal* 26 (3): 22–34.

Berg, Per Gustaf. 1981. *Svensk mystik: Anekdoter och historier* [. . .]. Facsimile ed. Suecica rediviva, 91. Stockholm: Rediviva. Orig. pub. 1871.

Bergh, Birger, Hans Aili, Ann-Mari Jönsson, and Carl-Gustaf Undhagen, eds. 1967–98. *Sancta Birgitta: Revelaciones.* SFSS. Ser. 2, Latinska skrifter, 7:1–7. Uppsala: Almqvist & Wiksell.

Bergljót Kristjánsdóttir. 1990. " 'Hvorki er eg fjölkunnig né vísindakona . . .' Um konur og kveðskap í Sturlungu." *Skáldskaparmál* 1: 241–54.

Berglund, Joel. 1982a. *Hvalsø: Kirkeplads og Stormandsgård.* Julianehåb: Qaqortoq Kommune.

———. 1982b. "Kirke, hal og status." *Grønland* 30: 275–85.

Berner, Ulrich. 2001. "The Notion of Syncretism in Historical and/or Empirical Research." *Historical Reflections/Reflexions Historiques* 27 (3): 499–509.

Bernström, John, and Monica Hedlund, eds. 1983. *Dyalogus Creaturarum Moralizatus 1483/Skapelsens sederlärande samtal 1483.* Uppsala: Michaelsgillet.

Berulfsen, Bjarne. 1948. *Kulturtradisjon fra en storhetstid: En kulturhistorisk studie pa grunn-lag av den private brevlitteratur i første halvdel av det 14. hundreår.* Oslo: Gyldendal.

Besserman, Lawrence L. 1979. *The Legend of Job in the Middle Ages.* Cambridge, Mass.: Harvard University Press.

Birkhan, H. 1989. "Popular and Elite Culture Interlacing in the Middle Ages." *History of European Ideas* 10 (1): 1–11.

Bjarne Larsson, Gabriela. 1992. "Det medeltida nordiska lagmaterialet och kvinnorna." In *Fokus på kvinner i middelalderkilder: Rapport fra symposiet "Kilder til kvinnehistoriske studier i nordisk middelalder," Isegran, september 1990,* ed. B. J. Sellevold, E. Mundal, and G. Steinsland. Skara: Viktoria Bokförlaget. Pp. 62–68.

Bjarni Aðalbjarnarson. 1936. *Om de norske kongers sagaer.* Skrifter utg. av det Norske videnskaps-akademi i Oslo. 2, Hist.-filos. kl., 4. Oslo: I kommisjon hos J. Dybwad.

———, ed. 1962. *Snorri Sturluson. Heimskringla I.* ÍF, 26. Reykjavík: Hið íslenzka forn-ritafélag. Orig. pub. 1941.

———, ed. 1979. *Snorri Sturluson. Heimskringla II.* ÍF, 27. Reykjavík: Hið íslenzka forn-ritafélag. Orig. pub. 1951.

Bjarni Einarsson, ed. 1984. *Ágrip af Noregskonunga sögum: Fagrskinna—Nóregs konunga tal.* ÍF, 29. Reykjavík: Hið íslenzka fornritafélag.

Bjarni Guðnason. 1977. "Theodoricus og íslenzkir sagnaritarar." In *Sjötíu ritgerðir hel-gaðar Jakobi Benediktssyni 20. júlí 1977,* ed. Einar G. Pétursson and Jónas Kristjánsson. Stofnun Árna Magnússonar á Íslandi Rit, 12. Vol. 1. Reykjavík: Stofnun Árna Mag-nússonar á Íslandi. Pp. 107–20.

———. 1981. "The Icelandic Sources of Saxo Grammaticus." In *Saxo Grammaticus: A Medieval Author between Norse and Latin Culture,* ed. K. Friis-Jensen. Danish Medie-val History and Saxo Grammaticus, 2. Copenhagen: Museum Tusculanum Press. Pp. 79–93.

Björn K. Þórólfsson and Guðni Jónsson, eds. 1972. *Vestfirðingasögur.* ÍF, 6. Reykjavík: Hið íslenzka fornritafélag. Orig. pub. 1943.

Björn M. Ólsen. 1916. "Hávamál v. 155 (Bugge): Efterslæt til afhandlingen om Hávamál i Arkiv XXXI." *ANF* 32: 71–83.

Björn Þorsteinsson. 1970. *Enska öldin í sögu íslendinga.* Reykjavík: Mál og Menning.

Björnsson, Árni. See Árni Björnsson.

Bloch, Maurice. 1998. "Why Trees, Too, Are Good to Think With: Towards an Anthro-pology of the Meaning of Life." In *The Social Life of Trees: Anthropological Perspectives on Tree Symbolism,* ed. L. Rival. Oxford: Berg. Pp. 39–55.

Blöndal, Sigfús. See Sigfús Blöndal.

Bø, Olav. 1982. "Amulettar." *KLNM* 1: 129–33.

Boberg, Inger M. 1953. *Folkemindeforskningens historie i Mellem- og Nordeuropa.* Danmarks Folkeminder, 60. Copenhagen: Munksgaard.

———, ed. 1966. *Motif-Index of Early Icelandic Literature.* Bibliotheca Arnamagæana, 27. Copenhagen: Munksgaard.

Bock, Gisela, and Margarete Zimmermann. 1997. "Die *Querrelle des Femmes* in Europa:

Eine begriffs- und forschungsgeschichtliche Einführung." *Querrelles*: Jahrbuch für Frauenforschung 2: 9–38.

Bøe, Arne. 1982. "Kristenrettar." *KLNM* 9: 297–304.

Boer, R. C., ed. 1888. *Örvar-Odds saga*. Leiden: E. J. Brill.

Boglioni, Pierre. 1977. "Some Methodological Reflections on the Study of Medieval Popular Religion." *Journal of Popular Culture* 11: 697–705.

Bolin, Sture. 1982. "Gesta Hammaburgensis ecclesiae pontificum." *KLNM* 5: 283–89.

Bolvig, Axel. 1994. *Bondens billeder: Om kirker og kunst i dansk senmiddelalder*. Copenhagen: Gyldendal.

———. 1999. *Kalkmalerier i Danmark*. N.p.: Sesam.

Boureau, Alain. 2006. *Satan the Heretic: The Birth of Demonology in the Medieval West*. Trans. T. L. Fagan. Chicago: University of Chicago Press.

Boyer, Paul, and Stephen Nissenbaum. 1974. *Salem Possessed: The Social Origins of Witchcraft*. Cambridge, Mass.: Harvard University Press.

Boyer, Régis. 1975. "Paganism and Literature: The So-Called 'Pagan Survivals' in the *samtíðarsögur*." *Gripla* 1: 135–67.

———. 1981. "Magie (*seiðr*) chez les Germains et Nordiques." In *Dictionnaire des mythologies et des religions des sociétés traditionnelles et du monde antique*, ed. Y. Bonnefoy. Vol. 2. Paris: Flammarion. Pp. 50–51.

———. 1986. *Le monde du double: La magie chez les anciens Scandinaves*. L'Ile verte. Paris: Berg International.

Bozóky, Edina. 2003. *Charmes et prières apotropaïques*. Typologie des sources du Moyen Age occidental, 86. Turnhout: Brepols.

Bragason, Úlfar. See Úlfar Bragason.

Brandt, Mette. 1976. "Mulier mala: Smørkernefremstillinger i dansk sengotisk kalkmaleri." In *Bild och betydelse: Föredrag vid det 4. nordiska symposiet för ikonografiska studier, Kvarnträsk, 19.–22. augusti 1974*, ed. L. Lillie and M. Thøgersen. Picta. Skrifter utgivna av Konsthistoriska institutionen vid Åbo Akademi, 2. Åbo: Åbo Akademi. Pp. 55–64.

Brate, Erik, ed. 1911. *Östergötlands runinskrifter*. 2 vols. Sveriges runinskrifter, 2. Stockholm: Kungl. Vitterhets Historie och Antikvitets Akademien.

Brauner, Sigrid. 1995. *Fearless Wives and Frightened Shrews: The Construction of the Witch in Early Modern Germany*. Amherst: University of Massachusetts Press.

Briem, Ólafur. 1963. *Vanir og Æsir*. Studia Islandica, 21. Reykjavík: Heimspekideild Háskóla Íslands: Bókaútgáfa Menningarsjóðs.

Brietzmann, Franz. 1912. *Die böse Frau in der deutschen Litteratur des Mittelalters*. Palaestra, 42. Berlin: Mayer & Müller.

Briggs, Robin. 1996a. "Many Reason Why: The Problem of Multiple Explanation." In *Witchcraft in Early Modern Europe: Studies in Culture and Belief*, ed. J. Barry, M. Hester, and G. Roberts. Cambridge: Cambridge University Press.

———. 1996b. *Witches & Neighbors: The Social and Cultural Context of European Witchcraft*. New York: Viking.

Brilioth, Yngve. 1941. "Den senare medeltiden 1274–1521." In *Svenska kyrkans historia,* ed. H. Holmquist and H. Pleijel. Vol. 2. Stockholm: Svenska Kyrkans Diakonistyrelses Bokförlag. Pp. 9–810.

———. 1959. *Medeltiden.* 2nd rev. ed. Handbok i Svensk kyrkohistoria, 1. Stockholm: Svenska Kyrkans Diakonistyrelses Bokförlag.

Brink, Stefan. 2005. "*Verba Volant, Scripta Manent?* Aspects of Early Scandinavian Oral Society." In *Literacy in Medieval and Early Modern Scandinavian Culture,* ed. P. Hermann. Viking Collection, 16. Odense: University Press of Southern Denmark. Pp. 77–135.

Brix, Hans. 1943. "Oldtidens og Middelalderens Litteratur i Danmark." In *Litteraturhistoria: A. Danmark, Finland och Sverige,* ed. Sigurður Nordal. Nordisk Kultur, 8:A. Stockholm: Albert Bonniers förlag. Pp. 3–63.

Broedel, Hans Peter. 2003. *The "Malleus Maleficarum" and the Construction of Witchcraft: Theology and Popular Belief.* Manchester: Manchester University Press.

Brøndum-Nielsen, Johannes, Poul Johannes Jørgensen, and Erik Buus, eds. 1920–42. *Danmarks gamle landskabslove med kirkelovene.* 10 vols. Copenhagen: Gyldendal for Danske sprog- og litteraturselskab.

Brown, Donald E. 1991. *Human Universals.* New York: McGraw-Hill.

Brown, Peter. 1981. *The Cult of the Saints: Its Rise and Function in Latin Christianity.* Haskell Lectures on History of Religions, n.s. 2. Chicago: University of Chicago Press.

Bruhn, Ole. 1999. *Tekstualisering: Bidrag til en litterær antropologi.* Århus: Aarhus universitetsforlag.

Brundage, James A. 1982. "The Problem of Impotence." In *Sexual Practices and the Medieval Church,* ed. V. L. Bullough and J. A. Brundage. Buffalo, N.Y.: Prometheus. Pp. 135–40.

———. 1988. "Impotence, Frigidity and Marital Nullity in the Decretists and the Early Decretalists." In *Proceedings of the Seventh International Congress of Medieval Canon Law, Cambridge, 23–27 July 1984,* ed. P. Linehan. Monumenta Iuris Canonici. Series C: Subsidia, 8. Vatican City: Biblioteca Apostolica Vaticana. Pp. 407–23.

———. 1995. *Medieval Canon Law.* London: Longman.

———. 2008. *The Medieval Origins of the Legal Profession: Canonists, Civilians, and Courts.* Chicago: University of Chicago Press.

Brynleifsson, Siglaugur. See Siglaugur Brynleifsson.

Buchholz, Peter. 1968. "Schamanistische Züge in der altisländischen Überlieferung." Inaugural-Dissertation zur Erlangung des Doktorsgrades, Westfälischen Wilhelms-Universität Münster. Bamberg.

———. 1971. "Shamanism: The Testimony of Old Icelandic Literary Tradition." *Mediaeval Scandinavia* 4: 7–20.

Buchner, R. 1968–. "Adam von Bremen." In *Reallexikon der germanischen Altertumskunde,* ed. H. Jankuhn, J. Hoops, and H. Beck. Vol. 1. Berlin: de Gruyter. Pp. 56–57.

Buck, Carl Darling. 1988. *A Dictionary of Selected Synonyms in the Principal Indo-European*

Languages: A Contribution to the History of Ideas. Chicago: University of Chicago Press. Orig. pub. 1949.

Bugge, Sophus. 1867. "Excurs til Grógaldr og Fjölsvinnsmál." In *Norrœn fornkvœði: Islandsk samling af folkelige oldtidsdigte om nordens guder og heroer, almindeligt kaldet Sæmundar Edda hins fróða.* Christiania: P. T. Mallings forlagsboghandel.

Burriss, Eli Edward. 1936. "The Terminology of Witchcraft." *Classical Philology* 31: 137–45.

Busk Sørensen, Bodil. 2004. *Ansgar og religionsmødet i Norden.* Frederiksberg: Alfa.

Butler, E. M. 1998. *Ritual Magic.* University Park: Pennsylvania State University Press. Orig. pub. 1949.

Butterfield, Herbert. 1931. *The Whig Interpretation of History.* London: G. Bell and Sons.

Bynum, Caroline Walker. 1997. "Wonder." *American Historical Review* 102 (1): 1–26.

Byock, Jesse L. 1984. "Saga Form, Oral Prehistory, and the Icelandic Social Context." *New Literary History* 16: 153–73.

———. 1990. "Sigurðr Fáfnisbani: An Eddic Hero Carved on Norwegian Stave Churches." In *Poetry in the Scandinavian Middle Ages: Proceedings of the Seventh International Saga Conference,* ed. T. Pàroli. Spoleto, Italy: Presso la Sede del Centro Studi. Pp. 619–28.

———. 1992. "History and the Sagas: The Effect of Nationalism." In *From Sagas to Society: Comparative Approaches to Early Iceland,* ed. Gísli Pálsson. Enfield Lock, Eng.: Hisarlik. Pp. 43–59.

———. 1994. "Modern Nationalism and the Medieval Sagas." In *Northern Antiquity: The Post-Medieval Reception of Edda and Saga,* ed. A. Wawn. London: Hisarlik Press. Pp. 163–87.

———. 2004. "Social Memory and the Sagas: The Case of *Egils saga.*" *SStudies* 76 (3): 299–31.

Byock, Jesse, et al. 2005. "A Viking-age Valley in Iceland: The Mosfell Archaeological Project." *Medieval Archaeology* 49: 197–220.

Caesar, Julius. 1970. *The Gallic War.* Trans. H. J. Edwards. Cambridge, Mass. and London: Harvard University Press & Wm. Heinemann. Orig. pub. 1917.

Campbell, Joseph. 1972. *Myths to Live By.* New York: Viking Press.

Canadé-Sautman, Francesca, et al. 1991. "Editorial: Medieval Folklore Today." *Medieval Folklore* 1 (1): 1–9.

Carlquist, Jonas. 1996. *De fornsvenska helgonlegenderna: Källor, stil och skriftmiljö.* SFSS, 82. Stockholm: Graphic Systems.

Carlsson, Gottfrid, ed. 1921–44. *Stockholms stads tänkeböcker 1483–92.* Stockholms stadsböcker från äldre tid. 2:a serien, 2. Stockholm: Kungl. Samfundet för utgivande af handskrifter rörande Skandinaviens historia med understöd af Stockholms stad och samfundet Sankt Erik.

Caro Baroja, Julio. 1964. *The World of the Witches.* Trans. O.N.V. Glendinning. Chicago: University of Chicago Press. Orig. pub. 1961.

Cavendish, Richard. 1967. *The Black Arts.* New York: Putnam.

Caviness, Madeline Harrison. 2001. *Visualizing Women in the Middle Ages: Sight, Spectacle, and Scopic Economy.* Philadelphia: University of Pennsylvania Press.

Celander, Hilding. 1943. "Oskoreien och besläktade föreställningar i äldre och nyare nordisk tradition." *Saga och sed*, 71–175.

———. 1955. *Förkristen jul enligt norröna källor*. Göteborgs universitets årsskrift, 61:3. Stockholm: Almqvist & Wiksell.

Chaves, Kelly K. 2008. "Ethnohistory: From Inception to Postmodernism and Beyond." *Historian* 70 (3): 486–513.

Christiansen, Reidar Thoralf, ed. 1958. *The Migratory Legends: A Proposed List of Types with a Systematic Catalogue of the Norwegian Variants*. FFC, 71, 1 (175). Helsinki: Suomalainen Tiedeakatemia.

Ciklamini, Marlene. 1978. *Snorri Sturluson*. Twayne's World Authors Series, 493. Boston: Twayne.

———. 1979. "The Folktale in *Heimskringla (Halfdanar saga Svarta—Hakonar Saga Goda)*." *Folklore* 90 (2): 204–16.

Clark, Stuart. 1991. "The 'Gendering' of Witchcraft in French Demonology: Misogyny or Polarity?" *French History* 5 (4): 426–37.

———. 1997. *Thinking with Demons: The Idea of Witchcraft in Early Modern Europe*. Oxford: Oxford University Press.

———. 2001. Introduction to *Languages of Witchcraft: Narrative, Ideology, and Meaning in Early Modern Culture*, ed. S. Clark. New York: St. Martin's Press. Pp. 1–18.

Clarke, D. E. Martin. 1923. *The Hávamál, with Selections from Other Poems of the Edda, Illustrating the Wisdom of the North in Heathen Times*. Cambridge: Cambridge University Press.

Cleasby, Richard, and Gudbrand Vigfusson, eds. 1982. *An Icelandic-English Dictionary*. 2nd ed. With a supplement by William Craigie. Oxford: Clarendon Press.

Clunies Ross, Margaret. 1994. *Prolonged Echoes*. Vol. 1, *Old Norse Myths in Northern Society*. Viking Collection, 7. Odense: Odense University Press.

———. 1998. *Prolonged Echoes*. Vol. 2, *The Reception of Norse Myths in Medieval Iceland*. Viking Collection, 10. Odense: Odense University Press.

Cnattingius, Hans. 1963. *Studies in the Order of St. Bridget of Sweden*. Vol. 1, *The Crisis in the 1420s*. Acta Universitatis Stockholmiensis. Stockholm Studies in History, 7. Stockholm: Almqvist & Wiksell.

Coffey, Jerome E. 1989. "The Drunnur-A Faroese Wedding Custom." *ARV* 45: 7–16.

Cohn, Norman. 1975. *Europe's Inner Demons: An Inquiry Inspired by the Great Witch-Hunt*. London: Sussex University Press.

Colbert, David. 1989. *The Birth of the Ballad: The Scandinavian Medieval Genre*. Skrifter utgivna av Svenskt Visarkiv, 10. Stockholm: Svenskt Visarkiv.

Cormack, Margaret. 1994. *The Saints in Iceland: Their Veneration from the Conversion to 1400*. Subsidia hagiographica, 78. Bruxelles: Société des Bollandistes.

Cornell, Henrik, and Sigurd Wallin. 1972. *Albertus Pictor, Sten Stures och Jacob Ulvssons målare. Hans ställning i den europeiska konsten. Hans betydelse i det konstnärliga och religiösa livet i Sverige*. Stockholm: Bonniers.

Cosgrove, Richard A. 2000. "Reflections on the Whig Interpretation of History." *Journal of Early Modern History* 4 (2): 147–67.

Cothren, Michael W. 1984. "The Iconography of Theophilus Windows in the First Half of the Thirteenth Century." *Speculum* 59 (2): 308–41.

Cournoyer, David E., and Barris P. Malcolm. 2004. "Evaluating Claims for Universals: A Method Analysis Approach." *Cross-Cultural Research* 38: 319–34.

Craigie, William A., ed. 1952. *Sýnisbók íslenzkra bókmennta til miðrar átjándu aldar: Specimens of Icelandic Rímur from the Fourteenth to the Nineteenth Century.* London: T. Nelson and Sons.

Cross, Frank L., and E. A. Livingston, eds. 1997. *The Oxford Dictionary of the Christian Church.* 3rd rev. ed. Oxford: Oxford University Press.

Cunningham, Graham. 1999. *Religion and Magic: Approaches and Theories.* Edinburgh: Edinburgh University Press.

Cusack, Carole M. 1999. *The Rise of Christianity in Northern Europe, 300–1000.* London: Cassell.

Dahlbäck, Göran, ed. 1987a. *I medeltidens Stockholm.* Monografier utgivna av Stockholms stad, 81. Stockholm: Stockholms medeltidsmuseum och Kommittén för Stockholmsforskning.

———. 1987b. *Svensk medeltidsforskning idag: En forskningsöversikt utarbetad på uppdrag av Humanistisk-samhällsvetenskapliga forskningsrådet.* Uppsala: Humanistisk-samhällsvetenskapliga forskningsrådet.

Dahlerup, Pil. 1998. *Dansk litteratur: Middelalder. 1 Religiøs litteratur. 2. Verldslig litteratur.* Copenhagen: Gyldendal.

Dahlerup, Troels. 1993. "Church Organization and Function. 1, Denmark." In *MScan.* Pp. 84–88.

Dahlgren, Fredrik August, ed. 1914–16. *Glossarium öfver föråldrade eller ovanliga ord och talesätt i svenska språket.* Lund: Gleerup.

Daly, Mary. 1978. *Gyn/ecology: The Metaethics of Radical Feminism.* Boston: Beacon Press.

Damico, Helen. 1984. *Beowulf's Wealhtheow and the Valkyrie Tradition.* Madison: University of Wisconsin Press.

Dasent, George Webbe. 1845. *Theophilus in Icelandic, Low German and Other Tongues from the Mss. in the Royal Library, Stockholm.* London: W. Pickering.

Davidsohn, Robert. 1888. *Philipp II, August von Frankreich und Ingeborg.* Stuttgart: J. G. Cotta.

Davidson, H. R. Ellis. 1943. *The Road to Hel: A Study of the Conception of the Dead in Old Norse Literature.* Cambridge: Cambridge University Press.

———. 1964. *Gods and Myths of Northern Europe.* Baltimore: Penguin.

———. 1976. *The Viking Road to Byzantium.* London: Allen & Unwin.

———, ed. 1979. *Saxo Grammaticus: The History of the Danes.* Vol. 1, *Text.* Trans. P. Fisher. Cambridge: D. S. Brewer.

———, ed. 1980. *Saxo Grammaticus: The History of the Danes.* Vol. 2, *Commentary.* Cambridge: D. S. Brewer.

———. 1998. *Roles of the Northern Goddess.* London: Routledge.

Daviðsson, Ólafur. See Ólafur Daviðsson.

Davies, Owen. 1999. *Witchcraft, Magic and Culture, 1736–1951.* Manchester: Manchester University Press.

de Vries, Jan. See Vries, Jan de.

Dégh, Linda, and Andrew Vázsonyi. 1983. "Does the Word 'Dog' Bite? Ostensive Action: A Means of Legend-Telling." *Journal of Folklore Research* 20: 5–34.

Delaborde, Henri François, ed. 1882. *Œuvres de Rigord et de Guillaume le Breton, historiens de Philippe-Auguste.* Société de l'histoire de France. Publications in octavo, 210, 224. Paris: Librairie Renouard H. Loones successeur.

Demos, John Putnam. 1982. *Entertaining Satan: Witchcraft and the Culture of Early New England.* Oxford: Oxford University Press.

Dennis, Andrew, Peter Foote, and Richard Perkins, eds. 1980–2000. *Laws of Early Iceland: Grágás, the Codex Regius of Grágás, with Material from Other Manuscripts.* 2 vols. University of Manitoba Icelandic Studies, 3, 5. Winnipeg: University of Manitoba Press.

Dillmann, François-Xavier. 1986. "Les magiciens dans l'Islande ancienne. Études sur la représentation de la magie islandaise et de ses agents dans les sources littéraires norroises." Thèse pour l'obtention du Doctorat d'État ès Lettres, Université de Caen. Caen.

———. 1992. "Seiður og shamanismi í *Íslendingasögum.*" *Skáldskaparmál* 11: 20–33.

———. 2006. *Les magiciens dans l'Islande ancienne. Études sur la représentation de la magie islandaise et de ses agents dans les sources littéraires norroises.* Acta Academiae Regiae Gustavi Adolphi, 92. Uppsala: Kungl. Gustav Adolfs Akademien för svensk folkkultur.

Douglas, Mary. 1970a. "Thirty Years after Witchcraft, Oracles and Magic." In *Witchcraft Confessions and Accusations,* ed. M. Douglas. Association of Social Anthropologists Monographs, 9. London: Tavistock. Pp. xiii–xxxviii.

———, ed. 1970b. *Witchcraft Confessions and Accusations.* Association of Social Anthropologists Monographs, 9. London: Tavistock.

Drobin, Ulf, and Marja-Liisa Keinänen. 2001. "Frey, Veralden olmai och Sampo." In *Kontinuitäten und Brüche in der Religionsgeschichte: Festschrift für Anders Hultgård zu seinem 65. Geburtstag am 23.12.2001,* ed. O. Sundqvist, A. van Nahl, and M. Stausberg. Reallexikon der germanischen Altertumskunde Ergänzungsbände, 31. Berlin: de Gruyter. Pp. 136–69.

DuBois, Thomas A. 1999. *Nordic Religions in the Viking Age.* Philadelphia: University of Pennsylvania Press.

———, ed. 2008. *Sanctity in the North: Saints, Lives, and Cults in Medieval Scandinavia.* Toronto: University of Toronto Press.

Dumézil, Georges. 1970. *Du mythe au roman: la saga de Hadingus (Saxo Grammaticus, I, v–viii) et autres essais.* Collection Hier. Paris: Presses universitaires de France.

Düwel, Klaus. 1992. "Runeninschriften als Quellen der germanischen Religionsgeschichte." In *Germanische Religionsgeschichte: Quellen und Quellenprobleme,* ed. H. Beck, D. Ellmers, and K. Schier. Ergänzungsbände zum Reallexikon der germanischen Altertumskunde, 5. Berlin: Walter de Gruyter. Pp. 336–64.

Edsman, Carl-Martin. 1982a. "Sibylla." *KLNM* 15: 169–73.

———. 1982b. "Trolldom. Kyrkligt. Sverige." *KLNM* 18: 661–67.

———. 2000. "Djävulspakt och besatthet: Ett 1700-talsdokument." In *Dialekter och folk-minnen: Hyllningsskrift till Maj Reinhammar den 17 maj 2000,* ed. L. Elmevik. Uppsala: Sällskapet för svensk dialektologi. Pp. 55–66.

Edwards, Paul, and Hermann Pálsson, eds. 1970. *Arrow-Odd: A Medieval Novel.* New York and London: New York University Press & University of London Press Ltd.

Egilsdóttir, Ásdís. See Ásdís Egilsdóttir.

Einar Ól. Sveinsson, ed. 1934. *Laxdæla saga. Halldórs þáttr Snorrasonar. Stúfs þáttr.* ÍF, 5. Reykjavík: Hið íslenzka fornritafélag.

———. 1937–38. "The Icelandic Sagas and the Period in Which Their Authors Lived." *Acta Philologica Scandinavica* 12: 71–90.

———, ed. 1939. *Vatnsdæla saga. Hallfreðar saga. Kormáks saga. Hrómundar þáttr halta. Hrafns þáttr Guðrúnarsonar.* ÍF, 8. Reykjavík: Hið íslenzka fornritafélag.

———, ed. 1954. *Brennu-Njáls saga.* ÍF, 12. Reykjavík: Hið íslenzka fornritafélag.

Einar Ól. Sveinsson and Matthías Þórðarson, eds. 1957. *Eyrbyggia saga. Brands þáttr örva. Eiríks saga rauða. Grœnlendinga saga. Grœnlendinga þáttr.* ÍF, 4. Reykjavík: Hið íslenzka fornritafélag. Orig. pub. 1935.

Einarsson, Bjarni. See Bjarni Einarsson.

Eiríkur Jónsson and Finnur Jónsson, eds. 1892–94. *Hauksbók udgiven efter De arnamag-næanske Håndskrifter N. 371, 544 og 675, 4to samt forskellige Papirshåndskrifter.* Copenhagen: Det kongelige nordiske Oldskrift-Selskab.

Ejdestam, Julius Eugen. 1975. *Svenskt folklivslexikon.* Stockholm: Rabén & Sjögren.

Ekholst, Christine. 2009. *För varje brottsling ett straff: Föreställningar om kön i de svenska medeltidslagarna.* Stockholm: Historiska institutionen, Stockholms unversitet.

Ekrem, Inger, Lars Boje Mortensen, and Peter Fisher, eds. 2003. *Historia Norwegie.* Copenhagen: Museum Tusculanum Press.

Elgqvist, Eric. 1955. *Ullvi och Ullinshov: Studier rörande ullkultens uppkomst och utbredning.* Lund: Olins antikvariat.

Elliott, Dyan. 2004. *Proving Woman: Female Spirituality and Inquisitional Culture in the Later Middle Ages.* Princeton, N.J.: Princeton University Press.

Ellis, Bill. 1989. "Death by Folklore: Ostension, Contemporary Legend, and Murder." *Western Folklore* 48 (1): 201–20.

———. 2000. *Raising the Devil: Satanism, New Religions and the Media.* Lexington: University Press of Kentucky.

———. 2001. *Aliens, Ghosts, and Cults: Legends We Live.* Jackson: University Press of Mississippi.

Elmevik, Lennart, and Lena Peterson. 1993–. *Samnordisk Rundatabas.* Institutionen för nordiska språk, Uppsala universitet. Available from www.nordiska.uu.se/forskn/samnord.htm

Eriksson, Bo. 1994. "Häx- och trolldomsforskning- Gamla och nya rön." *Folkets historia* 22 (4): 30–41.

Evans-Pritchard, E. E. 1937. *Witchcraft, Oracles and Magic among the Azande.* Oxford: Clarendon Press.

———. 1976. *Witchcraft, Oracles and Magic among the Azande.* Abridged by Eva Gillies. Oxford: Clarendon Press. Orig. pub. 1937.

Falk, Hjalmar. 1924. *Odensheite.* Skrifter utg. av Videnskabsselskapet i Kristiania. II, Historisk-filosofisk Klasse, 1924:10. Christiania: Dybwad.

Fanger, Claire. 1998. "Medieval Ritual Magic: What It Is and Why We Need to Know More about It." In *Conjuring Spirits: Texts and Traditions of Medieval Ritual Magic.* University Park: Pennsylvania State University Press. Pp. vii–xviii.

Fant, Ericus Michael, et al., eds. 1818–71. *Scriptores rerum Svecicarum medii aevi.* Uppsala: Palmblad.

Faulkes, Anthony. 1983. "Pagan Sympathy: Attitudes to Heathendom in the Prologue to Snorra Edda." In *Edda: A Collection of Essays,* ed. R. J. Glendinning and Haraldur Bessason. Manitoba: University of Manitoba Press. Pp. 283–314.

———. 1993. "Snorra edda." In *MScan.* Pp. 600–602.

Feilberg, Henning Frederik. 1910. *Bjærgtagen: Studie over en gruppe træk fra nordisk alfetro.* Danmarks folkeminder, 5. Copenhagen: Det Schonbergske forlag.

Fenger, Ole. 1979. Review of Elsa Sjöholm, *Gesetze als Quellen: Mittelalterlicher Geschichte des Nordens. Historisk Tidskrift (Denmark)* 79: 112–24.

———. 1983. *Gammeldansk ret: Dansk rets historie i oldtid og middelalder.* Viby: Centrum.

———. 1987. "Om kildeværdien af normative tekster." In *Tradition og historieskrivning: Kilderne til Nordens ældste historie,* ed. K. Hastrup and P. Meulengracht Sørensen. Acta jutlandica, 63:2. Humanistisk Serie, 61. Århus: Aarhus Universitetsforlag. Pp. 39–51.

———. 1993. "Laws. 1. Denmark." In *MScan.* Pp. 383–84.

Ferm, Olle. 2001. "Universitet och högskolor." In *Norden og Europa i middelalderen,* ed. P. Ingesman and T. Lindkvist. Skrifter udgivet af Jysk Selskab for Historie, 47. Århus: Aarhus Universitetsforlag. Pp. 93–129.

Fidjestøl, Bjarne. 1999. *The Dating of Eddic Poetry: A Historical Survey and Methodological Investigation.* Bibliotheca Arnamagnæana, 41. Copenhagen: C. A. Reitzel.

Filotas, Bernadette. 2005. *Pagan Survivals, Superstitions and Popular Cultures in Early Medieval Pastoral Literature.* Pontifical Institute of Mediaeval Studies. Studies and Texts, 151. Toronto: Pontifical Institute of Mediaeval Studies.

Fine, Gary Alan. 1991. "Redemption Rumors and the Power of Ostension." *Journal of American Folklore* 104: 179–81.

Finlay, Alison. 2001. "Monstrous Allegations: An Exchange of *ýki* in *Bjarnar saga Hítdœlakappa.*" *Alvíssmál* 10: 21–44.

Finnbogi Guðmundsson, ed. 1980. *Orkneyinga saga. Legenda de Sancto Magno. Magnúss saga skemmri. Magnúss saga lengri. Helga þáttr ok Úlfs.* ÍF, 34. Reykjavík: Hið íslenzka fornritafélag. Orig. pub. 1965.

Finnur Jónsson, ed. 1905–22. *Rímnasafn: Samling af de ældste islandske rimer.* SUGNL, 35. 2 vols. Copenhagen: S. L. Møllers bogtrykkeri.

————. 1920. *Den oldnorske og oldislandske Litteraturs Historie.* 2nd ed. Copenhagen: G. E. C. Gad.

————. 1922. "Mera om folkminnen och filologi." *Folkminnen och folktankar* 8: 129–32.

————, ed. 1931. *Edda Snorra Sturlusonar.* Copenhagen: Gyldendalske Boghandel/Nordisk Forlag.

————, ed. 1932. *Morkinskinna.* SUGNL, 53. Copenhagen: J. Jørgensen & Co.

————, ed. 1973. *Den norske-islandske Skjaldedigtning: B. Rettet Tekst.* Copenhagen: Rosenkilde og Bagger. Orig. pub. 1912–15.

Finnur Jónsson and Hannes Finnsson, eds. 1772. *Historia ecclesiastica Islandiæ, ex historiis, annalibus, legibus ecclesiasticis, aliisqve rerum septentrionalium monumentis congesta . . .* Copenhagen: G. G. Salicath.

Finnur Jónsson and Sveinbjörn Egilsson, eds. 1966. *Lexicon Poeticum Antiquæ Linguæ Septentrionalis: Ordbog over det norsk-islandske skjaldesprog.* 2nd rev. ed. (facsimile). Copenhagen: Atlas bogtryk. Orig. pub. 1931.

Finsen, Vilhjálmur. See Vilhjálmur Finsen.

Fix, Hans. 1993. "Laws. 2. Iceland." In *MScan.* Pp. 384–85.

Fleck, Jere. 1971a. "The 'Knowledge-Criterion' in the *Grímnismál:* The Case against Shamanism." *ANF* 86: 49–65

————. 1971b. "Óðinn's Self-Sacrifice: A New Interpretation. I. The Ritual Inversion II. The Ritual Landscape." *SStudies* 43: 119–42, 385–413.

Fleteren, Frederik Van. 1999. "Demons." In *Augustine through the Ages: An Encyclopedia,* ed. A. Fitzgerald and J. C. Cavadini. Grand Rapids, Mich.: W. B. Eerdmans. Pp. 266–68.

Flint, Valerie I. J. 1991. *The Rise of Magic in Early Medieval Europe.* Princeton, N.J.: Princeton University Press.

Flowers, Stephen E., trans. 1989. *The Galdrabók: An Icelandic Grimoire.* York Beach, Maine: Weiser.

Fogelklou Norlind, Emilia. See Norlind, Emilia Fogelklou.

Folin, Nina, and Göran Tegnér, eds. 1985. *Medeltidens ABC.* Stockholm: Gidlund, Statens historiska museum.

Foote, Peter. 1956. "Icelandic *sólarsteinn* and the Medieval Background." *ARV* 12: 26–40.

————. 1977. "Oral and Literary Tradition in Early Scandinavian Law: Aspects of a Problem." In *Oral Tradition, Literary Tradition: A Symposium,* ed. H. Bekker-Nielsen et al. Odense: Odense University Press. Pp. 47–55.

————. 1982. "Steinbøker." *KLNM* 17: 115–18.

————. 1984. "Observations on 'Syncretism' in Early Icelandic Christianity." In *Aurvandilstá: Norse Studies,* ed. M. Barnes, H. Bekker-Nielsen, and G. W. Weber. Viking Collection, 2. Odense: Odense University Press. Pp. 84–100.

————. 1986. "Law, Danish." In *Dictionary of the Middle Ages.* Vol. 7. New York: Charles Scribner's Sons. Pp. 431–33.

————. 1987. "Reflections on *Landbrigðisþáttr* and *Rekaþáttr* in *Grágás.*" In *Tradition og historieskrivning: Kilderne til Nordens ældste historie,* ed. K. Hastrup and P. Meulengracht Sørensen. Acta jutlandica, 63:2. Humanistisk Serie, 61. Århus: Aarhus Universitetsforlag. Pp. 53–64.

Fornmanna sögur eptir gömlum handritum. 1825–37. Copenhagen: Kongelige Nordiske Oldskriftselskab.

Foucault, Michel. 1975. *Surveiller et punir: Naissance de la prison.* Bibliothèque des histoires. Paris: Gallimard.

Frank, Roberta. 1982. "Merlínúspá." In *Dictionary of the Middle Ages,* ed. J. R. Strayer. Vol. 8. New York: Scribner. Pp. 275–76.

———. 1984. "Viking Atrocity and Skaldic Verse: The Rite of the Blood-Eagle." *English Historical Review* 99: 332–43.

Frazer, James George. 1890. *The Golden Bough: A Study in Comparative Religion.* London: Macmillan.

———. 1915. *The Golden Bough: A Study in Magic and Religion.* 3rd rev. ed. London: Macmillan.

Friðriksdóttir, Jóhanna Katrín. See Jóhanna Katrín Friðriksdóttir.

Friis-Jensen, Karsten, ed. 1981. *Saxo Grammaticus: A Medieval Author between Norse and Latin Culture.* Danish Medieval History and Saxo Grammaticus, 2. Copenhagen: Museum Tusculanum Press.

———. 1989. "Was Saxo Grammaticus a Canon of Lund?" *Cahiers del'Institut do moyen-âge grec et latin (Université de Copenhague)* 59: 331–57.

———. 2005a. "Inledning/Introduction." In *Saxo Grammaticus. Gesta Danorum. Danmarkshistorien,* ed. K. Friis-Jensen. Copenhagen: Det Danske Sprog- og Litteraturselskab/Gads forlag. Pp. 9–68.

———, ed. 2005b. *Saxo Grammaticus. Gesta Danorum. Danmarkshistorien.* Trans. P. Zeeberg. 2 vols. Copenhagen: Det Danske Sprog- og Litteraturselskab.

Fritzner, Johan. 1877. "Lappernes Hedenskab og Trolddomskunst sammen holdt med andre Folks, især Nordmændenes, Tro og Overtro." *Norsk Historisk Tidsskrift* 4: 136–217.

———. 1973. *Ordbok over Det gamle norske Sprog.* 4 vols. 4th rev. ed. Oslo: Universitetsforlaget. Orig. pub. 1886.

Fröjmark, Anders. 1992. *Mirakler och helgonkult: Linköpings biskopsdöme under senmedeltiden.* Studia historica Upsaliensia, 171. Uppsala: Almqvist & Wiksell International.

Fuglesang, Signe Horn. 1989. "Viking and Medieval Amulets in Scandinavia." *Fornvännen* 84: 15–25.

Gad, Tue. 1961. *Legenden i danske middelalder.* Copenhagen: Dansk Videnskabs Forlag A/S.

———. 1982. "Legende." *KLNM* 10: 413–23.

Gadelius, Bror Edvard. 1912–13. *Tro och öfvertro i gångna tider.* 2 vols. Stockholm: Geber.

Gallén, Jarl. 1982. "Kyrkorätt." *KLNM* 10: 1–5.

Ganzenmüller, Wilhelm. 1942. "Alchemie und Religion im Mittelalter." *Deutsches Archiv für die Geschichte des Mittelalters* 5: 329–46.

Garboe, Axel. 1982. "Guldmageri." *KLNM* 5: 576–77.

Garstein, Oskar, ed. 1993. *Vinjeboka: Den eldste svartebok fra norsk middelalder.* Oslo: Solum.

Geertz, Clifford. 1973. "Thick Description: Toward an Interpretive Theory of Culture." In *Interpretations of Culture.* New York: Basic. Pp. 3–30.

———. 2000. "Art as a Cultural System." In *Local Knowledge: Further Essays in Interpretive Anthropology.* 3rd ed. New York: Basic. Orig. pub. 1976. Pp. 94–120.

Geete, Robert. 1900. "Den vises sten: En hittils okänd rimdikt från 1300-talet; Efter en Upsalahandskrift från år 1379 (Bilaga til l Sv. Fornskr.-Sällsk:s årsmöte 1900)." In *Småstycken på forn svenska: Andra serien,* ed. R. Geete. SFSS. Stockholm: P. A. Norstedt & Söner. Pp. 1–16.

———, ed. 1904. *Skrifter till uppbyggelse från medeltiden.* SFSS, 36. Stockholm: P. A. Norstedt & Söner.

———, ed. 1907–09. *Svenska Böner från medeltiden efter gamla handskrifter.* SFSS, 38. Stockholm: P. A. Norstedt & Söner.

———, ed. 1913–15. *Peder Månssons skrifter på svenska.* SFSS, 43. Stockholm: P. A. Norstedt & Söner.

Gejrot, Claes, ed. 1988. *Diarium Vadstenense: The Memorial Book of Vadstena Abbey.* Acta Universitatis Stockholmensis. Studia Latina Stockholmensia, 33. Stockholm: Almqvist & Wiksell.

Gelsinger, Bruce E. 1981. *Icelandic Enterprise: Commerce and Economy in the Middle Ages.* Columbia: University of South Carolina Press.

Gering, Hugo, ed. 1882. *Islendzk aeventyri: Isländische Legenden, Novellen und Märchen.* Halle a.S.: Waisenhaus.

———. 1902. *Über Weissagung und Zauber im nordischen Altertum.* Kiel: Lipsius & Tischer.

Gertz, M. Cl., ed. 1908–12. *Vitae sanctorum danorum.* Novam editionem criticam. Copenhagen: Selskabet for Udgivelse af Kilder til dansk Historie.

———, ed. 1917–18. *Scriptores Minores Historiæ Danicæ Medii Ævi.* 2 vols. Copenhagen: Selskabet for Udgivelse af Kilder til dansk Historie.

Ginzburg, Carlo. 1984. "The Witches' Sabbat: Popular Cult or Inquisitorial Stereotype?" In *Understanding Popular Culture: Europe from the Middle Ages to the Nineteenth Century,* ed. S. L. Kaplan. Berlin: Mouton. Pp. 39–51.

———. 1985. *The Night Battles: Witchcraft and Agrarian Cults in the Sixteenth and Seventeenth Centuries.* Trans. J. and A. Tedeschi. New York: Penguin. Orig. pub. 1966 as *I benandanti: Stregoneria e culti agrari tra Cinquecento e Seicento.*

———. 1991. *Ecstasies: Deciphering the Witches' Sabbath.* Trans. R. Rosenthal. New York: Pantheon. Orig. pub. 1989 as *Storia notturna: Una decifrazione del sabba.*

———. 1992. *The Cheese and the Worms: The Cosmos of a Sixteenth-Century Miller.* Trans. J. and A. Tedeschi. New York: Penguin. Orig. pub. 1980 as *Formaggio e i vermi.*

———. 1993a. "Deciphering the Sabbath." In *Early Modern Witchcraft: Centres and Peripheries,* ed. B. Ankarloo and G. Henningsen. Oxford: Clarendon Press. Orig. pub. 1990. Pp. 121–37.

————. 1993b. "Witches and Shamans." *New Left Review* 200 (July–August): 75–85.

Gíslason, Konrað, et al., eds. 1883. See Konrað Gíslason et al., eds. 1883.

Gíslason, Konrað, et al., eds. 1889–94. See Konrað Gíslason et al., eds. 1889–94.

Gísli Pálsson. 1991. "The Name of the Witch: Sagas, Sorcery, and Social Context." In *Social Approaches to Viking Studies,* ed. R. Samson. Glasgow: Cruthine Press. Pp. 157–68.

Gísli Sigurðsson. 2002. *Túlkun íslendingasagna í ljósi munnlegrar hefðar: tilgáta um aðferð.* RIT/Stofnun Árna Magnússonar á Íslandi, 56. Reykjavík: Stofnun Árna Magnússonar á Íslandi.

————. 2004. *The Medieval Icelandic Saga and Oral Tradition: A Discourse on Method.* Trans. N. Jones. Publications of the Milman Parry Collection of Oral Literature, 2. Cambridge, Mass.: Harvard University Press.

Gísli Sigurðsson and Mitchell, Stephen A. 2008. "Translation of *Virgilessrímur.*" In *The Virgilian Tradition: The First Fifteen Hundred Years,* ed. J. M. Ziolkowski and M. C. J. Putnam. New Haven, Conn.: Yale University Press. Pp. 881–88.

Gísli Sigurðsson and Vésteinn Ólason, eds. 2004. *The Manuscripts of Iceland.* Culture House Editions, 2. Reykjavík: Árni Magnússon Institute in Iceland.

Gjerdman, Olof. 1941. "Hon som var värre än den onde: En saga och ett uppsvensk kyrkomålningsmotiv." *Saga och Sed,* 1–93.

Gjerløw, Lilli. 1982. "In principio." *KLNM* 7: 430–32.

Glauser, Jürg. 2000. "Sagas of Icelanders (*Íslendinga sögur*) and *þættir* as the Literary Representation of a New Social Space." In *Old Icelandic Literature and Society,* ed. M. C. Ross. Cambridge Studies in Medieval Literature, 42. Cambridge: Cambridge University Press. Pp. 203–20.

————. 2007. "The Speaking Bodies of Saga Texts." In *Learning and Understanding in the Old Norse World: Essays in Honour of Margaret Clunies Ross,* ed. J. Quinn, K. Heslop, and T. Wills. Medieval Texts and Cultures of Northern Europe, 18. Turnhout: Brepols. Pp. 13–26.

Glendinning, Robert James. 1974. *Träume und Vorbedeutung in der Islendinga Saga Sturla Thordarsons: Eine Form- und Stiluntersuchung.* Kanadische Studien zur deutschen Sprache und Literatur, 8. Bern: Herbert Lang.

Gollancz, Israel, ed. 1898. *Hamlet in Iceland.* Northern Library, 3. London: David Nutt.

Granlund, John. 1982. "Øl. Sverige." *KLNM* 20: 694–96.

Gräslund, Anne-Sofie. 1996a. "Arkeologin och kristnandet." In *Kristnandet i Sverige: Gamla källor och nya perspektiv,* ed. B. Nilsson. Projektet Sveriges kristnande. Publikationer, 5. Uppsala: Lunne böcker. Pp. 19–44.

————. 1996b. "Kristnandet ur ett kvinnoperspektiv." In *Kristnandet i Sverige: Gamla källor och nya perspektiv,* ed. B. Nilsson. Projektet Sveriges kristnande. Publikationer, 5. Uppsala: Lunne böcker. Pp. 313–34.

Grimm, Jacob. 1966. *Teutonic Mythology.* Trans. J. S. Stallybrass. New York: Dover. Orig. pub. 1882.

Grímsdóttir, Guðrún Ása. See Guðrún Ása Grímsdóttir.

Grønvik, Ottar. 1992. "En hedensk bønn: Runeinnskriften på en liten kobberplate fra Kvinneby på Öland." In *Eyvindarbók: Festskrift til Eyvind Fjeld Halvorsen, 4. mai 1992,* ed. E. F. Halvorsen and F. Hødnebø. Oslo: Institutt for nordistikk og litteraturvitenskap, Universitetet i Oslo. Pp. 71–85.

Grössinger, Christa. 1997. *Picturing Women in Late Medieval and Renaissance Art.* Manchester: Manchester University Press.

Guðbrandur Vigfússon and Unger, C. R., eds. 1860–68. *Flateyjarbok: En Samling af norske Konge-sagaer.* Norske historiske Kildeskriftfonds Skrifter, 4. Christiania: P. T. Malling.

Guðmundsson, Finnbogi. See Finnbogi Guðmundsson.

Guðnason, Bjarni. See Bjarni Guðnason.

Guðni Jónsson, ed. 1948. *Sturlunga saga.* 3 vols. Reykjavík: Íslendingasagnaútgáfan. Haukadalsútgáfan.

———, ed. 1954. *Fornaldar sögur Norðurlanda.* 4 vols. Reykjavík: Íslendingasagnaútgáfan.

———, ed. 1964. *Grettis saga Ásmundarsonar. Bandmanna saga. Odds þáttr Ófeigssonar.* ÍF, 7. Reykjavík: Hið íslenzka fornritafélag. Orig. pub. 1936.

Guðrún Ása Grímsdóttir, ed. 1998. *Biskupa sögur III. Árna saga biskups. Lárentíus saga biskups. Söguþáttur Jóns Halldórssonar biskups. Biskupa Ættir.* ÍF, 17. Reykjavík: Hið íslenzka fornritafélag.

Guðrún P. Helgadóttir. 1987. *Hrafns saga Sveinbjarnarsonar.* Oxford: Clarendon Press, Oxford University Press.

Gummerus, Jaakko, ed. 1900. *Beiträge zur Geschichte des Buss- und Beichtwesens in der schwedischen Kirche des Mittelalters.* Uppsala: Harald Wretman.

———, ed. 1902. *Synodalstatuter och andra kyrkorättsliga aktstycken från den svenska medeltidskyrkan.* Uppsala: Wretmens tryckeri.

Gumperz, John Joseph. 1982. *Discourse Strategies.* Studies in Interactional Sociolinguistics, 1. Cambridge: Cambridge University Press.

Gunnar Harðarson and Stefán Karlsson. 1993. "Hauksbók." In *MScan.* Pp. 271–72.

Gunnell, Terry. 1993. "Skírnisleikur og Freysmál: Endurmat eldri hugmynda um 'forna norræna helgileiki.'" *Skírnir* 167: 421–59.

———. 1995. *The Origins of Drama in Scandinavia.* Cambridge: D. S. Brewer.

———. 2005. "Eddic Poetry." In *CONILC.* Pp. 82–100.

Gunneng, Hedda, ed. 1989. *Kvinnors Rosengård: Medeltidskvinnors liv och hälsa, lust och barnafödande; Föredrag från nordiska tvärvetenskapliga symposier i Århus aug. 1985 och Visby sept. 1987.* Skriftserie från Centrum för kvinnoforskning vid Stockholms universitet, 1. Stockholm: Centrum för kvinnoforskning vid Stockholms universitet.

Gurevich, Aron. 1988. *Medieval Popular Culture: Problems of Belief and Perception.* Trans. J. M. Bak and P. A. Hollingsworth. Cambridge Studies in Oral and Literate Culture, 14. Cambridge: Cambridge University Press.

Haack, O. 1939a. "Om 'ægte' trolddom i Danmark i retshistorisk belysning." *Nordisk Tidsskrift for Strafferet* 27: 147–84.

———. 1939b. "Om den 'uægte' trolddom eller lavere grad af trolddom i Danmark." *Nordisk Tidsskrift for Strafferet* 27: 223–36.

Haastrup, Ulla. 1992. "Den umsømmelige Heks: Marie Magdelene kirke, o. 1515." In *Dansk kalkmaleri: Sengotik 1500–1536,* ed. U. Haastrup and R. Egevang. Copenhagen: Nationalmuseet. Pp. 204–5.

Hafström, Gerhard. 1965. *De svenska rättskällornas historia.* 2nd rev. ed. Lund: Studentlitteratur.

———. 1982a. "Dalalagen." *KLNM* 2: 623–26.

———. 1982b. "Lagsaga." *KLNM* 10: 166–67.

Hagen, Rune. 2002. "Harmløs dissenter eller djevelsk trollmann? Trolldomsprosessen mot samen Anders Poulsen i 1692." *Historisk Tidsskrift* 81 (2–3): 319–46.

Hall, Alaric. 2007. *Elves in Anglo-Saxon England: Matters of Belief, Health, Gender and Identity.* Woodbridge, Eng.: Boydell Press.

Hall, David D. 1990. *Worlds of Wonder, Days of Judgment: Popular Religious Belief in Early New England.* Cambridge, Mass.: Harvard University Press.

Hallberg, Peter. 1993. "Sturlunga saga." In *MScan.* Pp. 616–18.

Halldór Hermannsson, ed. 1911. *The Ancient Laws of Norway and Iceland.* Islandica, 4. Ithaca, N.Y.: Cornell University Library.

———. 1932. *Sæmund Sigfússon and the Oddaverjar.* Islandica, 22. Ithaca, N.Y.: Cornell University Press.

Halldórsson, Ólafur. See Ólafur Halldórsson.

Hallencreutz, Carl F. 1982. "Missionary Spirituality: The Case of Ansgar." *Studia theologica* 36 (2): 105–18.

———. 1996. "De berättande källorna, påvebreven och tidiga prov på inhemsk historieskrivning." In *Kristnandet i Sverige: Gamla källor och nya perspektiv,* ed. B. Nilsson. Projektet Sveriges kristnande. Publikationer, 5. Uppsala: Lunne böcker. Pp. 115–40.

Halvorsen, E. F. 1982. "Óðinn." *KLNM* 12: 503–9.

Hammond, Dorothy. 1970. "Magic: A Problem in Semantics." *American Anthropologist,* n.s. 72 (6): 1349–56.

Harðarson, Gunnar and Stefán Karlsson. See Gunnar Harðarson and Stefán Karlsson.

Harris, Joseph. 1975. "Cursing with the Thistle: 'Skírnismál' 31, 6–8, and OE Metrical Charm 9, 16–17." *Neuphilologische Mitteilungen* 76: 26–33.

———. 1976. "The Masterbuilder Tale in Snorri's *Edda* and Two Sagas." *ANF* 91: 66–101.

———. 1983. "Eddic Poetry as Oral Poetry: The Evidence of Parallel Passages in the Helgi Poems for Questions of Composition and Performance." In *Edda: A Collection of Essays,* ed. R. J. Glendinning and Haraldur Bessason. Manitoba: University of Manitoba Press. Pp. 210–42.

———. 1985. "Eddic Poetry." In *Old Norse-Icelandic Literature: A Critical Guide,* ed. C. Clover and J. Lindow. Islandica, 45. Ithaca, N.Y.: Cornell University Press. Pp. 68–156.

———. 1986. "Saga as Historical Novel." In *Structure and Meaning in Old Norse Literature: New Approaches to Textual Analysis and Literary Criticism,* ed. J. Lindow, L. Lönnroth, and G. W. Weber. Odense: Odense University Press. Pp. 187–219.

————. 2000a. "The Performance of Old Norse Eddic Poetry: A Retrospective." In *The Oral Epic: Performance and Music,* ed. K. Reichl. Berlin: Verlag für Wissenschaft und Bildung. Pp. 225–32.

————. 2000b. "Performance, Textualization, and Textuality of 'Elegy' in Old Norse." In *Textualization of Oral Epics,* ed. L. Honko. Trends in Linguistics: Studies and Monographs, 128. Berlin: Mouton de Gruyter. Pp. 89–99.

————. 2003. "'Ethnopaleography' and Recovered Performance: The Problematic Witnesses to 'Eddic Song.'" *Western Folklore* 62 (1–2): 97–117.

Harris, Marvin. 1974. *Cows, Pigs, Wars and Witches. The Riddles of Culture.* New York: Vintage.

Hasenfratz, Robert J., ed. 2000. *Ancrene wisse.* Middle English Texts. Kalamazoo.: Medieval Institute Publications, Western Michigan University. Available at www.lib. rochester.edu/camelot/teams/awintro.htm.

Hastrup, Kirsten. 1985. *Culture and History in Medieval Iceland: An Anthropological Analysis of Structure and Change.* Oxford: Clarendon Press.

————. 1990. *Island of Anthropology: Studies in Past and Present Iceland.* Viking Collection, 5. Odense: Odense University Press.

————. 1993. "Iceland: Sorcerers and Paganism." In *Early Modern European Witchcraft: Centres and Peripheries,* ed. B. Ankarloo and G. Henningsen. Oxford: Clarendon Press. Orig. pub. 1990. Pp. 403–22.

Haugen, Einar. 1950. "The Analysis of Linguistic Borrowing." *Language* 26: 210–31.

Haugen, Odd Einar, and Karl G. Johansson. 2009. "De nordiske versjonene av Barlaamlegenden." In *Barlaam i nord: Legenden om Barlaam och Josaphat i den nordiska medeltidslitteraturen,* ed. K. G. Johansson and M. Arvidsson. Bibliotheca nordica, 1. Oslo: Novus AS. Pp. 11–29.

Heide, Eldar. 2006. *Gand, seid og åndevind.* Bergen: Universitetet i Bergen.

Heikkinen, Antero, and Timo Kervinen. 1993. "Finland: The Male Domination." In *Early Modern European Witchcraft: Centres and Peripheries,* ed. Bengt Ankarloo and Gustav Henningsen. Oxford: Clarendon. Pp. 319–38.

Heinrichs, Anne. 1995. "Die jüngere und die ältere Þóra: Form und Bedeutung einer Episode in *Haukdœla þáttr" Alvíssmál* 5: 3–28.

————. 1997. "Der liebeskranke Freyr, euhemeristisch entmythisiert." *Alvíssmál* 7: 3–36.

Helga Kress. 2008. "'Óþarfar unnustur áttu': Um samband fjölkyngi, kvennfars og karlmennsku í *Íslendingasögum.*" In *Galdramenn: Galdrar og samfélag á miðöldum,* ed. Torfi H. Tulinius. Reykjavík: Hugvísindastofnun Háskóla Íslands. Pp. 21–49.

Helgadóttir, Guðrún P. See Guðrún P. Helgadóttir.

Helle, Knut. 1964. *Norge blir en stat 1130–1319.* Bergen: Universitetsforlaget.

————. 2001. *Gulatinget og Gulatingslova.* Leikanger: Skald.

————, ed. 2003. *The Cambridge History of Scandinavia.* Vol. 1, *Prehistory to 1520.* Cambridge: Cambridge University Press.

Hellqvist, Elof, ed. 1957. *Svensk etymologisk ordbok.* 3rd ed. Lund: C. W. K. Gleerup.

Helm, Karl. 1946. *Wodan: Ausbreitung und Wanderung seines Kultes.* Giessener Beiträge zur deutschen Philologie, 85. Giessen: Schmitz.

Hemmer, Ragnar. 1947. "De svenska medeltidslagarnas stadganden om skadlig trolldom och förgiftning." *Tidsskrift før rettsvitenskap*: 409–46.

Hen, Yitzhak. 1995. *Culture and Religion in Merovingian Gaul*, A.D. 481–751. Cultures, Beliefs, and Traditions, 1. Leiden: E. J. Brill.

Henning, Samuel, ed. 1954. *Siælinna thrøst*. SFSS, 59. Uppsala: Almqvist & Wiksell.

———. 1960. *Skrivarformer och vadstenaspråk i Siælinna thrøst: en textkritisk och filologisk undersökning*. SFSS, 66. Uppsala: Almqvist & Wiksell.

Henningsen, Gustav. 1969. "Trolddom og hjemmelige kunster." In *Dagligliv i Danmark i det syttende og attende århundrede*, ed. A. Steensberg. Copenhagen: Nyt Nordisk Forlag Arnold Busck. Pp. 161–97.

———. 1982. "Witch Hunting in Denmark." *Folklore* 93: 131–37.

———. 1983. "Hexenverfolgung und Hexenprozesse in Dänemark." In *Hexenprozesse: Deutsche und skandinavische Beiträge*, ed. C. Degn et al. Neumünster: K. Wachholtz. Pp. 143–49.

———. 1991–92. "White Sabbath and Other Archaic Patterns of Witchcraft." *Acta Ethnographica Hungaricae. Budapest* 37: 293–304.

———. 1992. Review of Jens Chr. V. Jensen, *Da Djævelen var ude . . . : Trolddom i det 17. århundredes Danmark. Historisk tidsskrift* 92 (1): 131–49.

———. 1993. "'The Ladies from Outside': An Archaic Pattern of the Witches' Sabbath." In *Early Modern European Witchcraft: Centres and Peripheries*, ed. B. Ankarloo and G. Henningsen. Oxford: Clarendon Press. Orig. pub. 1990. Pp. 219–55.

Hermann Pálsson. 1997. *Úr landnorðri: Samar og ystu rætur íslenskrar menningar*. Studia Islandica, 54. Reykjavík: Bókmenntafræðistofnun Háskóla Íslands.

———. 1999a. *Oral Tradition and Saga Writing*. Studia medievalia Septentrionalia, 3. Vienna: Fassbaender.

———. 1999b. "The Sami People in Old Norse Literature." *Nordlit: Arbeidstidsskrift i Litteratur* 5: 29–53.

Hermann Pálsson and Edwards, Paul, trans. 1968. *Gautrek's Saga and Other Medieval Tales*. New York: New York University Press.

———. 1985. *Seven Viking Romances*. Harmondsworth: Penguin.

———. 1989. *Eyrbyggja Saga*. Harmondsworth: Penguin. Orig. pub. 1972.

Hermann, Pernille. 2006. "Rimkrøniken: Tradition og erindring i senmiddelalder og tidlig renæssance." In *Renæssancens verden: Tænkning, kulturliv, dagligliv og efterliv*, ed. O. Høiris and J. Vellev. Århus: Aarhus universitetsforlag. Pp. 267–82.

———. 2007a. "*Íslendingabók* and History." In *Reflections on Old Norse Myths*, ed. P. Hermann, J. P. Schjødt, and R. T. Kristensen. Viking and Medieval Scandinavia Studies, 1. Turnhout: Brepols. Pp. 17–32.

———. 2007b. "Politiske og æstetiske aspekter i Rimkrøniken." *Historisk Tidskrift* 107 (2): 389–411.

———. 2009. "Concepts of Memory and Approaches to the Past in Medieval Icelandic Literature." *SStudies* 81 (3): 287–308.

Hermannsson, Halldór. See Halldór Hermannsson.

Herteig, Asbjørn. 1959. "The Excavation of 'Bryggen,' the old Hanseatic Wharf in Bergen." *Medieval Archaeology* 3: 177–86.

Hertzberg, Ebbe. 1905. "Vore aeldste Lovtexters oprindelige Nedskrivelsestid." In *Historiske Afhandlinger tilegnet Professor Dr. J. E. Sars . . .* Christiania: Aschehoug. Pp. 92–117.

Hesselman, Bengt, ed. 1917. *Samlade skrifter av Olaus Petri.* 4 vols. Uppsala: Almqvist och Wiksell.

Hester, Marianne. 1992. *Lewd Women and Wicked Witches: A Study in the Dynamics of Male Domination.* London: Routledge.

Hildebrand, Emil, ed. 1917. *Stockholms stads tänkeböcker 1474–1483 samt Burspråk.* Stockholms stadsböcker från äldre tid. 2: a serien. Tänkeböcker, 1. Stockholm: Kungl. Samfundet för utgivande af handskrifter rörande Skandinaviens historia med understöd af Stockholms stad och samfundet Sankt Erik.

Hildebrand, Hans. 1983. *Sveriges medeltid.* Stockholm: Gidlunds.

Hjørungdal, T. 1989. "Noen aspekter på tolkning av gravgods i eldre jernalder: Kan gravgods belyse kult?" In *Arkeologi och religion: Rapport från arkeologidagarna 16–18 januari 1989,* ed. L. Larsson and B. Wyszomirska. Institute of Archaeology. Report Series No. 34. Lund: University of Lund, Institute of Archaeology. Pp. 99–106.

Hødnebø, Finn. 1982a. "Tortur." *KLNM* 18: 518–19.

———. 1982b. "Trolldombøker." *KLNM* 18: 670–74.

———. 1995. "Tinget og loven." In *Den eldre Gulatingsloven,* ed. F. Hødnebø and M. Rindal. Corpus codicum Norvegicorum medii aevi. Quarto Series, 9. Oslo: Selskapet til utgivelse av gamle norske håndskrifter. Pp. 9–20.

Höfler, Otto. 1934. *Kultische Geheimbünde der Germanen.* Frankfurt am Main: M. Diesterweg.

Höjer, Torvald. 1905. *Studier i Vadstena Klosters och Birgittinordens historia intill midten af 1400-talet.* Uppsala: Almqvist & Wiksell.

Holbek, Bengt. 1992. Introduction to *Axel Olrik: Principles for Oral Narrative Research.* Bloomington: Indiana University Press. Pp. xv–xxviii.

Hollander, Lee M., trans. 1949. *The Sagas of Kormák and the Sworn Brothers.* Princeton, N.J.: Princeton University Press for the American-Scandinavian Foundation.

———. 1986. *The Poetic Edda.* 2nd rev. ed. Austin: University of Texas Press. Orig. pub. 1962.

———. 1991. *Heimskringla: History of the Kings of Norway by Snorri Sturluson.* Austin: University of Texas Press for the American-Scandinavian Foundation. Orig. pub. 1964.

Holmbäck, Åke, and Elias Wessén, eds. 1962. *Magnus Erikssons Landslag i nusvensk tolkning.* Skrifter utgivna av Institutet för Rättshistorisk Forskning, Serien 1. Rättshistorisk Bibliotek, 6. Stockholm: A.-B. Nordiska Bokhandeln.

———, eds. 1979. *Svenska landskapslagar.* 5 vols. Stockholm: AWE/Geber. Orig. pub. 1933–46.

Holm-Olsen, Ludvig. 1982. "Apostelsagaer." *KLNM* 1: 177–78.

Holmyard, Eric John. 1990. *Alchemy.* New York: Dover. Orig. pub. 1957.

Holtsmark, Anne. 1964. *Studier i Snorres mytologi.* Skrifter utg. av Norske videnskaps-akademi i Oslo. II, Hist.-filos. klasse, ns 4. Oslo: Univeritetsforlaget.

————. 1982a. "Historia Norvegiæ." *KLNM* 5: 585–87.

————. 1982b. "Hyndluljóð." *KLNM* 7: 200–201.

————. 1982c. "Svipdagsmál." *KLNM* 17: 585–87.

Homan, Theo. 1975. *Skidarima: An Inquiry into Written and Printed Texts, References and Commentaries.* Amsterdamer Publikationen zur Sprache und Literatur, 20. Amsterdam: Rodopi.

Honko, Laurie. 1989. "Nationalism and Internationalism in Folklore Research." *NIF Newsletter* 17 (2–3): 16–20.

Hooper, A. G. 1932. "Bragða-Ǫlvis Saga." *Leeds Studies in English and Kindred Languages* 1: 42–54.

Hughes, Shaun F. D. 1978. "'Völsunga rímur' and 'Sjúrðar kvæði': Romance and Ballad, Ballad and Dance." In *Ballads and Ballad Research,* ed. P. Conroy. Seattle: University of Washington Press. Pp. 37–45.

————. 1980. "Report on Rímur 1980." *Journal of English and Germanic Philology* 79: 477–98.

Hultgård, Anders. 1992. "Religiös förändring, kontinuitet och ackulturation/synkretism i vikingatidens och medeltidens skandinaviska religion." In *Kontinuitet i kult och tro från vikingatid till medeltid,* ed. S. Brink and B. Nilsson. Projektet Sveriges kristnande. Publikationer, 1. Uppsala: Lunne böcker. Pp. 49–103.

Hultkrantz, Åke. 2001. "Scandinavian and Saami Religious Relationships: Continuities and Discontinuities in the Academic Debate." In *Kontinuitäten und Brüche in der Religionsgeschichte: Festschrift für Anders Hultgård zu seinem 65. Geburtstag am 23.12.2001,* ed. O. Sundqvist, A. van Nahl, and M. Stausberg. Reallexikon der germanischen Altertumskunde Ergänzungsbände, 31. Berlin: de Gruyter. Pp. 412–23.

Hutchinson, Francis. 1718. *An Historical Essay Concerning Witchcraft . . .* London: Printed for R. Knaplock.

Hutchinson, Thomas. 1870. *The Witchcraft Delusion of 1692.* From an unpublished manuscript (an early draft of his *History of Massachusetts*). Reprinted from the *New-England Historical and Genealogical Register* for October, 1870. Boston: Privately printed.

Hutton, Ronald. 1996. Review of Diane Purkiss, *The Witch in History: Early Modern and Twentieth-Century Representations.* Institute of Historical Research. Available from http://ihr.sas.ac.uk/ihr/reviews/hutton.html.

————. 1999. *The Triumph of the Moon: A History of Modern Pagan Witchcraft.* Oxford: Oxford University Press.

Hyltén-Cavallius, Gunnar Olof. 1972. *Wärend och Wirdarne: Ett försök i svensk etnologi.* 3rd ed. Lund: Gleerup. Orig. pub. 1864.

Hymes, Dell. 1972. "Editorial Introduction to *Language in Society.*" *Language in Society* 1 (1): 1–14.

Indrebø, Gustav. 1931. *Gamal norsk homiliebok: Cod. AM 619 4*. Skrifter utgjevne for Kjeldeskriftfondet, 54. Oslo: Jacob Dybwad.

Inger, Göran. 1982. "Kyrkostraff." *KLNM* 10: 6–9.

Ingesman, Per. 2007. "Kirkelig disciplin og social kontrol i senmiddelalderens danske bondesamfund." In *Konge, kirke og samfund: De to øvrighedsmagter i dansk senmiddelalder*, ed. Agnes S. Arnórsdóttir, P. Ingesman, and B. Poulsen. Århus: Aarhus Universitetsforlag. Pp. 329–80.

Institoris, Heinrich. 2009. *The Hammer of the Witches. A Complete Translation of the Malleus Maleficarum*. Trans. C. Mackay. Cambridge: Cambridge University Press.

Iuul, Stig. 1982a. "Kyrkorätt. Danmark." *KLNM* 10: 5–6.

———. 1982b. "Kyrkostraff. Danmark." *KLNM* 10: 9–10.

Iversen, Tore. 1997. "Landskapslovene og kanonisk rett." In *Nordiske middelalderlover: Tekst og kontekst*, ed. A. Dybdahl and J. Sandnes. Rapport fra seminar ved Senter for middelalderstudier, 29.–30. nov. 1996. Senter for middelalderstudier. Skrifter, 5. Trondheim: Tapir. Pp. 69–86.

Jackson, Tatjana N. 2006. "The Fantastic in the Kings' Sagas." In *The Fantastic in Old Norse/Icelandic Literature*. Durham Saga Conference. Available at www.dur.ac.uk/medieval.www/sagaconf/jackson.htm.

Jacobsen, Grethe. 1986. *Kvindeskikkelser og kvindeliv i Danmarks middelalder*. Copenhagen: G. E. C. Gad.

———. 2007. "Køn og magt i dansk senmiddelalder." In *Konge, kirke og samfund: De to øvrighedsmagter i dansk senmiddelalder*, ed. Agnes S. Arnórsdóttir, P. Ingesman, and B. Poulsen. Århus: Aarhus Universitetsforlag. Pp. 151–77.

Jacobsen, Lis, and Erik Moltke, eds. 1941–42. *Danmarks runeindskrifter*. Copenhagen: Ejnar Munksgaards forlag.

Jahnkuhn, Herbert. 1967. "Das Missionsfeld Ansgars." *Frühmittelalterliche Studien* 1: 213–21.

Jakob Benediktsson, ed. 1968. *Íslendingabók. Landnámabók*. ÍF, 1. Reykjavík: Hið íslenzka fornritafélag.

———. 1974. "Landnám og upphaf allsherjarríkis." In *Saga Íslands*. Vol. 1, *Samin að tilhlutan þjóðhátíðarnefndar*, ed. Sigurður Líndal. Reykjavík: Hið íslenzka bókmenntefélag—Sögufélagi. Pp. 155–96.

———. 1982a. "Landnámabók." *KLNM* 10: 214–17.

———. 1982b. "Vergil: Island og Norge." *KLNM* 19: 654–59.

———. 1993. "Annals. 2. Iceland (and Norway)." In *MScan*. Pp. 15–16.

Jakobsson, Ármann. See Ármann Jakobsson.

Jansen, Wm. Hugh. 1959. "The Esoteric-Exoteric Factor in Folklore." *Fabula: Journal of Folklore Studies* 2: 205–11.

Jansson, Sven B. F. 1945. *Sagorna om Vinland*. Kungl. Vitterhets historie och antikvitets akademiens handlingar, 60:1. Stockholm: Wahlström & Widstrand.

Jansson, Sven-Bertil. 1971. *Medeltidens rimkrönikor: Studier i funktion, stoff, form*. Studia litterarum Upsaliensia, 8. Nyköping: Läromedelsförlaget.

Jansson, Valter. 1934. *Fornsvenska legendariet: Handskrifter och språk.* Nordiska texter och undersökningar, 4. Stockholm: H. Geber & Levin & Munkgaard.

———, ed. 1966. *Legendarium Suecanum ("Fornsvenska Legendariet").* Corpus Codicum Suecicorum Medii Aevi, 19. Copenhagen: Munksgaard.

———. 1982. "Fornsvenska Legendariet." *KLNM* 5: 518–22.

Jensen, Karsten Sejr. 1988. *Trolddom i Danmark 1500–1588.* Copenhagen: Nordisc.

Jesch, Judith. 1991. *Women in the Viking Age.* Woodbridge, Eng.: Boydell Press.

Jexlev, Thelma. 1991. "Anna Brahes Bønnebog: Ett birgittinsk håndskrift fra Maribo." In *Birgitta, hendes værk og hendes klostre i Norden,* ed. T. Nyberg. Odense University Studies in History and Social Sciences, 150. Odense: Odense Universitetsforlag. Pp. 323–28.

Jochens, Jenny. 1980. "The Church and Sexuality in Medieval Iceland." *Journal of Medieval History* 6: 377–92.

———. 1987. "The Female Inciter in the Kings' Sagas." *ANF* 102: 100–119.

———. 1990. "Old Norse Sources on Women." In *Medieval Women and the Sources of Medieval History,* ed. J. T. Rosenthal. Athens: University of Georgia Press. Pp. 155–88.

———. 1991. "Old Norse Magic and Gender: *Þáttr Þorvalds ens víðförla.*" *SStudies* 63: 305–17.

———. 1993. "Marching to a Different Drummer: New Trends in Medieval Icelandic Scholarship; A Review Article." *Comparative Studies in Society and History* 35 (1): 197–207.

———. 1995. *Women in Old Norse Society.* Ithaca, N.Y.: Cornell University Press.

———. 1996. *Old Norse Images of Women.* Philadelphia: University of Pennsylvania Press.

———. 2006. Review of Francois-Xavier Dillmann, *Les magiciens dans l'Islande ancienne: Études sur la représentation de la magie islandaise et de ses agents dans les sources litteraires norroises. SStudies* 78 (4): 488–92.

Joensen, Jóan Pauli. 2003. *I ærlige brudefolk: Bryllup på Færøerne.* Etnologiske studier, 10. Copenhagen: Museum Tusculanums Forlag.

Jóhanna Katrín Friðriksdóttir. 2009. "Women's Weapons. A Re-Evaluation of Magic in the *Íslendingasögur.*" *SStudies* 81 (4): 409–36.

Johannesson, Kurt. 1978. *Saxo Grammaticus: Komposition och världsbild i Gesta Danorum.* Lychnos-bibliotek, 31. Uppsala: Almqvist & Wiksell.

———. 1981. "Order in *Gesta Danorum* and Order in the Creation." In *Saxo Grammaticus: A Medieval Author between Norse and Latin Culture,* ed. K. Friis-Jensen. Danish Medieval History and Saxo Grammaticus, 2. Copenhagen: Museum Tusculanum. Pp. 95–104.

Johansen, Jens Christian V. 1989. "Danmark anklagelsernas sociologi. Häxans Europa." In *Med lov skal bygges og andre retshistoriske afhandlinger,* ed. I. Dübeck et al. N.p.: Jurist- og Økonomforbundets forlag. Pp. 196–217.

———. 1991. *Da djævelen var ude . . . : trolddom i det 17. århundredes Danmark.* Odense University Studies in History and Social Sciences, 129. Odense: Odense University Press.

————. 1993. "Denmark: The Sociology of Accusations." In *Early Modern European Witchcraft: Centres and Peripheries,* ed. B. Ankarloo and G. Henningsen. Oxford: Clarendon Press. Orig. pub. 1990. Pp. 339–65.

Johnsen, A. O. 1952. "Hvor studerte biskopbrødrene Arne og Audfinn?" *Historisk tidskrift* 36: 89–98.

Jolly, Karen Louise. 1996. *Popular Religion in Late Saxon England: Elf Charms in Context.* Chapel Hill: University of North Carolina Press.

Jón Árnason, ed. 1954–61. *Íslenzkar þjóðsögur og ævintýri.* 6 vols. 2nd rev. ed. Reykjavík: Bókaútgáfan þjóðsaga.

Jón Hnefill Aðalsteinsson. 1978. *Under the Cloak: The Acceptance of Christianity in Iceland with Particular Reference to the Religious Attitudes Prevailing at the Time.* Acta Universitatis Upsaliensis. Studia Ethnologica Upsaliensia, 4. Uppsala: Almqvist & Wiksell.

————. 1994. "Sæmundr Fróði: A Medieval Master of Magic." *ARV* 50: 117–32.

————. 1996. "Six Icelandic Magicians after the Time of Sæmundr Fróði." *ARV* 52: 46–61.

————. 1997. *Blót í norrænum sið: Rýnt í forn trúarbrögð með þjóðfræðilegri aðferð.* Reykjavík: Háskólaútgáfan: Félagsvísindastofnun.

Jón Viðar Sigurðsson. 1993. "Ólafr Tryggvason." In *MScan.* Pp. 446–47.

Jón Viðar Sigurðsson, Frederik Pedersen, and Anders Berge. 2008. "Making and Using the Law in the North, c. 900–1350." In *Making, Using and Resisting the Law in European History,* ed. G. Lottes, E. Medijainen, and Jón Viðar Sigurðsson. Pisa: PLUS-Pisa University Press. Pp. 37–64.

Jón Þorkelsson. 1888. *Om digtningen på Island i det 15. og 16. århundrede.* Copenhagen: Andr. Fred. Høst & søns forlag.

Jón Þorkelsson and Jón Sigurðsson, eds. 1857–1932. *Diplomatarium islandicum.* "gefið ut af Hinu íslenzka bókmentafélagi." Copenhagen: S. L. Møller.

Jónas Kristjánsson, ed. 1956. *Eyfirðinga sǫgur. Víga-Glúms saga. Qgmundar þáttr dytts. Þorvalds þáttr tasalda. Svarfdæla saga. Þorleifs þáttr jarlsskálds. Valla-Ljóts saga. Sneglu-Halla þáttr. Þorgríms þáttr Hallasona.* ÍF, 9. Reykjavík: Hið íslenzka fornritafélag.

Jones, Gwyn. 1968. *A History of the Vikings.* Oxford: Oxford University Press.

Jones, Prudence, and Nigel Pennick. 1995. *A History of Pagan Europe.* London: Routledge.

Jonsson, Bengt R. 1991. "Oral Literature, Written Literature, and the Ballad: Relations between Old Norse Genres." In *The Ballad and Oral Literature,* ed. J. Harris. Harvard English Studies, 17. Cambridge, Mass.: Harvard University Press. Pp. 139–70.

Jónsson, Eiríkur, and Finnur Jónsson, eds. See Eiríkur Jónsson and Finnur Jónsson, eds.

Jónsson, Finnur. See Finnur Jónsson.

Jónsson, Finnur, and Sveinbjörn Egilsson, eds. See Finnur Jónsson and Sveinbjörn Egilsson, eds.

Jónsson, Finnur, and Hannes Finnsson, eds. See Finnur Jónsson and Hannes Finnsson, eds.

Jónsson, Guðni, ed. See Guðni Jónsson, ed.

Jørgensen, Ellen, ed. 1920. *Annales danici medii ævi.* Copenhagen: Selskabet for Udgivelse af Kilder til dansk Historie.

Jorgensen, Peter A. 1994. "Four Literary Styles in Three Centuries: The Old Icelandic Theophilus Legend." In *Samtíðarsögur: The Contemporary Sagas; Pre-Prints of the 9th International Saga Conference.* Vol. 1. Akureyri: Stofnun Árna Magnússonar. Pp. 395–40.

Joys, Charles Louis André. 1948. *Biskop og konge: Bispevalg i Norge 1000–1350.* Oslo: H. Aschehoug.

Jungner, Hugo, and Elisabeth Svärdström, eds. 1940–70. *Västergötlands runinskrifter.* 2 vols. Sveriges runinskrifter, 5. Stockholm: Kungl. vitterhets historie och antikvitets akademien.

Kålund, Kristian. 1884–91. "En kontrakt med jomfru Marie." In *Småstykker.* Copenhagen: SUGNL. Pp. 127–30.

Kallestrup, Louise Nyholm. 2009. *I pagt med Djævelen: Trolddomsforestillinger og trolddomsforfølgelser i Italien og Danmark efter Reformationen.* Frederiksberg: Forlaget Anis.

Karras, Ruth Mazo. 1986. "Pagan Survivals and Syncretism in the Conversion of Saxony." *Catholic Historical Review* 72: 553–72.

———. 1988. *Slavery and Society in Medieval Scandinavia.* New Haven, Conn.: Yale University Press.

———. 1997. "God and Man in Medieval Scandinavia: Writing and Gendering the Conversion." In *Varieties of Religious Conversion in the Middle Ages,* ed. J. Muldoon. Gainesville: University Press of Florida. Pp. 100–114.

Kaspersen, Søren, et al. 1990. *Dansk litteraturhistorie.* Vol. 1, *Fra runer til ridderdigtning o. 800–1480.* Copenhagen: Gyldendal. Orig. pub. 1984.

Kearney, Michael. 1975. "World View Theory and Study." *Annual Review of Anthropology* 4: 247–70.

Kellogg, Robert L. 1991. "Literacy and Orality in the Poetic Edda." In *Vox intexta: Orality and Textuality in the Middle Ages,* ed. A. N. Doane and C. B. Pasternack. Madison: University of Wisconsin Press. Pp. 89–101.

Kempff, Margaret. 1992. "Kalkmålningar som källa till kvinnohistoria." In *Fokus på kvinner i middelalderkilder: Rapport fra symposiet "Kilder til kvinnehistoriske studier i nordisk middelalder," Isegran, September 1990,* ed. B. J. Sellevold, E. Mundal, and G. Steinsland. Skara: Viktoria Bokförlag. Pp. 52–61.

Kent, E. J. 2005. "Masculinity and Male Witches in Old and New England, 1593–1680." *History Workshop Journal* 60 (1): 69–92.

Keyser, R., and P. A. Munch, eds. 1846–95. *Norges gamle Love indtil 1387.* 5 vols. Oslo: Chr. Gröndahl.

Keyser, R., C. R. Unger, and P. A. Munch, eds. 1848. *Speculum Regale: Konungs skuggsjá. Konge-speilet.* Christiania: Carl C. Werner og Comp.

Kiær, Birgitta. 1982. "Rav." *KLNM* 13: 681–85.

Kick, Donata. 2006. "Old Norse Translations of Ælfric's *De falsis diis* and *De auguriis* in *Hauksbók.*" In *The Fantastic in Old Norse/Icelandic Literature.* Durham Saga Conference. Available at www.dur.ac.uk/medieval.www/sagaconf/kick.htm.

Kieckhefer, Richard. 1976. *European Witch Trials: Their Foundations in Popular and Learned Culture, 1300–1500*. Berkeley and Los Angeles: University of California Press.

———. 1989. *Magic in the Middle Ages*. Cambridge: Cambridge University Press.

———. 1994. "The Holy and the Unholy: Sainthood, Witchcraft, and Magic in Late Medieval Europe." *Journal of Medieval and Renaissance Studies* 24 (3): 355–85.

———. 1997. *Forbidden Rites: A Necromancer's Manual of the Fifteenth Century*. University Park: Pennsylvania State University Press.

Kienzle, Beverly Mayne. 2006. "Sermons and Preaching." In *Women and Gender in Medieval Europe: An Encyclopedia*, ed. M. Schaus. New York: Routledge. Pp. 736–40.

Kiessling, Nicholas K. 1968. "Grendel: A New Aspect." *Modern Philology* 65 (3): 191–201.

Kilström, Bengt Ingmar. 1957. *Villberga kyrka*. Upplands kyrkor, 86. Uppsala: Wretman.

Kirschenblatt-Gimblett, Barbara. 1991. "Objects of Ethnography." In *Exhibiting Cultures: The Poetics and Politics of Museum Display*, ed. I. Karp and S. D. Lavine. Washington, D.C.: Smithsonian Institution Press. Pp. 386–443.

Kittredge, George Lyman. 1929. *Witchcraft in Old and New England*. Cambridge, Mass.: Harvard University Press.

Klemming, Gustaf E., ed. 1856. *Skrå-ordningar*. SFSS, 13. Stockholm: P. A. Norstedt & Söner.

———, ed. 1857–84. *Heliga Birgittas Uppenbarelser efter gamla handskrifter*. 5 vols. SFSS, 14. Stockholm: P. A. Norstedt & Söner.

———, ed. 1862. *Konung Alexander*. SFSS, 12. Stockholm: P. A. Norstedt & Söner.

———, ed. 1866. *Svenska medeltidens rim-krönikor. II. Nya eller Karls-krönikan*. SFSS, 17. Stockholm: P. A. Norstedt & Söner.

———, ed. 1877–78. *Klosterläsning: Järteckensbok, Apostla gerningar, Helga manna lefverne, Legender, [och] Nichodemi evangelium, efter gammal handskrift*. SFSS, 22. Stockholm: P. A. Norstedt & Söner.

———, ed. 1883–86. *Läke- och örte-böcker från Sveriges medeltid*. SFSS, 26. Stockholm: P. A. Norstedt & Söner.

Klemming, Gustaf E., Robert Geete, and Bertil Ejder, eds. 1879–. *Svenska medeltids-postillor*. 6 vols. SFSS, 23. Stockholm: P. A. Norstedt.

Klockars, Birgit. 1967. "Medeltidens religiösa litteratur." In *Ny illustrerad svensk litteraturhistoria*. 2nd rev. ed., ed. E. N. Tigerstedt and E. H. Linder. Vol. 1. Stockholm: Natur och kultur. Orig. pub. 1952. Pp. 125–225.

Knight, K., ed. 2003. *The Catholic Encyclopedia: An International Work of Reference*. New York: Robert Appleton. Orig. pub. 1907. Available at www.newadvent.org/cathen/.

Knirk, James E. 1995. "Tor og Odin i runer på Bryggen i Bergen." *Arkeo* (1): 29–30.

Knudsen, Tryggve. 1982a. "Eidsivatingsloven." *KLNM* 3: 526–28.

———. 1982b. "Frostatingsloven." *KLNM* 4: 656–61.

———. 1982c. "Gulatinglovet." *KLNM* 5: 559–66.

———. 1982d. "Gullfjær." *KLNM* 5: 593–94.

Knutsen, Gunnar W. 2003. "Norwegian Witchcraft Trials: A Reassessment." *Continuity and Change* 18 (3): 185–200.

Knuuttila, Seppo. 1993. "Some Questions Concerning Mentalities, Ethnomethodology and Rhetorics in the Folkloristic Study of Community." In *Nordic Frontiers: Recent Issues in the Study of Modern Traditional Culture in the Nordic Countries,* ed. P. J. Anttonen and R. Kvideland. NIF Publications, 27. Turku: Nordic Institute of Folklore. Pp. 121–30.

————. 1995. "Mentalities and Modalities." *Suomen Antropologi* 20 (1): 18–25.

Kölbing, Eugen. 1876. *Beiträge zur vergleichenden Geschichte der romantischen Poesie und Prosa des Mittelalters, unter besonderer Berücksichtigung der englischen und nordischen Litteratur.* Breslau: W. Koebner.

Konrað Gíslason et al., eds. 1883. *Grágás: Stykker, som findes i det Arnamagnæanske Haandskrift Nr. 351 fol., Skálholtsbók, og en Række andre Haandskrifter.* Copenhagen: Gyldendal.

Konrað Gíslason et al., eds. 1889–94. *Katalog over Den arnamagnæanske Håndskriftsamling.* 2 vols. Copenhagen: Det arnamagnæanske Legat.

Kors, Alan C., and Edward Peters, eds. 2001. *Witchcraft in Europe, 400–1700: A Documentary History.* 2nd rev. ed. Philadelphia: University of Pennsylvania Press.

Krarup, Alfred, and William Norvin, eds. 1932. *Acta processus litium inter regem Danorum et archiepiscopum Lundensem.* Copenhagen: G. E. C. Gad.

Kress, Helga. See Helga Kress.

Kristensen, Marius, et al., eds. 1945. *Middelalderens danske bønnebøger.* 5 vols. Copenhagen: Gyldendal.

Kristjánsdóttir, Bergljót. See Bergljót Kristjánsdóttir.

Kristjánsson, Jónas, ed. See Jónas Kristjánsson, ed.

Kröningssvärd, C. C., ed. 1821. *Handlingar om trulldoms-wäsendet i Dalarne åren 1668–1673.* Fahlun: O.U. Arborelius..

Krötzl, Christian. 1994. *Pilger, Mirakel und Alltag: Formen des Verhaltens im skandinavischen Mittelalter, 12.-15. Jahrhundert.* Helsinki: Suomen Kirkkohistoriallinen Seura.

————. 2001. "Ad sanctos: Religion and Everyday Life in Scandinavian Later Middle Ages." In *Norden og Europa i middelalderen,* ed. P. Ingesman and T. Lindkvist. Skrifter udgivet af Jysk Selskab for Historie, 47. Århus: Aarhus Universitetsforlag. Pp. 203–15.

Kroman, Erik, ed. 1951–61. *Danmarks gamle købstadlovgivning.* 5 vols. Copenhagen: Rosenkilde og Bagger.

Kroon, Sigurd, et al., eds. 1993. *A Danish Teacher's Manual of the Mid-Fifteenth Century (Codex AM 76, 8to).* Vol. 1, *Transcription and Facsimile.* Skrifter utgivna av Vetenskapssocieteten i Lund, 85. Lund: Lund University Press.

Labouvie, Eva. 1990. "Männer im Hexenprozeß: Zur Sozialanthropologie eines 'männlichen' Verständnisses von Magie und Hexerei." *Geschichte und Gesellschaft* 16 (1): 56–78.

Läffler, Leopold Fredrik. 1916. "Till *Hávamáls* strof 155." *ANF* 32: 83–223.

Lagerlöf-Genetay, Birgitta. 1990. *De svenska häxprocessernas utbrottsskede 1668–1671. Bakgrund i Övre Dalarna: social och ecklesiastisk kontext.* Acta Universitatis Stockholmensis. Stockholm Studies in Comparative Religion, 29. Stockholm: Almqvist & Wiksell.

Langkilde, Birgitta. 2007. "Tiggerordnernes prædikenvirksomhed i dansk senmiddelalder." In *Konge, kirke og samfund: De to øvrighedsmagter i dansk senmiddelalder,* ed. Agnes S. Arnórsdóttir, P. Ingesman, and B. Poulsen. Århus: Aarhus Universitetsforlag. Pp. 471–98.

Larner, Christina. 1987. *Witchcraft and Religion: The Politics of Popular Belief.* Oxford: Basil Blackwell. Orig. pub. 1984.

Larrington, Carolyne. 1992. " 'What Does Woman Want?' Mær and munr in *Skírnismál.*" *Alvíssmál* 1: 3–16.

Larson, Laurence M., trans. 1935. *The Earliest Norwegian Laws: Being the Gulathing Law and the Frostathing Law.* New York: Columbia University Press.

Larsson, Ludvig. 1893. *Sagan ock rimora om Friðþiófr hinn frækni.* SUGNL, 22. Copenhagen: E. Malmströms bogtryckeri.

Lárusson, Magnús Már. See Magnús Már Lárusson.

Lárusson, Ólafur. See Ólafur Lárusson.

Lassen, Annette. 2006. "Gud eller djævel: Kristningen af Odin." *ANF* 121: 121–38.

———. forthcoming. "Hrafnagaldur Óðins/Forspjallsljóð: En tekstudgave med indledning, kommentar og oversættelse." In *Opuscula.* Bibliotheca Arnamagnæana. Copenhagen: C. A. Reitzel.

Lawrence, Duggan G. 1989. "Was Art Really the 'Book of the Illiterate'?" *Word and Image* 5: 227–51.

Layher, William. 2000. "Meister Rumelant & Co.: German Poets (Real and Imagined) in 13th-Century Denmark." *Zeitschrift für deutsche Philologie* 119: 143–66.

———. 2008. "The Big Splash: End-rhyme and Innovation in Medieval Scandinavian Poetics." *SStudies* 80: 407–36.

Lazar, Moshe. 1972. "Theophilus: Servant of Two Masters; The Pre-Faustian Theme of Despair and Revolt." *Modern Language Notes* 87 (6): 31–50.

Leach, Edmund Ronald. 1965. *Political Systems of Highland Burma.* Boston: Beacon Press. Orig. pub. 1954.

———. 1982. "Critical Introduction." In *Myth: The Icelandic Sagas and Eddas.* Ann Arbor, Mich.: Karoma. Pp. 1–20.

———. 1985. "Reflections on a Visit to Nemi: Did Frazer Get It Wrong?" *Anthropology Today* 1 (2): 2–3.

———. 1989. *Claude Lévi-Strauss.* Chicago: University of Chicago Press. Orig. pub. 1970.

Le Goff, Jacques. 1967. "Culture cléricale et traditions folkloriques dans la civilisation mérovingienne." *Annales, E.S.C.* 22: 780–91.

———. 1978. *Pour un autre Moyen Age: Temps, travail et culture en Occident.* Paris: Gallimard.

Lehmann, Alfred. 1920. *Overtro og trolddom: Fra de ældste tider til vore dage.* 2nd ed. Copenhagen: Frimodt. Orig. pub. 1893.

Lennersand, Marie. 1997. "Androm till sky och skräck: Den rättsliga behandlingen av trolldomprocesserna i Älvdalen och Mora 1668–68." In *Vägen till Blåkulla: Nya perspektiv på de stora svenska Häxprocesserna,* ed. L. Oja. Uppsala: Idé Tryck Grafiska Uppsala AB. Pp. 23–44.

Lévi-Strauss, Claude. 1963a. *Structural Anthropology.* Trans. C. Jacobson and B. G. Schoepf. New York: Basic.

———. 1963b. *Totemism.* Trans. R. Needham. Boston: Beacon Press.

Lid, Nils. 1950. *Trolldom. Nordiske Studiar.* Oslo: Cammermeyers Boghandel.

Lidén, Evald. 1914. "Ett par fornsvenska bidrag." In *Svenska studier tillägnade Gustaf Cederschiöld den 25 juni 1914.* Lund: C. W. K. Gleerup. Pp. 413–18.

———. 1933. "Till tydningen av Stockholms äldsta stadsböcker." *ANF* 49: 295–323.

Liedgren, Jan. 1982. "Landskabslove. Sverige." *KLNM* 10: 231–32.

Liestøl, Aslak. 1964. *Runer frå Bergen.* [rpt. from *Viking* 1963]. Bergen: Det midlertidige Bryggemuseum.

Liljegren, Joh. Gust., et al., eds. 1829–. *Svenskt diplomatarium.* 6 vols. Kungl. Vitterhets historie och antikvitets akademien and Riksarkivet. Stockholm: P. A. Norstedt & Söner.

Liljenroth, Gunnel, and Göran Liljenroth, eds. 1997. *Småländska antiqviteter av Petter Rudebeck—300-årigt manuskript uttytt, nedskrivet och varsamt redigerat.* Lidköping: AMA förlag.

Lind, Erik Henrik. 1920–21. *Norsk-isländska personbinamn från medeltiden.* Uppsala: A.-B. Lundquistska bokhandeln.

Líndal, Sigurður. See Sigurður Líndal.

Lindblom, Andreas. 1963. *Birgittas gyllene skrin.* Kungl. Vitterhets Historie och Antikvitets Akademiens Handlingar. Antikvariska serien, 10. Stockholm: Almqvist & Wiksell.

Linderholm, Emanuel. 1918a. *De stora häxprocesserna i Sverige: Bidrag till svensk kultur- och kyrkohistoria.* Uppsala: J. A. Lindblads Förlag.

———. 1918b. "Nordisk magi: Studier i nordisk religions- och kyrkohistoria." *Svenska landsmål och svenskt folkliv* B.20: 1–160.

Lindhe, Olof. 1978. *Rydaholms medeltidskyrka.* Småländksa kulturbilder. Meddelanden från Jönköpings läns hembygdsförbund, XLX [!]. Värnamo: Jönköpings läns hembygdsförbund och Stiftelsen Jönköpings läns museum.

Lindow, John. 1985. "Mythology and Mythography." In *Old Norse-Icelandic Literature: A Critical Guide,* ed. C. Clover and J. Lindow. Islandica, 45. Ithaca, N.Y.: Cornell University Press. Pp. 21–67.

———, ed. 1988. *Scandinavian Mythology: An Annotated Bibliography.* Garland Folklore Bibliographies, 13. New York: Garland.

———. 1997. *Murder and Vengeance among the Gods: Baldr in Scandinavian Mythology.* FFC, 262. Helsinki: Suomalainen tiedeakatemia.

———. 2002. *Norse Mythology: A Guide to the Gods, Heroes, Rituals, and Beliefs.* Oxford: Oxford University Press.

———. 2008. "St. Olaf and the Skalds." In *Sanctity in the North: Saints, Lives, and Cults in Medieval Scandinavia,* ed. T. A. DuBois. Toronto: University of Toronto Press. Pp. 103–27.

Lindquist, Ivar. 1923. *Galdrar: De gamla germanska trollsångernas stil undersökt i samband med en svensk runinskrift från folkvandringstiden.* Göteborgs Högskolas Årsskrift, 29. Gothenburg: Wettergren & Kerber.

———. 1956. *Die Urgestalt der* Hávamál: *Ein Versuch zur Bestimmung auf synthetischem Wege.* Lundastudier i nordisk språkvetenskap, Serie A, 11. Lund: Gleerup.

Lindquist, Ivar, and Gösta Holm. 1987. *Religiösa runtexter.* Skrifter utgivna av Vetenskapssocieteten i Lund, 79. Lund: Lund University Press.

Lindqvist, Mats. 1992. "Between Realism and Relativism: A Consideration of History in Modern Ethnology." *Ethnologia Scandinavica* 22: 3–16.

Lindqvist, Natan, ed. 1921. *En isländsk svartkonstbok från 1500-talet (Galdrabók).* Uppsala: Appelberg.

Lindroth, Sten. 1989. *Svensk lärdomshistoria. Medeltiden. Reformationstiden.* N.p.: Norstedt. Orig. pub. 1975.

Ljungberg, Helge. 1938. *Den nordiska religionen och kristendomen: Studier över det nordiska religionsskiftet under vikingatiden.* Nordiska texter och undersökningar, 11. Stockholm: H. Geber.

Lockhart, Paul Douglas. 2007. *Denmark, 1513–1660: The Rise and Decline of a Renaissance Monarchy.* Oxford: Oxford University Press.

Lönnroth, Lars. 1964. "Tesen om de två kultunrerna: Kritiska studier i den isländska sagaskrivningens sociala förutsåttningar." *Scripta Islandica* 15: 1–97.

———. 1969. "The Noble Heathen: A Theme in the Sagas." *SStudies* 41: 1–29.

———. 1971. "Hjálmar's Death-Song and the Delivery of Eddic Poetry." *Speculum* 46: 1–20.

———. 1976. *Njáls Saga: A Critical Introduction.* Berkeley: University of California Press.

———. 1977b. "*Skírnismál* och den fornisländska äktenskapsnormen." In *Opuscula Septentrionalia: Festskrift til Ole Widding. 10.10.1977,* ed. B. Chr. Jakobsen et al. Copenhagen: C. A. Reitzel. Pp. 154–78.

———. 1978. *Den dubbla scenen: Muntlig diktning från Eddan till ABBA.* Stockholm: Prisma.

———. 1996. "En fjärran spegel: Västnordiska berättande källor om svensk hedendom och om kristningsprocessen på svenskt område." In *Kristnandet i Sverige: Gamla källor och nya perspektiv,* ed. B. Nilsson. Projektet Sveriges kristnande. Publikationer, 5. Uppsala: Lunne böcker. Pp. 141–58.

———. 1999. "Saga and Jartegn. The Appeal of Mystery in Saga Texts." In *Die Aktualität der Saga: Festschrift für Hans Schottmann,* ed. S. T. Andersen. Berlin: de Gruyter. Pp. 111–23.

Loomis, C. Grant. 1948. *White Magic: An Introduction to the Folklore of Christian Legend.* Mediaeval Academy of America. Publication, 52. Cambridge, Mass.: Mediaeval Academy of America.

Lord, Albert Bates. 1991. "Words Heard and Words Seen." In *Epic Singers and Oral Tradition,* ed. G. Nagy. Ithaca, N.Y.: Cornell University Press. Pp. 15–37.

———. 2000. *The Singer of Tales.* 2nd ed., ed. S. A. Mitchell and G. Nagy. Harvard

Studies in Comparative Literature, 24. Cambridge, Mass.: Harvard University Press. Orig. pub. 1960.

Louis-Jensen, Jonna. 2001. "'Halt illu fran bufa!': Til Tolkningen af Kvinneby-amuletten fra Öland." In *Northern Lights: Following Folklore in Northwestern Europe,* ed. S. Ó. Catháin et al. Dublin: University College Dublin. Pp. 111–26.

Lundberg, Erik. 1961. *Albertus Pictor.* Sveriges allmänna konstförenings publikationer, 70. Stockholm: P. A. Norstedt & Söner.

Lundén, Tryggve, ed. 1950. *Frater Gregorius holmiensis O.P. Miracula defixionis Domini: En mirakelsamling från Stockholms dominikankloster.* Göteborgs högskolas årsskrift, 55. Göteborg: Elanders boktryckeri.

———. 1967. "Medeltidens religiösa litterature." In *Ny illustrerad svensk litteraturhistoria.* 2nd rev. ed, ed. E. N. Tigerstedt and E. H. Linder. Vol. 1. Stockholm: Natur och kultur. Orig. pub. 1952. Pp. 122–222.

———, ed. 1981. *Vita Katherine: Facsimile tryck av Bartholomeus Ghotans i Stockholm 1487 tryckta bok.* Uppsala: Bokförlaget Pro Veritate.

———. 1982. "Ingrid." *KLNM* 7: 406–7.

Macfarlane, Alan. 1991. *Witchcraft in Tudor and Stuart England: A Regional and Comparative Study.* Prospect Heights, Ill.: Waveland Press. Orig. pub. 1970.

MacLeod, Mindy, and Bernard Mees. 2006. *Runic Amulets and Magic Objects.* Woodbridge, Eng.: Boydell & Brewer.

Magerøy, Hallvard. 1982. "Ynglingatal." *KLNM* 20: 362–64.

Magnus, Olaus. 1555. *Historia de gentibus septentrionalibus.* Rome: apud Ioannem Mariam de Viottis Parmensem.

———. 1996–98. *Historia de gentibus septentrionalibus: Romæ 1555 = Description of the Northern Peoples: Rome 1555.* 3 vols. Trans. P. Fisher and H. Higgens. Ed. Peter Foote. Annotations by John Granlund. 2nd ser., 182, 187–88. London: Hakluyt Society.

Magnús Már Lárusson. 1982a. "Kristenrettar: Island." *KLNM* 9: 304–6.

———. 1982b. "Kyrkorätt: Island." *KLNM* 10: 13–15.

Magnús Rafnsson. 2003. *Angurgapi: Um galdramál á Íslandi.* Hólmavík: Strandagaldur.

Magnús Stefánsson. 1978. "Frá goðakirkju til biskupskirkju." In *Saga Íslands.* Vol. 3, *Samin að tilhlutan THjóðhátíðarnefndar 1974,* ed. Sigurður Líndal. Reykjavík: Hið íslenzka bókmenntefélag—Sögufélagið. Pp. 111–257.

———. 1993. "Church Organization and Function. 2. Norway." In *MScan.* Pp. 88–92.

Magnusson, Magnus, and Pálsson Hermann. 1965. *The Vinland Sagas, The Norse Discovery of America.* Baltimore: Penguin.

———. 1966. *Njal's Saga.* Baltimore: Penguin. Orig. pub. 1960.

Magnússon, Sigurður Gylfi. See Sigurður Gylfi Magnússon.

Mair, Lucy. 1963. "Some Current Terms in Social Anthropology." *British Journal of Sociology* 14 (1): 20–29.

Malinowski, Bronislaw. 1948. "Magic, Science and Religion." In *Magic, Science and Religion, and Other Essays.* Glencoe, Ill.: Free Press. Orig. pub. 1925. Pp. 17–92.

———. 1954. *Magic, Science and Religion, and Other Essays.* Doubleday Anchor Books, A23. Garden City, N.Y.: Doubleday.

Marold, Edith. 1993. "Merlínúspá." In *MScan*. Pp. 412–13.

Martène, E. and Durand, U., eds. 1717. *Thesaurus Novus Anecdotorum*. Paris: F. Delaulne.

Marwick, Max. 1967. "The Study of Witchcraft." In *The Craft of Social Anthropology*, ed. A. L. Epstein. London: Tavistock. Pp. 231–44.

Matras, Christian. 1957. "Drunnur." *Fróðarskaparrit* 6: 20–33.

———. 1958. "Atlantssiðir—atlantsorð." *Fróðarskaparrit* 1958 (7): 73–101.

Matthías Viðar Sæmundsson. 1996. *Galdur á brennuöld*. Reykjavík: Storð.

Maurer, Konrad von, and Ebbe Hertzberg. 1878. *Udsigt over de nordgermaniske Retskilders Historie: Historisk Tidsskrift*. Tillægsskrifter, 6. Christiania: A. W. Brøgger.

McGovern, Thomas H., et al. 2007. "Landscape of Settlement in Northern Iceland: Historical Ecology of Human Impact and Climate Fluctuation on the Millennial Scale." *American Anthropologist* 109 (1): 27–51.

McGrew, Julia H., and R. George Thomas, eds. 1970–74. *Sturlunga saga*. Library of Scandinavian Literature, 9–10. New York: Twayne and American-Scandinavian Foundation.

McKinnell, John. 2005. *Meeting the Other in Norse Myth and Legend*. Cambridge: D. S. Brewer.

McKinnell, John, Rudolf Simek, and Klaus Düwel, eds. 2004. *Runes, Magic and Religion: A Sourcebook*. Studia medievalia Septentrionalia, 10. Vienna: Fassbaender.

McNeill, J. T. 1933. "Folk Paganism in the Penitentials." *Journal of Religion* 13: 450–66.

Mebius, Hans. 2000. "Dag Strömbäck och den fornnordiska sejden." In *Sejd och andra studier i nordisk själsuppfattning av Dag Strömbäck*, ed. Gertrud Gidlund. Acta Academiae Regiae Gustavi Adolphi, 72. Hedemora: Kungl. Gustav Adolfs Akademien för svensk folkkultur/Gidlunds förlag. Pp. 273–306.

Meier, Christel. 1977. *Gemma spiritalis: Methode und Gebrauch der Edelsteinallegorese vom frühen Christentum bis ins 18. Jahrhundert*. Münstersche Mittelalter-Schriften, 34. Munich: Wilhelm Fink Verlag.

Mellor, Scott A. 2008. "The Life of Ansgar by Rimbert." In *Sanctity in the North: Saints, Lives, and Cults in Medieval Scandinavia*, ed. T. A. DuBois. Toronto: University of Toronto Press. Pp. 31–64.

Merback, Mitchell B. 1999. *The Thief, the Cross, and the Wheel: Pain and the Spectacle of Punishment in Medieval and Renaissance Europe*. Chicago: University of Chicago Press.

Metken, Sigrid. 1996. *Der Kampf um die Hose: Geschlechterstreit und die Macht im Haus, die Geschichte eines Symbols*. Frankfurt am Main: Campus.

Meulengracht Sørensen, Preben. 1977. *Saga og samfund: En indføring i oldislandsk litteratur*. Copenhagen: Berlingske.

———. 1980. *Norrønt nid: Forestillingen om den umandige mand i de islandske sagaer*. Odense: Odense Universitetsforlag.

———. 1983. *The Unmanly Man: Concepts of Sexual Defamation in Early Northern Society*. Viking Collection, 1. Odense: Odense University Press.

———. 1988. "Guðrún Gjúkadóttir in Miðjumdalr: Zur Aktualität nordischer Heldensage im Island des dreizehnten Jahrhunderts." In *Heldensage und Heldendichtung im Germanischen,* ed. H. Beck. Berlin: Walter de Gruyter. Pp. 183–96.

———. 1993. *Saga and Society: An Introduction to Old Norse literature.* Studia Borealia. Monograph Series, 1. Odense: Odense University Press.

Meyer, Poul. 1982. "Dødsstraf." *KLNM* 3: 455–59.

Michelet, Jules. 1862. *La Sorcière.* Paris: E. Dentu.

Midelfort, H. C. Erik. 1968. "Recent Witch Hunting Research, or Where Do We Go from Here?" *Paper of the Bibliographical Society of America* 62: 373–420.

———. 1972. *Witch Hunting in Southwestern Germany, 1562–1684. The Social and Intellectual Foundations.* Stanford, Calif.: Stanford University Press.

———. 1973. Review of Keith Thomas, *Religion and the Decline of Magic: Studies in Popular Beliefs in Sixteenth and Seventeenth-Century England. Journal of the American Academy of Religion* 41 (3): 432–34.

Migne, Jacques-Paul, ed. 1849. *Patrologiae cursus completus . . . Series Latina. 77. Sancti Gregorii magni.* Paris: Migne.

Milis, Ludo J. R., ed. 1998. *The Pagan Middle Ages.* Woodbridge, Eng.: Boydell Press. Orig. pub. 1991 as *De Heidense Middeleeuwen.*

Mitchell, Stephen A. 1983. "*Fǫr Scírnis* as Mythological Model: *frið at kaupa.*" *ANF* 98: 108–22.

———. 1984. "On the Composition and Function of *Gutasaga.*" *ANF* 99: 151–74.

———. 1985a. "'Nú gef ek þik Óðni': Attitudes toward Odin in the Mythical-Heroic Sagas." In *The Sixth International Saga Conference.* 2 vols. Copenhagen: Det Arnamagnæanske Institut. 2: 777–91.

———. 1985b. "The Whetstone as Symbol of Authority in Old English and Old Norse." *SStudies* 57: 1–31.

———. 1991a. "Heroic Legend, Parricide, and Istaby." In *The Eighth International Saga Conference: The Audience of the Sagas.* 2 vols. Gothenburg: Gothenburg University. 2: 113–19.

———. 1991b. *Heroic Sagas and Ballads.* Ithaca, N.Y.: Cornell University Press.

———. 1993. "*Skírnismál.*" In *MScan.* Pp. 596–97.

———. 1996. "Literature in Medieval Sweden." In *A History of Swedish Literature,* ed. L. Warme. A History of Scandinavian Literature, 3. Lincoln: University of Nebraska Press in cooperation with the American-Scandinavian Foundation. Pp. 1–57.

———. 1997a. "*Blåkulla* and Its Antecedents: Transvection and Conventicles in Nordic Witchcraft." *Alvíssmál* 7: 81–100.

———. 1997b. "Courts, Consorts, and the Transformation of Medieval Scandinavian Literature." In *Germanic Studies in Honor of Anatoly Liberman,* ed. M. Taylor. North-Western European Language Evolution, 31/32. Odense: Odense University Press. Pp. 229–41.

———. 1997c. "Nordic Witchcraft in Transition: Impotence, Heresy, and Diabolism in 14th-century Bergen." *Scandia* 63 (1): 17–33.

———. 1998. "Anaphrodisiac Charms in the Nordic Middle Ages: Impotence, Infertility, and Magic." *Norveg* 38: 19–42.

————. 2000a. "Folklore and Philology Revisited: Medieval Scandinavian Folklore?" In *Norden og Europa: Fagtradisjoner i nordisk etnologi og folkloristikk,* ed. B. Rogge and B. G. Alver. Occasional Papers from the Department of Cultural Studies, University of Oslo, 2. Oslo: Novus forlag. Pp. 286–94.

————. 2000b. "Gender and Nordic Witchcraft in the Later Middle Ages." *ARV* 56: 7–24.

————. 2000c. "Witchcraft Persecutions in the Post-Craze Era: The Case of Ann Izzard of Great Paxton, 1808." *Western Folklore* 59: 304–28.

————. 2001 (pub. 2004). "Warlocks, Valkyries and Varlets: A Prolegomenon to the Study of North Sea Witchcraft Terminology." *Cosmos* 17 (1): 59–81.

————. 2002a. "Performance and Norse Poetry: The Hydromel of Praise and the Effluvia of Scorn." *Oral Tradition* 16 (1): 168–202.

————. 2002b. "Women's Autobiographical Literature in the Swedish Baroque." In *Skandinavische Literaturen in der frühen Neuzeit,* ed. J. Glauser and B. Sabel. Beiträge zur Nordischen Philologie, 32. Tübingen: A. Francke Verlag. Pp. 269–90.

————. 2003a. "The *fornaldarsögur* and Nordic Balladry: The Sámsey Episode across Genres." In *Fornaldarsagornas struktur och ideologi,* ed. Ármann Jakobsson, A. Lassen, and A. Ney. Nordiska texter och undersökningar, 28. Uppsala: Uppsala Universitet, Institutionen för nordiska språk. Pp. 245–56.

————. 2003b. "*Gandr*-Göndul än en gång." In *Grammatik i fokus,* ed. L-O. Delsing et al. I. Lund: Lunds universitet, Institutionen för nordiska språk. Pp. 117–23.

————. 2003c. "Magic as Acquired Art and the Ethnographic Value of the Sagas." In *Old Norse Myths, Literature and Society,* ed. M. C. Ross. Viking Collection. Studies in Northern Civilization, 14. Viborg: University Press of Southern Denmark. Pp. 132–52.

————. 2003d (pub. 2004). "Reconstructing Old Norse Oral Tradition." *Oral Tradition* 18 (2): 203–6.

————. 2004. "A Case of Witchcraft Assault in Early Nineteenth-Century England as Ostensive Action." In *Witchcraft Continued: Popular Magic in Modern Europe,* ed. W. de Blécourt and O. Davies. Manchester: Manchester University Press. Pp. 14–28.

————. 2005. "'An Evil Woman Is the Devil's Door Nail': Probing the Proverbial and Pictorial Patriarchate in Medieval Scandinavia." In *Neue Wege in der Mittelalterphilologie,* ed. A. van Nahl and S. Kramarz-Bein. Beiträge zur Germanistik und Skandinavistik, 55. Frankfurt am Main/Basel: Peter Lang. Pp. 11–34.

————. 2007a. "DgF 526 'Lokket med runer,' Memory, and Magic." In *Emily Lyle: The Persistent Scholar,* ed. F. J. Fischer and S. Rieuwerts. Ballads and Songs International Studies, 5. Trier: Wissenschaftlicher Verlag. Pp. 206–11.

————. 2007b. "*Skírnismál* and Nordic Charm Magic." In *Reflections on Old Norse Myths,* ed. P. Hermann, J. P. Schjødt, and R. T. Kristensen. Viking and Medieval Scandinavia, Studies, 1. Turnhout: Brepols. Pp. 75–94.

————. 2008a. "The n-Rune and Nordic Charms." In *"Vi ska alla vara välkomna!" Nordiska studier tillägnade Kristinn Jóhannesson,* ed. Auður G. Magnúsdóttir et al.

Meijbergs Arkiv för svensk ordforskning, 35. Göteborg: Meijbergs Arkiv för svensk ordforskning. Pp. 219–29.

———. 2008b. "*Pactum cum diabolo* og galdur á Norðurlöndum." In *Galdramenn: Galdrar og samfélag á miðöldum,* ed. Torfi H. Tulinius. Reykjavík: Hugvísindastofnun Háskóla Íslands. Pp. 121–45.

———. 2008c. "Spirituality and Alchemy in *Den vises sten* (1379)." In *Lärdomber oc skämptan: Medieval Swedish Literature Reconsidered,* ed. M. Bampi and F. Ferrari. SFSS. Serie 3. Smärre texter och undersökningar, 5. Uppsala: Svenska Fornskrift-Sällskapet. Pp. 97–108.

———. 2009a. "Odin, Magic and a Swedish Trial from 1484." *SStudies* 81 (3): 263–86.

———. 2009b. "The Supernatural and the *fornaldarsögur:* The Case of *Ketils saga hængs.*" In *Fornaldarsagaerne: Myter og virkelighed; Studier i de oldislandske fornaldarsögur Norðurlanda,* ed. A. Ney, Ármann Jakobsson, and A. Lassen. Copenhagen: Museum Tusculanum Forlag, Københavns Universitet. Pp. 281–98.

Mitchell, Stephen A., Derek Collins, and Timothy R. Tangherlini. 2000. "Special Section: Witchcraft in Local and Global Perspectives (Introduction)." *Western Folklore* 59 (3–4): 246–328.

Mitchell, Stephen A., and Gregory Nagy. 2000. "Introduction to the Second Edition." In *The Singer of Tales,* by Albert B. Lord. 2nd ed. Harvard Studies in Comparative Literature, 24. Cambridge, Mass.: Harvard University Press. Pp. vii–xxix.

Molland, Einar. 1982a. "Predikan: Norge." *KLNM* 13: 427–29.

———. 1982b. "Trosskiftet." *KLNM* 18: 702–10.

Moltke, Erik. 1938. "Medieval Rune-amulets in Denmark." *Acta Etnologica* 3: 116–47.

———. 1976. *Runerne i Danmark og deras oprindelse.* Copenhagen: Forum.

Morgenstern, Gustav, ed. 1893. *Arnamagnæanische Fragmente (Cod. AM. 655 4to III–VIII, 238 fol. II, 921 4to IV 1.2): Ein supplement zu den Heilagra manna sögur nach den handschriften.* Leipzig: E. Gräfes Buchhandlung and Skandinavisk Antiquariat.

Morris, Bridget. 1999. *St. Birgitta of Sweden.* Studies in Medieval Mysticism, 1. Woodbridge, Eng.: Boydell Press.

Morris, Katherine. 1991. *Sorceress or Witch? The Image of Gender in Medieval Iceland and Northern Europe.* Lanham, Md.: University Press of America.

Muessig, Carolyn. 2002. "Sermon, Preacher and Society in the Middle Ages." *Journal of Medieval History* 28 (1): 73–91.

Munch, P. A. 1860. "Diplomatiske Bidrag til Erkebiskop Jens Grands Levnetshistorie." *Annaler for nordisk Oldkyndighed og Historie:* 62–189.

Mundal, Else, and Gro Steinsland. 1989. "Kvinner og medicinsk magi." In *Kvinnors rosengård: Medeltidens liv och hälsa, lust och barnafödande,* ed. H. Gunneng et al. Stockholm: Centrum för kvinnoforskning vid Stockholms Universitet. Pp. 97–121.

Murmel, Heinz. 1991. "Frazer oder Mauss: Bemerkungen zu Magiekonzeptionen." *Zeitschrift fur Missionswissenschaft und Religionswissenschaft* 75: 147–54.

Murray, Margaret Alice. 1971. *The Witch-cult in Western Europe.* Oxford Paperbacks, 53. Oxford: Clarendon Press. Orig. pub. 1921.

Næshagen, Ferdinand Linthoe. 2000. "Medieval Norwegian Religiosity: Historical Sources and Modern Social Science." *Scandinavian Journal of History* 25 (4): 297–316.

Næss, Hans Eyvind. 1982. *Trolldomsprosessene i Norge på 1500–1600-tallet: en retts- og sosialhistorisk undersøkelse.* Oslo: Universitetsforlaget.

———. 1983. "Die Hexenprozesse in Norwegen." In *Hexenprozesse: Deutsche und skandinavische Beiträge,* ed. C. Degn. Neumünster: K. Wachholtz. Pp. 167–71.

———. 1984. *Med bål og brann: Trolldomsprosessene i Norge.* Oslo: Universitetsforlaget.

———. 1990. "Norway: The Criminological Context." In *Early Modern European Witchcraft: Centres and Peripheries,* ed. B. Ankarloo and G. Henningsen. Oxford: Clarendon Press. Pp. 367–82.

Näsström, Britt-Mari. 1995. *Freyja: The Great Goddess of the North.* Lund Studies in [the] History of Religion, 5. Lund: Department of History of Religions.

———. 1996. "Från Fröja till Maria: det förkristna arvet speglat i en folklig föreställningsvärld." In *Kristnandet i Sverige: Gamla källor och nya perspektiv,* ed. B. Nilsson. Projektet Sveriges kristnande. Publikationer, 5. Uppsala: Lunne böcker. Pp. 335–48.

Nash, Manning. 1967. "Witchcraft as Social Process in a Tzeltal Community." In *Magic, Witchcraft, and Curing,* ed. J. Middleton. Garden City, N.Y.: Natural History Press. Orig. pub. 1961. Pp. 127–33.

Nationalmuseet. 1933–2008. *Danmarks kirker.* Copenhagen: G. E. C. Gad

Neckel, Gustav, and Hans Kuhn, eds. 1983. *Edda: Die Lieder des Codex Regius nebst verwandten Denkmälern. I. Text.* 5th rev. ed. Heidelberg: Carl Winter. Universitätsverlag.

Nedkvitne, Arnved. 2000. "Beyond Historical Anthropology in the Study of Medieval Mentalities." *Scandinavian Journal of History* 25 (1–2): 27–51.

Nelson, Marie. 1984. "'Wordsige and Worcsige': Speech Acts in Three Old English Charms." *Language and Style: An International Journal.* 17 (1): 57–66.

Nenonen, Marko. 1992. *Noituus, taikuus ja noitavainot Ala-Satakunnan, Pohjois-Pohjanmaan ja Viipurin Karjalan maaseudulla vuosina 1620–1700.* Historiallisia Tutkimuksia, 165. Helsinki: Suomen Historiallinen Seura.

———. 1993. "'Envious are all the people, witches watch at every gate': Finnish Witches and Witch Trials in the 17th century." *Scandinavian Journal of History* 18 (1): 77–91.

Ney, Agneta. 2004. *Drottningar och sköldmör: Gränsöverskridande kvinnor i medeltida myt och verklighet ca 400–1400.* Hedemora: Gidlund.

Nielsen, Karl Martin, et al. 1974. "Jelling Problems: A Discussion." *Mediaeval Scandinavia* 7: 156–234.

Nielsen, Niels Åge. 1983. *Danske runeindskrifter.* Copenhagen: Hernov.

Nielsen, Oluf, ed. 1872–87. *Kjøbenhavns Diplomatarium: Samling af Dokumenter, Breve og andre Kilder til Oplysning om Kjøbenhavns ældre Forhold før 1728.* 8 vols. Copenhagen: G. E. C. Gad.

Nilsén, Anna. 1986. *Program och function i senmedeltida kalkmåleri: Kyrkmålningar i Mälarlandskapen och Finland 1400–1534.* Stockholm: Kungl. vitterhets-, historie- och antikvitetsakademien.

Nilsson, Bertil. 1996a. "Christianization in Sweden: Concluding reflections." In *Kristnandet i Sverige: Gamla källor och nya perspektiv,* ed. B. Nilsson. Projektet Sveriges kristnande. Publikationer, 5. Uppsala: Lunne böcker. Pp. 431–41.

———, ed. 1996b. *Kristnandet i Sverige: Gamla källor och nya perspektiv.* Projektet Sveriges kristnande. Publikationer, 5. Uppsala: Lunne böcker.

Nilsson, Bruce E. 1976. "The Runic 'Fish-Amulet' from Öland: A Solution." *Mediaeval Scandinavia* 9: 236–45.

Nisbeth, Åke. 1985. *Bildernas predikan: Medeltida kalkmålningar i Sverige.* Värnamo: Gidlunds & Kungl. vitterhets-, historie-och antikvitetsakademien.

———. 1995. *Ordet som bild: Östgötskt kalkmåleri vid slutet av 1300-talet och början av 1400-talet.* Sällskapet Runica et mediævalia. Scripta maiora, 1. Stockholm: Sällskapet Runica et medivalia.

Norberg, Rune. 1988. *Dannemora kyrka.* 2nd ed. Upplands kyrkor, 130. Katrineholm: Kurir-Tryck for Ärkestiftets Stiftsråd.

Nordal, Sigurður. See Sigurður Nordal.

Nordland, Odd. 1969. *Brewing and Beer Traditions in Norway: The Social Anthropological Background of the Brewing Industry.* Oslo: Universitetsforlaget.

———. 1982. "Øl." *KLNM* 20: 689–94.

Noreen, Erik. 1941. "Bidrag till fornsvensk lexikografi." *Meijerbergs arkiv för svensk ordforskning* 3: 1–23.

Noreen, Erik, and Torsten Wennström, eds. 1935–. *Arboga stads tänkeböcker.* SFSS, 53. Uppsala: Almqvist & Wiksell.

Norlin, Theodor Arnold Valentin. 1858. *Blåkulla-färderna i Mockfjerd eller resorna till Josefsdal 1858: Ett sanningsenligt blad ur dagens religiösa krönika.* Uppsala.

Norlind, Emilia Fogelklou. 1942. "Nyare synpunkter på häxväsendet." *Kyrkohistorisk årsskrift* 42: 180–93.

Norseng, Per. 1987. "Lovmaterialet som kilde til tidlig nordisk middelalder." In *Kilderne til den tidlige middelalders historie: Rapporter til den XX nordiske historikerkongress Reykjavík 1987,* ed. Gunnar Karlsson. Ritsafn Sagnfræðistofnunar, 18. Reykjavík: Sagnfræðistofnun Háskóla Íslands. Pp. 48–77.

———. 1991. "Law Codes as a Source for Nordic History in the Early Middle Ages." *Scandinavian Journal of History* 16: 137–66.

Nuffel, Herman van. 1966. "Le pacte avec le diable dans la littérature médiévale." *Anciens pays et assemblées d'états* 39: 27–43.

Nyborg, Ebbe. 1978. *Fanden på væggen.* Århus: Wormianum.

Nyström, Per. 1974. "Landskapslagarna." In *Historieskrivningens dilemma och andra studier.* Stockholm: PAN/Norstedt. Orig. pub. 1934. Pp. 62–78.

Oakley, Thomas Pollock. 1940. "The Penitentials as Sources for Mediaeval History." *Speculum* 15: 210–23.

Ödeen, Nils. 1929–30. "Studier över den nordiska gudavärldens uppkomst." *Acta Philologica Scandinavica* 4: 122–71.

Odenius, Oloph. 1984. "'Hon var värre än den onde' i svensk tradition: En sagohistorisk och ikonografisk notis." In *Den ljusa medeltiden: Studier tillägnade Aron Andersson,* ed. H-Å. Nordström. Museum of National Antiquities Studies, 4. Stockholm: Statens Historiska Museum. Pp. 197–218.

Örn Ólafsson. 2000. "Var Njáll hommi?" *Morgunblaðið,* 30 June. www.mbl.is/mm/gagnasafn/grein.html?grein_id = 543908

Ogilvie, Astrid E. J., and Gísli Pálsson. 2003. "Mood, Magic and Metaphor: Allusions to Weather and Climate in the Sagas of Icelanders." In *Weather, Climate, Culture,* ed. S. Strauss and B. S. Orlove. Oxford: Berg. Pp. 251–74.

———. 2006. "Weather and Witchcraft in the Sagas of Icelanders." In *The Fantastic in Old Norse/Icelandic Literature.* Durham Saga Conference. Available at www.dur.ac.uk/medieval.www/sagaconf/ogilvie.htm.

Ogrinc, Will H. L. 1980. "Western Society and Alchemy from 1200 to 1500." *Journal of Medieval History* 6 (1): 103–32.

Ohlmarks, Åke. 1939. *Studien zum Problem des Schamanismus.* Lund: C. W. K. Gleerup.

Ohrt, Ferdinand, ed. 1917–21. *Danmarks Trylleformler.* Folklore Fellows Publications. Northern Series, 3. Copenhagen: Gyldendal, Nordisk forlag.

Oja, Linda. 1994. "Kvinnligt, manligt, magiskt: Genusperspektiv på folklig magi i 1600- och 1700-talets Sverige." *Kyrkohistorisk årsskrift:* 43–55.

———. 1999. *Varken Gud eller natur: Synen på magi i 1600- och 1700-talets Sverige.* Stockholm: Brutus Östlings bokförlag Symposion.

Ólafsson, Örn. See Örn Ólafsson.

Ólafur Davíðsson. 1940–43. *Galdur og galdramál á Íslandi.* Sögufélag Sögurit, 20. Reykjavík: Sögufélag.

Ólafur Halldórsson, ed. 1961. *Óláfs saga Tryggvasonar en mesta.* Editiones Arnamagnæanæ, Series A, 1–2. Copenhagen: Ejnar Munksgaard.

———, ed. 1970. *Jónsbók: Kong Magnus Hakonssons Lovbog for Island, vedtaget paa Altinget 1281 og Réttarboetr, de for Island givne retterbøder af 1294, 1305 og 1314.* Facsimile ed. Odense: Universitetsforlaget. Orig. pub. 1904.

———. 1993. "Óláfs saga Tryggvasonar." In *MScan.* Pp. 448–49.

Ólafur Lárusson. 1982a. "Grágás." *KLNM* 5: 410–12.

———. 1982b. "Járnsíða." *KLNM* 7: 566–68.

Ólason, Vésteinn. See Vésteinn Ólason.

Ólína Þorvarðardóttir. 2000. *Brennuöldin: Galdur og galdratrú í málskjölum og munnmælum.* Reykjavík: Háskólaútgáfan.

Ólsen, Björn M. See Björn M. Ólsen.

Olsen, Magnus. 1909. "Fra gammelnorsk myte og kultus." *Maal og Minne* 1: 17–36.

Olsen, Magnus, and Aslak Liestøl, eds. 1957. *Norges innskrifter med de yngre runer. 4. Hordalands fylke. Sogn og Fjordane fylke. Møre og Romsdal fylke.* Oslo: A/S Bokcentralen.

Olsen, Olaf. 1966. "Hørg, hov og kirke: Historiske og arkæologiske vikingetidsstudier." *Årbøger for nordisk oldkyndighed og historie:* 1–307.

Ordbog over det norrøne prosasprog: A Dictionary of Old Norse Prose. 1989. Copenhagen: Den arnamagnæanske kommission.

Orri Vésteinsson. 2000. *The Christianization of Iceland; Priests, Power, and Social Change, 1000–1300.* Oxford: Oxford University Press.

Óskarsdóttir, Svanhildur. See Svanhildur Óskarsdóttir.

Östling, Per-Anders. 2002. *Blåkulla, magi och trolldomsprocesser: En folkloristisk studie av folkliga trosföreställningar och av trolldomsprocesserna inom Svea hovrätts jurisdiktion 1597–1720.* Etnolore, 25. Uppsala: Uppsala universitet, Etnologiska institutionen.

Paasche, Fredrik. 1958. *Møtet mellom hedendom og kristendom i Norden,* ed. D. Strömbäck. Oslo: Aschehoug.

Page, R. I. 1995. "Anglo-Saxon Runes and Magic." In *Runes and Runic Inscriptions: Collected Essays on Anglo-Saxon and Viking Runes,* ed. D. Parsons. Woodbridge, Eng.: Boydell Press. Orig. pub. 1964. Pp. 105–25.

Palme, Sven Ulrik. 1969. "Die Kirche in der Gesellschaft der Landschaftsgesetze." In *Kirche und Gesellschaft im Ostseeraum und im Norden vor der Mitte des 13. Jahrhunderts,* ed. S. Ekdahl. Acta Visbyensia, 3. Visby: Museum Gotlands Fornsal. Pp. 55–63.

Pálsson, Gísli. See Gísli Pálsson.

Pálsson, Hermann. See Hermann Pálsson.

Pálsson, Hermann, and Paul Edwards. See Hermann Pálsson and Paul Edwards.

Pegelow, Ingalill. 1976. "Från Helga Lekamen—till Blåkulla. Vapenhusmålningar i uppländska kyrkor." In *Bild och betydelse. Föredrag vid det 4. nordiska symposiet för ikonografiska studier, Kvarnträsk, 19.–22. augusti 1974,* ed. L. Lillie and M. Thøgersen. Picta. Skrifter utgivna av Konsthistoriska institutionen vid Åbo Akademi, 2. Åbo: Åbo Akademi. Pp. 215–27.

Pertz, G. H., ed. 1846. *Adami Gesta hammaburgensis ecclesiae pontificum ex recensione Lappenbergii.* Scriptores rerum Germanicarum in usum scholarum ex Monumentis Germaniae historicis recusi. Hannover: Imprensis Bibliopolii Hahniani.

Peters, Edward. 1978. *The Magician, the Witch, and the Law.* Middle Ages Series. Philadelphia: University of Pennsylvania Press.

———. 1996. *Torture.* 2nd rev. ed. Philadelphia: University of Pennsylvania Press.

———. 2001. "The Medieval Church and State on Superstition, Magic and Witchcraft: From Augustine to the Sixteenth Century." In *Witchcraft and Magic in Europe: The Middle Ages,* ed. B. Ankarloo and S. Clark. Philadelphia: University of Pennsylvania Press. Pp. 173–245.

Petersen, E. Ladewig. 1970. "Preaching in Medieval Denmark." *Mediaeval Scandinavia* 3: 142–71.

Peterson, Lena. 1994. "Scandinavian Runic-text Data Base: A Presentation." In *Developments around the Baltic and the North Sea in the Viking Age,* ed. B. Ambrosiani and H. Clarke. Birka Studies, 3. Stockholm: Statens Historiska Museer. Pp. 305–9.

Piltz, Anders. 1974. *Prolegomena till en textkritisk edition av magister Mathias' Homo conditus.* Acta Universitatis Upsaliensis. Studia Latina Upsaliens 7. Uppsala: Uppsala universitet and Almqvist & Wiksell.

———, ed. 1984. *Magister Mathias: Homo conditus.* SFSS. Andra Serien. Latinska skrifter, 9:1. Angered: Graphic Systems.

Pipping, Hugo. 1915. "Fornsvenskt lagspråk. V. Studier över *Äldre Västgötalagen.*" *Studier i nordisk filologi* 7 (1): 1–100.

Pipping, Rolf. 1928. "Oden i galgen." *Studier i nordisk filologi* 18 (2).

———. 1943. "Den fornsvenska litteraturen." In *Litteraturhistoria. A. Danmark, Finland och Sverige,* ed. Sigurður Nordal. Nordisk Kultur, 8:A. Stockholm: Albert Bonniers förlag. Pp. 64–128.

Pócs, Éva. 1991–92. "Popular Foundations of the Witches' Sabbath and the Devil's Pact in Central and Southeastern Europe." *Acta Ethnographica Hungaricae.* Budapest 37: 305–70.

———. 1999. *Between the Living and the Dead: A Perspective on Witches and Seers in the Early Modern Age.* Trans. S. Rédey and M. Webb. Budapest: Central European University Press.

Pontoppidan, Erik, ed. 1741. *Annales ecclesiae Danicae diplomatici, oder nach Ordnung der Jahre abgefassete und mit Urkunden belegte Kirchen-Historie des Reichs Dännemarck.* Copenhagen: Christoph Georg Glasing.

Poulsen, Grete S. 1986. "The Complementarity of Magic in Nordic Mythology and in Archaeological Sources." In *Words and Objects: Towards a Dialogue between Archaeology and History of Religion,* ed. G. Steinsland. Instituttet for sammenlignende kulturforskning. Skrifter, 71. Olso: Norwegian University Press. Pp. 168–79.

Price, Neil S., ed. 2001. *The Archaeology of Shamanism.* London: Routledge.

———. 2002. *The Viking Way: Religion and War in Late Iron Age Scandinavia.* Aun, 31. Uppsala: Institutionen för arkeologi och antik historia, Uppsala universitet.

———. 2004. "The Archaeology of *seið r.* Circumpolar Traditions in Viking Pre-Christian Religion." *Brathair* 4 (2): 109–26.

———. 2008. "Sorcery and Circumpolar Traditions in Old Norse Belief." In *The Viking World,* ed. S. Brink and N. Price. New York: Routledge. Pp. 244–48.

Purkiss, Diane. 1996. *The Witch in History: Early Modern and Twentieth-Century Representations.* London: Routledge.

Quinn, Judy. 1998. "'Ok verðr henni ljóð á munni': Eddic Prophecy in the *fornaldarsögur.*" *Alvíssmál* 8: 29–50.

Rafn, Carl C., ed. 1829–30. *Fornaldar Sögur Nordrlanda, eptir gömlum handritum.* Copenhagen: n.p.

Rafnsson, Magnús. See Magnús Rafnsson.

Rafnsson, Sveinbjörn. See Sveinbjörn Rafnsson.

Raudvere, Catharina. 1993. *Föreställningar om maran i nordisk folktru.* Lund Studies in History of Religion, 1. Lund: Religionshistoriska avdelningen, Lunds universitet.

———. 2001. "*Trolldómr* in Early Medieval Scandinavia." In *Witchcraft and Magic in Europe: The Middle Ages,* ed. B. Ankarloo and S. Clark. Philadelphia: University of Pennsylvania Press. Pp. 73–171.

———. 2003. *Kunskap och insikt i norrön tradition: Mytologi, ritualer och trolldomsanklagelser.* Vägar till Midgård, 3. Lund: Nordic Academic Press.

Reichardt, Konstantin. 1939. "Die Liebesbeschwörung in *Fǫr Scírnis.*" *Journal of English and Germanic Philology* 38: 481–95.

Reu, M. De. 1998. "The Missionaries: The First Contact between Paganism and Christianity." In *The Pagan Middle Ages*, ed. L. J. R. Milis. Woodbridge, Eng.: Boydell Press. Orig. pub. 1991. Pp. 13–37.

Reuterdahl, Henrik, ed. 1841. *Statuta synodalia veteris ecclesiae sveogothicae.* Lund: Berling.

Rider, Catherine. 2006. *Magic and Impotence in the Middle Ages.* Oxford: Oxford University Press.

Rietz, Johan Ernst, ed. 1962. *Svenskt dialektlexikon: Ordbok öfver svenska allmogespråket.* Facsimile ed. Lund: C. W. K. Gleerups förlag. Orig. pub. 1862–67.

Riising, Anne. 1969. *Danmarks middelalderlige prædiken.* Copenhagen: Institut for Dansk Kirkehistorie. G. E. C. Gads Forlag.

———. 1982. "Predikan: Danmark." *KLNM* 13: 425–27.

Rindal, Magnus. 1983. "Introduction: The Legislation of King Magnus Håkonsson; Christian Laws." In *King Magnus Håkonsson's Laws of Norway and Other Legal Texts: Gl. kgl. saml. 1154 fol. in the Royal Library, Copenhagen,* ed. M. Rindal and K. Berg. Corpus codicum Norvegicorum medii aevi. Quarto Series, 7. Oslo: Society for Publication of Old Norwegian Manuscripts. Pp. 9–18.

———. 1993. "Laws. 3. Norway." In *MScan.* Pp. 385–86.

Robinson, Charles H., ed. 1921. *Ansgar: The Apostle of the North, 801–865.* London: Society for the Propagation of the Gospel in Foreign Parts.

Robinson, Fred C. 1984. "Medieval, the Middle Ages." *Speculum* 59 (4): 745–56.

Rodin, Kerstin. 1984. *Onda kvinnor och oregerliga hustrur: En etnologisk studie av kontroversiella kvinnobilder.* Uppsala: Almqvist & Wiksell.

Roesdahl, Else. 1982. *Viking Age Denmark.* Trans. S. Margeson and K. Williams. London: British Museum.

Romdahl, Axel L. 1914. "Rogslösadörren och en grupp romanska smiden i de gamla Götalandskapen." *Fornvännen* 9: 231–45.

Ronge, Hans H. 1957. *Konung Alexander: Filologiska studier i en fornsvensk text [Konung Alexander; philologische Studien zu einem altschwedischen Text].* Skrifter utg. av Institutionen för nordiska språk vid Uppsala Universitet, 3. Uppsala: Institutionen för nordiska språk vid Uppsala Universitet.

Rosenberg, Bruce A. 1980. "Was There a Popular Culture in the Middle Ages?" *Journal of Popular Culture* 14: 149–54.

Rosengren, Karl Erik. 1976. "Malinowski's Magic: The Riddle of the Empty Cell." *Current Anthropology* 17 (4): 667–85.

Rossel, Sven, ed. 1993–2007. *A History of Scandinavian Literature.* 4 vols. Lincoln: University of Nebraska Press in cooperation with the American-Scandinavian Foundation.

Rowe, Elizabeth Ashman. 2004. "Absent Mothers and the Sons of Fornjótr: Late-Thirteenth-Century Monarchist Ideology in *Þorsteins saga Víkingssonar.*" *Mediaeval Scandinavia* 14: 133–60.

———. 2005. *The Development of Flateyjarbók: Iceland and the Norwegian Dynastic Crisis of 1389.* Viking Collection: Studies in Northern Civilization, 15. Odense: University Press of Southern Denmark.

Rowlands, Alison. 1998. "Telling Witchcraft Stories: New Perspectives on Witchcraft and Witches in the Early Modern Period." *Gender and History* 10 (2): 294–302.

Rudwin, Maximilian J. 1973. *The Devil in Legend and Literature.* Chicago: Open Court. Orig. pub. 1931.

Runeberg, Arne. 1947. *Witches, Demons and Fertility Magic. Analysis of their Significance and Mutual Relations in West-European Folk Religion.* Societas Scientiarum Fennica. Commentationes Humanarum Litterarum, 14:4. Helsinki: Societas Scientiarum Fennica.

Russell, Jeffrey Burton. 1972. *Witchcraft in the Middle Ages.* Ithaca, N.Y.: Cornell University Press.

———. 1984. *Lucifer: The Devil in the Middle Ages.* Ithaca, N.Y.: Cornell University Press.

Såby, Viggo, ed. 1886. *Det arnamagnæanske Håndskrift Nr. 187 i oktav, indholdende en dansk Lægebog.* Copenhagen: Thieles Bogtrykkeri for Universitets-Jubilæets danske Samfund.

Sæmundsson, Matthías Viðar. See Matthías Viðar Sæmundsson.

Sahlgren, Jöran. 1915. "Blåkulla och blåkullafärderna: En språklig och mythistorisk undersökning." *Namn och Bygd* 3: 100–161.

Sahlin, Claire L. 2001. *Birgitta of Sweden and the Voice of Prophecy.* Studies in Medieval Mysticism, 3. Woodbridge, Eng.: Boydell Press.

Sandal, Aud-Jorunn. 1996. "Synd i Gamal Norsk Homiliebok." In *Til debatt: Innlegg ved Norske historiedagar 1996,* ed. Ø. Bjørnson, E. Nysæter, and A. K. Uthaug. 3. Bergen: Historisk institutt. Pp. 121–30.

Sandholm, Åke. 1965. *Primsigningsriten under nordisk medeltid.* Acta Academiae Aboensis. Ser. A, Humaniora, 29:3. Åbo: Åbo akademi.

Sands, Tracey. 2006. "The Cult of St. Eric, King and Martyr, in Medieval Sweden." In *Sanctity in the North: Saints, Lives, and Cults in Medieval Scandinavia,* ed. T. A. DuBois. Toronto: University of Toronto Press. Pp. 203–40.

———. 2010. *The Company She Keeps: The Medieval Swedish Cult of St. Katherine of Alexandria and Its Transformations.* Medieval and Renaissance Texts and Studies, 362. Tempe, Ariz.: ACMRS.

Sandvik, Gudmund, and Jón Viðar Sigurðsson. 2005. "Laws." In *CONILC.* Pp. 223–44.

Santino, Jack. 1994. *All Around the Year: Holidays and Celebrations in American Life.* Urbana: University of Illinois Press.

Sawin, Patricia E. 1998. "Performance." In *Encyclopedia of Folklore and Literature,* ed. M. E. Brown and B. A. Rosenberg. Santa Barbara, Calif.: Abc-Clio. Pp. 497–99.

Sawyer, Birgit Strand. 1980. *Kvinnor och män i Gesta Danorum.* Kvinnohistoriskt arkiv, 18. Göteborg: Historiska institutionen.

———. 1981. "Women in *Gesta Danorum.*" In *Saxo Grammaticus: A Medieval Author between Norse and Latin Culture,* ed. K. Friis-Jensen. Danish Medieval History and Saxo Grammaticus, 2. Copenhagen: Museum Tusculanum. Pp. 135–67.

———. 1992. *Kvinnor och familj i det forn- och medeltida Skandinavien.* Occasional Papers on Medieval Topics, 6. Skara: Viktoria Bokförlaget.

———. 2000. *The Viking-Age Rune-Stones: Custom and Commemoration in Early Medieval Scandinavia.* Oxford: Oxford University Press.

Sawyer, Birgit, and Peter Sawyer. 1993. *Medieval Scandinavia: From Conversion to Reformation, circa 800–1500.* Nordic Series, 17. Minneapolis: University of Minnesota Press.

———. 1999. "Confrontations between Pagans and Christians: The Contemporary Evidence." In *Religion och samhälle i det förkristna Norden: Et symposium,* ed. U. Drobin. Odense: Odense University Press. Pp. 181–94.

Sawyer, Peter. 1982. *Kings and Vikings: Scandinavia and Europe* AD 700–1100. London: Routledge.

Saxtorph, Niels M. 1997. *Danmarks kalkmalerier.* 2nd ed. Copenhagen: Politiken.

Schier, Kurt. 1977. "Edda." In *Enzyklopädie des Märchens: Handwörterbuch zur historischen und vergleichenden Erzählforschung,* ed. K. Ranke and H. Bausinger. Vol. 3. Berlin: de Gruyter. Pp. 979–1003.

Schjødt, Jens Peter. 2001. "Óðinn: Shaman eller fyrstegud?" In *Kontinuitäten und Brüche in der Religionsgeschichte: Festschrift für Anders Hultgård zu seinem 65. Geburtstag am 23.12.2001,* ed. O.Sundqvist, A. van Nahl, and M. Stausberg. Reallexikon der germanischen Altertumskunde Ergänzungsbände, 31. Berlin: de Gruyter. Pp. 562–77.

———. 2008. *Initiation between Two Worlds: Structure and Symbolism in Pre-Christian Scandinavian Religion.* Viking Collection, 17. Odense: University Press of Southern Denmark.

Schlauch, Margaret. 1934. *Romance in Iceland.* Princeton, N.J.: Princeton University Press for the American-Scandinavian Foundation.

Schlyter, D. C. J., ed. 1822–77. *Samling af Sweriges Gamla Lagar: Corpus iuris Sueco-Gotorum antiqui.* 13 vols. [vols. 1–2, ed. with D. H. S. Colin]. Vol. 1, Stockholm: Z. Haeggström; vols. 2–3, Stockholm: Norstedt & Söner; vols. 4–13, Lund: Gleerups.

Schmidt, Gary D. 1995. *The Iconography of the Mouth of Hell: Eighth-Century Britain to the Fifteenth Century.* Selinsgrove: Susquehanna University Press.

Schmidt, Kurt Dietrich. 1939. *Die Bekehrung der Germanen zum Christentum.* Göttingen: Vandenhoeck & Ruprecht.

Schnurbein, Stefanie V. 2003. "Shamanism in the Old Norse Tradition: A Theory between Ideological Camps." *History of Religions* 43 (2): 116–38.

Schück, Adolf. 1929. "S:ta Ingrids kloster." In *Skänninge stads historia,* ed. A. Schück et al. Linköping: "Efter uppdrag av stadsfullmäktige i Skänninge." Pp. 127–46.

Schück, Henrik. 1884. "Författarskapet till legendariet i Codex Bildstenianus." *Samlaren* 5.

———. 1951. *Stockholm vid fjortonhundra talets slut.* 2nd rev. ed. Tord Norberg. Stockholm: Hugo Gebers förlag.

Schück, Herman. 1959. *Ecclesia Lincopensis: Studier om Linköpingskyrkan under medeltiden och Gustav Vasa.* Acta Universitatis Stockholmiensis. Stockholm Studies in History, 4. Stockholm: Almqvist & Wiksell.

Schulz, Katja. 2004. *Riesen: Von Wissenshütern und Wildnisbewohnern in Edda und Saga.* Heidelberg: Winter.

Schumacher, Jan. 2005. "Kristendomen i tidlig middelalder." In *Norges religionshistorie,* ed. Arne Bugge Amundsen. Oslo: Universitetsforlaget. Pp. 63–104.

Seaver, Kirsten A. 1996. *The Frozen Echo: Greenland and the Exploration of North America, ca. A.D. 1000–1500.* Stanford, Calif.: Stanford University Press.

See, Klaus von. 1964. *Altnordische Rechtswörter: Philologische Studien zur Rechtsauffassung und Rechtsgesinnung der Germanen.* Tübingen: M. Niemeyer.

———. 1972. *Die Gestalt der* Hávamál: *Eine Studie zur eddischen Spruchdichtung.* Frankfurt am Main: Athenäum.

———. 1981. "Disticha Catonis und Hávamál." In *Edda, Saga, Skaldendichtung: Aufsätze zur skandinavischen Literatur des Mittelalters.* Skandinavistische Arbeiten, 6. Heidelberg: C. Winter. Orig. pub. 1972. Pp. 27–44.

See, Klaus von, et al., eds. 1997. *Kommentar zu den Liedern der Edda. Bd. 2: Götterlieder (Skírnismál, Hárbarðsljóð, Hymiskvíða, Lokasenna, Þrymskvíða).* Heidelberg: Winter.

Segev, Dror. 2001. *Medieval Magic and Magicians—in Norway and Elsewhere: Based upon 12th–15th centuries Manuscript and Runic Evidence.* Skriftserie/Senter for studier i vikingtid og nordisk middelalder, 2001:2. Oslo: Senter for studier i vikingtid og nordisk middelalder.

Seierstad, Andr. 1982. "Kyrkostraff: Noreg." *KLNM* 10: 10–13.

Seiferth, Wolfgang. 1952. "The Concept of the Devil and the Myth of the Pact in Literature Prior to Goethe." *Monatshefte* 44: 271–89.

Sellevold, Berit Jansen, Else Mundal, and Gro Steinsland, eds. 1992. *Fokus på kvinner i middelalderkilder: Rapport fra symposiet "Kilder til kvinnehistoriske studier i nordisk middelalder," Isegran, september 1990.* Skara: Viktoria Bokförlag.

Sigfús Blöndal et al., ed. 1980. *Islandsk-dansk Ordbog.* Reykjavík: Íslenska bókmenntafélag. Orig. pub. 1920–63.

Siglaugur Brynleifsson. 1976. *Galdrar og brennudómar.* Reykjavík: Mál og Menning.

Sigurður Gylfi Magnússon. 1997. *Menntun, ást og sorg: Einsögurannsókn á íslensku sveitasamfélagi 19. og 20. aldar.* Sagnfræðirannsóknir [= Studia historica], 13. Reykjavík: Sagnfræðistofnun Háskóla Íslands: Háskólaútgáfan.

Sigurður Líndal. 1969. "Sendiför Úlfljóts." *Skírnir* 143: 5–26.

———. 1974. "Upphaf kristni og kirkju." In *Saga Íslands.* Vol. 1, *Samin að tilhlutan þjóðhátíðarnefndar,* ed. Sigurður Líndal. Reykjavík: Hið íslenzka bókmenntefélag—Sögufélagi. Pp. 227–88.

Sigurðsson, Gísli. See Gísli Sigurðsson.

Sigurðsson, Gísli, and Stephen A. Mitchell. See Gísli Sigurðsson and Stephen A. Mitchell.

Sigurðsson, Gísli, and Vésteinn Ólason, eds. See Gísli Sigurðsson and Vésteinn Ólason, eds.

Sigurðsson, Jón Viðar. See Jón Viðar Sigurðsson.

Sigurðsson, Jón Viðar, Frederik Pedersen, and Anders Berge. See Jón Viðar Sigurðsson, Frederik Pedersen, and Anders Berge.

Sigurður Nordal.1940. *Hrafnkatla.* Íslenzk fræði, 7. Reykjavík: Ísafoldarprentsmiðja H.F.

———. 1941. "Gunnhildur konungamóðir." *Samtíð og saga* 1: 135–55.

———. 1953. "Sagalitteraturen." In *Litteraturhistoria: B. Norge og Island,* ed. Sigurður Nordal. Nordisk kultur, 8B. Stockholm: Bonniers. Pp. 180–288.

————, ed. 1979. *Egils saga Skalla-Grímssonar*. ÍF, 2. Reykjavík: Hið íslenzka fornritafélag. Orig. pub. 1933.

Sigurgeir Steingrímsson, Ólafur Halldórsson, and Peter Foote, eds. 2002. *Biskupa sögur 1:2 (sögutextar). Kristni saga. Kristni þættir (Þorvalds þáttr víðförla I; Þorvalds þáttr víðförla II; Stefnis þáttr Þorgilssonar; Af Þangbrandi; Af Þiðranda ok dísunum; Kristniboð Þangbrands; Þrír þættir; Kristnitakan). Jóns saga ins helga. Gísls þáttr Illugasonar. Sæmundar þáttr*. ÍF, 15. Reykjavík: Hið íslenzka fornritafélag.

Siikala, Anna-Leena. 2002. *Mythic Images and Shamanism: A Perspective on Kalevala Poetry*. FFC 280. Helsinki: Suomalainen Tiedeakatemia.

Silfverstolpe, Carl, ed. 1875–. *Svenskt diplomatarium från och med år 1401*. Stockholm: P. A. Norstedt & Söner.

Simek, Rudolf. 1993. *Dictionary of Northern Mythology*. Cambridge: D. S. Brewer.

Simpson, J. A., and E. S. C. Weiner, eds. 1993. *Oxford English Dictionary*. 2nd ed. Oxford: Clarendon Press and Oxford University Press.

Simpson, Jacqueline. 1973. "Olaf Tryggvason versus the Powers of Darkness." In *The Witch Figure*, ed. V. Newall. London: Routledge. Pp. 165–87.

————. 1979. "The King's Whetstone." *Antiquity* 53: 96–101.

————. 1994. "Margaret Murray: Who Believed Her, and Why?" *Folklore* 105 (1): 89–96.

Sjöholm, Elsa. 1976. *Gesetze als Quellen: Mittelalterlicher Geschichte des Nordens*. Stockholm Studies in History, 21. Stockholm: Almqvist & Wiksell International.

————. 1978. "Rättshistorisk metod och teoribildning." *Scandia* 44: 233–41.

————. 1988. *Sveriges medeltidslagar: Europeisk rättstradition i politisk omvandling*. Skrifter utgivna av Institutet for rättshistorisk forskning. Serien I, Rättshistoriskt bibliotek. Lund: Institutet for rättshistorisk forskning.

————. 1993. "Laws. 4. Sweden." In *MScan*. Pp. 386–87.

Skautrup, Peter, ed. and trans. 1933–41. *Den Jyske lov, text med oversaettelse og kommentar*. Copenhagen: C. A. Reitzels forlag.

Skovgaard-Petersen, Inge. 1975. "*Gesta Danorums* genremæssige placering." In *Saxostudier: Saxo-kollokvierne ved Københavns universitet*, ed. I. Boserup. Opuscula Graecolatina, 2. Copenhagen: Museum Tusculanum. Pp. 20–29.

————. 1981. "The Way to Byzantium: A Study in the First Three Books of Saxo's History of Denmark." In *Saxo Grammaticus: A Medieval Author between Norse and Latin Culture*, ed. K. Friis-Jensen. Danish Medieval History and Saxo Grammaticus, 2. Copenhagen: Museum Tusculanum Press. Pp. 121–34.

————. 1987. *Da Tidernes Herre var nær . . . : Studier i Saxos Historiesyn*. Copenhagen: Den danske historiske Forening.

Skre, Dagfinn. 1998. "Missionary Activity in Early Medieval Norway. Strategy, Organization and the Course of Events." *Scandinavian Journal of History* 23 (1–2): 1–19.

Skyum-Nielsen, Niels. 1971. *Kvinde og slave*. Copenhagen: Munksgaard.

————. 1994. *Fruer og vildmænd: Dansk middelalderhistorie*. Copenhagen: Akademisk forlag.

Sleumer, Albert, and Joseph Schmid, eds. 1990. *Kirchenlateinisches Wörterbuch*. Hildesheim: G. Olms Verlag. Orig. pub. 1926.

Söderberg, Barbro, and Inger Larsson. 1993. *Nordisk medeltidsliteracy i ett diglossiskt och digrafiskt perspektiv.* Meddelanden från Institutionen för nordiska språk vid Stockholms universitet (MINS), 39. Stockholm: Institutionen för nordiska språk.

Söderwall, Knut F., and Karl Gustav Ljunggren, eds. 1884–1973. *Ordbok öfver svenska medeltids-språket (& Supplement).* SFSS, 27. Lund: Berlingska boktryckeri- och stilg-juteri-aktiebolaget.

Sørensen, John Kousgård. 1982. "Lægebøger." *KLNM* 2:76–79.

Sørensen, Preben Meulengracht. See Meulengracht Sørensen, Preben.

Sörlin, Per. 1997. "The Blåkulla Story: Absurdity and Rationality." *ARV* 53: 131–52.

———. 1998. *Wicked Arts: Witchcraft and Magic Trials in Southern Sweden, 1635–1754.* Cultures, Beliefs, and Traditions, 7. Leiden: Brill.

Solli, Brit. 2002. *Seid: Myter, sjamanisme og kjønn i vikingenes tid.* Oslo: Pax Forlag A/S.

Sondén, Per et al. 1888–. *Rikskansleren Axel Oxenstiernas skrifter och brefvexling.* Stockholm: Kungl. Vitterhets historie och antikvitets akademien.

Ståhle, Carl Ivar. 1958. *Syntaktiska och stilistiska studier i fornnordiskt lagspråk.* Stockholm Studies in Scandinavian Philology, n.s. 2. Stockholm: Almqvist & Wiksell.

———. 1967. "Medeltidens profana litteratur." In *Ny illustrerad svensk litteraturhistoria.* 2nd rev. ed, ed. E. N. Tigerstedt and E. H. Linder. Vol. 1. Stockholm: Natur och kultur. Orig. pub. 1952. Pp. 37–124.

———. 1982. "Östgötalagen." *KLNM* 21: 50–53.

Stark, Rodney. 2001. "Reconceptualizing Religion, Magic, and Science." *Review of Religious Research* 43 (2): 101–20.

Stefánsson, Magnús. See Magnús Stefánsson.

Steingrímsson, Sigurgeir, Ólafur Halldórsson, and Peter Foote, eds. See Sigurgeir Steingrímsson, Ólafur Halldórsson, and Peter Foote, eds.

Steinsland, Gro. 1991. *Det hellige bryllup og norrøn kongeideologi: En analyse av hierogami-myten i Skírnismál, Ynglingatal, Háleygjatal og Hyndluljóð.* Oslo: Solum.

Steinsland, Gro, and Kari Vogt. 1981. "'Aukinn ertu Uolse ok vpp vm tekinn': En religions-historisk analyse av *Vǫlsaþáttr* i *Flateyjarbók.*" *ANF* 96: 87–106.

Stephens, George, and F. A. Dahlgren, eds. 1847–74. *Ett Forn-Svenskt Legendarium.* SFSS, 7. Stockholm: P. A. Norstedt och Söner.

Stevenson, Karen. 2001. "Hairy Business: Organizing the Gendered Self." In *Contested Bodies,* ed. R. Holliday and J. Hassard. London: Routledge. Pp. 137–52.

Stewart, Charles, and Rosalind Shaw, eds. 1994. *Syncretism/Anti-Syncretism: The Politics of Religious Synthesis.* European Association of Social Anthropologists. London: Routledge.

Storm, Gustav, ed. 1888. *Islandske Annaler indtil 1578.* Oslo: Det norske historiske Kilde-skriftfond.

———, ed. 1973. *Monumenta Historica Norvegiae.* Latinske Kildeskrifter til Norges Historie i Middelalderen, 14. Oslo: Norsk Historisk Kjeldeskrift-Institutt. Orig. pub. 1880.

Strand, Birgit. See Birgit Strand Sawyer.

Ström, Åke. 1969. "Tradition und Tendenz: Zur Frage des christlichen-vorchristlichen Synkretismus in der nordgermanischen Literatur." In *Syncretism: Based on Papers Read at the Symposium on Cultural Contact, Meeting of Religions, Syncretism Held at Åbo on the 8th–10th of September, 1966,* ed. S. S. Hartman. Scripta Instituti Donneriani Aboensis, 3. Stockholm: Almqvist & Wiksell. Pp. 240–62.

Ström, Folke. 1954. *Diser, norner, valkyrjor: Fruktbarhetskult och sakralt kungadöme i Norden.* Kungliga vitterhets historie och antikvitetsakademiens handlingar, filologisk-filosofiska serien, 1. Stockholm: Almqvist & Wiksell.

———. 1982. "År och fred." *KLNM* 20: 450–52.

Strömbäck, Dag. 1935. *Sejd: Textstudier i nordisk religionshistoria.* Nordiska Texter och Undersökningar, 5. Stockholm: Hugo Gebers förlag.

———. 1970. *Folklore och filologi: valda uppsatser.* Acta Academiae Regiae Gustavi Adolphi, 48. Uppsala: Kungl. Gustav Adolfs akademien.

———, ed. 1971. *Leading Folklorists of the North. Biographical Studies.* Oslo: Universitetsforlaget.

———. 1979a. "Folklore and Philology: Some Recollections." *ARV* 35: 13–23.

———. 1979b. "To the Readers of ARV." *ARV* 35: 9–11.

Stuart, Heather. 1985. "Utterance Instructions in the Anglo-Saxon Charms." *Parergon,* n.s. 3, 31–37.

Styers, Randall. 2004. *Making Magic: Religion, Magic, and Science in the Modern World.* Oxford: Oxford University Press.

Sullivan, Richard E. 1953. "The Carolingian Missionary and the Pagan." *Speculum* 28 (4): 705–40.

Sunde, Jørn Øyrehagen. 2002. "The Ploughman and the Flying Circus (review article)." *Scandinavian Journal of History* 27 (2): 115–24.

———. 2005. *Speculum legale—Rettsspegelen: Ein introduksjon til den norske rettskulturen si historie i eit europeisk perspektiv.* Bergen: Fagbokforlaget.

Svanhildur Óskarsdóttir. 2005. "Prose of Christian Instruction." In *CONILC.* Pp. 338–53.

Sveinbjörn Rafnsson. 1977. "Um Kristinsboðsþættina." *Gripla* 2: 19–31.

Sveinbjörnsson, Þórður, ed. See Þórður Sveinbjörnsson, ed.

Sveinsson, Einar Ól., ed. See Einar Ól. Sveinsson, ed.

Sveinsson, Einar Ól., and Matthías Þórðarson, eds. See Einar Ól. Sveinsson and Matthías Þórðarson, eds.

Svenska akademien. 1893–. *Ordbok öfver svenska språket.* Lund: C. W. K. Gleerup.

Sydow, Carl von. 1922a. "Folkminnesforskning och filologi." *Folkminnen och folktankar* 8: 75–123.

———. 1922b. "Mera om Folkminnen och filologi." *Folkminnen och folktankar* 8: 132–48.

———. 1944. "Folkminnesforskningens uppkomst och utveckling." *Folkkultur* 4: 5–35.

———. 1965. "Folktale Studies and Philology: Some Points of View." In *The Study of Folklore,* ed. A. Dundes. Englewood Cliffs, N.J.: Prentice Hall. Orig. pub. 1945. Pp. 219–42.

Tacitus, Cornelius. 1939. *Tacitus. Dialogus. Agricola. Germania.* Trans. W. Peterson and

M. Hutton. London and Cambridge, Mass.: W. Heinemann and Harvard University Press.

Tambiah, Stanley J. 1969. "Animals Are Good to Think and Good to Prohibit." *Ethnology* 8 (4): 423–59.

———. 1990. *Magic, Science, Religion, and the Scope of Rationality.* Cambridge: Cambridge University Press.

Tangherlini, Timothy R. 1990. "Some Old Norse Hang-Ups: Ritual Aspects of *Hávamál* 134." *Mankind Quarterly* 31: 87–108.

Taranger, Absalon. 1926. "De norske folkelovbøker (før 1263)." *Tidsskrift for retsvidenskap* 39: 183–211.

Taylor, A. R. 1969. "*Hauksbók* and Ælfric's *De Falsis Diis.*" *Leeds Studies in English* 3: 101–9.

Tedlock, Barbara. 2001. "Divination as a Way of Knowing: Embodiment, Visualisation, Narrative, and Interpretation." *Folklore* 112: 189–97.

Tegler, Kristina. 1997. "Till Blåkulla med kropp och själ: Schamanistiska föreställningar i svenska trolldomsprocessor." In *Vägen till Blåkulla: Nya perspektiv på de stora svenska häxprocesserna,* ed. L. Oja. Opuscula historica Upsaliensis, 18. Uppsala: Historiska institutionen. Pp. 47–72.

Tertullian. 1951. "On the Apparel of Women (*De cultu feminarum*)." In *The Ante-Nicene Fathers: Translations of the Writings of the Fathers down to* A.D. *325.* Vol. 4, *Fathers of the Third Century: Tertullian, Part Fourth; Minucius Felix; Commodian; Origen, Parts First and Second,* ed. A. C. Coxe. Trans. S. Thelwall. Grand Rapids, Mich.: Wm. B. Eerdmans. Pp. 14–25.

Thomas, Keith. 1970. "The Relevance of Social Anthropology to the Historical Study of English Witchcraft." In *Witchcraft Confessions and Accusations,* ed. M. Douglas. Association of Social Anthropologists Monographs, 9. London: Tavistock. Pp. 47–79.

———. 1971. *Religion and the Decline of Magic.* London: Weidenfeld & Nicolson.

Thompson, Claiborne W. 1978. "The Runes in *Bósa saga ok Herrauðs.*" *SStudies* 50 (1): 50–56.

Thompson, Stith, ed. 1966. *Motif-Index of Folk-Literature.* 6 vols. Bloomington: Indiana University Press.

Thorén, Ivar. 1942. *Studier över Själens tröst: Bidrag till kännedom om den litterära verksamheten i 1400-talets Vadstena.* Nordiska texter och undersökningar, 14. Stockholm: Hugo Gebers förlag.

Thorkelin, G. J., ed. 1781. *Samling af danske Kirke-Love.* Copenhagen: Godiches Arvingers Forlag.

Thorndike, Lynn. 1915. "Some Medieval Conceptions of Magic." *Monist* 25: 107–39.

———. 1944. *University Records and Life in the Middle Ages.* Records of Civilization, Sources and Studies, 38. New York: Columbia University Press.

Thunæus, Harald. 1968. *Ölets historia i Sverige.* Stockholm: Almqvist & Wiksell.

Thyregod, O. 1895–96. "Lovstridigt Hedenskab i Norden: Uddrag af gamle Love." *Dania* 3: 337–55.

Tjäder, Bertil. 1993. "Fornsvenska Legendariet." In *MScan.* Pp. 454–55.

Tolkien, Christopher, ed. 1960. *Saga Heiðreks konungs ins vitra: The Saga of King Heidrek the Wise.* London: Thomas Nelson and Sons.

Tolley, Clive. 1994. "The Shamanic Séance in the *Historia Norvegiae.*" *Shaman* 2 (2): 135–56.

———. 1996. "Sources for Snorri's Depiction of Óðinn in *Ynglinga saga*: Lappish Shamanism and the *Historia Norvegiae.*" *Maal og Minne*: 67–79.

———. 2009. *Shamanism in Norse Myth and Magic.* FFC, 296, 297. Helsinki: Suomalainen Tiedakatemia.

Tørnsø, Kim. 1986. *Djævletro og folkmagi: Trolddomsforfølgelse i 1500– og 1600-tallets Vestjylland.* Århus: Aarhus universitetsforlag.

Trevor-Roper, H. R. 1967. "Witches and Witchcraft." *Encounter* 38 (5): 3–25 and 38 (6): 13–34.

———. 1969. "The European Witch Craze of the Sixteenth and Seventeenth Centuries." In *The European Witch Craze of the Sixteenth and Seventeenth Centuries and Other Essays.* New York: Harper and Row. Pp. 90–192.

Troels-Lund, Troels Frederik. 1880–1901. *Dagligt Liv i Norden i Det 16de Aarhundrede.* 13 vols. Copenhagen: C. A. Reitzel.

Tubach, Frederic C. 1969. *Index Exemplorum: A Handbook of Medieval Religious Tales.* FFC, 204. Helsinki: Akademia Scientiarum Fennica.

Turner, Victor. 1967. "Witchcraft and Sorcery: Taxonomy versus Dynamics." In *Forest of Symbols.* Ithaca, N.Y.: Cornell University Press. Orig. pub. 1964. Pp. 112–27.

———. 1971. "An Anthropological Approach to the Icelandic Saga." In *The Translation of Culture,* ed. T. O. Beidelman. London: Tavistock. Pp. 349–74.

———. 1972. *Schism and Continuity in an African Society: A Study of Ndembu Village Life.* 2nd ed. Manchester: Manchester University Press. Orig. pub. 1957.

———. 1977. *The Ritual Process: Structure and Anti-Structure.* Ithaca, N.Y.: Cornell University Press.

Turville-Petre, E. O. G. 1953. *The Origins of Icelandic Literature.* Oxford: Clarendon Press.

———. 1964. *Myth and Religion of the North: The Religion of Ancient Scandinavia.* London: Weidenfeld and Nicolson.

Turville-Petre, Joan. 1960. "Sources of the Vernacular Homily in England, Norway and Iceland." *ANF* 75: 168–82.

Tuulse, Armin. 1963. *Kyrkor i Uppland. Håbo härad, mellersta delen: Konsthistoriskt inventarium.* Sveriges kyrkor, konsthistoriskt inventarium, 98. Uppland. Bd. 7:3. Stockholm: Kungl. Vitt. Hist. och Ant. Akademien.

Tveitane, Mattias. 1968. *Den lærde stil: Oversetterprosa i den norrøne versjonen av Vitæ Patrum.* Årbok for Universitetet i Bergen. Humanistisk serie; 1967, no. 2. Bergen: Norwegian Universities Press.

Úlfar Bragason. 2005. "Sagas of Contemporary History (*Sturlunga saga*): Texts and Research." In *CONILC.* Pp. 427–46.

Unger, C. R., ed. 1871. *Mariu saga: Legender om Jomfru Maria og hendes Jertegn.* Norske Oldskriftselskabs Samlinger, 11–12, 14, 16. Christiania: Brögger & Christie.

————, ed. 1874. *Postola sögur*. Christiania: B. M. Bentzen.

Unger, C. R., and H. J. Huitfeldt, eds. 1847–. *Diplomatarium Norvegicum*. Christiania: P. T. Malling.

Upham, Charles Wentworth. 1832. *Lectures on Witchcraft: Comprising a History of the Delusion in Salem in 1692*. 2nd ed. Boston: Carter Hendee & Babcock.

Van Engen, John. 1986. "The Christian Middle Ages as an Historiographical Problem." *American Historical Review* 91 (3): 519–52.

Van Gent, Jacqueline. 2008. *Magic, Body, and the Self in Eighteenth-Century Sweden*. Studies in Medieval and Reformation Traditions, 135. Leiden: Brill.

Vésteinn Ólason. 1982. *The Traditional Ballads of Iceland: Historical Studies*. Stofnun Árna Magnússonar á Íslandi. Rit, 22. Reykjavík: Stofnun Árna Magnússonar.

————. 2006. "Old Icelandic Poetry." In *A History of Icelandic Literature*, ed. D. L. Neijmann. 5. Lincoln: University of Nebraska Press, in cooperation with the American-Scandinavian Foundation. Pp. 1–63.

Vésteinsson, Orri. See Orri Vésteinsson.

Vigfússon, Guðbrandur, and C. R. Unger, eds. See Guðbrandur Vigfússon and C. R. Unger, eds.

Vilhjálmur Finsen, ed. 1974a. *Grágás, Konungsbók*. Facsimile ed. Odense: Universitetsforlag. Orig. pub. 1852.

————, ed. 1974b. *Grágás. Skálhóltsbók m.m.* Facsimile ed. Odense: Universitetsforlag. Orig. pub. 1883.

Vilmundarson, Þórhallur, and Bjarni Vilhjálmsson, eds. See Þórhallur Vilmundarson and Bjarni Vilhjálmsson, eds.

von Maurer, Konrad. See Maurer, Konrad von.

von See, Klaus. See See, Klaus von.

von Sydow, Carl. See Sydow, Carl von.

Vordemfelde, Hans. 1923. *Die germanische Religion in den deutschen Volksrechten*. Vol. 1, *Der religiöse Glaube*. Religionsgeschichtliche Versuche und Vorarbeiten, 18:1. Giessen: A. Töpelmann.

Vries, Jan de. 1928. "Over de dateering der *Þrymskviða*." *Tijdschrift voor nederlandse taal- en letterkunde* 47: 251–372.

————. 1934. "Om Eddaens Visdomsdigtning." *ANF* 50: 1–59.

————, ed. 1961. *Altnordisches etymologisches Wörterbuch*. Leiden: E. J. Brill.

————. 1962. "Wodan und die Wilde Jagd." *Die Nachbarn* 3: 31–59.

————. 1963. *Heroic Song and Heroic Legend*. Trans. B. J. Timmer. London: Oxford University Press.

————. 1964. *Altnordische Literaturgeschichte*. 2 vols. 2nd rev. ed. Grundriss der germanischen philologie, 15–16. Berlin: de Gruyter.

Wåhlin, Birgitte. 1974. "Retshistorisk metodik og teoridannelse." *Scandia* 40: 165–91.

Wainwright, F. T. 1975. "Early Scandinavian Settlement in Derbyshire." In *Scandinavian England: Collected Papers by F. T. Wainwright*, ed. H. P. R. Finberg. Chichester: Phillimore. Pp. 281–303.

Waitz, Georg, ed. 1977. *Vita Anskarii auctore Rimberto*. Monumenta Germaniae Historica. Scriptores rerum germanicarum, 55. Hannover: Hahn. Orig. pub. 1884.

Walberg, Carl Gustaf. 1815. *Blåkulla-assembléen, eller: Den gamle advokatens samvetsqval.* Stockholm: Carl Nyberg.

Wall, Jan. 1977–78. *Tjuvmjölkande väsen. I. Äldre nordisk tradition. II. Yngre nordisk tradition.* Acta universitatis Upsaliensis. Studia ethnologia Upsaliensis, 3, 5. Stockholm: Almqvist & Wiksell.

Warner, Marina. 1981. *Joan of Arc: The Image of Female Heroism.* New York: Alfred A. Knopf.

Wasserschleben, Hermann, ed. 1851. *Die Bussordnungen der abendländischen Kirche.* Halle: C. Graeger.

Watkins, Carl. 2004. " 'Folklore' and 'Popular Religion' in Britain during the Middle Ages." *Folklore* 115 (2): 140–50.

Wawn, Andrew. 2005. "The Post-Medieval Reception of Old Norse and Old Icelandic Literature." In *CONILC.* Pp. 320–37.

Wax, Murray, and Rosalie Wax. 1963. "The Notion of Magic." *Current Anthropology* 4 (5): 495–518.

Wax, Rosalie H. 1969. *Magic, Fate and History: The Changing Ethos of the Vikings.* Lawrence, Kans.: Coronado Press.

Wax, Rosalie, and Murray Wax. 1962. "The Magical World View." *Journal for the Scientific Study of Religion* 1: 179–88.

———. 1964. "Magic and Monotheism." In *Symposium on New Approaches to the Study of Religion: Proceedings of the 1964 Annual Spring Meeting of the American Ethnological Society,* ed. J. Helm. Seattle: University of Washington Press. Pp. 50–60.

Weber, Gerd Wolfgang. 1986. "Siðaskipti: Das religionsgeschichtliche Modell Snorri Sturlusons in *Edda* und *Heimskringla.*" In *Sagnaskemmtun: Studies in Honour of Hermann Pálsson on his 65th birthday, 26th May 1986,* ed. R. Simek, Jónas Kristjánsson, and H. Bekker-Nielsen. Philologica germanica, 8. Vienna: H. Bohlaus Nachf. Pp. 309–29.

Wegener, Caspar Frederik et al. 1864. "Otte Breve om Arven efter Biskop Bo af Aarhus (Efter Originalerne i Geheimearchivet)." *Danske Magazin* (Fjerde Række) 1 (4): 353–59.

Wessén, Elias, ed. 1964. *Lex Dalecarliae (Dalalagen) e Codice Membr. B54 Bibl. Reg. Holm.* Corpus codicum Suecicorum Medii Ævi, 17. Copenhagen: E. Munksgaard.

Wessén, Elias, and Sven B. F. Jansson. 1940. *Upplands runinskrifter.* 4 vols. Sveriges runinskrifter, 6–9. Stockholm: Kungl. Vitterhets historie och antikvitets akademien.

Westlund, Börje. 1989. "Kvinneby: en runinskrift med hittills okända gudanamn?" *Studia anthroponymica scandinavica: Tidskrift för nordisk personnamnsforskning* 7: 25–52.

Whitelock, Dorothy. 1937–45. "The Conversion of the Eastern Danelaw." *Saga-Book of the Viking Society* 12: 159–76.

Whitney, Elspeth. 1995. "International Trends: The Witch 'She'/The Historian 'He.' " *Journal of Women's History* 7 (3): 77–101.

Widding, Ole. 1996. "Norrøne Marialegender på europæisk baggrund." In *Opuscula* 10. Bibliotheca Arnamagnæana, 40. Copenhagen: Reitzel. Pp. 1–128.

Wieselgren, Harald, ed. 1966. *Helige Bernhards skrifter i svensk öfversättning från medeltiden efter gamla handskrifter.* SFSS, 16. Stockholm: P. A. Norstedt & Söner.

Wikman, K. Robert V., ed. 1946. *Johan J. Törners Samling af Widskeppelser.* Skrifter utgivna av Kungl. Gustav Adolfs akademien för folklivsforskning, 15. Uppsala: Almqvist och Wiksell.

Wiktorsson, Per-Axel. 1981. *Avskrifter och skrivare: Studier i fornsvenska lagtexter.* Acta Universitatis Upsaliensis. Studia philologiae Scandinavicae Upsaliensia, 17. Uppsala: Almqvist & Wiksell.

Williams, Henrik. 1996a. "Runtexternas teologi." In *Kristnandet i Sverige: Gamla källor och nya perspektiv,* ed. B. Nilsson. Projektet Sveriges kristnande. Publikationer, 5. Uppsala: Lunne böcker. Pp. 291–312.

———. 1996b. "Vad säger runstenarna om Sveriges kristnande?" In *Kristnandet i Sverige: Gamla källor och nya perspektiv,* ed. B. Nilsson. Projektet Sveriges kristnande. Publikationer, 5. Uppsala: Lunne Böcker. Pp. 45–83.

Wilson, Monica Hunter. 1982. "Witch-beliefs and Social Structure." In *Witchcraft and Sorcery. Selected Readings.* 2nd ed., ed. M. Marwick. Harmondsworth: Penguin. Orig. pub. 1951. Pp. 276–85.

Winberg, Christer. 1985. *Grenverket: Studier rörande jord, släktskapssystem och ståndsprivilegier.* Skrifter utgivna av Institutet för rättshistorisk forskning. Serien 1, Rättshistoriskt bibliotek, 38. Stockholm: Institutet för rättshistorisk forskning.

Winkelman, Michael. 1982. "Magic: A Theoretical Reassessment." *Current Anthropology* 23 (1): 37–66.

Witt, Lena. 1983. "Om kvinnors villkor i det senmedeltida Stockholm: Några iakttagelser i samband med filologiska studier i Stockholms stads tänkeböcker 1474–1500." In *Förändringar i kvinnors villkor under medeltiden,* ed. Silja Aðalsteinsdóttir and Helgi Þorláksson. Reykjavík: Sagnfræðistofnun Háskóla Íslands. Pp. 115–26.

Wolf, Kirsten. 1993. "Legenda." In *MScan.* Pp. 388–89.

———. 2008. "Pride and Politics in Iceland: Þorlákr Þórhallsson." In *Sanctity in the North: Saints, Lives, and Cults in Medieval Scandinavia,* ed. T. A. DuBois. Toronto: University of Toronto Press. Pp. 241–70.

Wolf-Knuts, Ulrika. 1991. *Människan och djävulen: En studie kring form, motiv, och funktion i folklig tradition.* Åbo: Åbo Academy Press.

Yalman, Nur. 1968. "Magic." In *International Encyclopedia of the Social Sciences,* ed. D. L. Sills. Vol. 9. New York: Macmillan. Pp. 521–28.

Zachrisson, Inger. 2008. "The Sámi and Their Interaction with the Nordic People." In *The Viking World,* ed. S. Brink and N. Price. New York: Routledge. Pp. 32–39.

Zeiten, Miriam Koktvedgaard. 1997. "Amulets and Amulet Use in Viking Age Denmark." *Acta Archaeologica* 68: 1–74.

Zimmerman, Tr. Odo John. 1959. *St. Gregory the Great, Dialogues.* New York: Fathers of the Church.

Zoëga, Geir T. 1975. *A Concise Dictionary of Old Icelandic.* Oxford: Clarendon Press. Orig. pub. 1910.

Þórður Sveinbjörnsson, ed. 1847. *Hin forna lögbók Íslendínga sem nefnist Járnsíða eðr Hákon-arbók: Codex juris Islandorum antiqvs, qvi nominatur Jarnsida seu Liber Haconis.* Copen-hagen: sumptibus Legati Arnæmagnæani.

Þorkelsson, Jón. See Jón Þorkelsson.

Þorkelsson, Jón, and Jón Sigurðsson, eds. See Jón Þorkelsson and Jón Sigurðsson, eds.

Þórólfsson, Björn K., and Guðni Jónsson, eds. See Björn K. Þórólfsson and Guðni Jóns-son, eds.

Þórhallur Vilmundarson and Bjarni Vilhjálmsson, eds. 1991. *Harðar saga; Bárðar saga; Þorskfirðinga saga; Flóamanna saga: Þórarins þáttr Nefjólssonar; Þorsteins þáttr Uxa-fóts; Egils þáttr Síðu-Hallssonar; Orms þáttr Stórólfssonar; Þorsteins þáttr tjaldstœðings; Þorsteins þáttr forvitna; Bergbúa þáttr; Kumlbúa þáttr; Stjörnu-Odda draumr.* ÍF, 13. Reykjavík: Hið íslenzka fornritafélag.

Þorsteinsson, Björn. See Björn Þorsteinsson.

Þorvarðardóttir, Ólína. See Ólína Þorvarðardóttir.

Index

Acknowledgments

I have been at this project for quite a while, and as I consider the very long list of people and institutions to whom I owe an immeasurable debt of gratitude for assistance of many different kinds, I am reminded of the story of one of Harvard's great men of letters, George Lyman Kittredge, who is said to have responded to a visiting Danish newspaperman's query as to how long it took him to prepare a lecture by saying, "Just my whole life, that's all, just my whole life."[1] I make no claim to "Kitty's" famed erudition, nor has this book taken my whole life (although it may have seemed that way to family and friends who know me best), yet it has taken a very long time.[2]

First and foremost, I express warmest thanks to two great and generous scholarly institutions, the Radcliffe Institute for Advanced Study at Harvard University and the University of Aarhus, Denmark, for providing me with that rarest of opportunities for an academic, namely, the chance to read, discuss, and contemplate simply for the sheer pleasure of learning and not just in order to write, as one of my colleagues has been heard to characterize our profession, another "furious footnote." It was during my fellow's year at Radcliffe that much of the background work on this book was done, and for the rigorous and helpful atmosphere provided by the Institute's leadership and its fellows, I am deeply grateful. I am equally (at the least) indebted to the supportive and invigorating research environment of the University of Aarhus, Denmark, and especially its Nordic Institute and Centre for Viking and Medieval Studies; colleagues there were of immeasurable help as I completed this project, listening to ideas and, in return, offering advice, support, and cheerful debate.

In addition, I have over the years received critical research assistance from Kungliga Gustav Adolfs Akademien, Uppsala; Stofnun Árna Magnússonar, Reykjavík; Uppsala universitetsbibliotek; Kungliga Biblioteket, Stockholm; Det Kongelige Bibliotek, Copenhagen; Sveriges medeltida personnamn (Institutet för språk och folkminnen), Uppsala; Antikvariskt-

topografiska arkivet, Stockholm; Stockholms stadsarkiv; Riksantikvarieämbetet, Stockholm; Landsarkivet i Vadstena; Svenska Akademiens Ordbok; Stats-
biblioteket, Århus; the British Library, London; the Public Records Office,
London; and, of course, my own home collection, Widener Library. For their
help, I thank all of these great and generous institutions, their archivists, and
their librarians; moreover, a number of local historians, church warders, parish priests, and parishioners have good-naturedly helped me gain access to
texts, traditions, and a variety of "photo ops." I could not have learned much
without their help. I express additional thanks to Kungliga Gustav Adolfs
Akademien for its assistance in subsidizing the publication of this book.

In working with the diverse materials at the heart of this study, I have
often been reminded of my debt to a number of teachers, particularly Alan
Dundes, Gösta Holm, Lauri Honko, and Lars Lönnroth. The insightful comments by several anonymous readers for the University of Pennsylvania Press
have helped shape the final product in important ways, and I thank them for
their insight, care, and courtesy, a point I would make about a number of
experts in the field who have been gracious in their exchanges with me over
the years, especially Owen Davies, François Xavier Dillman, Carlo Ginzburg,
Neil Price, Catharina Raudvere, and Clive Tolley. Three very gifted young
people, Maria Björg Águstsdóttir, Kaitlin Heller, and Casiana Ionata, assisted
me as research assistants during their undergraduate years at Harvard College.
And finally, among many other colleagues and friends, I am grateful to Agnes
Arnórsdóttir, Stefan Brink, Jürg Glauser, Kaaren Grimstad, Terry Gunnell,
Jens Peter Schjødt, and Gísli Sigurðsson, and especially Pernille Hermann
for their warm encouragement, sagacious advice, and much-appreciated colle-
giality—and, in some cases, for reading parts (or all) of various iterations of
this study; needless to say, the flaws that remain are certainly mine, not theirs.
But most of all, I want to thank more than a few of my closest colleagues for
putting aside, if all too briefly, scholarly matters and simply being friends,
making time to go *i veiðitúr* or on a fact-finding mission about the relative
merits of Wisby Klosteröl and *Gotlandsdricka*.